THE *SENTENCES* OF SEXTUS

Society of Biblical Literature

Wisdom Literature from the Ancient World

Leo G. Perdue, General Editor
Reinhard Gregor Kratz, Associate Editor

Area Editors

Bendt Alster
Pancratius C. Beentjes
Katharine Dell
Edward L. Greenstein
Victor Hurowitz
John Kloppenborg
Michael Kolarcik
Manfred Oeming
Bernd U. Schipper
Günter Stemberger
Loren T. Stuckenbruck

Number 1

THE *SENTENCES* OF SEXTUS

THE *SENTENCES* OF SEXTUS

By

Walter T. Wilson

Society of Biblical Literature
Atlanta

THE *SENTENCES* OF SEXTUS

Copyright © 2012 by the Society of Biblical Literature

All rights reserved. No part of this work may be reproduced or transmitted in any form or by any means, electronic or mechanical, including photocopying and recording, or by means of any information storage or retrieval system, except as may be expressly permitted by the 1976 Copyright Act or in writing from the publisher. Requests for permission should be addressed in writing to the Rights and Permissions Office, Society of Biblical Literature, 825 Houston Mill Road, Atlanta, GA 30329 USA.

Library of Congress Cataloging-in-Publication Data

Sentences of Sextus.
    The sentences of Sextus / Walter T. Wilson.
      p. cm. — (Wisdom literature from the ancient world ; number 1)
    ISBN 978-1-58983-719-5 (paper binding : alk. paper) — ISBN 978-1-58983-720-1 (electronic format)
    1. Christian life—Early works to 1800. 2. Sentences of Sextus. I. Sextus, Pythagoreus. II. Wilson, Walter T. III. Sentences of Sextus. English. 2012. IV. Sentences of Sextus. Greek. 2012. V. Title. VI. Series: Wisdom literature from the ancient world ; no. 1.
    BV4500.S4913 2012
    248.4—dc23
                                                                           2012041820

Printed on acid-free, recycled paper conforming to
ANSI/NISO Z39.48-1992 (R1997) and ISO 9706:1994
standards for paper permanence.

Contents

Acknowledgements vii
Abbreviations ix

Introduction 1
    Approaching the Text   1
    Versions   4
    Situating the Text   7
    Sources   11
    Morphology   29
    Orientation and Outlook   32

Text, Translation, and Commentary 41
    Sentences 1–5   41
    Sentences 6–14   46
    Sentences 15–21   54
    Sentences 22–30   61
    Sentences 31–36   69
    Sentences 37–40   74
    Sentences 41–50   77
    Sentences 51–62   88
    Sentences 63–66   99
    Sentences 67–75b   103
    Sentences 76–82d   112
    Sentences 82e–88   120
    Sentences 89–92   126
    Sentences 93–97   130
    Sentences 98–103   134
    Sentences 104–107   139
    Sentences 108a–111   143
    Sentences 112–121b   150

Sentences 122–128	159
Sentences 129–135	163
Sentences 136–148	167
Sentences 149–165g	176
Sentences 166–177	193
Sentences 178–187	202
Sentences 188–203	209
Sentences 204–209	220
Sentences 210a–214	226
Sentences 215–229	230
Sentences 230a–240	240
Sentences 241–253b	250
Sentences 254–257	261
Sentences 258–264b	264
Sentences 265–270	270
Sentences 271–277	276
Sentences 278–282	284
Sentences 283–292	287
Sentences 293–302	296
Sentences 303–311	305
Sentences 312–319	312
Sentences 320–324	319
Sentences 325–338	324
Sentences 339–349	336
Sentences 350–368	345
Sentences 369–376b	360
Sentences 377–382	367
Sentences 383–392	373
Sentences 393–399	381
Sentences 400–410	387
Sentences 411–425	394
Sentences 426–434	405
Sentences 435–440	412
Sentences 441–451	416

Bibliography ... 427
Index of Greek Words ... 437
Index of Texts Cited ... 446
Index of Authors ... 468
Index of Subjects ... 469

Acknowledgements

It is a pleasure to thank those who have helped with this project, especially my student research assistants, Ryan Bonfiglio, Edward Dixon, Meredyth Fleisher, Will Johnson, and Ryan Woods. I also owe a special debt of gratitude to the volume editor, John Kloppenborg (University of Toronto), the series editor, Leo Perdue (Brite Divinity School), and the Society of Biblical Literature's Editorial Director, Bob Buller, for their sage counsel.

On July 5, 2011, I presented a paper on Sextus at the Society of Biblical Literature International Meeting in London for the "Biblical Interpretation in Early Christianity" program unit. My thanks to Timothy Manor (University of Edinburgh) and the other participants for their feedback. On November 19, 2011, a session of the "Hellenistic Moral Philosophy and Early Christianity" program unit at the Society of Biblical Literature Annual Meeting was devoted to a discussion of my Sextus commentary. I especially want to thank Johan Thom (University of Stellenbosch), Daniele Pevarello (University of Cambridge), Pamela Gordon (University of Kansas), Teresa Morgan (University of Oxford), and David Konstan (New York University) for their feedback.

Research for this project was supported in part by the University Research Committee of Emory University.

In keeping with the format of the Wisdom Literature from the Ancient World series, in the commentary itself references to secondary literature have been kept to a minimum. Readers interested in learning more about Sextus and his world are encouraged to consult the items listed in the bibliography.

Walter T. Wilson

Abbreviations

Where available, abbreviations for Greek and Latin works are taken from David L. Petersen et al., eds., *The SBL Handbook of Style* (Peabody, Mass.: Hendrickson, 1999). Note also the following:

Act. Joan.	*Acta Joannis*
Act. Just. Sept. Sod.	*Acta Justini et Septem Sodalium*
Act. mart. Apoll.	*Acta et martyrium Apollonii*
Act. Phil.	*Acta Philippi*
Act. Thom.	*Acta Thomae*

Aesop
Fab.	*Fabulae*
Prov.	*Proverbia*
Sent.	*Sententiae*

Alexander of Aphrodisias
Anim. mant.	*De anima libri mantissa*

Ps.-Alexander of Aphrodisias
Prob.	*Problemata*

Alexander Filius Numenii
Fig.	*De figuris*

Ps.-Andronicus Rhodius
Pass.	*De passionibus*
Anec. Gr.	*Anecdota Graeca*
Anth. Gr.	*Anthologia Graeca*

Antoninus Liberalis
Metam. syn.	*Metamorphoseon synagoge*
Apoc. apocr. Joan.	*Apocalypsis apocrypha Joannis*
Apoc. Petr. graec.	*Apocalypsis Petri graeca*
Apophth. patr. [al.]	*Apophthegmata patrum* [collectio alphabetica]
Apophth. patr. [an.]	*Apophthegmata patrum* [collectio anonyma]
Apophth. patr. [sy.]	*Apophthegmata patrum* [collectio systematica]

Arius Didymus
    Lib. phil. sect.   *Liber de philosophorum sectis*
Arsenius
    Apophth.   *Apophthegmata*
Aspasius
    Eth. nic. comm.   *In ethica nichomachea commentaria*
Asterius
    Comm. Ps.   *Commentarii in Psalmos*
Athanasius
    Exp. Ps.   *Expositiones in Psalmos*
Ps.-Athanasius
    Ep. Cast.   *Epistulae ad Castorem*
Babrius
    Fab.   *Fabulae*
Basil of Caesarea
    Ascet. magn.   *Asceticon magnum sive quaestiones*
    Reg. mor.   *Regulae morales*
Ps.-Basil of Caesarea
    Const. ascet.   *Constitutiones asceticae*
Carm. aur.   *Carmen aureum*
Cat. ep. 2 Cor.   *Catena in epistulam ii ad Corinthios*
Ps.-Cato
    Dist.   *Collectio distichorum*
    Mon.   *Collectio monostichorum*
Chion. ep.   *Chionis epistulae*
Ps.-Clement
    Ep. virg.   *Epistulae de virginitate*
    Hom.   *Homiliae*
    Rec.   *Recognitiones*
Cyprian
    Quir.   *Ad Quirinum*
Diogenianus
    Paroem.   *Paroemiae*
Dioscorides Pedanius
    Mat. med.   *De materia medica*
Dorotheus
    Sent.   *Sententiae*
Ep. Apost.   *Epistula Apostolorum*
Ep. Barn.   *Barnabae epistula*

Ep. Diogn.	*Epistula ad Diognetum*
Ephraem Syrus	
Apol. frat. quen.	*Apologia ad fratrem quendam*
Corr. vit. viv.	*Ad correctionem eorum qui vitiose vivunt et honores appetunt*
Hom. meretr.	*Homilia in meretricem*
Imit. prov.	*Ad imitationem proverbiorum*
Inst. mon.	*Institutio ad monachos*
Iud. comp.	*De iudicio et compunctione*
Paen.	*De paenitentia*
Serm. adv. haer.	*Sermo adversus haereticos*
Serm. al. comp.	*Sermo alius compunctorius*
Serm. comm. res.	*Sermo de communi resurrectione*
Serm. comp.	*Sermo compunctorius*
Serm. paraen. mon.	*Sermones paraenetici ad monachos Aegypti*
Serm. virt. vit.	*Sermo de virtutibus et vitiis*
Virt.	*De virtute*
Epicurus	
Ep. frag.	*Epistularum fragmenta*
Ep. Men.	*Epistula ad Menoeceum*
Evagrius Ponticus	
Al. sent.	*Aliae sententiae*
Cap. paraen.	*Capita paraenetica*
Oct. spirit. malit.	*De octo spiritibus malitiae*
Orat.	*De oratione*
Pract.	*Practicus*
Sent. mon.	*Sententiae ad monachos*
Sent. virg.	*Sententiae ad virginem*
Serm. virt. vit.	*Sermo de virtutibus et vitiis*
Spirit. sent.	*Spirituales sententiae per alphabetum dispositae*
Evang. Bart.	*Evangelium Bartholomaei*
Galen	
Prop. an.	*De propriorum animi cuiuslibet affectuum dignotione et curatione*
Reb. bon. mal.	*De rebus boni malique suci*
Gnom. Democr.	*Gnomologium Democrateum*
Gnom. Vat.	*Gnomologium Vaticanum*
Gregory of Nyssa	
Diem lum.	*In diem luminum*

Eunom.	*Contra Eunomium*
Inst. Christ.	*De instituto Christiano*
Virg.	*De virginitate*

Ps.-Gregogry of Nyssa

Imag. dei sim.	*Ad imaginem dei et ad similitudinem*

Gregory Thaumaturgus

Met. Eccl. Sal.	*Metaphrasis in Ecclesiasten Salamonis*

Hierax

Just.	*De justitia*

Hierocles

In aur. carm.	*In aureum carmen*

Iamblichus

Comm. math. scien.	*De communi mathematica scientia*
Protr.	*Protrepticus*
Vit. Pythag.	*De vita Pythagorica*

Ps.-Ignatius

Ep. interp.	*Epistulae interpolatae*
Instr. Ankh.	*Instruction of Ankhsheshonqy*

Isidore of Seville

Vir. illust.	*De viris illustribus*

John Chrysostom

In Ps. 118	*In Psalmum 118*

Ps.-John Damascene

Sacr. par.	*Sacra parallela*

Ps.-Justin Martyr

Exp. rect. fid.	*Expositio rectae fidei*
Mon.	*De monarchia*
Quaest. Christ. gent.	*Quaestiones Christianorum ad gentiles*
Quaest. resp. orth.	*Quaestiones et responsiones ad orthodoxos*
Lib. Pont.	*Liber Pontificalis*

Lucian

Pod.	*Podagra*

Lycurgus

Leocr.	*Oratio in Leocratem*

Ps.-Lysias

Andoc.	*In Andocidem*

Ps.-Macarius

Serm.	*Sermones*

Macrobius
    Somn. Scip.   *Somnium Scipionis*
Manetho
    Apotel.   *Apotelesmatica*
Mant. prov.   *Mantissa proverbiorum*
Mart. Ptol. Luc.   *Martyrium Ptolemaei et Lucii*
Maximus Confessor
    Loc. comm.   *Loci communes*
    Schol. libr. myst. theol. *Scholia in librum De mystica theologia*
Maximus of Tyre
    Dial.   *Dialexeis*
Methodius
    Symp.   *Symposium sive Convivium decum virginum*
Nicolaus Catascepenus
    Vit. Cyr. Phil.   *Vita sancti Cyrilli Phileotae*
Nicomachus
    Theol. arith.   *Theologoumena arithmeticae*
Oribasius
    Coll. medic.   *Collectiones medicae*
Origen
    Frag. cat. 1 Cor.   *Fragmenta e catenis in Epistulam primam ad Corinthios*
    Hom. Jer.   *Homiliae in Jeremiam*
    Hom. Jer. II   *Homiliae in Jeremiam II* (latine Hieronymo interprete)
Palladius
    Dial. vit. Joan. Chrys. *Dialogus de vita Joannis Chrysostomi*
Pass. Pol.   *Passio Polycarpi*
Phal. ep.   *Phalaridis epistulae*
Philodemus
    Adul.   *De adulatione*
Philostratus
    Ep. et dial.   *Epistulae et dialexeis*
P. Iand.   Papyri Iandanae
P. Ins.   Papyrus Insinger
Pist. Soph.   *Pistis Sophia*
Proclus Diadochus
    Plat. rem publ. comm. *In Platonis rem publicam commentarii*
    Schol. Aesch. Eum.   *Scholia in Aeschylum Eumenides*

Secundus
    Sent.   *Sententiae*
    Sent. Pythag.   *Sententiae Pythagoreorum*
    Sent. Pythag. Dem.   *Sententiae Pythagoreorum* (fort. auctore vel collectore Demophilo)
Septem Sapientes
    Apophth.   *Apophthegmata*
    Praec.   *Praecepta*
    Sent.   *Sententiae*
Severian of Gabala
    Incarn. dom.   *In incarnationem domini*
Sext.   Sextus, *Sentences*
Socrat. ep.   *Socraticorum epistulae*
Tatian
    Orat. Graec.   *Oratio ad Graecos*
Themistius
    Protr. Nic.   Προτρεπτικὸς Νικομηδεῦσιν
Theodora Palaeologina
    Typ. mon. Lips   *Typicon monasterii Lips*
Aelius Theon
    Progym.   *Progymnasmata*
Theon Smyrnaeus
    Util. math.   *De utilitate mathematicae*
Vit. Aesop.   *Vitae Aesopi*
Vit. Pach.   *Vita Pachomii*
Vit. Sec.   *Vita Secundi*
Zenobius
    Paroem.   *Paroemiae*

Introduction

1. Approaching the Text

Described by Origen as a writing that "even the multitude of Christians read"[1] and by Jerome as a writing whose author was "a man without Christ,"[2] the *Sentences* of Sextus presents the student of antiquity not only with an intriguing interpretive history but also with distinctive insights relevant to at least three broad areas of scholarly inquiry.

First, originating in the late second or early third century C.E. and consisting of nearly five hundred Greek aphorisms,[3] the *Sentences* represents one of our earliest and longest examples of Christian Wisdom literature. In keeping with the conventions of such literature, the text addresses a range of stock moral topics (speech, moderation, education, marriage, wealth, death, etc.), utilizes a time-honored literary format (gnomic precepts and observations arranged anthologically), and draws on sapiential traditions familiar from a wide variety of sources, including Jewish (e.g., Ben Sira), Christian (e.g., the letter of James), Egyptian (e.g., the *Instruction* of Papyrus Insinger), Greek (e.g., the *Carmen aureum*, or "Golden Verses"), and Latin (e.g., the *Sentences* of Publilius Syrus) sources, not to mention more "popular" sources of wisdom such as the so-called schoolbook papyri.[4] Situated within such a comparative ambit, the study of Sextus's sayings can help us better understand how and why the ancient church developed its

---

1. *Cels.* 8.30.
2. *Ep.* 133.3.
3. Of the text's 451 numbered verses, 31 have been subdivided into a, b, c, etc., bringing the total to 490 sayings. The appendices (see below) add an additional 159 sayings.
4. Among such papyri, gnomic texts (sometimes referred to as gnomic "primers" or "copybooks") survive in greater quantities than any other kind of literature, apparently figuring in every stage of the curriculum, from elementary lessons in orthography to more advanced rhetorical exercises. See Cribiore 1996 and Morgan 1998.

own wisdom traditions, appropriating and adopting existing traditions to suit the distinctive needs of early Christian communities.[5] An appreciation for the dynamics informing such developments is of particular relevance for those interested in explicating the actual "life" of the ancient church insofar as the rhetorical posture of a gnomic text such as the *Sentences* is as fully practical as it is expressly instructional, the author's aim being to foster among his readers both habits of moral reasoning and capacities for moral action.

Second, even as the *Sentences* exemplifies a "traditional" mode of communication, there is something decidedly nontraditional about its basic social outlook and moral orientation, both of which are often described as ascetical.[6] As James Francis has observed, the starting point for most surveys of asceticism is the fourth century C.E., the time of the flowering of monasticism among Christians and of Neoplatonism among non-Christians. Consideration for the work of an author like Sextus provides an opportunity to study the character of this phenomenon at a more formative stage, at a time when the nature, rationale, and limits of ascetical practice were still under negotiation. Generally speaking, the activity of early ascetics, many of whom were non-Christian, was viewed with skepticism, the mistrust aimed at them being fueled in part by the perception that they were "advocating norms and values antithetical to the accepted social and political order, and claiming a personal authority independent of the traditional controls of their society."[7] In the case of the *Sentences*, the focal point for the establishment of such alternative authority—the "imaged final product of ascetical performance"[8]—is the sage, who in the author's imagining does not so much reject such roles as priest (e.g., vv. 46a–b), prophet (e.g., v. 441), patron (e.g., v. 176), and parent (e.g., v. 244) as usurp and combine the social functions with which such roles would have been associated, including their function as traditional (i.e., socially mandated) bearers of wisdom. In so doing, our author projects a social world wherein the readers' configuration of meaningful relationships and commitments has been not only significantly restructured, but also significantly restricted. Considered from this vantage point, the study of the

---

5. Cf. Küchler 1979, 553–92; Meeks 1993, 71–73.
6. E.g., Chadwick 1959, 161; Dodds 1965, 32; Edwards and Wild 1981, 1–2; Wisse 1988, 503; Meeks 1993, 147–49; Valantasis 2001, 187–88.
7. Francis 1995, xiii–xiv.
8. Valantasis 1995, 810.

Sentences can help to illumine both an underappreciated chapter in the history of asceticism as well as some of the factors associated with the emergence of ascetical sensibilities and identities in the early church.

Third, while it is apparent that the *Sentences* projects an eclectic intellectual profile,[9] what makes this writing most distinctive from an ideational standpoint is its author's reliance on two generically similar collections of Pythagorean sayings, documents that in turn are representative of a revival of Pythagoreanism that began in the first century B.C.E. Accordingly, the readers of the *Sentences* encounter a significant number of concepts and motifs consistent with the teaching of that movement. They are, for example, instructed:

- to practice silence (v. 427), brevity of speech (v. 156), and wariness in the dissemination of divine truths (vv. 350–352);
- to shun public discussions (v. 112) and the love of reputation (v. 188);
- to adopt a serious demeanor and avoid laughter (vv. 280a–282);
- to learn before acting (v. 290);
- to believe that insolence begets ruin (v. 203);
- to deem no material possessions their "own" (v. 227), but to have them in common with others (v. 228);
- to exercise discipline in sleep, so as to be "thrifty" with time (vv. 252 + 253b);
- in matters of diet, to prefer vegetarianism (v. 109) and avoid intoxication (v. 269);
- to keep "pure" not only the body (v. 346) but also the soul (v. 24) and the intellect (v. 57b);
- to understand that souls failing to observe this standard will be "claimed" by demons (v. 348);
- to cultivate friendships with others (v. 226), especially with the divine (v. 86b);
- to "follow" God (v. 421);

---

9. For examples of Platonic influence, see the commentary on vv. 44–45, 48, 103, 148, 165d–e, 168–170, 199, 391, 435. For examples of Stoic influence, see the commentary on vv. 31, 257, 272, 297, 323, 363a–364, 387–388. For examples of scriptural influence, see part 4 below.

- to consider that the best way to honor God is by making one's intellect like God (v. 44);
- to honor and emulate the sage as well (v. 376a), since he actually "images" God to humanity (v. 190).

Although Sextus would not have been the first or only Christian to demonstrate an acquaintance with Pythagoreanism,[10] the nature and extent of his interaction with this philosophical tradition make the *Sentences* a particularly fascinating test case for understanding how such appropriations would have been negotiated, especially at the practical level. While it would not be incorrect to see the *Sentences* as a conduit through which Pythagoreanism influenced the development of moral thought and practice in the early church, it is also the case, as we shall see, that Sextus does not simply replicate his source material but creatively adapts it to a new setting. Not coincidentally, the evaluation of such adaptations can contribute also to our knowledge of an underappreciated chapter in the history of philosophy.[11]

2. VERSIONS

The Greek text of the *Sentences* is preserved in two manuscripts, Patmiensis 263 (MS Π), from the tenth century C.E., and Vaticanus Graecus 742 (MS Υ) from the fourteenth century C.E.[12] Together they witness to over 600 Sextine sayings, though neither document comes close to preserving them all. Besides the title, MS Υ lacks vv. 59–60, 104, 157, 164b, 183, 208a, 211, 228, 310–311, 313, 341–342, 388, 410, 412, 414–415a, 416, 427–428, 434, 437, 440, 446, 448, 451–453, 455–456, 463–466, 470–471, 474–475, 478, 480–485, 491, 509–511, 516, 518, 530, 532, 535, 538–539, 552, and 555, while absent from MS Π are vv. 7a, 98, 107, 125, 127, 163b, 164b, 165b–g, 247, 279, 297b, 370, 398, 431–443, 458, 496, 556–568, 570–577, 580–582, 584, 587–590, 592, and 595–609.[13] A comparison of the two lists indicates

---

10. Cf. Justin Martyr, *Dial.* 2.4–5; Theophilus, *Autol.* 3.7; Clement, *Strom.* 5.5.27.1–5.5.31.5; Origen, *Cels.* 1.3; 5.49.

11. The evidence for Neopythagoreanism in the Hellenistic and early imperial periods has been little studied, though see Dörrie 1963 and van der Waerden 1979, 269–93.

12. For additional information, see Elter 1892, 3–4 and Chadwick 1959, 3–4.

13. In some cases, omissions in the Greek manuscripts (as well as in the transla-

that several sayings are missing from both manuscripts, their information being obtained either from the Latin translation of the *Sentences* (vv. 434, 437, and 444) or from a comparative source (v. 164b). Besides differences in length and content, the two manuscripts also differ as to the arrangement of material. The order of sayings in ms Υ is usually supported by that of the Latin, Coptic, Syriac, and Armenian translations, and so can safely be judged to better represent the order of the original text. Manuscript Π, on the other hand, organizes its sentences as follows: vv. 1–235, the first half of v. 262, the end of v. 379, vv. 380–405, 236–261, 428–430, 444–450, 569, 579, 578, 583, 585–586, 591, 593–594, 610, 452–454, 406–427, 455–488, the second half of v. 262, vv. 263–379, 489–555. In cases of textual variants within individual sayings, there is a tendency for the reading in ms Π to be supported by the Latin translation (e.g., vv. 13, 42, 154, 156, 166, 188, 191, 320, 326, 344) and for the reading preserved in ms Υ to be supported by the Syriac translation (e.g., vv. 10, 109, 155, 169, 173, 180, 207, 210a, 211, 228, 230b, 253a, 286, 342, 355, 414), though inversed configurations are also evident (e.g., vv. 32, 99, 130, 146, 169, 185, 271, 285, 344, 451).

The Latin version of the *Sentences*, prepared by Rufinus of Aquileia in the late fourth century C.E. (see part 3 below), is preserved in at least fifteen manuscripts, the earliest and most important of which is Salmasianus (Parisinus gr. 10318) from the seventh or eighth century C.E.[14] This version runs to 451 sayings and supports the arrangement of material in ms Υ over that of ms Π, supplying crucial evidence for both the extent and the ordering of the original text. Besides missing vv. 452–610, the Latin lacks vv. 7a, 82d–e, 91b, 163b, 164b, 165b–g, 171b, 210b, and 376b, while the text of vv. 265–266 and 389b–390 is deficient. Rufinus's translation overall is fairly literal, though there are places where it alters (e.g., v. 32), expands (e.g., v. 117), combines (e.g., vv. 82b–c), or misconstrues (e.g., v. 439) sayings in the Greek.

Approximately one quarter of Sextus's maxims, specifically vv. 157–180 (minus v. 162a) and vv. 307–397, is preserved in a fourth-century C.E. Coptic manuscript found at Nag Hammadi (NHC XII,1).[15] This transla-

---

tions) have the effect of eliminating duplications or near duplications of material; see part 5 below. Cf. Chadwick 1959, 153–54.

14. Gildemeister 1873; Chadwick 1959, 4–6; Silvestre 1963; Bogaert 1972; Bouffartigue 1979.

15. Wisse 1975; Poirier 1983; Wisse 1988.

tion is also fairly literal, departing significantly from the Greek on only a handful of occasions (e.g., vv. 325, 380, 392). In cases of textual variants within individual sayings, the Coptic version tends to agree slightly more often with ms ϒ and the Syriac version than with ms Π and the Latin version, and almost never agrees with ms Π against the other witnesses (cf. v. 354). As with the other translations, it generally supports the order of sayings as presented in ms ϒ.

Two different Syriac translations of the *Sentences* are preserved together in some eighteen manuscripts, the oldest of which dates from the sixth century c.e.[16] The shorter of these (sy[1]) is an epitome containing only 131 sayings, arranged in generally the same order as ms ϒ, and ranging as far as v. 555. The longer translation (sy[2]), by contrast, includes all of the sayings in vv. 1–587 except vv. 22, 36–77, 133, 170, 179, 202, 207, 211, 228, 235–239, 253b, 257, 288, 299, 324–325, 342, 350–354, 357–358, 360–363b, 367–369, 380–381, 405, 407, 414, 415b, 422–424, 447, 451, 456–460, 462, 466, 486–532, 535, and 544. Again, these sentences usually occur in the same order as in ms ϒ, though the sayings in two sections (vv. 231–258 and vv. 350–412) evidence significant differences in content and arrangement, the latter even incorporating material of a non-Sextine origin. By and large, the Syriac translation retains the core of the Greek sayings upon which it is based, thus making it useful for text-critical purposes, though it also demonstrates a tendency to expand individual sayings with explanatory material of a Christian character.[17]

Finally, included among a collection of sayings attributed to Evagrius Ponticus are about 130 Sextine sayings translated into Armenian, arranged in basically the same order as in ms ϒ.[18] Although this translation appears to have been based not on the Syriac but directly on the Greek, it has been but little studied and its evidence does not figure in critical editions of the text.[19]

---

16. Lagarde 1858; Ryssel 1895–1897; Baumstark 1922, 170.

17. Verse 36 ("To one who is faithful God gives authority befitting God; the authority he gives is therefore pure and sinless"), for instance, is rendered: "Now indeed power is given to him, the faithful person, as the power of God; to the person who has a clear conscience, being sinless, all power is given to him from God" (cf. 1 Tim 1:5, 19; 3:9; 2 Tim 1:3).

18. Conybeare 1910; Muyldermans 1929; Hermann 1938.

19. A number of Sextine sayings are also preserved in Georgian and Ethiopic translations; for the former, see Garitte 1959; Outtier 1978; for the latter, Poirier 1983, 17.

To conclude, the cumulative evidence furnished by the versions indicates that the *Sentences* consisted originally of 451 sayings, a finding that, as we will see, is corroborated by internal considerations (see especially n. 85 below). It is this collection, then, that constitutes the main focus of the commentary that follows. Sometime after the late fourth century c.e. (that is, sometime after Rufinus made his translation) but before the sixth century c.e. (that is, sometime before the Syriac translations were made) additional material (the so-called appendices) was added, eventually bringing the total to 610 sayings. This appended material can be further subdivided into appendix 1 (vv. 452–555), which is preserved by both Greek manuscripts and both Syriac translations, appendix 2 (vv. 556–587), which is preserved by ms Υ and sy², but only sporadically by ms Π and not at all by sy¹, and appendix 3 (vv. 588–610), which is preserved by ms Υ, but only sporadically by ms Π and not at all by the Syriac.[20]

3. Situating the Text

The earliest surviving references to our text are from the writings of Origen (c. 185–254 c.e.), references that furnish evidence regarding not only the identity of its author but also its date, provenance, and reputation, as well as some of the different uses to which its contents could be put.

The Alexandrian twice refers to the author and his work by name. In *Comm. Matt.* 15.3, he draws on vv. 13 and 273—material he says derives from "a book accepted by many as sound"—for evidence that certain Christians, inspired by a literal interpretation of Matt 19:12, endorse the practice of self-castration, a practice to which Origen explains he himself objects. In *Cels.* 8.30, meanwhile, he cites "a very graceful maxim" (i.e., v. 109)—one obtained from a writing that "even the multitude of Christians read"—in defense of the dietary mandates stipulated in Acts 15:29. On both occasions, Origen refers to the author of the book in question simply as Sextus (Σέξτος) and to the book itself as his maxims (γνῶμαι), designations that correspond with the title of the document preserved in ms Π (Σέξτου γνῶμαι).[21]

The *Sentences* is also cited three times in Origen's extant corpus without attribution.[22] In *Hom. Ezech.* 1.11, he cites the saying (i.e., v. 352) of

---

20. Chadwick 1959, 8. He prints the text of the appendices on pp. 64–72.
21. ms Υ lacks a title. ms Π repeats its title after v. 190 and again after v. 276.
22. See also the commentary on v. 152.

"a wise and believing man" (*sapiens et fidelis vir*), indeed, the saying of "a man I often quote," in support of his practice of deliberately withholding certain theological truths from those unworthy to hear them. The same verse is cited in support of the same practice in *Comm. Joan.* 20.6 and, together with v. 22, in the preface to Origen's commentary on the first psalm (*Sel. Ps.* 12.1080a [= Epiphanius, *Pan.* 2.416]).

We hear little of the *Sentences* until the end of the fourth century c.e.,[23] when, in response to a request from "the gracious and aristocratic Roman lady Avita," Rufinus of Aquileia (345–410 c.e.) translated the work into Latin.[24] In a preface to the text addressed to Avita's husband Apronianus, Rufinus expresses the hope that it will address her need for a theological treatise whose understanding "should not require any great effort." Indeed, the "very open and plain style" of the work that he has selected is, Rufinus believes, ideally suited to meet her needs, especially insofar as its entire contents are "expressed with such brevity that a vast meaning is unfolded in each verse, with such power that a sentence only a line long would suffice for a whole life's training." The collection, then, can be likened not only to "a necklace of the word and of wisdom" but also to a ring, one whose "seeds of instruction" can be kept "constantly at hand," the little book being aptly called in Greek the *Enchiridion* or in Latin the *Ring* (*anulus*).[25] As for the book's author, Rufinus refers to "Xystus, who is said to be the same man who at Rome is called Sixtus, and who gained the glory of being both bishop and martyr,"[26] a reference either to Pope Xystus I

---

23. Although he does not refer to it by name, the influence of the Greek version of our text was felt perhaps most profoundly by Evagrius Ponticus (345–399 c.e.), for whom the *Sentences* apparently served as both a source and a model. See the commentary on vv. 71a, 75a, 81, 88, 123, 125–26, 138, 141, 152, 189, 194, 204, 277, 305, 377, 393, 394, 413. Cf. Sinkewicz 2003, 228–32.

24. Chadwick 1959, 117. Murphy (1945, 119–23) dates the translation to 398–400 c.e. Even though certain sayings in the text (e.g., v. 238) assume a male readership, Rufinus provides evidence that its contents could be deemed appropriate for a female audience as well. Note that Porphyry's *Ad Marcellam*, a gnomic letter exhibiting numerous parallels with our *Sentences* (see part 4 below), is also addressed to a woman.

25. On Rufinus's prologue, see Bogaert 1972.

26. Rufinus's manner of reporting the ascription suggests that he is transmitting a tradition of some kind, though it is one that must have developed sometime after the first half of the third century c.e., since Origen betrays no knowledge of it.

(r. 117/119–126/128 c.e.)[27] or—more likely—to Pope Xystus II (r. 257–58 c.e.), who was martyred during the Valerian persecution.[28] Rufinus concludes the preface by explaining that he has appended to the received text some additional sayings, a reference not to the so-called appendices (see part 2 above), but to material from an unknown source that has not survived in the manuscript tradition.

It is worth noting that Rufinus was not the first or only person to render Sextine sayings into Latin. In 393 c.e., for example, Jerome had cited a certain saying of "Xystus" (i.e., v. 231) with approval.[29] Some twenty years later, he cited the same gnome (again, with approval), though now with the additional remark that its author's book had been "translated into Latin by a certain person who has tried to father it on the martyr Xystus, not observing that in the entire volume, which he purposelessly divided into two parts, the name of Christ and of the apostles is not mentioned."[30] Jerome's denigration of Rufinus becomes even more expansive in *Ep.* 133.3:[31]

> Who could adequately describe the rashness or rather the crack-headedness of a fellow who ascribed the book of Sextus the Pythagorean (a man without Christ and a heathen!) to Xystus the martyr-bishop of the Roman church? In this book much is said of perfection in accordance with the doctrine of the Pythagoreans, who make man equal to God and maintain that he is of God's substance. The result is that those who are ignorant that the volume is by a philosopher, supposing themselves to be reading the work of a martyr, drink from the golden cup of Babylon (cf. Jer 51:7). Furthermore, in that volume there is no mention of the prophets, of the patriarchs, of the apostles, or of Christ, so that he tries to make out that there was a bishop and a martyr who did not believe in Christ.

---

27. The fact that practically nothing is known about this figure (see *Lib. Pont.* 8; Irenaeus, *Haer.* 3.3.3) does not prevent Conybeare (1910, 123–24) from postulating him as the author of our *Sentences*.

28. For information on Xystus II, see *Lib. Pont.* 25; Cyprian, *Ep.* 80; Damasus, *Epigr.* 13.

29. *Jov.* 1.49.

30. *Comm. Ezech.* 6 (translation from Chadwick 1959, 119). Jerome's translations of v. 231 differ from one another as well as from the version offered by Rufinus. The "two parts" to which he alludes are presumably the original set of Sextine sayings and the now-lost material added by Rufinus.

31. Translation from Chadwick 1959, 120.

The man behind the *Sentences*, then, is not Xystus the Christian pope but Sextus the pagan philosopher, a reference perhaps to Quintus Sextius (fl. ca. 50 B.C.E.), a Stoic philosopher with Pythagorean leanings whose teaching greatly impressed Seneca.[32] Such ignorance regarding the work's authorship is particularly deplorable since, as Jerome complains elsewhere, this "ring" is being "widely read in many provinces, and especially by those who preach freedom from passion and sinless perfection."[33] For all its vitriol, Jerome's critique of the text's perfectionist associations was not entirely gratuitous, since, if the testimony of Augustine is to be trusted, Pelagius cited three of Xystus's precepts (vv. 36, 46a–b, and 60) in support of his doctrines.[34] Any heretical taint the collection may have thereby acquired[35] did not prevent Latin scribes responsible for copying the *Sentences* from attributing the text to Pope Xystus.[36] Nor did it prevent the work from becoming popular in monastic circles, where it is quoted, for example, in the *Rule* of the Master, the *Rule* of Saint Columban, and the *Rule* of Saint Benedict.[37]

While the debate between Rufinus and Jerome attests to the expanding popularity (or notoriety) of our text, their testimony (which is of a late and not altogether disinterested nature) is of little value in the task of identifying its author and his circumstances.[38] The evidence of Origen renders the former's (apparent) ascription to Pope Xystus II highly improbable,[39]

---

32. Seneca, *Ep.* 59.7–8; 64.2–5; 73.12–15; 98.13; 108.17–18. See also the commentary on Sext. 109.

33. *Comm. Jer.* 4.41 (translation from Chadwick 1959, 121).

34. *Nat. grat.* 64.77. Augustine here acknowledges the work as an authentic composition of the martyred bishop, though later (after exposure to Jerome's views) he will reverse himself (*Retract.* 2.68).

35. Cf. Isidore of Seville, *Vir. illust.* 1; Chadwick 1959, 120–21.

36. Most of the extant Latin manuscripts attribute the work to Pope Xystus (Gildemeister 1873, xiv–xxiii; Chadwick 1959, 5, 123–24), while the material in the Syriac version is organized under the title "Select Sayings of Saint Xystus bishop of Rome" (Lagarde 1858, iv; Gildemeister 1873, xxxi; Chadwick 1959, 6, 130).

37. See Vogüé 1973 and the commentary on vv. 145, 152, and 184. For citations of the *Sentences* in medieval literature, see Bogaert 1982; Evans 1983; Vogüé 1986.

38. As Chadwick (1959, 112–14, 135) discusses, indecision regarding Sextus's status as a Christian author has continued into modern times. Internal evidence led Chadwick himself to conclude that the compiler was Christian (1959, 137–40), though it is interesting that even among his own students the text is sometimes simply referred to as "a collection of Neopythagorean maxims" (Russell 2004, 118, cf. p. vii).

39. Chadwick (1959, 133–34) speculates that Xystus died an old man and there-

while internal evidence (see part IV below) renders an ascription to a non-Christian figure (or to any figure living before the second century C.E.) virtually impossible. It is best to conclude, then, that our author was simply, as Origen put it, "a wise and believing man,"[40] otherwise unknown, by the name of Sextus, writing sometime in the late second or early third century C.E.[41] The fact that Origen is the first author to demonstrate an acquaintance with the text raises the possibility that its originating provenance was Egyptian, a possibility that perhaps becomes a probability when we take into account the very large number of parallels between the *Sentences* and the writings of Clement of Alexandria (ca. 150–ca. 215 C.E.).[42]

4. SOURCES

The *Sentences* is familiar to modern readers especially from the work of Henry Chadwick, who, drawing on the contributions of Johann Gildemeister, Anton Elter, and others, published a critical edition of the Greek and Latin versions of the text in 1959, accompanied by a series of interpretive essays and explanatory notes. One of Chadwick's major contributions was to explicate Sextus's dependence on two generically similar collections of Pythagorean sayings, the *Sententiae Pythagoreorum* and the *Clitarchi sententiae*.[43] The former survives principally in three witnesses, the most important of which is a manuscript from the fifteenth century C.E., Vienna

---

fore could have published the *Sentences* early enough in the third century for the work to become popular by Origen's time.

40. *Hom. Ezech.* 1.11. Maximus Confessor (*Schol. libr. myst. theol.* 4.429) similarly refers to him as "Sextus the ecclesiastical philosopher" (see the commentary on vv. 27–29).

41. Among possible unattested ascriptions, mention may be made of the Sextus named by Eusebius (*Hist. eccl.* 5.27) as a Christian author active during the reign of Septimius Severus. While a date of 193–211 C.E. would tally with the evidence proffered by Origen, none of this figure's compositions (including a treatise on the resurrection—a topic, as we shall see, of no interest to our author) has survived, leaving us with no basis of comparison with the *Sentences* and therefore no basis for identifying him as its author.

42. Remember, too, that a copy was found at Nag Hammadi (see part 2 above), a document which Rubenson identifies as one of "the few texts that can be used as a bridge between late Egyptian wisdom literature and the early Egyptian monastic exhortations" (2004, 529).

43. Chadwick 1959 provides a critical edition of these texts on pp. 73–94.

cod. 225 (MS D), which contains 119 sayings organized alphabetically under the title αἱ γνῶμαι τῶν Πυθαγορείων.⁴⁴ Ninety-four of these sayings, plus another four sayings, are included also in Patmos cod. 263 (MS Π), a manuscript of the tenth century C.E. In addition, a Syriac version of the sixth or seventh century C.E. preserves ninety-eight aphorisms attributed to Pythagoras, ninety-four of which are also found (in the same order) in MS D.⁴⁵ The *Sentences* of Clitarchus, meanwhile, is present in four witnesses, the most substantial of which is Parisinus gr. 1630 (MS Φ),⁴⁶ a manuscript of the fourteenth century C.E., which has a collection of ninety-three unattributed aphorisms, twenty-two of which are also found in Vaticanus gr. 1144 (MS Λ), a manuscript from the fifteenth century C.E., which contains fifty-nine maxims under the title ἐκ τῶν Κλειτάρχου πραγματικῶν χρειῶν συναγωγή. In addition, there is Bodleianus Auct. F. 6.26 (MS Σ), also from the fifteenth century C.E., which has thirty-eight sayings under the heading παραινετικά, all of which are also found in MS Φ, and Parisinus gr. 1168 (MS Θ) from the thirteenth century C.E., which has twenty-three sayings under the title Κλειτάρχου, seven of which are also found in MS Φ and/or MS Λ. While MSS Φ, Λ, and Σ generally agree as to the order of the sayings that they have in common, MS Θ presents a different, and presumably secondary, arrangement.⁴⁷ As Chadwick also observed, there is one final writing whose study is relevant to explicating the source-critical history of Sextus's *Sentences*, namely, Porphyry's *Ad Marcellam*, a gnomic letter written around 300 C.E. in part to provide the Neoplatonic philosopher's wife spiritual guidance in his absence. This text is preserved in a single manuscript, Ambrosianus Q. 13, from the late fifteenth century C.E.⁴⁸

---

44. See Schenkl 1886.
45. Printed by Lagarde 1858, 195–201. Cf. Gildemeister 1870. Many of the Greek gnomes are preserved also by Stobaeus, including especially a collection of fifteen alphabetically organized sayings in *Anth*. 3.1.30–44 introduced with the heading Πυθαγόρου γνῶμαι. Forty-five sayings (again, alphabetically organized) from the Vienna collection are also found in a manuscript from the sixteenth century C.E. (Vaticanus gr. 743), though these are ascribed by editors to Demophilus (Mullach 1860–1881, 1.497–99).
46. Printed in Boissonade 1833, 1.127–34.
47. Elter 1892, 37–43; Chadwick 1959, 73–74. In analyzing this text, then, it is important to bear in mind that many of its sayings are preserved by only one witness. It appears that each copyist created an epitome of sayings from a now-lost source.
48. Rocca-Serra 1971; Wicker 1987.

Viewed synoptically, the literary parallels that the *Sentences* manifests with these three comparative texts are seen to be not only numerous but also pervasive:[49]

Sextus	Clitarchus	Sent. Pythag.	Marc.
4		40	(15)
10	66		
14		6a	
17		97	
18–19		(30a–b)	
22		(112)	(15)
23	(6)		
24	17		(11)
35			(11)
36			11
41		(79)	
44			(11)
46a		(66a)	(11, 19)
49	4	39a	11
50	11		
51	5		
53	137		
55	7		
57a	8		
61–62			(21)
71b	10		
74			34
75a	(86)	21	34
75b	85	71	34
76		110c	(14)
86a	13		

---

49. What follows is a corrected and expanded version of the catalogue provided by Chadwick 1959, 144–46.

88	14		
92	15	(3b)	(12)
93	16		
97	17		11
102			(9)
113	18		(12)
114	19		(12)
120	20		
122			12
124			12
125	21		12
126			12
127		121a	12
128	22	3a	12
134			13
136			13
137	23		
138	24	(110d)	
140	143a		
141	25, 143b		
142	143c		
145		(92)	13
146	26		
149	27		
152	28	(7)	(14)
153	29		
154	30		
156	31		
157	32		
159	34		
162a–b	36		
163a	37		
163b	35		
164a	39a		

164b	38		
165a–c			14
165d	40		
165f	41		
165g	39[b]		
168	42		
169	43		
171a	44		
174	45		
176	(63, 134)		
177	48		(8)
178		6	
181			9
182		13[c]	
186	53		
190	9		
191		(17)	
198		86	
202			(9)
204			(9)
205		2[b], (116)	(9)
207–208a			9
209		(2[c])	(9)
214	64		
227		(62, 80)	
231	71		
232			(35)
236	69		
238	72		
240	73		
245		(113[a])	
253b	(87)		
255	76		
265	(94, 97)		

270	95		
273			34
274a			34
274b		30ᶜ	
283		84	
285		64	
290	(50)		
294		(89)	
295	105	(32)	
299	(106)	111ᵇ	
301		95	(32)
303			(12)
304			16
305	(126b)	49	16
312			16
313			16
314			(16)
316		(107)	
319	134	105	
325	132	(47)	
326a		11ᶜ	
327		11ᵃ	
328		104	
333	109		
334–335			(35)
343	110		
345	114	(103)	(35)
350			15
351		55ᵃ	15
352	(144)	55ᵇ	15
356			15
359		56	15
360			15
362		(7), 115	15

INTRODUCTION 17

366			(15)
371		51	35
376a		4	15
378		70^b	
381		102^a	16
382		70^{c-d}	
385	120		
387	121		
399	123		
400		35	
402		(102^c)	(16)
404	15, (122)		
406		(94)	(17)
408		83^a	
409	126a		
416			16
417			16
418			16
421	(1)		
422			16
423			16
424	(135)		16
426		14^a	16
427		14^b	16
429		15^a	16
430		10^a, (16)	20
431		10^b	
443		(20^c)	

While the overall situation is obviously complex, comparative analysis yields the following general observations:

- Sextus has sixty-six sayings with parallels in the *Sentences of Clitarchus*. This represents 13 percent of all the sayings in

Sextus and 46 percent of all the sayings in Clitarchus. Of these sixty-six sayings, four also have parallels in the *Ad Marcellam*.

- Sextus has thirty-nine sayings with parallels in the *Sententiae Pythagoreorum*.[50] This represents 8 percent of all the sayings in Sextus and 31 percent of all the sayings in the Pythagorean collection. Of these thirty-nine sayings, eighteen also have parallels in the *Ad Marcellam*.
- Apart from the parallels that they have in common with Clitarchus and/or the *Sententiae Pythagoreorum*, Sextus and the *Ad Marcellam* have twenty-five parallel sayings. This represents 5 percent of all the sayings in Sextus and less than 1 percent of all the sayings in the *Ad Marcellam*.[51] The *Ad Marcellam* also exhibits a number of parallels with Clitarchus and (especially) the *Sententiae Pythagoreorum* that are not found in Sextus.
- There are nine occasions when the parallels between Sextus and Clitarchus exhibit exact verbal agreement.[52] More often, the parallels exhibit minor differences in wording, word order, or both.
- There are two occasions when the parallels between Sextus and the *Sententiae Pythagoreorum* exhibit exact verbal agreement.[53] Everywhere else, the parallels exhibit minor differences in wording, word order, or both.
- The twenty-five parallels that Sextus and Porphyry have apart from the parallels that they also share with Clitarchus and/ or the *Sententiae Pythagoreorum* never exhibit exact verbal

---

50. Counted twice in this reckoning are four sayings that the *Sententiae Pythagoreorum* has in common with both Sextus and Clitarchus. See the commentary on Sext. 49, 75b, 128, and 319.

51. Thus of all the sayings in Sextus, 26 percent (13 + 8 + 5 percent) have parallels in one or more of the comparative sources, meaning that nearly three-quarters of the Sextine sayings lack such parallels, a fact that renders Chadwick's favorite designation for our author (i.e., "the compiler," e.g., pp. 138–39, 152, 154, 157) somewhat misleading.

52. Sext. 10 = Clitarchus, *Sent.* 66; Sext. 114 = Clitarchus, *Sent.* 19; Sext. 128 = Clitarchus, *Sent.* 22; Sext. 137 = Clitarchus, *Sent.* 23; Sext. 140 = Clitarchus, *Sent.* 143[a]; Sext. 156 = Clitarchus, *Sent.* 31; Sext. 157 = Clitarchus, *Sent.* 32; Sext. 164a = Clitarchus, *Sent.* 39[a]; Sext. 385 = Clitarchus, *Sent.* 120.

53. Sext. 128 = *Sent. Pythag.* 3[a]; Sext. 305 = *Sent. Pythag.* 49 (ms Π).

agreement. Overall, differences between Sextus and Porphyry in wording and word order tend to be more substantial than those between Sextus and Clitarchus or those between Sextus and the *Sententiae Pythagoreorum*.

- On those occasions when both Sextus and Porphyry have a parallel with the same saying in the *Sententiae Pythagoreorum*, it is more common for Porphyry and the Pythagorean collection to agree against Sextus in the saying's wording or word order than for Porphyry and Sextus to agree against the version of the saying in the *Sententiae Pythagoreorum*.[54] Similarly, on those (far fewer) occasions when both Sextus and Porphyry have a parallel with the same saying in Clitarchus, it is more common for Porphyry and Clitarchus to agree against Sextus in the saying's wording or word order than for Porphyry and Sextus to agree against the version of the saying in Clitarchus.[55]
- The correspondence in the arrangement of sayings is higher between Sextus and Clitarchus than it is between Sextus and the *Ad Marcellam*, and much higher between Sextus and Clitarchus than it is between Sextus and the *Sententiae Pythagoreorum*. In addition, while the parallels that Sextus exhibits with Clitarchus are strewn throughout the text, they tend to be concentrated in the first half of the *Sentences*, with forty-four of the sixty-six sayings that Sextus has in common with Clitarchus occurring between Sext. 49 and Sext. 177. On the other hand, nineteen of the thirty-nine sayings that Sextus has in common with the *Sententiae Pythagoreorum* occur between Sext. 274b and Sext. 382. Most of the sayings that Sextus has in common with Porphyry, finally, are concentrated in clus-

---

54. See especially Sext. 127 = *Sent. Pythag.* 121^a = *Marc.* 12; Sext. 205 = *Sent. Pythag.* 2^b = *Marc.* 9; Sext. 371 = *Sent. Pythag.* 51 = *Marc.* 35; Sext. 381 = *Sent. Pythag.* 102^a = *Marc.* 16; Sext. 429 = *Sent. Pythag.* 15^a = *Marc.* 16. More complicated scenarios are presented by Sext. 4 = *Sent. Pythag.* 40 = *Marc.* 15 and Sext. 352 = *Sent. Pythag.* 55^b = *Marc.* 15. Cf. also Sext. 22 = *Sent. Pythag.* 112 = *Marc.* 15; Sext. 402 = *Sent. Pythag.* 102^c = *Marc.* 16; Sext. 406 = *Sent. Pythag.* 94 = *Marc.* 17.

55. See Sext. 49 = Clitarchus, *Sent.* 4 = *Marc.* 11; Sext. 97 = Clitarchus, *Sent.* 17 = *Marc.* 11.

ters (e.g., Sext. 122–136, 350–362, 416–429), wherein we sometimes find agreements in relative order.
- Even as Sextus often agrees with Clitarchus in the general order of shared material, there are occasions where Porphyry agrees with Clitarchus against Sextus in the arrangement of sayings.[56] There are also occasions where Porphyry agrees with the *Sententiae Pythagoreorum* against Sextus in the arrangement of sayings.[57]
- Besides the parallels discussed so far, Sextus also exhibits a fair number of partial parallels with the comparative texts (indicated in the chart above by the numbers in parentheses), places where verbatim agreement is limited to one or two words and/or short phrases. Sextus exhibits more partial parallels with the *Ad Marcellam* than with the *Sententiae Pythagoreorum*, and more partial parallels with the *Sententiae Pythagoreorum* than with Clitarchus. Obviously, a certain amount of subjectivity on the interpreter's part figures into the identification of such partial parallels. Nevertheless, their presence in any quantity, especially beside so many "full" parallels, raises the possibility of indirect as well as direct literary influence among the four texts.
- As we shall see, Sextus contains some twenty sayings of biblical origin or character. None of these sayings have parallels in Clitarchus, Porphyry, or the *Sententiae Pythagoreorum*.

Consideration of these factors led Chadwick to a conclusion regarding the literary relationship of these four texts—indeed, a conclusion he found "impossible to resist"—namely, that Sextus and Porphyry independently utilized the *Clitarchi sententiae* and the *Sententiae Pythagoreorum*

---

56. For example, the sayings in Clitarchus, *Sent.* 48 and 49 occur together and in the same order in *Marc.* 8, while Clitarchus, *Sent.* 48 has a parallel in Sext. 177, and Clitarchus, *Sent.* 49 has a parallel in Sext. 547.

57. For example, the three members of *Sent. Pythag.* 102 occur in the same order and (essentially) the same wording in *Marc.* 16, while *Sent. Pythag.* 102[a] has a parallel in Sext. 381 and *Sent. Pythag.* 102[c] has a partial parallel in Sext. 402. Similarly, the six members of *Sent. Pythag.* 110 occur in the same order and (essentially) the same wording in *Marc.* 14, while *Sent. Pythag.* 110[c] has a parallel in Sext. 76 and *Sent. Pythag.* 110[d] has a partial parallel in Sext. 138.

as sources for their compositions.[58] This would best account both for Porphyry's tendency to agree with the two Pythagorean collections against Sextus and for the absence in the *Ad Marcellam* of Sextus's distinctively Christian material. For his part, Sextus favored the *Clitarchi sententiae* over the *Sententiae Pythagoreorum*, drawing on the former more frequently, citing it without alteration more frequently, following its arrangement of sayings more closely, and using up a greater portion of its material (almost one-half, compared to less than one-third of the material in the *Sententiae Pythagoreorum*).[59]

As compelling as this explanation is, it leaves unaccounted the parallels (and partial parallels) that Sextus has with the *Ad Marcellam* apart from what the two have in common with Clitarchus and the Pythagorean collection. One possibility would be to posit a now-lost text, one that (like the *Clitarchi sententiae* and the *Sententiae Pythagoreorum*) Sextus and Porphyry accessed independently of one another. The number and nature of the parallels, however, make the reconstruction of such a source problematic, to say the least. An alternative explanation suggests itself when passages such as the following are considered:

Sent. Pythag. 49: κακῶν πράξεων κακὸς δαίμων ἡγεμών ἐστιν.
Sext. 304: ὁ θεὸς ἀνθρώπων βεβαιοῖ καλὰς πράξεις.
Sext. 305: κακῶν πράξεων κακὸς δαίμων ἡγεμών ἐστιν.
Marc. 16a: θεὸς δὲ ἄνθρωπον βεβαιοῖ πράσσοντα καλά.
Marc. 16b: κακῶν δὲ πράξεων κακὸς δαίμων ἡγεμών.

While the wording varies slightly, Sextus and Porphyry agree in presenting together and consecutively two gnomes, only one of which has an analogue in the *Sententiae Pythagoreorum*.

Sent. Pythag. 55ᵃ: λόγον περὶ θεοῦ τοῖς ὑπὸ δόξης διεφθαρμένοις λέγειν οὐκ ἀσφαλές.
Sent. Pythag. 55ᵇ: καὶ γὰρ τὰ ἀληθῆ λέγειν ἐπὶ τούτων καὶ τὰ ψευδῆ κίνδυνον φέρει.
Sext. 350: λόγου περὶ θεοῦ μὴ παντὶ κοινώνει.
Sext. 351: οὐκ ἀσφαλὲς ἀκούειν περὶ θεοῦ τοῖς ὑπὸ δόξης διεφθαρμένοις.

---

58. Chadwick 1959, 148, cf. 158.
59. Chadwick's (1959, 144–59) presentation of the evidence obscures this fact.

22   THE *SENTENCES* OF SEXTUS

> Sext. 352: περὶ θεοῦ καὶ τἀληθῆ λέγειν κίνδυνος οὐ μικρός.
> Marc. 15a: μήτε βίου μήτε λόγου τοῦ περὶ θεοῦ κοινώνει.
> Marc. 15b: λόγον γὰρ περὶ θεοῦ τοῖς ὑπὸ δόξης διεφθαρμένοις λέγειν οὐκ ἀσφαλές.
> Marc. 15c: καὶ γὰρ καὶ τἀληθῆ λέγειν ἐπὶ τούτων περὶ θεοῦ καὶ τὰ ψευδῆ κίνδυνον ἴσον φέρει.

Again, while the wording varies (sometimes significantly), Sextus and Porphyry agree in presenting together and consecutively three gnomes, only two of which (the second and the third) have analogues in their source material. In addition, Sextus and Porphyry agree against the *Sententiae Pythagoreorum* in adding περὶ θεοῦ to the third saying (though they do so in different places).

> *Sent. Pythag.* 56: λόγου τοῦ περὶ θεοῦ προηγείσθω τὰ θεοφιλῆ ἔργα.
> Sext. 359: τὰ ἔργα σου θεοφιλῆ προηγείσθω παντὸς λόγου περὶ θεοῦ.
> Sext. 360: ἐπὶ πλήθους λέγειν περὶ θεοῦ μὴ ἐπιτήδευε.
> Marc. 15d: προηγείσθω οὖν τοῦ περὶ θεοῦ λόγου τὰ θεοφιλῆ ἔργα.
> Marc. 15e: σιγάσθω ὁ περὶ αὐτοῦ λόγος ἐπὶ πλήθους.

Again, while the wording varies, Sextus and Porphyry agree in presenting together and consecutively two gnomes, only one of which has an analogue in their source material. Note further that Sext. 362 = *Marc.* 15 = *Sent. Pythag.* 115, so that Sextus and Porphyry further agree in bringing *Sent. Pythag.* 56 and *Sent. Pythag.* 115 into close proximity with one another.

Analysis of such examples,[60] then, raises the prospect that what we are dealing with is not a now-lost source, but a now-lost edition of the *Sententiae Pythagoreorum*, one that contained not only different versions of the sayings preserved in the extant manuscripts but also more sayings and that organized its contents differently.[61] Here it is important to bear in mind that aphoristic anthologies generally lend themselves to complex editorial

---

60. Sext. 127–128 and *Marc.* 12 agree in conjoining *Sent. Pythag.* 3[a] and *Sent. Pythag.* 121[a]. A more complicated scenario is presented by Sext. 75a-b = *Marc.* 34, where Sextus and Porphyry agree in conjoining *Sent. Pythag.* 21 and *Sent. Pythag.* 71, though they may be doing so under the influence of Clitarchus, *Sent.* 85–86. See the commentary on vv. 75a–b.

61. Cf. Chadwick 1959, 149–53.

trajectories, as an inspection of the ancient witnesses to Clitarchus, the *Sententiae Pythagoreorum*, and, of course, Sextus himself attests.

While the sample size is smaller, similar phenomena can be observed when attention is turned to parallels involving Clitarchus; for example:

> Clitarchus, *Sent.* 21: ὧν ἡγεμόνες οἱ πόνοι, ταῦτα εὔχου σοι γενέσθαι μετὰ τοὺς πόνους.
> Sext. 125: ὧν ἡγεμόνες οἱ πόνοι, ταῦτά σοι εὔχου γενέσθαι μετὰ τοὺς πόνους.
> Sext. 126: εὐχὴ ῥᾳθύμου μάταιος λόγος.
> Marc. 12a: ὧν ἡγεμόνες οἱ μετ' ἀρετῆς πόνοι, ταῦτα εὐχώμεθα γενέσθαι μετὰ τοὺς πόνους.
> Marc. 12b: εὐχὴ γὰρ ῥᾳθύμου μάταιος λόγος.

Even as the wording varies, Sextus and Porphyry agree in presenting together and consecutively two gnomes, only one of which has an analogue in their source material, the same sort of pattern detected above.[62]

Consideration for such editorial patterns yields the following stemma diagram:

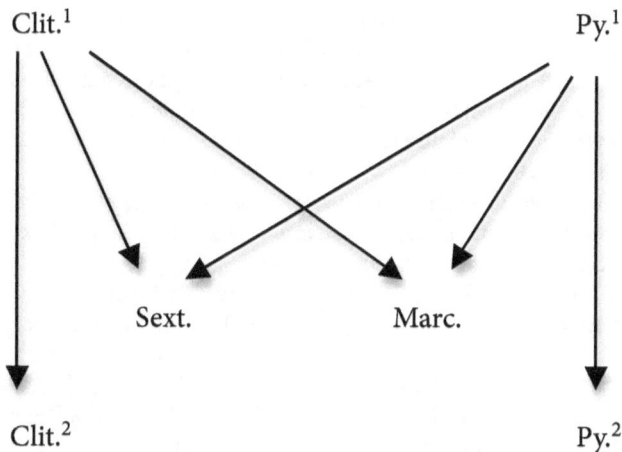

Here Clit.¹ and Py.¹ refer respectively to the now-lost editions of the *Clitarchi sententiae* and the *Sententiae Pythagoreorum* utilized independently

---

62. For another example, see the commentary on v. 177.

by Sextus (Sext.) and by Porphyry in the *Ad Marcellam* (Marc.), while Clit.² and Py.² refer respectively to the versions of these texts as they can be reconstructed from the extant manuscripts. See further the commentary on vv. 36, 170, 177, 204, 273, 350, 356, and 360.

As for the nature of his interactions with the source material, our author's approach can be fairly described as both active and variable. For example, Sextine redactional activity often results in the expansion of a saying,[63] though it is almost as likely to result in a saying's contraction.[64] Changes in wording,[65] word order,[66] or a combination of the two[67] are quite common, sometimes resulting in the reformulation of a saying.[68] On other occasions it appears that our author is not so much rewriting a received saying as he is composing one of his own, drawing on the source material for inspiration.[69] On still other occasions, he seems to combine elements from different sayings.[70] There are also more than a few instances where it appears that Sextus has redacted certain gnomes in order to make them align better with the surrounding text.[71] Perhaps the most distinctive edi-

---

63. E.g., κρεῖττον ἀποθανεῖν ἢ διὰ γαστρὸς ἀκρασίαν ψυχὴν ἀμαυρῶσαι (Clitarchus, *Sent.* 114) becomes κρεῖττον ἀποθανεῖν λιμῷ ἢ διὰ γαστρὸς ἀκρασίαν ψυχὴν ἀμαυρῶσαι (Sext. 345). Cf. the commentary on vv. 36, 50, 146, 165d, 171a, 177, 236, 325, 422–423.

64. E.g., ἄξιος ἄνθρωπος θεοῦ θεὸς ἂν εἴη ἐν ἀνθρώποις (*Sent. Pythag.* 4) becomes ἄξιος ἄνθρωπος θεοῦ θεὸς ἐν ἀνθρώποις (Sext. 376a). Cf. the commentary on vv. 127, 168, 181, 350, 352, 371. A more extreme case is represented by Sext. 429 = *Sent. Pythag.* 15ᵃ.

65. E.g., ἐκ φιληδονίας ἀκολασία φύεται (Clitarchus, *Sent.* 10) becomes ἐκ φιληδονίας ἀκολασίαν οὐκ ἐκφεύξῃ (Sext. 71b). Cf. the commentary on vv. 49, 138, 153, 163a, 174, 178, 182, 205, 231, 240, 270, 274b, 283, 399.

66. E.g., ἄνθρωπον μὲν ἀπατῆσαι δυνατὸν λόγῳ, θεὸν δὲ ἀδύνατον (Clitarchus, *Sent.* 53) becomes δυνατὸν ἀπατῆσαι λόγῳ ἄνθρωπον, θεὸν μέντοι ἀδύνατον (Sext. 186). Cf. the commentary on vv. 125, 152, 159, 198, 328, 359.

67. E.g., πρᾶττε μεγάλα, μὴ ὑπισχνούμενος μεγάλα (*Sent. Pythag.* 86) becomes ποίει μεγάλα μὴ μεγάλα ὑπισχνούμενος (Sext. 198). Cf. the commentary on vv. 182, 214, 351.

68. E.g., ὁ γὰρ μὴ μεταδιδοὺς ἀγαθοῖς δεομένοις οὐ λήψεται δεόμενος παρὰ θεῶν (*Sent. Pythag.* 70ᵇ) becomes μὴ διδοὺς δεομένοις δυνατὸς ὢν οὐ λήψῃ δεόμενος παρὰ θεοῦ (Sext. 378). Cf. the commentary on vv. 17, 202, 333, 360, 381, 382.

69. E.g., Sext. 253b (ἔστιν σοφοῦ καὶ ὕπνος ἐγκράτεια) appears to have been prompted by Clitarchus, *Sent.* 87 (ὕπνον προσίεσο διὰ τὸ ἀναγκαῖον), even though the two sayings have only one word in common. Cf. the commentary on vv. 176, 191, 227, 245, 273, 294, 408.

70. See the commentary on vv. 92, 178, 295, 299, 304, 319.

71. E.g., in v. 301 Sextus replaces συνετός in his source (*Sent. Pythag.* 95) with σοφός, creating a catchword with σοφόν in v. 302. Cf. the commentary on vv. 53, 57a,

torial feature of our *Sentences* is its author's proclivity for inserting πιστός and related terms into received sayings,⁷² especially since πιστός represents what Chadwick deemed to be the best example of Sextus's "characteristically Christian" vocabulary. As he notes, this is one of the more important ways in which our author adapts his "pagan" sources to an ideational environment more amenable to his intended audience.⁷³

Also characteristically Christian is Sextus's reliance on biblical sources, which can be catalogued as follows:⁷⁴

v. 6	(cf. Matt 6:30; 8:26; 14:31; 16:8)
v. 9	Luke 16:10 (cf. Matt 5:19)
vv. 12–13	Matt 5:29–30; 18:8–9 (cf. Mark 9:43–48)
v. 15	Luke 6:30
v. 20	Matt 22:21
v. 30	(cf. 1 John 1:5)
v. 32	(cf. Heb 1:14)
v. 39	Matt 5:26 (cf. Matt 18:34; Luke 12:59)
v. 41	(cf. Luke 12:34)
v. 77	Matt 6:20; Luke 12:33
v. 87	Lev 19:18
v. 89	Matt 7:12; Luke 6:31
vv. 106a–b	Matt 22:37, 39; Mark 12:30–31; Luke 10:27
v. 110	Matt 15:11; Mark 7:15
v. 130	(cf. Matt 6:19–20)
v. 141	(cf. Matt 6:24; Luke 16:13)
v. 155	Prov 10:19a

86a, 97, 149, 162a–b, 163b, 190, 304–305, 430. It is interesting that even as he contextualizes sayings in this manner, Sextus also demonstrates a propensity to drop connecting particles like δέ and οὖν, e.g., ἀπλήρωτον γὰρ ἐπιθυμία, διὰ τοῦτο καὶ ἄπορον (Clitarchus, *Sent.* 26) becomes ἀπλήρωτος ἐπιθυμία, διὰ τοῦτο καὶ ἄπορος (Sext. 146). Cf. the commentary on vv. 165f, 165g, 207, 208a, 230a, 274a, 344, 422, 427, 431. For exceptions, see on vv. 51, 55, 255, 274b, 283.

72. E.g., οὐδεμία προσποίησις ἐπὶ πολὺν χρόνον λανθάνει (Clitarchus, *Sent.* 132) becomes οὐδεμία προσποίησις ἐπὶ πολὺν χρόνον λανθάνει, μάλιστα δὲ ἐν πίστει (Sext. 325). Cf. the commentary on vv. 36, 49, 169, 171a, 209, 400, 409. Note that πιστός occurs 32 times in Sextus but never in the *Sententiae Pythagoreorum* and only once in Clitarchus.

73. Chadwick 1959, 138, 154.

74. Cf. Chadwick 1959, 139–40; Delling 1961.

v. 175	(cf. Rom 2:24)
v. 190	(cf. Gen 1:26–27)
v. 192	(cf. Mark 10:23; Luke 18:24)
v. 193	Matt 19:23
v. 201	(cf. 1 Pet 4:6)
v. 210b	Matt 7:12; Luke 6:31
v. 213	Matt 5:44; Luke 6:27–28
v. 226	(cf. Lev 19:18)
vv. 227–228	(cf. Acts 2:44–47)
v. 233	Matt 5:28
v. 242	(cf. Matt 10:8)
v. 264a	Matt 19:21 (cf. Mark 10:21; Luke 18:22)
v. 271	Rom 7:18
v. 303	(cf. 2 Cor 1:23)
v. 316	(cf. Matt 6:21; Luke 12:34)
v. 320	2 Cor 5:4
v. 329	(cf. Luke 6:30)
v. 336	(cf. Matt 20:26–27; Mark 10:43–44)
v. 340	Sir 4:10
vv. 341–342	Matt 6:1–2
v. 347	(cf. Jas 5:3)
v. 372	(cf. 1 Tim 2:1)
v. 386	(cf. Isa 54:14)

Altogether there are twenty sayings in the *Sentences* that incorporate allusions to scripture, the most popular text being the Gospel of Matthew.[75] Verse 39 ("After his release from the body, one who lives an evil life is called to account by an evil demon until the last penny is paid up"), for example, draws on Matt 5:26 ("Truly I tell you, you will never get out until you have paid the last penny"). Here, as elsewhere, biblical material is not cited verbatim (in this case only τὸν ἔσχατον κοδράντην is retained) but is accommodated to the aphoristic form and philosophical argot of the author's nonbiblical sources. Likewise typical is vv. 12–14:

Sext. 12: It is neither eye nor hand that sins, nor anything of that sort, but one who uses hand and eye wrongly.

---

75. Cf. Köhler 1987, 508.

Sext. 13: Every part of the body that persuades you not to observe moderation, throw away; for it is better to live moderately without the part than to live ruinously with it.

Sext. 14: Consider that both the rewards and the punishments given to you at the judgment will be unending.

This cluster is clearly based on Matt 5:29–30; 18:8–9 (cf. Mark 9:43–48). Observe, however, that the final line (Sext. 14), even as it projects a scenario consistent with that of the biblical source (note especially τὸ πῦρ τὸ αἰώνιον in Matt 18:8), is derived not from any gospel text but from *Sent. Pythag.* 6a, which Sextus cites with virtually no change. Similar again is vv. 155–156:

Prov 10:19a: ἐκ πολυλογίας οὐκ ἐκφεύξῃ ἁμαρτίαν.
Prov 10:19b: φειδόμενος δὲ χειλέων νοήμων ἔσῃ.
Sext. 155: πολυλογία οὐκ ἐκφεύγει ἁμαρτίαν.
Sext. 156: βραχυλογίᾳ σοφία παρακολουθεῖ.

Upon recognizing the allusion to the first clause of Prov 10:19 in Sext. 155, the reader might be excused for assuming that Sext. 156 is based on its second clause. The line's actual source, however, is not a biblical proverb but Clitarchus, *Sent.* 31, which Sextus reproduces exactly. Such integration is typical of the sort of hermeneutic Sextus models for his readers.[76] In still other cases, what the Sextine evidence reflects is not so much a particular biblical text as the particular appropriation of that text in early Christian circles. For example, the saying in v. 316 ("Where your ability to reason is, there is your good") appears to be based not on the dominical logion in Matt 6:21 but on a noetic version of the logion circulating in the ancient church. Compare, for example, Justin Martyr, *1 Apol.* 15.16: "For where the treasure is, there also is the mind of a human being."[77]

In addition to these twenty sayings, there are twenty more sayings that entail possible or indirect allusions to scripture (indicated in the chart above by the references in parentheses). For instance, v. 30 ("God is

---

76. Cf. Clement, *Strom.* 1.1.18.1: "My miscellanies will embrace the truth which is mixed in with the dogmas of philosophy—or rather which is covered and hidden with them, as the edible part of the nut is covered by the shell. In my view, only the farmers of faith are fit to protect the seeds of truth." Cf. also below, nn. 89–90.

77. Delling 1961, 231.

a wise light not admitting of its opposite") can be compared with 1 John 1:5 ("God is light and in him there is no darkness at all"), v. 130 ("Honor none of the things that an evil man might take from you") with Matt 6:19 ("Do not store up for yourselves treasures on earth, where ... thieves break in and steal"), v. 201 (τέλος ἡγοῦ βίου τὸ ζῆν κατὰ θεόν) with 1 Pet 4:6 (ζῶσι δὲ κατὰ θεὸν πνεύματι), v. 226 ("The one who does not love a sage does not love himself") with Lev 19:18 ("You shall love your neighbor as yourself"), v. 242 ("What you freely receive from God, freely give as well") with Matt 10:8 ("You received without payment; give without payment"), and v. 336 ("It is better to serve others than to be served by others") with Matt 20:26 ("Whoever wishes to become great among you shall be your servant"). Of course, care must be observed when drawing conclusions from such parallels. For instance, even if Chadwick includes v. 190 (σέβου σοφὸν ἄνδρα ὡς εἰκόνα θεοῦ ζῶσαν) in his list of Sextus's "characteristically Christian" features,[78] it should be noted that its content derives not from any biblical source (cf. Gen 1:26–27) but from Clitarchus, *Sent.* 9: δίκαιος ἀνὴρ εἰκὼν θεοῦ. Similar issues arise when considering a case such as the following:

> Matt 5:29: "If your right eye causes you to sin, tear it out and cast it from you; it is better for you to lose one of your members than for your whole body to be thrown into hell."
> Sext. 13: "Every member of the body that persuades you not to observe moderation, throw away; for it is better to live moderately without the part than to live ruinously with it."
> Porphyry, *Marc.* 34: "Often people cut some limb to save their lives; you should be prepared to cut off the whole body to save your soul."
> Sext. 273: "You may see people cutting off and throwing away their own limbs in order to keep the rest of the body strong. Is it not much better to do this in order to observe moderation?"

At different points in the collection we find a pair of similar sayings, one whose formulation is more familiar from a biblical or Christian context, and another whose formulation is more familiar from one of the author's non-Christian sources. This phenomenon—one that requires of the knowing reader a certain mediating reflection—is something that occurs else-

---

78. Chadwick 1959, 154.

where in the *Sentences*. Verse 15, for example, has a counterpart in v. 91b, v. 16 in v. 38, vv. 33–34 in v. 176, v. 65 in v. 189, v. 166 in v. 305, v. 175 in v. 396, and v. 389b in v. 433.

Finally, there are another dozen or so additional places where Sextus is seen to be utilizing specific biblical images or concepts, including, most notably, the image of God as father (vv. 58–60, 135, 221–222, 225, 228, 376b). See further the commentary on vv. 158, 166, 184, 210a, 292, 311, and 425. Chadwick also identified a small number of specific terms, including ἐκλεκτός (vv. 1–2, 35, 433), κόσμος (vv. 15, 16, 20, 37, 82b, 235, 405), and, of course, πιστός (see above), that are employed in a manner consistent with Christian usage.[79]

5. Morphology

The *Sentences* of Sextus is a typical example of a gnomic anthology, or gnomologium, and as such can be compared not only with the two Pythagorean anthologies upon which it relies but also with a variety of other ancient texts, including the *Instruction* of Papyrus Insinger,[80] the *Sentences* of Menander, the *Sentences* of Syriac Menander, and the *Sentences* of Publilius Syrus.[81] The monostichic form predominates, some sayings being as short as two or three words (e.g., vv. 68–70), though multisegmented sayings can also be found (e.g., vv. 28, 230b). Admonitions (e.g., vv. 82b, 338), jussives (e.g., vv. 91a, 177), conditionals (e.g., vv. 247, 262), and wisdom sentences (e.g., vv. 176, 337) are all well represented, sometimes in isolation (as in the examples just given), sometimes bundled in various combinations so as to create rhetorically coherent exhortatory clusters, for example, vv. 141–142 (matching conditionals), vv. 190–191 (admonition + jussive), vv. 268–270 (jussive + admonition + wisdom sentence), vv. 295–296 (admonition + wisdom sentence), vv. 310–311 (complementary wisdom sentences), vv. 341–342 (wisdom sentence + conditional), etc. In some cases, groupings are based on structural as well as thematic affinities, as with this pair of matching admonitions:

Sext. 178: ὃ μὴ δεῖ ποιεῖν, μηδ' ὑπονοοῦ ποιεῖν.
Sext. 179: ἃ μὴ θέλεις παθεῖν, μηδὲ ποίει.

---

79. Chadwick 1959, 154.
80. For a comparison of this text with Sextus, see Lichtheim 1983, 187–91.
81. Cf. Küchler 1979, 256–58.

While the *Sentences* as a whole exhibits an assortment of text-structuring techniques, by far the most common is catchword composition, the types of which include simple (e.g., vv. 167–168, 186–187), compound (e.g., vv. 417–418, 422–423), anaphoric (e.g., vv. 143–144, 415b–417), epistrophic (e.g., vv. 7a–b, 430–431), and extended (e.g., vv. 350–362, 411–418) catchword. Another common structuring device is antithetical juxtaposition (e.g., vv. 61–62, 113–114). We also find examples of interlocking structures (e.g., vv. 6–8, 94–97). Connectors like δέ and γάρ are used to link sayings as well (e.g., vv. 29, 255), though rather sparingly. Like other gnomic anthologists, Sextus is unafraid of repetition, sometimes reusing the same saying in different contexts and combinations. Note in particular the following: v. 59 = v. 222 (ms Υ omits the former), v. 89 = v. 210b (Rufinus omits the latter), v. 92 = v. 404 (with a slight difference), v. 98 = v. 334 (ms Π omits the former).[82] As to their length and complexity, the exhortatory units vary, most containing two or three verses, though some can extend to several lines, as we see, for example, with vv. 204–209:

Sext. 204: οὐκ ἀναβήσεται πάθος ἐπὶ καρδίαν πιστοῦ.
Sext. 205: πᾶν πάθος ψυχῆς λόγῳ πολέμιον.
Sext. 206: ὃ ἂν πράξῃς ἐν πάθει ὤν, μετανοήσεις.
Sext. 207: πάθη νοσημάτων ἀρχαί.
Sext. 208a: κακία νόσος ψυχῆς.
Sext. 208b: ἀδικία ψυχῆς θάνατος.
Sext. 209: τότε δόκει πιστὸς εἶναι, ὅταν τῶν τῆς ψυχῆς παθῶν ἀπαλλαγῇς.

The term πάθος functions as a keyword for the unit, forms of the word occurring in five of its seven lines, while the catchword ψυχῆς binds the structurally similar pair of wisdom sentences in vv. 208a–b with v. 209, and, to a lesser extent, with v. 205. The saying in v. 207, meanwhile, is joined to the couplet that follows by the use of the similar terms νοσημάτων (v. 207) and νόσος (v. 208a). Note finally the *inclusio* created by the repeti-

---

82. Note also that a fairly large number of sayings in the original collection have repetitions or near repetitions in the appendices: v. 115 = v. 602, v. 117 = v. 603, v. 227 = v. 594, v. 241 = v. 570, v. 282 = v. 573, v. 386 = v. 608, v. 427 = v. 589, v. 428 = v. 588, v. 443 = v. 592. Cf. Chadwick 1959, 153–54.

tion of πιστός (as well as πάθος) in v. 204 and v. 209: what begins as an assertion concludes as an appeal.[83]

Like the other examples of its genre, the *Sentences* evidences no overall literary structure, though a significant number of sayings in the collection have been similarly grouped by subject matter. In this regard, it is noteworthy that the text opens with a series of coordinated units, as if the author were alerting his readers to key themes in the instruction that follows. Thus, after an impressive introductory sorites (vv. 1–5), we have units on sin (vv. 6–14), on "the world" (vv. 15–21), on the nature of God (vv. 25–30), on God's relationship with humanity (vv. 31–36), and on honoring God (vv. 41–50). Evidence of topical organization is less consistent after this point, though the reader still encounters a significant number of coherent compositions, many of them unified by the use of keyword,[84] including units on the sage's thoughts (vv. 54–62), on justice (vv. 63–66), on moderation (vv. 67–75b), on piety and impiety (vv. 82e–88), on moral action (vv. 93–97), on self-sufficiency (vv. 98–103), on food (vv. 108a–111), on acquisitiveness (vv. 115–121b), on prayer (vv. 122–128), on speech-ethics (vv. 149–165g), on passion (vv. 204–209), on benefaction (vv. 210a–214), on marriage (vv. 230a–240), on learning (vv. 248–251), on children (vv. 254–257), on diet (vv. 265–270), on seriousness (vv. 278–282), on the sage (vv. 306–311), on death (vv. 320–324), on the soul (vv. 345–349), and on caution in making theological statements (vv. 350–368).[85] Sextus not only repeats individual sayings, then, he also repeats topical units (e.g., compare vv. 108a–111 with vv. 265–270). Perhaps most interesting in this regard are the two major instructions on speech, vv. 149–165g and vv. 350–368. The former (based substantially on Clitarchus) offers a "secular"

---

83. Kirk (1998, 121–25) helpfully analyzes the morphology of several instructional units in the *Sentences*, including vv. 67–72, 93–98, and 307–311. See also Lazaridis 2007, 230–236.

84. See especially the commentary on vv. 54–62, 63–66, 67–75b, 93–97, 108a–111, 122–128, 204–209, 248–251, 254–257, 265–270, 306–311.

85. Many sayings in the appendices are also organized by subject matter, e.g., there are sections on ruling well (vv. 452–460), on Cynic self-sufficiency (vv. 461–464), on citizenship (vv. 481–485), on parents (vv. 486–495), on siblings (vv. 496–498), on marriage (vv. 499–517), on children (vv. 518–523), on human nature (vv. 524–529), on education (vv. 540–547), on ruling well (vv. 548–555), and on the nature of God (vv. 556–569). Both the consistency with which their sayings have been arranged as well as some of the specific topics represented (citizenship, parents, etc.) distinguish the appendices from the original collection.

view on the subject, its twenty-six sayings including not a single reference to God, while the latter (virtually free of Clitarchan influence) offers a more "theological" perspective, the phrase περὶ θεοῦ occurring no less than seventeen times. Taken as a whole, the priorities indicated by these various topical units in the *Sentences* are of obvious import for constructing the text's ideational profile, a task to which we now turn.

6. Orientation and Outlook

Although the *Sentences* is properly characterized as a wisdom writing, its focus is not on wisdom as such (σοφία), but on the person who embodies wisdom most fully, the sage (σοφός). Nevertheless, in assessing the content of the *Sentences*,[86] it is appropriate to begin with ontology, this being determinative for both the text's epistemology and its soteriology. Consideration of these topics, in turn, sets the stage for a discussion of the text's anthropology, which can be seen to exhibit social, theological, and moral dimensions. In evaluating these dimensions, it is important to bear in mind the text's rhetorical posture: Sextus's objective is not simply to show what the sage is "like" (vv. 44–45, 381, etc.) but also to show how it is possible to become a sage oneself.

The divine exists as mind (v. 26), ineffable (vv. 27–28), incoercible (v. 306), omniscient (v. 57a, 66), and self-sufficient (vv. 49–50, 382), the creator of all things (v. 31). It is particularly in the being of the divine as wisdom (v. 30) that the various roles adopted by God in relation to creation are best appreciated, just as the execution of such roles most fully manifests the nature of wisdom itself. This is because the exercise of such wisdom is understood above all to be "illuminating" (vv. 30, 95a–b), that is, it is understood as the means by which God becomes not only knowable (v. 406) but also approachable (v. 167) and imitable (vv. 147–148). The God thus apprehended is perceived to be the source, guide, and validator of everything that is truly and abidingly good (vv. 131, 404) or—to use a favorite Sextine term—"noble" (καλός) in existence (vv. 104, 113, 215, 304, 390), including salvation (v. 373), God functioning as the originating and preeminent agent in a vast regime of benefaction and generosity (vv. 33, 47, 176, 242). Because the wisdom that characterizes God is "pure" (vv. 30, 36), the divine is both inimical to evil (v. 314) and utterly disassoci-

---

86. Cf. Chadwick 1959, 97–106.

ated from evil (v. 440), the source of evil being something that is itself evil, namely, the demonic (v. 305). God, then, does not cause evil (v. 114); God judges evil (v. 347), thereby instantiating yet another aspect of divine providence (vv. 312, 380).

God is also defined over against "the world" (vv. 19–20, cf. v. 55), the latter signifying the realm of existence associated with the human body. Participation in corporeity is not itself evil, however, but becomes the occasion for evil when things of the body become the object of desire, rendering one vulnerable to the corrupting infiltration and influence of demonic entities (vv. 62, 305, 348). Any "goods" that the world has to offer, then, are as deceptive as they are transitory (vv. 271, 274b, 317, 405).

While the divine self exists in a perfect unity, the human self exists as a composite of disparate and potentially contentious elements. For its part, the body "belongs" to the world, while the soul belongs to God (v. 55), the soul being the element of the human personality that not only originates with God but can return to God upon its separation from the body at death (vv. 21, 39–40, 127, 347–349), this being possible because it possesses the capacity to "join" with God (vv. 416–419). Despite their different natures, the body and the soul are interconnected (vv. 320, 346, 449), however, especially insofar as it is through the former that the latter is tested (vv. 347, 425). Even though the body was created to cause little disturbance for the soul (v. 139a, cf. v. 276), its legitimate needs being finite (vv. 19, 115, 412–413), the pleasures of the body can insult (v. 448), burden (v. 335), torture (v. 411), enslave (vv. 75a–b, 322), defile (vv. 108a–b, 111), debilitate (vv. 207–209, 345), dehumanize (v. 270), and even destroy (v. 397) the soul if not vigilantly checked—bodily longings making it impossible for the soul to realize its purpose of knowing God (v. 136, cf. v. 72). Mere physical existence, then, regardless of its quality, is insufficient for human thriving. Like the body, the soul requires certain "nourishment." Unlike the body, however, what the soul requires is not something material but something divine (v. 413). Only those who relinquish the things of the body become free to acquire the things of the soul (vv. 77–78), things that make it possible not only to know God but to become like God. Indeed, the individual who excels in the testing that accompanies somatic existence acquires attributes associated with the divine so completely that he can be described as "a god in a living human body" (v. 7a, cf. v. 82d). Insofar as the divine is manifested through wisdom (σοφία), it stands to reason that such an individual is ordinarily referred to as a sage (σοφός) or a philosopher (φιλόσοφος). Similarly, insofar as the divine exists as mind (νοῦς), the element of the human personality with which the philosopher-sage occupies himself, and which he cultivates more fully than anyone else, is the power of the mind (τὸ νοοῦν) that has been established within him (vv. 26, 394), the "something godlike" within the human constitution (v. 35) that has the greatest affinity for the divine, variously identified as the mind (e.g., v. 181), the intellect (e.g., v. 381), reason (e.g., v. 363a), and the ability to reason (e.g., vv. 315–316). It is the exercise of this faculty that enables the soul to control the passions of the body and achieve a "greatness" commensurate with its divine nature (v. 403).

Knowledge of the divine, then, is presented as a matter of self-knowledge, while assimilation to the divine is conceived as a matter of self-actualization, the domain of the noetic serving both as the medium mediating between the realm of the transcendent and the realm of the soul and as the modality by which the soul recognizes its essential kinship with the divine and realizes its potential for deification. This is more than a matter of acquiring learning (vv. 251, 290, 353, 384) or knowledge (vv. 148, 250, 406, 439) about the divine, however, but also of establishing habits of thought that free the mind of sin and cultivate its capacities for moral reasoning. This helps to account for the importance attached to prayer in our text, this representing one of the sage's most fundamental practices (e.g., vv. 122, 124–125, 128). This also helps to account for the rather large number of appeals in the text to "think" only divine things (e.g., vv. 54, 56, 82e, 95a, 233, 289) or to imagine the divine as actually present in the mind, scrutinizing its deliberations (e.g., vv. 66, 57a, 143–144). The complementarity of form, function, and content evidenced by the *Sentences* in this regard is noteworthy. Insofar as its short, striking sayings lend themselves to easy recitation and memorization, engagement with the text itself fosters such noetic habits both by reshaping one's patterns of thought and by facilitating the translation of thought into action.[87] In addition, as with most gnomic compositions, the logic of the *Sentences* presents something of a rhetorical paradox, for while its ostensible purpose is to advance a particular moral perspective, the aphoristic progression of thought is actually fractured and unsystematic, jolting the reader from one judgment or topic to the next. The seemingly random character of the text's organization underscores the underdetermined nature of the

---

87. Cf. Galen, *Prop. an.* 6: "You may be sure that I have grown accustomed to ponder twice a day the exhortations attributed to Pythagoras. First I read them over, then I recite them aloud."

sayings themselves, compelling the reader to make connections, ponder relevant applications, and discern unifying patterns. In this manner, the text not only shapes moral comportment; it also develops capacities of moral reasoning and imagination.

In support of his agenda, the author has amassed an impressive array of metaphorical fields, which together serve both to clarify the nature of his anthropological ideal and to motivate his readers to embrace this ideal as their own. Wisdom, for example, is spoken of as "leading" the soul (v. 167, cf. v. 402), which, "guided" by reason (v. 74, cf. vv. 95b, 104), "follows" God (v. 421, cf. v. 264a) in its "journey" to the divine (vv. 40, 420). Images of movement are supplemented by images of proximity and perception. The soul of the sage is always "with" God (vv. 55, 82a, 143, 444), inseparably "joined" to God (vv. 418, 423), "hearing" (v. 415b) and "seeing" (vv. 417, 446–447) God, who "dwells" within his intellect (v. 144, cf. vv. 46a, 61). A variety of relational images is employed as well. The sage can be described as God's "servant" (v. 319), for instance, indeed, as the ideal servant, his will being so closely aligned with divine reason that he is instinctively "ruled" (v. 41) and "governed" (v. 422) by God in everything that he does, thereby achieving the ultimate form of freedom, that is, freedom from worldly constraints, desires, and deceptions (v. 264b, cf. vv. 43, 275, 309, 392). The sage, then, not only "works" for God (vv. 359, 383–384); he himself becomes the "work" of which God is most proud (vv. 308, 395). Because he shares all things with God (vv. 310–311), the sage can also be understood as God's friend, φιλία with God representing the goal of his spiritual life (v. 86b), a life based on the principle that what is like God is "dear" (φίλος) to God (v. 443, cf. vv. 45, 147) and that in order to become like God it is necessary for him to love (φιλεῖν, ἀγαπᾶν) the aspect of himself that is most like God (vv. 106a–b, 141, 442, 444). A fair number of the priorities already mentioned (likeness, obedience, affection, etc.) are implied by yet another image, that of God as father. Whatever authority the sage wields he possesses by virtue of his status as God's son (v. 60, cf. vv. 36, 375), who, as such, not only honors God (cf. vv. 355, 427, 439) but honors only what God also honors (v. 135), in the knowledge that the best way to honor God is to conform oneself to God as much as possible (vv. 44, 381). Thus he not only confesses God as father (v. 225); he remembers this confession in all of his actions (vv. 59, 221–222), thereby making himself worthy (v. 58) of one who, as God's son, is "nearest to the best" (v. 376b). Recognizing that he is μετὰ θεόν (vv. 34, 82c, 129, 292), then, he organizes his entire existence so as to live κατὰ θεόν (vv. 48, 201, 216, 399, 433).[88] Indeed, the sage assimilates himself to God so completely that he not only "sees" God himself, he actually "presents" (v. 307), "images" (v. 190), and "mirrors" (v. 450) God to others (cf. vv. 7a, 82d, 376a). For his part, God, much like a father, provides and cares for the sage (vv. 419, 423–424), taking pleasure in the sage's accomplishments (vv. 48, 340, 382, 422).

It is important to note that participation in the life of the mind determines not only the nature of the sage's relationship with God but also his place in an anthropological hierarchy. While God may have created everything—even the angels—for the sake of humankind (vv. 31–32), this does not mean that God relates to all people equally. The divine "abides" not in the human intellect as such but only in an intellect that is "pious" (v. 46a), "pure" (v. 57b), and "good" (v. 61), that is, in the intellect of the sage (vv. 143–144, 450), while an intellect deficient in these qualities becomes the abode of evil things (v. 62). Goodness, in fact, is rare (v. 243), the majority of people failing not only to meet the sage's standards (vv. 7b, 400) but even to recognize the sage for who he is (vv. 53, 145) and what he can do (v. 214). And even among the faithful, that is, among those pledged to remain sinless (vv. 8, 247), there will be those who sometimes fail to act in accord with reason (v. 331, cf. v. 285). Within this context, the relationship of the sage to those around him is analogous to that of the mind to the body, which in turn is analogous to that of God to the world. On one hand, the sage self-consciously differentiates himself from the faithless "masses" (v. 214), making little effort to ingratiate himself with them (vv. 112, 360), even to the point of scorning their approval (vv. 241, 299, cf. v. 188), cognizant of the fact that it is not only worldly things but also worldly people that can deceive (vv. 186, 338, 367–368, 409–410). By the same token, he avoids anything that might bring public disrepute upon himself or his message (vv. 16, 51, 343, 396), implicitly acknowledging the judgment of nonbelievers as a measure of how his godlike life comes to expression. Moreover, insofar as it takes the activity of God as its model, the vocation of the sage requires that he interact with a broad range of people in a variety of ways. At the risk of oversimplification, the priorities attendant upon this vocation can be evaluated under three broad and overlapping categories, each of which can be understood as both an articulation of practical

---

88. For these distinctively Sextine phrases, see the commentary on vv. 82c and 201.

self-formation and a configuration through which the sage is manifested to the world as a vessel of divinity.

1. To begin with, the sage commits himself to a life of *personal holiness*, one defined especially by disciplined deportment in matters of diet (vv. 108a–111, 265–270), sexual activity (vv. 231, 239–240), social intercourse (v. 112), sleep (v. 253b), and the accumulation of material possessions (vv. 137, 264a, 274b). A regimen organized around such somatic austerities represents an essential means of training the soul, whose pleasures (vv. 70–72, 111, 139b, 172, 232, 272, 411), desires (vv. 146, 274b, 437, 448), passions (vv. 75a–b, 204–209), and longings (v. 136) for the things of the world must be restrained, such discipline extending to the control of one's thoughts and intentions (vv. 12, 178, 181, 233). By divesting himself of material possessions (vv. 78, 81, 82b, 121a, 264a); by observing the standards of moderation (vv. 13, 67, 273, 399, 412), self-sufficiency (vv. 98, 263, 334), and self-control (vv. 86a, 239, 253b, 294, 438); and by remaining unperturbed at the loss of physical things (vv. 15, 91b, 130), even his own body (v. 321), the sage both practices and demonstrates his freedom from worldly concerns. Indeed, even though he accepts the experience of certain physical pleasures as necessary for survival (v. 276), the sage endeavors to "conquer the body in everything" (v. 71a, cf. v. 274a), refusing to consider anything in the physical world as his "own" (v. 227), that is, as something whose acquisition contributes to his identity as a person worthy of the divine. By maintaining this regimen and reducing his needs as much as possible (cf. vv. 19, 115, 140), the sage emulates God (vv. 18, 49–50), who needs nothing, encratism constituting the very foundation of one's relationship with God (v. 86a, cf. vv. 428, 438) since it represents the means by which one avoids sins like greed (v. 137), intemperance (vv. 68, 71b, 231, 451), and the love of money (v. 76), which, like any sins, must be meticulously checked (vv. 8–13, 181, 233–234, 247, 283, 297–298). Insofar as it represents a path to godliness, then, this encratism is appropriately conceptualized not only in terms of piety (vv. 49, 204, 209, 428, 437–438) but also in terms of purity (vv. 81, 102, 108b, 111, 429). Both body (v. 346) and mind (vv. 57b, 181) must be purged of carnal contaminants so that the latter can serve as God's "temple" (vv. 35, 46a), that is, as a venue of divine revelation. From this perspective, the entire existence of the sage can be understood as a modulation of sacred power, one that provides the world not only with a model of the godly life but also with a living norm and effusion of the holy.

2. Like anyone else, the sage is expected to observe the golden rule (vv. 89–90, 179, 210b–212, 327) and refrain from wronging others (vv. 23, 64–66, 138, 208b, 370, 386), the mistreatment of a fellow human being constituting the greatest act of impiety that one can commit against God (v. 96). Beyond this, the sage has a particular role to play as steward and imitator of divine benefaction (vv. 33–34). In fact, as a *common benefactor* of all humanity (vv. 210a, 260) the sage ranks second only to God (v. 176), surpassing all humankind in his goodwill toward humankind (v. 332), the love of humanity serving as an expression of his reverence for God (v. 371). Convinced that "nothing is good that is unshared" (v. 296, cf. v. 377), the sage not only prays for everyone (v. 372), he freely shares what he has freely received (v. 242, cf. v. 82b) with everyone (v. 266, cf. v. 228), even with enemies (v. 213) and the ungrateful (v. 328). Insofar as they represent a special object of divine concern, the principal beneficiaries of the sage's largesse are the poor (v. 267), the needy (vv. 52, 330, 378–379, 382), and other socially vulnerable groups (v. 340). Although he understands that God ignores those who ignore the poor (vv. 217, 378), the sage gives not for his own sake (v. 342) but for the sake of God and for the sake of being like God, convinced that such beneficence is the only offering acceptable to God (v. 47, cf. vv. 52, 340, 379, 382). He therefore gives willingly (vv. 300, 379) and promptly (v. 329), whenever he can (v. 378), without discrimination (v. 266) or reproach (v. 339) or in order to attract attention (v. 342), deeming it more important, as befits God's servant (v. 319), to serve others than to be served by them (v. 336). The sage's beneficence to humanity is evidenced further in his teaching, especially in his teaching about God (vv. 357–358, 410), which takes the form of leading (v. 182), guiding (v. 166), praising (v. 298), persuading (v. 331), correcting (vv. 24, 103), reproving (v. 245), censuring (vv. 90, 298), and judging (vv. 63, 183, 258, 261) those under his protection (v. 331), even the ignorant (v. 285), the sage's authority over other people being an extension of God's authority over the sage (vv. 182, 288, 422–424).

3. This leads to the third category, one which, if for no other reason, demands consideration by virtue of the sheer volume of material that Sextus devotes to it. As a rule, the sage is more concerned with acts of faith than with words of faith (v. 383), and prefers hearing such words to speaking them (vv. 171a–b). This is due in part to the fact that a great deal of power—and therefore a great deal of risk—is implicated in any speech act, which therefore requires of the sage particular attention to the problem of *speech ethics*, which represents yet another area in which he com-

municates God to the world. Words can "purify" the soul (vv. 24, 103), to be sure, but words can also be used to harm (vv. 152, 185) and deceive (vv. 165a–b, f, 186, 393). The sage is leery, then, of anything that unbelievers have to say (vv. 241, 299, cf. vv. 408–410), even (or perhaps especially) when this consists of praise for the sage's speech (v. 286). For his part, the sage refrains from saying anything that is false (vv. 158–159, 165c–d, 168, 393, cf. v. 165e), deceptive (vv. 165a–b, f, 186), hurtful (v. 185), slanderous (v. 259), blasphemous (vv. 83–85, 223), obsequious (vv. 149–150), ill-timed (vv. 160–163a), or excessive in length (vv. 155–157, 431). He refrains also from overpromising (v. 198), self-assertion (vv. 389b, 433), and boastfulness (vv. 284, 432), convinced that no imposture can remain hidden for long (v. 325) since faith is a matter not of speech but of speech informed by thought (vv. 93, 153–154) and confirmed by action (vv. 177, 356, 359), that is, of actually "being" faithful (vv. 188–189, cf. v. 220). Particular power—and therefore particular risk—is attached to speech about God, even when such speech is truthful (v. 352). This is because a word about God must be accorded the same reverence as God himself (v. 355, cf. v. 439), that is, it must be approached in a state of purity, a state that applies to the speaker, who as he talks about God is being judged by God (v. 22), as well as his listeners, whose souls have been commended to the speaker as a trust (v. 195, cf. v. 361). Accordingly, declarations about God uttered by those who have not been "cleansed" of sin must be ignored (v. 356, cf. v. 173), since even listening to a questionable opinion is dangerous (v. 338), and those who speak falsely about God are forsaken by God (vv. 367–368), the ability to speak truthfully about God having been granted exclusively to the righteous (v. 410), that is, to those who not only say but also do what is pleasing to God (vv. 358–359). Likewise, it is never acceptable for the sage to speak a word about God to those who are "unclean" (v. 407), that is, to the multitudes (vv. 350, 360), to the ungodly (v. 354), or to those corrupted by fame (v. 351), sordidness (v. 401), or overindulgence (v. 451), such speech acts, even when committed unintentionally (v. 401), constituting a betrayal of God himself (v. 365).

In evaluating the significance of such statements, it is helpful to make comparison with the *Stromata*, wherein the practice of esotericism (for which see the commentary on vv. 350–368) represents an expressed strategy. As Clement explains in passages like *Strom.* 1.1.14.2–1.1.15.1, 1.12.55.1–3, and 7.18.110.1–4, in an effort to protect his message from those morally and intellectually unworthy of it, in writing he has not only refrained from openly expressing certain biblical truths; he has deliberately presented his material in an enigmatic and unsystematic fashion.[89] Turning back to the *Sentences*, if we bear in mind the random character of its organization, the veiled manner in which it alludes to biblical texts, and the underdetermined nature of its gnomic contents generally, then it is possible to recognize esotericism not only as a major theme (again, see the commentary on vv. 350–368) but also as a priority that informs its form and mode of communication as well.[90]

Consideration for this priority pertains to one final observation regarding the rhetorical posture of our text, which has to do with the indeterminacy surrounding the relationship between the text's projected reader and the text's anthropological ideal. Certain sayings in the collection address the reader as though he were already a sage, leading and teaching others (e.g., vv. 182, 285, 331), while other sayings present the sage as someone to whom the reader relates as a student in need of correction (e.g., vv. 244–246, 298), while still other sayings address the reader as though he may not yet be "pure" enough to speak or even hear a word about God (e.g., vv. 211, 356). Such discrepancies have the effect of leaving the reader's actual status vis-à-vis the sage uncertain and unresolved, the implication being that becoming a sage is more a process than a goal, one attended not only by constant effort but also by constant self-scrutiny. It is from this perspective that it is possible to see how within every description that the text provides of the sage there is an implied imperative, just as within every imperative to think or act like a sage there is an element that contributes to the sage's overall description, the author simultaneously commending a moral and anthropological ideal for his readers while challenging them to realize that ideal for themselves.

---

89. *Strom.* 1.12.56.3: "My present outline of memoranda contains the truth in a kind of sporadic and dispersed fashion, so as to avoid the attention of those who pick up ideas like jackdaws. When it lights on good farmers, each of the germs of truth will grow and show the full-grown grain."

90. In *Strom.* 5.4.22.1–5.4.23.1, Clement refers to the gnomes of the Greek sages as representative of the esoteric style; cf. Origen, *Cels.* 3.45.

Text, Translation, and Commentary

Sentences 1–5

Text

^aΣΕΞΤΟΥ ΓΝΩΜΑΙ^a
1 πιστὸς ἄνθρωπος ἐκλεκτός ἐστιν ἄνθρωπος.
2 ἐκλεκτὸς ἄνθρωπος ἄνθρωπός ἐστι θεοῦ.
3 θεοῦ ἄνθρωπος ὁ^a ἄξιος θεοῦ.
4 θεοῦ^a ^bἄξιος ὁ μηδὲν ἀνάξιον^b θεοῦ πράττων.
5 ἐπιτηδεύων οὖν πιστὸς εἶναι μηδὲν ἀνάξιον θεοῦ πράξῃς.

Translation

1 A faithful person is a chosen person.
2 A chosen person is a person who belongs to God.
3 A person who belongs to God is one who is worthy of God.
4 Worthy of God is one who does nothing unworthy of God.
5 So if you are striving to be faithful, do nothing unworthy of God.

Textual Notes

0^{a–a} omit Υ • 3^a omit Υ • 4^a omit Υ • 4^{b–b} ἀνάξιος ὁ μηδὲν ἄξιον: Υ

Commentary

As Chadwick (1959, 138–39) notes, the initial sections of the *Sentences* contain a relatively large number of sayings whose tone can be described as "specifically and unambiguously Christian" (besides vv. 1–2, 5, he mentions vv. 6–8, 13, 15–16, 19–20), an editorial feature that has the effect of both projecting an ideal readership for the text and providing a basic introduction to its contents. In the case of vv. 1–5, this feature is evident not only in the choice of terminology (πιστός in vv. 1, 5; ἐκλεκτός in vv. 1–2) but also in the manner in which v. 4, drawn from one of the author's Pythagorean sources, has been integrated into the unit by means of sorites, a rhetorical device consisting of a series of propositions, arranged so that the predicate of each proposition is the subject of the next, followed by a conclusion, which combines the subject of the first proposition with the predicate of the last. Here we have a five-member sorites, beginning in v. 1 and culminating in v. 5, the latter drawing a conclusion from the preceding affirmations (note the οὖν) in the form of a direct appeal, one that is foundational for understanding the rhetorical orientation of the text as whole: to be a believer—that is, to be the sort of person to whom the *Sentences* is addressed—is to "do" something, namely, to do nothing unworthy of God. In an important sense, everything that follows functions as a guide to this end.

The sorites was popular with both sapiential and paraenetic authors in antiquity. Wisdom 6:17–21, for example, articulates a similarly broad moral agenda through a succession of declarations culminating (like Sext. 5) in a command expressed as a conditional sentence. Comparison can also be made with Seneca, *Ep.* 85.2, which offers a progressive list of moral appellations (cf. Sext. 1–3) concluding with a reference to the *summum bonum*: "He that possesses prudence is also self-restrained; he that possesses self-restraint is also unwavering; he that is unwavering is unperturbed; he that is unperturbed is free from sadness; he that is free from sadness is happy. Therefore, the prudent man is happy, and prudence is sufficient to constitute the happy life." See also the quotation of *Teach. Silv.* 108.18–30 below under v. 5.

Title

The title Σέξτου γνῶμαι is preserved in Π, which also inserts the title after v. 190 and again after v. 276. The information it conveys is confirmed by Origen, who in *Cels.* 8.30 and *Comm. Matt.* 15.3 refers to sayings in our collection as γνῶμαι and to their author as Σέξτος (the Latin and Syriac manuscript traditions, meanwhile, name the author as Xystus; see part 3 of the introduction to this volume). While γνῶμαι is used as a title for other gnomologia (e.g., the *Gnomologium Democrateum*; see also Jaekel 1964, xiv), our author's direct inspiration probably comes from the *Sententiae Pythagoreorum*, whose contents are introduced in D as αἱ γνῶμαι τῶν Πυθαγορείων (note that the small collection of Pythagorean sayings preserved in Stobaeus, *Anth.* 3.1.30–44 is similarly introduced with the heading Πυθαγόρου γνῶμαι). For the γνώμη as a literary form, see especially Aristotle, *Rhet.* 2.21.1–16 (cf. Ps.-Cicero, *Rhet. Her.* 4.17; Quintilian, *Inst.* 8.5.1–35).

Sentences 1–3
With the opening words of his composition, πιστὸς ἄνθρωπος, Sextus simultaneously indicates the status and the goal of his prospective reader. The material that follows expands on this epithet by promptly linking it with other identity markers, much as Clement does in *Quis div.* 36.1, which groups together the labels "faithful," "chosen," "godlike," and "worthy" as a way of depicting the different facets of the ideal Christian self (cf. Eusebius, *Comm. Ps.* 23.632.1–3). Like other Jewish and Christian authors, Sextus and Clement agree in construing faith as an implication and correlate of election (cf. Wis 3:9; Sir 45:4; Jas 2:5; Rev 17:14; *Sib. Or.* 2.169, 175; 3.69). As Wilken (1975, 159) notes, while Sextus generally uses σοφός, φιλόσοφος, and πιστός interchangeably to name his anthropological model, it is significant that to begin the work he chooses to focus on the term that would have been most congenial to a Christian audience. Note that πιστός, used some thirty times by Sextus, never occurs in *Sententiae Pythagoreorum* or Porphyry's *Ad Marcellam* (cf. Clitarchus, *Sent.* 75), while ἐκλεκτός, found four times in Sextus (vv. 1–2, 35, 433), never occurs in any of these related documents. The positioning of the former is particularly significant insofar as it brings the *Sentences* into alignment with other wisdom texts from the Judeo-Christian tradition that similarly open with references to faith (Sir 1:14; Jas 1:3, 5) and/or to an analogous concept, the fear of the Lord (Prov 1:7; Sir 1:11–13; *Syr. Men.* Epit. 1). The application of such terms, then, represents a means by which the text projects a recognizably Christian idiom and context.

For Philo, it is only upon someone who has been "chosen" (ἐκλεκτός) and purified through divine grace that the designation ἄνθρωπος θεοῦ can be properly conferred (*Gig.* 63–64). For Sextus, to be chosen is a function of having something within the self that is godlike (v. 35). This would appear to be the basis according to which one "belongs" to God in v. 2 (for the title ἄνθρωπος θεοῦ, cf. 1 Tim 6:11; *Mart. Paul.* 7). At the same time, in wisdom literature it is often the case that election is expressly predicated upon particular qualifications that the chosen are thought to embody in a particularly rigorous or distinctive manner. Accordingly, a sapiential author like ours concentrates less on delineating the characteristics of the chosen as a group and more on delineating the moral demand imposed upon individuals who would identify with that group. In the *Sentences*, this is presented as the obligation that each of the chosen has to "purify" and venerate the divine within themselves as though it were a temple dedicated to God (v. 35), thereby "doing all things in accord with God," that is, in accord with one's election by God (v. 433).

If the readers are to "belong" to God, then, they must prove themselves "worthy" of God (ἄξιος θεοῦ). As Origen explains in *Cels*. 8.25, "not all men are called men of God, but only those who are worthy of God (οἱ ἄξιοι τοῦ θεοῦ)," exemplars of such worthiness including Moses (cf. Deut 33:1) and Elijah (cf. 4 Kgdms 1:10). For the most part, the appellation "worthy of God" tends to be used in contexts where it is suggestive of a certain kind of comportment, for example, Wis 3:5 (see on Sext. 7a); 1 Thess 2:12; Ign. *Eph*. 2.1; 4.1; Justin Martyr, *Dial*. 5.3; Epictetus, *Ench*. 15; cf. Col 1:10; Origen, *Mart*. 39: "By doing the will of God you become worthy of the One." According to Philo, since the thing most worthy of God that the sage possesses is his soul, it is this that he must consecrate to God by purifying the soul of the body's passions (*Leg*. 3.141; cf. Sext. 75b, 136, 209).

Sentences 4–5

The moral requirement of faith, implicit in the concept of worthiness, is now made explicit with a pair of sayings joined by the repetition of the verb πράττω. The believer is not simply someone who "is" (an accumulation of identities) but someone who "does" (an integration of identity and action). Indeed, actions "worthy" of God not only meet human standards of morality (v. 132), they actually render the subject godlike (v. 376a), thereby confirming one's status as a child of God (v. 58). The aspiration to observe this standard expressly informs the performance of specific practices, including prayer (v. 122) and study (v. 248).

Although Sext. 4 and the version of *Sent. Pythag*. 40 preserved in D (θεοῦ ἄξιος ἄνθρωπος ὁ θεοῦ ἄξια πράττων) share the same final term, the more likely source for both Sext. 4 and Porphyry, *Marc*. 15 ("Neither to speak nor to do nor to ask to know anything at all unworthy of God will make you worthy of God") is the version of *Sent. Pythag*. 40 preserved in Π: θεοῦ ἄξιόν σε ποιεῖ τὸ μηδὲν ἀνάξιον θεοῦ εἰπεῖν ἢ πρᾶξαι. Note in particular how the three sayings agree in casting the defining action in negative (μηδὲν ἀνάξιον θεοῦ) rather than positive (θεοῦ ἄξια) terms, in contrast to the version of the saying in *Sent. Pythag*. 40 (D). The versions of the saying in *Sent. Pythag*. 40 (Π) and Porphyry, *Marc*. 15 agree against Sext. 4 in including the terms "make" and "speak," while Porphyry, *Marc.* 15 further expands the gnome to create a triad of thought, word, and deed (cf. Philo, *Mut.* 236–239) that better integrates the gnome with the surrounding material in *Marc.* 15–16. By contrast, it appears that our author wanted to make his version of the saying as pointed and forceful as possible. Note further that Sext. 4 lacks the ἄνθρωπος of *Sent. Pythag.* 40 (D), even though the term's presence would have strengthened its soritical connection with the sayings in vv. 1–3.

The version of the saying in Porphyry, *Marc.* 15 is immediately followed by a saying that parallels Sext. 376a (= *Sent. Pythag.* 4), while *Marc.* 17 has a similar ἀνάξιος saying, "May you never adopt any thought that is unworthy of God or of his blessedness and immortality" (cf. Sext. 46a, 181, 233, 381). *Sententiae Pythagoreorum* 40 (Π), meanwhile, has close parallels in Ps.-Democritus, frag. 302.185 (θεοῦ ἄξιόν σε ποιήσει τὸ μηδὲν ἀνάξιον πράττειν), as well as in two later sources, Nicolaus Catascepenus, *Vit. Cyril. Phil.* 5.2; 38.1 and Arsenius, *Apophth.* 8.89l. For the variant of v. 4 preserved in Υ (ἀνάξιος ὁ μηδὲν ἄξιον θεοῦ πράττων), cf. Ps.-Clement, *Hom.* 13.10.

Having moved from identity to action, Sextus next moves from description to prescription, in essence extending an invitation for anyone who endeavors to be faithful (for this use of ἐπιτηδεύω, cf. *Cat. ep. 2 Cor.* 441) to comply with a standard of comportment that centers on the nature of God and thereby embrace the hortatory agenda set forth by the ensuing text. Formally, then, the final line of the sorites turns the indicative of v. 4 ("does") into an imperative ("do"), specifically, a conditional + imperative, one of our author's favorite grammatical constructions (cf. vv. 15, 91b, 173, 247, 262, 356). The aim here is formulated negatively, effectively anticipating the theme and tone of the next section (vv. 6–14), though it is important to note that in the *Sentences* as whole the task of living faithfully is explicated in both its positive and negative dimensions. In examining Sextus's sorites as a whole, and v. 5 in particular, comparison can be made with *Teach. Silv.* 108.18–30, which links the obligation to do nothing unworthy of God with the aim of becoming like God, a critical theme for our author as well, indeed, one that he will mention very shortly (see below on v. 7a): "The rational man is he who fears God. He who fears God does nothing insolent. And he who guards himself against doing anything insolent is one who keeps his guiding principle. Although he is a man who exists on earth, he makes himself like God. But he who makes himself like God is one who does nothing unworthy of God."

Sentences 6–14

Text

6   ὀλιγόπιστος ἐν πίστει ἄπιστος.
7a πιστὸς ἐν δοκιμῇ πίστεως θεὸς ἐν ἀνθρώπου σώματι ζῶντι.
7b ἄπιστος ἐν πίστει νεκρὸς ἄνθρωπος ἐν σώματι ζῶντι.
8   ᵃπιστὸς ἀληθείᾳᵃ ὁ ἀναμάρτητος.
9   μέχρι καὶᵃ τῶν ἐλαχίστων ἀκριβῶς βίου.
10 οὐᵃ μικρὸν ἐν βίῳ τὸ παρὰ μικρόν.
11 πᾶν ἁμάρτημα ἀσέβημα ἡγοῦ.
12 οὐκ ὀφθαλμὸς οὐδὲ χεὶρ ἁμαρτάνει οὐδέ τι τῶν ὁμοίων, ᵃἀλλ' ὁ κακῶς χρώμενοςᵃ χειρὶ καὶ ὀφθαλμῷ.
13 πᾶν μέλος τοῦ σώματος ᵃἀναπεῖθόν σεᵃ μὴ σωφρονεῖν ῥῖψον· ἄμεινον γὰρ χωρὶς τοῦ μέλους ζῆν σωφρόνωςᵇ ἢ μετὰ τοῦᶜ μέλους ὀλεθρίωςᵈ.
14 ἀθανάτους σοιᵃ νόμιζε παρὰ τῇ κρίσει καὶ τὰς τιμὰς ἔσεσθαι καὶ τὰς τιμωρίας.

Translation

6   In faith, one with little faith is one without faith.
7a One who is faithful in a test of faith is a god in a living human body.
7b In faith, one without faith is a dead person in a living body.
8   Truly faithful is the one who is sinless.
9   Regarding even the least of matters, live strictly.
10 In life, a small shortfall is not small.
11 Deem every sin an impious act.
12 It is neither eye nor hand that sins, nor anything of that sort, but one who uses hand and eye wrongly.
13 Every part of the body that persuades you not to observe moderation, throw away; for it is better to live moderately without the part than to live ruinously with it.
14 Consider that both the rewards and the punishments given to you at the judgment will be unending.

Textual Notes

7a omit Π, lat • 8ᵃ⁻ᵃ πιστὸς ἐν ἀληθείᾳ: Υ; μὴ ἁμαρτάνων: Π • 9ᵃ omit Π • 10ᵃ οὐ γὰρ: Υ, sy² • 12ᵃ⁻ᵃ ἀλλὰ τὸ κακῶς ὁρώμενον ἐν: Υ • 13ᵃ⁻ᵃ ᾧ τι ἀναίτιον: Π • 13ᵇ omit Π, lat • 13ᶜ omit Π • 13ᵈ ὀλεθρίως ζῆν: Υ • 14ᵃ omit Υ

Commentary

Having concluded that the faithful will do nothing unworthy of God (v. 5), the author proceeds to address a prominent category of such conduct, namely, sin. Note especially ἀναμάρτητος (v. 8), ἁμάρτημα (v. 11) and ἁμαρτάνει (v. 12), as well as κακῶς χρώμενος (v. 12). References to πιστός in vv. 1, 5, 7a, and 8 help to integrate the two sections lexically; note also πίστις (vv. 6, 7a, 7b), ὀλιγόπιστος (v. 6), and ἄπιστος (vv. 6, 7b). The general outlook reflected in vv. 1–14 as a whole is effectively summarized by two sayings found later in the collection, v. 234 ("In calling yourself faithful, you have pledged not to sin against God") and v. 247 ("If you want to be faithful above all do not sin; but if you do, do not commit the same one twice"). Given such priorities, it is not surprising that in vv. 6–14 an emphasis is placed on moral stringency and meticulousness. The faithful must endeavor to achieve a sinlessness that is practically godlike, scrutinizing even the most trivial of moral decisions, especially when it comes to controlling the body.

Sentence 6

The four precepts in vv. 6–8 are joined by an interlocking structure, vv. 6 and 7b describing the ἄπιστος (note also the parallel positioning of ἐν πίστει), vv. 7a and 8 the πιστός, that word occupying the first position in each line. The term ὀλιγόπιστος, meanwhile, appears to be of Christian derivation, familiar especially from Matt 6:30; 8:26 (cf. Mark 4:40); 14:31; 16:8; cf. Luke 12:28. In contrast to its usage in the first gospel, for Sextus the term refers not to insufficient or anxious faith but to the absence of faith, something that is a matter for reproach (v. 400, cf. v. 241). The uncompromising nature of his position on faith is redolent of the moral rigor espoused in such texts as *T. Ash.* 2.1–10 (cf. on Sext. 9). Comparison may also be made with *Strom.* 4.7.42.4, where Clement insists that members of the church who deny their status as Christians should be referred to not as people of little faith but as faithless hypocrites.

Sentence 7a

For the idea that a person's worthiness (see on vv. 4–5) is demonstrated through the experience of various trials, see Wis 3:5: "Having been disciplined a little, (the righteous) will receive great good, because God tested them and found them worthy of himself." Statements like this are representative of a broader trend among moralists of the time, according to which the superiority of the sage is depicted in terms of his ability to overcome hardships. The immediate context (see vv. 8, 11, 12) suggests that for Sextus what makes such trials tests "of faith" is that they occur especially when one is tempted to sin. For the expression *test of faith*, compare Jas 1:3 and 1 Pet 1:7. Martyrdom, of course, would represent an extreme instance of such testing (e.g., Eusebius, *Hist. eccl.* 6.4.2), though what Sextus intends appears to be more comprehensive, encompassing not just the sort of "drastic situation" mentioned in v. 200, but all occasions for sin, even the seemingly most minor (vv. 9–10). Cf. Sir 2:1–11.

It is important to bear in mind, however, that for the person striving to be worthy of God, resistance to sin is not simply a matter of obeying God but constitutes a means of becoming like God. See v. 190 ("Revere a wise man as a living image of God"), v. 307 ("A wise man presents God to human beings"), and v. 376a ("A human being worthy of God is a god among human beings"). That such godlike status is manifested specifically in "a living human body" is appropriate insofar as it is through the body that the faithful are tested by God (v. 425). Cf. v. 82d: "The soul of a God-fearing person is a god in a body." In this regard, the somatic demonstration envisaged by the precept in v. 7a brings to mind 2 Cor 4:7–11 and its description of the Pauline body, which in contending with various hardships is said to manifest something divine. While what the apostolic body bears is the death and life of Jesus, however, what the body of the Sextine sage bears is a divine impassivity (see on v. 15). In the same vein, it is important to note that for our author it is not the body itself that is capable of becoming godlike, but the intellect, the aspect of the self in which the divine is said to "dwell" (v. 144, cf. vv. 46a, 450). Both the concept and the language are illustrated by Seneca in *Ep.* 41.4: "If you see a man who is unafraid in the midst of dangers, untouched by desires, happy in adversity, peaceful amid the storm … will not a feeling of reverence for him steal over you? Will you not say, 'This quality is too great and too lofty to be regarded as resembling this petty body in which it dwells? A divine power has descended upon that man.'" Similarly, in *Ep.* 31.11, he lauds the soul that, because it is "upright, good, and great," never yields to the power of fortune: "What else could you call such a soul than a god dwelling as a guest in a human body?" That the concept of deification penetrated early Christian circles at this time is evidenced by Clement, according to whom all those worthy of being called faithful are properly called "noble and godlike" (*Quis div.* 36.1) owing to the fact that the one who obeys God "is fully perfected after the likeness of his teacher, and thus becomes a god while still moving about in the flesh" (*Strom.* 7.16.101.4; cf. *Protr.* 1.8.4; 11.114.4; *Paed.* 1.6.26.1; also the quotation of *Teach. Silv.* 108.18–30 above under v. 5).

Sentence 7b

The antithetical juxtaposition of v. 7a and v. 7b is reinforced by the lines' similar endings: ἐν ἀνθρώπου σώματι ζῶντι in the former and ἄνθρωπος ἐν σώματι ζῶντι in the latter. Just as faith is seen to have moral connotations, the way that faithlessness corrupts human existence is construed in moral terms as well. The faithlessness under discussion here comes to expression for our author especially in the form of a sinful life. It is this, according to v. 397, and not physical death, that "destroys the soul" (cf. vv. 175, 208b). The sinner can therefore be properly described as physically alive but morally dead: "a dead human being in a living body." Cf. Porphyry, *Abst.* 4.21 (= Democritus, frag. 160): "To live badly, without intelligence or temperance or piety, is not bad life, but long death." For the concept of moral or spiritual death, see also 1 Tim 5:6; Rev 3:1; Herm. *Sim.* 9.21.2–4; 9.28.6; Musonius Rufus, frag. 53. Related are the Philonic concept of the death of the soul (e.g., *Her.* 290; *Fug.* 54–61; *Spec.* 1.345; *QG* 1.51) and the Pauline concept of being dead in one's sins (Col 2:13; Eph 2:1, 5). See also Philo, *QG* 1.70: "But from the prayers of evil men he turns away his face, considering that—even though they enjoy the prime of life—they are dead to true life and bear their body with them like a tomb that they may bury their unhappy soul in it" (for the Pythagorean conception of the σῶμα as σῆμα, see Plato, *Crat.* 400b–c; *Gorg.* 493a). A common denominator for all of these texts is a basic anthropological assumption: just as the body depends on the soul for its life, the soul itself depends on something for its proper existence and functioning. In the case of Sextus, this psychic life principle is the intellect and its capacity for virtue and assimilation to the divine (see on vv. 35, 44–46a). Bodily existence, then, regardless of its character, is not sufficient for human thriving (cf. vv. 133, 201), a point made also by one of Sextus's sources: "If you do not rise above the flesh, you will bury the soul in the flesh" (*Sent. Pythag.* 108).

Sentence 8

The faithful person, having received "sinless" power from God (v. 36, cf. v. 60), dedicates his "sinless" heart to God (v. 46b), the use of καρδία suggesting that the sage's participation in sinlessness extends even into the realm of his inner thoughts and intentions (see on v. 12); cf. v. 596: "Consider even the intention to sin to be for you a sin." As Clement explains in *Paed.* 1.2.4.3, to never sin in any way is a form of perfection that belongs to God alone. To never sin deliberately, however, a state proper to the sage, places one in an order next to the divine (cf. Philo, *Fug.* 157; *Abr.* 26; *Virt.* 176–177). It is in the latter sense that the person of faith would appear to be "a god in a living human body" (v. 7a). Elsewhere Sextus adopts a more realistic posture toward sin, for example, in v. 247 ("If you want to be faithful above all do not sin; but if you do, do not commit the same one twice"), v. 283 ("It is best not to sin, but having sinned, it is better to acknowledge it than to ignore it"), and v. 298 (cf. v. 572). This can be contrasted with the ideal sage as envisaged by Stoic thinkers: incapable of error or of assenting to anything false (Diogenes Laertius, *Vit. phil.* 7.121–122), even Zeus cannot surpass him in virtue (Plutarch, *Comm. not.* 1076a); cf. *SVF* 3:548–566.

Sentences 9–10

The reader of the *Sentences* is called upon not only to live "well" (v. 196), that is, in accordance with God's will (v. 201), but to live as one who ranks among all things second only to God (v. 34). Given the comments made above, it is obvious that such a life requires meticulousness, especially with regard to sin. As Clement explains in *Paed.* 1.2.4.2, the faithful must strive to the best of their ability to sin as little as possible (ἐλάχιστα ἁμαρτάνειν), since there is nothing more urgent than eliminating the soul's passions and blocking its sinful proclivities. Especially in light of the reference to πιστός in v. 8, it is probably safe to conclude that Sextus's formulation of this sentiment draws on Luke 16:10: "One who is faithful in very little (ὁ πιστὸς ἐν ἐλαχίστῳ) is faithful also in much; and one who is unjust in very little is unjust also in much." Cf. Matt 25:21; Luke 19:17; 2 *Clem.* 8.5; Basil of Caesarea, *Reg. mor.* 31.713. Comparison may also be made with texts that enjoin strictness in observance of the law, such as Matt 5:19 (also with ἐλαχίστων); Jas 2:10; 4 Macc 5:20 ("To transgress the law in matters either small or great is of equal seriousness"); and Philo, *Leg.* 3.241; *m. Avot* 2:1 ("Be as meticulous in a small religious duty as in a large one"). A similar spirit of moral perfectionism is evident in the Stoic paradox that "whoever has one vice has them all" (e.g., Seneca, *Ben.* 5.15.1; Augustine, *Ep.* 167.4; see further on v. 297). For the criterion of "strictness" in life, see also Sir 51:19; Diogenes Laertius, *Vit. phil.* 9.12; Gregory of Nyssa, *Virg.*

6.n.1–2; Ps.-Basil of Caesarea, *Const. ascet.* 31.1388. As Eusebius explains, those who observe a strict way of life "cut away the very roots of every base passion from the mind itself" (*Praep. ev.* 1.4.9).

The explanatory statement in v. 10 (note the use of γάρ in Υ) supports the appeal of v. 9, the two lines being bound by the catchword βίος. For the latter, Sextus draws on Clitarchus, *Sent.* 66 (Φ), which he reproduces exactly: οὐ μικρὸν ἐν βίῳ τὸ παρὰ μικρόν. Philo deploys a similar wordplay in *Spec.* 4.191: "For the genuine ministers of God have carefully sharpened their intellect, deeming the smallest error not to be small (τὸ παρὰ μικρὸν οὐ μικρὸν σφάλμα ἡγούμενοι)." This is because in every matter they have consideration for the surpassing greatness of the one to whom they owe service. Cf. Sir 19:1 ("One who despises small things will fail little by little"); Dorotheus, *Sent.* 10; Menander, *Mon.* 245: "If you do not guard the small you will lose the great."

Sentence 11

This gnome is repeated as v. 297b in one of the Greek manuscripts. There the saying appears to be added by way of commentary on v. 297, which uses language similar to that of v. 10: "Do not consider one sin smaller (μικρότερον) than another." In biblical wisdom, sin is frequently associated with both impiety and the impious, for example, Job 34:8; Prov 8:36; 10:16; 11:31 (cf. 1 Pet 4:18); 21:4; 29:16; Sir 12:6; 41:5 (cf. Origen, *Exp. Prov.* 17.185). The same kind of equivalence is asserted by Musonius Rufus, though the scope of impious sins under his purview is more circumscribed than it is for Sextus: "For just as one who is unjust to strangers sins against Zeus, god of hospitality, and one who is unjust to friends sins against Zeus, god of friendship, so whoever is unjust to his own family sins against the gods of his fathers and against Zeus, guardian of the family, from whom wrongs done to the family are not hidden, and surely one who sins against the gods is impious" (frag. 15.96.28–15.98.1). In the *Sentences*, sinful actions render one morally impure (v. 102) and therefore unfit to approach the divine (v. 370, cf. v. 46b), the greatest impiety against God consisting of actions that harm fellow human beings (v. 96, cf. v. 491).

Sentences 12–14

This cluster of sayings is based on Matt 5:29–30 and 18:8–9 (cf. Mark 9:43–48). Verse 12 introduces the principle of interpretation: moral outcomes are determined not by the body and its impulses, but by the will of the agent who has power over them. The admonition of v. 13 then applies this principle to the readers' moral performance, buttressed by a motive sentence in the form of a "better" saying. A reminder about the final judgment in v. 14 serves as a divine sanction.

The chiastic structure of the first line in the cluster (eye/hand//hand/eye) contributes to its internal unity. The order of the first pair corresponds with Matt 5:29–30 (though there each part is designated as belonging to the body's right side), while Matt 18:8–9 has hand or foot/eye (Mark 9:43–47 has hand/foot/eye). In lieu of σκανδαλίζω in Matt 5:29–30 and 18:8–9, Sextus has ἁμαρτάνω (cf. vv. 8, 11). It is the nature of the body to cause few troubles for the soul (v. 139a), bodily members becoming burdensome only to those who do not know how to make proper use of them (v. 335). Cf. Clement, *Quis div.* 18.3: "Neither strength nor greatness of body confers life, nor does insignificance of the limbs (μελῶν) destroy, but the soul by its use (χρωμένη) of these provides the cause leading to either result." From this perspective, doing something like amputating body parts would be pointless, since the source of sin is not the body, but one's thoughts and intentions, which must be purified (v. 181, cf. vv. 46b, 174, 233, 596).

The initial words of v. 13 seem to be based on μελός and σῶμα in Matt 5:29–30 (cf. v. 273). Here in lieu of σκανδαλίζω our author supplies μὴ σωφρονεῖν, thereby introducing an important theme for the text and implicitly correlating sin with intemperance. Indeed, one of the highest priorities set upon readers of the *Sentences* involves training themselves "to provide ... for the body with moderation" (v. 412, cf. vv. 67, 235, 237, 273, 399, 499, 508). Verse 13 also replaces βάλε (Matt 5:29–30; 18:8–9) with ῥῖψον (cf. v. 273) and changes the wording of the "better" saying from συμφέρει γάρ σοι κτλ (Matt 5:29–30) or καλόν σοί ἐστιν κτλ (Matt 18:8–9) to ἄμεινον γάρ κτλ (cf. vv. 165a, 283, 366). The assertion regarding how one ought to live (ζῆν), meanwhile, appears to draw on the reference to entering (eternal) life in Matt 18:8–9 (τὴν ζωὴν εἰσελθεῖν), though what Sextus is contrasting at this point are not different eschatological outcomes (as in v. 14), but different moral directions, that is, either living moderately (σωφρόνως) or living ὀλεθρίως, the latter referring to a manner of life that leads to ruin, death, or both—immoderation generally being understood as one of the leading causes of ὄλεθρος (e.g., Dionysius of Halicarnassus, *Ant. or.* 1; Josephus, *Ant.* 19.210; Cassius Dio, *Hist. rom.* 52.14.5; Ps.-Clement, *Hom.* 13.13).

In *Comm. Matt.* 15.3, Origen cites v. 13 (changing μέλος to μέρος and dropping τοῦ σώματος) together with a parallel saying in v. 273 as evidence that certain Christians endorse a literal interpretation of Matt 19:12 (see

Chadwick 1959, 109–12). However, given the "mild" form of asceticism embraced by Sextus generally (see for example the discussion of vv. 230a–240 below) as well as the specific principle advanced in v. 12 (note how v. 273 is attached to a similar principle in v. 274a), our author would probably have agreed with Origen that what the Christian ought to amputate are not the members of the body but "the passions of the soul" (*Comm. Matt.* 15.4). The problem for Sextus is not with the body as such but with the moral agency of its owner, who must set aside not the body but the "things" of the body as much as possible (v. 78, cf. vv. 71a, 101, 115, 274a). Clement similarly interprets Matt 5:29–30 as a command to cast off lust (*Paed.* 3.11.70.1) or riches (*Quis div.* 24.1–2). Cf. Ps.-Clement, *Rec.* 7.37: "But let none of you think, brethren, that the Lord commended the cutting off of members. His meaning is that the purpose should be cut off, not the members, and the causes that allure to sin."

Despite the evidence proffered by Origen in *Comm. Matt.* 15.3 (cf. Justin Martyr, *1 Apol.* 29.1–2; and for Origen's alleged self-mutilation, Eusebius, *Hist. eccl.* 6.8.1–5), it does not appear that the practice of self-castration emerged as a problem for the church until the fourth century. In Christian circles during Sextus's time one would have been more likely to encounter a "spiritual" eunuch than a real one (e.g., Athenagoras, *Leg.* 33.2–4; Clement, *Strom.* 3.1.1.1–4; 3.15.99.1), and certain authors even condemn the practice (e.g., *Act. Joan.* 53–54). With regard to the patristic reception of Matt 19:12, as Daniel Caner has shown, "none of the exegeses that have come down to us advocate a literal interpretation of the passage" (1997, 404). For the type of "persuading" Sextus has in mind here, comparison may be made with Xenophon, *Mem.* 1.2.23: "So it certainly seems to me that everything that is noble and good is the result of training, especially when it comes to moderation. For in the same body along with the soul are planted pleasures that plead (πείθουσιν) with her, 'Don't observe moderation (μὴ σωφρονεῖν), but make haste to gratify us and the body.'" Cf. Didymus Caecus, *Comm. Eccl.* 336.

Although v. 14 belongs to a cluster based on Matt 5:29–30; 18:8–9, its language is derived not from the biblical text but from *Sent. Pythag.* 6a (Π): ἀθανάτους σοι πίστευε παρὰ τῇ κρίσει καὶ τὰς τιμὰς καὶ τὰς τιμωρίας. Note, however, that the eternality of eschatological rewards and (especially) punishments is reflected in Matt 18:8 (τὸ πῦρ τὸ αἰώνιον) as well; cf. Mark 9:43, 48. Comparison can also be made with a saying ascribed to the sage Periander by Diogenes Laertius: αἱ μὲν ἡδοναὶ φθαρταί, αἱ δὲ τιμαὶ ἀθάνατοι (*Vit. phil.* 1.97). For the pairing of τιμή and τιμωρία, cf. Polybius,

Hist. 6.14.4; Dio Chrysostom, *Or.* 31.24; Cassius Dio, *Hist. Rom.* 53.10.2. The soul may be released from the body at death (vv. 127, 320–322), but whatever the soul pursued while inhabiting the body accompanies it as evidence when it goes to judgment (v. 347). At that point, the soul, depending on its moral character, encounters either God or an evil demon (vv. 39–40).

Sentences 15–21

Text

15 ᵃὁπόσα τοῦ κόσμου ἔχεις, κἂν ἀφέληταίᵃ ᵇσού τιςᵇ, μὴ ἀγανάκτει.
16 σεαυτὸν ἐπιλήψιμον μὴ πάρεχε τῷ κόσμῳ.
17 χωρὶς τῆς ἐλευθερίας πάνταᵃ ἀφαιρουμένῳ σε τῷ πέλας ὕπεικε.
18 σοφὸς ἀκτήμων ὅμοιος θεῷ.
19 τοῖς κοσμικοῖς πράγμασιν εἰς αὐτὰ τὰ ἀναγκαῖα χρῶ.
20 τὰ μὲν τοῦ κόσμου τῷ κόσμῳ, τὰ δὲ τοῦ θεοῦ τῷ θεῷ ἀκριβῶς ἀποδίδου.
21 τὴν ψυχήν σου νόμιζε παραθήκην ἔχειν παρὰ θεοῦᵃ.

Translation

15 Even if someone takes from you however much of the world you possess, do not be indignant.
16 Do not give the world reason to condemn you.
17 To the neighbor who would take from you yield everything except your freedom.
18 A sage without property is like God.
19 Use worldly things only for essential needs.
20 Be strict in rendering the things of the world to the world and the things of God to God.
21 Consider your soul to be a deposit you have from God.

Textual Notes

15ᵃ⁻ᵃ ὅπως τὰ τοῦ κόσμου ἔχῃς ὅταν ἀφαιρῆταί: Υ • 15ᵇ⁻ᵇ τίς σου: Π • 17ᵃ παντὶ τῷ: Π • 21ᵃ τοῦ θεοῦ: Π

Commentary

The theme of this section can be discerned by comparing v. 15 with v. 91b, v. 16 with v. 38, v. 19 with *Sent. Pythag.* 30^b, and v. 20 with Matt 22:21. In each instance the version of the saying found in vv. 15–21 is distinguished by the use of κόσμος or κοσμικός, terms that together function as keywords for the unit. Insofar as such language exhibits a "characteristically Christian" connotation (Chadwick 1959, 154), this apparent redaction renders both the individual sayings (several of which are derived from one of the author's Pythagorean sources) and the section as a whole more congenial to a Christian context (see above on vv. 1–5; and for parallels to this use of κόσμος in New Testament literature, see John 15:19; 1 Cor 1:20–21; 2:12; Eph 2:2; 1 Tim 1:15; Jas 1:27; 4:4). The section consists of two subunits. The first, vv. 15–18, is organized around a pair of similar commands (vv. 15 and 17, both with ἀφαιρέω) on the sage's proper stance towards material possessions. The second, vv. 19–21, contrasts what the sage owes to his body with what he owes to his most precious possession, his soul.

Sentence 15

This saying can be read against the background of various New Testament commands to endure unjust treatment with patience (e.g., Rom 12:12; Heb 12:7; 1 Pet 2:20; 3:14–17; cf. Ign. *Eph.* 10.3). In commenting on the verse, Chadwick (1959, 163) refers to Luke 12:33 (cf. Matt 6:19–20; Mark 10:21), though a more likely allusion is to Luke 6:30 (cf. Matt 5:40; *Did.* 1.4): "Give to everyone who asks of you, and from the one who takes away your things, do not demand them back (ἀπὸ τοῦ αἴροντες τὰ σὰ μὴ ἀπαίτει)." According to Irenaeus, this logion teaches Christians not to grieve when they are defrauded but to "rejoice as those who have given willingly ... conferring a favor upon our neighbors," thereby assimilating themselves to God (*Haer.* 4.13.3). Cf. Ps.-Clement, *Hom.* 15.9: "To all of us possessions are sins. The deprivation of these, in whatever way it may take place, is the removal of sins."

A different, and perhaps more original (Chadwick 1959, 155), version of this maxim occurs in v. 91b: "Even if someone takes from you what has been given you, do not be indignant." The use of κόσμος here not only connects the line with the injunction in v. 16; it also anticipates the distinction drawn in v. 20 between the things of the world and the things of God. Since none of the things of the world are in fact his own (v. 227), at least not for long (vv. 128, 405), even his own body (vv. 321–322), the Sextine sage assigns to them no value (vv. 130, 192) and so faces their loss with equanimity. Instead, he demonstrates his contempt for wealth by giving or throwing it away (vv. 81, 82b, 228, 264a, 329–330), concentrating instead on what God provides, of which no one can deprive him (vv. 92, 118, 404). Indeed, he actually welcomes the divestment of material goods insofar as it represents a means of assimilating himself to God (v. 18).

In *Diatr.* 4.1.103, Epictetus constructs a scenario similar to that of v. 15, though for him the perpetrator is not an anonymous "someone" or the "evil man" of v. 130 but the deity: "Having received everything, then, from another, even your very self, are you indignant (ἀγανακτεῖς) and blame the giver if he takes something away from you?" In other texts, the culprit is fortune—for example, *Sent. Pythag.* 120: "You will not need anything which sovereign chance gives then takes away" (similar sayings occur in Clitarchus, *Sent.* 122 and Porphyry, *Marc.* 12). For an additional Pythagorean perspective on the theme, we have *Carm. aur.* 15–18: "Know that death has been destined for all, and that property is wont to be acquired now, lost tomorrow. But whatever pains mortals suffer through the divine workings of fate, whatever lot you have, bear it and do not be indignant (μηδ' ἀγανάκτει)." Cf. P.Ins. 27.9: "When a wise man is stripped, he gives his clothes and blesses."

Sentence 16

Chadwick (1959, 154–55) suggests that v. 16 "looks like a Christian version of the maxim preserved in its original pagan form" at v. 38: "Give no one reason to condemn you." That saying, in turn, has been "Christianized" by its attachment to v. 37: "Let the world revere your way of life." A common motivating strategy in early Christian moral discourse involved reminding readers that their behavior was being scrutinized by the non-Christian world (e.g., Rom 12:17–18; Col 4:5–6; 1 Thess 4:12; 1 Tim 3:7; Titus 2:7–8; 1 Pet 2:15, 20; 3:14–15; Ign. *Eph.* 10.1–3; Pol. *Phil.* 10.2). Particular emphasis was placed on avoiding anything that might incur the negative judgment of outsiders (e.g., 1 Cor 10:32; Phil 2:14–15; 1 Pet 3:15–17; 2 Pet 2:2; *1 Clem.* 47.6–7; Ign. *Trall.* 8.2). A similar concern for conspicuousness is evident in Sext. 15–17 (cf. vv. 37–38, 51, 396). This has the effect of drawing attention to the sage's status as a public figure, though in contrast to texts like 1 Pet 2:12 ("Conduct yourselves honorably among the Gentiles, so that, though they malign you as evildoers, they may see your honorable deeds and glorify God") or 3:14 ("But even if you should suffer for the sake of righteousness, you are blessed. And do not fear their intimidation, and do not be troubled"), the objective is not conduct that conforms generally with prevailing expectations of what is right but a demonstration of one's unflappable superiority to worldly concerns and the caprice of fortune.

Insofar as it functions as a motivating adjunct to v. 15, this line creates something of a gnomic paradox: the sage should not demonstrate an overattachment to things of "the world" since to do so would provide "the world" with reason to censure him. As texts such as those cited under the discussion of v. 15 indicate, imperturbability (often ἀταραξία) was an ingredient of the philosopher's public persona. It is only natural to become indignant when deprived of one's property (e.g., Cassius Dio, *Hist. rom.* 48.6.3). The sage, however, remains dispassionate and content when confronted with such misfortunes, proof of his freedom (see v. 17) from any preoccupation with worldly ambitions or the vicissitudes of life. Consequently, he is both unaffected by adversity and insusceptible to distress (e.g., Cicero, *Tusc.* 3.7.14–15). In fact, he is incapable of receiving either injury or insult, since he refuses to allow inconsequential things to annoy him (e.g., Musonius Rufus, frag. 10). Because he is the most self-sufficient of all people in the art of living well, it is less dreadful for him to be deprived of his possessions than it is for anyone else (Plato, *Resp.* 387d–e; cf. Epictetus, *Diatr.* 4.1.59–60). To quote Seneca: "He has invested everything in himself ... for the only possession he has is virtue, and of this he is never robbed" (*Const.* 5.4–5). Therefore when faced with the loss of material possessions he refuses to succumb to anger, or to emotional agitation of any kind (*Const.* 9.3). As the speech ascribed by Epictetus to the ideal sage in *Diatr.* 3.22.47–49 highlights, the sage's visibility in this regard is something to which he actually aspires: "Look at me," he says, "I am without home, city, property, or slaves.... Yet what do I lack? Am I not free from pain and fear, am I not free? ... When have I ever found fault with either God or man? When have I ever blamed anyone? ... Who, when he lays eyes upon me, does not feel that he is seeing his king and his master?" In *Pat.* 7, Tertullian draws on these traditions in a way that makes a contrast with "the world" comparable to the one at work in this section of the *Sentences*: "If our spirit is aroused by the loss of property, it is admonished by the Lord's scriptures in almost every place to a scorning of the world.... He who is greatly stirred with impatience of a loss does, by giving things earthly precedence over things heavenly, sin directly against God."

Sentence 17

This line is a reformulation of *Sent. Pythag.* 97: συγγενεῖ καὶ ἄρχοντι καὶ φίλῳ πάντα εἶχε πλὴν ἐλευθερίας. Sextus drops the threefold reference in favor of the more generic "neighbor," the topics of friends and relatives being of little interest to him (συγγενής, for instance, occurs five times in the *Sententiae Pythagoreorum* but never in Sextus). In its current context, the saying complements the similar command in v. 15: since freedom from possessions is necessary for the sage's assimilation to God (v. 18), it represents the one "possession" to which he must cling. This freedom is not a matter of legal status (v. 392), but of freeing oneself from service to everything except God (v. 264b), thereby achieving a freedom that is second only to that of God (v. 309). This is the freedom of the philosopher, which no one can take away (v. 275). That freedom is the most precious of commodities was a Stoic tenet (e.g., Epictetus, *Diatr.* 1.12.15; Dionysius of Halicarnassus, *Ant. rom.* 19.18.3; Philo, *Spec.* 4.15). Of special interest is the extended treatment accorded the theme by Epictetus in *Diatr.* 4.1, entitled Περὶ ἐλευθερίας. True freedom is achieved only when one is unhampered by the concern for worldly things, things over which one has no control: "Therefore, the body is not our own, its members are not our own, property is not our own. If, then, you conceive a strong passion for some one of these things, as though it were your immediate possession, you will be punished as he should be who fixes his aim upon what is not his own. This is the road which leads to freedom" (*Diatr.* 4.1.130–131). Since he alone recognizes and abides by this code, the sage alone is free (e.g., Diogenes Laertius, *Vit. phil.* 7.121; cf. 6.71). Indeed, all things belong to him, even if he lacks money or possessions (e.g., Philo, *Plant.* 69), since he wants for nothing (e.g., Musonius Rufus, frag. 34).

Sentences 18–19

God needs nothing (v. 382) and no one (v. 49). The person who emulates God needs next to nothing (v. 50) and no one but God (v. 49). The sage, therefore, out of a desire to live as far as possible in accord with the nature of God (vv. 44, 45, 48, 381), not only refuses to think of anything as his own property (v. 227), he also divests himself of material things in order to achieve a higher state of purity (v. 81).

The basic material for these lines is to be found in *Sent. Pythag.* 30^{a-b} (for *Sent. Pythag.* 30^c, see on v. 274b): "The one who truly lives like (ὁμοίως) God is the one who is self-sufficient and without property (ἀκτήμων) and a philosopher and regards not to have need of anything, even necessities (ἀναγκαίων), as the greatest wealth." Like other texts (cf. *Anecd. Gr.* 3.470: ὡς ἀληθῶς ὅμοιος θεῷ ὁ αὐτάρκης καὶ ἀκτήμων ἄνθρωπος), this saying associates the goal of assimilating oneself to God with the goal of achieving a godlike self-sufficiency, or αὐτάρκεια (cf. vv. 98, 263, 334). The Philonic sage, for instance, because he is "completely sufficient in himself," needs very little, "standing on the boundary between immortal and mortal nature, having certain wants on account of a body that is mortal, but not having many wants on account of a soul set on immortality" (*Virt.* 8–9). According to Porphyry, in his effort to become like the divine, a philosopher commits himself to "living a life suited to that which he seeks to resemble, a simple, self-sufficient life, involved as little as possible with mortal things" (*Abst.* 1.37.4; cf. 1.54.6). Such perspectives resonate with Cynic teachings on material wealth as well, for example, Ps.-Crates, *Ep.* 11: "Practice being in need of only a few things, for this is the closest thing to God, while the opposite is the farthest."

For its part, v. 19 not only extends and applies the thought of v. 18; it also anticipates the first half of v. 20, in effect explaining to the readers how it is that they are to "render" the things of the world to the world. Cf. Origen, *Comm. Matt.* 17.27:

> We are composed of soul and body ... and we are under an obligation to render as it were the tribute of our bodies to the ruler named Caesar, that is, to give the body its necessary requirements which bear the physical image of the Ruler of bodies; these needs are food and clothing and necessary rest and periods of sleep. And since the soul is by nature in the image of God, we owe other things to God its king, which are expedient and conformed to the nature and essence of the soul; these are the ways that lead to virtue and virtuous actions.

This text also helps to explain the relation of v. 21 to the second half of v. 20: the "things" that one must render to God have to do with the soul, which one has from God. Cf. Clement, *Ecl.* 24.

As noted above, Sextus's inspiration for this line, *Sent. Pythag.* 30[b], suggests that to have need of nothing, even necessities, represents an appropriate aim for the sage. Our author, by contrast, embraces neither the austerity of this gnome nor that of an author like Evagrius Ponticus, for whom the voluntary abandonment of worldly things constitutes the first and most basic form of renunciation necessary for obtaining knowledge of God (*Mal. cogit.* 26). Instead, his position more clearly approximates that of Clement in *Strom.* 6.12.99.6–6.12.100.1: "For the possession and use of necessities (τῶν ἀναγκαίων) are not harmful in quality, but in quantity, when in excess. For this reason the gnostic circumscribes his desires in reference to both possession and use, not exceeding the limit of necessity." For the individual who accepts these priorities, the Alexandrian goes on to explain, the love of God, the acquisition of knowledge, and the demands of righteousness will take precedence over such things as familial responsibilities. The Sextine sage similarly puts aside material things not altogether, but as much as possible (v. 78), acquiring just enough to meet the body's basic requirements (v. 115, cf. v. 276).

Sentence 20

For inspiration our author shifts from a Pythagorean source to a biblical one, Matt 22:21: ἀπόδοτε οὖν τὰ Καίσαρος Καίσαρι καὶ τὰ τοῦ θεοῦ τῷ θεῷ (cf. Mark 12:17; Luke 20:25). Sextus retains τὰ τοῦ θεοῦ τῷ θεῷ as well as the verb ἀποδίδωμι, changing its form to the present singular and shifting its position to the end of the sentence. Besides the introduction of κόσμος (see the comments above on vv. 15–21), the most notable addition is that of ἀκριβῶς, for which see on v. 9. For the line's relationship to those that immediately precede and follow, see on v. 19. As vv. 412–413 explain, the sage provides for the needs of the body moderately, for example, with plain food, but for the needs of the soul with devotion, that is, by nourishing it with the divine word. Cf. v. 55: "Let your body alone be at home on the earth; let your soul always be with God." For Sextus, "the world" signifies in particular the realm of bodily needs and concerns that distracts one from "the things of God." Reliance on this sort of antithetical construction represents one of the more conspicuous ways in which the outlook of the *Sentences* departs from that of its Pythagorean counterparts, as represented, for instance, by Clitarchus, *Sent.* 3: πατρίδα τὸν κόσμον ἡγοῦ (cf. Sext. 464). Chadwick (1959, 74) notes that the Syriac version expands v. 20 by adding "But know well that you are the slave of that which you desire" (cf. Clitarchus, *Sent.* 12; Sext. 75a, 600).

Sentence 21

The soul is one of the "things of God" mentioned in the preceding verse, specifically, the "deposit" (v. 21) that one "renders" (v. 20) to God through a way of life that tends to the soul (for ἀποδίδωμι + παραθήκη, cf. Sextus Empiricus, *Pyr.* 3.243; Clement, *Quis div.* 42.8; Diogenes Laertius, *Vit. phil.* 3.83). This is only appropriate since the soul originates from God (v. 449) and after death returns to God (v. 40).

The observation that the human soul or spirit is only a "loan" from the deity was a cliché especially of ancient consolation literature, offered by way of encouragement to the bereaved so that they might accept the inevitability of death with resignation (e.g., Ps.-Plutarch, *Cons. Apoll.* 106f-7a; Seneca, *Polyb.* 10.4-5; *Marc.* 10.1-2; Ps.-Ovid, *Cons. Liv.* 369-370; cf. Lucretius, *De rerum nat.* 3.970-971). For Sextus, by contrast, the metaphor is used as a reminder that one's soul is not one's own, to be used only as one sees fit, but should be cared for as a trust from God. Similar sentiments are expressed in Athanasius, *Vit. Ant.* 20.9: "Since we have received the soul as a deposit, let us protect it (i.e., from filthy thoughts) for the Lord, that he may acknowledge his work—that is, the soul—as being the same as when he created it." Compare also Ps.-Philo, *L.A.B.* 33.2-3: "Only direct your heart to the Lord your God during the time of your life, because after your death you cannot repent of those things in which you live. For then death is sealed up and brought to an end, and the measure and the time and the years have returned their deposit." See further Epictetus, *Diatr.* 1.1.32; Philo, *Her.* 104; *Spec.* 1.295; Josephus, *Bell.* 3.372; Asterius, *Comm. Ps.* 12.12-14. For the theme in wisdom literature, see Wis 15:8; Ps.-Phoc. 106-108 (cf. Luke 12:20). For a different use of the metaphor, see on v. 195.

Sentences 22-30

Text

22 ὅτε λέγεις περὶ θεοῦ, κρίνῃ ὑπὸ θεοῦ.
23 ἄριστον ἡγοῦ καθαρμὸν τὸ μηδένα[a] ἀδικεῖν.
24 ψυχὴ καθαίρεται λόγῳ θεοῦ ὑπὸ σοφοῦ.
25 ἀναίσθητον οὐσίαν μὴ πεισθῇς εἶναί ποτε θεοῦ[a].
26 ὁ θεὸς καθὸ νοῦς ἐστιν αὐτοκίνητος, κατ' αὐτὸ τοῦτο καὶ ὑφέστηκεν.
27 θεοῦ μέγεθος οὐκ ἂν ἐξεύροις πτεροῖς πετόμενος.
28 θεοῦ ὄνομα μὴ ζήτει, οὐ γὰρ εὑρήσεις· πᾶν τὸ ὀνομαζόμενον ὀνομάζεται ὑπὸ τοῦ κρείττονος, ἵνα τὸ μὲν καλῇ, τὸ δὲ ὑπακούῃ· τίς οὖν ὁ ὀνομάσας θεόν; θεὸς οὐκ ὄνομα θεοῦ, ἀλλὰ δόξα περὶ θεοῦ[a].
29 μηθὲν οὖν ἐν θεῷ ὃ μὴ ἔστι ζήτει.
30 θεὸς αὐγὴ σοφὴ τοῦ ἐναντίου ἀνεπίδεκτος.

Translation

22 When you speak about God, you are judged by God.
23 Realize that that the best purification is to wrong no one.

24 A soul is purified by a word of God from a sage.
25 Do not ever be persuaded that the being of God is incapable of perception.
26 God as mind is self-moved; as such he also subsists.
27 Even flying with wings you would not discover the greatness of God.
28 Do not seek God's name, for you will not find it. Everything with a name is named by someone stronger, so that one might call and the other obey. Who then has named God? 'God' is not God's name, but an opinion about God.
29 Therefore do not seek anything in God that does not exist.
30 God is a wise light not admitting of its opposite.

Textual Notes
23ᵃ μηδέν: Υ • 25ᵃ θεόν: Υ • 28ᵃ θεόν: Π

Commentary

As Chadwick (1959, 153) observes, vv. 25–30 is a unified section on the nature of God, one that balances negative and positive statements. God is not an insensate being but is subsistent, self-moving νοῦς (vv. 25–26), a pure source of illuminating wisdom (v. 30). God's greatness is so ineffable that even God's name lies beyond the power of human comprehension (vv. 27–28). The relation of vv. 22–24 to this unit is not immediately obvious, though v. 22 may provide the key. If it is advisable to avoid attributing to God anything that might be inappropriate or contrary to the nature of the divine (v. 29), then discretion must be observed in any situation where one is called upon to speak about God. The unstated premise connecting vv. 23–24 with v. 22, in turn, appears to be provided by the statement in v. 356 (cf. v. 590): only those who are first cleansed should be permitted to offer such speech.

Sentence 22

This line (together with v. 352) appears in the preface to Origen's commentary on the first psalm (*Sel. Ps.* 12.1080 [= Epiphanius, *Pan.* 2.416]) in support of his argument that one ought to observe discretion when speaking and (especially) writing about sacred matters (see Chadwick 1959, 115). Sextus's warning may be based indirectly on *Sent. Pythag.* 112: χρὴ καὶ λέγειν καὶ ἀκροᾶσθαι τὸν περὶ θεῶν λόγον ὡς ἐπὶ θεοῦ. Cf. Porphyry,

Marc. 15: "It is fitting to hear and speak the word about God as though in the presence of God." The rendition here lacks the reference to hearing (cf. vv. 171a–b, 338) and heightens the degree of consequentiality by injecting the theme of divine judgment (cf. vv. 14, 183–184, 347).

The first Christians were well aware that speaking about God can be a perilous enterprise—for example, Jas 3:1 ("we who teach will receive a stricter judgment"); cf. Matt 12:36–37; 2 Pet 2:1–3; Justin Martyr, *Dial.* 82.3 ("We know that everyone who can speak the truth but does not speak it shall be judged by God"). According to v. 195, the souls of the teacher's listeners have been entrusted to him—presumably by God—and for that reason Sextus may think that such a person will be judged with particular scrutiny (cf. v. 177). At any rate, it is apparent that the need for discretion in speech generally represents a major concern for our author; see on vv. 149–165g. Of particular interest for the interpretation of v. 22 is vv. 350–368, an extended section on the risks accompanying theological discourse, concerns being raised with regard to the fitness of both the speaker (e.g., v. 358) and the audience (e.g., v. 354), as well as the nature of what the former communicates to the latter (e.g., v. 353). Note in particular Sext. 352 ("To speak even the truth about God entails no small risk") and Sext. 368: "A human being having nothing true to say about God is bereft of God." See further vv. 223, 407, 410, 431, 451. For the problem of blasphemous speech, see vv. 83–85.

Sentence 23
  In *Phaed.* 69b–c, Plato likens the effect of justice and the other virtues to that of a purification, one that purges the soul of its vices. Philo similarly speaks of how "the soul should receive a cleansing from its unutterable wrongdoings by washing away and purging its defilements after the fashion of a sacred purification" (*Det.* 170; cf. *Deus* 7–9; *Spec.* 1.257–260, 269–270; 3.209). Such tropes were a stock-in-trade of ancient moral discourse. Solon, for example, was reported as arguing that in the matter of righteousness the best way to keep oneself "pure" is to become so self-sufficient (see above on vv. 18–19) that it never becomes necessary to wrong others by taking what rightfully belongs to them (Plutarch, *Sept. sap. conv.* 159c). From the corpus of Wisdom literature, perhaps the best parallel to the formulation here comes from Sir 35:3: "To keep from wickedness is pleasing to the Lord, and to refrain from wrongdoing (ἀπὸ ἀδικίας) an atonement." Cf. Prov 15:27; Clitarchus, *Sent.* 6: εὐσεβὴς οὐχ ὁ πολλὰ θύων, ἀλλ' ὁ μηδὲν ἀδικῶν. For Christian appropriations of the theme, see Clem-

ent, *Paed.* 3.11.76.2 and *Strom.* 7.4.27.4: "For in reality there is no other purity but abstinence from sins." In our author's eyes, injustice not only constitutes a source of defilement (vv. 102, 110); it also represents a form of impiety, indeed, the greatest form of impiety (v. 96). In vv. 370–371, we have a saying that spells out one of the implications of such impure conduct ("It is not possible that someone could revere God while wronging a human being") coupled with a saying that can be interpreted as a positive counterpart to the counsel offered here ("The foundation of reverence for God is love for humanity"). If the best purification is to harm no one, then the best offering consists of actions that do others good (v. 47). Mention in this context can also be made of Pythagoras, who is reported as insisting that those approaching the altar for sacrifice "should appear before the gods with not only a body pure of every wrongful deed but also a soul that is undefiled" (Diodorus Siculus, *Bibl. hist.* 10.9.6). This idea of complementary cleansings may inform the relationship between vv. 23 and 24 in our text: refraining from injustice purifies the body, while hearing the divine word cleanses the soul (note καθαρμόν in v. 23 and καθαίρεται in v. 24). On the importance of keeping the body "unstained," see vv. 346, 449; cf. Porphyry, *Marc.* 13.

Sentence 24

Just as the tongue can pollute and corrupt (e.g., Matt 15:11; Jas 3:8), it can also cleanse, assuming that what it conveys comes from the right source. This is actually the first of two maxims that Sextus has derived from Clitarchus, *Sent.* 17: ψυχὴ καθαίρεται ἐννοίᾳ θεοῦ (cf. Porphyry, *Marc.* 11: καθαίρεται μὲν ἄνθρωπος ἐννοίᾳ θεοῦ). Verse 24 utilizes the first part of the saying, while the second part is developed in v. 97. For our author, the agent of the soul's purification is not a divine thought, as it is for Clitarchus, nor is it the divine Logos, as Origen maintains in *Cels.* 7.8. Rather, Sextus's view better approximates that of Plato, according to whom it is the work of the moral educator that effects a cleansing of the soul (e.g., *Soph.* 231b). In the same vein, to his disciples, the teachings of Pythagoras effected "many and great cleansings and purifications of the soul" (Iamblichus, *Vit. Pythag.* 17.74; cf. Philo, *Somn.* 1.198; Ps.-Clement, *Hom.* 16.21). As we learn from v. 103, one of the principal means by which this cleansing is accomplished is through the refutation of false opinions (cf. Plato, *Soph.* 230d). Presumably, the sage's "purifying" word is a manifestation of the "pure," that is, sinless, power he has received from God (v. 36), a power that enables him to declare the word of God (cf. vv. 361–362, 413, 420) in a morally worthy fashion (cf. vv. 356, 359, 590). For the concept of a pure or cleansed soul, see *Sent. Pythag.* 97, 119; Clitarchus, *Sent.* 125 (ψυχὴ καθαίρεται κακίας ἀπαλλαγῇ). Elsewhere the language of purity is applied not only to the soul (v. 441) but also to the heart (v. 46b), the mind (v. 57b), and the thoughts (v. 181).

Sentences 25–26

Accusing idols of being "senseless" is a regular component of Christian antipagan rhetoric, for example, in *Ep. Diogn.* 2.4; Origen, *Cels.* 8.20; Ps.-Clement, *Hom.* 10.21. For a Greco-Roman perspective, consider Plutarch, *Is. Os.* 382b:

> In general we must hold it true that nothing inanimate is superior to what is animate, and nothing without the power of perception (ἀναίσθητον) is superior to that which has that power.... The divine is not engendered in colors or forms or polished surfaces, but whatsoever things have no share in life ... have a portion of less honor than that of the dead. But the nature that lives and sees and has within itself the source of movement and a knowledge of what belongs to it and what belongs to others has drawn to itself an efflux and portion of beauty from the intelligence "by which the universe is guided," as Heraclitus puts it.

The saying in Sext. 25 is consistent with statements elsewhere in the collection that assert the reality of divine providence (v. 312), divine judgment (v. 373), and divine grace (vv. 436a–b, cf. v. 380). Further observations regarding the οὐσία of God are made in the appendices, specifically vv. 560 and 566. For the form of the saying, cf. v. 91a.

Antipagan rhetoric also sometimes included the observation that idols are incapable of movement, for example, Isa 46:7; Ep. Jer. 26–27; Wis 13:16–19; *Act. mart. Apoll.* 14. The theological axiom in v. 26 is repeated verbatim in the appendices as v. 562, except for the addition of δὴ after κατ' αὐτό. Cf. also v. 559: "The mind of God is self-moved and ever-moved." In its position here, the saying can be interpreted as a counterpoint to v. 25: the nature and activity of God are not insensate because God is mind. For a comparable though more expansive affirmation, see Clement, *Strom.* 4.25.162.5: "God, who is without being, is the perfect beginning of all things, and the producer of the beginning. As being, then, he is the first principle of physics, as good, the first principle of ethics, as mind, the first principle of logic and judgment" (cf. *Strom.* 4.25.155.2; and for the *philosophia tripertita*, see *SVF* 2:35, 42). While not altogether absent in Stoicism (e.g., Epictetus, *Diatr.* 2.8.2: "What, then, is the true being of God? ... It is mind, knowledge, right reason"), such assertions are familiar especially from Middle Platonism and Neopythagoreanism, where identifying the Demiurge (or active causal principle of the universe) as mind was the prevailing view (Dillon 1977, 7, 120–21, 157, 283–84, 316, 355). Some of the fullest Christian expositions of the doctrine are located in the writings of Origen—for example, *Princ.* 1.1.6: "God therefore must not be thought to be any kind of body, nor to exist in a body, but to be a simple intellectual existence, admitting in himself of no addition whatever, so that he cannot be believed to have in himself a more or a less, but is Unity or, if I may say so, Oneness throughout, and the mind and fount from which originates all intellectual existence or mind." Also *Cels.* 8.38: "Since we affirm that the God of the universe is mind ... we would maintain that God is not comprehended by any being other than that made in the image of that mind." As with the Alexandrian, for Sextus this ontology determines the direction of both his epistemology and his soteriology, v. 26 providing the theological basis for statements later in the collection according to which the affinity that the sage achieves with God is one of the mind (vv. 46a, 61, 144, 394, 450). Cf. Menander, *Mon.* 531: "God is mind; it is noble to have this mind."

Sentences 27–29

These three verses are cited in the *Passio* of Babylas of Antioch (Bolland 1734, 574), where they are attributed to the saint himself. The first line entails a probable allusion to the myth of the charioteer. If the wings of the soul's horses are in perfect condition, Plato explains, it is able to "fly high," (*Phaedr.* 246c), achieving a vision of heaven and the place beyond heaven, that is, a vision of reality as it truly is, "visible only to mind, the soul's steersman" (247c). Even from such a lofty vantage point, Sextus seems to say, one cannot comprehend the immensity of God, or, as Minucius Felix puts it: "God is beyond all sense, infinite, measureless, his dimensions known to himself alone" (*Oct.* 18.8). For Sextus's language, compare Clement, *Strom.* 5.12.81.5–6: "No one can rightly express him wholly. For on account of his greatness (μέγεθος) he is ranked as the All, and is the father of the universe. Nor are any parts to be predicated of him. For the One is indivisible; therefore it is infinite, not considered with reference to inscrutability, but with reference to its being without dimensions, and not having a limit." See further Irenaeus, *Haer.* 4.20.1; Theophilus, *Autol.* 1.3: God is "in glory uncontainable, in greatness (μέγεθος) incomprehensible, in loftiness inconceivable, in wisdom unteachable, in goodness inimitable, in beneficence inexpressible." Inasmuch as his mind is an abode for God (vv. 46a, 144, 394), the soul of the Sextine sage is similarly ungraspable in its magnitude (v. 403).

The multisegmented entry in v. 28, unusual in the collection for its length and complexity (cf. vv. 13, 230b, 273), is alluded to as a teaching of Σέξτος ὁ ἐκκλησιαστικὸς φιλόσοφος by Maximus Confessor, *Schol. libr. myst. theol.* 4.429 (see Chadwick 1959, 164). An actual citation of the line can be found in Ps.-John Damascene, *Sacr. par.* 96.533, though there it is attributed to Saint Babylas, the reference being drawn from his martyrology (see above). The latter is very close to our version, adding a γάρ and changing the word order slightly. As for the saying's content, we can turn to Justin Martyr, who is similarly aware of the power dynamics involved when assigning someone a name: "The father of all has no given name, since he is unbegotten. For whoever is addressed by some name has as older than him the one who gave him the name. But 'father' and 'god' and 'creator' and 'lord' and 'master' are not names but appellations (προσρήσεις) derived from his beneficence and works ... just as the designation 'god' is not a name but an opinion (δόξα) implanted in the nature of human beings about something difficult to set forth" (*2 Apol.* 5.1–3). For God as father, see vv. 59, 222, 225, and 228. For further ruminations on the namelessness of God, cf. *Gos. Truth* 38.24–39.28; *Eugnostos* 3.72.1–3; Justin Martyr, *1 Apol.* 61.11; Clement, *Strom.* 5.12.82.1–2; Origen, *Cels.* 6.65; 7.42; Cicero, *Nat. deor.* 1.12.30; Dio Chrysostom, *Or.* 12.78; Maximus of Tyre, *Or.* 2.10; Philo, *Mut.* 13: "For those who are born into mortality necessarily need some substitute for the divine name, so that they may approach if not the fact at least the name of supreme excellence and be brought into relation with it" (cf. *Somn.* 1.67). Even though it is only an opinion, the name of God nevertheless must not be reviled (v. 175).

Verse 29, connected to the line that precedes it by οὖν and by catchword (ζήτει), draws a generalizing inference from the cluster's first two lines. Caution must be observed whenever attributing something to God, since doing so entails the risk that what is being claimed will fall short of God's awesome dignity (v. 27). This applies especially to the practice of naming God, which can be understood as a species of speaking about God, which always must be carried out with discretion (see on v. 22). Above all, to God one must never attribute anything evil or base (vv. 114, 314, 440).

Sentence 30

This prohibition is relevant to the interpretation of the next line as well. If a biblical basis were to be ascribed to v. 30, the most likely candidate would be 1 John 1:5: ὁ θεὸς φῶς ἐστιν καὶ σκοτία ἐν αὐτῷ οὐκ ἔστιν οὐδεμία. Antithetical constructions of this sort (cf. John 1:5; Jas 1:17; Rev 22:5) attempt to describe the mystery of divine being and activity by drawing attention to the absoluteness of God's nature. From this perspective, it is possible to read v. 30 as an elucidation in support of the command in v. 29: what "does not exist" in God, and therefore what should not be sought by those who endeavor to know God, is anything that contradicts the affirmation that God is only and fully illuminating wisdom. In the course of discussing the 1 John text in *Comm. Joan.* 2.23.149–151, Origen observes that while Christ is "the true light" (cf. John 1:9; 1 John 2:8), "in proportion as God, since he is the father of truth, is more and greater than truth, and since he as the father of wisdom is greater and more excellent than wisdom, in the same proportion God is more than the true light" (cf. *Comm. Joan.* 2.25.162; *Cels.* 5.11). Cf. Athenagoras, *Legat.* 16.3 ("God is Himself everything to Himself—light unapproachable, a perfect world, spirit, power, reason"); Theophilus, *Autol.* 2.15: "Just as the sun always remains full and does not wane, so God always remains perfect and is full of all power, intelligence, wisdom, immortality, and all good things." The quotations from Origen and Theophilus are also reflective of traditions that employ the imagery of light to describe the power of σοφία (e.g., Wis 7:26; Bar 3:14; Philo, *Migr.* 40; *Congr.* 47–48; *Spec.* 3.6; Origen, *Cels.* 5.10). Such texts, in turn, belong to a larger metaphorical field, one in which light is associated both with God himself (e.g., Isa 60:1–3, 19–20) and with the different vehicles through which God is made known to humankind, for example, God's word (e.g., Ps 119:105 [118:105]) or God's commandment (e.g., Prov 6:23). The symbolism of light also plays a prominent role in the writings of Philo, who for his part appears to have been inspired especially by Plato's metaphor of the sun (*Resp.* 507b–509c), a typical illustration occurring in *Virt.* 164: "For just as when the sun rises the darkness departs, and everything is full of light, so in the same way when God, the intelligible sun (ὁ νοητὸς ἥλιος), appears and shines upon the soul, the gloom of the passions and vices is dispelled, and that purest and most venerable form, the form of exceedingly brilliant virtue, reveals itself." Cf. *Opif.* 30; *Somn.* 1.75; *Ebr.* 44; also *Deus* 3, which describes how the αὐγαὶ φρονήσεως facilitate for the soul of the sage a vision of God. Similarly, in the *Sentences*, the imagery of illumination is important for conveying not simply the knowability of God, but the relevance of such knowability for ethics (v. 95b: "Let your light guide your actions"), the concept of wisdom playing a pivotal role in both epistemology (v. 406: "Divine wisdom is the knowledge of God") and soteriology (v. 167: "Wisdom leads a soul to God").

Sentences 31–36

Text

31 ὁᵃ θεὸς ὅσα ἐποίησεν, ὑπὲρ ἀνθρώπων αὐτὰᵇ ἐποίησεν.
32 ἄγγελος ὑπηρέτης θεοῦ πρὸς ἄνθρωπονᵃ, οὐ γὰρ δὴ πρὸς ᵇοὐδένα ἄλλονᵇ· τιμιώτερον οὖν ἄνθρωπος ἀγγέλου παρὰ θεῷ.
33 τὸ μὲν πρῶτον εὐεργετοῦν ὁᵃ θεόςᵇ, τὸ δὲ δεύτερον εὐεργετούμενον ἄνθρωποςᶜ.
34 βίου τοιγαροῦν ὡς ὢν μετὰ θεόνᵃ.
35 ἐκλεκτὸς ὢν ἔχεις τι ἐν τῇ συστάσει ᵃσου ὁποῖον θεός· χρῶ οὖν τῇ συστάσει σου ὡς ἱερῷ θεοῦᵃ.
36 ἐξουσίαν ᵃπιστῷ ὁ θεὸς δίδωσι τὴν κατὰ θεόνᵃ· καθαρὰν οὖν δίδωσι καὶ ἀναμάρτητον.

Translation

31 Whatever God created, he created for the sake of human beings.
32 An angel is God's servant to humanity, for he is such to no one else; thus a human being is more honored before God than an angel.
33 First there is God giving benefits; second there is humanity receiving benefits.
34 Accordingly, live as one who is next after God.
35 Being chosen, you have within the constitution of yourself something godlike; therefore treat yourself as God's temple.
36 To one who is faithful God gives power that accords with God; what he gives, therefore, is pure and sinless.

Textual Notes

31ᵃ omit Υ • 31ᵇ omit Π • 32ᵃ ἀνθρώπους: Π, sy² • 32ᵇ⁻ᵇ οὐδέν: Π; οὐδὲν ἄλλο: sy² • 33ᵃ omit Π • 33ᵇ θεός ἐστιν: Π • 33ᶜ ἄγγελος, τὸ δὲ τρίτον ἄνθρωπος: Π • 34ᵃ θεοῦ: Π • 35ᵃ⁻ᵃ ὡς υἱὸς θεοῦ ἀνύσιμον: Υ • 36ᵃ⁻ᵃ πίστεως δίδωσι ὁ θεός: Υ

Commentary

Balancing the preceding section, on the nature of God (vv. 22–30), is a series of sayings on the nature of God's relationship to humanity (note ἄνθρωπος in vv. 31, 32, 33). This relationship is delineated specifically as a regime of benefaction, one whose particulars establish both the nature of humanity's dependency on God and—more important for Sextus's purposes here—the nature of humanity's exalted status, one that exceeds even that of the angels (v. 32). Through the progression of statements in the section an implicit anthropological hierarchy within this regime is conveyed: in creating the world God confers benefits on humanity as such (v. 31), but the most godlike benefits are bestowed on those whose conduct is most godlike, the faithful elect (vv. 35–36). Direct commands in vv. 34 and 35 draw attention to the implications of the section's anthropocentric affirmations for the readers' moral purpose, while modifications Sextus appears to have made to his source material in vv. 35 and 36 (see below) contribute to the development of their self-understanding as agents in a continuum of moral power and purity; cf. Justin Martyr, *1 Apol.* 21.6: "We have been taught that only those who live holy and virtuous lives close to God are made divine."

Sentence 31

In *Cels.* 4.74–99, Origen exposits on Celsus's charge that "they assert that God made all things for humankind." The apologist is quick to point out that the Christian position on this question actually approximates that of the Stoics, who not only deem the rational superior to the irrational but contend that "providence has made everything primarily for the sake of the rational nature" (*Cels.* 4.74). For the Stoic tenet that all things exist to sustain, benefit, and/or serve humanity, see Cicero, *Fin.* 3.67; Epictetus, *Diatr.* 1.6.12–22; 1.16.1–21; 2.8.6–8; *SVF* 2:1152–1167. A similar teleological anthropocentrism is developed in Philo's oeuvre as well (e.g., *Mos.* 1.60–62; 2.22; *Spec.* 2.69; 4.119–121; *Virt.* 154), and figures especially in his account of the creation (e.g., *Opif.* 77–78). For the idea that God created everything for the sake of humankind, see also Justin Martyr, *1 Apol.* 10.2; *2 Apol.* 3.2.

Sentence 32

In scripture, angels minister to God (e.g., Ps 103:20–21 [102:20–21]), to Christ (e.g., Matt 4:11), and, in Heb 1:14, to the saints: "Are they not all ministering spirits, sent out to render service (εἰς διακονίαν) for the sake of those who will inherit salvation?" In his defense of Christian anthropocentrism (see above), Origen cites as evidence the fact that at the beginning of the world people received help from "angels of God who came to visit them ... looking after them and caring for them" (*Cels.* 4.80). Elsewhere, in an exposition of Heb 1:14, he explains that in their role as ministers, angels continue to make important (albeit less miraculous) appearances, dwelling in the souls of those who practice virtue and holiness, guiding them with heavenly counsels (*Princ.* 3.3.6; cf. Athanasius, *C. Ar.* 1.62; 3.14; Origen, *Cels.* 5.4; 8.34; *Princ.* 1.5.1).

The question of humankind's standing vis-à-vis the angels was a matter of some debate in the early church. Tertullian, for one, takes texts like 1 Cor 6:3 and Heb 1:14 as evidence that human beings are superior (*Marc.* 2.9.7; cf. *Teach. Silv.* 115.30–35), while Origen interprets the former to mean that the saints will judge some but not all of the angels (*Comm. Matt.* 10.13; cf. Clement, *Ecl.* 56–57). In *Quis div.* 29, Clement explains that the angels have been ordered "to serve us for great reward," though only until "they too shall be freed from the vanity of the world at the revelation of the glory of the sons of God" (cf. Rom 8:19–21). The diversity of opinion regarding this issue is evidenced further by Rufinus, who in his translation of v. 32 (*tam pretiosus*, etc.) modifies the text to state that human beings are of *equal* value before God as the angels, a position expressed elsewhere in *Apoc. apocr. Joan.* 26 and Clement, *Strom.* 7.12.78.6; 7.18.84.2 (cf. Luke 20:36).

Taken together with v. 319 (cf. v. 519), this line suggests a hierarchy of servanthood: angels minister to the sage, while the sage ministers to God (note also v. 33 v.l.). What kind of angelic ministering Sextus has in mind is difficult to say, though stories like Tob 5:4–7 and Acts 12:6–11 could be interpreted as examples of angelic "service" to humankind. For ἄγγελος ὑπηρέτης θεοῦ, cf. Philo, *Gig.* 12; *Mut.* 87; Clement, *Exc.* 72.2; Origen, *Cels.* 8.13.

Sentences 33–34

Chadwick (1959, 155) describes vv. 33–34 as "a Christian form of the simple pagan saying" preserved in v. 176 ("A wise man is a benefactor next after God"), though here the high ranking accorded human beings is due not to the fact that they follow God's example in granting benefits to others (cf. vv. 47, 542) but to the fact that they enjoy a special place as the beneficiaries of God's actions, as indicated by vv. 31–32. Compare v. 82c

("Remember that you are next after God"), v. 129 ("After God, accustom your soul to have confidence in itself"), v. 376b ("God is the best, and God's son is nearest to the best"), and v. 580 ("After God, respect yourself"). For the image of a divine εὐεργέτης, see Diodorus Siculus, *Bibl. hist.* 5.67.5; 5.71.5; Plutarch, *Is. Os.* 355e, 368b; Ps.-Clement, *Hom.* 3.7; Hippolytus, *Haer.* 1 prol. 6. The concept is especially common in Philo's writings, for example, *Opif.* 169; *Leg.* 1.96; 2.56; *Deus* 110; *Dec.* 41. Subsequent sayings reveal that for Sextus humankind is ideally not only the recipient, but also the imitator of God's beneficent activity (see the commentary on v. 47 and v. 176), a fact that helps to account for the injunction in v. 34. The formula κατὰ θεόν, one of our author's favorites, identifies not only humankind's status but, more important, humankind's purpose (v. 201, cf. vv. 48, 63, 216, 399, 433). The statements in vv. 31–33, then, are not simply anthropological affirmations, but assertions intended to shape the readers' moral self-awareness. Sextus elaborates on the implications of this command elsewhere (again, see v. 176), though vv. 35–36 immediately identify one priority: the need to remain pure. Cf. Epictetus, *Diatr.* 2.8.11–13: "But you are a being of primary importance; you are a fragment of God; you have within you a part of him.... It is within yourself that you bear him, and you do not perceive that you are defiling him with impure thoughts and filthy actions."

Sentence 35

As it is used here, σύστασις refers to the constitution or "makeup" of the human self (cf. Plato, *Tim.* 36d; Ps.-Plato, *Epin.* 981a; Plutarch, *An. procr.* 1027d). The godlike "something" (τι) within whose presence renders the self comparable to a temple of God is left unspecified here, though it will be identified shortly, in v. 46a ("A pious person's intellect is a holy temple of God"); cf. vv. 61, 144, 394, 448; Porphyry, *Marc.* 11: "The divine is entirely present everywhere, but its sanctuary among humanity has been firmly established only in the intellect of the sage ... and let a temple (ἱερόν) be adorned for him because of wisdom in his judgment, one with a living statue, the mind, for God imparts his form to the one who honors him." No doubt our author would agree that, among all the benefits conferred by God upon humanity (see v. 33), the foremost is the intellect, its functioning representing the principal reason for humanity's exalted status (see v. 34). In his explicit statements, however, Sextus's focus is not on the intellect as such (though cf. v. 315) but on the intellect in which God dwells, the intellect that is "good" (v. 61), that is, the intellect of the pious person (v. 46a), otherwise known as the sage (v. 144). By the same token, it should be noted that what concerns Sextus more at this particular juncture is naming not the something divine within the self but the someone in whom it resides. Thus he speaks of the divine element within the human self not in terms of one's intellectual capacities but in terms of one's chosenness, a status that, as vv. 2–4 have established, is defined principally with reference to moral comportment. As v. 433 puts it, someone who is chosen "does all things in accord with God (κατὰ θεόν)." This emphasis helps to account for the presence of the final, imperatival element of the sentence here: "treat yourself as God's temple." Imagery of this sort was applied variously in ancient anthropological speculations. In 1 Cor 6:19, for instance, Paul refers to the human body as a temple (cf. *2 Clem.* 9.3; Ign. *Phld.* 7.2; *Act. Thom.* 12; *Const. ap.* 4.14). The soul, especially the rational part of the soul, could be described similarly—for example, in Philo, *Somn.* 1.149, 215; Clement, *Strom.* 7.5.28.1–7.5.29.8; Origen, *Cels.* 6.63: "The body of the man who has assumed characteristics of God, in that part which is made in the image of God, is a temple, since he possesses a soul of this character and has God in his soul because of that which is in his image." Temples, of course, are venues not only of piety and power but also of purity. From this perspective, the moral implications of the command in v. 35 are enunciated not only in vv. 46a–47, where similar imagery is employed, but also in the verse that immediately follows.

Sentence 36

It is likely that this line derives from now-lost source material shared with Porphyry, *Marc.* 11 (cf. the quotation above): ἀνθρώπῳ δὲ σοφῷ θεὸς θεοῦ δίδωσιν ἐξουσίαν (for more on this source-critical question, see part 4 of the introduction.) As Chadwick (1959, 156) observes, "Sextus has given a moral content to the saying with the insistence that it is purity and sinlessness, rather than intellectual wisdom as such, which confers a freedom comparable to that of God." The epithet *faithful* certainly communicates moral content for our author (e.g., vv. 5, 7a, 8). At the same time, it is noteworthy that the Sextine version of this saying highlights not only the moral character of the recipients of divine authority but also the moral nature of the authority that they receive. Indeed, within the broader context of the *Sentences* as a whole, this precept serves as an important reminder regarding the origin and nature of the sage's authority. What confers authority upon the faithful is not human sinlessness but God. Having asked for and received ἐξουσία ("power, authority") from God (v. 375), the sage is governed by God (vv. 182, 422, 424) and under God's authority (though note that Υ lacks τὴν κατὰ θεόν). Indeed, everything he does is under God's control (v. 288). It is through the exercise of this rule that God and the sage are inseparably bound (v. 423). In this regard Rufinus's translation represents a significant departure from the original: "God has granted men freedom of will in order that by living purely and without sin they may become like God." This is the first of three sayings that according to Augustine (*Nat. grat.* 64.77) Pelagius borrowed from Sextus. Cf. on vv. 46a–b, 60.

Sentences 37–40

Text

37 αἰδείσθω σου τὸν βίον ὁ κόσμος.
38 μηδενὶ σεαυτὸν ἐπιλήψιμον δίδου^a.
39 κακῶς ζῶντα^a μετὰ τὴν ἀπαλλαγὴν τοῦ σώματος ^bεὐθύνει κακὸς^b δαίμων μέχρις οὗ καὶ τὸν ἔσχατον κοδράντην ἀπολάβῃ.
40 μακάριος ἀνήρ, οὗ τῆς ψυχῆς οὐδεὶς ἐπιλήψεται ^aεἰς θεὸν πορευομένης^a.

Translation

37 Let the world revere your way of life.
38 Give no one reason to condemn you.
39 After his release from the body, one who lives an evil life is called to account by an evil demon until the last penny is paid up.
40 Blessed is the man whose soul no one will seize when it journeys to God.

Textual Notes

38^a ποίει: Π • 39^a ζῶντι: Π • 39^{b–b} εὐθύνοι κακῶς: Υ; εὐθυνεῖ κακός: lat • 40^{a–a} πορευομένης παρὰ θεῷ: Υ

Commentary

The sayings in this short passage all have something to do with judgment, either in this life (vv. 37–38) or in the life to come (vv. 39–40). The latter connects the segment loosely with the preceding unit (vv. 31–36), which addressed the theme of God's relationship to humanity.

Sentences 37–38

In Chadwick's view (1959, 155), v. 16 ("Do not give the world reason to condemn you") represents "a Christian version of the maxim preserved in its original pagan form" at v. 38. With regard to the latter, Sextus has created a "Christian version" of the saying, or at least a Christian setting for it, by appending it to v. 37, which, like v. 16, also includes a reference to κόσμος. The desirability of avoiding the world's condemnation, which had been the focus previously, is balanced here with the aspiration of earning its approval as well. The sort of godlike life just extolled (note βίου in v. 34), one achieved by recognizing the "something godlike" within, should be deserving of the world's respect. Compare *Sent. Pythag.* 42a ("Want your neighbors to revere you rather than fear you"); Musonius Rufus, frag. 30 ("You will be worthy of reverence from all if first you begin to revere yourself"); and 1 Pet 2:12: "Conduct yourselves honorably among the Gentiles, so that … they may see your honorable deeds and glorify God." By including the world's sense of reverence as an object of the readers' concern, Sextus implicitly acknowledges the judgment of outsiders as a measure of how their godlike life comes to expression. The whole matter of the sage's relationship to the general population, however, remains ambiguous. To be sure, he avoids anything that might bring disrepute on himself or his message (vv. 51, 343, 396), yet he finds it shameful to be praised by the unfaithful (v. 241, cf. vv. 112, 188). During his lifetime, the sage will achieve a certain amount of recognition (vv. 53, 145), not on account of his public speaking (v. 360) but apparently because of the consideration and beneficence he extends to all people (vv. 210a, 260, 372). Nevertheless, to the masses he will appear to be useless (v. 214).

Sentences 39–40

Ancient authors often conceptualize postmortem existence as a journey in which the soul encounters daemonic forces. The Platonic soul, for example, after its release (ἀπαλλαγή) from the body at death (*Phaed.* 64c), leaves for a "journey abroad" (61e, 67b–d; cf. *Apol.* 40e), led by a daemon to a certain place for judgment. The soul that is "well-ordered and wise" follows its guide without difficulty, but the soul that has committed impure or unjust acts "hovers around … the visible world for a long time, struggling and suffering much until it is led away by force and with difficulty" by its daemon to its final abode (*Phaed.* 107e–108c). Elsewhere, Plato describes how a wicked soul is seized (ἐπιλαμβάνειν) by a postmortem judge and sent "straight to the guardhouse," ending up in "the prison of payment" (*Gorg.* 523b, 524e–525a).

In Christian thought, the role of beings inhabiting this realm becomes even more insidious. According to Ps.-Clement, *Hom.* 9.9, for example, during its earthly life, demons attempt to infiltrate and corrupt the soul through the body. If someone commits many evil deeds, a demon is able to blend its essence with the soul to such an extent that even after the soul's release (ἀπαλλαγή) from the body the demon becomes "the strong chain of the soul," witnessing the soul's horrible punishments with pleasure. In some cases, along its journey the soul encounters otherworldly "toll keepers," as we hear, for example, in Clement, *Strom.* 4.18.117.2: "For those who demand toll detain (κατέχουσιν οἱ τὸ τέλος ἀπαιτοῦντες) those who bring in any worldly things, burdened with their own passions. But one that is free of all things that are subject to toll, and is full of knowledge and the righteousness of works, they pass on with their good wishes, blessing the man with his work" (cf. *Strom.* 7.13.83.1). Sextus similarly assumes that, even though it has been released from the body, the postmortem soul will be judged according to what it pursued while in the body (v. 347). For the corrupting power of demons in human life, see on vv. 305 and 348–349 (cf. v. 604). For the combination of being seized and called to account, see *Vit. Ant.* 65.3, where Athanasius recounts a vision of Anthony's heavenly ascent in which the latter sees "standing in the air some terrible and bitter beings who wanted to prevent him from passing by" and "attempted to take an accounting of him, to see whether or not he was accountable to them." Cf. *Vit. Ant.* 66.5: "Anthony understood that this was the pathway for souls and that the giant standing there was the Enemy, who envies the faithful. He was seizing those who were accountable to him and preventing them from passing by."

From this sort of perspective, it is not surprising that the interpretation of Matt 5:26 (cf. Matt 18:34; Luke 12:59; *Did.* 1.5) expressed in v. 39 (Sextus retains only τὸν ἔσχατον κοδράντην) is reflected in a variety of other early Christian texts. According to Origen, for example, the "adversary" of Luke 12:57–59 is a wicked angel who always accompanies the soul, rejoicing when it sins. After death, the souls of sinners are "dragged reluctantly and unwillingly" by their adversaries before the Lord for final judgment (*Hom. Luc.* 35.9). As Irenaeus, *Haer.* 1.25.4 indicates, the Matthean text also appears to have been popular in Gnostic circles, as we see, for example, in *Testim. Truth* 30.12–17: because they are "assisting the world" those who "[turn] away from the light … are unable [to pass by] the archon of [darkness] until they pay the last [penny]." Comparison can also be made with the commentary on Matt 5:25–26 offered in *Pist. Soph.* 113:

> Concerning this (text), the word is clear: every soul which comes forth from the body, and proceeds upon the way with the spirit counterpart and does not find the mystery of the releasing of all the seals and all the bonds, so that it releases itself from the spirit counterpart which is bound to it ... the spirit counterpart takes that soul to the presence of the Virgin of the Light. And that Virgin of the Light and judge gives that soul into the hands of one of her *paralemptai*, and her *paralemptes* casts it into the sphere of the aeons.

For the use of ἀπαλλαγή in v. 39 (the verb ἀπαλλάττω is used of release from bodily life in vv. 127 and 337), see also Porphyry, *Marc.* 2; Origen, *Cels.* 8.32; *Act. Thom.* 160. For the form of v. 40 (μακάριος ἀνήρ κτλ), cf. Ps 1:1; Prov 8:34; 28:14; Sir 14:1, 20; Jas 1:12. Like other ancient makarisms, this one announces an anticipated eschatological verdict; cf. *1 En.* 81.4: "Blessed is the man who dies righteous and upright, against whom no record of oppression has been written, and who received no judgment on that day."

Sentences 41–50

Text

41 ᵃὃ ἂν τιμήσῃςᵃ ὑπὲρ πάντα, ἐκεῖνόᵇ σου κυριεύσει.
42 τίμα τὸᵃ ἄριστον, ἵνα καὶ ἄρχῃ ὑπὸ τοῦ ἀρίστου.
43 ἀρχόμενος ὑπὸ τοῦ ἀρίστου αὐτὸςᵃ ἄρξεις ὧν ἂν προαιρῇ.
44 τιμὴ μεγίστη θεῷ θεοῦ γνῶσις καὶ ὁμοίωμα.
45 ᵃὅμοιον μὲν οὐδὲν θεῷᵃ, προσφιλέστατον δὲ τὸ εἰς δύναμιν ἐξομοιούμενον.
46a ἱερὸν ἅγιον θεοῦ διάνοια εὐσεβοῦς.
46b ἄριστον θυσιαστήριον θεῷ καρδία καθαρὰ καὶ ἀναμάρτητος.
47 θυσία θεῷ μόνη καὶᵃ προσηνὴς ἡᵇ ᶜἀνθρώποις εὐεργεσία διὰ θεόνᶜ.
48 ἄνθρωπος κεχαρισμένα θεῷ πράττει ὁ ζῶν εἰς δύναμιν κατὰ θεόν.
49 ὁ μὲν θεὸς οὐδενὸς δεῖται, ὁ δὲ πιστόςᵃ μόνου θεοῦᵇ.
50 ζηλοῖ τὸν οὐδενὸς δεόμενον ὁ τῶν ὀλίγωνᵃ ἀναγκαίως δεόμενος.

78   THE *SENTENCES* OF SEXTUS

Translation

41   That which you honor above all things will rule you.
42   Honor what is best so that you may also be governed by what is best.
43   If you are governed by what is best, you yourself will govern what you choose.
44   The greatest honor to offer God is to know and become like God.
45   Nothing is like God, but dearest to him is that which becomes like him as much as possible.
46a   A pious person's intellect is a holy temple of God.
46b   The best altar for God is a heart pure and sinless.
47   The only offering suitable for God is beneficence to humanity for God's sake.
48   A person who lives as much as possible in accord with God has earned favor with God.
49   God has need of nothing; the faithful one has need only of God.
50   The one who has need of few things for his necessities emulates the one who has need of nothing.

Textual Notes

41ᵃ⁻ᵃ ὃ ἐὰν τιμήσεις [*sic*]: Π • 41ᵇ ἐκεῖνός: Π • 42ᵃ τὸν: Π, lat • 43ᵃ omit Π • 45ᵃ⁻ᵃ ἐλέου ὅμοιον μὲν οὐδέν: Υ • 47ᵃ ἡ: Υ • 47ᵇ omit Π • 47ᶜ⁻ᶜ ὑπὸ ἀνθρώπου εἰς ἄνθρωπον διὰ θεὸν εὐεργεσία: Υ • 49ᵃ πιστὸς καὶ σοφός: Π • 49ᵇ τοῦ θεοῦ: Υ • 50ᵃ ἐλαχίστων: Υ

Commentary

This unit opens with sayings (in vv. 41–45) connected by the theme of honor. Note τιμάω in vv. 41 and 42, and τιμή in v. 44. These sayings have attracted others by way of catchword, v. 43 being linked to v. 42 by the repetition of ἄριστος and ἄρχω, and v. 45 being linked to v. 44 by the similarity of ὁμοίωμα and ὅμοιος. The unit begins with a rule on the dynamics of honor and subordination (v. 41), followed by a specific recommendation based on that rule. Lines 42–43 then extend the theme with a short *gradatio*: honor/governed/governed/govern. This crescendos to an effective rhetorical conclusion: the readers possess the ability to choose not only what to honor but, if they choose wisely, what to govern. The underdetermined nature of vv. 41–43 is then resolved by v. 44, which stipulates both the object of the readers' honor and the form that it takes. Finally, a rider in v. 45 offers both a qualification of and motivation for the objective identified in v. 44. The logic of the section is perhaps best grasped by reading its lines in reverse order: to imitate God means to honor God, and to honor God is to be governed by God, which in turn enables one to govern whatever one chooses. The formulation of the Platonic *telos* in vv. 44–45, in turn, has attracted a different formulation of the *telos* in vv. 48–50. Nestled in between are three temple-imagery sayings that develop in its support an implicit anthropology: if assimilation to God is to involve the whole person, it must involve thoughts (v. 46a), intentions (v. 46b), and deeds (v. 47). The temple imagery draws attention both to the need for moral purity, so that the self becomes a fit place for the divine to dwell, and to the need for moral exclusiveness, so that the only activity deemed fit for the sage is that which focuses on God.

Sentences 41–42

For v. 41, Chadwick (1959, 165) and Wilken (1975, 155–56) point to Luke 12:34 (cf. Matt 6:21) as a parallel, though note that the gospel text lacks Sextus's emphasis on being ruled by what one honors, an idea that connects this saying with the two that follow (for a more likely instance of reliance on Luke 12:34, see v. 316). Of course what the readers of the *Sentences* are expected to honor above all else is God (vv. 44, 244, 319). This means that they are expected to assign honor not according to worldly criteria (vv. 130, 192) but, in keeping with their status as God's children, according to what God himself honors (v. 135, cf. vv. 65, 583), thereby imitating God (see below). This includes honoring a fellow sage (vv. 219, 244, 319) as well as a word about God (vv. 355, 439), even though ultimately honor is less about words than actions (v. 427). Cf. *Sent. Pythag.* 79 ("Every person is worthy to the extent that the things he knows or thinks are worthy"); Marcus Aurelius, *Med.* 7.3 ("Someone is worth only as much as the things about which he is serious are worth").

In negotiating their roles as both moral and political agents, it would have been the natural aspiration of every ancient person to be governed by "the best" (e.g., Aristotle, *Eth. nic.* 9.6.2; *Pol.* 3.10.3–4), even if the exigencies of human affairs made achieving such a scenario virtually impossible. In the moral world projected by v. 42, however, the sage possesses the ability to choose that by which he will be governed. In order to be governed by something, however, one must honor it; that is, one must endeavor to know and imitate it to the best of one's ability (vv. 44–45). It was a point of agreement that τιμή demands not just expressions of respect but concrete acts of obedience. According to Clement, for instance, Prov 7:1 teaches that people show honor to God through fidelity to God's commands (*Strom.* 2.8.39.5). Similarly, for Origen it is obvious that the best way to honor God is to observe God's law (*Cels.* 8.10). Cf. Philo, *Somn.* 2.100: "Of all things in creation that one can hold in honor, servitude to God is best."

Sentence 43

Verse 36 described the sort of authority that the faithful receive from God. Something of the relational nature of this authority is indicated in vv. 43–45. Here Sextus not only articulates for his readers a basic principle of governance; he also summons them to recognize how this principle informs both (1) how and by whom they are ruled, and (2) how and whom they themselves rule. From this perspective, the configuration of power relations set forth for the sage can be compared with that of a political state. According to Aristotle, for example, while different types of constitutional arrangements for a city are possible, "in relation to the best form, a citizen is one who has the capacity and the will both to be governed and to govern with a view to the life in harmony with virtue" (*Pol.* 3.7.13). Accordingly, if there is an individual in the state who is "so greatly distinguished in outstanding virtue" that no one else can compare, it is no longer proper to consider that person a part of the state; rather, "such a man will naturally be as a god among men" (*Pol.* 3.8.1). While the criterion that determines the arrangement of power in the Aristotelian system is the possession of virtue, in the *Sentences* it is, as we will soon learn, the imitation of God. Specifically, the sage honors (i.e., imitates) God to such an extent that in being governed by God he in turn governs whatever he chooses. Implicated in a divine continuum of governance, he can be thought of as a godlike man (vv. 7a, 82d, 376a), exercising control not only over other human beings (v. 182) but also over his body (v. 274a) and desires (v. 240), thus doing everything under the control of God (v. 288, cf. v. 264b).

Sentences 44–45

Among ancient educators it was understood that people emulate what they honor and honor what they emulate. Therefore, if students hope to make progress in their moral development by emulating the character and deeds of a worthy role model, such imitation needs to be accompanied by feelings not of envy or jealousy but of honor and goodwill (e.g., Plutarch,

Virt. prof. 84e). It is only at this point in the *Sentences* that the identity of the "best" and the manner in which it is "best" honored becomes plain. A similar thought is expressed by Porphyry in *Marc.* 11: "Appropriate honor (τιμή) has been rendered to God by the one who has firm knowledge (ἐγνωκότος) of God." Cf. Hierocles, *In aur. carm.* 1.17: "For as the Pythagoreans say, you will honor (τιμήσεις) God best if you make your intellect like God (τῷ θεῷ τὴν διάνοιαν ὁμοιώσῃς)." The Sextine sage honors God not only by growing in the knowledge of God (v. 439) but also by forming himself in God's likeness, which, according to vv. 41–43, means being governed by God. As Sextus argues in v. 148, it is the knowledge and ὁμοίωμα of God together that ought to constitute for his readers the *summum bonum* (cf. vv. 201, 216).

Such statements invite comparison with middle Platonic and Neoplatonic identifications of the *telos*, which were derived especially from Plato, *Theaet.* 176a–b: "One should make all haste to escape from earth to heaven; and escape means becoming as much like God as possible (ὁμοίωσις θεῷ κατὰ τὸ δυνατόν); and one becomes like God when he becomes just and pious, with understanding" (cf. *Tim.* 90c–d; *Resp.* 500c, 613a–b). By the early imperial period, the doctrine of assimilation (ἐξομοίωσις) had taken on various permutations, though the interpretation advanced in the *corpus Philonicum* is fairly representative, particularly insofar as it depicts the process of becoming like the divine as an exercise in choosing and following the way of the virtues (*Opif.* 144, cf. 151; *Deus* 48; *Fug.* 63; *Abr.* 60–61, 87; *Decal.* 100–101; *Spec.* 4.188). Since "God, being One, is alone and unique, and like God there is nothing," such assimilation must take the dissimilarities between God and humankind into account (*Leg.* 2.1; cf. Sext. 45). Philo is also instructive insofar as he anticipates the work of later, Christian authors by integrating the Platonic goal of assimilation with the biblical affirmation that humankind was created after the image and likeness (καθ' ὁμοίωσιν) of God (Gen 1:26). Cf. Clement, *Strom.* 2.19.97.1: "He is the gnostic, who is after the image and likeness of God, who imitates God as far as possible." Since it is possible to speak of the image of God in humankind only with respect to the mind, Philo (e.g., *Det.* 83) and Clement (e.g., *Strom.* 2.19.102.6) would have further agreed both with one another and with the Pythagorean tradition (see the quote of Hierocles, *In aur. carm.* 1.17 above) that any progress in human assimilation to that image necessitates the involvement of the faculty of reason. Cf. Marcus Aurelius, *Med.* 10.8: "It is not flattery (the gods) crave but for all rational things to be conformed to their likeness." This basic perspective informs the version of Sext. 44–45 preserved in v. 381 ("The one who makes his intellect like God as much as possible honors God best"), which confines the process of assimilation to the work of the διάνοια, that part of the human self that has the greatest affinity for the divine (vv. 46a, 61, 144, 147, 450, 533); cf. v. 447: "If you see God you will make the ability to reason within of the same sort as God's." In vv. 44–45, the anthropological scope for conforming to God is potentially much broader, though it should be emphasized that the reference to γνῶσις in a context of this kind is hardly gratuitous. After all, one can conform to the nature of the divine only to the extent that the nature of the divine can be known (v. 439). In this regard, comparison can again be made with Clement, in whose regimen of assimilation becoming like God and growing in the true knowledge of God are not only concomitant processes but also mutually implicating and mutually reinforcing activities (e.g., *Strom.* 3.5.42.1; 4.26.168.2; 7.14.86.5). Accordingly, the regimen is actualized through a combination of moral and contemplative practices. As he puts it in *Strom.* 3.5.42.5, to become like the Lord means that "we are, as far as possible, to purify ourselves from pleasures and lusts, and to take care of our soul, which should continue to be engaged solely with the divine."

In order to appreciate one final dimension of Sextus's pronouncement in v. 45, it is necessary to consider a different formulation of the *telos*, this one articulated by Plato in *Leg.* 716c–d: "What conduct is dear to God and in his steps? One kind of conduct, expressed in an ancient phrase, namely, 'like is dear to like.' … So the one who is to become dear (προσφιλῆ) to God must become, as much as possible, of a like character." As we know from v. 443, Sextus is also familiar with the philosophical appropriation of Homer, *Od.* 17.218, and his use of προσφιλής here similarly defines the affinity between God and the sage in terms of likeness. The goal of pleasing God will appear again in v. 48 (cf. vv. 358–359). As vv. 422–424 suggest, pleasing God is also a product of being governed by God, a point that connects v. 45 with vv. 41–43 earlier in the unit. Cf. Epictetus, *Diatr.* 2.14.12: "Next we must learn what the gods are like; for whatever their character is discovered to be, the one who is going to please and obey them must endeavor as much as possible to become like (ἐξομοιοῦσθαι) them." A counterpart to Sextus's thought here can be found in v. 579: ὁμοίωσις θεοῦ παντὸς τοὐναντίου ἀποφυγή (note the use of φυγή in Plato, *Theaet.* 176a–b; cf. Philo, *Fug.* 63; Clement, *Strom.* 2.22.133.3; Plotinus, *Enn.* 1.2.3; Methodius, *Symp.* 1.5: ὁμοίωσις γὰρ θεῷ φθορᾶς ἀποφυγή).

Sentence 46a

Imitating God entails honoring God with appropriate devotion, as Porphyry explains: "We shall worship him in pure silence and with pure thoughts about him. We must, then, be joined with him and made like him, and must offer our own uplifting as a holy sacrifice" (*Abst.* 2.34.2–3; cf. Augustine, *Civ.* 19.23; Minucius Felix, *Oct.* 32: "The best sacrifice is a good disposition, a pure mind, and a sincere judgment"). From this perspective, it stands to reason that a precept about conforming to God would be joined to an observation regarding the intellect, since the intellect is that part of the human self that has the greatest affinity for the divine. God is νοῦς (v. 26), and that which is godlike (vv. 35, 442) is τὸ νοοῦν (v. 394). It is therefore possible to speak of the intellect not only as the mirror of God (v. 450) but also as the abode of God (v. 61), the very place where the divine dwells (v. 144). This is not the intellect as such, however, but the intellect that is "pure" (v. 57b) and "good" (v. 61), that is, the intellect of the sage (vv. 143–144, 450). For the logic connecting v. 46a with vv. 44–45, see especially v. 381 ("The one who makes his intellect like God as much as possible honors God best") and v. 447: "If you see God you will make the ability to reason within of the same sort as God's."

It would have been natural, of course, to utilize temple imagery in the context of instruction about how best to honor the deity. Chadwick (1959, 144, 147) suggests as parallels to v. 46a *Sent. Pythag.* 66ᵃ (νεὼς θεοῦ σοφὸς νοῦς) and Porphyry, *Marc.* 19 (νεὼς μὲν ἔστω τοῦ θεοῦ ὁ ἐν σοὶ νοῦς), though Sextus's actual terminology is better reflected in Porphyry, *Marc.* 11: "The divine is entirely present everywhere, but its sanctuary among humanity has been firmly established only in the intellect (διάνοια) of the sage … and let a temple (ἱερόν) be adorned for him because of wisdom in his judgment, one with a living statue, the mind, for God imparts his form to the one who honors him" (note that this passage is preceded in *Marc.* 11 by a sentence that parallels Sext. 44 and followed in *Marc.* 11 by a sentence that parallels Sext. 49). Cf. Porphyry, *Abst.* 2.45.4: "Holiness (ἁγνεία), both internal and external, belongs to a godly man (ἀνδρὸς … θείου) … who feeds on wisdom about the gods and becomes like them (ὁμοιουμένου) through right thoughts (διανοίαις) about the divine, a man sanctified by intellectual sacrifice." Whatever his inspiration, what makes our author's formulation distinctive is its use of εὐσεβής, the Sextine sage being particularly noteworthy for his piety (vv. 82d, 86b, 287). For the temple imagery, see further on v. 35.

Sext. 46a–b is the second of three sayings that according to Augustine (*Nat. grat.* 64.77) Pelagius borrowed from the *Sentences*. Cf. on vv. 36, 60. For v. 46a, Augustine has *templum sanctum est Deo mens pura*. His version of v. 46b is the same as that offered by Rufinus.

Sentence 46b

It is not simply the intellect but also the heart that must be "pure of all evil" (v. 57b, cf. v. 181). In scriptural contexts, the pure heart is a symbol of moral integrity and singleness of intention (e.g., Pss 24:4 [23:4]; 51:10 [50:12]; Matt 5:8; 1 Tim 1:5; 2 Tim 2:22). Perhaps more to the point for our author is the idea that the one who is pure of heart is pure from sins (Prov 20:9; Sir 38:10; Jas 4:8). For the expression "pure and sinless," see also v. 36, cf. vv. 60, 204: "Passion will not arise in a faithful person's heart." Within the context of vv. 41–50, the altar-heart metaphor of v. 46b can be interpreted as an effort to encourage moral introspection. Compare Pol. *Phil.* 4.3: "The widows must think soberly about the faith … knowing that they are God's altar, and that all sacrifices are carefully inspected and nothing escapes him, whether thoughts or intentions or secrets of the heart." As Ps.-Macarius states, the human heart is an altar of the Holy Spirit only if it is indeed holy, that is, pure of desire, hatred, anger, and passion (*Serm.* 7.18.3). For comparable imagery, see Ps 51:17 [50:19] ("A broken spirit is an offering to God, a broken and humbled heart God will not despise"), a verse that is cited in different variations by *Ep. Barn.* 2.10 and Clement, *Strom.* 2.18.79.1. See further *Let. Aris.* 234 ("Honoring God: this is not done with gifts or sacrifices, but with purity of heart and a devout disposition"); Philo, *Spec.* 1.287 ("The true altar of God is the thankful soul of the sage"); *Ep. Barn.* 6.15 ("For the dwelling place of our heart … is a holy temple dedicated to the Lord"); Clement, *Strom.* 7.6.32.5 ("The truly hallowed altar is the righteous soul, and the incense which ascends from it, the prayer of holiness"); Origen, *Cels.* 8.17: "Our altars are the mind of each righteous person, from which true and intelligible incense with a sweet savor is sent up, prayers from a pure conscience."

Sentence 47

If the best purification is to do no harm (v. 23, cf. v. 370), then the best offering is to do good. The sage bestows benefits "for God's sake" both because he, like all of humanity, is the recipient of God's beneficence (v. 33) and because, in conforming himself to God, he distinguishes himself by becoming a benefactor second only to God (v. 176, cf. v. 542), that is, a common benefactor of all humanity (vv. 210a, 260, cf. vv. 213, 328). Compare Clitarchus, *Sent.* 63 (ἄνθρωπος ὅμοιον ἔχει θεῷ τὸ εὐεργετεῖν), 134; *Sent. Pythag.* 105. As Clement explains in *Strom.* 2.19.97.1, those who endeavor to become like God must live righteously, control their passions, and share their possessions, "conferring benefits in word and deed (εὐεργετῶν καὶ λόγῳ καὶ ἔργῳ)." In this they imitate God best by offering gifts similar to those God offers, that is, gifts "available for the benefit of all" (*Strom.* 2.19.97.2).

It was a commonplace among ancient Christian moralists that the only offering worthy of the divine was an upright life, and that ritual practices were acceptable to the deity only if accompanied by moral integrity. According to Clement, *Strom.* 6.7.60.2–3, for example, the temple-like purity of the body in which the gnostic soul dwells is achieved not only by abstaining from evil deeds but also through "the fixed habit of doing good after the likeness of God (εὐποιίας καθ' ὁμοίωσιν τοῦ θεοῦ)." Elsewhere in the same document he explains that the only things that are "acceptable sacrifice in God's sight" are "gentleness, philanthropy, and magnanimous piety" (*Strom.* 7.3.14.1). Cf. *Act. mart. Apoll.* 44 ("By almsgiving and a philanthropic manner of life you might send up prayers to God alone as a bloodless and pure sacrifice"); Minucius Felix, *Oct.* 32 ("He who cultivates justice makes offerings to God"); Origen, *Hom. Num.* 11.9: "If one gives to the poor, if one performs any good work, he has offered to God a present according to the commandment." Sextus assumes that devotion to God expresses itself not only in helping humanity, but also in loving humanity (v. 371; cf. *Sent. Pythag.* 51; Porphyry, *Marc.* 35).

Sentence 48

This version of the Platonic *telos* is similar to the one conveyed in v. 45, though it lacks the latter's proviso that "nothing is like God" and uses different language to describe the divine approval conferred on the sage (κεχαρισμένα ... πράττει). More important, the process of assimilation is expressed here as a matter of how one "lives," specifically, ζῶν εἰς δύναμιν κατὰ θεόν. This formulation is reminiscent especially of *Phaedr.* 273e, where Plato explains how people who are sensible exert themselves "so as to be able to speak and to act (πράττειν) in a way that pleases (κεχαρισμένα) the gods as much as possible (εἰς δύναμιν)" (cf. Clement, *Strom.* 1.28.176.3). Sextus is convinced that individuals possess the freedom to live well (v. 255, cf. v. 262), that is, to live with God (v. 215), to live in a way that expresses one's faith in God and reverence for God (vv. 196, 326b). Since living κατὰ θεόν is the ultimate form of human existence (v. 201), the sage will endure "everything" in order to achieve it (v. 216). Living in accordance with God means acting in accordance with the virtues (v. 399).

With his reference to the goal of earning divine favor, Sextus taps into an important theme of biblical spirituality. The lives of the patriarchs in particular were deemed "well pleasing" to God (Gen 5:22, 24; 6:9; 17:1; Wis 4:10; Sir 44:16; Heb 11:5; Justin Martyr, *Dial*. 45.4; Ps.-Clement, *Hom*. 18.14). Indeed, according to Philo the one thing that the patriarchs all had in common was the view that pleasing God constitutes the *telos* of human life (*Praem*. 24; cf. *Mut*. 41–42; *Abr*. 235). As he puts it elsewhere, all the words and actions of those whose goal is assimilation to God are "undertaken in order to please the father and king" (*Opif*. 144). For variations on the εὐάρεστος theme, see Rom 12:1–2; 2 Cor 5:9; Eph 5:10; Heb 13:21; *1 Clem*. 21.1; 35.5; Herm. *Man*. 12.3.1; *Sim*. 5.3.2; Theophilus, *Autol*. 2.38; *Act. Thom*. 85.

Sentences 49–50

For the progression of thought linking vv. 49–50 with v. 48, see vv. 381–382: "The one who makes his intellect like God as much as possible honors God best. God needs nothing in any way, but rejoices in those who share with those in need." The objective of emulating God in the area of necessities (ἀναγκαῖα) is raised also in vv. 18–19: "A sage without property is like God. Use worldly things only for essential needs." The sage not only limits his need for such things: since they do not feed the life of the soul, he finds them to be despicable (v. 127).

As a parallel to v. 49, Chadwick (1959, 147, 166) cites *Sent. Pythag*. 39[a]: θεὸς δεῖται οὐδενός· σοφὸς δὲ μόνου δεῖται θεοῦ. However, seeing how Sext. 51 is paralleled by Clitarchus, *Sent*. 5 (see below), a more likely source for Sext. 49 (and one that accords more closely with the actual wording) is Clitarchus, *Sent*. 4 (ὁ μὲν θεὸς οὐδενὸς δεῖται, ὁ δὲ σοφὸς μόνου θεοῦ), while the source for the first part of Sext. 50 appears to be Clitarchus, *Sent*. 11: ζήλου τὸν μηδενὸς δεόμενον. With its μέν ... δέ ... construction, the version of the former preserved in Porphyry, *Marc*. 11 (θεὸς μὲν γὰρ δεῖται οὐδενός, σοφὸς δὲ μόνου θεοῦ) resembles the sayings in Clitarchus, *Sent*. 4 and Sext. 49, though it agrees with *Sent. Pythag*. 39[a] in eschewing the definite article (note that the parallel for v. 49 in *Marc*. 11 follows the passage in *Marc*. 11 quoted above as a parallel for v. 46a). Whatever his inspiration, it is apparent that our author has replaced the reference to σοφός in his source with πιστός. This conforms with redactional proclivities evident elsewhere in the text (see part 4 of the introduction) and brings the gnome into alignment with declarations about the pious person earlier in the section (vv. 46a–47).

As Wicker (1987, 97) notes, the sentiment expressed in Sext. 49–50 and so forth constitutes a gnomic *topos*. Cf. Xenophon, *Mem.* 1.6.10: "To have no wants is divine; to have as few as possible comes next to the divine." As befits his assimilation to God, the Philonic sage "is in want of little, standing on the boundary between immortal and mortal nature," since "God, being in need of nothing, is in want of nothing, but he himself is completely sufficient in himself" (*Virt.* 8–9). From a Pythagorean context we have Ps.-Ecphantus, *Regn.* 82.7–30: God alone achieves perfect self-sufficiency. However, insofar as the king is the likeness of God and assimilates himself to God, he participates in the self-sufficiency of God and models it for others: "Indeed, the imitation of God is the self-sufficiency of everything else." The subject was also a favorite of Clement's— for example, *Protr.* 10.105.3: "An adherent of the one who needs nothing is himself in need of little." In *Paed.* 3.1.1.1, he explains that people become like God, "by having as few needs as possible. For God alone has no needs, and he rejoices especially when he sees … our bodies clothed with the adornment of moderation" (cf. Plato, *Leg.* 716c–d). The divine to which the faithful endeavor to assimilate themselves "is free alike from need and passion" (*Strom.* 2.18.80.5–2.18.81.1; cf. 2.6.28.3). See further Porphyry, *Abst.* 1.37.4: the philosopher commits himself to "living a life suited to that which he seeks to resemble (i.e., the divine), a simple, self-sufficient life, involved as little as possible with mortal things" (cf. 1.54.6). Also see *Sent. Pythag.* 30, cited above under vv. 18–19. The theme not unexpectedly also makes an appearance in Cynic sources, for example, Ps.-Crates, *Ep.* 11: "Practice being in need of only a few things, for this is the closest thing to God" (cf. Diogenes Laertius, *Vit. phil.* 6.104). Manifestations of self-sufficiency are of particular importance in establishing the philosopher's moral and social pre-eminence: "For the gods need nothing. But, so that you may learn more exactly what is involved in having few needs … reflect that children have more needs than adults, women than men, invalids than the healthy, and, in general, the inferior everywhere has more needs than the superior. Therefore the gods have need of nothing and those nearest to them have the fewest needs" (Ps.-Lucian, *Cyn.* 12). Sext. 49–50 is distinct from such pronouncements in stipulating not only that the sage has few needs but that he has in fact only one need, namely, God (cf. v. 148).

To be ζῆλος θεοῦ is an important dimension of biblical piety (e.g., Num 25:13; 3 Kgdms 19:10, 14; Jdt 9:4; Sir 45:23; Acts 22:3; Rom 10:2). For various developments of the theme, see *T. Ash.* 4.5; Philo, *Leg.* 3.242; *Post.* 183; Epiphanius, *Pan.* 70.1.1. For a parallel from Greco-Roman literature, cf. Epictetus, *Diatr.* 2.14.13: in everything he says and does, the philosopher must be a ζηλωτὴς θεοῦ.

Sentences 51–62

Text

51 ἄσκει ᵃμέγας μὲνᵃ εἶναι παρὰ θεῷ, παρὰ δὲ ἀνθρώποις ἀνεπίφθονος.
52 χρηστὸς ὢν εἰς τοὺς δεομένουςᵃ μέγας ἂν εἴης παρὰ θεῷ.
53 ἀνδρὸς σοφοῦ ᵃζῶντος μὲνᵃ ᵇὀλίγος ὁ λόγοςᵇ παρὰ ἀνθρώποις, τελευτήσαντος δὲ τὸ κλέος ᾄδεται.
54 τὸν χρόνον ὃν ἂν μὴ νοήσῃςᵃ τὸν θεόν, τοῦτον νόμιζέ σοι ἀπολωλέναιᵇ.
55 τὸ μὲν σῶμά σου μόνονᵃ ἐπιδημείτω τῇ γῇ, ἡ δὲ ψυχὴᵇ ἀεὶ ἔστω παρὰ θεῷ.
56 νόει τὰ καλά, ἵνα καὶ πράττῃςᵃ τὰ καλά.
57a ἔννοια ἀνθρώπου ᵃθεὸν οὐᵃ λανθάνει.
57b ἔστω σου ἡ διάνοια καθαρὰ κακοῦ παντός.
58 ἄξιος ἔσοᵃ τοῦ ἀξιώσαντός σε εἰπεῖνᵇ υἱόνᶜ ᵈκαὶ πράττε πάνταᵈ ὡς υἱὸς θεοῦ.
59 θεὸν πατέρα καλῶν ἐν οἷς πράττεις τούτου μέμνησο.
60 ἁγνὸς ἀνὴρ καὶ ἀναμάρτητος ἐξουσίαν ἔχειᵃ παρὰ θεῷ ὡς υἱὸς θεοῦ.
61 ἀγαθὴ διάνοια χῶροςᵃ θεοῦ.
62 κακὴ διάνοια χῶρόςᵃ ἐστιν κακῶν.

Translation

51 Practice being great with God while not arousing envy with people.
52 If you are kind to those in need, you will be great with God.
53 While he lives a wise man is of little account among the people, but after he dies his fame is praised.
54 Whatever time you do not spend thinking about God, consider this to be lost to you.

55 Let your body alone be at home on the earth; let your soul always be with God.
56 Think about noble things, so that you may also do noble things.
57a What a person is thinking does not escape God's attention.
57b Let your intellect be pure of every evil.
58 Be worthy of the one who deems you worthy to be called son and act always as God's son.
59 In the things you do remember this, that you call God "father."
60 A man holy and sinless has power before God as God's son.
61 A good intellect is the abode of God.
62 An evil intellect is the abode of evil things.

Textual Notes

51ᵃ⁻ᵃ μὲν μέγας: Υ • 52ᵃ δεηθέντας: Υ • 53ᵃ⁻ᵃ omit Υ • 53ᵇ⁻ᵇ ὁ λόγος ὀλίγος: Π • 54ᵃ νοῇς: Π • 54ᵇ ἀπολελωκέναι: Π • 55ᵃ omit lat • 55ᵇ ψυχή σου: Υ • 56ᵃ πράττεις: Π • 57aᵃ⁻ᵃ omit Υ • 58ᵃ ἔσῃ: Π; ἔσω: Υ • 58ᵇ καὶ εἰπόντος: Υ • 58ᶜ υἱὸν θεοῦ: Π • 58ᵈ⁻ᵈ πρᾶττε οὖν πάντα: Π; καὶ πάντα πρᾶττε: Υ • 59 omit Υ • 60 omit Υ • 60ᵃ ἔχῃ: Π • 61ᵃ χορὸς: lat • 62ᵃ χορός: lat

COMMENTARY

This section contains two units. The first and shorter unit (vv. 51–53) concerns the dual standing of the sage, that is, his reputation before God and his reputation among other people. Note μέγας ... παρὰ θεῷ in vv. 51 and 52, and παρὰ ... ἀνθρώποις in vv. 51 and 53. While attending to the former is obviously more urgent, both are presented as matters of concern (see on v. 16). The second unit (vv. 54–62) presents a rather complex sequence of sayings expounding largely on the nature of the sage's thoughts. Note the linking words νοέω (vv. 54, 56), ἔννοια (v. 57a), and διάνοια (vv. 57b, 61–62); cf. μιμνήσκω in v. 59. Most of the initial gnomes are commands, with the observation in v. 57a serving as a motive sentence for the jussive in v. 57b, while the final three sayings take the form of pronouncements. The first two sayings establish priorities for the sage's noetic activity in terms of time (v. 54) and place (v. 55), while v. 56 elucidates the purpose of such activity. Contrasts between good and evil thoughts, expressed in vv. 56–57b through commands and in vv. 60–61 through precepts, juxtapose the basic alternatives. Within this discussion, vv. 58–60, on the sage's status as a son of God the father, has the appearance of a digression or interruption. To be sure, the lexical connection between these verses and the surrounding material is weak (though note πράττω in vv. 56, 58, 59). By the same token, in terms of content the section can be seen to lend some specificity to the thought–action process delineated in vv. 53–57b, 61–62, especially by introducing the theme of remembrance. Time spent thinking about God (v. 54) should include remembering that God is the father (v. 59), while purifying the mind of all evil (v. 57b) is a means of becoming the sort of ἁγνὸς ἀνήρ who receives authority as God's son (v. 60).

Sentence 51

The source for this gnome is Clitarchus, *Sent.* 5: ἄσκει μέγας εἶναι παρὰ τῷ θεῷ, παρὰ δὲ ἀνθρώποις ἀνεπίφθονος. Sextus adds μέν after μέγας and drops τῷ. Even as the sage endeavors to know and become like God (cf. on vv. 41–50), he must also make a practice of being ἀπενίφθονος, that is, of not causing resentment or envy in others. Among ancient moralists, envy ranked among the most destructive and intractable of the vices (cf. vv. 463, 477, 497). Attracting envy was a problem for virtually anyone who had achieved a certain level of success or prominence. As Josephus puts it, "even if one restrains his lawless passions, it is difficult, especially in a position of high authority, to escape the calumnies of envy" (*Vita* 80). Philosophers would hardly have been immune from this, especially given their role in society as moral authorities and guides. For example, although Pythagoras and his followers conferred many benefits on the states of Greece, "still they did not escape the envy which besmirches all noble things" (Diodorus Siculus, *Bibl. hist.* 10.10.2). Some people were envious of Socrates as well, "at his receiving greater favors even from the gods than they had" (Xenophon, *Apol.* 14). A somewhat different view is expressed by Maximus of Tyre, according to whom Socrates was rather exceptional in that, although "he conversed with the divine in his mind," he ordered his life in such a way that his interactions with others did not arouse envy or anything inappropriate (*Dial.* 8.3). This reflects the idea that various strategies could be adopted for minimizing behavior conducive of envy. The elder Cato, for example, is reported as saying that the person least likely to be envied is the one who is careful to live ἐπιεικῶς καὶ μετρίως (Plutarch, *Reg. imp. apophth.* 199a; cf. Ps.-Plutarch, *Lib. ed.* 7f). Similar remedies were prescribed within Pythagorean circles as well. According to Porphyry, for example, Pythagoras "urged everyone to avoid the love of honors and praise, which particularly occasions envy, and to shun public discussions" (*Vit. Pythag.* 32). Also from the Pythagorean tradition is *Carm. aur.* 35–36: "Become accustomed to have a pure way of life, not an enervated one, and guard against doing the kind of thing that incurs envy."

Sextus's admonition here would seem to be a specific application of the advice given in vv. 16 and 38: do not give anyone, including anyone in "the world," reason to censure you (cf. v. 37). This includes eschewing any behavior that might anger the people (v. 343) or anything that might give the sage's message a bad reputation (v. 396). It is important to remember that in the ancient world the business of becoming ἀπενίφθονος applied especially to one's habits of speech. Plutarch's treatise *De laude ipsius* (Περὶ τοῦ ἑαυτοῦ ἐπαινεῖν ἀνεπιφθόνως), for example, is replete with instructions on how the public speaker can avoid inciting envy in his listeners (540b–d, 542f, 543d, 544b, etc.). Read against this background, the discretion Sextus urges in matters of speech would be particularly apt for someone intent on not incurring the envy of others. The sage is to refrain from all boasting (e.g., vv. 284, 432), especially when it comes to his status as one of the chosen (v. 433). In concert with this, he avoids speaking to the multitudes (v. 360, cf. v. 164a), neither seeking nor valuing public approval (v. 112). Indeed, he views praise with scorn when it comes from individuals he does not respect (vv. 241, 299). Thus the fame enjoyed by the sage during his lifetime will be limited, owing, at least in part, to his belief that "a love of reputation is the foremost cause of a bad reputation" (v. 188). Immunizing oneself from attracting envy (often associated with the evil eye) is a priority with a variety of patristic authors; see especially Basil of Caesarea's *De invidia*.

Sentence 52

Aiding those in need constitutes one of the fundamental practices of sapiential piety. In some cases, compliance is encouraged with reminders of how such actions bring the agent into a positive relationship with God—for example, Prov 14:31; 19:17 ("The one who has mercy on a poor person lends to God, and he will repay him according to his gift"); 22:9; 28:7; Tob 4:7 ("Do not turn your face away from any poor person, and the face of God shall not be turned away from you"), 11; Sir 17:22 ("The almsgiving of a man is as a signet ring with him, and he will keep someone's kindness as the apple of his eye"); cf. *T. Zeb.* 6.6; Matt 6:3–4; 19:21; 25:34–40; Mark 10:21; Luke 12:33; 18:22; Acts 10:4 ("Your prayers and your alms have ascended as a memorial before God"); *2 Clem.* 16.4. In some texts, what is redemptive is not the act of aid itself, but the resulting intercessory prayer offered by the recipient of the aid; for examples, see on v. 217.

The obligation to share, which is mentioned repeatedly in our text (e.g., vv. 82b, 227-228, 295-296, 377), represents one aspect of the sage's participation in a regime of benefaction (e.g., vv. 33, 176, 210a, 260): what he has freely received from God, he freely gives to others (v. 242). Thus he shares his possessions with the needy (v. 330, cf. v. 264a) and his food with everyone, especially with the poor (vv. 266-267). While he does not give in order to attract attention (v. 342), he is aware that such actions meet with the approval of God, who rejoices when someone shares with the needy (v. 382) and loves those who care for orphans (v. 340). It is not what one shares or how much one shares that is "great" before God, but rather the readiness to share (v. 379). Conversely, those who do not help the poor when they are able cannot expect God's help in their time of need (vv. 217, 378).

Sentence 53

The source for this line is Clitarchus, *Sent.* 137: σοφοῦ ζῶντος δόξα μὲν ὀλίγη, μετὰ δὲ τὴν τελευτὴν τὸ κλέος ᾄδεται. Sextus adds ἀνδρός and παρὰ ἀνθρώποις, replaces δόξα with ὁ λόγος (which is in a slightly different position), and uses the participle τελευτήσαντος in lieu of μετὰ δὲ τὴν τελευτήν. Perhaps the most important difference is the addition of παρὰ ἀνθρώποις, which aligns the gnome with vv. 51-52, for which v. 53 serves as a kind of qualification. Cf. *Sent. Pythag.* 9: "Do you wish to be known to the gods? Then above all be unknown to the people." The virtuous deeds of the sage may be recognized by God as soon as they occur, but the sort of reputation they earn him in heaven will be acknowledged fully on earth only after his death (to have enjoyed κλέος for one's wisdom was a common epithet, e.g., *Anth. Gr.* 7.54.3-4; 8.98.3-4; 8.125.3-4; cf. Plutarch, *Tranq. an.* 471b; Philostratus, *Vit. Apoll.* 4.1). The Sextine sage understands not only that during his lifetime he will be recognized by few (v. 145) but that to most people his life will appear to be quite useless (v. 214). This is due in part to the fact that he neither desires nor expects fame (see on v. 51) and avoids those who have been corrupted by it (v. 351, cf. v. 188). Since he does not seek public approval (vv. 112, 241, cf. v. 299) but rather takes it upon himself to refute foolishness (v. 103, cf. vv. 182, 331) and sees the life of the faithless as a disgrace (v. 400), it is not surprising that his is the sort of life that might incur the disrespect, indifference, or even animosity of outsiders. Accordingly, sayings in the collection suggest that under certain circumstances the sage may be slandered (v. 259) or censured (v. 299), or that there are certain individuals who are simply unable to endure the sage's presence (v. 246, cf. v. 229). Someone, perhaps a tyrant (vv. 363b–364), might deprive him of his possessions (vv. 15, 17) or even his life (vv. 321–322). He must therefore be careful to avoid doing anything that might anger the people (v. 343).

The second half of the saying promises the sage that, despite all this, after his death his praises will be sung. For a typically philosophical perspective on the topic, comparison may be made with Diodorus Siculus's comments about the legacy of Pythagoras in *Bibl. hist.* 10.12.2–3. Those things that are most worthy of remembrance about someone after he dies, we hear, are "reason and the virtues in general which range everywhere upon the lips of fame. Time, which withers all else, preserves for these virtues an immortality, and the further it may itself advance in age, the fresher the youth it imparts to them." Since sages exceed all others in virtue, their renown is not only great—it is multiplied with each successive generation, "for though they were of the distant past, everyone remembers them as though they were present here and now." As Seneca explains, the vice of envy (a topic raised by Sextus in v. 51) has a role to play in this regard, insofar as the virtuous dead are less likely to be envied than the virtuous living: "malice may have imposed silence upon the mouths of all who were alive in your day; but there will come people who will judge you without prejudice and without favor. If there is any reward that virtue receives at the hands of fame, not even this can pass away." Thus, in the end, "virtue is never lost to view.... There will come a day which will reveal her, though hidden away or suppressed by the spite of her contemporaries" (*Ep.* 79.17). It is for this reason that there are many "whose progress toward virtue has come to light only after their death" (*Ep.* 79.14).

Sentence 54

According to Eph 5:15–16, time lost is time not spent living wisely. According to the *Sentences*, time lost is time not spent thinking wisely about God. Insofar as the intellect is that aspect of the human personality that has the greatest affinity for the divine (vv. 46a, 61, 144, 394, 450, etc.), it is through the exercise of one's noetic capacities that one becomes like God (vv. 381, 447). The highest form of such activity, then, focuses on the divine, on growing in one's knowledge of God (v. 44). Accordingly, having trained himself to look constantly to God (vv. 224, 445), the sage does not do anything before thinking about God (v. 95a). In fact, he thinks about God more often than he breathes (v. 289), the time spent reflecting on God serving to enlighten his soul (v. 97, cf. v. 30) to such an extent that his intellect actually reflects the divine to others (v. 450). Cf. *Gnom. Democr.* 112: "It is a mark of a divine mind always to be thinking of something noble."

Sentence 55

The second half of this verse is based on Clitarchus, *Sent.* 7: ἡ ψυχή σου ἀεὶ ἔστω παρὰ θεῷ. Sextus moves σου to after σῶμα in the first half of the line and connects the two strophes with a μέν ... δέ ... construction. Like his intellect (v. 143), the sage's soul is always παρὰ θεῷ. For the unity of the sage's soul with God, see especially on vv. 415b–418: his soul hearkens to God, is attuned to God, always perceives God, and is always in union with God. The implication of this unity spelled out here is that the sage's soul does not, like the body, have as its proper place the earth (γῆ), a term that appears to function as the equivalent of κόσμος (see on vv. 15, 19, 20), that is, as a symbol for the realm of bodily needs and concerns that distracts one's attention from God. As v. 402 explains, the goal of the life of faith is to guide the soul from earth to God. By contrast, the σῶμα of the sage is at home on the earth, and insofar as the body is implicated in "earthly" matters, especially the desire for material possessions and physical pleasures, it can prevent his soul from knowing God (v. 136, cf. v. 411). The body has legitimate needs, but these must be provided for with moderation, so that the soul can devote itself as fully as possible to God (vv. 412–413). In this much, v. 54 is familiar from the description of the philosophical vocation offered by Plato in *Theaet.* 173d-e, a passage that Clement cites with approval in *Strom.* 5.14.98.5–8. The sage, we hear, has little knowledge of the marketplace, the courts, or the places of public assembly. Indeed, "in all these matters, he knows not even that he knows not; for he does not hold himself aloof from them in order to gain a reputation, but because in reality it is only his body that resides and is at home (ἐπιδημεῖ) in the city. His intellect, having come to the conclusion that all these things are of little or no account, spurns them and pursues its winged way ... throughout the universe." By the same token, during the course of one's "earthly" life the body and soul are for Sextus intimately connected. The body bears the imprint of the soul (v. 346) and the soul is tested through the body (v. 425, cf. v. 411), whatever the soul pursued while inhabiting the body accompanying the soul as evidence when it goes to judgment (v. 347). For other body–soul sayings in the collection, see vv. 77–78, 82d, 139a, 301, and 449.

Sentence 56

Excellence in thought is accompanied by excellence in deeds (e.g.,

Aristotle, *Eth. nic.* 8.1.2); cf. P.Ins. 30.3: "One who thinks of the good is one who masters it." For Sextus, thinking about God (v. 54) means thinking noble thoughts, and nothing but noble thoughts (cf. vv. 82e, 178, 233), since this is what befits God (v. 197). Being noble, these thoughts are not ends in themselves but must be translated into actions, that is, actions sanctioned by God (v. 304, cf. vv. 104, 113, 390, 399). Consequently, the only actions that should be undertaken by the sage are those guided by reason (vv. 74, 123, 151, cf. v. 95b). Insofar as such actions are necessarily embodied, the priority identified here sheds some light on the nature of the mind–body connection addressed in the preceding gnomes. The higher aspects of the self, the mind and the soul, should be occupied solely with God. By the same token, the vocation of the sage does not consist solely of intellectual pursuits. Such pursuits, in fact, direct themselves towards a higher purpose: the sage focuses his thoughts appropriately so that (ἵνα) he might act appropriately. For a negative version of the command here, see v. 178: "What must not be done, do not even consider doing."

Sentence 57a

The source for this maxim is Clitarchus, *Sent.* 8: διάνοια ἀνθρώπου θεὸν οὐ λανθάνει. Retaining διάνοια would have made the connection with the admonition in v. 57b clearer (Rufinus's translation has *cogitatio* in both lines), though Sextus may have replaced it with ἔννοια in order to create an alignment with νόει in v. 56, which also occupies the first position in the line. As that verse implied, one's thoughts inform one's actions and, as v. 66 asserts, neither of these can be hidden from God (cf. vv. 94, 186, 303–304, 569). In keeping with the general thrust of the unit (vv. 54–57b), the focus here is on the former. Belief in divine omniscience was widespread: "Nothing escapes his notice (λέληθεν), whether intentions or thoughts (ἐννοιῶν) or the secrets of the heart" (Pol. *Phil.* 4.3). Cf. *T. Gad* 5.3; Philo, *Ios.* 265; *Prov.* 35; Matt 6:4; *Sent. Pythag.* 26; Porphyry, *Marc.* 20–21; Diogenes Laertius, *Vit. phil.* 1.36. From the canon of wisdom literature, perhaps the most sweeping pronouncements on this theme come from Ben Sira: "He searches out the abyss and the heart; he understands the innermost secrets. For the Lord knows all that can be known.... No thought escapes him, and no word is hidden from him" (Sir 42:18, 20; cf. Prov 15:11). See also P.Ins. 5.8: "(The god) knows the impious man and the man of god by his heart." For Stoic reflections on the topic, see especially Epictetus, *Diatr.* 1.14 ("Ὅτι πάντας ἐφορᾷ τὸ θεῖον).

Sentence 57b

Since all of one's thoughts are exposed to God's scrutiny (v. 57a), it is necessary to make those thoughts as acceptable to God as possible. As *Let. Aris.* 132–133 declares, the power and sovereignty of the divine fill the world to such an extent that "even if someone thinks of doing evil he will not escape." Or, as *1 Clem.* 21.8–9 puts it, one must live "in holiness with a pure intellect, for (God) is the searcher of thoughts and desires."

Plato distinguished two types of cleansing, one type dealing with the body, the other type dealing with the soul, that is, with "the cleansing that concerns thinking" (*Soph.* 227c). Sextus busies himself with the latter. For him, it is not only food (e.g., v. 111) or speech (e.g., v. 159) or actions (e.g., v. 102) but also thoughts that can defile. If the intellect, then, is to be the temple and abode of God (vv. 46a, 61, 144), it must be purged of all evil: "Cleanse even your mind of sins" (v. 181, cf. v. 46b). Compare Ign. *Eph.* 15.3: "Nothing is hidden from the Lord; even our secrets are close to him. Therefore let us do everything with the knowledge that he dwells in us in order that we may be his temples." The *Sentences* encourages a general appreciation for the corrupting power of thought: even to think of committing a sin makes one a sinner (v. 233, cf. v. 178); certain thoughts are so evil that they can defile even God (v. 82e). For the desirability of making the intellect morally "pure," see Plato, *Phaed.* 67c; *T. Reub.* 6.1–3; Josephus, *Ant.* 8.120; Porphyry, *Marc.* 23; Marcus Aurelius, *Med.* 8.51; Athanasius, *Vit. Ant.* 34.2. The regimen prescribed by Pythagoras for the training of souls could be described as a κάθαρσις τῆς διανοίας (Iamblichus, *Vit. Pythag.* 16.68–70).

Sentences 58–59

Similar father–son imagery is deployed in vv. 221–222 (v. 222 actually replicates v. 59). While the two members of the couplet there are united by the theme of remembrance, the two here are united by the theme of action. References to the faithful as God's children are strewn throughout the New Testament (e.g., Matt 5:45; Luke 6:35; John 1:12; Rom 8:14–19; Gal 3:26; 4:6–7; Eph 1:5; Heb 12:5–8; 1 Pet 1:14–17; Rev 21:7). The language in v. 58 of being "called" a son by God is redolent especially of passages like Matt 5:9; Rom 9:26; and 1 John 3:1. Reminders of this sort could also provide an incentive for ethical conduct, for example, Eph 5:1 ("Therefore be imitators of God, as beloved children") and Justin Martyr, *Dial.* 123.9 ("We who observe the commandments of Christ are called genuine children of God"). For Sextus, divine filiation is similarly both adoptive and deserved. The father-son imagery (found nowhere in Clitarchus, the *Sententiae Pythagoreorum*, or Porphyry's *Ad Marcellam*) contributes to the broader processes of identity formation fostered by the *Sentences* insofar as it implies and supports a variety of other categorizations for explicating the nature of the reader's relationship to God, including categorizations relating to authority (e.g., v. 182), ranking (e.g., v. 376b), obedience (e.g., v. 288), love, (e.g., vv. 106a-b), and likeness (e.g., vv. 44-45). The categorization mentioned explicitly at this juncture is worthiness. As vv. 3-4 had established, to be ἄξιος of God is a matter of moral action, a point underscored in both members of the couplet. What v. 58 contributes to the development of this theme is the idea that the worthy life is predicated upon and a response to the divine declaration of worthiness. Cf. *2 Clem.* 1.3-4: "What repayment, then, shall we give to him, or what fruit worthy of what he has given us? And how many holy acts do we owe him? For he has given us the light; as a father he has called us children." The principal occasion on which Christians would call God "father" (v. 59), of course, would be when reciting the Lord's prayer (Matt 6:9; Luke 11:2; *Did.* 8.2; cf. Matt 23:9), though it would have been common in other kinds of prayers as well (e.g., *Did.* 9.2, 3; 10.2).

Sentence 60

This line would seem to shed some light on the sort of comportment advocated in vv. 58-59. Deeds worthy of a son of God, one who in his actions remembers that he has God as a father, are holy, that is, sinless. A parallel pronouncement had been made in v. 36: "To one who is faithful God gives power that accords with God; what he gives, then, is pure and sinless." Here the focus shifts from the nature of the authority that God gives to the attributes of the one who receives that authority. As v. 28 had suggested, the act of conferring a name is an act of power. Whatever authority the sage wields, he does so in his capacity as God's son, that is, as one who has been named as such by God (v. 58). His power, then, is granted to the sage by God, especially through prayer (v. 375). Since it derives from God, it is therefore subordinate to God's (v. 182: "In governing human beings, remember that you are governed by God"). As one would expect of an obedient son, everything the sage does reflects God's will (vv. 287-288), and it is through the exercise of this control that God and the sage are considered to be intimately bound (v. 423, cf. vv. 422, 424). The correspondence of "pure and sinless" to characterize the nature of the ἐξουσία God bestows in v. 36 and "holy and sinless" here to characterize the one upon whom it is bestowed (cf. v. 46b) suggests the lexical equivalence of καθαρός and ἁγνός, in which case the proximity of our line to v. 57b becomes meaningful: purifying the intellect of all evil, that is, of all sin (see v. 181), represents the means by which one becomes truly sinless. For Sextus's concept of holiness, see further on vv. 67, 108a–b, and 441.

Verse 60 is the third of three sayings that according to Augustine (*Nat. grat.* 64.77) Pelagius borrowed from the *Sentences*. Cf. on vv. 36 and 46a–b. To Augustine's version of the saying (which matches Rufinus's exactly) is appended the following explanation:

> Xystus designed his words to be an admonition that, on any man's attaining such a high character, and thereby being rightly reckoned to be among the sons of God, the attainment must not be thought to have been the work of his own power. This indeed he, through grace, received from God, since he did not have it in a nature that had become corrupted and depraved—even as we read in the gospel, "But as many as received him, to them he gave power to become the sons of God." (John 1:12)

Sentences 61–62

The closing to the unit in vv. 54–62 draws on the same antithesis of good vs. evil found in vv. 56–57b. What had been presented as contrasting options for the intellect now takes the form of pronouncements on the contrasting repercussions that await it, cast in metaphysical terms. Sextus has already established that the sage's intellect is a holy temple for God (v. 46a, cf. v. 35). Purified of sin (v. 181), it becomes a place for the indwelling of the divine (v. 144, cf. v. 394). Thus it is not just the case that the sage possesses authority appropriate to the status of one who is God's son (see on v. 60) but that God is actually at work in the sage, the former being manifested to others through the working of the latter's intellect (v. 450). Cf. P.Ins. 30.19: "Heart and tongue of the wise man, the greatness of their dwelling place is being that of the god." The principal contribution vv. 61–62 makes to this set of affirmations is the juxtaposition of the "good" intellect (i.e., the intellect pure of sin; see on v. 57b) with its opposite. Thinking evil of God defiles God (v. 82e), leaving the soul unfit for interaction with the divine (cf. v. 313). The "evil things" that take up residence in such an intellect as a result are not identified here, though as a counterpart to the personal subject θεός in v. 61 the unclean demons of v. 348 (which lay claim to unclean souls; cf. vv. 305, 604) are likely candidates (note that Rufinus translates *daemonum malorum*). In this case comparison can be made with texts that visualize demons "residing" in human beings, for example, *T. Naph.* 8.6; Matt 12:43–45; Luke 11:24–26; *Ep. Barn.* 16.7; *Act. Thom.* 46; Ps.-Justin Martyr, *Quaest. resp. orth.* 415b. The term that Sextus has chosen to designate this dwelling place, χῶρος θεοῦ, is appropriate inasmuch as it and related expressions could be used of a sacred grove or precinct (e.g., Sophocles, *Oed. Col.* 38; Plutarch, *Nic.* 3.6; Diodorus Siculus, *Bibl. hist.* 17.50.2; Pausanias, *Graec. descr.* 10.37.5). Attention should be paid in particular to Porphyry, *Marc.* 21, which presents alternative possibilities similar to those in Sext. 61–62 (cf. vv. 304–305): "But the evil daemon must necessarily dwell wherever forgetfulness of God sneaks in, for, as you have learned, the soul is a dwelling place (χώρημα) either of gods or daemons. Accordingly, when gods are present it will do good in both words and deeds, but if it receives the evil partner, the soul does everything in a state of wickedness" (cf. *Marc.* 19).

Sentences 63–66

Text

63   τὸν ἀδικοῦντα τοῦ ἀδικεῖν ἀπαλλάττων κολάζοις ἄν[a] κατὰ θεόν.
64   ἄσκει [a]μὴ τὸ[a] δοκεῖν ἀλλὰ τὸ εἶναι δίκαιος· τὸ δοκεῖν γὰρ[b] ἕκαστον τοῦ εἶναι ἀφαιρεῖται.
65   τίμα τὸ δίκαιον δι' αὐτό.
66   οὐκ ἂν λάθοις θεὸν πράττων ἄδικα, [a]οὐδὲ γὰρ διανοούμενος[a].

Translation

63   By releasing the unjust person from his unjust act you would punish him in accord with God.
64   Practice not seeming but being just, for seeming always usurps being.
65   Honor justice for its own sake.
66   You cannot hide your doing unjust acts from God any more than you can hide your intending them.

Textual Notes

63[a] ἐάν: Π • 64[a-a] τὸ μὴ: Π • 64[b] omit Υ • 66[a-a] οὐ γὰρ διανοούμενος ἐκφεύξῃ: Υ

Commentary

Binding together the cluster of sayings in this segment is the subject of righteousness. Note δίκαιος in vv. 64 and 65 as well as ἀδικέω in v. 63 and ἄδικος in v. 66. The unit begins by addressing the reader's response to injustice committed by others (v. 63) and ends by addressing how he responds to his own acts of injustice (v. 66). Sandwiched in between are exhortations on the need for pure motives when pursuing justice (vv. 64–65), a concept that functions as a major theme for our text (vv. 23, 138, 208b, 261, 370, 399, 410, cf. vv. 452, 569, 582). For gnomic paragraphs similarly organized around the δικ- stem, cf. Hesiod, *Op.* 213–224, 274–285; Theognis, *El.* 731–752; Ps.-Phoc. 9–21.

Sentence 63

In the world of ordinary human justice, punishing offenders and releasing offenders represent mutually exclusive activities. Upon assuming the throne, Claudius, for example, "released those who had been imprisoned for *maiestas* and similar charges, but punished those who were guilty of actual wrongdoing" (Cassius Dio, *Hist. rom.* 60.4.2) Indeed, it is by punishing the unjust that the just are "released" both from danger (e.g., Lycurgus, *Leocr.* 114) and from the fear of wrongful conviction (e.g., Ps.-Lysias, *Andoc.* 13). The Sextine sage is similarly positioned to pass judgment on others, though because his authority is of divine origin (vv. 36, 60) he is aware that when he acts as judge he himself is being judged by God (vv. 182–184). Accordingly, he strives to align his standards of judgment with God's, just as he strives to do everything κατὰ θεόν (v. 201). For the early Christian belief that God "releases" wrongdoers from their sins, see Clement, *Ecl.* 20.1; Origen, *Cels.* 4.19; *Comm. Joan.* 13.15.94; Athanasius, *Exp. Ps.* 27.297. The sage understands that injustice corrupts human life (v. 208b), and that sinners will be punished by God after they die (vv. 14, 347). However, in this life even to punish a wrongdoer justly is something that he finds offensive (v. 261), since ultimately the fate of human souls is a matter of divine grace (vv. 373, 436a–b). The habit of imitating divine clemency towards malefactors, then, can be interpreted as one of the means by which the sage conforms himself to God (vv. 44–45, 48, 148, 381, etc.). It can also be seen as a specific application both of the golden rule (cf. vv. 89, 179, 210b, 211; Ps.-Clement, *Hom.* 12.32) and of the sage's aspiration to do good even to his enemies (v. 213, cf. vv. 105, 321). Cf. v. 607: "Do what is right even to those who try to wrong you." Given his reliance on other passages from the Sermon on the Mount (see part 4 of the introduction), it is possible that in the background of the author's thought lies Matt 5:39 (μὴ ἀντιστῆναι τῷ πονηρῷ), a dictum illustrative of how to "be perfect as your heavenly father is perfect" (Matt 5:48). As Davies and Allison (1988–1997, 1.543) note, ἀνθίστημι in the gospel text "could … have a forensic meaning: 'Do not oppose in court.'" Cf. Rom 12:17–19; 1 Cor 6:7.

Sentences 64–65

Discerning the difference between appearance and reality is a gnomic *topos*—for example, Prov 14:12; 16:25; 17:28; 26:12; Gnom. Democr. 97; Gnom. Vat. 54; Publilius Syrus, Sent. 722; Clitarchus, Sent. 115; Menander, Mon. 20; and, in our text, cf. vv. 214, 325, 392, 537 (ἐν παντὶ τοῦ δοκεῖν τὸ εἶναι λυσιτελέστερον). See also Cicero, *Off.* 1.65: "True and philosophical greatness of spirit regards the moral goodness to which nature most aspires as consisting in deeds, not in fame, and prefers to be first in reality rather than in name." Here the relevance of such discernment is applied to the need to "practice" (ἀσκεῖν) justice correctly, a moral ambition expressed in various venues (e.g., Isocrates, *Nic.* 2; Dionysius of Halicarnassus, *Ant. rom.* 6.6.2; *Let. Aris.* 168; Herm. *Mand.* 8.10), including Pythagorean circles (e.g., *Carm. aur.* 13; Iamblichus, *Vit. Pythag.* 30.186); cf. Sext. 606: δικαιοσύνην ἔργῳ μᾶλλον ἢ λόγῳ ἄσκει. Ingredient to the correct practice of justice is that one practices it with the correct intention. According to 2 Clem. 20.4, for example, those who perform acts of justice in order to receive "the wages of the righteous immediately" are "pursuing not piety but profit." Approaching morality as though they were engaged with God in a business transaction, such persons only appear to be righteous.

For an early and influential treatment of the idea that seeming to be just "usurps" (ἀφαιρεῖται) being just, we can turn to book 2 of Plato's *Respublica*. The author observes that most people "do not praise justice itself, only the high reputation it leads to and the consequences of being thought to be just" (*Resp.* 362e). Given this reality, a problem arises when we consider the "fully unjust" person, the person who is so successful at injustice that he not only conceals his acts of injustice but, in committing such crimes, he actually achieves the greatest reputation for justice, resulting in the paradox that "the extreme of injustice is believed to be just without being just" (*Resp.* 361a). Conversely, the truly just person, one who "does not want to be believed to be good but to be so," will not only receive no recognition for being just, he will actually earn the greatest reputation for injustice. Indeed, what makes him "fully" just is that he continues to act justly even though every just acts he performs (that is, every act he performs, since he is a just person) gives him a reputation for being unjust (*Resp.* 361b–c). Thus, in order to prove that someone is truly just, the ordinary way in which appearances usurp reality must be reversed: "we must deprive him of seeming" (ἀφαιρετέον δὴ τὸ δοκεῖν) to be just, since otherwise it would not be clear "whether he is just for the sake of justice itself" or for the sake of the honors that accompany a reputation for justice (*Resp.* 361b–c, cf. 367b–c). Such a person is able "to honor justice" (δικαιοσύνην τιμᾶν) appropriately because he recognizes it as one of the goods worth obtaining "for their own sake," on account of the benefits they confer on the soul (*Resp.* 366c–e, 367d). For subsequent discussions of these themes, see Aristotle, *Rhet.* 1.7.36–41; Teles, frag. 1 (Περὶ τοῦ δοκεῖν καὶ τοῦ εἶναι); Plutarch, *Adul. amic.* 50f; Clement, *Strom.* 4.22.143.4–4.22.144.2; Eusebius, *Praep. ev.* 12.10.1–7. For the goal of honoring, that is, obeying (see vv. 41–42) justice, cf. *Sib. Or.* 3.630; *Chion. ep.* 16.6; Philo, *Spec.* 1.300; Eusebius, *Comm. Ps.* 23.316. This would be one of the things that the sage honors in his role as God's son (v. 135, cf. v. 58). See also on v. 189.

Sentence 66
The most fundamental of philosophical principles, proclaims Epictetus, is the belief "that there is a God, and that he provides for the universe, and that it is impossible for someone to hide (λαθεῖν) from him not only what one is doing, but even what one is intending (διανοούμενον) or thinking" (*Diatr.* 2.14.11). An apophthegmatic version of v. 66 is attributed to the sage Thales by Diogenes Laertius: ἠρώτησέ τις αὐτὸν εἰ λήθοι θεοὺς ἄνθρωπος ἀδικῶν· ἀλλ᾽ οὐδὲ διανοούμενος, ἔφη (*Vit. phil.* 1.36; a similar saying is ascribed to Pittacus in Aelius Theon, *Progym.* 97). In its Sextine version, the gnome can be read in concert with vv. 57a–b: "What a person is thinking does not escape (λανθάνει) God's attention. Let your intellect be pure of every evil." Sext. 66 extends these assertions with an *a minore ad maius* argument: if it is impossible to conceal even one's unjust thoughts and intentions from God (cf. vv. 596–597, 601), the same applies more so when such intentions are actually carried out. As v. 94 explains, the only way to keep improper actions from coming to God's attention is not to do them in the first place. It may be possible to deceive others, but God can never be deceived (v. 186, cf. vv. 178, 181, 569). It is imperative, therefore, to have God in mind before doing anything (v. 95a, cf. vv. 224, 303). Sextus is convinced that God is somehow "involved" in all moral actions, either

guiding good ones (e.g., vv. 95b, 104, 113, 288, 304, cf. v. 582) or, as here, scrutinizing evil ones (cf. vv. 14, 39–40, 347). Similar sentiments about the nature and scope of divine omniscience are expressed by Porphyry in *Marc.* 21: "Everything is known in advance by God.... divine angels and good daemons are overseers of actions (τῶν πραττομένων), and it is impossible to elude (λαθεῖν) them." The moral standard guiding such divine superintendence is indicated in the paragraph that follows: it is impossible "to escape or elude (λαθεῖν) the gods or justice, the attendant of the gods" (*Marc.* 22). For Sextus, justice is one of the sage's defining virtues. Indeed, it is impossible to live κατὰ θεόν (v. 399) or even speak truthfully about God (v. 410) without acting righteously. Conversely, the sage repudiates injustice (vv. 138, 208b, 212, cf. v. 452), since harming someone else is the greatest act of impiety he could commit against God (vv. 96, 370, cf. v. 23). See also P.Ins. 31.3: "(The god) knows the impious man who thinks of evil."

Sentences 67–75b

Text

67   σώφρων[a] ἀνὴρ ἁγνὸς[b] παρὰ τῷ[c] θεῷ.
68   ἀκολασίαν φεῦγε.
69   εὐλογιστίαν ἄσκει.
70   κράτει τῶν ἡδονῶν.
71a νίκα τὸ σῶμα ἐν παντί.
71b ἐκ φιληδονίας ἀκολασίαν οὐκ ἐκφεύξῃ.
72   φιληδόνου ὁ θεὸς οὐκ ἀκούει.
73   τρυφῆς πέρας[a] ὄλεθρος.
74   ὁ λόγος σου τῶν [a]ὁρμῶν σου[a] προηγείσθω.
75a δεινότατόν ἐστιν πάθεσι δουλεύειν.
75b ὅσα πάθη ψυχῆς[a], τοσοῦτοι δεσπόται.

Translation

67   A moderate man is holy before God.
68   Flee intemperance.
69   Practice sound reasoning.
70   Control pleasures.
71a Conquer the body in everything.

71b You will not escape intemperance while longing for pleasure.
72 God does not listen to one who longs for pleasure.
73 The result of luxury is ruin.
74 Let your reason guide your impulses.
75a To be enslaved to passions is most dire.
75b All the soul's passions are just so many despots.

Textual Notes
67ᵃ σοφὸς: lat • 67ᵇ ἀγαθὸς: Π • 67ᶜ omit Υ • 73ᵃ πέλας: sy¹ • 74ᵃ⁻ᵃ πράξεων: Π, lat • 75bᵃ τῆς ψυχῆς: Π

Commentary

Kirk (1998, 122) identifies vv. 67–72 as an example of a topical grouping introduced by a programmatic maxim announcing the general theme (v. 67), followed by a series of short admonitions on more specific subjects offered by way of elaboration (vv. 68–71a), then a motive (v. 71b) + sanction (v. 72) offered by way of support. As the commentary will show, the unit draws on a moral lexicon of mutually implicating concepts familiar from the ancient discourse of moderation. Note in particular the following linkwords: ἀκολασία (vv. 68, 71b); ἡδονή (v. 70), φιληδονία (v. 71b), φιλήδονος (v. 72); φεύγω (v. 68), ἐκφεύγω (v. 71b). Seeing how the goal of possessing a soul governed by λόγος and not by πάθος or τρυφή also appears to be an integral part of such discourse, it is probably best to include vv. 73–75b in the unit as well.

Sentence 67
In the myth of the chariot, Plato imagines the virtue of moderation sitting enthroned "upon a pedestal of holiness" (*Phaedr.* 254b; cf. Plotinus, *Enn.* 1.6.9). In Jewish and Christian moral literature, terms used to express moderation (σώφρων, σωφροσύνη) and holiness (ἁγνός, ἁγνεία) are sometimes found paired together (e.g., Philo, *Mos.* 2.137; Ign. *Eph.* 10.3) or adjacent to one another in lists of virtues (e.g., Titus 2:5; *1 Clem.* 64.1; *Const. ap.* 3.3; 4.14). Cf. Clement, *Paed.* 3.1.1.1: "minds and bodies clothed with the adornment of the holy garment of moderation." For the element of divine approval, see *T. Jos.* 10.1: "You also, if you pursue moderation and holiness with patience and prayer with fasting in humility of heart, the Lord will dwell among you, because he loves moderation." For Sextus, moderation is one of the virtues without which life in accord with God

would be impossible (v. 399). It is as important a virtue for the believing wife as it is for the believing husband (vv. 235, 237, cf. vv. 499, 508). In both cases, living moderately is principally a problem of the body and how it should be used (vv. 12–13, 273, 412). Providing it with too much food, for instance, causes impurity and hinders holiness (vv. 108a–111).

Sentence 68

A series of staccato commands in vv. 68–71a provides the reader with specific guidance on how to become moderate, and therefore holy (v. 67). The conditional sentence in v. 71b then elaborates on the first of these commands (v. 68) by identifying a potential obstacle to its fulfillment.

Ancient writers frequently present σωφροσύνη and ἀκολασία as opposites—for example, Plato, *Leg.* 733e–734a; Dionysius of Halicarnassus, *Ant. rom.* 5.66.4; Philo, *Mut.* 153; Epictetus, *Diatr.* 3.1.8; Dio Chrysostom, *Or.* 3.7; Plutarch, *Adul. amic.* 74b. Given the importance assigned to the former in marriage (vv. 235, 237), it is not surprising that a warning against the latter (v. 231) is included in a block of sayings dealing with that particular institution (vv. 230a–240). In the Aristotelian classification of virtues and vices, moderation and intemperance are related insofar as each is displayed with respect to the pleasures (ἡδοναί; cf. vv. 70, 71b) that human beings share with animals, that is, the pleasures of touch and taste (*Eth. nic.* 3.10.8). Those who indulge such pleasures excessively are intemperate, while those who refrain from them are moderate (*Eth. nic.* 7.7.2). Moderation can also be defined as the mean between intemperance and insensibility (ἀναισθησία) to pleasures (*Eth. nic.* 2.7.3; cf. *Magn. mor.* 1.21.1–4).

The verb φεύγω is often used in a moral sense, for example, in Sir 21:2; 1 Cor 6:18; 2 Tim 2:22; *1 Clem.* 30.1; Porphyry, *Marc.* 10, 33; cf. Sext. 313, 435. For the line of thought connecting v. 67 with v. 68 (cf. v. 71b), see especially Musonius Rufus, frag. 4.44.21–22: "The only way we escape from intemperance is through moderation" (διὰ γὰρ σωφροσύνης μόνης ἐκφεύγομεν ἀκολασίαν). As Aristotle observes, while it is true that he will experience certain bodily pleasures, the moderate man, unlike the intemperate man, flees (φεύγει) from those that are excessive (*Eth. nic.* 7.12.7). See also on v. 451.

Sentence 69

A particularly instructive parallel for understanding the lexical configurations at work in vv. 67–75b is 4 Maccabees. In the moral world projected by that text, a special place is accorded the concept of εὐλογιστία. In 4 Macc 5:22–23, for example, the author assumes that sound reasoning informs σωφροσύνη (cf. Marcus Aurelius, *Med.* 8.32.1), the exercise of which involves controlling pleasures: "You scoff at our philosophy as though living by it did not accord with sound reasoning (οὐ μετὰ εὐλογιστίας), but it teaches us moderation (σωφροσύνη), so that we control all the pleasures and desires (πασῶν τῶν ἡδονῶν καὶ ἐπιθυμιῶν κρατεῖν)." In 4 Macc 6:35, meanwhile, it is the power of reasoning as such (ὁ λογισμός) that enables one to control pleasures (τῶν ἡδονῶν κρατεῖν). Later, in 4 Macc 13:7, the same text narrates an example of how εὐλογιστία, fortified by piety, "conquered the intemperance of the passions (τὴν τῶν παθῶν ἐνίκησεν ἀκολασίαν)." For Sextus, the capacity for such reasoning is something that can only be achieved through the sort of "practice" that makes it habitual. The importance assigned to this objective here anticipates the maxim in v. 74 (see below). For other appeals to make moral decisions εὐλόγως, see vv. 81 and 121a–b; cf. v. 480.

Sentence 70

The saying ἡδονῆς κρατεῖν is attributed to the sage Cleobulus in Diogenes Laertius, *Vit. phil.* 1.92. A very similar gnome is found among the Praecepta Delphica: ἡδονῆς κράτει (*SIG* 3.1268.1.5). Moderation is a matter of "controlling" pleasures and desires: besides 4 Macc 5:22–23 and 6:35 (cited above), see Clement, *Strom.* 5.11.69.3; Ps.-Clement, *Hom.* 1.4; Iamblichus, *Protr.* 66. On the other hand, excessive indulgence in pleasures is a sign of ἀκολασία (cf. v. 68), as in Aristotle, *Eth. nic.* 3.11.5; Plutarch, *Superst.* 165a. Those who fail to control their pleasures are certain to be controlled by them (Plato, *Leg.* 633e; Dio Chrysostom, *Or.* 8.26; 16.1). For Sextus, since self-control (ἐγκράτεια) is the foundation of piety (vv. 86a, 438, cf. v. 574), exercising control over one's physical and sexual appetites can be understood as an expression of faith (vv. 239–240, 428, cf. vv. 507–509). Self-control is the sage's most prized asset (v. 294) to such an extent that even sleep is a matter for self-control (v. 253b), while succumbing to pleasure leads to defilement and disgrace: ἄνθρωπος ἀκρατὴς μιαίνει τὸν θεόν (v. 429, cf. vv. 108b, 111, 270, 272, 604). Therefore nothing should ever be done for the sake of pleasure (v. 232).

Sentence 71a

While human beings may experience various kinds of pleasures, the pleasures that must be controlled are those of the body, for example, Xenophon, *Mem.* 1.5.6 (τῶν διὰ τοῦ σώματος ἡδονῶν ἐκράτει); Clement, *Strom.* 3.5.41.2. For the use of νικάω here, see Plato, *Phil.* 12a; 4 Macc 3:17 ("The moderate mind can conquer the drives of the passions"); 6:33; 13:7 (cited above); *2 Clem.* 16.2; Theophilus, *Autol.* 2.12. As Philo puts it in *Leg.* 3.242, those who lack strength to contend with the body (σώματι ... ἀγωνίσασθαι) will not be able to conquer pleasure (νικῆσαι τὴν ἡδονήν). As with most ancient authors, Sextus understands moderation to be primarily a somatic affair, that is, a matter of disciplining one's bodily needs and the desires these needs can engender (vv. 12–13, 273, 412, cf. v. 335). As the imprint (v. 346) and garment (v. 449) of the soul, the body must be kept pure. If the body is overcome by desire, the soul cannot know God (v. 136, cf. v. 425). On the other hand, nothing good can derive from the flesh (vv. 271, 317). The sage, then, not only resists forming attachments to the body (vv. 78, 101, 115, 291): he actually despises anything that he will not need after being released from the body (v. 127). For him, then, gaining control over the body represents a major feat of learning (v. 274a). Cf. Evagrius Ponticus, *Cap. paraen.* 20: ὑπὲρ πάντα καταχρῶ τῷ σώματι.

Sentence 71b

The source for this line is Clitarchus, *Sent.* 10: ἐκ φιληδονίας ἀκολασία φύεται. By replacing the verb with οὐκ ἐκφεύξῃ, Sextus transforms a statement about moral genealogy into an elaboration of v. 68: if the readers are to shun intemperance, they must renounce any longing for pleasures. To be afflicted by ἀκολασία (cf. on v. 68) is to be mastered by one's pleasures (Plato, *Phaed.* 68e; Plutarch, *Tu. san.* 136c), and "the only way we escape from intemperance (ἐκφεύγομεν ἀκολασίαν) is through moderation" (Musonius Rufus, frag. 4.44.21–22; cf. Clement, *Paed.* 2.10.93.3). Accordingly, it is incumbent upon anyone intending to curtail intemperance and the longing for pleasures to adopt a regimen with respect to food and sex that is moderate in nature (Plutarch, *Is. Os.* 351f–352a; cf. Sext. 231). For this use of ἐκφεύγω, see also vv. 155 and 598.

Sentence 72

Prayer represents one of the sage's most basic practices (vv. 88, 124–125, 128, 213, 372, 374). Through prayer one articulates both that which is worthy of God (v. 122) and the sort of person one desires to be in the presence of God (v. 80). The granting of prayers is one of the means by which God bequeaths divine power on the sage (v. 375), the only effective prayers being uttered by persons who have a share in divine reason (v. 277). The prayers of the pleasure lover, on the other hand, fall into the same category as those of the lazy man (v. 126) and those of the man who ignores the needy (v. 217): all go unheeded.

Origen would have agreed that pleasure and prayer should not mix: "There are always many who are pleasure-loving rather than God-loving in their seeming prayer, who debauch prayer amid banqueting and carousing" (*Orat.* 19.3; cf. 2 Tim 3:4). Christians, by contrast, "drive out all lust from their mind when they worship God with prayers" (*Cels.* 7.48). For Sextus, the φιλήδονος is so distracted by the burden of bodily pleasures (v. 139) that he cannot apprehend the divine (v. 136), a deficiency that renders his entire life useless (v. 172). For similar assessments of the φιλήδονος, see Philo, *Leg.* 3.237; Origen, *Exp. Prov.* 17.208.

Sentence 73

Believed to engender all manner of moral corruption, τρυφή ("opulence, luxury") is the target of criticism in a wide range of moral writings, for example, Ps.-Phoc. 61 ("Great luxury leads to ignoble desires"); Musonius Rufus, frag. 20.126.15–17 ("Luxury destroys both body and soul, causing weakness and impotence in the body, self-indulgence and cowardice in the soul"). Its association with φιληδονία would have been a natural one, as Clement, *Strom.* 2.20.119.5 suggests: "Luxury is simply a form of longing for pleasures, an excessive superfluity on the part of those dedicated to the passion of pleasure" (cf. Plutarch, *Galb.* 19.2). In Sextus's view, living in opulence contradicts God's plan for human thriving (v. 117, cf. v. 603). For the conviction that τρυφή ultimately brings disaster upon those who embrace it, see Ps.-Crates, *Ep.* 34.3; Dio Chrysostom, *Or.* 33.28; Ps.-Cato, *Dist.* 2.19; Jas 5:5; Herm. *Sim.* 6.4.1–6.5.7; and especially Iamblichus, *Vit. Pythag.* 30.171: "The first of evils usually to slip unawares into households and cities is called luxury (τρυφή), second insolence, third ruin (ὄλεθρος)" (cf. Sext. 203). The following comments from Musonius Rufus are also apt, insofar as they illustrate not only how such avoidance would have contributed to some of the broader objectives communicated in vv. 67–75b but also how such avoidance would have represented a particular concern of moral leaders and role models:

> The king himself must observe moderation (σωφρονεῖν) himself and demand it of his subjects so that with moderate rule and seemly submission there shall be no luxury on either's part. For luxury is ruinous (λυμαντικός) to ruler and citizen alike. For how could anyone be moder-

ate himself without making an effort to curb his desires, or how could someone who is intemperate (ἀκόλαστος) make others moderate? One can mention no study except philosophy that fosters moderation. For it teaches one to be above pleasure (ἐπάνω ἡδονῆς), etc." (frag. 8.62.10–16; cf. Epictetus, *Gnom*. 16)

Excursus: The Sources for *Sentences* 74–75b

With v. 75a, Chadwick (1959, 166) compares *Sent. Pythag*. 21 (δουλεύειν πάθεσι χαλεπώτερον ἢ τυράννοις). In lieu of the final three words, Sextus opens with δεινότατόν ἐστιν. With v. 75b, Chadwick (1959, 167) compares *Sent. Pythag*. 71 (ὅσα πάθη ψυχῆς, τοσοῦτοι καὶ ὠμοὶ δεσπόται), the Sextine version lacking the fifth and sixth words. While Chadwick's observation ("It is noteworthy that Sextus and Porphyry agree in bringing together in the same order two maxims which occur separately in the Pythagorean maxims") is correct, this only begins to describe the source-critical challenges confronting the interpreter at this juncture. For ease of comparison, the relevant section in Porphyry, *Marc*. 34 can be divided into four components:

34a: "Therefore, let reason guide every impulse (ἡγείσθω τοίνυν πάσης ὁρμῆς ὁ λόγος) as it banishes those dread (δεινοὺς) and ungodly despots (δεσπότας) from us..."

34b: "...because it is even more difficult to be enslaved to one's passions (δουλεύειν πάθεσιν) than to tyrants."

34c: "But it is impossible for the one governed (κρατούμενον) by the passions to be free..."

34d: "...for all the passions of the soul are just so many cruel despots (ὅσα γὰρ πάθη ψυχῆς τοσοῦτοι καὶ ὠμοὶ δεσπόται)."

In terms of Porphyry's reliance on *Sententiae Pythagoreorum*, *Marc*. 34b approximates *Sent. Pythag*. 21 (doing so more closely than Sext. 75a), while *Marc*. 34c is an abbreviated version of a nearly adjacent saying, *Sent. Pythag*. 23 (ἐλεύθερον ἀδύνατον εἶναι τὸν πάθεσι δουλεύοντα καὶ ὑπὸ παθῶν κρατούμενον), and *Marc*. 34d matches *Sent. Pythag*. 71. At the same time, the beginning of *Marc*. 34a (ἡγείσθω τοίνυν πάσης ὁρμῆς ὁ λόγος) closely resembles Sext. 74, and both *Marc*. 34a and Sext. 75a have δεινός, a term found nowhere in *Sententiae Pythagoreorum*, raising the possibility that the two rely on some other (or different) source. In addition, consideration must be given to Clitarchus, *Sent.* 85 (ὅσα πάθη ψυχῆς, τοσοῦτοι δεσπόται) and 86 (οὐκ ἔστιν ἐλεύθερον εἶναι κρατούμενον ὑπὸ παθῶν), the former a version of *Sent. Pythag.* 71, Porphyry, *Marc.* 34d, and Sext. 75b, the latter a partial parallel to *Sent. Pythag.* 23, Porphyry, *Marc.* 34c, and (less so) Sext. 75a. This raises the possibility that the connection between Porphyry, *Marc.* 34c + 34d, and perhaps also Sext. 75a + 75b, may have been inspired by Clitarchus, *Sent.* 85–86 (note that the order of Clitarchus, *Sent.* 85 and 86 in Σ is inversed). The possibility of Clitarchan influence on Sextus at this point is strengthened by the fact that Sext. 75b exactly matches Clitarchus, *Sent.* 85, while *Sent. Pythag.* 71 and Porphyry, *Marc.* 34d add καὶ ὠμοὶ before δεσπόται.

Sentence 74

This line can be interpreted as a commentary on v. 69: one practices sound reasoning by ensuring that reason guides one's every impulse. These two verses, in turn, contribute to the section's general theme of moderation. A person who is moderate, as Aristotle asserts, "is so constituted as to take no pleasure in things that are contrary to reason" (*Eth. nic.* 7.9.6). Moderation could also be envisioned as a struggle through which reason gains ascendancy over the passions in controlling the soul, in which case it is also appropriate to read v. 74 in conjunction with vv. 75a–b. Once again comparison with 4 Maccabees is instructive, especially 1:3 ("Reason rules over those passions that hinder moderation") and 1:30–31 ("Reason is sovereign over the passions by virtue of the restraining power of moderation"); cf. 1:1, 9, 13–14, 33–35; 2:6–9, 15, 18; 3:1; 6:31–35; and so forth. In the same vein, reason could be imaged as leading or directing the passions, for example, Plutarch, *Virt. mor.* 445b: "Moderation belongs to the sphere where reason steers and manages the passionate element, like a gentle animal obedient to the reins, making it yielding in its desires" (cf. Plato, *Phaedr.* 246a–b, 253c–254e). Clement likens reason to a κυβερνήτης: "Reason, that is, the guiding power within us, remains infallible as it takes charge of the soul, and is called its pilot" (*Strom.* 2.11.51.6). See further 4 Macc 7:1; Clement, *Paed.* 1.12.99.1; *Sent. Pythag.* 57 (λόγῳ ἡγεμόνι ἐν παντὶ χρώμενος οὐχ ἁμαρτήσεις); Porphyry, *Marc.* 6; Menander, *Mon.* 68: ἀρχῆς ἁπάσης ἡγεμὼν ἔστω λόγος. Given the proximity of v. 74 to vv. 75a–b, it is probable that Sextus (or his source) was familiar with the Stoic definition of πάθος as an ἄλογος ὁρμή, for which see *SVF* 3:378, 386, 462. As Philo explains, "the starting point of pleasure (ἡδονή, cf. vv. 70, 71b, 72) is passion, an irrational impulse" (*Leg.* 3.185). It is in the nature of impulse and pleasure, then, to oppose reason (*Somn.* 2.276). In response, it is the business of moderation "to alleviate the unbounded impulses of the passions" (*Opif.* 81). This occurs when reason is set over the impulses of the passions "as a charioteer and pilot," curbing and controlling them (*Leg.* 3.118). Compare Plotinus, *Enn.* 3.1.9: "When in its impulse (ὁρμᾷ) the soul has as a guide (ἡγεμόνα) pure and untroubled reason (λόγον), then this impulse alone is said to be in our own power and free … not suffering error from ignorance or defeat from the violence of the passions." Plutarch expresses similar views in *Virt. mor.* 444b: "The impulse of passion springs from moral virtue; but it needs reason to keep it within moderate bounds and to prevent its exceeding or falling short of its proper season." Cf. Clement, *Paed.* 3.11.53.1; 3.11.57.3. Setting reason over the impulses as a guide, then, would address one of the root problems associated with achieving moderation. Goodness is to be sought out not in the desires of the flesh but in the ability to reason, since the latter is the essence of one's God-given humanity (vv. 315–317). For those who would realize their full potential as human beings, then, reason serves as a norm in every aspect of their lives (v. 123). Since it is divine in nature (v. 277), reason constitutes a power within the self that no one can restrain (v. 363a).

Given the relationship between vv. 74–75b and Porphyry, *Marc.* 34 detailed above, ὁρμῶν σου in Υ is most likely the correct reading. Later copyists changed the unanticipated term (ὁρμή is attested nowhere else in the *Sentences*) to πράξεων, perhaps in order to bring the gnome into alignment with v. 95b: "Let your light guide your actions." Cf. Sir 37:16: "Reason (λόγος) is the beginning of every work, and counsel comes before every action (πρὸ πάσης πράξεως)."

Sentences 75a–b

The σώφρων is to be distinguished from individuals who have become "mastered by passion" to such a degree that they cannot act in accord with reason (Aristotle, *Eth. nic.* 7.8.4–5). The former "frees his soul of the passions" (Clement, *Strom.* 3.5.41.2) and so overcomes their drives (4 Macc 3:17). This is critical, because "to yield in subjection to the passions is the lowest form of slavery, just as to conquer them is the only true freedom" (Clement, *Strom.* 2.23.144.3). Sextus elaborates on the danger of the passions especially in vv. 204–209: there is no passion that does not oppose the operation of reason in the soul (v. 205), debilitating the soul like an illness (v. 207). Liberating oneself from the passions is therefore an act of faith (vv. 204, 209), while allowing an act to be dictated by passion leads only to regret (v. 206).

For depictions of the passions as masters or tyrants enslaving the soul, see Aesop, *Sent.* 40 (ἐλεύθερον ἀδύνατον εἶναι τὸν πάθεσι δουλεύοντα); Philo, *Migr.* 26; *Her.* 186; *Abr.* 164; Origen, *Hom. Luc.* 37.211; Seneca, *Ep.* 14.1 ("He will have many masters who makes his body his master"). As Philo observes, the soul becomes a slave of passion only after its reason has been "trussed and pinioned" (*Mos.* 1.299). For parallels in *Sent. Pythag.* 21, 23, 71; Clitarchus, *Sent.* 85; and Porphyry, *Marc.* 34, see the excursus above on Sext. 74–75b. Note also Clitarchus, *Sent.* 12 (ὧν ἐπιθυμεῖ τις δοῦλός ἐστιν) and Sext. 600 (ὧν ἂν ἐπιθυμήσῃς, τούτων νόμιζε δοῦλος εἶναι). The formulation of v. 75a is reflected especially in two sayings attributed to Evagrius Ponticus, namely, *Cap. paraen.* 10 (κάκιστόν ἐστι πάθεσι δουλεύειν αἰσχροῖς) and *Al. sent.* 54 (δεινόν ἐστι πάθεσι δουλεύειν σαρκός).

Sentences 76–82d

Text

76 φιλοχρηματία φιλοσωματίας ἔλεγχος.
77 κτῶ τὰ τῆς ψυχῆς ὡς βέβαια.
78 ἀποτάττου τοῖς τοῦ σώματος, ἐφ' ὅσον δυνατὸς εἶ.
79 μόνον[a] οἰκεῖον ἡγοῦ τὸ ἀγαθόν.
80 ὁποῖος θέλεις εὐχόμενος εἶναι, ἀεὶ ἔσο.
81 ὅταν τὰ κάλλιστα τῶν κτημάτων εὐλόγως εἰς[a] βόβορον ῥίψῃς, τότε καθαρὸς ὢν αἰτοῦ τι παρὰ τοῦ[b] θεοῦ.
82a ὁποῖος θέλεις εἶναι παρὰ θεῷ, ἤδη ἔσο.
82b τῶν τοῦ κόσμου μεταδιδοὺς καταφρόνει.
82c μέμνησο ὧν μετὰ θεόν[a].
82d ψυχὴ ἀνθρώπου θεοσεβοῦς θεὸς ἐν σώματι.

Translation

76 Love of money is proof of love of body.
77 Acquire the things of the soul since they are secure.
78 Renounce the things of the body as much as you are able.
79 Deem only the good to be your own.
80 Whatever you want to be when praying, be such always.

81   When you intentionally throw the finest of your possessions into the mud, then, being pure, ask for something from God.
82a Whatever you want to be before God, be such now.
82b Despise the things of the world by sharing them.
82c Remember that you are next after God.
82d The soul of a God-fearing person is a god in a body.

Textual Notes

79ᵃ νόμον: sy² • 81ᵃ ὡς: sy² • 81ᵇ omit Υ • 82cᵃ θεοῦ: Υ

COMMENTARY

Most of the sayings in this paragraph concern possessions. Corresponding priorities are set forth in the first three lines: the readers are urged to acquire the things of the soul (v. 77) while eschewing the things of the body (v. 78), especially money (v. 76). These priorities are re-expressed in vv. 79 and 82b, "the good" of the former referring to the spiritual goods of v. 77, the worldly things of the latter referring back to the bodily things of v. 78. The body–soul dichotomy with which the unit begins figures in its conclusion as well. The body is not something to be loved (cf. v. 76)—that is, it is not something to be served by acquiring possessions for it; rather, it itself serves as a means by which the godlike soul of the sage is manifested (v. 82d). Within this context, v. 82c functions as a reminder to the readers that, in their freedom from the body and desires for worldly wealth, they approximate the self-sufficiency of God. Embedded in the unit is a cluster of sayings on prayer (vv. 80–82a), verbally linked to the sayings on possessions by v. 81 (κτάομαι: v. 77; κτῆμα: v. 81).

Sentence 76

This line is based on *Sent. Pythag.* 110ᶜ: ὁ δὲ φιλοσώματος καὶ φιλοχρήματος. The Sextine version presents abstract concepts in lieu of character types. *Sententiae Pythagoreorum* 110ᶜ (together with the other five members of *Sent. Pythag.* 110) is cited in Porphyry, *Marc.* 14, with πάντως placed after φιλοσώματος. *Sent. Pythag.* 110ᵃ⁻ᵉ are also cited by Arsenius, *Apophth.* 17.86f and Maximus Confessor, *Loc. comm.* 91.729b (where the sayings are attributed to Pythagoras), while *Sent. Pythag.* 110ᶜ⁻ᵈ are cited in Asterius, *Hom.* 14.12.3.

It was a Platonic dictum that a lover of the body is not only a lover of wisdom but "also a lover of wealth or of honors, either or both"

(*Phaed.* 68c). In the *Sentences*, the love of body constitutes a significant moral threat. One should not love anything that belongs to the body (v. 101). Instead, the body is something to be subjugated (v. 274a), its needs despised (v. 127), since the body constrains and burdens the soul (v. 322). See further on v. 78. The love of money, meanwhile, is often singled out by ancient moralists as a source of personal and social ills; see *Sib. Or.* 3.235; 1 Tim 6:10; Pol. *Phil.* 4.1; *Asc. Isa.* 3.25–28; Diogenes Laertius, *Vit. phil.* 6.50; etc. In his depiction of the lover of money (*Or.* 4.91–100), Dio Chrysostom notes that it is difficult for such an individual to master his soul in anything like a consistent fashion, since "wealth is the handmaid and the willing ministrant to every appetite and interest" (*Or.* 4.99).

Sentence 77

No doubt the dominical admonition in Matt 6:20/Luke 12:33 stands in the background of the author's thought here (cf. Heb 6:19). Worldly goods are insecure (v. 405, cf. vv. 15, 91b, 128) and money is of no value to the soul (v. 116). Therefore the sage does not concern himself with such things (v. 130) and does not think of them as his own (v. 227), recognizing that acquisitiveness can be an obstacle to salvation (vv. 193, 264a). Instead, the sage possesses whatever God possesses (v. 310), confident in the reliable and abiding character of such assets, since "what God gives, no one takes away" (v. 92, cf. v. 118). The only thing that he needs is God (v. 49) and the only thing necessary for his happiness is the knowledge of God (v. 148). As Plutarch explains, the soul has more inherent "security" than the body because it is able to achieve perfection of its own accord, without the aid of anything else (*Suav. viv.* 1088d–e). The content of τὰ τῆς ψυχῆς for Sextus is left unspecified, though Origen contends that "the only secure realities in the world are knowledge and truth, which are derived from wisdom" (*Cels.* 3.72; cf. Philo, *Sacr.* 126; *Spec.* 1.191). Conversely, one of the sayings from the *Sententiae Pythagoreorum* specifies items that are not secure: "Do not be quick to call someone blessed who depends on friends or children or some other fleeting things for his preservation; for all such things are perilous, while the only thing that endures secure of itself is of God" (*Sent. Pythag.* 91).

Sentence 78

Body and soul represent the basic components of the human self (vv. 55, 82d, 139a, 301, 449, cf. vv. 19–20). Verses 77–78 address their relative importance in terms of the decision one makes regarding which to furnish with "possessions." While Matt 6:19–20 draws a contrast between earthly and heavenly "treasures," Sext. 77–78 draws a contrast between τὰ τῆς ψυχῆς and τὰ τοῦ σώματος, for which see Plutarch, frag. 144; Iamblichus, *Myst.* 2.9. The soul that exercises self-control "renounces the things that accord with the body" (ἀποτάξηται τοῖς κατὰ τὸ σῶμα) so that the soul can attend to that to which it properly belongs, namely, the activities of the soul (Philo, *Leg.* 3.238; cf. Ephraem Syrus, *Serm. comp.* 114). Similarly, in our text self-control is the "wealth" of the sage (v. 294) since it represents the means by which he subdues (v. 71a) and controls (v. 274a) the body. Sextus concedes that the body has certain requirements (v. 276), but these must be provided for with moderation (vv. 412–413), that is, with nothing beyond what the body actually needs (v. 15, cf. v. 19). This is because the body can lead one to intemperance (vv. 13, 273), and a body filled with desire cannot know God (v. 136). Conversely, the practice of relinquishing the things of the body brings one closer to God by allowing one both to emulate God (vv. 18, 50) and to concentrate on following God (vv. 264a–b). The sage therefore responds with indifference to the loss of such things (vv. 15, 130, 329), even the loss of the body itself (vv. 321–322).

Sentence 79

As Aristotle observes, it is in the nature of each species of living thing to obtain the good for its "own," that is, to obtain whatever is appropriate and necessary for the flourishing of its own kind (*Eth. nic.* 10.2.4). In the *Sentences*, the task is to identify the good that is the sage's "own." Goodness in this sense is that which befits not the body (vv. 271, 317) but God (vv. 131, 197), which would include especially the ability to reason in accord with God (v. 316). This exemplifies a true "good" in the sense that one can share it with others and still possess it oneself (vv. 295–296). Goodness according to this definition is rare, since it can be found only among the faithful (v. 243) and (particularly) in the sage, the latter representing the very embodiment of goodness (v. 246, cf. v. 132) insofar as he does not think of anything as his "own" (v. 227) except what he has received from God (vv. 128, 277, 310). Such endowments are truly his own because no one can take them from him (vv. 17, 92, 118, 404). Cf. Clement, *Strom.* 7.7.44.3–4: "But as for the things that are actually good, that is, those pertaining to the soul, the gnostic's prayer is that they may both be granted to him and that they may continue. Thus he does not desire anything which he has not, being contented with his present circumstances. For he is not lacking in the good things that are proper to him (τῶν οἰκείων ἀγαθῶν), being already sufficient to himself through divine grace and knowledge." See also Epictetus, *Diatr.* 4.1.130–131: "Therefore, the body is not our own, its members are not our own, property is not our own. If, then, you conceive a strong passion for some one of these things, as though it were your immediate possession, you will be punished as he should be who fixes his aim upon what is not his own. This is the road that leads to freedom."

Verse 79 is repeated as v. 593 in the appendices, where it is immediately followed (v. 594) by a version of the maxim in v. 227.

Sentence 80

This saying exhibits the same basic structure (ὁποῖος θέλεις ... εἶναι ... ἔσο) as v. 82a. The implication to be drawn from the correlation of the two lines seems clear enough: whatever one desires to be in the presence of God is what one should desire to be when praying to God (note Rufinus's use of *deum* in both verses).

The correct understanding and practice of prayer represent major priorities for our text. It is proper to pray to God not for what the world gives (v. 128) but for what God alone can give (v. 124, cf. vv. 88, 374). Thus, when praying to God, one articulates that which is worthy of God (v. 122) including, here in v. 80, a self that is worthy of God. This is the sort of self whose prayers are heeded by God, someone who eschews bodily pleasures (v. 72) and participates in divine reason (v. 277), conferring benefits on those in need of them (v. 217), including, at least through prayer, all of humanity (v. 372).

The particular contribution of this line to the text's reflections on prayer is in its assumption that the practice represents an exercise in self-visualization and self-formation. When the sage prays for opportunities to do good to his enemies (v. 213), for example, if he follows the principle articulated here, in the course of doing so he must both envision himself being the sort of person who would act in such a way and then practice actualizing this vision. One of the implications of the process is that the sage becomes more fully aware of any discrepancies that exist between the self as it is envisioned and the self as it actually is, thus opening up a space for moral scrutiny and progress. As we learn elsewhere, resolving such discrepancies is understood as entailing a synergy of human effort (vv. 125–126) and divine aid, the latter conceptualized as "power from God" (v. 375). It is from this perspective that the moral life itself can be conceptualized as continuous prayer, as we see, for example, in Origen, *Orat.*

12.2: "The one who links together his prayer with deeds of duty and fits seemly actions with his prayer is the one who prays without ceasing, for his virtuous deeds or the commandments he has fulfilled are taken up as a part of his prayer.... The whole life of the saint is one mighty integrated prayer." Cf. *Orat.* 8.2: "He is greatly helped who is intent in his mind on his prayer, through his very intentness in prayer adapting himself to the presence of God."

Sentence 81

If prayer is not conducted in a state of purity, effective communication cannot take place: "Just as it is impossible to see someone's face in murky water, so it is not possible for the soul to pray if it is not cleansed of unseemly things" (*Apophth. patr.* [an.] 379). What constitutes such a state could be expressed variously, for example, as having a clean conscience when praying (e.g., Philo, *Praem.* 84; Origen, *Cels.* 8.17) or as having a heart pure of enmity (e.g., *Const. ap.* 2.53) or of wicked thoughts (e.g., Evagrius Ponticus, *Sent. virg.* 38). For Clement, such preparation applies to the entirety of one's life: "Both in eating and drinking, and in marrying, if reason so dictates, and even in his dreams, the gnostic's actions and thoughts are holy, so that he is always purified for prayer" (*Strom.* 7.12.78.5). Similarly, for Porphyry the only prayer that is pure is one accompanied by good deeds (*Marc.* 24; cf. Sext. 356). In Sext. 81, emphasis is placed on cleansing oneself of material possessions. As our author has just advised, such "things of the body" are to be renounced (v. 78, cf. v. 264a). It is the case not simply that one should refrain from asking God for such things (v. 128) but that to approach God in prayer while possessed of them renders both oneself and one's prayer impure. Cf. *Sent. Pythag.* 17: "God listens only to the one unencumbered with extraneous burdens." The incongruity of καθαρός and βόρβορος in v.81 dramatizes the meaning of the symbolic action being prescribed: what matters in prayer is the purity of the self, not of the self's possessions. The basic idea here finds expression in later monastic instructions on prayer, the *De oratione* of Evagrius Ponticus being representative, for example, *Orat.* 17 ("Go, sell your possessions and give to the poor, take up your cross and deny yourself utterly so that you may be able to pray uninterruptedly") and 37 ("If you yearn to pray, abandon everything so that you can inherit everything"). As Sext. 82b will soon remind us, the principle way in which the sage divests himself of worldly goods is by sharing them with others. Cf. *Gnom. Vat.* 67: "A free life cannot acquire many possessions, because this is not easy to do without servility to mobs or monarchs, yet it possesses all things in unfailing abundance; and if by chance it obtains many possessions, it is easy to distribute them so as to win the gratitude of neighbors."

Sentence 82a

This saying complements v. 80 formally and conceptually: prayer is a practice performed παρὰ θεῷ (e.g., Origen, *Comm. Matt.* 16.22; Ps.-Athanasius, *Ep. Cast.* 28.865). Put differently, the one who prays is "adapting himself to the presence of God, and to speech with him who is present as with one who both looks upon him and is present" (Origen, *Orat.* 8.2; cf. Matt 6:6). God is ever-present in the thoughts of the sage (vv. 95a, 143, 289), witnessing his deeds (vv. 224, 303). Cognizant of the fact that he is already being judged by God (vv. 22, 183, cf. vv. 14, 39–40), the sage therefore does not postpone trying to be great (v. 51) and holy (v. 60) παρὰ θεῷ, but endeavors to realize these ideals in every aspect of his comportment, for example, by being good to the needy (vv. 52, 379).

The sort of conceptualization employed here is familiar from traditions of ancient moral guidance, according to which students were encouraged to imagine their mentor or spiritual guide as being actually present, observing and evaluating their conduct, for example, Seneca, *Ep.* 11.8–10; Clement, *Strom.* 7.7.35.4: "If the presence of some good man always moulds for the better one who converses with him, owing to the respect and reverence that he inspires, with much more reason must he, who is always in the uninterrupted presence of God by means of his knowledge and his life and his thankful spirit, be raised above himself on every occasion, both in regard to his actions and his words" (cf. Philo, *Mut.* 217). The power of such imagining for moral self-awareness and guidance is acknowledged by Porphyry as well, for example, in *Marc.* 12: "Let God be present as overseer and guardian of every deed and word."

Sentence 82b

Readers of the New Testament are encouraged to share (μεταδιδόναι) such things as clothes (Luke 3:11) and alms (Eph 4:28), thereby demonstrating their generosity (Rom 12:8; cf. Herm. *Vis.* 3.9.2, 4). Readers of the *Sentences* are encouraged to share the things of the world, thereby demonstrating their contempt for the world. The sage signals his freedom from and disregard for the things of the world by remaining untroubled at their loss (vv. 15, 91b, 130), by limiting his body's need for them (vv.

18-19, 50, 78), by throwing them away (vv. 81, 264a), and by sharing them with the poor. Indeed, in Sextus's opinion the last of these constitutes the best possible use of possessions (vv. 329-330), since even the willingness to share with others is something that is great in God's sight (v. 379, cf. v. 382). From this perspective sharing possessions can be considered an act of piety (v. 228). The sage is also eager to share his wisdom and other spiritual gifts, since these represent true "goods" (vv. 295-296, cf. v. 131). For the sage's contempt for material things, see also vv. 121a and 127.

Sentences 82c-d

Verse 82c is probably best read together with v. 82d: the reason why the sage ranks second after God (μετὰ θεόν) is that within himself he possesses something divine, namely, his soul (cf. v. 292). Verses 82c-d, in turn, with their juxtaposition of ψυχή and σῶμα, may be read in conjunction with the unit's opening lines, vv. 76-78: the godlike freedom of the sage's soul (cf. v. 309) is evident especially in his freedom from the things of the body. In eschewing any dependence on such things, the sage emulates God (v. 50) and becomes like God (v. 18), depending solely on God (v. 49). The reminder in vv. 82c-d (cf. vv. 59, 222), then, serves as a motivation for the reader to adopt the sort of attitude toward possessions that is advocated in the preceding verses. Insofar as this attitude takes the form of distinct body versus soul obligations, the gist of the unit is effectively summarized by v. 412: "Accustom yourself to provide the things of the body for the body with moderation, and the things of the soul for the soul with reverence (θεοσεβῶς)." That the sage's status as θεοσεβής (a term largely interchangeable with εὐσεβής, for which see vv. 86a-87, cf. on v. 371) becomes explicit here is not unexpected, since it is especially through trials of faith that his godlike status is revealed (v. 7a, cf. vv. 190, 307, 376a). A similar description of the θεοσεβής and his relationship to God is provided by Clement in *Strom.* 7.1.3.4-6: "For he alone is truly God-fearing who ministers to God rightly and without blame in respect to human affairs.... And the God-fearing one alone is dear to God. As such he is someone who knows what is fitting both in theory and in life, as to how one should live who will one day become god, and indeed is even now being made like God." For more on the sage's exalted status, see vv. 34, 176, 244, 319, 376b, 542, 580.

Sentences 82e–88

Text

82e μιαίνει^a τὸν θεὸν ὁ κακῶς νοῶν τὸν θεόν.
83 γλῶσσα βλάσφημος διανοίας ^aἔλεγχος κακῆς^a.
84 γλῶσσαν εὔφημον κέκτησο, μάλιστα δὲ^a περὶ θεοῦ.
85 κακῶς μὲν ποιῆσαι ^aθεὸν δυνατὸς οὐδείς^a, ἀσεβέστατος δὲ ὁ βλασφημῶν· ^bδυνατὸς γὰρ ὢν κἂν ἐποίησεν^b.
86a κρηπὶς^a εὐσεβείας ἐγκράτεια.
86b τέλος εὐσεβείας φιλία πρὸς θεόν.
87 χρῶ τῷ εὐσεβεῖ ὡς σαυτῷ.
88 εὔχου σοι γενέσθαι^a μὴ ἃ βούλει, ἀλλ᾽ ἃ^b δεῖ ^cκαὶ^d συμφέρει^c.

Translation

82e The one who thinks evil of God defiles God.
83 A blasphemous tongue is proof of an evil intellect.
84 Have a reverent tongue, especially concerning God.
85 No one is able to inflict evil upon God; but the blasphemer is most impious, for, if he was able, he would do so.
86a The foundation of piety is self-control.
86b The goal of piety is friendship with God.
87 Treat a pious person as yourself.
88 Pray that what will come to pass for you are not things that you want but things that are necessary and advantageous.

Textual Notes

82e^a μηαίνει: Π • 83^{a–a} κακῆς ἔλεγχος: Υ • 84^a omit Π • 85^{a–a} ἀδύνατον οὐδεὶς θεόν: Π • 85^{b–b} omit Υ • 86a^a κριτὴς: Υ • 88^a γίνεσθαι: Π • 88^b ὡς: Π • 88^{c–c} omit lat • 88^d ἤ: Υ

Commentary

The sayings in this unit have to do with piety and impiety. Three of the four sayings in the first cluster of sayings (vv. 82e–85) construct a gnomic characterization of the "most impious" of all human beings, the blasphemer (vv. 82e, 83, 85, with κακός in each). This is offset by a cluster of four sayings on piety (vv. 86a–88). Note the keywords εὐσέβεια in vv. 86a, 86b and εὐσεβής in v. 87. The first two sayings in the latter cluster indicate the basis and purpose of piety, while the third prescribes the correct treatment of a person embodying this virtue, who stands as an antitype to the blasphemer. While the blasphemer would defile and harm God (vv. 82e, 85), the pious person would befriend God (v. 86b). Embedded within each cluster is an appeal regarding proper speech. In the first cluster, the reader is implored to have a tongue that is not βλάσφημος but εὔφημος (v. 84), and in the second he is instructed to pray for what is appropriate, just the sort of thing one would expect of a pious person.

Sentence 82e
This verse briefly considers a negative implication of the theological anthropology first announced in v. 35: "Being chosen, you have within the constitution of yourself something godlike; therefore treat yourself as God's temple." If God is mind (v. 26) and dwells within the mind (vv. 143–144, 394), then it is necessary to keep the mind holy (vv. 35, 46a), cleansing its thoughts and intentions (vv. 46b, 181) so that it is free of all evil (vv. 57a–b). Otherwise, according to the statement here, God is rendered susceptible to impurities that infiltrate the mind in the form of defiling thoughts. Having been informed that God dwells only in a mind that is "good" (v. 61), we can infer that the divine will not abide in the mind when it becomes corrupted by such thoughts, and it is presumably under such conditions that its owner becomes vulnerable to the influence of demonic forces (vv. 305, 348–349). As v. 429 will explain, what "defiles" God is not only improper thinking but also improper behavior.

For the idea that even one's thoughts have the capacity to corrupt the divine, see Epictetus, *Diatr.* 2.8.13: "Do you suppose that I am speaking of some external God, made of silver or gold? It is within yourself that you bear him, and you do not perceive that you are defiling him with impure thoughts and filthy actions." To "think evil of God" is to attribute evil to God (v. 440, cf. vv. 29–30, 114, 314), which entails finding fault with God (v. 194) and denying divine providence (v. 312, cf. v. 380). Those who utter falsehoods of this kind slander God (v. 367) and are abandoned by God (v. 368, cf. v. 175). Conversely, the refutation of such opinions cleanses the soul (v. 103).

Sentence 83
The blasphemer is now presented as the specific manifestation of one who defiles God with evil thoughts (note the catchword κακός). He fits

such a categorization on account of the essential correspondence that exists between thoughts and words, the latter serving as "proof" (ἔλεγχος) of the former. This correspondence informs the composition of other sayings in the collection (e.g., v. 163a: "An untimely word is proof of an evil intellect") as well as the condemnation of blasphemy in Wis 1:6: "For wisdom is a kindly spirit, but will not free blasphemers from the guilt of their words; because God is witness of their inmost feelings, and a true observer of their hearts, and a hearer of their tongues." Cf. *Did.* 3.6: "Do not be arrogant or evil-minded (πονηρόφρων), for all these things breed blasphemies."

Most early Christians would probably have agreed with Justin Martyr that blasphemous talk is "unclean" in the sense that it proceeds from an unclean, that is, demonic source (*Dial.* 82.3; cf. *Vit. Pach.* 96; Ephraem Syrus, *Serm. comm. res.* 65; Severian of Gabala, *Incarn. dom.* 321–330). The souls of blasphemers are so mired in immorality, says Philo, that they are "hardly capable of cleansing and purifying" (*Fug.* 85). Cf. *Sent. Pythag.* 65ª: "Do not let some grievous and blasphemous word stain your tongue." For the expression γλῶσσα βλάσφημος, see Hippolytus, *Antichr.* 1; Gregory of Nyssa, *Eumon.* 3.10.34. Just as the soul must be purified of lawlessness and the body of pollution, the tongue must be cleansed of blasphemy (Philo, *Dec.* 93). Verse 83 is cited (with the order of the last two words reversed) in Arsenius, *Apophth.* 5.53b and in Maximus Confessor, *Loc. comm.* 91.784d, where the saying is attributed to Plutarch.

Sentence 84

This line serves as the positive counterpart to the one that precedes it; note the anaphoric catchword with γλῶσσα. When adjudicating between different opinions about God, "we ought to attribute to God whichever one of them is more reverential" (Ps.-Clement, *Hom.* 19.8). As evidence of his piety (see below), it was said of Pythagoras that "he used reverential language toward the higher powers and on every occasion remembered and honored the gods" (Iamblichus, *Vit. Pythag.* 28.149). As with most gnomic texts, the problem of speech occupies a central place in the *Sentences*, for example, in vv. 151–165g. The particular problem of speech about God is raised especially in vv. 350–368. It is critical for Sextus that every aspect of the speech-act be worthy: not only those who speak (e.g., v. 356) and hear (e.g., v. 354) words about God, but also the words themselves. Since a word about God is "God's word" (v. 357), that word must be accorded the same honor as God's very self (v. 355). Given the importance assigned in that unit to the criterion of truth (vv. 352, 355, 357), it is likely that for Sextus to have a "reverent tongue" concerning God means to make statements about God that are true, not false (cf. vv. 367–368), that is, statements that one has "learned from God" (v. 353). Cf. v. 223: "Let your words of faith be full of much piety."

Sentence 85

This line functions in part as a proviso to v. 82e: the blasphemer may defile the divine with his evil thoughts, but there is nothing he can do to inflict evil upon the divine. By establishing an antithesis of ἀσεβής (v. 85) versus εὐσέβεια (vv. 86a, b) and εὐσεβής (v. 87), it also has the function of connecting the cluster in vv. 82e–85 thematically with the cluster that follows in vv. 86a–88.

Blasphemy is condemned as an act of impiety in various Greek (e.g., Dio Chrysostom, *Or.* 3.53), Jewish (e.g., *m. Sanh.* 7:4–5), and Christian (e.g., Justin Martyr, *Dial.* 80.3) sources. What makes the blasphemer "most impious" in the eyes of our author (cf. v. 96) is not his capacity to cause God harm but his meaning to cause God harm, the issue of intentionality representing a significant concern for the *Sentences* generally (cf. vv. 46b, 56–57b, 134, 178, 181, 233, 342, 379). While it may be within one's power to hurt other people with deceitful words (cf. Ps.-Clement, *Hom.* 2.38), it is not possible to harm God (vv. 185–186, cf. v. 165f). Quite the contrary: whenever one speaks about God, one is being judged by God (v. 22). Therefore such speech must be conducted with the utmost care. Cf. *Sent. Pythag.* 115: "Consider it more desirable to let slip a soul than a blasphemous word concerning God." A similar assertion regarding divine impermeability is found in Porphyry, *Marc.* 18: "Do not, therefore, defile the divine with human delusions for you will not harm it, since it is eternally blessed and every harm has been expelled from its immortality." The person who has evil thoughts about God inflicts harm not on God but only on himself: "The fool makes himself impious and unacceptable to God, not by suffering evil at the hands of God—since the divine can do only good—but at his own hands in many things, especially in the evil opinion he has about God" (*Marc.* 17). Cf. *Const. ap.* 6.5: "For those are most certainly to be avoided who blaspheme God. The greatest part of the impious, indeed, are ignorant of God; but these men, as fighters against God, are possessed with a willful evil disposition, as with a disease."

Sentence 86a

The source for this line is Clitarchus, *Sent.* 13: ἐγκράτεια δὲ κρηπὶς εὐσεβείας, which is cited without change in Arsenius, *Apophth.* 6.48i, together with Clitarchus, *Sent.* 23-24 (= Sext. 137-138). The difference in word order here (κρηπὶς εὐσεβείας κτλ) creates better parallelism with v. 86b (τέλος εὐσεβείας κτλ). Ancient moralists placed a premium on self-control (e.g., Aristotle, *Eth. nic.* 7.1.1–7.14.9; Clement, *Strom.* 3.7.57.1–3.7.60.4). In some cases the need for ἐγκράτεια is seen as so fundamental that it is posited as the basis of morality itself—for example, in Xenophon, *Mem.* 1.5.4: "Should not every man consider self-control to be the foundation of all virtue, and first lay this foundation firmly in his soul?" (cf. Stobaeus, *Anth.* 3.17.31). Philo makes a similar statement in *Somn.* 1.124, where he speaks of men "who have laid down as the foundation, so to speak, of their whole life self-control, self-discipline, and endurance, which are the safe underpinnings of the soul" (cf. *Somn.* 2.106; *Spec.* 1.193). In the *Sentences*, the disciplines associated with self-control constitute the basis of a particular virtue, εὐσέβεια (cf. vv. 46a, 223, 228, 374, 489, 493), inasmuch as they guide the process of living in accord with God by freeing the soul of bodily desires and distractions (vv. 399, 412). Conversely, those who fail to exercise self-control are enslaved (vv. 75a–b) and defiled (vv. 108a–b, 111) by their passions. The pollution brought on by a lack of self-control is of such a nature that it defiles the very essence of the divine (v. 429), thus impairing one's relationship with God. Indeed, the desires of the body actually cut a person off from God: such a person cannot know God (v. 136), and God will not listen to him (v. 72). The sage, on the other hand, having made the control of the body a major priority for his life (vv. 274a, 294), through his temperance becomes pure in God's sight (v. 67). Faithfulness to God, then, can be expressed as a matter of exercising control over bodily desires (vv. 437–438), especially over the desire for food and sex (v. 428). For the conceptualization of ἐγκράτεια as a means of pious purification, cf. Clement, *Strom.* 2.18.80.5 ("If we exercise self-control we continue on our journey in purity toward piety") and Porphyry, *Marc.* 28: "Even the gods have prescribed remaining pure by abstinence from food and sex. This leads those who are pursuing piety towards nature's intent, which the gods themselves have constituted." A positive relationship between the two virtues is established also in 2 Pet 1:5–6: "Make every effort to support your faith with goodness, and goodness with knowledge, and knowledge with self-control, and self-control with endurance, and endurance with piety," and so forth (cf. *1 Clem.* 1.2). For the form of v. 86a, see v. 371: κρηπὶς θεοσεβείας φιλανθρωπία.

Sentence 86b

Sages were often referred to as friends of God (e.g., Wis 7:14, 27; Philo, *Her.* 21; *Prob.* 44; Epictetus, *Diatr.* 3.22.95; 3.24.60; Ps.-Apollonius, *Ep.* 52; Diogenes Laertius, *Vit. phil.* 6.72), though the appellation could also be applied to persons renowned for their piety (e.g., Diodorus Siculus, *Bibl. hist.* 5.7.7; cf. Jas 2:23). The particular formulation here resonates especially with Pythagorean views on the subject, as we learn, for example, from Iamblichus, *Vit. Pythag.* 33.229 (cf. 16.69): friendship between human beings and the gods occurs "by means of piety and scientific worship" (cf. Clement, *Strom.* 2.19.102.1, citing a statement of Hippodamus the Pythagorean). Iamblichus goes on to explain that "all of the Pythagoreans' zeal for friendship, both in words and deeds, aimed at some kind of mingling and union with God" (*Vit. Pythag.* 33.240). It was generally agreed that friendship is predicated on ὁμοιότης, "likeness" (Plutarch, *Amic. mult.* 96d). Aristotle, however, held that the similarities between human beings and the gods were insufficient for them to be united by such a bond (*Eth. nic.* 8.7.4–5; cf. 8.1.6). For Sextus, however, the whole point of the sage's existence is to become like God (vv. 18, 44–45, 147–148, 381), and "like is friend (φίλον) to like" (v. 443). Another principle of friendship was conveyed by the precept κοινὰ τὰ φίλων, a principle that was sometimes attributed to Pythagoras (e.g., Iamblichus, *Vit. Pythag.* 6.32; Diogenes Laertius, *Vit. phil.* 8.10). The Sextine sage fulfills this qualification for divine friendship as well. Indeed, whatever belongs to God belongs also to the sage (v. 310), who shares the same kingdom with God (v. 311) and the same desires as God (vv. 134–135). Yet another friendship *topos* is summarized in the idea that friends share "one soul" (e.g., Aristotle, *Eth. nic.* 9.8.2; Plutarch, *Amic. mult.* 96f). Insofar as the soul of the sage is always with God and united to God (vv. 55, 416, 418), his relationship with God approximates friendship according to this criterion as well. Cf. Maximus of Tyre, *Or.* 14.6: "The pious man is a friend to the gods, the superstitious man a flatterer."

Sentence 87

Lev 19:18 (ἀγαπήσεις τὸν πλησίον σου ὡς σεαυτόν) is cited as expressing a fundamental moral obligation in a variety of early Christian contexts, including Matt 19:19; 22:39; Mark 12:31, 33; Luke 10:37; Rom 13:9; Gal 5:14; Jas 2:8; *Did.* 1.2; Justin Martyr, *Dial.* 93.2; *Didasc. apost.* 9. Clement cites the verse frequently, for example, *Strom.* 2.15.71.1. Sextus's variation of the precept uses "pious person" in lieu of "neighbor" as the object of the reader's action (for the treatment of neighbors, see on v. 89), and "treat" in lieu of "love" as the verb (cf. vv. 101, 106a–b, 158, 419, 442–444), for which cf. v. 226: "The one who does not love (μὴ φιλῶν) a sage does not love himself." To the extent that the pious are like their friend God (see above), they are also like one another. It follows that each should treat the other "like" himself, especially since they have a common friend in God. As comparison with v. 106a suggests, the sage may treat all people fairly, but he only "loves" that which is akin to himself, that is, God and other sages.

Sentence 88

This line is based on Clitarchus, *Sent.* 14: εὔχου σοι γενέσθαι μὴ ἃ βούλει ἀλλ' ἃ δεῖ. Sextus appends καὶ συμφέρει, for which see on v. 165g. As he indicates elsewhere, what one should ask for in prayer are the sorts of "good things" worthy of those who have a share in divine reason (v. 277), that is, whatever is worthy of God (v. 122), including whatever is necessary for the salvation of oneself (v. 374, cf. v. 80) and of all humanity (v. 372). It would be improper to pray for what one wishes, since this may be at variance with what God deems necessary. Compare Evagrius Ponticus, *Orat.* 31: "Do not pray that your will be done—for it is not always in accord with God's desire. Instead, pray as you have been taught, saying, 'Your will be done' in me (cf. Matt 6:10). And ask him thus in every situation so that his will be done—for he wills what is good and advantageous (συμφέρον) for your soul, whereas that is not always what you seek." In some cases, what is advantageous may in fact appear to be undesirable: "We pray for advantageous things, feeling that it is unfitting for us to ask of thee the highest rewards. Even though they may seem to be evil, we will receive as advantageous all the trials that meet us, whatever they may be, which thy ordering employs for our training in steadfastness" (Clement, *Strom.* 7.12.72.6, cf. 7.12.73.2). For similar instructions on prayer, see *Act. Thom.* 30; Origen, *Orat.* 6.4.

SENTENCES 89–92

TEXT

89   ὡς θέλεις χρήσασθαί σοι τοὺς πέλας, καὶ σὺ χρῶ αὐτοῖς.
90   ἃ ψέγεις, [a]μηδὲ ποίει[a].

91a μηδείς σε πειθέτω ποιεῖν[a] τι παρὰ τὸ βέλτιον[b].
91b [a]ἃ δέδοταί σοι[a], κἂν ἀφέληταί [b]σού τις[b], μὴ ἀγανάκτει.
92 ἃ δίδωσιν ὁ θεός, οὐδεὶς ἀφαιρεῖται.

Translation

89 As you want your neighbors to treat you, so you treat them.
90 Things that you censure, do not do.
91a Let no one persuade you to do something other than what is best.
91b Even if someone takes from you things that have been given to you, do not be indignant.
92 Things that God gives, no one takes away.

Textual Notes

90[a-a] omit Υ (which combines vv. 90 + 91a into a single saying) • 91a[a] omit Υ • 91a[b] βέλτιστον: Π • 91b[a-a] ἃ δίδωσιν ὁ θεός: Π • 91b[b-b] omit Π

Commentary

Lines 89–92 present two loosely connected clusters of sayings. The first, vv. 89–91a, is on what the reader should do (note ποιέω in vv. 90, 91). The second, vv. 91b–92, is on what has been given to the reader: note the anaphoric ἃ δέδοται (v. 91b) and ἃ δίδωσιν (v. 92). The former is loosely connected to the unit that precedes (vv. 82e–88) by the theme of treating others (vv. 87, 89) and to the unit that follows (vv. 93–97) by the theme of doing, or acting (note especially ποιέω in v. 93).

Sentence 89

Shortly after offering a version of Lev 19:18 that omits its reference to the neighbor (v. 87), our author offers here a version of Matt 7:12/Luke 6:31 that inserts such a reference (note χράομαι in both lines), which has the effect of bringing the two biblical precepts into alignment. The actual wording of v. 89 bears little resemblance to its source, though Sextus's ὡς θέλεις may be compared with Luke's καθὼς θέλετε. In ancient literature, negative forms of the golden rule predominate (see on v. 179), though the positive form can be found in *Let. Aris.* 207; Dio Cassius, *Bibl. hist.* 52.34.1; Diogenes Laertius, *Vit. phil.* 5.21; Seneca, *Ep.* 94.43; *Ben.* 2.1.1. Generally speaking, the latter both places a greater burden on the moral agent to initiate action and governs a greater range of actions; see further on vv. 105 and 213. For the reference to neighbor, compare Sir 31:15 ("Judge your neighbor's feelings by your own, and in every matter be thoughtful") and Publilius Syrus, *Sent.* 2 ("As you treat a neighbor, expect another to treat you"). Jesus' proclamation of the rule had a profound impact on the development of Christian ethics, early allusions to Matt 7:12/Luke 6:31 including *Did.* 1.2; *Act. Thom.* 83; *Ep. Apost.* 18; Theophilus, *Autol.* 2.34; Irenaeus, *Haer.* 4.13.3; Clement, *Paed.* 3.12.88.1; Ps.-Clement, *Hom.* 11.4; 12.32; *Rec.* 5.23; 8.56.

The saying in Sext. 89 is repeated in v. 210b, where it is preceded by a plea to become a benefactor of all humanity (v. 210a) and followed by a negative form of the golden rule (v. 211).

Sentence 90

To the extent that actions they do not want others perpetrating against them are among the sorts of things people criticize, this verse can be interpreted as a negative form of the golden rule. The element of reciprocity, however, is not made explicit, as it is in vv. 179 and 211 (cf. vv. 327, 386). Attention is drawn instead to the problem of hypocrisy, of doing oneself what one condemns in others. Addressing such a problem is relevant to the instruction of the *Sentences* insofar as it is assumed that the sage will be involved in both offering and receiving correction (vv. 103, 245, 298, 331, cf. vv. 194, 299). Judging others, however, carries with it a certain amount of risk, since it is an act that invites divine scrutiny (vv. 183–184). Integrity of word and deed for the sage is therefore essential (v. 177). The theme raised in v. 90 is a favorite among gnomic authors, for example, *Gnom. Democr.* 60; Ps.-Cato, *Dist.* 1.30 ("What you are wont to blame do not do yourself"); 3.7; Epictetus, *Ench.* 5 ("It is the part of an uneducated person to blame others in matters where he himself acts wrongly"); Epictetus, *Gnom.* 52; Menander, *Mon.* 7: "Let us not imitate those things that we censure (ψέγομεν)." Similarly, to the question, "How shall we lead the best and most righteous life?" Thales is reported to have replied, "By refraining from doing what we blame in others" (Diogenes Laertius, *Vit. phil.* 1.36). Aristotle reverses the logic of the equation in *Rhet.* 2.6.19: "A person is supposed not to reproach others with what he does himself, so it is clear that what he reproaches them with is what he does not do himself." As he remarks a bit later on, "generally it is ridiculous for a man to reproach others for what he does or would do himself" (*Rhet.* 2.23.7).

Sentence 91a

Comparison with vv. 25–26 of the *Carmen aureum* suggests a Pythagorean pedigree for this saying: "Let no one persuade (παρείπῃ) you either by word or even by deed to do or say whatever is not best (μὴ βέλτερον) for you." Both teaching and correction are often matters of persuasion, that is, of developing appropriate arguments of one's own, as well as of responding to the arguments of others. As v. 331 indicates, believers have an obligation to "persuade" one another not to act out of ignorance (cf. vv. 25, 358). But, as sayings like vv. 353, 356, and 408–410 indicate, believers also have an obligation to accept as instructors only those who both know and follow God's word. Discrimination therefore must be observed both in terms of who teaches and (as we learn here) what is taught. As Abba Agathon said, "If someone were very specially dear to me, but I realized that he was leading me to do something less good, I should put him from me" (*Apophth. patr.* [al.] 116.22–24).

Sentences 91b–92

Chadwick (1959, 155) believes v. 91b preserves the more original version of the appeal made in v. 15 (ὁπόσα τοῦ κόσμου ἔχεις, κἂν ἀφέληταί σού τις, μὴ ἀγανάκτει). There the point was to encourage the reader's indifference to and disassociation from the things of "the world" (cf. vv. 16, 20). Here the point is to draw a contrast between what can and cannot be taken away from the reader, the same sort of contrast that is drawn using a nearly identical version of v. 92 in vv. 404–405: "Whatever God gives, no one takes away. What the world provides, it does not keep secure." The similar openings for v. 91b (ἃ δέδοται) and v. 92 (ἃ δίδωσιν) not only indicate that the two lines should be read in conjunction with one another (note also how they both use ἀφαιρέω); they also draw attention to the fact that the things in question are not inherently one's own (cf. v. 227) but originate from elsewhere. Things of divine origin, the "things of the soul," are secure and therefore worth acquiring (vv. 77, 118, 128, cf. v. 21). The loss of physical things, including even one's body (v. 321) should not be a source of consternation, since they are of no true or abiding value to the self (v. 130). Cf. *Sent. Pythag.* 120 ("You will not need anything which sovereign chance gives then takes away"); Clitarchus, *Sent.* 122 ("Whatever fortune gives, these things circumstances take away"); Porphyry, *Marc.* 12 ("You will not need anything which fortune often gives and then takes away again").

The source for v. 92 is Clitarchus, *Sent.* 15: ἃ δίδωσι παιδεία, ταῦτα οὐδείς σε ἀφαιρήσεται (note that the source for v. 93 is Clitarchus, *Sent.*

16). Sextus drops ταῦτα and σε, alters the tense of the second verb, and, most important, replaces παιδεία with ὁ θεός, perhaps under the influence of *Sent. Pythag.* 3ᵇ (δῶρον γὰρ θεοῦ πᾶν ἀναφαίρετον), which, together with the other two elements of *Sent. Pythag.* 3 (for v. 3ᵃ, see on Sext. 128), is also cited in Porphyry, *Marc.* 12 and, as a saying of Pythagoras, in Stobaeus (see Wachsmuth and Hense 1884–1912, 5.viii; cf. Chadwick 1959, 149, 156–57). For a similar editorial move, see on v. 285.

Sentences 93–97

Text

93   σκέπτου πρὸ τοῦ πράττειν ἃ πράττεις, ἵνα μὴ δὶς ποιῇς ἃ μὴ δεῖ.
94   ὃ πράττωνᵃ οὐκ ἂν θέλοιςᵇ εἰδέναι τὸν θεόν, τοῦτο μὴ πράξῃς.
95a πρὸ παντὸς οὗ πράττεις νόει τὸν θεόν.
95b φῶςᵃ σου τῶν πράξεων προηγείσθω.
96   μεγίστη ἀσέβεια εἰς θεὸν ἀνθρώπουᵃ κάκωσις.
97   ψυχὴ φωτίζεται ἐννοίᾳ θεοῦ.

Translation

93   Deliberate before taking the actions that you take, so that you do not repeat doing things you should not.
94   Whatever action you do not want God to know, this do not do.
95a Before every action you take, think about God.
95b Let your light guide your actions.
96   The greatest impiety against God is the mistreatment of a human being.
97   A soul is enlightened by a thought about God.

Textual Notes

94ᵃ omit lat, sy² • 94ᵇ ἔχοις: Υ • 95bᵃ ὅπως γνῷς ἀνθρώπων κάκωσιν φῶς: Υ • 96ᵃ ἀνθρώπων: Π

Commentary

In this unit Sextus draws attention to the reader's actions. Note πράττω in vv. 93, 94, and 95a, and πρᾶξις in v. 95b. The opening for the section (v. 93)

expresses a moral commonplace: think before you act, lest you regret the outcome. This "text" (borrowed from Clitarchus, *Sent.* 16) is then elaborated by a chain of admonitions (vv. 94–95b) and a pair of concluding maxims (vv. 96–97) that specify the nature of both the thinking and acting involved. To think before one acts means to think about God (v. 95a), who is the "light" that should illuminate all of one's thoughts and deeds (note φῶς in v. 95b and φωτίζω in v. 97). Regrettable actions, meanwhile, are defined as anything that the reader would not want coming to God's attention (v. 94), including especially the mistreatment of another person (v. 96). The composition, then, exhibits an interlocking structure, the maxim in v. 96 supporting the admonition in v. 94, and the maxim in v. 97 supporting the admonitions in vv. 95a + 95b (note also νόει in v. 95a and ἐννοίᾳ in v. 97). See further Kirk 1998, 122–24.

Sentence 93

The maxim in v. 93 as printed by Elter (1892, 10) and Chadwick (1959, 22) replicates Clitarchus, *Sent.* 16 (σκέπτου πρὸ τοῦ πράττειν καὶ ἃ πράττεις ἐξέταζε, ἵνα μηδὲν ποιῇς ὃ μὴ δεῖ), though the (somewhat shorter) line preserved in both Greek manuscripts (see above) makes sense as it is. The Latin version, meanwhile, appears to ignore the second, negative part of the saying: "Deliberate before you act, and before you act bear in mind what kind of act it will be." For ἃ μὴ δεῖ, cf. vv. 141 and 153.

As Marcus Aurelius explains, before commencing any action, the wise are careful to deliberate about what should be done (σκοπεῖν τί δεῖ πραχθῆναι), taking into account whether the action "is just or unjust, the work of a good person or a bad one" (*Med.* 7.44.1; 10.12.1; cf. Plato, *Apol.* 28b; Dio Chrysostom, *Or.* 31.32). Among gnomic authors, Publilius Syrus perhaps addresses the danger of acting before thinking most frequently— for example, in *Sent.* 32 ("Hasty judgment means speedy repentance"), 125, 151, 518, 734. Other contributions to the theme of predeliberation include Sir 32:19; 37:16 ("Let reason go before every deed, and counsel before every action"); *Instr. Ankh.* 8.4 ("Do not do a thing that you have not first examined"); *Gnom. Democr.* 66 ("It is better to plan before one's actions than to repent later"); Diogenes Laertius, *Vit. phil.* 1.92 ("When anyone leaves the house, let him first inquire what he means to do"); Menander, *Mon.* 111; and, from a Pythagorean context, *Carm. aur.* 27: "Reflect before the deed, lest foolish things result from it." That the readers should think before they speak is a recommendation of v. 153, which exhibits a similar structure: "Deliberate before speaking, so that you do not say things you should not."

Sentences 94–95a

Human beings cannot hide their actions from God any more than they can hide their thoughts from God (v. 66, cf. v. 57a). All of one's actions in life will be counted as evidence when the time comes to stand before God in judgment (v. 347, cf. v. 39), and nothing one can assert about those actions will deceive God regarding their true nature (v. 186, cf. v. 569). Knowing this, the sage always imagines himself standing in God's presence (vv. 82a, 224), calling upon God to witness and confirm his good deeds (vv. 303–304). Against this background, v. 94 offers prudential counsel: the only way to keep God from having knowledge of a misdeed is not to commit such an act in the first place.

The advice of v. 95a supports that of v. 94: if the reader thinks about God before doing anything, he will not do anything he does not want coming to God's attention. Verse 95a also serves to clarify the content of v. 93: the sort of prior deliberation that prevents people from doing what they should not entails thinking about God. For Sextus an essential connection exists between thinking and acting. If one wishes to accomplish noble things, it is necessary to think noble things (v. 56). Toward this end, the sage strives to think constantly about God (vv. 54, 289, cf. vv. 143–144), which means never thinking about what should not be done (vv. 178, 233, cf. vv. 57b, 181).

Sentence 95b

The parallelism that this line exhibits with vv. 95a, 97, and 104 ("God is the guide of humanity's noble actions") indicates that the light in question here is God, which would accord with the identification of God as the "wise light" in v. 30 (for more on the background of Sextus's light imagery, see the commentary on that verse). The imagery employed here is reminiscent especially of early Christian texts that speak of the faithful as "walking" in the light (e.g., John 8:12; 11:9; 12:35; Eph 5:8; 1 John 1:7; Rev 21:24; Clement, *Strom.* 3.4.32.2) or walking in the "way" of light (e.g., *Ep. Barn.* 19.1; Clement, *Strom.* 1.29.181.3; Ps.-Clement, *Ep. virg.* 1.2.4), or being summoned to perform good works "in the light" (e.g., Matt 5:16; John 3:21; *Act. Thom.* 34; Gregory of Nyssa, *Diem lum.* 9.238; Evagrius Ponticus, *Serm. virt. vit.* 23). To allow one's actions to be guided by God (cf. v. 582) means to allow one's actions to be guided by reason (vv. 74, 123), that is, by the something godlike within (vv. 35, 46a, 61, 144, 394). The actions of those who fail in this regard are guided instead by an evil demon (v. 305).

Sentence 96

This line clarifies the nature of the actions proscribed by v. 94: while the greatest impiety one can commit against God with words is blasphemy (v. 85), the greatest impiety one can commit against God with actions is to mistreat another human being. To paraphrase Philo, those who sow injustice reap impiety (*Conf.* 152; cf. *Spec.* 1.215; *Virt.* 94; *Praem.* 105). Impiety and injustice are frequently found paired together (e.g., Plato, *Protag.* 324a; Rom 1:18; Josephus, *Bell.* 7.260; Justin Martyr, *1 Apol.* 4.7; *Dial.* 46.5; Ps.-Apollonius, *Ep.* 58.6; Diogenes Laertius, *Vit. phil.* 6.17), the implication being that those guilty of the former are also guilty of the latter. Cf. Prov 12:21 (οἱ δὲ ἀσεβεῖς πλησθήσονται κακῶν); Ps.-Justin Martyr, *Quaest. Christ. gent.* 161b (ἐξ ἀνάγκης πᾶσαν κακίας ὑπερβολὴν ἡ ἀσέβεια ἔχουσα); Marcus Aurelius, *Med.* 9.1.1: "Injustice is impiety. For in that the nature of the universe has fashioned rational creatures for the sake of one another ... the transgressor of her will acts with obvious impiety against the most venerable of deities." Porphyry also issues several statements on the topic, for example, *Marc.* 35 ("For there is certainly no way that an unjust person can be pious towards god") and *Abst.* 3.26.1: "Someone who did not refrain from injustice towards relatives would rightly be judged impious." Of the ideal king, Dio Chrysostom writes, "virtue he regards as holiness and vice as utter impiety, being firmly persuaded that not only those who rob temples or blaspheme the gods are sinners and accursed but, much more so, the cowardly, the unjust, the licentious, the fools, and, in general, those who act contrary to the power and will of the gods" (*Or.* 3.53). In Ps.-Clement, *Rec.* 5.23, the principle informing v. 96 is expressed with reference to Gen 1:26–27: "Be assured that whoever commits murder or adultery, or anything that causes suffering or injury to others, in all these the image of God is violated. For to injure others is a great impiety toward God. Whenever, therefore, you do to another what you would not have another do to you, you defile the image of God." Similarly, for Sextus every sin is an act of impiety (v. 11) that renders the perpetrator impure (v. 102) and unfit to worship God (v. 370). Conversely, the best purification that people can perform for themselves is to refrain from harming others (v. 23), and the best offering one can render to God is to do good for others (v. 47).

Sentence 97

This line is based on Clitarchus, *Sent.* 17: ψυχὴ καθαίρεται ἐννοίᾳ θεοῦ. Cf. Porphyry, *Marc.* 11: καθαίρεται μὲν ἄνθρωπος ἐννοίᾳ θεοῦ. The former appears to have influenced the composition of Sext. 24 as well: ψυχὴ καθαίρεται λόγῳ θεοῦ ὑπὸ σοφοῦ. Presumably Sextus changes the verb here to φωτίζεται in order to create a connection with φῶς in v. 95b: the "light" that should guide one's actions is generated by reflection upon God. In addition, the phrase ἐννοίᾳ θεοῦ in v. 97 matches up with νόει τὸν θεόν in v. 95a: the illumination of the soul is not an end in itself but ought to precede and inform all of one's actions. Similar is *Marc.* 20, though there Porphyry applies the principle not to the reader's actions but to her words: "Therefore, even if your lips utter some statement about another topic, let your intellect and heart be turned toward God. For in this way even your speech will be god-filled, illumined by the light of God's truth." Early Christians often described themselves as those who had been enlightened (e.g., John 1:9; 2 Cor 4:6; Eph 1:18; Heb 6:4; Rev 22:5; Ign. *Rom.* prol. 1; Origen, *Cels.* 6.5; 7.21; *Princ.* 4.2.8; *Comm. Joan.* 13.23.132–137), though the illumination of the soul is an aspiration of Neoplatonic philosophy as well, as in Plotinus, *Enn.* 3.9.3; 5.1.2; 5.3.8; 5.3.17. Cf. Ps.-Clement, *Hom.* 11.29: "When the mind is enlightened by knowledge, the disciple is able to be good, and thereupon purity follows; for from the understanding within a good care of the body without is produced."

Sentences 98–103

Text

98 αὐτάρκειαν ἄσκει.
99 τῶν ἀτόπων[a] μὴ ὀρέγου.
100 τῶν καλῶν ἐκπόνει τὰ αἴτια.
101 τὰ τοῦ σώματος μὴ ἀγάπα.
102 ἀκάθαρτον ἄνθρωπον ποιεῖ πρᾶξις αἰσχρά[a].
103 [a]καθαίρει ψυχὴν[a] ἀνοήτου δόξης ἔλεγχος.

Translation

98 Practice self-sufficiency.
99 Do not long for inappropriate things.
100 Search out the causes of noble things.
101 Do not love the things of the body.
102 A shameful action makes a person impure.

103   Refutation of a senseless opinion purifies a soul.

Textual Notes

98 omit Π • 99ª ἁπάντων: Υ, lat • 102ª ἀχρεία: sy² • 103ª⁻ª καθαιρεῖ ψυχῆς: Π

Commentary

Verse 98 announces the topic of this section, αὐτάρκεια, with vv. 99–103 providing some specifics on how the virtue ought to be practiced. The preferred comportment is expounded largely in negative terms: those who aspire to self-sufficiency should refrain from wanting things that are unnatural (v. 99), that belong to the body (v. 101), that are shameful (v. 102) and foolish (v. 103). Countering this for Sextus is v. 100, which raises the possibility that the virtue has a positive dimension as well. In this case, self-sufficiency is a matter not simply of contracting one's needs for material things but also of discovering the nature of "good things," things upon which it is presumably suitable for the sage to rely.

Sentence 98

This verse is repeated as v. 334 (note that Π omits the line here), where it is attached to a saying about the burdensome nature of the body and its members (v. 335, cf. on v. 101 below). As they become more self-sufficient, people become more like God, who is entirely self-sufficient (vv. 49–50), and becoming like God is "sufficient" for their well-being (v. 148); see also on v. 263. For the form of the saying, cf. vv. 69 and 120.

Famous for their contentment, frugality, and detachment from society, the Cynics were among those who took the need "to strive for self-sufficiency" (*Socrat. ep.* 8.1) most seriously (cf. Teles, frag. 2). Of more immediate relevance for the interpretation of our text is *Sent. Pythag.* 30ª⁻ᵇ: "The one who truly lives like God is the one who is self-sufficient and without property and a philosopher and regards not to have need of anything, even necessities, as the greatest wealth." Cf. Porphyry, *Marc.* 28: "The philosophers say that nothing is as necessary as perceiving clearly what is not necessary, and that the greatest wealth of all is self-sufficiency." Such "wealth" is not simply to be had, however, but must be cultivated over time and with much effort. As Paul explains in Phil 4:11, being self-sufficient is something that he has "learned" to do. For Clement, training in self-sufficiency is compulsory for those who wish to complete life's journey successfully: "God seeks to train us to the condition of a wayfarer, that is, to make us well-girded and unimpeded by provisions, that we might be self-sufficient of life and practice a moderate frugality in our journey toward the good life of eternity" (*Paed.* 1.12.98.4). He goes so far as to claim as a "first principle" that "the universe is made for the sake of self-sufficiency" (*Paed.* 2.3.39.1). For other discussions of αὐτάρκεια in early Christian discourse, see 2 Cor 9:8; 1 Tim 6:6; Herm. *Sim.* 1.6; Tatian, *Orat.* 2.1; 19.1; Clement, *Paed.* 2.1.7.3; *Strom.* 2.22.133.7; 3.12.89.1.

Sentence 99

Developing self-sufficiency requires exercising control over one's longings, since, as Clement explains, "natural longings have a limit set to them by self-sufficiency" (*Paed.* 2.1.16.4). Compare also Porphyry, *Marc.* 27: "The person who follows nature and not empty false opinions is self-sufficient in everything. For satisfying nature any possession is wealth, but for satisfying unlimited longings even the greatest wealth is nothing." As these examples illustrate, assertions regarding αὐτάρκεια often rested on certain assumptions regarding the natural limits of human ὄρεξις (cf. Epicurus, *Ep. Men.* 130; Plutarch, *Comp. Arist. Cat.* 4.3; Alexander of Aphrodisias, *Anim. mant.* 163). To long for things that are "strange" or inappropriate (ἄτοποι) would be taken as a sign of illness, desperation, or irrationality (e.g., Plutarch, *Frat. amor.* 479b; *Them.* 23.2; for the Stoic definition of ἐπιθυμία as an irrational longing, see *SVF* 3:391, 394, 396, 438, 463, 464, etc.). In a Sextine context, the inappropriate objects of human longing include in the first place worldly possessions (vv. 128, 130, 137, 274b). Such things ought to be scorned, not desired (vv. 82b, 121a, 127). Of material aids the sage acquires nothing that exceeds his actual physical requirements (vv. 19, 115), endeavoring instead to bring his desires into alignment with God's (vv. 134–135). Sentence 99 can also be read in concert with warnings elsewhere in the text regarding ἐπιθυμία (vv. 146, 274b), ἡδονή (vv. 70, 111, 232, 272, 276, 342, 411, cf. vv. 71b–72, 139b, 172), and πάθος (vv. 75a–b, 204–207, 209).

Sentence 100

Cf. Porphyry, *Marc.* 29: "Let us neither censure the flesh as cause (αἰτίαν) of great evils nor attribute our distress to external circumstances. Rather let us seek their causes in the soul, and, by breaking away from every vain longing (ὄρεξιν) and hope for fleeting fancies, let us become totally in control of ourselves." In contrast to the Neoplatonic philosopher, who encourages his reader to search for the causes of evil things by looking within (cf. Epictetus, *Diatr.* 2.5.5; 3.22.44), Sextus encourages his reader to search out the causes of noble things, which, in his view, are to be found with God alone (vv. 104, 113, 197, 390), since by definition only that which befits God is noble (v. 197, cf. v. 104). Investigating such noble things is not an end in itself but entails thinking about them with the intent of doing them (v. 56). In its current context, the reference to τὰ καλά serves as a counterpoint to the inappropriate, bodily, shameful, and foolish things denigrated by the surrounding gnomes (vv. 99, 101–103). As v. 142 explains, those who strive for such base things are wont to overlook that which is noble.

Moral philosophy could be defined as "searching for the good," trying "to find out what exactly it can be" (Aristotle, *Eth. nic.* 1.7.1; cf. 1.2.3; 1.5.4). Specifically, the moral philosopher "seeks to know the things that are good for human beings" (*Eth. nic.* 6.7.5). Clement, citing a modified version of Wis 6:13, expresses confidence regarding the successful outcome of such a quest: "Goodness is found by him who seeks it, and is easily seen by him that has found her" (*Paed.* 1.10.91.3; cf. Origen, *Cels.* 4.44). The verb Sextus employs here, ἐκπονέω, often means to "work at" or "work through" something, and so draws attention to the element of toil and striving involved. Wanting to be noble is not enough, as Epictetus explains; rather, one must "work at" being noble, that is, work at acquiring the virtue appropriate to a human being (*Diatr.* 3.1.7; cf. Xenophon, *Cyr.* 2.3.4; Clement, *Protr.* 10.95.3). Cf. Amos 5:14: ἐκζητήσατε τὸ καλόν.

Sentence 101

The relation of this verse to the one that precedes it is suggested by v. 317: "Do not seek goodness in the flesh." In the search for what is good and noble, the things of the body have no part, since nothing good can derive from the flesh (v. 271). The sage understands that if he loves what he should not, he will be unable to love what he should (v. 141, cf. v. 136). Therefore he loves not the flesh (v. 291) but that which is akin to his true self (v. 106a, cf. vv. 442, 448), that is, God, whom he loves more than his own soul (vv. 106b, 292, cf. v. 444). The body and its pleasures, on the other hand, are not things to be loved (cf. vv. 71b, 101, 139b) but things to be renounced (v. 78), conquered (v. 71a), and controlled (v. 274a) since they are burdensome to the soul (vv. 322, 335, 411) and can lead to spiritual ruin (v. 13).

Ancient moralists agreed that training in self-sufficiency makes demands on the whole person: "The soul that does not take account of the self-sufficiency of the body cannot make itself self-sufficient" (Ps.-Apollonius, *Ep.* 82; cf. Plutarch, *Cohib. ira* 461c; Aspasius, *Eth. nic. comm.* 16; Basil of Caesarea, *Ascet. magn.* 31.973). Just as those who long for inappropriate things can be described as irrational (see on v. 99), the same can be said of those who long for things of the body: "So a human being is set on the boundaries between rational and irrational nature, and if he sinks toward the body and loves the things of the body very much, he clings to the life of the irrational things and is reckoned among them" (Posidonius, frag. 309a).

Sentence 102

In searching out the causes of noble things (v. 100), one would eschew not only anything that is corporal (v. 101) but also anything that is shameful. This is because, as Porphyry, *Marc.* 9 explains, "the shameful is the opposite of the noble. Since the divine is noble, it is impossible for it to come into contact with evil; for Plato says that 'It is not at all lawful for the impure to partake of the pure' (cf. *Phaed.* 67a–b)." As this quotation also indicates, participation in what is shameful leaves one "impure" and therefore unfit for communion with the divine. Ancient Christians would have agreed that shameful acts render their perpetrators impure (e.g., Origen, *Frag. Eph.* 24), or, as Clement puts it, "Purity is a quality that keeps a person's life innocent and free of shameful deeds" (*Paed.* 3.11.55.2). Because it involves the purging of excessive desires, self-sufficiency (see on v. 98) represents one of the means by which the soul can be purified of evils (Ps.-Diogenes, *Ep.* 46; for the association of self-sufficiency with purity, see also Herm. *Mand.* 6.2.3; Plutarch, *Sept. sap. conv.* 159c; Porphyry, *Abst.* 1.57.3). It is not surprising that those who indulge in shameful deeds eschew and even disparage the need for self-sufficiency (Plutarch, *Adul. am.* 57c–d). In the *Sentences*, it is acts resulting from an evil character, for example, overindulgence in food (v. 108b), that are thought to be defiling (v. 110, cf. v. 469). Those whose souls have not been cleansed of such "unholy deeds" are unfit to utter or even hear a word about God (vv. 356, 407). Indeed, the person who lacks self-control (in many respects the opposite of the person who practices self-sufficiency) defiles not only himself but also God (v. 429), his unclean soul serving as a conduit for unclean demons (v. 348).

Sentence 103

This verse balances the one that precedes it: note the juxtaposition of anaphoric ἀκάθαρτον and καθαίρει. Sextus not only identifies what makes a person impure; he also stipulates how such impurity can be removed. The "best" purification may be to refrain from harming others (v. 23, cf. v. 81), but, as *Sent. Pythag.* 55 and Porphyry, *Marc.* 15 attest, a person can be defiled by opinions as well as by actions. The procedure advocated here is derived from *Soph.* 230d, where Plato describes ἔλεγχος as "the principal and most important kind of purification." This is because a soul will gain no benefit from instruction until someone "removes the opinions that interfere with learning and exhibits it cleansed, believing that it knows only those things that it does not know, and nothing more." In *Paed.* 1.9.82.3, Clement declares that Plato's statement "echoes the Word when he claims that one who is notably lacking in purification becomes undisciplined and shameful (cf. v. 102) when he is left uncorrected." Such refutation ought to have the effect of "leading those enslaved by intemperance back to moderation" (*Paed.* 1.9.82.2). Taken in isolation, the "senseless" opinions of v. 103 (cf. Clitarchus, *Sent.* 118) could refer to incorrect theological conceptions generally (cf. vv. 28, 410), though read together with vv. 98–102 (see above), it is possible that a more specific reference is being made, namely, to opinions that might inhibit one from practicing self-sufficiency. Presumably the refutation under discussion is issued by the sage, whose discourse about God has the power to purify the soul (v. 24), though this power must be used with discretion (v. 407). While such words are an expected, even welcomed, component of moral education (vv. 245, 298, cf. v. 543), they must only be uttered by those who have been properly prepared—that is, properly cleansed (v. 356)—to do so.

Sentences 104–107

Text

104 ὁ θεὸς ἀνθρώπων[a] καλῶν πράξεων ἡγεμών ἐστιν.
105 μηδένα ἐχθρὸν ἡγοῦ.
106a ἀγάπα τὸ ὁμόφυλον.
106b ἀγάπα τὸν θεὸν καὶ πρὸ τῆς ψυχῆς σου[a].
107 οὐ[a] χαλεπὸν ἁμαρτωλοὺς ἐπὶ τὸ αὐτὸ γενέσθαι μὴ[b] ἁμαρτάνοντας.

Translation

104 God is the guide of humanity's noble actions.

105 Deem no one an enemy.
106a Love what is akin to you.
106b Love God even more than your soul.
107 It is not difficult for sinners to be together if they do not sin.

Textual Notes
104 omit Υ • 104ᵃ ἀνθρώποις: lat, sy¹ • 106bᵃ omit Π • 107 omit Π • 107ᵃ omit lat • 107ᵇ omit lat

COMMENTARY

At the center of this loose assortment of sayings is a pair of precepts based on the great commandment (vv. 106a–b). Flanking these are precepts that incorporate some rather sanguine references to typical moral "outsiders" (enemies in v. 105, sinners in v. 107), and a pronouncement familiar from a previous saying in the collection (v. 104, cf. v. 95b).

Sentence 104

Those who aspire to noble deeds have God as their "guide and counselor" (Josephus, *C. Ap.* 2.160), or, as Philo puts it: "Whenever a human being acts rightly in decisions and actions that are beyond reproach, these can be assigned to God's account as universal guide" (*Opif.* 75). According to Clement, individuals are said to have God as their "leader and guide" when in their actions they follow the norms set down by the virtues of moderation and justice (*Strom.* 4.20.127.2; cf. Sext. 399). The formulation here essentially restates the jussive of v. 95b ("Let your light guide your actions") in the form of a precept. In order to live in accord with God one must act nobly (v. 399), and only that which befits God is noble (v. 197). Since it is impossible to live nobly without God (v. 215), whenever the sage performs a noble deed he understands God to be its ultimate cause (vv. 113, 390, cf. v. 582). The person whose actions are guided by God, that is, by the divine reason that dwells within (vv. 74, 123, 264a), can become a guide to noble action for others (v. 166). Conversely, the guide of an evil action is an evil demon (v. 305).

Sentence 105

Pythagoras bade his disciples to interact with other people in such a way "as not to make friends into enemies but to turn enemies into friends" (Diogenes Laertius, *Vit. phil.* 8.23); cf. Iamblichus, *Vit. Pythag.* 8.40; Ps.-

Zaleucus, frag. 226.18–21; 227.29–228.1; *Sent. Pythag.* 76 ("Whomever you judge to be a friend you have kept from becoming an enemy"); Sir 6:1 ("Do not become an enemy instead of a friend, for a bad name inherits shame and reproach"); Ps.-Phoc. 142 ("It is better to make a gracious friend instead of an enemy"); *Chion. ep.* 16.7 ("I have learned ... to avoid acquiring enemies and, if I have an enemy, to make him my friend"); Philo, *Virt.* 152; Diogenes Laertius, *Vit. phil.* 1.87, 91. While Sextus's counsel here is not inconsistent with such statements, it also differs from them in lacking the explicit goal of turning enemies into friends. Cf. Dio Chrysostom, *Or.* 1.35 ("Whose life is safer than his whom all alike protect, whose is happier than his who deems no one his enemy, and whose is freer from vexation than his who has no cause to blame himself?") and Hierocles, *In aur. carm.* 7.11 (οὐδεὶς ἐχθρὸς τῷ σπουδαίῳ). While the sage will pray that he may do good to his enemies (v. 213, cf. v. 372) and strives to benefit as many people as possible (vv. 210a, 260, cf. v. 371), his friendships are reserved for those who are "like" himself (v. 443, and see vv. 106a–b below), that is, God (v. 86b) and other sages (v. 226).

Sentences 106a–b

This pair of sayings reformulates Jesus' teaching on the great commandment in Matt 22:37, 39; Mark 12:30–31; Luke 10:27 (cf. Lev 19:18; Deut 6:5). The command to love God "with all your soul" is changed into a command to love God "more than your own soul" (v. 106b), while the command to love the neighbor as oneself is changed into a command to love "what is akin to you" (v. 106a). As we have seen, in v. 87 Sextus similarly converts the command on neighbor love into a command to "treat a pious person as yourself." The sage may consider no one to be his enemy (v. 105), but his love is directed solely toward that which is akin to his truest and highest self, namely, God.

For an example of the like-loves-like theme from ancient wisdom literature, mention may be made of Sir 13:15–16: "Every creature loves its like, and every person his neighbor. All living things associate with their own kind, and a man sticks close to his like." While Ben Sira utilizes the theme to support the argument that there is no common interest between the rich and the poor (see 13:18–23), here the theme is used to encourage reflection on what the reader is and ought to be "like." Compare Plato, *Leg.* 716c: "What conduct, then, is dear to God and in his steps? One kind of conduct, expressed in one ancient saying, 'like is dear to like'" (cf. Homer, *Od.* 17.218). In a Sextine context, to "love" God means to commit oneself to becoming as much like God as possible through one's conduct, a goal the author urges his readers to take upon themselves at various points in the text (vv. 44–45, 48, 148). Such conduct is often presented in relational terms: it honors God (v. 44), pleases God (v. 45), and earns God's favor (v. 48), having as its goal friendship with God (v. 86b). The more like God one becomes through such conduct the more dear (φίλος) one becomes to God (v. 443). This is predicated in part on the natural affinity that those who are wise have with one another (v. 147). Presupposed throughout is the idea that the part of a human being that should love what is akin to itself is the "something godlike" within (v. 35, cf. vv. 394, 448), as opposed to the body (v. 101) or the flesh (v. 291). Indeed, it is impossible to love God without having something "of God within yourself" (v. 442). To the extent that this divine element is "like" God, the sage can be described as the image of God (v. 190) and as actually presenting God to humanity (vv. 7a, 307, 376a). In support of this agenda, the language of love is appropriate insofar as the sort of commitment expected allows of no compromises (v. 141). While he loves his own soul (cf. v. 129) as well as the soul of another sage (vv. 226, 292), the sage loves God more, because God is the ultimate source and destination of all souls (vv. 21, 40, 349) and the heart of one who loves God is secure in God's hands (v. 419; cf. Clement, *Quis div.* 28.1: "God therefore you must love more than yourself"). On the other hand, those who fail to love God can never be "with" God (v. 444).

Sentence 107

As a group, aphoristic authors take a dim view of sinners, statements such as Sir 16:6 ("In an assembly of sinners a fire is kindled") and Menander, *Mon.* 383 ("Evil acquaintances make an evil man") being representative (cf. Sir 12:14; 19:22; 21:9; Menander, *Mon.* 722). In the same vein, Sextus elsewhere describes the life of the faithless as a "disgrace" (v. 400). Against this backdrop it is not difficult to understand why interpreters both ancient and modern have struggled to understand the sentiment being expressed in the current verse. In his translation, Rufinus dropped both οὐ and μή, resulting in a rather banal assertion, while the copyist responsible for Π dropped the line altogether. The Syriac, meanwhile, adds an explanatory gloss: "It is not disgraceful for sinful people to be gathered as one when they desire to repent and to cease from their sins." In his critical edition, Elter (1892, 10) suggests dropping οὐ, though, as Chadwick (1959, 168) points out, this simply creates a different set of problems. (His assertion that no other gnome in the collection begins with χαλεπόν is incorrect; see

v. 193, cf. *Sent. Pythag.* 114. For a gnome beginning with οὐ χαλεπόν, see v. 187.) It is probably best, then, to eschew such emendations and interpret the text as it stands. After all, Jesus had conceded that under certain circumstances even sinners can abide by an ethic of (exact) reciprocity (Luke 6:32-33; cf. Matt 5:46-47). See also Publilius Syrus, *Sent.* 175: "Even in crime loyalty is rightly displayed." In pointing out that not everything sinners say and do among themselves is a sin, the author may be encouraging for the sage a more merciful and godlike attitude in dealing with wrongdoers (see on v. 63). This would apply perhaps most particularly to situations where he carries out his responsibility to correct others (vv. 103, 183-184, 331). In this case, comparison can be made with a formally similar saying attributed to Pythagoras in Stobaeus, *Anth.* 3.13.54: "It is not so difficult to sin, as not to reprove one who sins" (οὐχ οὕτω χαλεπὸν ἁμαρτάνειν ὡς τὸν ἁμαρτάνοντα μὴ ἐξελέγχειν).

Sentences 108a-111

Text

108a τροφαὶ πολλαὶ ἁγνείαν[a] ἐμποδίζουσιν.
108b ἀκρασία σιτίων ἀκάθαρτον ποιεῖ.
109 ἐμψύχων ἁπάντων χρῆσις μὲν[a] ἀδιάφορον[b], ἀποχὴ δὲ λογικώτερον[c].
110 οὐ τὰ εἰσιόντα διὰ τοῦ στόματος σιτία [a]καὶ ποτὰ[a] μιαίνει[b] τὸν ἄνθρωπον, ἀλλὰ τὰ ἀπὸ[c] κακοῦ ἤθους ἐξιόντα.
111 ὃ ἂν <ἡδονῇ>[a] ἡττώμενος σιτίον προσφέρῃ μιαίνει σε.

Translation

108a Too much food impedes holiness.
108b Overindulgence in food creates impurity.
109 The consumption of living things is morally indifferent, but abstinence is more rational.
110 It is not food and drink going in through the mouth that defile a person but things going forth from an evil character.
111 Whatever you consume while yielding to pleasure defiles you.

Textual Notes

108a[a] ἄγνοιαν: Υ; ἁγνίαν: Π • 109[a] μόνον: Π • 109[b] ἀδιάφορος: Π • 109[c] χρησιμώτερον: Υ, sy² • 110ᵃ⁻ᵃ omit lat • 110ᵇ κοινοῖ: Π • 110ᶜ τοῦ: Υ • 111ᵃ omit Π, Υ

COMMENTARY

This is the first of two sections in the *Sentences* dealing with food (cf. vv. 265–270), the repetition of σιτίον in vv. 108b and 110–111 contributing to the section's verbal unity. Here Sextus addresses first the question of the amount of food one consumes (vv. 108a–b), then the type of food one consumes (v. 109), then the moral conditions under which food is consumed (vv. 110–111). Self-restraint in eating, drinking, and banqueting represents one of the stock themes of gnomic literature. See Prov 23:20–21, 29–35; Sir 31:12–32:13; *Syr. Men.* 52–66; Ps.-Phoc. 68–69b; Theognis, *El.* 467–510; *Carm. aur.* 32–34; Epictetus, *Gnom.* 17–26; P.Ins. 6.8–19. In the *Sentences*, this theme is combined with the religious idea that certain foods render one unclean (vv. 108a–b, 110–111).

Sentences 108a–b

For Ben Sira, overeating leads to sickness (Sir 37:29–31), while for Clement it leads to "pain and lethargy and shallow-mindedness" (*Paed.* 2.1.17.3). For our author it leads to impurity, the claim in v. 108b serving as a stronger counterpart to the one in v. 108a. In a biblical setting, food contaminates the person who consumes it if it comes from an unclean animal (e.g., Acts 10:12–14), if it has come in contact with something unclean (e.g., Lev 7:19), or if it is somehow associated with pagan idolatry (e.g., 1 Cor 8:7). That defilement can be the result of overindulgence in eating is a view endorsed also by Clement in *Paed.* 2.1.4.1–5, though there the primary concern is that such unseemly conduct desecrates the Agape feast, while here the point appears to be that it desecrates the individual who overeats. Comparison can also be made with Plutarch, frag. 200, which laments lives made "sullied and impure by love of pleasure and gluttony" (θολερούς καὶ ἀκαθάρτους ὑπὸ φιληδονίας καὶ γαστριμαργίας). Cf. Clement, *Paed.* 3.7.37.3; Ephraem Syrus, *Serm. al. comp.* 397; Clitarchus, *Sent.* 113: ψυχὴν σιτίοις μὴ ἐπιθολοῦ μηδὲ ἀμέτροι[ς…].

Those undertaking philosophical ἄσκησις were often encouraged to adapt themselves to various forms of alimentary discipline. In frag. 18a–b, for example, Musonius Rufus condemns ἀκρασία περὶ τροφήν as a form of harmful excess that demonstrates an irrational and shameful lack of self-control (frag. 18b.116.4–22). Conversely, self-restraint in eating and drinking is the foundation of σωφροσύνη. Refraining from sumptuous fare benefits not only the body, he says, by making it more rigorous, but also the soul, since the soul will be "the lightest and purest" if it is fed by pure and "natural" foods, such as water, vegetables, and cheese (frag. 18a.112.8–29). Pythagoras had similarly suggested that the renunciation of excessive eating contributes to "purity of soul" (Iamblichus, *Vit. Pythag.* 3.13). Referring to his teacher Attalus, Seneca writes: "Whenever he castigated our pleasure-seeking lives, and extolled personal purity, moderation in diet, and a mind free from unnecessary, not to speak of unlawful, pleasures, the desire came upon me to limit my food and drink" (*Ep.* 108.14). For Sextus, moderation is the path to holiness (v. 67) and every excess is to be shunned (v. 140), as one endeavors to conquer and control the body in every way (vv. 71a, 274a) and as much as possible (v. 78). This involves controlling the stomach (vv. 240, 428) and refraining from overindulgence, since this can both pollute the body and impair the soul (vv. 345–346). Instead, bodily hunger should be assuaged with moderation, that is, with plain food (vv. 412–413). By limiting his bodily needs to a bare minimum (v. 115), the sage emulates God, who needs nothing (v. 50). Similar objectives inform Porphyry's comments in *Abst.* 1.54.5–6: "We must also make the body unaccustomed, as far as possible, to pleasure from satiety (cf. Sext. 111), but accustomed to the repletion which comes from satisfying hunger … and take as our limit not the unlimited, but the necessary. Thus it too, by self-sufficiency and assimilation to the divine, can obtain the good that is possible for it." Compare also Porphyry, *Abst.* 2.45.4 ("Holiness, both internal and external, belongs to a godly man, who strives to fast from the passions of the soul just as he fasts from those foods which arouse passions, who feeds on wisdom about the gods and becomes like them by right thinking about the divine") and *Marc.* 28: "Even the gods have prescribed remaining pure by abstinence from food and sex … as though any excess, by being contrary to nature's intent, is defiled and deadly."

Sentence 109

The Stoics included among moral indifferents (ἀδιάφορα) matters relating to life, wealth, pleasure, beauty, strength, wealth, fame, and noble birth (Diogenes Laertius, *Vit. phil.* 7.102; cf. *SVF* 3:118–123). Sextus sees the eating of animal flesh as morally indifferent but quickly adds that it is more in keeping with reason to abstain. Clement similarly connects the observation that eating meat is morally indifferent with a reference to Matt 15:11

(see on v. 110) in *Paed.* 2.1.16.3: "The use (χρῆσις) of these foods is a matter of moral indifference (ἀδιάφορος) for us, too, 'for not that which goes into the mouth defiles a person.'" Cf. also *Paed.* 2.1.8.4–2.1.9.1: "'Nor does what goes into a person defile him, but what comes out of the mouth,' in the words of scripture. The physical use (χρῆσις) of the food is morally indifferent (ἀδιάφορος)." At the same time, Clement also agrees that abstaining from such food is reasonable; see *Strom.* 7.6.32.8: "If any of the righteous refuses to weigh down his soul by the eating of flesh, he has the advantage of a rational reason (λόγῳ τινὶ εὐλόγῳ)." According to some thinkers, one of the reasons why it reasonable to refrain from meat is that is helps preserve the power of reason itself. Musonius Rufus, for example, held that eating meat "darkens the soul" because it is "a heavy food and an obstacle to thinking and reasoning" (frag. 18a.112.20–22). For Sextus, what makes abstaining from meat a reasonable practice is that it is consistent with efforts to limit and simplify the body's needs and desires, thus facilitating assimilation to the divine (see above on vv. 108a–b). He may also have been familiar with the idea that a meatless diet curbs the libido; see on v. 240 and cf. Clement, *Strom.* 7.6.33.6: "A gnostic might therefore abstain from flesh, both for the sake of discipline and to weaken the sexual appetite."

While vegetarianism was not widely observed in the ancient world, there is evidence for the practice in certain philosophical circles including, most famously, Pythagorean circles. Indeed, according to Iamblichus, Pythagoras "led people to virtue beginning with food," instructing his most advanced students never to eat anything animate, though "to eat certain animals he permitted the rest, whose way of life was not entirely purified, holy, and philosophical" (*Vit. Pythag.* 24.107–109; cf. 16.68; 31.187; 32.225). For more on the (conflicting) traditions regarding Pythagoras's dietary restrictions, see Diodorus Siculus, *Bibl. hist.* 10.6.1; Origen, *Cels.* 5.41; 8.28; Porphyry, *Vit. Pythag.* 34; *Abst.* 1.3.3; 1.26.3; 2.28.2; Diogenes Laertius, *Vit. phil.* 8.19; cf. Plato, *Leg.* 782c–d. Pythagorean influence in this area continued well into the imperial period. According to Seneca, for example, one of his teachers, the Pythagorean philosopher Sextius, encouraged abstinence from meat, advice that Seneca himself followed for a time (*Ep.* 108.17–22). Apollonius of Tyana, meanwhile, claimed to be following Pythagoras's example when he "refused the meat of animals as impure and dulling the mind" (Philostratus, *Vit. Apoll.* 1.8.1; cf. Ps.-Apollonius, *Ep.* 43).

Generally speaking, ancient philosophers adduced three different kinds of argument in favor of vegetarianism: first, there was the religious argument, informed by the doctrine of the transmigration of souls; second, there was the moral argument, informed by the idea that animals are possessed of a rational soul and therefore participate in a community of justice with humankind; and third, there was the medical argument, informed by the idea that abstaining from meat is conducive to physical health. For systematic defenses of the practice, see especially Plutarch's *Bruta animalia ratione uti* and *De esu carnium*, and Porphyry's *De abstinentia*. Evidence also exists for the practice of vegetarianism in early Christianity. According to Clement, with his statement in Rom 14:21 ("It is good not to eat meat and not to drink wine") Paul was speaking "just as the Pythagoreans say" (*Paed.* 2.1.11.1; cf. 2.1.16.1; *Strom.* 7.6.33.4). Tertullian, meanwhile, accused both Marcion and Tatian of requiring vegetarianism of their followers (*Jejun.* 15.1). Of particular interest is *Cels.* 8.28–30, where Origen cites Sext. 109 in his reply to the criticism that Christians are inconsistent in their dietetics, insofar as they abstain from eating sacrificial meat but not, like the Pythagoreans, from eating meat altogether. Origen explains that what is sinful is not animal flesh as such but only flesh that has become "the food of demons" (*Cels.* 8.30). At the same time, biblical precepts like Rom 14:15, 21 and 1 Cor 8:13 teach that abstaining from meat and wine is preferable, though not because of any belief in the transmigration of souls but "for the sake of a safer and purer life" (*Cels.* 8.28). Jesus' instruction in Matt 15:11 indicates that the ultimate criterion guiding decisions in such matters is the cultivation of moral character. Specifically, Christians avoid any sort of alimentary practice that might be "associated with evil and its consequences" (*Cels.* 8.30; cf. Sext. 110). Thus it is incumbent upon them "to abstain from eating with gluttonous motives (cf. Sext. 108a–b) or merely because of a desire for pleasure (cf. Sext. 111), without having in view the health of the body and its restoration" (*Cels.* 8.30). As these parallels suggest, it is possible that Origen had not only v. 109 but also vv. 108a–111 at his disposal when writing this passage.

Sentence 110

Sextus here offers his rendition of Matt 15:11: οὐ τὸ εἰσερχόμενον εἰς τὸ στόμα κοινοῖ τὸν ἄνθρωπον, ἀλλὰ τὸ ἐκπορευόμενον ἐκ τοῦ στόματος τοῦτο κοινοῖ τὸν ἄνθρωπον. Our author simplifies the sentence's structure by eliminating some of the repetition created by the last seven words, replacing ἐκ τοῦ στόματος with ἀπὸ κακοῦ ἤθους. For Matthew that which defiles comes out of the mouth, that is, words (though cf. Matt 15:19), while for Sextus that which defiles derives from a person's ἦθος, a term familiar from his

Pythagorean sources (*Sent. Pythag.* 11, 18; Clitarchus, *Sent.* 139) as well as from Porphyry, *Marc.* 14 (see on v. 326a). In this respect, v. 110 better approximates the version of the dominical saying in Mark 7:15. Sextus also renders certain aspects of the saying more explicit, replacing κοινοῖ with μιαίνει (the former is retained in Π) and specifying "food and drink" as that which goes into a person. Finally, he substitutes εἰσιόντα for εἰσερχόμενον and ἐξιόντα for ἐκπορευόμενον. As noted above, in *Paed.* 2.1.8.4–2.1.9.1, Clement agrees with Sextus in linking a reference to Matt 15:11 with an observation that eating meat is morally indifferent. It is also noteworthy that the Alexandrian's (highly simplified) reformulation of the scriptural quotation also employs these two participles: οὐδὲ τὰ εἰσιόντα κοινοῖ τὸν ἄνθρωπον, ἀλλὰ τὰ ἐξιόντα, φησί, τοῦ στόματος (cf. *Paed.* 2.6.49.1).

Wilken (1975, 154–55) suggests that a certain inconsistency can be detected between the thought of this line and the one that precedes—v. 109 encouraging abstention from certain kinds of food as reasonable, while v. 110 "suggests that what one eats and drinks is of little consequence." Insofar as the language of defilement is deployed in our text to signify that which inhibits one's assimilation to the divine (see on vv. 23–24, 46b–47, 57b, 181, 429), the point here may be that "true" defilement should be construed as a function not of food itself but of the moral choices and dispositions that accompany the use of material things of this kind. In this case, v. 110 anticipates v. 111. Presumably, the defiling "things" proceeding from an evil character mentioned here include the shameful actions that render one impure in v. 102 and the "unholy deeds" of which one must be cleansed before speaking about God in v. 356. For the basic sentiment, compare *Const. ap.* 6.27: "Neither the burial of a man, nor a dead man's bone, nor a sepulcher, nor any particular sort of food, nor the nocturnal pollution, can defile a person's soul, but only impiety towards God and transgression and injustice towards one's neighbor." For a gnomic sentiment, see Publilius Syrus, *Sent.* 710: "The will, not the body, makes impurity." For the idea of an "unclean" ἦθος, see Philo, *Spec.* 3.208; Origen, *Cels.* 3.25.

Sentence 111

Cf. Clement, *Paed.* 2.1.1.4: "Eating is not our main occupation, nor is pleasure our chief ambition." Chadwick (1959, 24) conjectures <ἡδονῇ> before ἡττώμενος, based on Rufinus's translation, which has *cupiditate ... acceperis*, and the Syriac version, which has "All food that you approve because of desire, when you eat it, it makes your body unclean." If this is correct, then the reference to ἡδονή helps to clarify the meaning of other precepts in the unit (note how the verse is linked to what precedes by the catchwords σιτίον and μιαίνω). What creates impurity in excessive eating (vv. 108a–b) is not the food itself, or even the quantity of food, but the fact that such overindulgence betrays a desire for bodily pleasures. Similarly, our author may think that it is more in keeping with reason to abstain from meat (v. 109) not because the flesh itself is a source of pollution but because the consumption of such food is more likely to be accompanied by pleasure than the consumption of "plain" food (v. 413). A contrast between reason and pleasure informs Porphyry's argument in *Abst.* 1.46.1: "Reason, then, will quite properly reject abundant or excessive food, and will restrict what is necessary to a small amount, if the intention is neither, when making provision, to have problems because more is needed; nor, when preparing the meal, to need more servants; nor, when eating, to reach out for more pleasures" (in *Abst.* 1.24.1, he notes that eating meat is a "pleasure"). The sort of defiling comportment that manifests an evil character (v. 110), then, would include in the first place actions motivated by the desire for pleasure. As Porphyry explains, when the soul is "dragged down into pleasure," it is "defiled by the passions on account of their involvement with unreason" (*Abst.* 4.20.3–4). In this case, the assertions made in vv. 108a–111 regarding the moral problem of food can be seen as contributing to Sextus's advice elsewhere for the reader to exercise control over bodily pleasures in general (v. 70, cf. v. 232), the assumption being that curbing one's appetite and curbing one's other physical drives are mutually informing endeavors (vv. 240, 428, 435). Those who fail in this regard are so far from assimilating themselves to the divine that their presence actually defiles God (v. 429). They are therefore rightly the subject of reproach (v. 272). Indeed, the person found yielding (ἡττώμενος) to his stomach is no better than an animal (v. 270). For pleasure as a source of defilement, see Philo, *Leg.* 3.148; Seneca, *Ep.* 108.14 (quoted above); Plutarch, frag. 200 (quoted above); Philostratus, *Ep. et dial.* 1.48; Evagrius Ponticus, *Pract.* 89. As Musonius Rufus explains, the pleasure associated with eating is in many respects the most intractable: "Although there are many pleasures that lure people into wrongdoing and force them to yield to the contrary of what is good, pleasure in eating is probably the hardest of all to combat." This is because other types of pleasures are encountered less frequently or can even be avoided altogether, but it is impossible to put off eating for very long: "Thus the more often we are tempted by pleasure in eating, the more dangers there are involved. And indeed at each meal there is not one hazard for going wrong, but many" (frag. 18b.116.22–32).

Sentences 112–121b

Text

112 πλήθει ἀρέσκειν μὴ ἐπιτήδευε.
113 παντὸς οὗ καλῶς πράττεις αἴτιον ἡγοῦ τὸν θεόν.
114 κακῶν θεὸς ἀναίτιος.
115 μὴ ᵃπλέον κτῶᵃ ὧν τὸ σῶμα ἐπιζητεῖ.
116 ψυχὴν χρυσὸς οὐ ῥύεται κακῶν.
117 οὐ γέγονας ἐντρυφήσωνᵃ τῇ τοῦ θεοῦ παρασκευῇ.
118 κτῶ ἃ μηδείς σουᵃ ἀφαιρεῖταιᵇ.
119 φέρε τὰ ἀναγκαῖα ὡς ἀναγκαῖα.
120 μεγαλοψυχίαν ἄσκει.
121a ὧν καταφρονῶν ᵃἐπαινῇ εὐλόγως, τούτωνᵃ μὴ περιέχουᵇ.
121b ἐφ' οἷς εὐλόγως μεγαλοφρονεῖςᵃ, ταῦτα κέκτησο.

Translation

112 Do not strive to please a multitude.
113 Deem God to be the cause of everything you do nobly.
114 God is not the cause of evil things.
115 Do not acquire more than what the body requires.
116 Gold cannot rescue a soul from evil things.
117 You were not born to indulge in what is provided by God.
118 Acquire things that no one can take from you.
119 Bear the things that must be as things that must be.
120 Practice greatness of soul.
121a Do not cling to those things that, if you despised them, would rightly bring you praise.
121b Acquire those things in which you are rightly confident.

Textual Notes

115ᵃ⁻ᵃ πλεονεκτῶ: Υ • 116 χρυσὸς οὐ ῥύεται κακῶν τὴν ψυχήν: Υ • 117ᵃ ἐν τρυφῇ ὤν: Π, lat, sy² • 118ᵃ omit Υ • 118ᵇ ἀφαιρήσεται: Υ • 121aᵃ⁻ᵃ ἐπαινεῖ, εὐλόγως τούτων: Π • 121aᵇ ἀντέχου: Υ • 121bᵃ μέγα φρονεῖς: Υ

Commentary

If Chadwick's (1959, 24, 168) emendation for v. 111 is correct, then the first member in this group of sayings (v. 112) is loosely connected to the last saying of the previous unit by the theme of pleasure. Verses 113–114, meanwhile, present contrasting maxims regarding God's involvement in good and evil (note the juxtaposition of αἴτιον and ἀναίτιος). Most of the sayings here belong to a segment on acquisitiveness (vv. 115–121b), with forms of κτάομαι present in vv. 115, 118, and 121b. A negative admonition in v. 115 is supported by two motive clauses (vv. 116–117), and then counterbalanced by a positive admonition in v. 118. A similar contrast of negative and positive admonitions is repeated in vv. 121a–b: note the wordplay created by καταφρονῶν (v. 121a) and μεγαλοφρονεῖς (v. 121b). Inserted into the unit are a pair of sayings on greatness of soul (vv. 119–120), loosely connected to v. 118 by the idea that possessions can be taken away, μεγαλοψυχία in such a context referring primarily to the state of being superior to material wealth (see below). The question of what the reader should or should not acquire will be raised in the ensuing section as well, especially vv. 122, 124, 125, and 128 (also with κτάομαι).

Sentence 112

The gnome πλήθει ἄρεσκε, attributed in some traditions to the sage Chilon (Septem Sapientes, *Sent.* 216.32; cf. *Sent.* 215.4; Septem Sapientes, *Praec.* 218.11; Diogenes Laertius, *Vit. phil.* 1.85), appears to have been the inspiration for longer maxims like Menander, *Mon.* 59 (ἄρεσκε πᾶσι καὶ σὺ μὴ σαυτῷ μόνῳ), 78 (ἄρεσκε πλήθει καθ' ἕνα φιλοτιμούμενος), and 102 (βούλου δ' ἀρέσκειν πᾶσι, μὴ σαυτῷ μόνῳ). Such general encouragement to be affable and accommodating in one's public transactions (cf. 1 Cor 10:33) can be contrasted with a more philosophical perspective on the topic, like the one expressed by Epicurus in *Ep. frag.* 131: "I never aspired to please the multitudes, for what is pleasing to them I do not teach, and what I know is beyond their understanding." Cf. Ps.-Plutarch, *Lib. ed.* 6b: "To please the multitude is to displease the wise." Pythagoras reportedly went so far as to shun public discussions altogether, and encouraged others to do the same (Porphyry, *Vit. Pythag.* 32). Statements of this sort, in turn, can be read against the background of the philosophical critique of obsequiousness, or ἀρεσκεία, a vice associated especially with sophists, sycophants, and demagogues (e.g., Diodorus Siculus, *Bibl. hist.* 25.8.1), each of which represents a different kind of antitype to Sextus's sage. Aristotle, for example, defines the obsequious as "people who complaisantly approve of everything and never raise objections, but think it a duty to avoid giving pain to those with whom they come in contact" (*Eth. nic.* 4.6.1). Because they want to befriend everyone, they end up befriending no one (*Eth. nic.* 9.10.6). Much like flatterers, the obsequious exhibit "a sort of behavior which provides pleasure (ἡδονῆς), but not with the best of intentions" (Theophrastus, *Char.* 5.1; cf. Aristotle, *Eth. nic.* 10.3.11; *Eth. eud.* 2.3.8; Ps.-Diogenes, *Ep.* 11; Maximus of Tyre, *Dial.* 14.6). In an effort to ingratiate himself to everyone, the obsequious person offers praise indiscriminately. But his willingness to abase himself and compromise his principles in such a manner demonstrates a character that is servile and distracted: "You tremble, lie awake, take counsel with everyone, and, if your plans are not likely to please everyone, you think that your deliberations have been faulty" (Epictetus, *Diatr.* 3.26.20). Because it can create an obstacle to speaking frankly and critically to those in need of moral amendment, the problem of obsequiousness is sometimes raised in discussions of moral guidance and education (e.g., Philodemus, *Adul.* P. Herc. 1457 cols. V, VIII–X).

Such a background is appropriate for interpreting the advice here, insofar as the Sextine sage is implicated in practices of mutual correction (vv. 245, 298, 331). While he strives to benefit as many people as possible (vv. 210a, 260), the sage exercises caution whenever he speaks (vv. 151–165g), especially when he speaks in public (v. 164a). Most of all, he does not try to speak to the multitudes about God (v. 360), since such gatherings will consist largely of unbelievers (v. 243), who are unworthy to hear such a message (vv. 354, 365). While he avoids saying anything to anger the crowd (v. 343), he will probably avoid saying anything to praise the crowd either, knowing that "When flattered wicked people become worse" (v. 149) and "Praise makes wickedness intolerable" (v. 150). For his own part, he is wary of approval when it comes from unbelievers (v. 241), since their way of life is, by definition, disgraceful (v. 400). For this reason, the sage will not have much of a public reputation (vv. 145, 214). Cf. v. 534: "The one who tries to please the many is like the many."

Sextus was not the only early Christian author to address the issue of ἀρεσκεία and public discourse. For example, to the charge that the apostles were not skilled in the rhetorical arts, Origen replies: "It seems to me that if Jesus had chosen some men who were wise in the eyes of the multitude, and who were capable of thinking and speaking acceptably to the crowds … he might on very good grounds have been suspected of making use of a method similar to that of philosophers who are leaders of some particular sect" (*Cels.* 1.62). Our author probably would have agreed with the assertion in Ps.-Clement, *Hom.* 18.10 that when addressing the multitudes, the man of integrity speaks "not to please them but to tell them the truth" (cf. Sext. 158, 168). Christians ought to be more concerned with pleasing God than with pleasing people (Ps.-Clement, *Hom.* 3.64; cf. 1 Thess 2:4; Ign. *Rom.* 2.1).

Sentences 113–114

This pair of sayings is taken over with only minor modifications from Clitarchus, *Sent.* 18–19: παντὸς οὗ καλῶς πράττεις θεὸν ἡγοῦ αἴτιον. κακῶν θεὸς ἀναίτιος. In the first line, Sextus reverses the position of θεόν and αἴτιον, adding a definite article to the former. Cf. Porphyry, *Marc.* 12 ("Let us deem God the cause of all the good things we do. But as for the evils, we who have chosen them are the causes; God is not the cause") and 24 ("No god causes evils for a man; rather he himself causes them by the choices he makes for himself"). The inspiration for Clitarchus, *Sent.* 18–19, in turn, comes from Plato, *Resp.* 379b–c: since God "is good in reality and must be described as such," and "the good is not the cause of all things, but the source of the things that go well and not the source of evils (κακῶν ἀναίτιον)," then "God alone is the cause of good things, and we must find some other cause for the evil ones" (cf. 380b, 617e). For a more succinct expression of this affirmation, see Plutarch, *Per.* 39.2: "We do firmly hold that those who control and rule the universe are the source only of good things and not the source of evil things." For evidence of the theme's influence on early Christian texts, see Clement, *Strom.* 5.14.136.4; 7.4.22.2; Origen, *Philoc.* 24.1–5; Ps.-Clement, *Hom.* 15.8. Our author is more explicit about identifying the actual cause of evil when composing a similar juxtaposition of sayings later in the collection: "God confirms the noble actions of human beings. An evil demon is a guide of evil deeds" (vv. 304–305).

Sext. 113 is restated in an only slightly different form in v. 390 (cf. v. 104). In both versions, attributing what is noble to God is presented not as an abstract notion but as something that ought to inform moral self-reflection and self-understanding. For a similar effort to put the thought into gnomic form, comparison may be made with a saying attributed to the sage Bias: "Whatever good you do (πράττῃς), ascribe it to the gods" (Diogenes Laertius, *Vit. phil.* 1.88). In order to live a godly life, one must act nobly (v. 399). It is therefore incumbent upon the sage to seek out the sources of noble things (v. 100). Since the noble is only that which befits God (v. 197), what such a quest reveals is that it is not possible to live nobly without God (v. 215). Conversely, that God is not responsible for human

154   THE *SENTENCES* OF SEXTUS

sin and misfortune is asserted by a wide range of ancient authors; see Sir 15:11–13, 20; Jas 1:13; Philo, *Conf.* 180; *Det.* 122; *Prov.* 2.53; Ps.-Clement, *Hom.* 19.6; Plutarch, *An. procr.* 1015c; Dio Chrysostom, *Or.* 38.20; Maximus of Tyre, *Or.* 13.8–9; *Teach. Silv.* 115.27–29: The "divine is not pleased with anything evil. For it is this which teaches all men what is good." For Sextus, it is wrong to assign evil to God or even to think evil of God, since God's nature is "not admitting of its opposite" (vv. 29–30, cf. vv. 82e, 314, 440: "Regard nothing that is evil as belonging to God"). God does not cause evil; God judges evil (vv. 14, 39–40, 347). Evil things, meanwhile, derive from evil demons abiding in evil souls and guiding evil deeds (vv. 62, 305, 348, cf. v. 604). The souls most vulnerable to such infiltration, and thus most likely to sin, are those that misuse the body and the things of the body (vv. 12, 136, 346, 448). Cf. Iamblichus, *Vit. Pythag.* 32.218: "Noblest of all, (Pythagoras) showed that the gods are blameless of evils, and that sickness and the whole gamut of bodily problems are seeds of licentiousness."

Sentence 115

This line is repeated in the appendices as v. 602 (with πλείονα in lieu of πλέον), accompanied in v. 603 with a slightly modified version of v. 117 (see below). For a gnomic but nonascetical perspective on the topic of acquisitions, comparison can be made with Publilius Syrus, *Sent.* 603: "Any possession beyond the needful overburdens you." Our author, by contrast, defines what is "needful" with reference to the body. Even an ascetic like Hierax would concede that one should acquire for the body what has been determined by φύσις as necessary to maintain its health and strength (*Just.* frag. 2 = Stobaeus, *Anth.* 3.9.54). As Sextus points out in v. 139a, the body by nature ought to cause little disturbance for the soul. By the same token, in his effort to emulate God, the sage curtails his involvement with the physical world to the greatest extent possible (v. 50), recognizing that excess (τὸ πλέον) of every kind in this matter is detrimental to human flourishing (v. 140). Since the body is what drives the desire to acquire physical possessions, it must be controlled at all costs and in all ways (vv. 274a–b, cf. vv. 71a, 240, 428). Toward this end, the sage relinquishes himself of such possessions to the greatest extent that he can (vv. 78, 81, 264a), using them only to meet his essential requirements (v. 19), requirements that are determined by the standards of moderation (vv. 13, 67, 273, 399, 412), self-sufficiency (vv. 98, 148, 263, 334), and self-control (vv. 86a, 239, 253b, 294, 438). Indeed, the sage does not consider anything in the physical world as his "own" (v. 227), that is, as something whose acquisition contributes to his identity as a human being worthy of God. Conversely, surrendering to the body's longing for physical possessions leads not to the knowledge of God but to πλεονεξία (vv. 136–137). Cf. Philo, *Somn.* 1.124 (the virtuous are "men superior to the temptations of money, pleasure, popularity, having no regard for meat and drink and the actual necessities of life, so long as lack of food does not begin to threaten their health"); Clement, *Paed.* 3.7.39.2 ("Just as the foot is the measure of the sandal, so the physical needs of each person are the measure of what he should possess"); Athanasius, *Vit. Ant.* 45.5: "He used to say that it is necessary to give all one's time to the soul rather than to the body, but to concede a little time to the body for its necessities; all the rest of the time, however, one ought to devote to the soul and what is profitable for it."

Sentence 116

This line is the first of two motive sentences for v. 115. Gold exemplifies the sort of thing the readers should not seek to acquire because it cannot save them from evil. Gold might be offered to ransom a prisoner from captivity (e.g., Plutarch, *Reg. imp. apophth.* 194f–195a), but for the sage it represents not a means of rescue, but something from which one needs to be rescued (cf. Plato, *Resp.* 417a), since avarice manifests a passion for the body that enslaves the soul (vv. 75a–76). However, as Porphyry explains, gaining "release from the bondage of gold" can cause considerable distress to those accustomed to wealth "on account of the pleasure it provides" (*Marc.* 7). Gnomic authors frequently inveigh against both the allure and the destructiveness of gold, for example, Sir 8:2; 31:6 ("Many have come to ruin because of gold, and their destruction has met them face to face"); Ps.-Phoc. 43 ("Gold and silver are always a delusion for people"); Menander, *Mon.* 131; Ps.-Anacharsis, *Ep.* 9; *Anth. Gr.* 9.394; *Anec. Gr.* 1.96 ("Gold, you cause of evils, terror to the one who possesses you, grief to the one who does not!"); cf. Theognis, *El.* 523–524 ("Not to no purpose, Wealth, do mortals honor you most of all, for you readily put up with evil"); Seneca, *Ben.* 7.10.1.

By contrast, Sextus's gnome focuses not on the misery gold can bring into people's lives but on its irrelevance for the life of the soul. The sage assigns no value to money and material wealth, not only because such things are insecure (vv. 128, 130, 405) but because that which enlightens the soul is a thought about God (v. 97), and the only source of salvation for the soul is knowing and becoming like God (v. 148, cf. vv. 44–45). This is what saves the soul from the thing that can destroy it, namely, an evil life (v. 397). Having riches, on the other hand, is contrary to philosophy (v. 300), which means that it is difficult for the rich to be saved (v. 193), the only true "wealth" being self-control (v. 294).

Sentence 117

This line is repeated in the appendices as v. 603, with τοῦ κόσμου written in lieu of τοῦ θεοῦ (cf. vv. 19–20, 82b, 405). Verse 117 is the second of two motive sentences offered in support of the admonition in v. 115. Here acquiring more than the body needs is interpreted as contributing to a type of luxury (τρυφή) contrary to what God intends for human thriving. Cf. v. 73: "The result of luxury is ruin." The things provided by God for human survival are meant to be used with moderation, that is, only when and as necessary (vv. 13, 19, 88, 273, 276, 412–413). Anything beyond what one needs should be shared with those who do in fact have a need (vv. 330, 378–379, 382). The dictum in v. 117 can also be interpreted against the background of assertions that τρυφή is contrary to nature—for example, Clement, *Paed.* 2.10.99.2; Ps.-Lucian, *Amor.* 20; Oribasius, *Coll. medic.* 24.31.13; Themistius, *Protr. Nic.* 303c. Of course, opinions as to what constitutes "luxury" could vary. Epictetus, for one, recommends that "in things pertaining to the body, take only as much as your bare need requires, I mean such things as food, drink, clothing, shelter, and household slaves; but cut down everything which is for outward show or luxury" (*Ench.* 33.7).

Sentence 118

This admonition offers a positive counterbalance to the command in v. 115. Because worldly goods can be lost or taken away (vv. 15, 17, 91b, 130, 405), the sage does not think of them as his own (v. 227, cf. vv. 81, 228, 264a). Instead he concentrates on acquiring goods that are secure, that is, the things of the soul (v. 77), things can be acquired only from God (vv. 128, 277). These are possessions of which he is rightly proud (v. 121b) because they belong also to God (v. 310). See also vv. 92, 404: "Whatever God gives, no one takes away." As *Sent. Pythag.* 80 teaches, the sage's true possessions are not those that he finds within his house but those that he finds within his mind. Cf. further *Sent. Pythag.* 3, 120; Porphyry, *Marc.* 12.

Sentence 119

Appeals for composure and perseverance in facing the exigencies of life are commonplace in gnomic literature, for example, Sir 2:4 ("Accept whatever befalls you, and in times of humiliation be patient"); Ps.-Phoc. 55–56, 118–121; Theognis, *El.* 591–592 ("We ought to endure what the gods give to mortals, and bear in patience either lot"), 657–658; *Carm. aur.* 17–18; Menander, *Mon.* 15, 223, 392 ("We must bear lightly the things fortune presents us"), 721, 813; Publilius Syrus, *Sent.* 206, 411 ("What you cannot change, you should bear as it comes"), 473, 479; Diogenes Laertius, *Vit. phil.* 1.93; cf. *Ceb. Tab.* 31.1–6; Philo, *Cher.* 78. Set within the immediate vicinity of several sayings on possessions (vv. 115–118, 121a–b), it is tempting to read v. 119 principally in the light of vv. 15 and 91b (cf. vv. 17, 130), which counsel the reader not to see the dispossession of worldly goods as a source of consternation. At the same time, Sextus emphasizes that the sage will endure "everything" for the sake of living in accord with God (v. 216), including things pertaining to both the body and the soul (v. 301). He will, for example, endure the ignorance (v. 285) and anger (v. 293, cf. v. 493) of others, bearing even the loss of loved ones gratefully (v. 257, cf. v. 523). Even though it binds his soul like chains, the sage is not vexed by the body, yet neither is he angry at the one who would deprive him of his body (vv. 320–322, 337). While present in the body, he accepts that certain bodily pleasures will be unavoidable (note the similarly structured v. 276: ἡδονὰς ἡγοῦ τὰς ἀναγκαίας ὡς ἀναγκαίας). Adept at adjusting to circumstances (v. 385), he is content knowing that his life is secure in God's hands (v. 419).

Sentence 120

For this precept Sextus copies Clitarchus, *Sent.* 20 without modification. In its Clitarchan context, the line is immediately preceded by a maxim that parallels Sext. 114 and immediately followed by a maxim that parallels Sext. 125. In its Sextine context, the line can be read in conjunction with v. 119. The Stoics included μεγαλοψυχία in their canon of virtues, defining it as "the knowledge or habit of mind which makes one superior to anything that happens, whether good or evil equally" (Diogenes Laertius, *Vit. phil.* 7.93; cf. *SVF* 3:264, 269–270, 274). For evidence that this definition circulated in early Christian circles, see Clement, *Strom.* 2.18.79.5; cf. Origen, *Cels.* 2.24, 42. Epictetus generally uses the term with this sense: "Come, have you not received faculties that enable you to bear whatever happens? Have you not received greatness of soul? Have you not received courage? Have you not received fortitude?" (*Diatr.* 1.6.28; cf. 1.12.30; 2.16.14; 3.8.6; 4.1.109; 4 Macc 15:10). Earlier, Aristotle had noted that one of the defining traits of the great-souled man is that "he will not rejoice overmuch in prosperity, nor grieve overmuch at adversity" (*Eth. nic.* 4.3.18). From this perspective, v. 119 can be seen as explicating what it means to "practice" this virtue. For the form of the saying in v. 120, cf. vv. 69, 98, and 334. The one who practices greatness of soul to the greatest extent, of course, is the sage, for whom see the commentary on v. 403.

Sentences 121a–b

These two complementary admonitions on possessions, the first negative and the second positive, are conjoined verbally by the repetition of εὐλόγως as well as by the juxtaposition of καταφρονῶν and μεγαλοφρονεῖς. A similar wordplay is employed by Clement in *Paed.* 2.3.39.4: "True confidence (μεγαλοφροσύνη) means not to have confidence in wealth (ἐπὶ πλούτῳ μεγαλοφρονεῖν) but to have contempt for it (καταφρονεῖν)" (cf. *Paed.* 3.2.12.4; 3.8.41.1; *Quis div.* 12.2). As Plutarch explains, to have contempt for wealth (τὸ πλούτου καταφρονεῖν) means having a spirit that is superior to wealth, guided by an understanding that "possessions cannot buy peace of mind, confidence (μεγαλοφροσύνη), serenity, courage, and self-sufficiency" (*Cupid. divit.* 523d–e; cf. *Chion. ep.* 16.8; Epictetus, *Diatr.* 4.9.3). The wealthy citizens of a particular city, for example, could be said to embody μεγαλοφροσύνη when they show contempt for possessions (χρημάτων κατεφρόνησαν) by drawing on their own resources to alleviate the plight of the poor (Aelian, *Var. hist.* 14.24). The readers of the *Sentences* are similarly expected to demonstrate contempt for worldly goods by sharing them with those in need (v. 82b), though they are also summoned to despise everything associated with the body and its desires (v. 127). Presumably, the commendation they receive for doing so comes principally from God (e.g., vv. 304, 308, 422) and not from nonbelievers (vv. 241, 299), though sayings like vv. 16, 37, 51, and 53 indicate that "the world's" opinion of him is something that the sage takes into consideration, while v. 298 suggests that he even desires praise for his good deeds from others, presumably from other sages. If the things of the body are to be renounced as insecure (see on v. 118), then the possessions in which the sage places his trust are his soul (v. 129, also with μεγαλοφρονέω), the "trust" that he has received from God (v. 21), and whatever belongs to the soul (v. 77). He derives confidence from such things because they also belong to God (vv. 310–311).

Sentences 122–128

Text

122 εὔχου τῷ θεῷ τὰ ἄξια τοῦ θεοῦ.
123 τὸν ἐν σοὶ λόγον τοῦ βίου σου[a] νόμον[b] ποίει.
124 αἰτοῦ παρὰ θεοῦ ἃ μὴ λάβοις ἂν [a]παρὰ ἀνθρώπου[a].
125 ὧν ἡγεμόνες[a] οἱ πόνοι, ταῦτά σοι εὔχου γενέσθαι μετὰ τοὺς πόνους.
126 εὐχὴ ῥᾳθύμου μάταιος λόγος.
127 [a]ὧν τοῦ[a] σώματος ἀπαλλαγεὶς οὐ δεήσῃ, καταφρόνει.
128 ὃ κτησάμενος[a] οὐ καθέξεις, μὴ αἰτοῦ παρὰ[b] θεοῦ.

Translation

122 Pray to God for things worthy of God.
123 Make the reason within you a norm for your life.
124 Ask from God for things you cannot obtain from a human being.
125 Pray that after your labors those things to which labors lead might be yours.
126 A lazy person's prayer is idle talk.
127 Despise those things you will not need after being released from the body.
128 Do not ask from God for that which once acquired you will not keep.

Textual Notes

123[a] σοι: Υ • 123[b] νόμιμον: Π • 124[a-a] παρ' ἄλλου: Π • 125 omit Π • 125[a] οἱγεμόνες: Υ • 127 omit Π • 127[a-a] ὧν τῶν τοῦ: Υ • 128[a] κτώμενος: Υ • 128[b] τοῦ: Π

Commentary

Verses 122–128 impart instruction on prayer (Chadwick 1959, 153), particular emphasis being placed on petitionary prayer. Besides εὔχομαι in vv. 122, 125 and εὐχή in v. 126, note αἰτέω in vv. 124, 128. With this focus on clarifying what the readers should endeavor to obtain from God, the topic of acquisitiveness carries over from the preceding section (vv. 115–121b; note κτάομαι in vv. 115, 118, 121b, 128; also καταφρονέω in vv.

121a, 127). Should they take reason as their guide in making such determinations (v. 123), the readers will pray for what is divine (v. 122) rather than what is human (v. 124), bodily (v. 127), and insecure (v. 128). The gnomic observation in v. 126 identifies a negative moral model supporting the admonition in v. 125: things worthy of God are not simply theirs for the asking but are acquired only through hard work.

Sentence 122

This verse has a close parallel in Porphyry, *Marc.* 12: ὅθεν καὶ εὐκτέον θεῷ τὰ ἄξια θεοῦ. For the thought, compare Origen, *Orat.* 17.2: "We must pray for those things that are chiefly and truly great and heavenly" (cf. *Orat.* 27.1; *Comm. Matt.* 16.29). More often the question of worthiness in prayer focuses not on what but on whom, for example, Clement, *Strom.* 7.7.41.5 ("For God knows generally those who are worthy to receive good things and those who are not; he accordingly gives to each what belongs to him"); Origen, *Orat.* 2.3; 13.5; 14.6; 19.2; 26.2 ("What we pray for can be true for us if we make ourselves worthy of obtaining God who hears our prayer for all these things"); 27.13, 16; Ps.-Ignatius, *Ep. interp.* 6.4.5 (for a non-Christian perspective on the subject, see Maximus of Tyre, *Dial.* 5.3). Sextus also expresses a concern for the "worthiness" of his readers (vv. 3–4, 58, 376a). Presumably, the things worthy of God that they are to ask for in prayer here are those things that will empower them (v. 375) to become worthy of God, especially since "what is worthy of God is also worthy of a good man." (v. 132). According to Evagrius Ponticus, the only things that one should seek in prayer are "righteousness and the kingdom—that is, virtue and knowledge—and all the rest will be added to you" (*Orat.* 39; cf. Matt 6:33).

Sentence 123

Cf. v. 74: "Let your reason guide your impulses." The logic informing the decision to include a similar saying in a unit on prayer is provided by v. 277: "All pray to have good things, but those who truly partake of divine reason possess them." God is νοῦς (v. 26), and it is through the life of the mind that the divine is present in the sage (vv. 46a, 61, 144, 394, cf. vv. 315–316, 450), directing his actions (vv. 95b, 104). Reason, then, constitutes both the medium of effective prayer and the basis for any petition the sage makes to God in prayer (see vv. 122, 124–125), which can be understood as one of the means by which divine reason guides his life. Compare Evagrius Ponticus, *Orat.* 84: "Prayer is activity that befits the dig-

nity of the mind, that is, its best and uncontaminated activity and use."
For comparable gnomic expressions, see *Sent. Pythag.* 57 (λόγῳ ἡγεμόνι ἐν παντὶ χρώμενος οὐχ ἁμαρτήσεις); Menander, *Mon.* 68 (ἀρχῆς ἁπάσης ἡγεμὼν ἔστω λόγος), 438 (λόγος διοικεῖ τὸν βροτῶν βίον μόνος), 540 (νοῦς ἐστι πάντων ἡγεμὼν τῶν χρησίμων); Clement, *Strom.* 5.14.118.2 (ὁ λόγος ἀνθρώπους κυβερνᾷ, κατὰ τρόπου σῴζει).

Sentence 124

The parallel to this line in Porphyry, *Marc.* 12 (καὶ αἰτώμεθα ἃ μὴ λάβοιμεν ἂν παρ' ἑτέρου) follows immediately upon a saying that matches v. 122, continuing its instruction on prayer (see above). Sextus's formulation, with its juxtaposition of παρὰ θεοῦ and παρὰ ἀνθρώπου, highlights the contrast of divine and human options for acquiring assets. From other people, the readers can acquire material possessions, though, of course, other people can also take these things away (vv. 15, 17, 91b, 130, cf. v. 405). From God, the readers ought to pray for salvation (vv. 372, 374) and a share in God's kingdom (v. 311), things that no one can take away (vv. 118, 404). The sage will also pray for divine power (v. 375), including the power to live nobly (v. 215, cf. v. 390) and benefit others, including even enemies (v. 213). As v. 81 indicates, it is not simply the case that one should not pray for material possessions but that divesting oneself of such possessions is the best means of preparing oneself to ask God for what is truly "necessary" (v. 88).

Sentences 125–126

The parallels for these two lines in Porphyry, *Marc.* 12 (ὧν ἡγεμόνες οἱ μετ' ἀρετῆς πόνοι, ταῦτα εὐχώμεθα γενέσθαι μετὰ τοὺς πόνους. εὐχὴ γὰρ ῥᾳθύμου μάταιος λόγος) follow immediately upon the saying that parallels v. 124. The source for the first maxim is Clitarchus, *Sent.* 21 (ὧν ἡγεμόνες οἱ πόνοι, ταῦτα εὔχου σοι γενέσθαι μετὰ τοὺς πόνους), which Sextus reproduces exactly (except for reversing the order of εὔχου and σοι), while Porphyry limits the toils involved to those that contribute to virtue (note the parallelism of μετ' ἀρετῆς with μετὰ τοὺς πόνους). The second saying, meanwhile, is expressed in the same form by Porphyry and Sextus, except that the former adds γάρ. For a "synergistic" interpretation of prayer, see Clement, *Strom.* 7.7.38.4: "The gnostic makes his prayer and request for the things that are truly good, that is, those pertaining to the soul, and he prays, and joins his own efforts as well (συνεργῶν), that he may no longer have his good things attached to him like ornaments, but may be himself good." Cf.

Carm. aur. 48–49 ("But get to work and pray for the gods to grant fulfullment"); Evagrius Ponticus, *Orat.* 19 ("At the hour of prayer, you will find the fruit of whatever hardship you endure philosophically"); and Marcus Aurelius, *Med.* 9.40: "Who told you that the gods do not co-operate with us even in the things that are in our power? Begin at any rate with prayers for such things and you will see."

As Sextus explains in v. 301, becoming wise entails toiling on behalf of both the body and the soul (cf. vv. 539, 548). Conversely, the prayer of a lazy man falls under the category of idle speech (cf. *Const. ap.* 4.3; Ps.-Justin Martyr, *Mon.* 108e; Ephraem Syrus, *Orat.* 419; *Iud. comp.* 399; *Serm. virt. vit.* 9; Ps.-Athanasius, *Ep. Cast.* 28.852). For a Greco-Roman perspective on the ineffectiveness of prayers offered by idle people, see Maximus of Tyre, *Dial.* 5.1. A more popular opinion on the subject is offered by Babrius, *Fab.* 1.20: "Pray to the gods only when you are doing something to help yourself. Otherwise your prayers will be useless." For the early Christian critique of ματαιολογία, see 1 Tim 1:6; Titus 1:10; Pol. *Phil.* 2.1; Clement, *Strom.* 1.8.41.3; Origen, *Cels.* 3.48; *Philoc.* 18.19. A different type of unanswered prayer is discussed in v. 217 (cf. v. 492).

Sentences 127–128

An expanded version of v. 127 is found in *Sent. Pythag.* 121[a] (ὧν τοῦ σώματος ἀπαλλαγεὶς οὐ δεήσῃ, ἐκείνων καταφρόνει πάντων), while v. 128 has identical parallels in both *Sent. Pythag.* 3[a] and Clitarchus, *Sent.* 22 (recall that Clitarchus, *Sent.* 21 parallels Sext. 125). In addition, close parallels to both v. 127 and v. 128 are found in Porphyry, *Marc.* 12, though in reversed order and with the remaining elements of *Sent. Pythag.* 3 (i.e., *Sent. Pythag.* 3[b-c]) intervening: ἃ δὲ κτησαμένη οὐ καθέξεις, μὴ αἰτοῦ παρὰ θεοῦ· δῶρον γὰρ θεοῦ πᾶν ἀναφαίρετον· ὥστε οὐ δώσει, ὃ μὴ καθέξεις. ὧν δὴ τοῦ σώματος ἀπαλλαγεῖσα οὐ δεηθήσῃ, ἐκείνων καταφρόνει. Note also that the last of these sayings in *Marc.* 12 better approximates the version in *Sent. Pythag.* 121[a] (both having ἐκείνων before καταφρόνει) than does the version in Sext. 127. Finally, *Sent. Pythag.* 121[a-b] is cited as a dictum of Pythagoras in Stobaeus, *Anth.* 3.1.43.

In its current location, the saying in v. 127 prescribes the sentiment informing the instruction on prayer in v. 128. The things that one cannot keep are the things of the body, since at death the soul will be "released" from both the body (for the language, see on vv. 39, 337, cf. v. 322) and the need for bodily things. Harboring the sort of contempt advised in v. 127 (for καταφρονέω, cf. vv. 82b, 121a, 299, 539) also facilitates certain priorities identified elsewhere in the text, such as conquering the body's passions (vv. 71a, 448), deliberately relinquishing the things of the body (vv. 78, 81, 264a), and remaining unperturbed at the loss of such things (vv. 15, 91b). Recognizing that nothing good can derive from the flesh (v. 271), the sage not only avoids any attraction to the flesh (v. 291, cf. vv. 99, 141)— he actively despises the flesh and even envisions the possibility of being rightly commended for doing so (v. 121a). One of the ways in which he demonstrates his scorn for physical things is by sharing them with others (v. 82b). Verse 128, meanwhile, can be interpreted as a negative version of v. 118 cast in the form of instruction on prayer (cf. v. 124, also with αἰτοῦ). The way that one acquires things that cannot be lost is by asking God for them, since "what God gives, no one takes away" (v. 92, cf. v. 404). These things of the soul, things that are truly "good" and secure, are what the sage endeavors to acquire for himself (vv. 77, 277, cf. v. 121b). Conversely, the sage refrains from asking God for material things, things that can be taken away (vv. 15, 17, 91b, 130), since his aim is to acquire them only to the extent that his body needs them to survive (v. 115).

Sentences 129–135

Text

129 ἔθιζε τὴν ψυχήν σου μετὰ θεὸν ᵃἐφ' ἑαυτῇ μεγαλοφρονεῖνᵃ.
130 μηθὲνᵃ ὧν ἀφαιρήσεταίᵇ σε κακὸς ἀνὴρ τίμα.
131 μόνον ἀγαθὸν ἡγοῦ τὸ πρέπον θεῷᵃ.
132 τὸ ἄξιον θεοῦᵃ καὶ ἀνδρὸς ἀγαθοῦ.
133 ὃ οὐᵃ συμβάλλεται πρὸς εὐδαιμονίαν θεῷ, οὐδὲᵇ ἀνθρώπῳ.
134 ταῦτα θέλε ἃ ᵃθέλοι ἂνᵃ καὶᵇ ὁ θεός.
135 υἱὸς θεοῦ ὁ ταῦτα μόναᵃ τιμῶν ἃ καὶ ὁ θεός.

Translation

129 After God, accustom your soul to have confidence in itself.
130 Honor none of the things that an evil man might take from you.
131 Deem to be good only that which befits God.
132 What is worthy of God is also worthy of a good man.
133 That which does not contribute to happiness for God does not contribute to happiness for a human being.

134   Want those things that God would also want.
135   A son of God is the one who honors only those things that God also honors.

Textual Notes

129ᵃ⁻ᵃ μέγα φρονεῖν ἐφ' ἑαυτῇ: Υ • 130ᵃ μηδὲν: Υ • 130ᵇ ἀφαιρεῖται: Π, sy² • 131ᵃ τῷ θεῷ: Π • 132ᵃ τοῦ θεοῦ: Π • 133ᵃ omit Π • 133ᵇ καὶ: Π • 134ᵃ⁻ᵃ θέλοιεν: Υ • 134ᵇ omit Υ • 135ᵃ μόνον: Υ

Commentary

The sayings in this section are bound together by an accumulation of analogous expressions: "to have confidence in" (v. 129), "to honor" (τιμάω in vv. 130, 135), to "deem good" (v. 131), to be "worthy" (v. 132), to "want" (v. 134). In each case, some issue is raised regarding how and to what the readers should (vv. 129, 131–132, 134–135) or should not (vv. 130, 133) assign value, and, in each case, they are instructed to take God as their point of reference when making such determinations. By bringing their value judgments into compliance with those of God, the readers express their status as sons of God (v. 135), an important identity marker for our text. Note that v. 131 and v. 132 are further connected by the catchword ἀγαθός, which in turn is juxtaposed with κακός in v. 130.

Sentence 129

Cf. v. 580: ἑαυτὸν αἰδοῦ μετὰ θεόν. If the readers learn to put their trust in God first (cf. v. 106b), and next also in their own souls, then they will be more likely to pursue things of the soul (vv. 77, 118, 121b, etc.) and less likely to rely on wealth, possessions, or things of the body (vv. 78, 127, 264a, etc.); cf. Clement, *Paed.* 2.3.39.4. This reflects a Platonic perspective, according to which the "chief occupation" of the philosopher is "to accustom (ἐθίσαι) the soul to gather itself and collect itself out of every part of the body and to dwell by itself as far as it can both now and in the future, freed, as it were, from the bonds of the body" (*Phaed.* 67c–d; cf. Philo, *Prob.* 107; Dio Chrysostom, *Or.* 20.13–16). For Sextus, it is in the life of the soul, and particularly by cultivating godliness in the soul, that the readers achieve a godlike status: "Remember that you are next after God. The soul of a God-fearing person is a god in a body" (vv. 82c–d, cf. vv. 376a–b). Sayings like this encourage the readers to accord their own souls the same sort of reverence they accord the soul of a sage (cf. vv. 244, 292, 319).

Sentences 130–132

A similar progression of thought occurs in vv. 15–20, though the underlying distinction there is between things of God and things of "the world," while here we have a contrast between good and evil. The reference in v. 130 to the κακὸς ἀνήρ (cf. v. 387) is redolent of Matt 6:19–20: "Do not store up for yourselves treasures on earth, where … thieves break in and steal; but store up for yourselves treasures in heaven, where … thieves do not break in and steal." Cf. Origen, *Hom. Jer.* 14.12.2: "For each man stores up treasures on earth if he is evil, in heaven if he is good." The sage assigns no importance to earthly treasures because they can impede the life of the soul (see on vv. 127–128). He therefore honors not those who have much wealth (v. 192), but those who have much wisdom (vv. 219, 244, 319, cf. v. 135), above all, God (vv. 42, 244, 319, 427, 439), whose gifts no one can take away (vv. 92, 118, 404). As a consequence, the sage remains impervious to the criminal activity of evil people in the world, since such persons have no power over what contributes to his well-being (vv. 322, 387).

An expanded version of the next saying, v. 131, is found in v. 197, with τὸ καλόν inserted as a middle term: "Deem only what is noble to be good and only what befits God to be noble" (ἀγαθός and καλός appear to be largely synonymous for our author; see v. 395). According to Origen, what is "fit for God" and therefore worthy of being offered to God is a life informed by virtue (*Cels.* 8.17; *Hom. Luc.* 8.51). Given the priorities he identifies in vv. 44–45, 148, 201, and 381, Sextus's viewpoint on the subject would probably accord more with the one expressed by Clement in *Strom.* 7.1.3.6: "If by godliness (θεοπρέπεια) we mean the habit of mind which preserves that which befits God (τὸ πρέπον τῷ θεῷ), then the godly person alone is dear to God. And such would he be who knows what is fitting (τὸ πρέπον) both in theory and in life, as to how one should live who will some day become a god, and indeed is even now becoming like God" (cf. *Strom.* 7.1.2.1). What befits God, then, is that which is like God. It is this alone that the readers should judge to be "good," that is, the sort of thing to which honor and value ought to be assigned (see on v. 79), as opposed to things of the body, from which no "good" can derive (vv. 271, 317). Cf. Matt 19:17/Mark 10:18/Luke 18:19.

An example of something that is like God and therefore ought to be considered good is mentioned in the verse that follows (v. 132), namely, the good man. Since the goodness he embodies (see on v. 246) is rare (v. 243), such a person should be looked upon as "a work of God" (v. 395). The things that are worthy of such a man, then, are things that are worthy of someone who would be called God's son (v. 58, cf. v. 135), someone who would do nothing unworthy of his father, the one to whom he belongs (vv. 3–5). Insofar as he participates in things that are worthy of God, this person himself becomes something worthy of God, and in this capacity actually presents God to humankind (v. 376a).

Sentences 133–135

No doubt our author would have concurred with the notion that the deity alone participates in the highest and most complete form of εὐδαιμονία (e.g., Ps.-Plato, *Def.* 411a; Philo, *Abr.* 208; Ps.-Clement, *Hom.* 10.19; Diogenes Laertius, *Vit. phil.* 7.147; 10.121). There is therefore nothing that anyone can do to augment God's happiness, just as there is nothing that anyone can do to cause God harm (v. 85, cf. vv. 49, 382). As Philo puts it, "since his nature is most perfect, God himself is the summit, end, and limit of happiness, partaking of nothing outside of himself to increase his excellence" (*Cher.* 86). By the same token, Sextus can speak of the readers doing things that please God and earn God's favor (vv. 45, 48, 382, cf. vv. 308, 422). Presumably, such actions correspond with what God "wants" (v. 134) and what God "honors" (v. 135), and as such accord best with divine εὐδαιμονία. Specifically, what is most pleasing or "dearest" to God is the imitation of God (v. 45), which, as v. 148 stipulates, is sufficient for human εὐδαιμονία (cf. v. 466) and therefore what Sextus's readers must learn how to do (v. 344). Clement advances a similarly Platonic perspective on the theme in *Strom.* 2.19.100.3, where he states that the goal of εὐδαιμονία consists in achieving "the greatest possible likeness to God" (cf. *Strom.* 2.22.131.5; Plato, *Leg.* 716c–d). As the extended version of the saying in v. 134 found in Porphyry, *Marc.* 13 (ταῦτ' οὖν θέλε καὶ αἰτοῦ τὸν θεὸν ἃ θέλει τε καὶ ἔστιν αὐτός) indicates, wanting what God wants entails wanting what God is. Texts of this kind, in turn, reflect another widespread notion, namely, that God not only partakes of happiness—God makes it possible for human beings to partake of happiness as well. Indeed, as Aristotle, explains, since it represents "the greatest and best of human goods" (*Eth. eud.* 1.7.2; cf. *Eth. nic.* 1.7.1–16), when it is realized, happiness is of all human possessions the one most likely to be of divine origin (*Eth. nic.* 1.9.2). Epictetus can even aver that "God made all humankind to be happy" (*Diatr.* 3.24.2). Such happiness is not simply to be had, however, but must be attained through actions that are pleasing to God (*Diatr.* 4.4.48). Cf. Josephus, *Ant.* 1.14: "Those who conform to the will of God … are offered happiness by God for their reward."

Insofar as one wants what one honors, v. 135 expands on the thought of v. 134 (note the similar endings: καὶ ὁ θεός). It also serves as a positive counterpart to v. 130. Early Christians have an obligation not only to honor God as father (e.g., John 5:23; Ps.-Clement, *Hom.* 11.27; Clement, *Strom.* 7.1.4.1; cf. Exod 20:12; Deut 5:16), but, according to Sextus, also to honor whatever the father honors. Wanting and honoring what God also wants and honors thus serve together as evidence of one's divine sonship, a status second only to that of God (v. 376b, cf. v. 221), one that comes to expression especially in one's actions (vv. 58–60, 222). Honoring God above all else represents a foundational practice for the sage (vv. 244, 319, 355, 427, 439), who, as v. 381 states, conforms his intellect to the divine as much as humanly possible. Cf. Sophocles, frag. 247: σοφὸς γὰρ οὐδεὶς πλὴν ὃν ἂν τιμᾷ θεός.

Sentences 136–148

Text

136   ἐφ' ὅσον ποθεῖ τὸ σῶμα, ἡ ψυχὴ τὸν[a] θεὸν ἀγνοεῖ.
137   ὄρεξις κτήσεως ἀρχὴ πλεονεξίας.
138   ἐκ φιλαυτίας ἀδικία[a] φύεται[b].
139a ὀλίγα πέφυκεν τῇ ψυχῇ [a]τὸ σῶμα[a] ἐνοχλεῖν.
139b φιληδονία ποιεῖ σῶμα ἀφόρητον[a].
140   πᾶν τὸ πλέον ἀνθρώπῳ πολέμιον[a].
141   φιλῶν ἃ μὴ δεῖ οὐ φιλήσεις ἃ δεῖ.
142   σπουδάζοντά σε περὶ [a]τὰ μὴ καλὰ[a] λήσεται[b] τὰ καλά.
143   σοφοῦ διάνοια ἀεὶ παρὰ θεῷ[a].
144   σοφοῦ διανοίᾳ θεὸς ἐνοικεῖ.
145   σοφὸς ὀλίγοις γινώσκεται.
146   ἀπλήρωτος [a]ἐπιθυμία, διὰ τοῦτο καὶ ἄπορος[a].
147   τὸ σοφὸν ἀεὶ [a]ἑαυτῷ ὅμοιον[a].
148   αὔταρκες πρὸς εὐδαιμονίαν θεοῦ γνῶσις [a]καὶ ὁμοίωμα[a].

Translation

136   Insofar as the body has longings, the soul is ignorant of God.
137   Craving for property is the beginning of greed.
138   Injustice springs from self-love.

168   THE *SENTENCES* OF SEXTUS

139a It is the nature of the body to cause few troubles for the soul.
139b Longing for pleasure makes a body intolerable.
140 Every excess is hostile to humanity.
141 If you love things you should not, you will not love things you should.
142 If you concern yourself with the things that are not noble, the things that are noble will go unnoticed.
143 A sage's intellect is always with God.
144 God dwells in a sage's intellect.
145 A sage is acknowledged by few.
146 Desire is insatiable, and thus uncontrollable.
147 What is wise is always like itself.
148 Sufficient for happiness is to know and become like God.

Textual Notes
136ᵃ omit Π • 138ᵃ ἡ ἀδικία: Υ; κακία: Π • 138ᵇ γίνεται: Υ • 139aᵃ⁻ᵃ omit sy² • 139bᵃ ἀκόρεστον: sy² • 140ᵃ ἀφόρητον: Υ • 142ᵃ⁻ᵃ τὰ κακά: Υ, sy² • 142ᵇ λήσῃ: Π; λήσεταί σε: Υ; λήξεται: sy² • 143ᵃ τῷ θεῷ: Υ • 146ᵃ⁻ᵃ ἐπιθυμία ἅπασα παντός: Π, sy² • 147 ὁ σοφός...ὅμοιος: lat, sy² • 147ᵃ⁻ᵃ ὅμοιον ἑαυτῷ: Υ • 148ᵃ⁻ᵃ omit Υ

COMMENTARY

Evidence of thematic unity in this section of the text is not extensive, though several sayings make reference to the body (vv. 136, 139a–b) and to the sorts of yearnings generally associated with physical needs (vv. 136–138, 139b, 141, 146; note the use of words beginning with φιλ– in vv. 138, 139b, 141), all of which are characterized as harmful, extreme, distracting, or some combination thereof. Nestled within this presentation are two small clusters of sayings on the sage and his wisdom, vv. 143–145 and vv. 147–148 (note σοφός in vv. 143–145, 147).

Sentences 136
Among the conditions that can impede one's knowledge of God are a mind set on worldly things (e.g., Theophilus, *Autol.* 2.17), demonic influence (e.g., Origen, *Cels.* 8.33), false beliefs (e.g., Ps.-Justin Martyr, *Quaest. Christ. gent.* 161a–168b), or, here, bodily longings. Cf. Clement, *Strom.* 3.5.43.1: "It is impossible for those who are still under the direction of their passions to receive true knowledge of God." Knowledge of God is

a sine qua non for one who would become like God (vv. 44, 148), and so the sage strives to know not only God's words and works (v. 439) but also who God is (v. 394, cf. vv. 250, 406, 430, 432). Given this priority, the assertion made in v. 136 offers a strong motivation for directives issued elsewhere regarding the need to see both the body as something to be subdued (vv. 71a, 78, 274a, etc.) and self-control as the basis for one's relationship with God (v. 86a), since "God does not listen to one who longs for pleasure" (v. 72, cf. v. 569). The parallel to v. 136 in Porphyry, *Marc.* 13 reads as follows: "To the extent anyone longs for the body and the things related to the body, to that extent is he ignorant of God." In the shorter version offered by Sextus, the body is not the object of one's longings but is itself consumed with longing. His rendition also has the effect of creating a polarity of ψυχή and σῶμα, in which case comparison can be made with other body–soul sayings in the collection, including vv. 55, 82d, 139a, 301, 347, 411–413, 425, and 449. Although this is the only occasion on which our author has recourse to either ποθέω or πόθος, in the moral syntax of the time both terms were associated with ἐπιθυμία (e.g., *SVF* 3:395, 397), ἡδονή (e.g., Philo, *Opif.* 152), and πάθος (e.g., Arius Didymus, *Lib. phil. sect.* 95.2), and so this verse can be interpreted as buttressing warnings issued regarding those vices in vv. 70, 71b, 75a–b, 111, 139b, 146, 172, 204–207, 209, 232, 272, 274b, 342, and 411.

Sentence 137

Verses 137 and 138 bring together a pair of cause-and-effect sayings, for which see also vv. 188, 210b, and 327. The first line reproduces Clitarchus, *Sent.* 23 without change. It is cited as a saying of Clitarchus— along with *Sent.* 13 (= Sext. 86a) and 24 (= Sext. 138)—in Arsenius, *Apophth.* 6.48i. While the source may be Pythagorean, its critique of greed is at home in an early Christian setting. Athenagoras, for instance, classifies πλεονεξία (together with licentiousness and covetousness) as a craving (ὄρεξις) of the body (*Res.* 21.3; cf. Philo, *Spec.* 4.5), while *Act. Phil.* 111 identifies the ἀρχή of greed as the ἐπιθυμία of "the enemy." Greed is also frequently included in early Christian vice lists (e.g., Mark 7:22; Rom 1:29; Eph 4:19; Col 3:5; *1 Clem.* 35.5; *Did.* 5.1; *Ep. Barn.* 10.4; 20.1; Pol. *Phil.* 2.2; Herm. *Mand.* 6.2.5; 8.1.5). Greed naturally focuses on the accumulation of property (e.g., Luke 12:15; Ps.-Clement, *Hom.* 15.7; Plutarch, *Quaest. conv.* 644c), but the Sextine sage practices indifference toward such things (e.g., vv. 15, 91b, 227), his principal inclination being not to acquire possessions but to share them (e.g., vv. 82b, 228, 330, 377). Rather than praying for material wealth (v. 128), therefore, he strives not to crave (ὀρέγειν) anything that is improper (v. 99), recognizing that "the possession of goods will not stop a desire for possessions" (v. 274b, cf. v. 300). For the form of the saying, cf. Sir 10:13: ἀρχὴ ὑπερηφανίας ἁμαρτία. Cf. Juvenal, Sat. 14.138–140: "While your purse is full to bursting, your love of gain grows as much as the money itself has grown, and the man who has none of it covets it the least." For Seneca, craving for possessions is provocative not of greed but of lust (*Ep.* 110.14).

Sentence 138

The preceding line was based on Clitarchus, *Sent.* 23, while this one is based on Clitarchus, *Sent.* 24: ἐκ γὰρ φιλαργυρίας ἀδικία φύεται. Cf. *Sent. Pythag.* 110ᵈ: ὁ δὲ φιλοχρήματος ἐξ ἀνάγκης καὶ ἄδικος. Sextus replaces φιλαργυρία ("love of money") with φιλαυτία ("love of self"), a relation of some kind between the two concepts being implied by 2 Tim 3:2: ἔσονται γὰρ οἱ ἄνθρωποι φίλαυτοι, φιλάργυροι, κτλ. For the form of the saying, compare v. 271 and Menander, *Mon.* 250: ἐξ ἡδονῆς γὰρ φύεται τὸ δυστυχεῖν. Cf. Evagrius Ponticus, *Spirit. sent.* 48: ὦ ἀπὸ τῆς φιλαυτίας τῆς πάντα μισούσης.

For those intent on sustaining the life of the soul, injustice poses a serious threat (see on v. 208b), and so understanding its cause represents a matter of some importance. Among ancient moralists, Philo discourses on the problem of self-love perhaps most frequently, even going so far as to brand it "the greatest of evils" (*Congr.* 130). The φίλαυτος takes self-seeking to such an extreme that obligations to family, law, and God are nothing to him (*Deus* 16). His actions are therefore opposed by justice (*Conf.* 128). According to Plutarch, the vice is conducive of insatiable desires (*Tranq. an.* 471d) and anger (*Cohib. ira* 461a), while for Clement it is the pagan philosophers who are especially guilty of self-love, since they are more interested in understanding themselves than in understanding God (*Strom.* 6.7.56.2–6.7.58.3; cf. *Paed.* 3.2.13.4; 3.6.34.1). Aristotle had argued that the noble man will possess a certain type of self-love (*Eth. nic.* 9.8.1–11), though he also admitted that ordinarily φιλαυτία is used as a term of reproach, to describe individuals who "assign to themselves the greater share of money, honors, or bodily pleasures" (*Eth. nic.* 9.8.4).

Sentences 139a–b

The first of these sayings is connected to v. 138 by the catchword φύω, while v. 139a and v. 139b are connected to each other by the repetition of σῶμα. As Dio Chrysostom explains, nature fitted the human body not to trouble (ἐνοχλεῖν) but to protect its owner (*Or.* 6.27). Cf. Porphyry, *Marc.* 29: "Let us neither censure the flesh as cause of great evils nor attribute our distress to external circumstances." Although he is convinced that "nothing good stems from the flesh" (v. 271), according to Sextus what causes trouble for the soul is not the body as such, but the body's vices. After all, it is not the members of the body but the one who uses those members wrongly that sins (v. 12, cf. v. 335). Life in the body, then, should not be seen as an annoyance (v. 337). Ancient moralists differed somewhat as to the principle source of what "troubles" the soul: longings (Athenagoras, *Res.* 21.2; cf. Sext. 136), passions (Origen, *Cels.* 8.51), "uncouth thoughts and desires" (Maximus of Tyre, *Dial.* 11.10), bodily wickedness in general (Plotinus, *Enn.* 2.9.8). Here, reading v. 139a with v. 139b, the principal source is identified as the love of pleasure. Cf. v. 411: "Do not torture the body with your soul nor your soul with the pleasures of the body." Since bodily pleasures engender disgrace (v. 272) and defilement (v. 111), anyone who longs for them is cut off from God (v. 72, cf. v. 574) and thus becomes "useless in all things" (v. 172). The readers, then, must learn not only to exercise control over the pleasures (v. 70, cf. v. 71b) but also to do nothing for the sake of pleasure (v. 232). As Philo observes, φιληδονία can do more than make the body unbearable: "The longing for pleasure ... enervates the bodies of those who entertain it, relaxes the sinews of the soul and wastes away the means of subsistence, consuming like an unquenchable fire all that it touches and leaving nothing wholesome in human life" (*Dec.* 122). According to Origen, the danger in φιληδονία becomes evident when it prevents the faithful from observing their obligation to use the body properly, allowing it instead to waste away (*Orat.* 28.2).

Sentences 140–142

These three sayings are presented together and in the same order by Clitarchus, *Sent.* 143: πᾶν τὸ πλεῖον ἀνθρώπῳ πολέμιον. φιλῶν ἃ μὴ δεῖ [*sic*] λήσεταί σε τὰ καλὰ σπουδάσοντα περὶ τὰ μὴ καλά. Cf. Clitarchus, *Sent.* 25: φιλῶν ἃ μὴ δεῖ οὐ φιλήσεις ἃ δεῖ. Apparently, the second half of v. 143[b] has fallen out, owing to *homoioteleuton* (note the repetition of δεῖ in v. 25). The first saying, meanwhile, which Sextus reproduces in v. 140 exactly, is a variation on the Delphic maxim μηδὲν ἄγαν (e.g., Plato, *Charm.* 164d–165a; *Protag.* 343b; Ps.-Plato, *Hipp.* 228d–e; Plutarch, *Sept. sap. conv.* 163d–164c; *E Delph.* 385d; *Pyth. orac.* 408e; Ps.-Plutarch, *Cons. Apoll.* 116d; Clement, *Strom.* 5.8.45.4), which, as Clement notes in *Strom.* 1.14.61.1, is attributed to various sages, including Chilon (Diogenes Laertius, *Vit. phil.* 1.41; Diodorus Siculus, *Bibl. hist.* 9.10.1), Solon (Diogenes Laertius, *Vit. phil.* 1.63; Septem Sapientes, *Apophth.* 2.1), and Pittacus (Septem Sapientes, *Sent.* 216.9). In its current position the gnome can be interpreted as a commentary on v. 139b, in which case comparison may be made with Plato, *Phil.* 45e: "Moderate people somehow always stand under the guidance of the proverbial maxim 'Nothing too much' and obey it. But as to foolish people and those given to depravity, the excesses of their pleasures drive them to the brink of madness." While Sextus concedes that the experience of certain pleasures is unavoidable (v. 276), the point of a saying like this is that a surfeit of anything, even something that might appear to be agreeable, is harmful. As Pseudo-Phocylides observes, "A good that is excessive is for mortals no gain" (v. 60) and "Of all things moderation is best, but excesses are grievous" (v. 69b). For similar variations, see *Gnom. Democr.* 102; Theognis, *El.* 1.335, 401; Philo, *Mos.* 2.13; Plutarch, *Comm. not.* 1076c (= Menander, frag. 724); Ps.-Cato, *Dist.* 2.6. For this use of πολέμιος, cf. vv. 205, 314. Sextus is particularly concerned, of course, with any excess that has to do with the body; see on v. 115.

Verse 141 reproduces Clitarchus, *Sent.* 25 exactly (see above). The same saying is found also in Evagrius Ponticus, *Spirit. sent.* 45. This maxim resembles its predecessor insofar as it adopts an uncompromising position towards its subject matter. In v. 140 no room was allowed for any kind of excess, while here no room is allowed for any kind of split loyalty. The idea of exclusive commitment being expressed here may be indebted to Matt 6:24/Luke 16:13 (with ἀγαπήσει), though it is found in other sayings as well, for example, Plato, *Resp.* 555c ("It is impossible for a city to honor wealth and at the same time for its citizens to acquire moderation, but one or the other is inevitably neglected"); Philo, frag. 2.649 ("It is impossible for love of the world to coexist with the love of God"); *Corp. herm.* 4.6 ("It is not possible, my son, to attach yourself both to things mortal and to things divine"); *Gnom. Democr.* 72 ("Violent desires for anything blind the soul to the other things"). That the readers will "love" something is taken for granted (cf. vv. 86b, 226, 497), though alternatives exist as to the moral direction of their desires, as Arius Didymus explains: "The erotic man ... is spoken of in two senses; in one sense with regard to virtue as a type of worthwhile person, in the other with regard to vice as a reproach" (*Epit.* 5b9). For the form of the saying in v. 141, see vv. 388–389a: ὃ δεῖ ποιεῖν, ἑκὼν ποίει. ὃ μὴ δεῖ ποιεῖν, μηδενὶ τρόπῳ ποίει. For Sextus's conception of what is "necessary," see also on vv. 88 and 178.

Verse 142 (based on Clitarchus, *Sent.* 143ᶜ; see above) essentially restates v. 141 (for the parallelism of φιλέω and σπουδάζω, cf. Epictetus, *Diatr.* 2.22.2-3; Marcus Aurelius, *Med.* 9.34.1), though the juxtaposition of τὰ καλά and τὰ μὴ καλά supplies further clarity as to the potential objects of the readers' aspirations. Individuals "who are especially concerned with noble actions (περὶ τὰς καλὰς πράξεις ... σπουδάζοντας)," as Aristotle observes, "are universally approved and commended" (*Eth. nic.* 9.8.7; cf. Epictetus, *Diatr.* 4.11.29). Zeal for what is noble is commendable from Sextus's vantage point insofar as it expresses one's zeal for God, since only that which befits God is considered to be noble (v. 197), God functioning as both the source (v. 390, cf. v. 100) and the guide (v. 104, cf. v. 215) of all noble deeds. Those who aspire to obey and imitate God must both think and do noble things (v. 56). Cf. Menander, *Mon.* 324 ("If you want to live nobly, do not have thoughts about what is base"); Origen, *Hom. Jer.* 17.4.5: "If you are seeking what is on earth you are not seeking what is in heaven."

Sentences 143–145

This triad of sayings on the sage and his intellect (each beginning with either σοφοῦ or σοφός) contrasts with the surrounding material, which focuses on the body and its desires. Verse 144 provides the explanation for v. 143. According to the *Sentences*, where God "dwells" is not among the people, as various biblical texts had promised (Exod 29:45–46; Lev 26:11–12; Num 35:34; etc.), but in the intellect of the sage. It is in this sense that the sage is always "with" God (cf. v. 444). Such presence is possible because the sage honors God by conforming his intellect to the divine as much as possible (v. 381, cf. v. 447), rendering it morally and spiritually acceptable to God. Similar claims are made elsewhere, especially in v. 46a ("A pious person's intellect is a holy temple of God") and v. 61 ("A good intellect is the abode of God"). Cf. Philo, *Praem.* 123 ("For in truth the sage's intellect is a palace and house of God"); Porphyry, *Marc.* 11 ("The divine is entirely present everywhere, but its temple among humankind has been firmly established only in the intellect of the sage"). It is through this process of assimilation and participation that the διάνοια of the sage reflects the divine to others (v. 450, cf. v. 582). In v. 55, it is not the intellect but the soul that is said to be παρὰ θεῷ (cf. v. 418).

In v. 145, the sage's standing before God is seen to contrast with his standing before the people. The inspiration for this line may come from *Sent. Pythag.* 92 ("A person who is wise and venerates God is known by

God; he therefore pays no heed even when ignored by all the people"), though a closer parallel is located in Porphyry, *Marc.* 13: "A wise person, though known by few (σοφὸς δὲ ἄνθρωπος ὀλίγοις γινωσκόμενος) or, if you will, even ignored by all, is known by God" (note that vv. 134 and 136 have parallels in *Marc.* 13 as well). Although the sage is a living image of God (v. 190, cf. vv. 7a, 82d, 376a) and a benefactor of humanity second only to God (v. 176, cf. vv. 210a, 260, 372), his reputation among the people is ὀλίγος (v. 53). This represents another way in which the sage is "like" God, since there are not many people who honor God appropriately, goodness among humankind being rare (v. 243). While he avoids doing anything that might offend others (vv. 51, 343), the sage has little standing with the masses since, as God's son, he honors only what God honors (v. 135), his true and higher self being directed exclusively toward God (v. 55). Cognizant of fame's corrupting influence (v. 351, cf. v. 188), he avoids speaking in public (vv. 354, 360) and has no interest in trying to win public approval (v. 112, cf. v. 241). To most people, then, he is not only largely unknown but also largely useless (v. 214). Cf. Isocrates, *Phil.* 22: "I am not highly esteemed by the masses or those who form their opinions offhand, but … am misunderstood and disliked by them … because I lay claim to a wisdom greater than their own."

Verse 145 is the first of two Sextine aphorisms quoted in the *Regula Magistri* (cf. on v. 152). In this case, the citation comes from 10.81: *sicut scriptum est, Sapiens paucis verbis innotescit* (corresponding exactly with Rufinus's translation). It is cited also in chapter 7 (*De humilitate*) of the *Regula Sancti Benedicti* in a slightly different form: … *sicut scriptum est, Sapiens verbis innotescit paucis* (7.61).

Sentence 146

This line is based on Clitarchus, *Sent.* 26: ἀπλήρωτον γὰρ ἐπιθυμία, διὰ τοῦτο καὶ ἄπορον. Sextus drops the γάρ connecting the saying to Clitarchus, *Sent.* 25 (= Sext. 141; Clitarchus, *Sent.* 25 + 26 is cited as a saying of Philo in *Mant. prov.* 3.38). Π (cf. the Syriac) also extends the range of potential application with the addition of ἅπασα παντός after ἐπιθυμία—not simply desire as such but desire in all its different manifestations is ἀπλήρωτος. In the Stoic taxonomy of passions, the different forms of desire are listed as anger, love, resentment, and so forth (*SVF* 3:394–397), while for Philo the "insatiable" desires include especially drunkenness, gluttony, and lewdness (*Mos.* 1.185; cf. *Leg.* 3.148; *Legat.* 14) and Secundus, *Sent.* 16 defines wealth as an ἀπλήρωτος ἐπιθυμία. Desires of this sort are most likely to become insatiable among those who are unintelligent and easily swayed by others (Dionysius of Halicarnassus, *Ant. rom.* 5.67.2). Elsewhere Sextus specifically mentions the ἐπιθυμία for possessions (v. 274b; cf. Epictetus, *Diatr.* 3.9.18–22) as well as the desires of the body, the latter possessing the power to abuse and debase that which is within (v. 448). No doubt such desires also figure among the forces that can enslave the soul (vv. 75b, 270) and make the body unbearable (v. 139b). Since desire is also ἄπορος (cf. Plotinus, *Enn.* 4.4.17), it requires control in the same way as any of the body's passions or drives (e.g., vv. 70, 239–240, 274a, 428). For the form of the saying, cf. vv. 424, 533.

Sentences 147–148

Verses 147 and 148 are linked, just as vv. 44 and 45 had been linked, by the language of likeness: ὅμοιον (v. 147, cf. v. 45), ὁμοίωμα (v. 148, cf. v. 44). The previous pair of statements had established that those who are "dearest" to God are those who know and become like God as best they can, and it was a basic principle that "like is dear to like" (v. 443). The relevance of the assertion in v. 147, that what is wise is like itself, becomes clear with v. 148. God is all-wise (v. 30), the knowledge of God is divine wisdom (v. 406), and it is through wisdom that a soul is led to God (v. 167). It is therefore incumbent upon those who would become like God to grow in wisdom (cf. v. 533). Verses 44–45 had also established that becoming like God brings honor to God (cf. v. 381). Here we learn that it also brings happiness to humankind. Indeed it is "sufficient" for human happiness, since it conforms with divine εὐδαιμονία (see on v. 133).

The formulation in v. 148 has the effect of combining two major tenets associated with Plato: "He maintained that the goal is becoming like God, and that virtue is sufficient for happiness" (Diogenes Laertius, *Vit. phil.* 3.78; cf. Plato, *Theaet.* 176b). For the idea that Plato identified becoming like God as the key to εὐδαιμονία, see Theon Smyrnaeus, *Util. math.* 16; Clement, *Strom.* 2.19.100.3 ("Plato puts forward happiness as the goal of life and says it consists in the greatest possible likeness to God"); 2.22.131.5; Hippolytus, *Haer.* 1.19.17: "Happiness, (Plato) says, is becoming like God, as far as this is possible." Cf. Philo, *Dec.* 73: "The best of prayers and the goal of happiness is to become like God."

Sentences 149–165g

Text

149 κακοὶ κολακευόμενοι κακίους γίνονται.
150 ἀφόρητον^a γίνεται κακία ἐπαινουμένη.
151 ἡ γλῶσσά σου^a τῷ νοΐ σου^b ἐπέσθω.
152 αἱρετώτερον λίθον εἰκῇ βάλλειν^a ἢ λόγον.
153 σκέπτου ^aπρὸ τοῦ^a λέγειν ^bἵνα μὴ λέγῃς^b ἃ μὴ δεῖ.
154 ῥήματα ἄνευ νοῦ ψόφος^a.
155 ^aπολυλογία οὐκ ἐκφεύγει^a ἁμαρτίαν.
156 ^aβραχυλογίᾳ σοφία^a παρακολουθεῖ^b.
157 μακρολογία σημεῖον ἀμαθίας.
158 τὸ ἀληθὲς ἀγάπα.
159 τῷ ψεύδει χρῶ ὡς φαρμάκῳ^a.
160 καιρὸς τῶν λόγων σου προηγείσθω.
161 λέγε ὅτε σιγᾶν οὐ καθήκει.
162a περὶ ὧν οὐκ οἶδας σιώπα.
162b περὶ ὧν οἶδας, ὅτε δεῖ λέγε.
163a λόγος παρὰ καιρὸν διανοίας ἔλεγχος κακῆς.
163b ὁπότε δεῖ πράττειν, λόγῳ μὴ χρῶ.
164a ἐν συλλόγῳ πρῶτος λέγειν μὴ ἐπιτήδευε.
164b ἡ αὐτὴ ἐπιστήμη ἐστὶ τοῦ λέγειν καὶ τοῦ σιωπᾶν.
165a ἄμεινον ἡττᾶσθαι τἀληθῆ λέγοντα τοῦ περιγενέσθαι μετὰ ἀπάτης.
165b ὁ νικῶν τῷ ἀπατᾶν νικᾶται ἐν ἤθει^a.
165c μάρτυρες κακῶν γίνονται λόγοι ψευδεῖς.
165d μεγάλη περίστασις ᾗ πρέπει ψεῦδος.
165e ὁπότε ἁμαρτάνων εἶ^a τἀληθῆ λέγων, ἀναγκαίως τότε ψευδῆ λέγων οὐχ ἁμαρτήσεις.
165f μηδένα ἀπάτα, μάλιστα τὸν συμβουλίας δεόμενον.
165g μετὰ πλειόνων λέγων μᾶλλον ὄψει τὰ συμφέροντα.

Translation

149 When flattered wicked people become more wicked.
150 Praise makes wickedness intolerable.
151 Let your tongue obey your mind.
152 It is better to throw a stone without purpose than a word.

153 Deliberate before speaking, so that you do not say things you should not.
154 Words without thought are blameworthy.
155 Excessive speech does not escape sin.
156 Wisdom accompanies brevity of speech.
157 Prolonged speech is a sign of ignorance.
158 Love the truth.
159 Treat lying like poison.
160 Let the occasion guide your words.
161 Speak when it is not appropriate to keep silent.
162a Regarding things you do not know, be silent.
162b Regarding things you know, speak when necessary.
163a An untimely word is proof of an evil intellect.
163b When it is necessary to act, do not resort to speech.
164a In an assembly do not strive to speak first.
164b The same understanding that is needed to speak is needed to keep silent.
165a It is better to be defeated while speaking the truth than to overcome with deceit.
165b The one who conquers with deceit is conquered in character.
165c False words are attestations of evil things.
165d It is an extreme situation in which a lie is fitting.
165e When you would sin by speaking the truth, then you would surely not sin by speaking falsely.
165f Deceive no one, especially one in need of advice.
165g By speaking with many others you will better see the things that are beneficial.

Textual Notes

150ᵃ ἀόριστον: sy² • 151ᵃ omit Π • 151ᵇ omit Π • 152ᵃ βαλεῖν: Υ • 153ᵃ⁻ᵃ πρὶν ἤ: Υ • 153ᵇ⁻ᵇ μὴ δὶς λέγῃς: Υ • 154ᵃ ψόγος: Π, lat; φόβος: Υ • 155ᵃ⁻ᵃ πολυλογίᾳ οὐκ ἐκφεύξῃ: Υ, sy¹, sy² • 156ᵃ⁻ᵃ βραχυλογία σοφία: Π, lat • 156ᵇ ἀκολουθεῖ: Π • 157 omit Υ • 159ᵃ φαρμάκῶι (sic): Π • 163b omit Π, lat • 164b omit Π, Υ, lat • 165b-g omit Π, lat • 165bᵃ ἀληθείᾳ: co • 165eᵃ εἷς: Υ

Commentary

Constituting one of the longest thematic sections in the collection, the twenty-six sayings above form a unit on verbal integrity and the control of speech. While these represent two of the most ordinary of gnomic *topoi*, within the context of the Sentences this section is remarkable for its complete absence of references to God, the topic of discretion in religious speech being postponed until vv. 350–368. Sextus's instruction here is conveyed in a predominantly antithetical mode: talkativeness is contrasted with taciturnity (vv. 155–157), timely speech with untimely (vv. 160, 163a), speech with action (v. 163b), and, most important, truthfulness with falsehood (vv. 158–159, 165a–f). Given his noetic proclivities, it is not surprising that in developing these themes particular attention is drawn to the relation of speech to reason (vv. 151–154), to knowledge (vv. 162a–b), and to understanding (v. 164b), while a distinctively Pythagorean perspective is evident in sayings that mention silence (vv. 161–162a, 164b).

As a whole, aphoristic authors were preoccupied with sins of the tongue, stressing the need for discipline and discretion in one's speech. Proverbs 18:21 spells out just how high the stakes involved were thought to be: "Life and death are in the power of the tongue; they that control it shall eat its fruit."

Sentences 149–150

Verses 149–150 are a couplet of matching sayings on flattery, flatterers being known for the indiscriminate ways in which they distribute praise (note also the catchword with κακίους and κακία). Among Greco-Roman moralists, the flatterer (ὁ κόλαξ) was a stock figure, reviled for his obsequiousness, voracity, and guile (e.g., Theophrastus, *Char.* 2.1–13; Maximus of Tyre, *Or.* 14; Stobaeus, *Anth.* 3.14). In Plutarch's *Quomodo adulator ab amico internoscatur*, for example, flatterers emerge as purveyors of moral corruption, capable of stimulating in their victims a whole range of immoderate passions, including malice, fear, wrath, envy, and erotic desire (*Adul. amic.* 61d–62b). Flattery is particularly despicable when conferred on the wicked, since it encourages them to act on their inclinations, thereby fostering vice (*Adul. amic.* 57c–58b). Thus, as Philostratus explains in *Vit. Apoll.* 7.3.2, "Someone who flatters bad people with praise (κολακεύων ἐπαίνοις) shares the responsibility for their crimes, since the wicked become worse when praised (οἱ γὰρ κακοὶ κακίους ἐπαινούμενοι)." See further Diodorus Siculus, *Bibl. hist.* 33.4.1; Plutarch, *Dem.* 9.1; *Vit. pud.* 536b.

The first line of our couplet is derived from Clitarchus, *Sent.* 27: κακοὶ κολακευόμενοι κακίους. Sextus adds γίνονται, perhaps to strengthen the connection with v. 150 (with γίνεται), which both parallels and intensifies the assertion made in v. 149. Flattery not only exacerbates wickedness; it makes it intolerable (cf. v. 139b). What wickedness deserves is not praise but censure (v. 298; cf. Plutarch, *Vit. pud.* 531c). See further Sext. 571 ("How many have been ruined by praise!"); *Gnom. Democr.* 113 ("People who praise the unintelligent do great harm"); Ps.-Cato, *Mon.* 50: "Praise voted to the bad disgusts the good." As we learn from v. 241 (cf. vv. 299, 530–531), our author disapproves not only of praising the wicked but also of accepting praise from the wicked.

Sentence 151

The cluster of sayings in vv. 151–154 takes up the relationship between speech and the reasoning faculties (note the use of νοῦς in vv. 151 and 154, and of σκέπτομαι in v. 153). In keeping with prevailing anthropological ideals, this relationship is construed in strictly hierarchical terms, with the mind directing and (especially) restraining the tongue, vigilance in maintaining such arrangements being necessary on account of the latter's capacity for mischief (e.g., vv. 155, 163a, 165c) and carried out in concert with the demands of rationality and self-control more generally (cf. Cicero, *Fin.* 2.46–47; see also on Sext. 74). Parallels to the first saying in the cluster abound, for example, Isocrates, *Demon.* 41: "Always when you are about to say anything, first weigh it in your mind, for with many the tongue outruns the thought." The saying ἡ γλῶττα μὴ προτρεχέτω τοῦ νοῦ ("Let not your tongue outrun your mind"), in turn, is attributed to Pittacus in Septem Sapientes, *Sent.* 216.7–8 and to Chilon in Diogenes Laertius, *Vit. phil.* 1.70. See also Theognis, *El.* 1185–1186 ("The mind is a good thing and so is the tongue, but they are found in few men who have control over them both"); Ps.-Phoc. 20 (γλώσσῃ νοῦν ἐχέμεν); Plutarch, *Garr.* 510a ("The tongue must be fenced in, and reason must ever lie, like a barrier, in the tongue's way"); Ps.-Cato, *Dist.* 1.10 ("Speech is bestowed on all, sound sense on few"); Publilius Syrus, *Sent.* 226 ("Conscience sets a bridle on the tongue"); and Clement's description of the true gnostic: "Whatever he has in his mind he has also on his tongue" (*Strom.* 7.9.53.1). Cf. Sext. 426: "It is not the sage's tongue that is honored before God, but his prudence."

Sentence 152

The source for vv. 152–154 is Clitarchus, *Sent.* 28–30. Sextus cites the first of the maxims from his source with no alteration, except for reversing the order of the second and third words. Comparison can also be made both with Sent. Pythag. 7 (αἱρετώτερόν σοι ἔστω λίθον εἰκῇ βάλλειν ἢ λόγον ἀργόν), which is cited as a saying of Pythagoras in Stobaeus, Anth. 3.34.11, as well as with Porphyry, Marc. 14: αἱρετωτέρου σοι ὄντος λίθον εἰκῇ βαλεῖν ἢ λόγον (note that the latter is part of a longer saying whose continuation parallels Sext. 165a–c). For the wordplay, cf. Stobaeus, Anth. 3.36.14a (attributed to Menander): οὔτ᾽ ἐκ χερὸς μεθέντα καρτερὸν λίθον ῥᾷον κατασχεῖν, οὔτ᾽ ἀπὸ γλώσσης λόγον.

The power of speech or, more properly, speech governed by reason, is often imaged as a weapon and means of defense. Indeed, according to Menander, "The greatest weapon for people is *logos*" (*Mon.* 621); cf. Prov 10:13; 14:7; Ps.-Phoc. 124; Philo, *Somn.* 1.103–108; Josephus, *Bell.* 5.361. Like any weapon, of course, speech can be used to harm as well as to protect: "There are some who wound when they speak, like swords; but the tongues of sages heal" (Prov 12:18; cf. 25:18; 26:18–19; Sir 28:17–18; Menander, *Mon.* 546; Ps.-Cato, *Dist.* 1.12). Our author was well aware of how words can be used to hurt others (v. 185). The point of the saying here is that, when it is done "without purpose" (cf. v. 362), speaking becomes a reckless and potentially damaging activity. For a similar "better" saying, see Sir 20:18 ("A slip on the pavement is better than a slip of the tongue"), and note the similar construction in Sext. 362: ψυχὴν αἱρετώτερον ἢ λόγον εἰκῇ προέσθαι περὶ θεοῦ.

Verse 152 is the second of two Sextine aphorisms quoted in the *Regula Magistri* (cf. on v. 145). This time the citation occurs in 11.62: *Nam et Originis sententia sapiens dicit, Melius est lapidem in vanum iactare quam verbum*. The reference to Origen suggests that the Master's source is not Rufinus's translation (which has *frustra*, not *in vanum*) but a translation of one of the Alexandrian's now-lost writings, where the gnome was presumably used without attribution. Verse 152 is also the likely inspiration for Evagrius Ponticus, *Cap. paraen.* 2: βέλτιον λίθον εἰκῇ βαλεῖν ἢ λόγον.

Sentence 153

The positive counterpart to v. 152 follows in this line, which replicates Clitarchus, *Sent.* 29 (σκέπτου πρὸ τοῦ λέγειν ἵνα μὴ λέγῃς εἰκῇ), except that Sextus replaces the final word, εἰκῇ (which helps to link Clitarchus, *Sent.* 29 with Clitarchus, *Sent.* 28 = Sext. 152), with ἃ μὴ δεῖ (cf. v. 141 = Clitarchus, *Sent.* 25). This change has the effect of reinforcing the line's parallelism with a previous saying in the collection, Sext. 93 (= Clitarchus, *Sent.* 16): "Deliberate before taking the actions that you take, so that you do not repeat doing something you should not." Note in particular how σκέπτου πρὸ τοῦ + ἵνα μή/μηδέν + ἃ/ὃ μὴ δεῖ structures both lines. Thinking before speaking is just as important as thinking before acting. Cf. Sir 18:19 ("Before you speak, learn"); 33:4 ("Prepare what to say, and then you will be listened to"); Ps.-Apollonius, *Ep.* 92: "Take great care not to say things you should not (ἃ μὴ δεῖ). For it is the absolute mark of an uncultured person not to be able to stay silent and to blurt out improprieties." For the use of σκέπτομαι here, compare Demosthenes, *Aristog.* 1.14; Dio Chrysostom, *Or.* 60.2; Ps.-Plutarch, *Reg. imp. apophth.* 187f. Thoughtless speech, of course, can have all manner of negative consequences: "Babblers are derided for telling what everyone knows, they are hated for bearing bad news, they run into danger since they cannot refrain from telling secrets" (Plutarch, *Garr.* 504f). For Sextus, the "things you should not say" include speech that is false (v. 165c), hurtful (v. 185), inopportune (v. 163a), slanderous (v. 259), and boastful (v. 284); cf. v. 171a: "Being faithful, do not honor speaking things that are necessary above hearing them." Verses 350–368 recount various forms of inappropriate theological speech as well (cf. vv. 83, 401, 407, 410).

Sentence 154

The final line in the cluster offers a motivation for the preceding three: those who speak before they think deserve reproach. Cf. Sir 9:18 ("The one who is reckless in speech is hated") and *Instr. Ankh.* 7.23–24 ("Do not hasten when you speak, lest you give offense. Do not say right away what comes out of your heart"). Verse 154 is derived from Clitarchus, *Sent.* 30 (ῥήματα ἄνευ νοῦ ψόφοι), though it is unclear what choice Sextus made regarding the last word for his version of the precept. Elter (1892, 13) retains Clitarchus's ψόφοι, while Chadwick (1959, 30) prints ψόφος ("noise"), although neither term is present in either of the Greek manuscripts, Π reading ψόγος, while Υ has φόβος. Seeing how the former is supported by *obprobria* in Rufinus's translation, it is probably best to follow Edwards and Wild (1981, 34) and propose that our author altered ψόφοι in his source to the more ethically pertinent ψόγος (for which cf. v. 299; Clitarchus, *Sent.* 106; *Sent. Pythag.* 111[b]; and note the reference to ἁμαρτία in the following line). For its part, the Syriac reads: "All words that do not go out from just knowledge are empty and idle."

Sentence 155

The next cluster (vv. 155–157) contains alternating precepts on talkativeness (vv. 155, 157) and taciturnity (v. 156), the topic in each line being announced by an opening term with the –λογια stem. A discussion of elementary education attributed to Plutarch suggests something of the logic connecting this group of sayings with the one that immediately precedes: "Apart from all the other errors, those who speak on the impulse of the moment fall from a dreadful disregard of limit into talkativeness (πολυλογίαν). Deliberation (σκέψις, cf. σκέπτου in Sext. 153), on the other hand, prevents a discourse from exceeding the due limits of proportion" (*Lib. ed.* 6c).

Inserted into a section that draws extensively on the *Sentences* of Clitarchus for its material (see on vv. 149, 152–154, 156–157, 159) is a saying based on a biblical source, namely, Prov 10:19a: ἐκ πολυλογίας οὐκ ἐκφεύξῃ ἁμαρτίαν. Sextus creates a more abstract statement, dropping the ἐκ reinforcing the verb and changing its subject from "you" to πολυλογία itself (cf. v. 598). Cf. *m. Avot* 1:17: "Whoso multiplies words occasions sin." For a Greco-Roman parallel, see Ps.-Apollonius, *Ep.* 93: "Talkativeness causes many mistakes (πολυλογία πολλὰ σφάλματα ἔχει), but silence is safe." Plutarch also reports as a saying of Simonides "that he had often repented of speaking, but never of holding his tongue" (*Garr.* 515a). Early Christian texts associate verbosity with various other vices (e.g., Herm. *Mand.* 11.12; *Const. ap.* 3.5), while Matt 6:7 presents it as a characteristic of pagan piety. Clement weaves Prov 10:19 as well as other traditional sayings into his instruction at *Paed.* 2.6.52.4: "Nonsensical chatter should also be silenced, for 'by talking much,' it says, 'you shall not escape sin.' Loquaciousness will draw down upon itself judgment of some kind. 'There is one who keeps silent and is found wise, while another becomes hateful from much speech.' And already the chatterer is a boor even to himself, for 'he who uses many words shall abominate his own soul'" (cf. Sir 20:5, 8). Origen investigates the problem of πολυλογία on numerous occasions, for example, *Comm. Joan.* 4.1; 5.1, 4–5; *Orat.* 21.2; *Philoc.* 5.3–4. Sextus will identify one of the causes of excessive talk in v. 431.

Sentence 156

Like its predecessor, the thought informing this line would be at home in the book of Proverbs. Indeed, it parallels the continuation of the precept that Sextus has just cited, Prov 10:19b: "But if you refrain your lips you will be prudent." See also Prov 17:27–28: "One who refrains from uttering a hard word is knowledgeable, and a patient man is prudent. Wisdom shall be reckoned to a fool who asks after wisdom, and the one who holds his peace shall seem prudent." The line's actual source, however, is Clitarchus,

Sent. 31, which Sextus reproduces exactly. In Greco-Roman antiquity, brevity of speech (βραχυλογία) was associated especially with the seven sages, Spartan culture, and the Delphic oracle (e.g., Plato, *Prot.* 343a–b; Plutarch, *Pyth. orac.* 408e; *Garr.* 511a–b; Clement, *Strom.* 1.14.60.2–3; Diogenes Laertius, *Vit. phil.* 1.72; Ps.-Demetrius, *Eloc.* 242–243). Iamblichus explains that in many of his teachings Pythagoras "hid the embers of truth for those able to kindle them, storing up in brevity of speech a limitless and vast extent for contemplation" (*Vit. Pythag.* 29.162; cf. Maximus of Tyre, *Dial.* 25.2). Among Pythagorean philosophers, Apollonius of Tyana was probably best known for his laconic brevity (e.g., Philostratus, *Vit. Apoll.* 1.17; 4.33; 5.32; 7.35; Ps.-Apollonius, *Ep.* 8.2). Origen, meanwhile, thinks that Solomon ought to be admired for the way he was able to "express profound thoughts in terse phrases" (*Cels.* 3.45; cf. *Philoc.* 18.16). In general, "those who can speak concisely and briefly and those who can pack much sense into a short speech are more admired and loved, and are considered to be wiser, than unbridled and headstrong talkers" (Plutarch, *Garr.* 510e; cf. *Praec. ger. rei publ.* 803e). Sextus identifies one of the causes of taciturnity in v. 430.

Sentence 157

Verse 157 reproduces Clitarchus, *Sent.* 32 exactly. For the form of the saying, cf. Sext. 280a. Prolonged speech (μακρολογία) involves "expounding on matters that are not pertinent or germane to the question at hand" (Dio Chrysostom, *Or.* 7.132). Such prolixity is associated especially with old men (e.g., Isocrates, *Panath.* 88) and with people who like to talk about themselves (e.g., Aristotle, *Rhet.* 3.17.16). To certain ambassadors who were speaking at length (μακρολογοῦσιν) about a matter of state, the Spartan king Cleomenes replied, "What you said at the beginning I do not remember; for that reason I did not understand the middle part; and the conclusion I do not approve" (Plutarch, *Apophth. lac.* 223d, cf. 216a, 224c, 232d). Among gnomic authors, meanwhile, loquaciousness functions as a signifier of ignorance, for example, Sir 21:25 ("The lips of babblers speak of what is not their concern, but the words of the prudent are weighed in the balance"); Theognis, *El.* 295–297 ("For a chatterbox the hardest burden to bear is silence, but when he talks he is a bore to those present and everyone dislikes him"); Ps.-Cato, *Dist.* 2.20 ("Trust not those who forever news relate; Slight faith is due to tongues that glibly prate"); Stobaeus, *Anth.* 2.15.28 (attributed to Menander): "The one who has no wisdom but who chatters much on every point exhibits his character in his words." Note also a saying attributed to the sage Thales: "Many words do not declare an understanding heart" (Diogenes Laertius, *Vit. phil.* 1.35).

Sentences 158–159

While the contrast drawn in vv. 155–157 was between taciturnity and talkativeness, here it is between truth and falsehood. Parallels abound: Prov 14:25 ("A truthful witness saves lives, but one who utters lies is a betrayer"); Eph 4:25 ("So then, putting away falsehood, let all of us speak the truth to our neighbors, for we are members of one another"); *Instr. Ankh.* 13.14–15 ("Do not acquire two voices. Speak truth to all men; let it cleave to your speech"); Septem Sapientes, *Apophth.* 2.6 ("Do not lie, but tell the truth"); Ps.-Apollonius, *Ep.* 83 ("To lie is illiberal, while the truth is illustrious"); *SVF* 3:554 ("It is said that the sage does not lie, but in everything tells the truth"). Among the many acclamations made of truth in Greek literature, the one found in Plato, *Resp.* 730c is perhaps most effusive in its praise: "Truth heads the list of all things good, for gods and mortals alike. Let anyone who intends to be happy and blessed be its partner from the start, so that he may live as much of his life as possible a man of truth." Biblical literature asserts that God "loves the truth" (Ps 51:6 [50:8]; cf. *1 Clem.* 18.6), and both Jewish (e.g., *T. Reub.* 3.9; *T. Dan* 2.1; 6.8) and Christian (e.g., Herm. *Mand.* 3.1; Clement, *Paed.* 3.11.54.2; Ps.-Clement, *Hom.* 16.14) authors expect their readers to do the same. A "lying tongue," meanwhile, "hates truth" (Prov 26:28) and persecutors of the faithful "hate truth and love a lie" (*Did.* 5.2; *Ep. Barn.* 20.2). Cf. 2 Thess 2:10: "Those who are perishing ... did not receive the love of the truth (τὴν ἀγάπην τῆς ἀληθείας) so as to be saved." One who loves the truth can be counted on to embrace it under all circumstances: "For the person fond of truth (ὁ φιλαλήθης), who is truthful even when nothing depends on it, will *a fortiori* be truthful when some interest is at stake, since having all along avoided falsehood for its own stake, he will assuredly avoid it when it is morally base; and this is a disposition that we praise" (Aristotle, *Eth. nic.* 4.7.8). Being "fond of truth" is something that early Christians found praiseworthy as well, for example, *Mart. Ptol. Luc.* 11; Justin Martyr, *1 Apol.* 2.1; 12.11; Theophilus, *Autol.* 3.17; Ps.-Clement, *Hom.* 1.10–11; 1.18; 1.20.7.

If the sage "has a love of truth and is a friend of truth" (Clement, *Strom.* 2.9.45.3), then it is also true that "every wise and honest person hates a lie" (Menander, *Mon.* 846), since "a lie is the greatest evil for humankind" (*Mon.* 849). Verse 159 replicates Clitarchus, *Sent.* 34 (τῷ ψεύδει ὡς φαρμάκῳ χρῶ) with a slight change in word order. The power of speech can be compared not only to that of a weapon (v. 152) but also to that of a φάρμακον. Like a drug, it can be used for good, as in Menander, *Mon.* 840: "To an ailing soul speech is a drug" (for the doctrine of the "medicinal" lie, see on v. 165d). Given the juxtaposition with v. 158 (cf. vv. 168–169), however, it is more likely that φάρμακον here carries a negative connotation: loving the truth means refraining from lies as though they were lethal (cf. v. 393: ψεύδεσθαι φυλάττου). In this case, the line can be classed with a variety of sayings that liken the insidious and corrupting effects of false speech to those of poison or venom, for example, LXX Pss 13:3 ("With their tongues they have used deceit; the venom of asps is under their lips"); 139:4 (quoted in Rom 3:13); Jas 3:8 ("No one can tame the tongue—a restless evil, full of deadly poison"); Publilius Syrus, *Sent.* 251: "Flattering speech contains its special poison." Plutarch graphically describes the effect of a poisonous falsehood after it has taken hold of its victim: "It feeds upon his soul, distracts him, does not allow him to sleep, fills him with stinging desires, pushes him over precipices, chokes him, and takes from him his freedom of speech" (*Superst.* 164f-165a). The figurative use of φάρμακον is evidenced also in *Trall.* 6.2, where Ignatius compares heretics to "those who administer a deadly drug mixed with wine, which the unsuspecting victim accepts without fear" (cf. Herm. *Vis.* 3.9.7).

Sentences 160–161

The sage knows the right moment to speak (note καιρός in vv. 160, 163a); otherwise, he keeps silent (note σιγάω in v. 161 and σιωπάω in vv. 162a, 164b). As Solon declares in Diogenes Laertius, *Vit. phil.* 1.58, "Speech ought to be sealed by silence (σιγῇ), and silence by the occasion (καιρῷ)." Ben Sira communicates similar priorities in Sir 20:6-7 by contrasting the conduct of the sage with that of his opposites: "There is one who keeps silent (σιωπῶν) because he has no answer, and there is one who keeps silent, knowing the occasion (καιρόν). A wise person will keep silent (σιγήσει) until there is an opportunity (ἕως καιροῦ), but a babbler and a fool disregard such opportunity" (cf. Qoh 3:7; Sir 1:23–24). Indeed, even if they are wise, the words of a fool will be rejected, since "he does not speak at the proper moment (ἐν καιρῷ)" (Sir 20:20). Likewise, a rogue is unable to "say something at the proper moment (καιρόν) and for the common good" (Prov 15:23). Concerning the chatterer, Plutarch observes how "the untimeliness of his words destroys and annuls all gratitude for any deed" (*Garr.* 504c). Menander can even go so far as to declare that "a word said at the wrong time (παρὰ καιρόν) overturns a life" (*Mon.* 690). Thus the need for admonitions like *Instr. Ankh.* 12.24: "Do not say something when it is not the time for it." For a Christian perspective, we can turn to Clement, *Strom.* 6.15.116.3: "It is the prerogative of the gnostic to know how to make use of speech, and when, and to whom" (cf. *Strom.* 2.7.58.1). The need for good judgment in such matters is emphasized also by Epictetus in *Diatr.* 2.23.15; 4.12.17.

This would include for Sextus recognizing those times when it is not appropriate (οὐ καθήκει) to keep silent (v. 161). Sir 4:23 suggests one such occasion: "Don't hold back your word in a moment of need (ἐν καιρῷ χρείας)." Compare Sir 20:7: "The wise remain silent until the right moment, but a boasting fool misses the right moment." Epictetus uses similar language: "Be silent for the most part, or else comment only on the most necessary matters (τὰ ἀναγκαῖα), and then only in a few words" (*Ench.* 33.2). Didymus Caecus provides somewhat more specific criteria: "Speaking is not as beneficial as keeping silent in all situations; for to the one who is able to open his mouth with a word of God it is not appropriate to keep silent (οὐ καθήκει σιωπᾶν), but to the one who utters idle speech and words condemning the good there should be silence" (*Frag. Ps.* 1229). Of course, as Epictetus points out, what constitutes "appropriate" speech will vary depending on an individual's particular point of view (*Ench.* 42.1). We can probably assume that for Sextus the time when it is most appropriate to break one's silence is when there is a need to speak the truth about God (e.g., vv. 352, 410), though even this must be done with great care. Cf. v. 366: "It is better to keep silent with a word about God than to utter it recklessly." For Pythagorean practices of silence, see the commentary on v. 427.

Sentences 162a–b

With the importance of καιρός in speech established, vv. 162a + b then attach an additional criterion: it is important not only to know the right moment to speak but also to know what one is speaking about. Cf. Plutarch, *Lyc.* 20.2: "The one who knows what to say also knows when to say it." Sextus's couplet (note the similar openings: περὶ ὧν οὐκ οἶδα and περὶ ὧν οἶδα) reproduces Clitarchus, *Sent.* 36 exactly, except for replacing ὃ δεῖ (for which cf. Xenophon, *Symp.* 6.10) with ὅτε δεῖ, which has the effect of creating greater continuity with the thought of vv. 160–161: one should speak about what one knows only "when" it is necessary to do so. This agrees with the counsel of Isocrates, who argued that there should be "but two occasions for speech: when the subject is one you know thoroughly and when it is one on which you are compelled to speak. On these occasions alone is speech better than silence" (*Demon.* 41). A similarly structured gnome occurs in Sir 5:12: "If you have understanding, answer your neighbor; if not, put your hand over your mouth." See further Sir 4:25; 11:8; *Instr. Ankh.* 15.16; Dio Chrysostom, *Or.* 36.19 ("Those who are educated make it their business to know the meaning of everything of which they speak"); Menander, *Mon.* 409, 710: "Better to be silent than to speak unfittingly." For Sextus, the need to know of what one speaks applies especially to speech about God (vv. 353, 367–368, 410). This is because what God values about the sage is not his tongue but his mind, which honors God even when the sage is silent (vv. 426–427), since "knowledge of God produces a man of few words" (v. 430).

Sentence 163a

This line is based on Clitarchus, *Sent.* 37: λόγος παρὰ καιρὸν ἀνοίας ἔλεγχος. In its original setting, the gnome supplements Clitarchus, *Sent.* 36 (see above): ignorance in one's speech is exposed not only by speaking about what one does not know but also by speaking at the wrong time (cf. Plato, *Phaedr.* 272a). In adapting the saying to its current setting, our author replaces ἀνοίας with a much stronger designation, διανοίας ... κακῆς (cf. v. 83). Inopportune speech, then, reveals not merely an intellectual problem but also an ethical one. Most often, ill-timed words are simply condemned as ineffective, unwelcomed, or both (e.g., Plutarch, *Garr.* 504c; *Quaest. conv.* 716e–f; Dio Chrysostom, *Or.* 38.5). But in the moral world of the *Sentences*, such words are every bit as malicious as blasphemous ones (see on v. 83) or false ones (see on v. 165c). In this, Sextus would seem to part ways with the author of 2 Tim 4:2: "Proclaim the message; be persistent whether the time is favorable or unfavorable (ἀκαίρως)." By the same token, we have the gnomic concept that something coming at the wrong time, even something good, can be bad, for example, Menander, *Mon.* 144 v.l. ("Ill-timed laughter among mortals is a terrible evil"), 690 (cited above); Zenobius, *Paroem.* 1.50 ("An ill-timed kindness does not differ from hostility").

Sentence 163b

Just as there is a time when it is necessary to speak (v. 162b), there is a time when it is necessary to act. Verse 163b reproduces Clitarchus, *Sent.* 35 exactly, though our author alters the sequence of sayings, borrowing from *Sent.* 35 after he has borrowed from both *Sent.* 36 (= vv. 162a + b) and *Sent.*

37 (= v. 163a). This adjustment has the effect of bringing the saying in v. 163a into closer proximity to the saying in v. 160, which also has καιρός. The current line supplements the preceding instruction on timeliness with a case in point: one of the moments when it is not right to speak is when action is required. That acting ought to take precedence over speaking is argued in a variety of moral texts, for example, 1 John 3:18: "Let us love, not in word or speech, but in truth and action." In Jas 1:22–27, meanwhile, acting is a priority over hearing as well as speaking. It was something of a philosophical cliché to castigate teachers who were proficient in the rhetorical arts but useless when it came to transforming words into actions (e.g., Philo, *Det.* 43–44; Seneca, *Ep.* 108.36–37). Conversely, Maximus of Tyre notes of Pythagoras that while his discourses "were short and concise, like laws, the lengthy sequence of his deeds saw no interruption" (*Dial.* 25.2). For an aphoristic formulation, see Sir 4:29: "Do not be hasty with your tongue but slack and remiss with your deeds." Similarly, in the *Sentences*, the true measure of the readers' faith is what they do, not what they promise to do (v. 198, cf. v. 408). Their deeds, then, should be many, but their words few (v. 383). In particular, appropriate deeds must precede any speech about God (vv. 356, 359).

Sentence 164a

This line replicates Clitarchus, *Sent.* 39[a] exactly (for *Sent.* 39[b], see on vv. 165f–g). In its current location, the admonition parallels the preceding verse, supplementing the instruction on καιρός in vv. 160–163a with another case in point: when in an assembly, one should not vie with others to speak first. Prudence and decorum suggest that it is best to bide one's time until the proper moment. Compare P.Ins. 22.20–21 ("Do not give way often to your tongue to counsel when you have not been asked. He who hastens with his word when he speaks gives a false answer"); Sir 11:7–9 ("Do not find fault before you investigate; examine first, and then criticize. Do not answer before you listen, and do not interrupt when another is speaking. Do not argue about a matter that does not concern you"); 32:9 ("Among the great do not act as their equal; and when another is speaking, do not babble"); *m. Avot* 5:7: "A sage does not speak before someone greater than he in wisdom. And he does not interrupt his fellow." Sextus's readers are urged to be discrete and respectful in their outspokenness (v. 253a). This applies especially to their conduct in public venues (v. 112), where caution should be observed especially when speaking about God (v. 360). Even when in the company of believers it is better to listen than to speak (vv. 171a–b), striving to surpass others not in fine speech but in good judgment (v. 332). The story is told of Demonax that once, when there was party strife in Athens, "he went into the assembly and simply by showing himself reduced them to silence. Then, seeing that they had already repented, he went away without a word" (Lucian, *Dem.* 64).

Sentence 164b

This line is absent from both Greek manuscripts as well as from Rufinus's translation, though it is present in the Coptic and Syriac versions, both of which correspond closely to Clitarchus, *Sent.* 38, whose text Elter (1892, 13) and Chadwick (1959, 30) print as v. 164b. Note also that Sextus reverses the order of Clitarchus, *Sent.* 38 and 39ª (= v. 164a), thus positioning a general statement on silence at the end of the subunit in vv. 160–164b.

The value and wisdom of silence are affirmed by a host of gnomic statements, for example, Prov 18:18 ("A silent man quells strifes and determines between great powers"); Sir 20:5 ("There is one who stays silent and is found wise, and there is another who talks much and is hated"); *Syr. Men.* 312 ("Being silent is at all times a virtue"); Menander, *Mon.* 597 ("Nothing is more useful than silence"); *m. Avot* 1:17 ("All my days I have grown up among the wise, and I have not found anything better for one than silence"). Cf. Plutarch, *Garr.* 502e (= Sophocles, frag. 78): "In silence lie many noble things." Elsewhere in *De garrulitate*, Plutarch suggests that such wisdom in the area of speech-ethics is not instinctive, but must be acquired through training. Indeed, "those who have received a noble and truly royal education learn first to be silent, and then to speak" (*Garr.* 506c). Such instruction can even be said to be divine in its source and nature: "No spoken word, it is true, has ever done such service as have in many cases words unspoken.... Thus, I think, in speaking we have men as teachers, but in keeping silent we have the gods, and we receive from them this lesson of silence at initiations into the mysteries" (*Garr.* 505f). Against such a background, it is not surprising to hear our author aver that "a wise man honors God even while silent" (v. 427). As other statements in the unit suggest, the content of the relevant "understanding" (ἐπιστήμη) for Sextus probably has to do with the ability to recognize the καιρός (vv. 160, 163a). Cf. *Vit. Aesop.* (G) 88: "Just as I understand (ἐπίσταμαι) when to speak, I also know when to keep silent, for the height of wisdom is to recognize the proper moment (καιρόν)." Also compare *Schol. Aesch. Eum.* 278: "I understand (ἐπίσταμαι) when it is necessary to keep silent and when it is necessary to speak, knowing the proper moment (καιρόν) for each."

Sentences 165a–c

The subunit in vv. 165a–f conveys warnings concerning falsehood and deception. Note ἀπάτη in v. 165a, ἀπατάω in vv. 165b, f, ψευδής in vv. 165c, e, and ψεῦδος in v. 165d. The first three lines in the subunit are paralleled by three sayings that occur in the same order in Porphyry, *Marc.* 14. The first of these matches a saying in Porphyry, *Marc.* 14 that is the continuation of a saying that parallels v. 152: "It is preferable for you to throw a stone without purpose than a word, and to be defeated while telling the truth than to win by being deceitful (τὸ ἡττᾶσθαι τἀληθῆ λέγοντα ἢ νικᾶν ἀπατῶντα)." Most likely, Sextus's wording is closer to that of the original saying with περιγενέσθαι, which Porphyry has changed to νικᾶν so as to create greater continuity with the saying that immediate follows in *Marc.* 14: τὸ γὰρ νικῆσαν ἀπάτῃ ἐν τῷ ἤθει ἥττηται (= Sext. 165b).

If wisdom leads a soul to God, and nothing is closer to wisdom than the truth (vv. 167–168), then those who seek God must love the truth and avoid lying (vv. 158–159). As a practical matter, this means refraining from deception in all of one's personal interactions (v. 165f). Indeed, as vv. 186–187 explain, in an argument it is better to lose because one lacks knowledge than to win by resorting to deception, since such an offense will not go unnoticed by God, who cannot be deceived. Verses 165a–b similarly warn against ἀπάτη, though here it presented as a matter not of θεός but of ἦθος (cf. Philo, *Det.* 38). Any victory achieved with deception is only apparent, since it comes at the cost of something far more valuable than winning an argument, namely, one's moral integrity. The act of deception, then, implicates itself in a certain irony: those who deceive others actually deceive themselves, insofar as they fail to recognize this cost (v. 393, cf. v. 327). The stakes in such matters are high, since duplicity in speech can ruin a person's reputation: "Honor and dishonor come from speaking, and the tongue of mortals may be their downfall. Do not be called double-tongued and do not lay traps with your tongue; for shame comes to the thief, and severe condemnation to the double-tongued. In great and small matters cause no harm, and do not become an enemy instead of a friend; for a bad name incurs shame and reproach; so it is with the double-tongued sinner" (Sir 5:13–6:1). With the thought conveyed in v. 165a, comparison can be made with a saying attributed to Chilon in Diogenes Laertius, *Vit. phil.* 1.70: "Prefer a loss to a dishonest gain, for one brings pain at the moment, the other for all time." The form and language of Epictetus, *Gnom.* 28 are also comparable, though here what opposes truth is not deception but δόξα: "It is better (ἄμεινον), by yielding to truth, to conquer (νικᾶν) opinion than, by yielding to opinion, to be defeated (ἡττᾶσθαι) by truth." Cf. P.Ins. 12.5: "The stupid man who seeks to deceive, his tongue brings him harm."

Like the first two lines, the third line in the subunit (v. 165c) is paralleled by a saying on falsehood found in Porphyry, *Marc.* 14: μάρτυρες δὲ κακῶν ψευδεῖς λόγων. Not only does an act of deception compromise one's integrity, but the false words through which it is accomplished attest to the presence of evil—that is, they bring to expression the evil things that lurk in an evil mind (vv. 62, 83, 163a). As illustrated by the quotation of Sir 5:13–6:1 above, duplicity in speech was often interpreted as proof of malevolent intentions (cf. Prov 26:23–26; Sir 12:16; Theognis, *El.* 91–92; Plutarch, *Vit. pud.* 533d). For Sextus, however, lying represents more than a demonstration of personal malice, since things flowing through the mouth from an evil ἦθος have the capacity to defile a soul (v. 110, cf. v. 165b), leaving it vulnerable to the infiltration of polluting, demonic forces (v. 348), which in turn prompt one to commit evil deeds (v. 305).

Sentences 165d–e

The first line in this couplet is based on Clitarchus, *Sent.* 40: μεγάλῃ περιστάσει πρέπει ψεῦδος (note the similar ending in v. 165c). Sextus inserts ἤ and changes the first two words to the nominative.

In the *Respublica*, Plato famously argued that under certain circumstances falsehoods are not only undeserving of condemnation but can in fact be helpful—for example, when one lies in order to confound one's enemies (see above) or when one lies in order to dissuade a friend from making a mistake. Of particular relevance to his argument is the concept of the "noble" lie, according to which the Guardians will propagate myths they know to be false in order to ensure the stability of the state (*Resp.* 382c–d, 389b–c, 414b–c). Indeed, "it looks as though our rulers will have to make considerable use of falsehood and deception for the benefit of those they rule" (*Resp.* 459c). In such cases, the effects of the lie can be likened to those of a φάρμακον, or drug (cf. v. 159). Clement alludes to this doctrine in *Strom.* 7.9.53.2, where he describes how the gnostic always speaks truthfully, "except on occasion, when he speaks medicinally, just as a physician, with a view to the safety of his patients, will practice deception or use deceptive language" (cf. Xenophon, *Mem.* 4.2.17). Origen will even claim that God employs deceit in order to help humanity, and that the faithful ought to "pray to be deceived by God" rather than by Satan (*Hom. Jer.* 20.3.5; cf. 19.15.2–7; 20.4.1; *Cels.* 4.19). In a very different setting, we have the Stoic sage. Guided by an innate sense of true and false, he remains unconcerned about how his statements might be evaluated by others (Epictetus, *Diatr.* 4.6.28–38). Indeed, according to *SVF* 3:554, the Stoics "think that (the sage) will upon occasion employ falsehood in different ways without being conscious of it: as a stratagem against adversaries, out of foresight for what is beneficial, and for the sake of many other considerations in life" (cf. Plutarch, *Stoic. rep.* 1055f–1056a). According to Aristotle, a person who is magnanimous always speaks the truth, "except when he speaks in a self-deprecating way to the many" (*Eth. nic.* 4.3.28). Publilius Syrus identifies yet another pretext for lying: "Falsehood for safety's sake is true" (*Sent.* 706).

Verse 165e proceeds to give an example of the sort of extreme situation mentioned by v. 165d, the sort of situation that "reveals" a faithful person (v. 200). Sextus's concern may be that the reader will say something that might lead others to sin, perhaps in the context of correcting them, and therefore share in their culpability (cf. v. 174). Alternatively, he might be concerned that the reader will sin by telling the truth about God to those who are unworthy of it (vv. 350–352, 401, 407, 451), though the lack of theological language here or anywhere in the section opens the door to other interpretative possibilities as well.

Sentences 165f–g

The first line in this couplet reproduces Clitarchus, *Sent.* 41 precisely, except for dropping the δέ after μάλιστα. Integrity of speech when offering advice represents a particular priority for gnomic authors, P.Ins. 25.21 being representative: "Do not let your tongue differ from your heart in counsel." These authors are also worldly enough to recognize that those who proffer advice do not always do so out of pure motives, for example, Prov 12:26 ("The righteous gives good advice to friends, but the way of the wicked leads astray"); Sir 37:7–8: "All counselors praise the counsel they give, but some give counsel in their own interest. Be wary of a counselor, and learn first what is his interest, for he will take thought for himself." For his part, Clement voices concern not only over the direct effects of duplicitous speech, but also over the sort of example it sets for others. In his opinion, loving the truth ought to be an expression of loving the neighbor: "We must never adulterate the truth … gratifying our own desires and ambitions with a view to the deception of our neighbors, whom we ought to love above everything and teach to cling to the truth itself" (*Strom.* 7.16.105.5). The current line can be interpreted as a specification of the warnings against deceit that had been issued earlier in the section (vv.

165a–b, cf. vv. 185–186). To a person in need of advice, one should offer not words of deception but words of guidance that will help him mend his ways (v. 331).

Verse 165g reproduces Clitarchus, *Sent.* 39[b], reversing the order of ὄψει and μᾶλλον and, more notably, dropping the γάρ. This is necessary because Sextus has separated the two members of Clitarchus, *Sent.* 39, postponing the use of v. 39[b] until this point, where it is combined instead with Clitarchus, *Sent.* 41 (= v. 165f) so as to create a couplet on consultativeness. One implication of this new arrangement is that the "many" people to be consulted in v. 165g are no longer (necessarily) members of the "assembly" mentioned in Clitarchus, *Sent.* 39[a] (= v. 164a). When in need of advice themselves, the readers ought to turn not to just anyone (cf. v. 400), but to fellow believers (v. 171b), and especially to a fellow sage (v. 218), whose words can purify the soul (v. 24). For comparable sayings, see Prov 11:14 ("In much counsel there is safety"); 12:15; 15:22; 24:6–7; Tob 4:18 ("Seek advice from every wise person and do not despise any useful counsel"); Sir 21:13; 37:16; *Let. Aris.* 255; Septem Sapientes, *Praec.* 217.15; P. Louvre 2377 no. 2 ("Listen to the voice of every man, that you may discover what is good to say"); Menander, *Mon.* 109; Ps.-Cato, *Dist.* 4.13; Publilius Syrus, *Sent.* 141: "In a crisis the prudent man's remedy is counsel."

Sentences 166–177

Text

166 πιστὸς[a] ἁπασῶν καλῶν[b] πράξεων ἡγεμών ἐστιν.
167 σοφία ψυχὴν ὁδηγεῖ [a]πρὸς θεόν[a].
168 οὐδὲν οἰκειότερον σοφία ἀληθείας.
169 οὐ δυνατὸν τὴν αὐτὴν[a] φύσιν πιστήν τε[b] εἶναι καὶ[c] φιλοψευδῆ[d].
170 δειλῇ καὶ ἀνελευθέρῳ φύσει πίστις οὐκ ἂν μετείη.
171a τὸ λέγειν [a]ἃ δεῖ[a] τοῦ ἀκούειν πιστὸς ὢν μὴ προτίμα.
171b ἐν πιστοῖς ὢν μᾶλλον ἄκουε ἤπερ λέγε.
172 φιλήδονος[a] ἀνὴρ ἄχρηστος ἐν παντί.
173 ἀνεύθυνος ὢν λόγοις μὴ[a] χρῶ περὶ θεοῦ.
174 τὰ τῶν ἀγνοούντων ἁμαρτήματα τῶν[a] διδαξάντων αὐτοὺς ὀνείδη.
175 νεκροὶ παρὰ θεῷ δι' οὓς τὸ ὄνομα τοῦ θεοῦ λοιδορεῖται.
176 σοφὸς ἀνὴρ εὐεργέτης μετὰ θεόν.
177 τοὺς λόγους σου ὁ βίος βεβαιούτω παρὰ τοῖς ἀκούουσιν.

Translation

166 A faithful person is a guide for all noble actions.
167 Wisdom leads a soul to God.
168 Nothing is more akin to wisdom than truth.
169 It is not possible for the same nature to be both faithful and fond of falsehood.
170 Faith could have no part in a cowardly and illiberal nature.
171a Being faithful, do not honor speaking things that are necessary above hearing them.
171b Among the faithful, listen rather than speak.
172 A man who longs for pleasure is useless in all things.
173 If you are not accountable, do not utter words about God.
174 The sins of the ignorant are a reproach to those who teach them.
175 Dead before God are those through whom the name of God is reviled.
176 A wise man is a benefactor next after God.
177 Let your life confirm your words among those who hear you.

Textual Notes

166ᵃ πίστις: lat • 166ᵇ τῶν: Π, lat • 167ᵃ⁻ᵃ παρὰ θεῷ πρὸς θεόν: Π • 169ᵃ omit Υ, lat • 169ᵇ omit Υ, lat • 169ᶜ καὶ μὴ: Π • 169ᵈ ψευδῆ: Υ, sy¹, sy² • 171aᵃ⁻ᵃ ἀεί: Π • 172ᵃ ἄπιστος: Υ • 173ᵃ omit Υ, sy² • 174ᵃ τῶν μὴ: Υ

Commentary

The material here is not grouped in such a way as to suggest an overall theme, though it is noteworthy that a fair number of the sayings (vv. 168, 169, 171a–b, 173, 177) carry over themes from the preceding section (vv. 149–165g), which dealt with integrity in speech. In contrast to that block of material, however, some of these sayings incorporate references to God (v. 173, cf. vv. 167 + 168) or to the faithful (vv. 169, 171a–b). Indeed, faith language figures rather prominently in the first part of the section (vv. 166, 169, 170–171b), while references to sinners become more conspicuous in the latter part (vv. 172, 174–175).

Sentence 166

In scripture, God (e.g., Exod 15:13), God's wisdom (e.g., Wis 9:11), and God's people (e.g., Rom 2:19) can be described as guides. For the thought here, see especially Heb 13:7: "Remember your leaders, those who spoke the word of God to you; consider the outcome of their way of life, and imitate their faith." Theophilus draws on a precept similar to Sextus's (note that the Latin witness for v. 166 reads πίστις rather than πιστός) in *Autol.* 1.8: "But why do you disbelieve? Do you not know that faith leads the way in all matters (ἁπάντων πραγμάτων ἡ πίστις προηγεῖται)? What farmer can harvest unless he first entrusts the seed to the earth? Who can cross the sea unless he first entrusts himself to the ship and the pilot? What sick man can be cured unless he first entrusts himself to the physician? What art or science can anyone learn unless he first delivers and entrusts himself to the teacher?" Cf. Origen, *Sel. Jes. Nave* 12.820; Ephraem Syrus, *Imit. prov.* 186.

The full meaning of v. 166 comes into view when it is read together with the line that immediately follows. A faithful person serves as a guide for noble actions to the extent that he is a σοφός, that is, to the extent that he participates in the σοφία that guides a soul to God (cf. Prov 15:24: "The thoughts of the wise are paths of life"). This would appear to be one of the principal ways in which the sage "presents" or "images" God to others (vv. 190, 307, cf. vv. 7a, 82d, 376a). It is God, then, who functions as the ultimate source (vv. 113, 390), guide (v. 104, cf. v. 582), and confirmer (v. 304) of humankind's noble actions. Compare Philo, *Prob.* 20: "He who has God alone for his guide, he alone is free, though to my thinking he is also the guide of all others, having received charge over earthly things from the great, the immortal king, whom he, the mortal, serves as regent." Since it is impossible to live nobly without God (v. 215, cf. vv. 197, 399), the faithful must let God guide their actions (v. 95b, cf. v. 30). That which guides evil actions, on the other hand, is an evil demon (v. 305; cf. Chadwick 1959, 156).

Sentence 167

Biblical authors will on occasion speak of following the "ways" (ὁδοί) of wisdom (e.g., Prov 3:6; 4:11; Bar 3:23; cf. Clement, *Strom.* 2.19.101.2; Ps.-Origen, *Frag. Ps.* 110:10; Evagrius Ponticus, *Pract.* 73), and in the book of Wisdom σοφία is said to "guide" the actions of the wise (Wis 9:11), even as wisdom itself is guided by God (Wis 7:15). According to Origen, σοφία was manifested "so that people might be led (ὁδηγήσωσιν) from vice to virtue, and from ignorance to the knowledge of God" (*Exp. Prov.* 17.201; cf. Ps.-Macarius, *Serm.* 18.4.13). The appropriation of this imagery informs the linkage of v. 167 with the preceding line: just as a faithful person guides others to what is noble (v. 166), wisdom guides a soul to God (v. 167), the source of all that is noble (vv. 113, 390). For Sextus, this is the same as declaring that faith guides a soul to God (v. 402, cf. v. 349), since for him a soul that is wise is also faithful (v. 441). By definition, wisdom in the *Sentences* is divine wisdom, that is, the knowledge of God (v. 406), the means by which human beings honor and imitate God (vv. 44, 439) and thereby thrive (v. 148). The faithful allow the illumination cast by this wisdom to guide their actions (v. 95b, cf. v. 30), just as they adopt for their guide and norm divine reason (vv. 74, 123), which can also be described as the means by which the soul "journeys" to God (v. 420).

Sentences 168–169

The source for this couplet (note the antithesis of ἀλήθεια and φιλοψευδής) is Clitarchus, *Sent.* 42–43. The first line replicates *Sent.* 42 precisely, except for dropping the ἤ before ἀλήθεια. The second line evidences a more significant alteration, with Sextus replacing φιλόσοφον in his source with πιστήν (cf. vv. 166, 170–171b). This has the effect of ruining the maxim's internal wordplay (φιλόσοφον … φιλοψευδῆ) as well as the connection between φιλόσοφον and the reference to σοφία in the first line. The material for Clitarchus's couplet, in turn, comes from Plato's *Respublica*: "So can you find anything more akin to wisdom than truth (οἰκειότερον σοφίᾳ τι ἀληθείας)? Certainly not. Then is it possible for the same nature to be both fond of wisdom and fond of falsehood (δυνατὸν εἶναι τὴν αὐτὴν φύσιν φιλόσοφόν τε καὶ φιλοψευδῆ)? Not at all. Then someone who loves learning must above all strive for every kind of truth from childhood on" (*Resp.* 485c–d).

In its Sextine context, the saying in v. 168 is linked to the one that precedes it by the catchword σοφία. Those who are led to God by wisdom will be accompanied on their journey by that which is most closely related to wisdom, the truth, as suggested by Clement, *Strom.* 2.2.4.2: "The paths of wisdom are diverse, but they lead directly to the path of truth, and that path is faith." The faithful person not only knows and speaks the truth, above all, the truth about God (vv. 352, 355, 357, 368, 410), he is also a "worker" (v. 384) and prophet (v. 441) of truth. The juxtaposition of truth and falsehood informs the structure of vv. 158–159 as well, though here embracing the former and rejecting the latter are presented as expressions of faith: abiding by these standards is one of the ways in which a faithful person guides others to noble actions (v. 166). Cf. Plutarch, *Adul. amic.* 61d: "Our soul has two sides: on one side are truthfulness, fondness for what is noble, and power to reason, and on the other side irrationality, fondness for falsehood, and the emotional element." For the critique of φιλοψευδία, see Aristotle, *Eth. eud.* 3.7.6; Posidonius, frag. 423; Irenaeus, *Haer.* 1.1.8; and Lucian's *Philopseudes sive incredulus*.

Sentence 170

The saying in this line is modeled after Plato, *Resp.* 486b: δειλῇ δὴ καὶ ἀνελευθέρῳ φύσει φιλοσοφίας ἀληθινῆς, ὡς ἔοικεν, οὐκ ἂν μετείη. The Sextine version drops δή plus ἀληθινῆς, ὡς ἔοικεν, and, more important, changes φιλοσοφίας to πίστις, much like φιλόσοφον had been changed to πιστήν in v. 169. Thus this line is linked to the one that precedes it by a compound catchword: φύσιν πιστήν (v. 169) and φύσει πίστις (v. 170). Our author, apparently recognizing the dependence of Clitarchus, *Sent.* 42–43 on *Resp.* 485c–d, expands by drawing on material that occurs shortly after that passage in the *Respublica*. (Alternatively, v. 170 is based on a version of the saying, one presumably closer to the Platonic text in wording, that was originally in Clitarchus's collection but that later fell out of the manuscript tradition; see part 4 of the introduction.) Coming on the heels of vv. 168–169, v. 170 would seem to imply that fondness for falsehood is what demonstrates a nature that is "cowardly and illiberal." Cf. Ps.-Apollonius, *Ep.* 83: "To lie is illiberal (ἀνελεύθερον), while truth is illustrious." Similarly, Dio Chrysostom's good king holds that "unscrupulousness and deceit are for the fool and the slave, for he observes that among the wild beasts also it is the most cowardly (δειλότατα) and ignoble that surpass all the rest in lying and deceit" (*Or.* 1.26). More often, δειλός and ἀνελεύθερος are used as terms of contempt for vice in general (e.g., Teles, frag. 4a.36; Dio Chrysostom, *Or.* 4.22; 8.8), while in the New Testament the former is denounced as the opposite of faith or as an obstacle to the exercise of faith, which may account for the particular wording of Sextus's precept. See especially Matt 8:26; Mark 4:40 (τί δειλοί ἐστε; οὔπω ἔχετε πίστιν;); John 14:27; 2 Tim 1:7; Rev 21:8. Cf. further Herm. *Sim.* 9.1.3; 9.21.3; 9.28.4; *Const. ap.* 4.4; Evagrius Ponticus, *Sent. virg.* 27.

Sentences 171a–b

In the New Testament, hearing is the basis of faith (John 5:24; Acts 4:4; Rom 10:17; etc.). In the *Sentences*, hearing is a practice of faith. The most appropriate posture for the believer is not one of speaking but one of listening, especially to God (vv. 353, 415b), though the sage will also welcome instruction (v. 290), advice (v. 165g), commendation (v. 298), and correction (v. 245) from others. The source for the first line of this couplet is Clitarchus, *Sent.* 44: "Honor hearing things that are necessary above speaking them" (τοῦ λέγειν ἃ δεῖ τὸ ἀκούειν προτίμα). Sextus inserts πιστὸς ὢν μή before προτίμα and switches the placement of the definite articles. Besides the insertion of faith language, the effect of this revision is to turn a positive command into a negative one. For Sextus, resisting the impulse to honor the act of speaking is a higher priority than indulging the impulse to honor the act of listening. This emphasis is consistent with warnings issued elsewhere regarding excessive talk (vv. 155–157, 430–431), striving to speak first (v. 164a), and speaking about God (vv. 22, 173, 195, 352, 356). Yet, just as there are things that should not be spoken (v. 153), there are also things that are "necessary" to both speak and hear, that is, things about which the speaker knows (v. 162b) and about which it would be inappropriate to keep silent (v. 161). The second line of the couplet applies this priority to the readers' own speech practices. They should not only prefer hearing to speaking generally: they should model such behavior to other believers. Note the chiastic arrangement of catchwords: λέγειν … ἀκούειν πιστός (v. 171a), πιστοῖς … ἄκουε … λέγε (v. 171b).

Sentence 172

A soul that succumbs to ἡδονή is "impotent to achieve the good, bereft of function, the plaything of the pleasures that nurture it" (Maximus of Tyre, *Dial.* 33.6; cf. Euripides, frag. 282; Ps.-Andronicus Rhodius, *Pass.* 4.1; Plutarch, *Cons. ux.* 609a). In terms of their value to the church, those ensnared by evil desires are not to be considered anything more than "useless servants" (Ps.-Clement, *Hom.* 11.3). Indeed, according to Ephraem Syrus, those fond of pleasure are so "constrained by useless passions (ὑπὸ ἀχρείων παθῶν)" that they cannot even repent of their sins (*Virt.* 3). While a wise man *appears* useless to the masses (v. 214), his opposite, the man fond of pleasure, truly is useless, and not only to the masses, but in every respect. Ensnared by the vice of intemperance (v. 71b), his body becomes an "intolerable" distraction from the life of faith (v. 139b, cf. v. 411). The fact that his prayers go unheeded (v. 72) provides an additional explanation for why such an individual is ἄχρηστος, since responding to prayer is a means by which God grants humankind power and authority (v. 375).

Sentence 173

Elter (1892, 14) and Chadwick (1959, 32) print μή before χρῶ even though the former is found only in Π (see the text-critical notes). Given that it is more customary for ἀνεύθυνος to mean "not accountable" or "irresponsible" (e.g., Josephus, *Ant.* 19.179; Plutarch, *Rect. rat. aud.* 45e; Epictetus, frag. 25; Clement, *Strom.* 3.5.40.4) rather than "blameless" (e.g., Ps.-Clement, *Hom.* 5.8; 8.15), this reading is probably correct, and it appears to be supported by the Coptic witness: "When there is no [(accounting of) sin, do not speak] in anything (which is) from [God]." Note also the partial parallel in v. 541 (ἀνεύθυνος ὢν μὴ ἐπιχείρει νέων ἄρχειν), where μή is omitted by Υ, but supported by Π as well as by the Syriac and Armenian witnesses. The version with μή also better fits the negative characterizations of vv. 172 and 174–175. If Elter and Chadwick are correct, then v. 173 expresses the same basic thought as v. 356: "If you are not cleansed of unholy works, do not utter a word about God." See also v. 410: "To speculate about God is easy, but to speak the truth has been granted the just one alone." The one who speaks about God is "accountable" both to God, who passes judgment on all theological discourse (v. 22), and to the souls of his listeners, which have been entrusted to him (v. 195). For more on the responsibilities accompanying theological discourse, see the commentary on vv. 350–368.

Sentence 174

Plato had named ignorance "the cause of sins" (*Leg.* 863c; cf. Aristotle, *Eth. nic.* 5.8.12; Epictetus, *Diatr.* 1.26.6–7; Ps.-Clement, *Hom.* 10.12: "ignorance, the cause of evils"). For our author, what the ignorant lack specifically is knowledge about God, the sort of knowledge that makes it possible for one to become like God (vv. 44, 148, cf. v. 250) and ascend to God (v. 167). The source for this line is Clitarchus, *Sent.* 45: τὰ τῶν παιδευομένων ἁμαρτήματα τῶν παιδευόντων ὀνείδη. Sextus's alterations raise some questions concerning how he envisions the social dynamics of the pedagogical process. Is τῶν ἀγνοούντων in his version of the saying equivalent to τῶν παιδευομένων in the same manner that τῶν διδαξάντων appears to be the equivalent of τῶν παιδευόντων, or are "the ignorant" a particular subgroup of learners, namely, those most likely to sin? Either way, insofar as their sins are a matter for reproach, the actions of the ignorant are no different than those of faithless outsiders, whose whole way of life is an ὄνειδος (v. 400). Other questions can be raised regarding the reason and responsibility for their ignorance. As v. 285 indicates, ignorance results from a lack of learning. But if the ignorant have teachers, who shoulders the blame if they commit sins on account of a failure to learn? According to v. 174, the "reproach" is said to fall not on the former (cf. Philo, *Migr.* 116; Josephus, *Ant.* 4.263) but on the latter. This is a matter of some concern for the readers, since, according to v. 331, they have an obligation not only to tolerate the ignorant in their midst (cf. v. 285), but to protect a brother who lacks judgment from acting out of ignorance (cf. v. 103). See further Clement, *Strom.* 7.13.82.1 (quoting from the *Traditions of Matthias*): "If the neighbor of an elect person sins, it is the fault of the elect; for if he had conducted himself as reason dictates, his neighbor's reverence for such a life would have prevented him from sinning." For the opinion that teachers ought to be held responsible for their students' mistakes, see Xenophon, *Mem.* 1.2.27; Plato, *Euth.* 5b; Epictetus, *Diatr.* 1.26.13–14. For the opposing view, cf. Plato, *Ep.* 341a; *Gorg.* 456e–457c.

Sentence 175

This line is loosely connected to the one that precedes it by the use of strongly negative language: ὄνειδος (v. 174), νεκρός, λοιδορέω (v. 175). The lives of the ignorant who sin even though they have teachers would presumably be included among the sorts of things that cause God's name to be reviled (cf. Ps 74:18 [73:18]: "An enemy reproaches the Lord, and a senseless people provoke your name"). By the same token, the reference to ὄνομα draws attention to the particular sin of blasphemy, in which case there is the possibility of an allusion (as Chadwick 1959, 170 suggests) to Rom 2:24: "The name of God is blasphemed among the Gentiles because of you" (citing Isa 52:5; cf. Lev 24:16; 1 Tim 6:1; Jas 2:7). The act of reviling God, of course, could be interpreted as a manifestation of blasphemous speech. According to Origen, for instance, the λοίδοροι condemned by Paul in 1 Cor 6:10 are "people who are utter atheists and deny providence" (*Cels.* 8.38). Sextus takes up the problem of blasphemy especially in vv. 82e–85 (cf. v. 367): the evil thoughts informing the blasphemer's speech defile God, evidencing an intention to inflict evil upon God, an intention that is "most impious" (v. 85). Even though it in fact only expresses an "opinion" about God (v. 28), the name of God must not be reviled. The person who does so is as good as dead, that is, as good as a person without faith (v. 7b), a verdict that accords with Clement's description of the blasphemer as νεκρὸς τῇ φύσει (*Quis div.* 23.1; cf. Jude 10–12). In a comparably structured saying preserved in v. 396 (ἄθλιοι δι' οὓς ὁ λόγος ἀκούει κακῶς), somewhat less damning language is applied to those who bring "the word" into disrepute.

Sentence 176

In vv. 33–34, a person's status μετὰ θεόν is a matter of receiving benefits, while here it is a matter of bestowing them. The inspiration for this line may come from Clitarchus, *Sent.* 63 ("A human being who bestows benefactions is like God." Cf. *Sent. Pythag.* 43) and/or Clitarchus, *Sent.* 134 ("After God, honor the person who benefits you as a servant of God." Cf. *Sent. Pythag.* 105; Sext. 319). The idea that certain individuals particularly resemble or serve God in the distribution of benefits, however, is a common one, familiar especially from ancient kingship literature (e.g., Strabo, *Geogr.* 17.2.3; Dio Chrysostom, *Or.* 1.37–46; 3.52; *Let. Aris.* 188, 210, 281: "As God showers blessings upon all, you too in imitation of him are a benefactor to your subjects"). A Pythagorean tractate attributed to Diotogenes, for example, proclaims that "a king whose rule is beneficent ... exhibits the form of God among men" (*Regn.* 2.72.22-23). In the *Sentences*, this place is occupied by the sage, since he receives more from God than anyone else (e.g., vv. 36, 277, 310–311) and is like God more than anyone else (e.g., vv. 18, 50, 82d, 190). Having God as both his benefactor and model, the sage confers manifold benefits on others: he prays for humanity's salvation (v. 372), he teaches the truth about God (vv. 357–358), he shares what he has with the needy (vv. 266–267), and, most important, he provides a model of the godly life. Indeed, the conferral of benefits is one of the chief ways in which he presents God to humanity (v. 307). Cf. Clement, *Strom.* 2.19.102.2: "The real image of God is a human being who does good to others, and in so doing receives a benefit." The sage endeavors to become a benefactor to all humanity (vv. 210a, 260, cf. v. 484), even to his enemies (v. 213), and even in the face of ingratitude (v. 328), believing that benefiting others for God's sake is the only offering fit for God (v. 47). Cf. v. 542: παιδευτικὸς ἀνὴρ οὗτος εὐεργέτης μετὰ θεόν.

Sentence 177
Just as a buyer must offer a deposit (βεβαίωσις) when purchasing a property, to be credible an orator must offer confirmation for his words with a worthy βίος (Aeschines, *Ctes.* 249). The source for this line is Clitarchus, *Sent.* 48: τοὺς λόγους σου ὁ βίος βεβαιούτω. The Sextine version adds παρὰ τοῖς ἀκούουσιν, for which comparison can be made with *Marc.* 8, where Porphyry appears to be drawing on Clitarchus, *Sent.* 48 together with *Sent.* 49 (τῶν δογμάτων σου τὰ ἔργα ἀπόδειξις ἔστω. = Sext. 547): "It is no small thing to remember the divine doctrines by which you were initiated into the right philosophy. Your actions have been wont to prove your steadfast (βεβαίαν) obedience to them. For deeds provide the positive demonstration of each person's beliefs; and whoever has acquired certainty must live (βιοῦν) in such a way that he himself can be a faithful witness

to the things about which he speaks to his listeners (τοῖς ἀκροωμένοις)." While the addition of παρὰ τοῖς ἀκούουσιν in v. 177 conforms with priorities expressed elsewhere in the *Sentences* (e.g., v. 195, where listeners are likened to a "deposit" entrusted to their speaker), the fact that Sextus and Porphyry make reference to listeners independently of Clitarchus suggests that they are utilizing common source material now lost to us, perhaps a different version of the *Clitarchi sententiae* (see part 4 of the introduction). Cf. *Syr. Men.* 2 ("Prior to the words of a man are all his activities"); Musonius Rufus, frag. 32 ("Do not try to enjoin actions that are right on those who know that your actions are wrong"); *Gnom. Democr.* 82; Seneca, *Ep.* 20.1–2. From a Christian context, mention can be made of *Did.* 2.5: "Your word must not be false or meaningless, but confirmed by action." For our author, integrity of word and deed is a standard that informs not only practices of self-scrutiny (vv. 90, 359, 383, cf. v. 123) but how one ought to evaluate others as well (v. 408).

Sentences 178–187

Text

178   ὃ μὴ δεῖ ποιεῖν, μηδ' ὑπονοοῦ^a ποιεῖν.
179   ἃ μὴ θέλεις παθεῖν, μηδὲ^a ποίει.
180   ἃ ποιεῖν αἰσχρόν, καὶ προστάττειν ^aἑτέρῳ αἰσχρόν^a.
181   μέχρι καὶ ^aτοῦ νοῦ^a καθάρευε τῶν^b ἁμαρτημάτων.
182   ἄρχων ἀνθρώπων μέμνησο^a ἄρχεσθαι παρὰ^b θεοῦ.
183   ὁ κρίνων ἄνθρωπον κρίνεται ὑπὸ τοῦ θεοῦ.
184   μείζων ὁ κίνδυνος δικαζομένου δικαστῇ.
185   ἅπασι^a μᾶλλον ἢ λόγῳ βλάπτε ἄνθρωπον^b.
186   ^aδυνατὸν ἀπατῆσαι λόγῳ ἄνθρωπον^a, θεὸν μέντοι ἀδύνατον.
187   οὐ χαλεπὸν ἐπίστασθαι καὶ ἐν λόγῳ νενικῆσθαι.

Translation

178   What should not be done, do not even consider doing.
179   Things that you do not want to experience, do not do.
180   Things that are shameful to do are also shameful to command of another.
181   Cleanse even your mind of sins.

182 In governing human beings remember that you are governed by God.
183 The one who judges a human being is judged by God.
184 The danger is greater in being a judge than in facing a judge.
185 Harm a human being with anything but speech.
186 It is possible to deceive a human being with speech, but to do this to God is not possible.
187 It is no hardship to have knowledge and yet to be conquered in speech.

Textual Notes

178 ὑποπτεύου ποιεῖν μήτε ὑπονόει: Π • 178ᵃ ὑπονόει: co, sy² • 179ᵃ μήτε: Π • 180ᵃ⁻ᵃ ἄλλῳ αἰσχρότερόν ἐστιν: Π • 181ᵃ⁻ᵃ τῷ νῷ: Π; τοῦ λαλεῖν: Υ • 181ᵇ omit Υ • 182ᵃ νόμιζε: Π • 182ᵇ ὑπὸ: Π • 183 omit Υ • 185ᵃ πᾶσι: Υ • 185ᵇ omit Υ, lat • 186ᵃ⁻ᵃ ἀπατῆσαι λόγῳ δυνατὸν ἄνθρωπον: Υ

Commentary

This section of text presents the reader with three short units. The first, vv. 178–181, treats the problem of immoral conduct in broad terms (recall the references to sinners in vv. 172, 174–175). The first three lines of the unit are bound together by the catchword ποιέω, as well as by similar openings: ὅ (v. 178), ἅ (v. 179), and ἅ (v. 180). Next comes a triad of sayings on accountability in judging (vv. 182–184), followed by a triad of sayings on speech (vv. 185–187), the latter bound by the catchword λόγῳ.

Sentence 178

This line reproduces *Sent. Pythag.* 6 exactly, except for changing the initial ἅ to ὅ, perhaps under the influence of the saying in v. 389a: ὃ μὴ δεῖ ποιεῖν, μηδενὶ τρόπῳ ποίει. One should refrain not only from doing "what is wrong to do" but from contemplating it as well, the thought here anticipating that of v. 181 (cf. vv. 327, 601). For similar sayings, see Tob 4:5 ("Do not be willing to sin.... do not follow the ways of wrongdoing"); *Let. Aris.* 133; Menander, *Mon.* 37–38; *Gnom. Democr.* 62: "It is good, not to do no wrong, but not even to wish to." According to *T. Gad* 5.5, the just man "is completely unwillingly to wrong anyone, even in his thoughts." Motivation for Sextus's injunction is provided in v. 233: a person will be deemed a sinner even if he only thinks about sinning (cf. v. 596). For a positive form of the command here, as well as an assertion of the mind-body connection, see v. 56: "Think about noble things, so that you may also do noble things."

The version of the saying in v. 178 preserved in *Sent. Pythag.* 6 is cited as a maxim of Pythagoras by Stobaeus (*Anth.* 3.1.32) and Arsenius (*Apophth.* 2.53a), and as an anonymous gnome by Palladius (*Dial. vit. Joan. Chrys.* 94) and Isidorus (*Ep.* 1540).

Sentence 179

For Sextus's positive version of the golden rule, see on v. 89 (cf. v. 210b). Illustrations of the negative version abound, for instance, Herodotus, *Hist.* 3.142; Isocrates, *Nic.* 61; Septem Sapientes, *Apophth.* 5.4; *Instr. Ankh.* 12.6; 15.23; P.Ins. 30.10; Tob 4:15; *Syr. Men.* 250–251; Ps.-Clement, *Rec.* 5.23; *b. Sabb.* 31a (Hillel). Philo's formulation of the rule in *Hypoth.* 7.6 is particularly close to the one found here: "What someone would hate to experience he must not do to another" (ἅ τις παθεῖν ἐχθαίρει, μὴ ποιεῖν αὐτόν). Cf. also Acts 15:20 v.l.; 15:29 v.l. (both also with θέλω).

Sayings elsewhere in the collection postulate a certain innate logic of reciprocity governing the commission of misdeeds. In mistreating others one in fact mistreats oneself (v. 211); those who intend evil for others are the first to experience evil themselves (v. 327, also with πάσχω). In Ps.-Clement, *Rec.* 8.56, this logic is enumerated with reference to the second table of the Decalogue: "For almost the whole rule of our actions is summed up in this, that what we are unwilling to suffer we should not do to others. For as you would not be killed, you must beware of killing another; and as you would not have your own marriage violated, you must not defile another's bed; you would not be stolen from, neither must you steal; and every matter of humanity's actions is comprehended within this rule."

Sentence 180

Just as the readers must not allow anyone to persuade them to act immorally (v. 91a, cf. v. 306), they must not impose immoral acts on others. Cf. v. 549: "It is shameful to enjoin things you do not do yourself." In a discussion of involuntary actions, Aristotle gives the example of a tyrant who, having a man's parents and children in his power, "orders him to do something shameful" (προστάττοι αἰσχρόν τι πρᾶξαι). If the man complies, it is, in the Stagirite's view, open to question whether he should be held responsible for his actions or not. Either way, it would be correct to say that anyone forcing such a moral dilemma on another person would be acting like a tyrant (*Eth. nic.* 3.1.4; cf. vv. 363b–364, 387). Given that at least some of Sextus's readers are assumed to have families (see vv. 230a–239, 254–257), the scenarios sketched by Musonius Rufus in his tract, "Must One Obey One's Parents in all Circumstances?" (frag. 16), are perhaps more apropos: for example, the scenario of the father who orders his son to steal, or to engage in prostitution. He concludes, "Therefore whether one's father or the magistrate or even the tyrant orders something wrong or unjust or shameful, and one does not carry out the order, he is in no way disobeying" (frag. 16.102.14–16). This is because in disobeying he neither does anything wrong nor fails to do something right, and it was wrong of the father to make the command in the first place. As Dio Chrysostom points out, certainly a god would never command someone to commit a heinous or disgraceful act (*Or.* 10.27; cf. Sir 15:20).

Sentence 181

Since even sinful thoughts are defiling (v. 82e) and make one a sinner (v. 233, cf. v. 596), it is not sufficient to purify the body of moral pollution (v. 346, cf. vv. 23, 356). The heart (v. 46b) and the mind must be purified as well. Only a mind thus purged can serve as the temple and abode of God (vv. 46a, 61, 144). This line has a close parallel in Porphyry, *Marc.* 9: μέχρι τοῦ νοῦ καθαρεύειν δεῖ τῶν παθῶν τε καὶ τῶν διὰ τὸ πάθος ἁμαρτημάτων ("It is necessary to cleanse even the mind of both the passions and the sins that result from passion"). In *Mos.* 2.24, Philo similarly describes a cleansed intellect as one "untroubled by any bodily passion" (cf. *Mut.* 247; *Virt.* 189). In its Sextine context, the gnome both supports the thought of v. 178 (see above) and essentially restates v. 57b: ἔστω σου ἡ διάνοια καθαρὰ κακοῦ παντός ("Let your intellect be pure of every evil"). The regimen that Pythagoras prescribed for the training of souls could be likened to a κάθαρσις τῆς διανοίας (Iamblichus, *Vit. Pythag.* 16.68–70). Compare also Iamblichus, *Protr.* 2.10.1–3: "We worship God correctly when we keep the mind in us pure from all evil as from a defilement." The concept of an intellect cleansed of sins is found frequently in the writings of Ephraem Syrus, for example, *Paen.* 60; *Apol. frat. quen.* 90; *Inst. mon.* 309.

Sentences 182–184

The most likely source for the first line in this cluster is *Sent. Pythag.* 13c: βασιλεύων γάρ τις ἀνθρώπων καλῶς, οὗτος ὑπὸ θεοῦ βασιλεύεται. Sextus eschews its royal overtones (cf. *Sent. Pythag.* 13a–b: βασιλέα φρόνησις οὐ διάδημα ποιεῖ. νοῦς γάρ ἐστιν ὁ ἄρχων) in favor of more general language. For the insertion of μέμνησο, cf. vv. 59, 82c, 221–222, and 364. It was a commonplace of ancient ethics that those incapable of making correct decisions on their own need someone to "govern" them (e.g., Ps.-Crates, *Ep.* 34.4; Philo, *Prob.* 29–31). For his part, the Sextine sage is governed by God in the sense that he constantly strives to know, honor, and emulate God (vv. 41–44, 288), who, being "inseparable" from what he governs, watches over and cares for the sage, rejoicing in his accomplishments (vv. 422–424). In turn, the sage governs those in need of moral guidance by offering instruction (vv. 358, 410), correction (vv. 24, 103), and a model of the godly life (vv. 190, 307, 359). He has a particular responsibility to care for and protect fellow members of the faith who have a tendency to act out of ignorance (v. 331, cf. vv. 174, 285). He will also have certain responsibilities to his family members, if any (vv. 230a–b), since it is expected that a husband will "govern" his wife (v. 236). Whatever the situation, this verse suggests that God's governance of the sage furnishes the basis and standard for the sage's governance of other people. Clement's comments on the true gnostic evidence similar priorities: "In imitation of the divine plan," he "does good to such as are willing, as far as he can. And if ever placed in authority (ἀρχή), like Moses, he will rule for the salvation of the governed; and he will tame wildness and faithlessness, by recording honor for the best, and punishment for the wicked" (*Strom.* 7.3.16.3–4).

As this citation indicates, providing governance entails making judgments. In this respect the symmetry of v. 182 (ἄρχων ἀνθρώπων ... ἄρχεσθαι ... θεοῦ) and v. 183 (κρίνων ἄνθρωπον κρίνεται ... θεοῦ) is noteworthy: the same hierarchy that determines how the sage will govern others determines also how the sage will judge others. The specific manner in which this criterion shapes the sage's deportment as judge is suggested by v. 63: "By releasing the unjust person from his unjust act you would punish him in accord with God." The sage, then, is generally cautious about meting out judgment, not only because this accords with God's example, or because even the just punishment of an offender is deplorable (v. 261), but also out of an awareness than when doing so he runs the risk of exposing himself to special scrutiny. The gnomic paradox of "the judged judge" informs a wide range of ancient sayings, for example, Ps.-Phoc. 11 ("If you judge evilly, God will afterwards judge you"); Matt 7:2 ("With the judgment you make you will be judged"); Epictetus, *Gnom.* 55 ("It is shameful for the judge to be judged by others"); cf. Ezek 7:27; Matt 7:1; Luke 6:37; Rom 2:1; Jas 2:13; 4:12; *1 Clem.* 13.2; Pol. *Phil.* 2.3; Justin Martyr, *Dial.* 47.5; *Teach. Silv.* 87; Publilius Syrus, *Sent.* 673 (Sext. 572 recommends forestalling divine scrutiny by practicing self-scrutiny: κρῖνε σεαυτὸν ὡς μηδὲν ἁμαρτεῖν καὶ οὐ μὴ κριθῇς). Sextus encourages his readers to have a robust appreciation for the reality of divine judgment in their lives (vv. 14, 22, 39, 347). They must therefore keep God before their eyes as a witness to everything that they do (vv. 224, 303). For the danger (κίνδυνος) that attends unjust judgments, cf. Philostratus, *Vit. Apoll.* 2.39.1. Verse 352 presents speaking about God as another potentially "dangerous" situation.

Verse 184 is cited in the ninth chapter of the *Regula monachorum* of Saint Columban, in the same form as Rufinus's translation: *maius est periculum iudicantis quam eius qui iudicatur.*

Sentence 185

Both qualitatively and quantitatively, the capacity of speech to wreak havoc exceeds even that of physical weapons: "The blow of a whip raises a welt, but a blow of the tongue crushes the bones. Many have fallen by the edge of the sword, but not as many as have fallen because of the tongue" (Sir 28:17–18). See further Philo, *Somn.* 2.239–240 and Menander, *Mon.* 546: "A sword can wound a body, speech the mind." Since his is the life of the soul, the sage is impervious to harm from fellow human beings (vv. 302, 318) or from anything censorious they might have to say about him (v. 299). In his own conduct, however, he must be careful not to harm others, particularly in his speech, something that is apt to happen when words are uttered "without purpose" (v. 152). By setting this prohibition adjacent to a unit on accountability in judging (vv. 182–184), our author may be suggesting that there is a particular temptation to utilize hurtful language when one assumes the role of judge. Elsewhere Sextus advises that care be observed when talking about God, since the souls of the speaker's listeners have been entrusted to him (v. 195) and, as Plutarch points out, it is often the case that listeners will unintentionally consent to false and harmful teachings when the speaker is someone they trust (*Rect. rat. aud.* 41b). The possibility of inflicting harm with words is increased, of course, with public speaking (e.g., Isocrates, *Antid.* 51, 75), which represents yet another area in which the readers are urged to proceed with caution (e.g., vv. 164a, 360).

Sentence 186

Insofar as deceitful speech can be understood as a type of harmful speech (e.g., Ps.-Demosthenes, *Philip.* 4.76), this line forms a natural tandem with v. 185. Note the catchwords λόγῳ ... ἄνθρωπον (v. 185) and λόγῳ ἄνθρωπον (v. 186). Cf. Prov 26:18-19: "Like a maniac who shoots deadly firebrands and arrows, so is one who deceives a neighbor." The source for the saying here is Clitarchus, *Sent*. 53: ἄνθρωπον μὲν ἀπατῆσαι δυνατὸν λόγῳ, θεὸν δὲ ἀδύνατον. Sextus rearranges the word order of the first part of the saying (most notably moving ἄνθρωπον from the first to the final position) and drops the μέν ... δέ ... construction in favor of μέντοι. With its warning against ἀπάτη, the dictum picks up on a major theme of the extended instruction on speech in vv. 149–165g (see especially on vv. 165a–b, f). At the same time, v. 186 departs from the material in that unit by incorporating a divine warrant, and so accords more with the thrust of vv. 182–184, where God is imaged as the ideal judge. In so doing, the saying may provide a relevant perspective from which to interpret the warning issued in v. 393: the one who deceives others only deceives himself if he thinks that the deception will go unnoticed by God. God cannot be deceived by human beings because nothing a human being thinks escapes God's attention (v. 57a). Sextus would agree with Philo, then, that "it surely would be the height of folly to think that the Existent could be deceived, and that his most certain purpose could be upset by the devices of human beings" (*Conf*. 65; cf. Theognis, *El*. 197–208).

Sentence 187

Perhaps the best-known example of a sage who "had knowledge" and yet was defeated in speech is Socrates, who at his trial deemed it more important to preserve his integrity and tell the truth about himself and his vocation than to be acquitted. To the jury that has just sentenced him, he proclaims: "I was convicted because I lacked not words but boldness and shamelessness and a willingness to say to you what you would have most gladly have heard from me, lamentations and tears and my saying and doing many things that I say are unworthy of me but that you are accustomed to hear from others" (Plato, *Apol*. 38d–e). If v. 187 is read together with v. 186 (note the catchword λόγῳ), then the couplet can be interpreted as reinforcing the claims made in vv. 165a–b, which utilize similar language: "It is better to be defeated while speaking the truth than to overcome with deceit (μετὰ ἀπάτης). The one who conquers (ὁ νικῶν) with deceit (τῷ ἀπατᾶν) is conquered (νικᾶται) in character." The instruction here departs from that of the previous unit by presenting deceitful speech as a matter not of ἦθος but of θεός. To lose an argument because one did not resort to deception is no "hardship" because God is the ultimate arbiter of such affairs and God requires the truth, especially when God himself is the subject of discussion (vv. 355, 357, 410, 441, cf. vv. 158–159, 167–168). The sage strives to conquer others not in speech but in good judgment (v. 332). Cf. *Gnom. Vat.* 74: "In a philosophical discussion he who is worsted gains more in proportion as he learns more."

Sentences 188–203

Text

188 κακοδοξίας αἰτιώτατον ἥ[a] ἐν πίστει φιλοδοξία.
189 τίμα τὸ πιστὸς εἶναι διὰ τοῦ εἶναι.
190 σέβου σοφὸν ἄνδρα ὡς εἰκόνα θεοῦ ζῶσαν.
191 σοφὸς ἀνὴρ καὶ γυμνὸς ὤν[a] δοκείτω σοι σοφὸς εἶναι[b].
192 διὰ τὸ πολλὰ ἔχειν χρήματα [a]<μὴ> τιμήσῃς[a] μηδένα.
193 χαλεπόν ἐστιν πλουτοῦντα σωθῆναι.
194 ψέγειν ἄνδρα σοφὸν καὶ θεὸν ἴσον ἁμάρτημα.
195 λόγον χειρίζων περὶ[a] θεοῦ παραθήκην σοι[b] δεδόσθαι νόμιζε τὰς ψυχὰς τῶν ἀκουόντων[c].
196 οὐκ ἔστιν βιῶναι[a] καλῶς μὴ πεπιστευκότα γνησίως.
197 μόνον τὸ καλὸν ἀγαθὸν ἡγοῦ καὶ καλὸν μόνον[a] τὸ πρέπον θεῷ.
198 ποίει μεγάλα [a]μὴ μεγάλα ὑπισχνούμενος[a].
199 οὐ γενήσῃ[a] σοφὸς οἰόμενος εἶναι[b] πρὸ τοῦ εἶναι.
200 μεγάλη περίστασις πιστὸν ἄνδρα δείκνυσι.
201 τέλος ἡγοῦ βίου τὸ ζῆν κατὰ θεόν.
202 μηδὲν ἡγοῦ κακόν, ὃ μή ἐστιν αἰσχρόν.
203 κακοῦ[a] πέρας ὕβρις, ὕβρεως δὲ ὄλεθρος.

Translation

188 In faith, a love of reputation is the foremost cause of a bad reputation.
189 Honor being faithful by being faithful.
190 Revere a wise man as a living image of God.
191 Let a wise man seem to you wise even when he is naked.
192 Do not honor anyone because he has many possessions.
193 It is difficult for a rich person to be saved.
194 It is just as much a sin to censure a wise man as it is to censure God.

195 When making a statement about God, consider the souls of your listeners to be a deposit that has been given to you.
196 It is not possible to live nobly without truly having faith.
197 Deem only what is noble to be good and only what befits God to be noble.
198 Do great things without promising great things.
199ª You will not become wise thinking that you are wise before you are.
200 An extreme situation reveals a faithful man.
201 Deem the purpose of life to live in accord with God.
202 Do not deem that which is not shameful to be evil.
203 The result of evil is insolence, and the result of insolence is ruin.

Textual Notes
188ª omit Π, lat • 191ª omit Υ • 191ᵇ omit Π, lat • 192ᵃ⁻ᵃ τιμήσεις: Π, Υ • 195ᵃ⁻ᵃ παρὰ: Υ • 195ᵇ omit Υ • 195ᶜ ἀκουόντων περὶ θεοῦ: Π • 196ª σοι βιῶσαι: Π • 197ª omit Υ • 198ᵃ⁻ᵃ joined to the beginning of v. 199: Π • 199ª γενήσῃ: Π • 199ᵇ omit Υ • 202–203 joined as a single maxim: Π • 203ª κόρου: sy²

Commentary

Taken as a whole, the lines in this block demonstrate little thematic coherence. It is possible to construe vv. 190–194 as a unit contrasting the humble but godlike σοφὸς ἀνήρ (vv. 190–191, 194), who is deserving of honor, with the rich man, who is not (vv. 192–193). Surrounding this are couplets of sayings on faith (vv. 188–189), on living nobly (vv. 196–197), and on humility (vv. 198–199), as well as some miscellaneous sayings (vv. 195, 200–203).

Sentences 188–189

Vaingloriousness, or love of reputation (φιλοδοξία), was seen as a manifestation of pride and hubris (e.g., Esth 4:17d) and is often included in vice lists, for example, 4 Macc 1:26: "arrogance, love of money, love of reputation, love of contentiousness, faithlessness, malice" (cf. Philo, *Spec.* 1.281; *Prob.* 21; Plutarch, *Garr.* 502e; Justin Martyr, *Dial.* 82.4). Clement's comments in *Strom.* 7.11.67.2 indicate the actual sort of "reputation" Christians afflicted by φιλοδοξία might expect to achieve: "For those that abide (by the confession of their calling) for the love of reputation, or from fear of some severer punishment, or with a view to any joys or pleasures after death, these are mere children in the faith, blessed indeed, but not having attained to adulthood, like the gnostic, in their love of God." According to Origen, in his teaching Jesus attacked vaingloriousness as though it were a fatal disease (*Orat.* 19.2; cf. Diogenes Laertius, *Vit. phil.* 7.115), while Porphyry reports that Pythagoras "urged everyone to avoid the love of honor and the love of reputation, which particularly occasions envy, and to shun public discussions" (*Vit. Pythag.* 32; for avoiding actions that incite envy, see on v. 51). Theophrastus puts the matter even more succinctly: "Nothing is so unprofitable as the love of reputation" (Diogenes Laertius, *Vit. phil.* 5.41); cf. *m. Avot* 1:13: "A name made great is a name destroyed." As Plutarch notes, the vice often manifests itself in public contexts (*Quaest. conv.* 622b), in which case the warning in v. 188 would be relevant to counsel Sextus offers elsewhere regarding the dangers of public speaking (vv. 164a, 360) and public acclaim (v. 241). Cognizant of fame's power to corrupt (v. 351), the sage refrains from boasting about himself (vv. 284, 389b, 432–433) or trying to please the crowds (v. 112). His reputation with the people, then, is rather poor (vv. 53, 145, 214), though with God it is great (vv. 51, 308, 422).

Verse 189 is connected to v. 188 by catchword (πίστει/πιστός): faith is a matter of being faithful, not of having a reputation for being faithful. That reality ought to trump appearance was established as a principle for the readers' moral comportment by a previous couplet in the collection: "Practice not seeming but being just, for seeming always usurps being. Honor justice for its own sake" (vv. 64–65). As Chadwick (1959, 156) notes, v. 189 in fact appears to be a Christian adaptation of v. 65, which exhibits a comparable structure: τίμα τὸ δίκαιον δι' αὐτό (cf. Evagrius Ponticus, *Cap. paraen.* 13: "In honoring the law you shall live according to the law"). For the thought, see also v. 325: "No pretense escapes notice for very long, especially in faith." To honor something means to be ruled by it (vv. 41–42) and to conform to it (v. 381). The readers, then, are to honor not what the world honors (v. 192), but only God (vv. 244, 319, 355, 427, 439) and what God honors (v. 135). In the realm of faith, this means doing nothing unworthy of God (v. 5), that is, nothing sinful (v. 247). For the concept of "honoring" faithfulness, cf. Plutarch, *Frat. amor.* 479d; Clement, *Quis div.* 30; Cassius Dio, *Hist. rom.* 38.44.4.

Sentence 190

Among those things that the readers are called upon to honor is the sage (vv. 219, 244, 319, cf. v. 226). This is only appropriate, given his status as a servant of God (v. 319), a benefactor second only to God (v. 176), and the greatest of all God's works (v. 308, cf. v. 403), possessed of anything that God possesses (vv. 310–311). Moreover, since he participates with God in the life of the mind (vv. 143–144, cf. vv. 415b–418, 421), his intellect can be said to "mirror" God (v. 450), and through words and actions guided by this intellect he actually exhibits God to humanity (v. 307). He is therefore deserving of the same sort of "reverence" as God (cf. vv. 369–370) or a holy temple of God (v. 46a, cf. v. 35). This is the only place in the *Sentences* where the sage (or anyone else) is described as the "image" of God. The saying does not derive directly from Gen 1:26–27, as might be expected of a Christian author, but from Clitarchus, *Sent.* 9: δίκαιος ἀνὴρ εἰκὼν θεοῦ. Sextus alters the first word to σοφόν, perhaps to create better continuity with vv. 191 and 194, and inserts σέβου, perhaps to create better continuity with v. 189. For the addition of ζῶσαν, cf. v. 7a. A statement similar to Clitarchus's is attributed to Diogenes the Cynic: "Good men he called images of the gods" (Diogenes Laertius, *Vit. phil.* 6.51). A statement similar to Sextus's can be found in Porphyry, *Marc.* 11, which also takes the sage as its subject: "The person by whom the divine must be honored because of wisdom is reasonably the sage alone, and a shrine must be adorned for him because of wisdom in his heart, a shrine with a living statue, the intellect, for God imparts his image (ἐνεικονισαμένου) to the one who honors him."

It was a convention of Hellenistic ruler ideology to assert that the king ought to be honored as an image of God (e.g., Plutarch, *Princ. iner.* 780e–f; *Them.* 27.1–3; cf. Menander, *Mon.* 264: εἰκὼν δὲ βασιλεύς ἐστιν ἔμψυχος θεοῦ). There are a number of Pythagorean texts that contribute to the *topos* (e.g., Ps.-Ecphantus, *De regno*), though they also broaden its application to include the virtuous (e.g., Hierocles, *In aur. carm.* 21.5) or even humankind in general (Diodorus Aspendius, frag. 1). Thinkers influenced by other philosophical schools reflect this trend as well. According to Cicero, for example, the person who has wisdom recognizes "that he has a divine element within him, and will think of his own inner nature as a kind of consecrated image of God; and so he will always act and think in a way worthy of so great a gift of the gods" (*Leg.* 1.59; cf. Lucian, *Pro imag.* 28; Porphyry, *Christ.* frag. 76; Menander, *Mon.* frag. 2.3: γέροντα τίμα τοῦ θεοῦ τὴν εἰκόνα). The Christian appropriation of the motif is evidenced also by Clement, *Strom.* 7.3.16.5 ("The soul of a just man is an image divine"); 7.5.29.4; 7.11.64.6: "The gnostic soul is an earthly image of the divine power, adorned with perfect virtue, built up by the combined action of nature, discipline, and reason."

Sentences 191-192

When asked to explain the difference between a person who is wise and a person who is not, Aristippus replied, "Strip them both and send them among strangers and you will know" (Diogenes Laertius, *Vit. phil.* 2.73). Sextus agrees that wisdom is properly ascertained not from externals (v. 192), which can be a source of distraction (v. 193), but from conduct. Seneca makes the same point with illustrations from daily life: "When you buy a horse, you order its blanket to be removed; you pull off the garments from slaves that are up for sale, so that no bodily flaws may escape your notice. When you judge a man, do you judge him when he is wrapped in a disguise? ... Do you see yonder Scythian or Sarmatian king, his head adorned with the badge of his office? If you wish to see what he amounts to, and know his full worth, take off his diadem; much evil lurks beneath it." He continues by applying these lessons to the readers themselves: "But why do I speak of others? If you wish to set a value on yourself, put away your money, your estates, your honors, and look into your own soul" (*Ep.* 80.9–10). For Sextus, such externals are not only unnecessary to the life of virtue (cf. v. 554, also with γυμνός), they actually make it difficult to be saved (v. 193), since they impede the task of knowing and emulating God. Instead, the sage purges himself of material possessions as much as possible, so that he can entreat God in a state of purity (v. 81, cf. vv. 18, 78, 264a, etc.). In this, comparison can be made with *Sent. Pythag.* 17 (cf. Porphyry, *Marc.* 33), which may have prompted the reference here: "Sent away naked, the sage in his nakedness will call on the one who sent him, for God listens only to the one not encumbered with extraneous burdens." The sage, then, refuses to honor (cf. v. 189) others on account of their wealth, since material possessions are something that he not only disregards but actually scorns (v. 127), his only "wealth" being self-control (v. 294). Verse 192 can be compared with a saying attributed to the sage Bias: "If a man is unworthy, do not praise him because of his wealth" (Diogenes Laertius, *Vit. phil.* 1.88). As Clement argues, those who praise the rich should be condemned as both impious and insidious: impious because they ought to be praising God instead, and insidious because they encourage the rich to become even more avaricious (*Quis div.* 1.1–3). For Philo's concept of "naked" philosophy (i.e., a way of life unencumbered by bodily distractions), see *Leg.* 2.54–59; *Prob.* 43. This most likely entails an allusion to the Gymnosophists of India, for which see his comments in *Somn.* 2.56; *Abr.* 182; *Prob.* 74, 93; and, further, Strabo, *Geogr.* 16.2.39; Plutarch, *Alex.* 64; Lucian, *Fug.* 7; Clement, *Strom.* 1.15.71.4; 3.7.60.4; 4.4.17.3; 6.4.38.2;

Diogenes Laertius, *Vit. phil.* 1.1, 6, 9; 9.35, 61; Porphyry, *Abst.* 4.17. The μή printed by Chadwick (1959, 34) for v. 192 is missing from both Greek manuscripts but is supported by the Latin and Syriac versions.

Sentence 193

Having many possessions is not only irrelevant in the Sextine scheme of honor: it may represent an impediment to being saved (cf. vv. 373–374). This line is based on Matt 19:23: "It will be hard for a rich person (πλούσιος δυσκόλως) to enter the kingdom of heaven." The version of the saying preserved in Mark 10:23 and Luke 18:24, meanwhile, with οἱ τὰ χρήματα ἔχοντες in lieu of πλούσιος, appears to have influenced the wording of v. 192 (ἔχειν χρήματα).

According to Clement, the reason why salvation seems to be more difficult for Christians with wealth than for those without it is twofold: some, upon hearing comments like the one Jesus makes in Matt 19:24, despair of themselves and give up hope of achieving eternal life, while others, though they understand the saying correctly, fail to take the demands of discipleship seriously (*Quis div.* 2.1–4). In *Paed.* 3.7.37.2–3, he adds that a rich man only rarely inherits the kingdom because his fondness for worldly goods disorientates his sense of moral direction, ironically "robbing" him of all shame when in the presence of dishonorable things, while in *Strom.* 5.5.28.3, he proposes that the Pythagorean *akousma*, "Don't sail on land," is congruent with the thought behind Matt 19:23 insofar as it shows that "taxes and similar contracts, being troublesome and fluctuating, ought to be declined." Hermas, meanwhile, suggests that it is difficult for the rich to enter the kingdom because it is difficult for them to associate with God's servants, "for they are afraid that they may be asked for something by them" (*Sim.* 9.20.2). Origen, finally, contends that the rich person of the biblical text can refer either to those who are preoccupied with wealth or to those who are "rich in false opinions" (*Cels.* 7.23; cf. *Comm. Matt.* 15.20). Cf. Sir 31:5: "One who loves gold will not be justified; one who pursues money will be led astray by it."

Sentence 194

Cf. Evagrius Ponticus, *Cap. paraen.* 23: ψέγειν τὸν ἀνεπίληπτον εἰς θεὸν ἁμαρτία. Sextus assumes that people should and will be censured for their sins (v. 298; cf. Aristotle, *Eth. eud.* 3.2.14; Clement, *Paed.* 1.8.74.2). He also assumes that since God's nature is inimical to everything associated with sin (vv. 30, 114, 314), it would be sinful to censure God (cf. vv. 29, 440), or even to think evil of God (v. 82e). As the living image of God (see on v. 190) and someone who has proven himself to be trustworthy (v. 258), the sage is deserving of honor (vv. 219, 226, 244, 319), the sort of honor appropriate to an individual whose "holy and sinless" self (v. 60, cf. vv. 8, 46b) reflects the "pure and sinless" authority that God has bestowed on him (v. 36). Those who fail to show proper gratitude for the sage, then, are actually showing ingratitude to God (v. 229). Instead, the readers have a responsibility not only to refrain from censuring the sage, as we learn here, but to endure the correction he offers them with thanks, since this is a manifestation of his innate goodness (vv. 245–246). According to v. 259, they have an additional responsibility to disregard any slander aimed at the sage, a likely problem, given that to most people he appears to be useless (v. 214). In Ps.-Plato, *Min.* 318e–319a, Socrates cautions his interlocutor against perpetrating the same sort of impiety as "the mass of people" are wont to commit. In fact, "than this there cannot be anything more impious"—that is, doing something "mistaken in word and deed with regard to the gods, and in second place, with regard to divine humans.... For god vents his anger when anyone censures (ψέγῃ) someone similar to himself."

Sentence 195

While Paul speaks of converts being "entrusted" to the teaching that they have received (Rom 6:17), Sextus speaks of them being entrusted to the one who teaches them. This line can be interpreted as a counterpart to the one that precedes it: just as the reader should not say anything that might be detrimental about his superiors, he should not say anything that might be detrimental to those dependent on him. Sextus is familiar with the power of words both to harm (vv. 152, 185) and to instruct (v. 103), words that attempt to instruct others about God being especially puissant (v. 357). Indeed, coming to a correct understanding about God is so critical for salvation that whenever someone speaks about God, the souls that his listeners have received as a deposit from God (v. 21) are committed to his care. As Plutarch explains in *Rect. rat. aud.* 41b, the stakes in a speech-act are particularly high when the listeners have feelings of goodwill and confidence towards the speaker, since under such conditions it is possible that they will unwittingly accept into their minds "a great many false and vicious doctrines." For Sextus, the corrupting effects accompanying improper theological discourse can be so insidious (vv. 85, 367–368) that it is actually better to squander a soul than a word about God (v. 362). It is therefore imperative in any communication about God that the moral worthiness of the speaker (vv. 173, 177, 358–359, 408, 410) and the listeners (vv. 350–351, 354, 360, 365, 401, 451) be scrutinized, not to mention the reverence and truthfulness of what is being spoken (vv. 84, 353, 355, 410), all with an awareness that "even to speak the truth about God involves no small risk" (v. 352), since those who do so are judged by God (v. 22). In most situations, a concern for piety will dictate that it is better to listen than to speak (vv. 171a–b, 366, cf. vv. 153–154). For the unusual locution χειρίζω + λόγος, cf. Clement, *Strom.* 5.1.5.3.

Sentence 196–197

These lines create a couplet linked verbally by the catchword καλός. It is not possible, according to the first saying, to live nobly without faith, which is the same as claiming that it is not possible to live nobly without God (v. 215), since faith leads a soul to God (v. 402). Faith, then, is the only possible basis of a life worth living, since the purpose of life is to live according to God (v. 201), and living according to God means living a life that is noble (v. 399), avoiding sin as much as possible (v. 247; cf. Origen, *Princ.* 3.1.1).

The second saying is an expanded version of v. 131: μόνον ἀγαθὸν ἡγοῦ τὸ πρέπον θεῷ. That "only the noble is good" was a tenet popularized by the Stoics; besides *SVF* 3:29–36, see Clement, *Paed.* 2.12.121.3; *Strom.* 3.5.43.2; 5.14.96.5; 5.14.97.6. Sextus amends the principle by defining the noble as consisting only of that which "befits" God, in other words, only of that which is like God (see on v. 131). Those who search out the causes of noble things (v. 100) will discover that God is not only the source but also the guide and confirmer of both noble deeds and noble persons (vv. 104, 304, 395, cf. v. 166). The readers should therefore give God credit for whatever they do nobly (vv. 113, 390). It is only such actions that ought to be considered "good," that is, appropriate as the object of one's moral efforts and aspirations (cf. vv. 79, 246, 277, 316).

Sentence 198

Those who are sensible guard against making inflated promises, aware that, as Aesop puts it, "Many people promise great things (μεγάλα ἐπαγγέλλονται) without even being able to do small things" (*Fab.* 56.3). For the theme, see also Theognis, *El.* 159–160, 1031–1032 ("Do not add to your grief and shame by boasting of deeds that cannot be done"); Menander, *Mon.* 175; Ps.-Cato, *Dist.* 1.13, 25; Cassius Dio, *Hist. rom.* 4.17.4; *Act. Thom.* 123; Ign. *Eph.* 14.2: "Those who profess to be Christ's will be recognized by their actions. For the work is a matter not of what one promises now, but of persevering to the end in the power of faith." The source for this line is *Sent. Pythag.* 86 (πρᾶττε μεγάλα, μὴ ὑπισχνούμενος μεγάλα), which is cited as a saying of Pythagoras in Stobaeus, *Anth.* 3.1.37. Sextus alters the word order slightly and substitutes ποίει for πρᾶττε. In the current context, "great things" would refer in the first instance to that which befits God, that which is good and noble (v. 197). The sage observes caution and humility in the claims that he makes (vv. 284, 432, cf. vv. 64, 171a, 325), especially about himself (see vv. 389b and 433, both also with ὑπισχνέομαι, cf. v. 470), preferring instead to give God the credit for any good that he does (v. 390).

Sentence 199

Among the type of person inclined to promising "great" things would be a person who holds an inflated opinion of himself. Circumspection is counseled, then, not only in one's habits of making promises but also in one's habits of self-perception. Those wary of deceit (vv. 165a-b, f, 169, 186, 393) must also be wary of self-deceit, especially when it comes to wisdom. Indeed, according to Sextus, it is acceptable to claim "anything" except that one is wise (v. 389b). The sage is reluctant to make boasts (vv. 284, 432), including boasts about his own status in the scheme of election (v. 433). Instead, like any believer he remains anxious about his soul until he actually attains to God (v. 434), cognizant of the fact that the clearest path to knowledge is the awareness that one does not possess it (v. 333). What he seeks is not the appearance of wisdom or a reputation for wisdom, but the reality (cf. vv. 53, 64, 145, 214).

In the Greco-Roman world, not "to think oneself wise when one is not" was a principle associated chiefly with the life and teaching of Socrates (Plato, *Apol.* 29a). His characteristic approach was to examine a man who "appeared wise to many people and especially to himself," and to try to show him that "he thought himself wise (οἴοιτο ... εἶναι σοφός), but that he was not" (*Apol.* 21c). At the conclusion of such a dialogue, Socrates would reflect to himself, "he thinks he knows something when he does not, whereas when I do not know, neither do I think I know; so I am likely to be wiser than he is to this small extent" (*Apol.* 21d, cf. 22c, 23a-b, 33c; *Phaed.* 90b-c; *Theaet.* 173a-b; *Soph.* 230a; *Hipp. min.* 369d-e; *Epin.* 979d). For subsequent developments of the theme, see Aristotle, *Soph. elench.* 165a; Maximus of Tyre, *Dial.* 25.1; Porphyry, *Abst.* 2.40; Plotinus, *Enn.* 2.9.18; and in Christian literature: Justin Martyr, *Dial.* 2.6; Theophilus,

Autol. 2.35; Clement, *Protr.* 6.67. Warnings against self-conceit in wisdom are conveyed in various gnomic texts as well, for example, Prov 3:7; 26:12 ("Do you see persons wise in their own eyes? There is more hope for fools than for them"); 28:11; Qoh 7:16; Ps.-Phoc. 53; *Teach. Silv.* 91; Menander, *Mon.* 1, 246, 336, 350, 606; Publilius Syrus, *Sent.* 451. Such warnings also figure prominently in some of Paul's writings, for example, Rom 11:25; 12:16; 1 Cor 3:18; 8:2; cf. Clement, *Strom.* 1.11.54.1–4; Origen, *Cels.* 7.66; *Frag. cat. 1 Cor.* 16.

Sentence 200

When does the sage know that he is truly wise? Verse 200 provides one possible answer: when he shows himself to be faithful in the midst of "extreme" circumstances. Compare Epictetus, *Diatr.* 1.24.1: αἱ περιστάσεις εἰσὶν αἱ τοὺς ἄνδρας δεικνύουσαι (and see further *Diatr.* 1.6.37; 1.29.33–34; 3.22.59). A person's worth is tested not in words but in works (vv. 177, 408, 425), and one must endure "everything" in order to live according to God (v. 216, cf. v. 201). The one who is faithful in a test of faith is, according to our author, "a god in a living human body" (v. 7a).

It is probably safe to assume that for Sextus what makes an extreme situation something that demonstrates πίστις in particular is that it occurs when one is tempted to sin, since a truly faithful person will avoid sin altogether (vv. 8, 234, 247). Presumably this includes especially sins against other people, since the greatest impiety that one can commit is the mistreatment of a fellow human being (v. 96), and a faithful person will not harm anyone (v. 212). In the biblical ambit, certain individuals are venerated as heroes in regard to testing, especially Abraham (1 Macc 2:52; Sir 44:20; Heb 11:17; Jas 2:21; etc.), though it is also assumed that eventually every believer will be called upon to endure a faith trial of some sort (e.g., Luke 8:13; 1 Cor 10:13; Jas 1:2–3; 1 Pet 1:6–7).

Sentence 201

The *telos* of piety is friendship with God (v. 86b), but the *telos* of life itself is conduct that accords with God. The bearing of this line on the one that precedes it becomes apparent when comparison is made with v. 216: the readers should "endure everything," even a dire situation, "in order to live according to God" (κατὰ θεὸν ζῆν), an aspiration that can be construed as the ultimate goal and standard of faith (cf. vv. 5, 49, 349, 402). As we know from v. 400, a βίος lived without faith is an object of reproach (cf. vv. 196, 215). Those who are chosen, on the other hand, do all things κατὰ θεόν (v. 433), an expression that communicates an important and distinctive principle within the *Sentences* (note that it is found nowhere in Clitarchus, the *Sententiae Pythagoreorum*, or Porphyry's *Ad Marcellam*). Those who abide by this standard act "moderately, nobly, and righteously" (v. 399), earning God's favor by striving for such virtues to the best of their abilities (v. 48, cf. vv. 36, 63). As Chadwick (1959, 171) suggests, the use of the expression here may be inspired by 1 Pet 4:6 (ζῶσι δὲ κατὰ θεὸν πνεύματι), though see also Eph 4:24 ("and put on the new self, which in the likeness of God has been created in righteousness and holiness"). In *Post*. 69, Philo defines living in accord with God as loving God, referring to Deut 30:19-20, while Ignatius explains to the Ephesians that they will live in accord with God once they have uprooted any "dissention capable of tormenting you" (*Eph*. 8.1); cf. Clement, *Quis div*. 18.2; Origen, *Cels*. 8.75; *Frag. Luc*. 180.

Sentence 202

This line is connected to the preceding one by the catchword ἡγοῦ, which is absent from the parallel saying in v. 475: οὐδὲν κακόν, ὃ μὴ αἰσχρόν. According to Porphyry, *Marc*. 9 (cf. below on vv. 205, 207, 208a), "all evil is shameful" (κακία δὲ πᾶσα αἰσχρόν). By inverting the respective positions of "evil" and "shameful" in the saying (cf. Epictetus, *Diatr*. 4.1.133: τὰ ἄδικα καὶ αἰσχρὰ κακά) and formulating it logically as a double negative (μηδέν ... μή ...), Sextus's version of the maxim creates an ambiguity: that which is not shameful is not to be considered evil, but is it therefore to be considered good? Because no answer is provided to this question, our author opens up the possibility of a category of acts that could be described as amoral or morally neutral, even as he elsewhere urges meticulousness in assessing moral comportment (vv. 9-10, 297, etc.). Within the context of the *Sentences*, perhaps the best illustration of a moral indifferent is the consumption of meat. While it is more rational to abstain (v. 109), it is also the case that food cannot defile a person (v. 110) and, according to v. 102, what makes an action shameful is its capacity to render a person impure. Such an action, then, should be considered neither good nor bad. For other possibilities, see on vv. 230a and 276.

Sentence 203

In v. 73 it is luxury that is said to result in ruin. Here it is insolence (cf. vv. 339, 509). The dictum "Overindulgence is bred by wealth, and insolence by overindulgence" (ὁ μὲν κόρος ὑπὸ τοῦ πλούτου γεννᾶται ὕβρις δὲ ὑπὸ τοῦ κόρου) is attributed to the sage Solon in Diogenes Laertius, *Vit. phil.* 1.59. Philo was particularly fond of the sentiment expressed in the second part of the saying, of which he offers sundry versions in *Post.* 98; *Agr.* 32; *Abr.* 228; *Mos.* 2.13, 164; *Spec.* 3.43; *Virt.* 162; *Flacc.* 91 (cf. Theognis, *El.* 153; Clement, *Strom.* 6.2.8.7–8; Diogenianus, *Paroem.* 8.22). In *Bibl. hist.* 34/35.2.35, Diodorus Siculus says of a certain tyrant that he "bred first overindulgence, then insolence, and finally ruin" (πρῶτον κόρον ἐγέννησεν, εἶθ᾽ ὕβριν, τὸ δὲ τελευταῖον ὄλεθρον). That insolence begets ruin is reflected also in several sayings from the Pythagorean tradition, such as Iamblichus, *Vit. Pythag.* 30.171: "The first of evils (πρῶτον τῶν κακῶν) usually to slip unawares into households and cities is that called luxury (τρυφή), second insolence (ὕβρις), third ruin (ὄλεθρος)." A precept attributed to Pythagoras in Stobaeus, *Anth.* 4.1.80 expands the sequence to include four elements: "The first thing to enter into cities is luxury, then overindulgence, then insolence, then ruin." Noteworthy for their use of πέρας are a pair of precepts of Pythagorean provenance, one attributed by Stobaeus, *Anth.* 4.23.61 to Phintys (ὕβριος δὲ πάσας πέρας ὄλεθρος), the other attributed by Stobaeus, *Anth.* 4.34.71 to Hippodamus: "For the result (πέρας) of overindulgence and insolence is ruin."

Chadwick (1959, 34), apparently influenced by the form of the saying in Stobaeus, *Anth.* 4.1.80 (which he cites on p. 171), follows the Syriac and prints κόρου, even though both Greek manuscripts and Rufinus's translation support Elter's reading (1892, 15) of κακοῦ (printed also by Edwards and Wild 1981, 38). Given the weight of the textual evidence, as well the variations noted above (note in particular the reference to "evils" in Iamblichus's version), the latter is to be preferred. Either Sextus had access to a now-lost version of the saying with κακοῦ, or he changed κόρου in his source to κακοῦ in order to strengthen the continuity with v. 202, which has κακόν.

SENTENCES 204–209

TEXT

204   οὐκ ἀναβήσεται πάθος ἐπὶ καρδίαν πιστοῦ.
205   πᾶν πάθος ψυχῆς λόγῳ πολέμιον.
206   ὃ ἂν πράξῃς ἐν πάθει ὤν, μετανοήσεις.
207   πάθη νοσημάτων ἀρχαί[a].

208a κακία νόσος ψυχῆς.
208b ἀδικία ψυχῆς θάνατος.
209 τότε δόκει πιστὸς εἶναι, ὅταν τῶν τῆς ψυχῆς παθῶν ἀπαλλαγῇς.

Translation

204 Passion will not arise in a faithful person's heart.
205 Every passion of the soul is hostile to reason.
206 You will repent of whatever you do while in a state of passion.
207 Passions are foremost among illnesses.
208a Wickedness is a soul's disease.
208b Injustice is a soul's death.
209 When you rid your soul of its passions, then consider yourself to be faithful.

Textual Notes
207ª ἀρχή: Υ, sy¹ • 208a omit Υ

Commentary

These six lines constitute a unit on passion (note πάθος in vv. 204, 205, 206, 207, 209), with the first and last sayings creating an *inclusio* relating this topic to the theme of faith (note πιστός in vv. 204 and 209). Verse 208a is bound to v. 207 (with νόσημα) by the catchword νόσος, while v. 208b is bound to the lines that both precede and follow it by the repetition of ψυχῆς.

Sentence 204

The doctrine of impassibility or "passionlessness" (ἀπάθεια) dominates the writings of Clement, for whom achieving spiritual perfection involves passing from mere moderation of the passions (μετριοπάθεια) to complete liberation from their oppressive influences, facilitating the process of becoming like God, who is ἀπαθής (e.g., Strom. 2.20.103.1; 6.9.72.1; 6.9.74.1; 7.12.72.1; 7.14.84.2). As he explains in Strom. 7.2.10.1, the commandments that God gave to humankind "ordained that the soul which at any time improved as regards the knowledge of virtue and increase in righteousness should obtain an improved position in the universe, pressing onwards at every step to a passionless state, until it comes to a perfect man." For such an individual, passions such as desire, anger, lust, and grief are simply "inadmissible" (*Strom.* 6.9.71.4). This is because, as we learn in *Strom.* 7.3.13.3, he "assimilates to that which is by nature free from passion (i.e., God) that which has been subdued by training to a passionless state (i.e., the soul)." Insofar as this "laying aside of our passions and becoming free from sin" constitutes a process of spiritual development, one predicated on the knowledge and love of God, it can be correctly described (in *Strom.* 7.3.14.3) as the "impassibility that comes from faith" (ἡ ἐκ πίστεως ἀπάθεια). Thus "the fear of the God who is free from passions is itself free from passions" (*Strom.* 2.8.40.2).

While Clement appears to be indebted primarily to Stoic (cf. *SVF* 3:443–455; Epictetus, *Diatr.* 2.17.29–33; 3.13.9–13; 4.10.25–30; Seneca, *Ep.* 116.1–8; etc.) and Philonic (e.g., *Leg.* 2.99–102; 3.129–137; *Plant.* 98; *Abr.* 257) sources for his teaching on impassibility, it is important to note that the theme is present in Pythagorean texts as well (e.g., Iamblichus, *Vit. Pythag.* 33.234); in the midst of his instruction on πάθη in *Marc.* 9, the reader is not surprised to hear Porphyry proclaim how "it is necessary to free oneself of passions." Given the extended parallels between vv. 202–209 and *Marc.* 9, it is possible that Sextus's inspiration for v. 204 may have come from now-lost source material he shares with Porphyry (see part 4 of the introduction). For more on the problem of passion in the *Sentences*, see on vv. 75a–b. Being purged of the passions would appear to be one of the principal ways in which a person's heart becomes "pure and sinless" (v. 46b) or, as Evagrius Ponticus puts it, "without impassibility (χωρὶς ἀπαθείας) the heart cannot be raised to the heights" (*Sent. mon.* 66).

Sentence 205

This line is based on *Sent. Pythag.* 2ᵇ: πᾶν δὲ πάθος ψυχῆς εἰς σωτηρίαν πολεμιώτατον. Cf. Porphyry, *Marc.* 9: πᾶν πάθος ψυχῆς εἰς σωτηρίαν αὐτῆς πολεμιώτατον (note that Porphyry's quotation includes *Sent. Pythag.* 2ᵃ and 2ᶜ as well, in the order *bac*). The version of the maxim preserved in *Sent. Pythag.* 116 (ψυχῆς πᾶν πάθος εἰς σωτηρίαν αὐτῆς πολεμιώτατον) is quoted as a saying of Pythagoras in Stobaeus, *Anth.* 3.1.41. Sextus softens the force of the saying's final term with πολέμιον and, more important, replaces εἰς σωτηρίαν with λόγῳ. In *Strom.* 2.13.59.6 (= *SVF* 3:377), Clement, reflecting standard Stoic dogma (cf. *SVF* 3:378, 386, 391, 412, 462, 465), defines passion as "an excessive impulse (ὁρμή) exceeding the measures of reason, or an impulse unbridled and disobedient to reason (ἀπειθὴς λόγῳ). The passions, then, are an unnatural movement of the soul in disobedience to reason. This revolt (ἀπόστασις), this disaffection, this disobedience is in our control, just as obedience is in our control." As the language here suggests, the stance of the passions toward reason is one not just of defiance but of active opposition. In order for someone to be faithful, therefore, the latter must subjugate the former. For the martial imagery, comparison can be made with Philo, *Abr.* 223 (cf. *Her.* 284): "For a time the soul was in a state of war and was the scene of conflict, for as yet it was not perfectly purified, but its passions and illnesses (νοσημάτων, cf. Sext. 207) still prevailed over its healthy principles." The same point is made without martial imagery in v. 74: "Let your reason guide your impulses (ὁρμῶν)." See also v. 123: "Make the reason within you a norm for your life."

Sentence 206

Those incapable of governing their passions are bound to experience feelings of remorse and regret (e.g., Philo, *Opif.* 167; Josephus, *Bell.* 1.444; Clement, *Strom.* 6.14.109.3; Plutarch, *Comp. Aem. Tim.* 2.11; Maximus of Tyre, *Dial.* 3.2; Stobaeus, *Anth.* 4.56.36). Indeed, for Plutarch passion and regret are so closely bound together that it is more accurate to say that regret is actually present in an act inspired by passion than something that occurs as a result of the act (*Vit. pud.* 533d; cf. *Sera* 554b). The only recourse open to someone who has acted in such a way is repentance (μετάνοια), though even this is not necessarily assured. As he explains elsewhere, we can only presume that God "distinguishes whether the passions of the sick soul to which he administers his justice will in any way yield and make room for repentance, and for those in whose nature vice is not unrelieved or intractable, he fixes a period of grace" (*Sera* 551d; cf. Philo, *Spec.* 1.239). If they follow his advice, Sextus's readers will have few regrets, since they will be quick to acknowledge any sins that they have committed (v. 283, cf. v. 247) and will avoid repeating their mistakes by making it a point to deliberate carefully and think about God before undertaking any action (vv. 93–95b). If v. 206 is read together with vv. 207–208a, then it is possible that our author imagines repentance as a process similar to that of being cured of a disease, a notion familiar from Philo's writings, for example, *Leg.* 2.60; 3.211; *Ios.* 87; *Spec.* 1.236, 239, 253; *Virt.* 176; *Praem.* 21 (cf. Plutarch, *Lat. viv.* 1128d–e).

Sentences 207–208a

These verses have a close parallel in Porphyry, *Marc.* 9: πάθη δὲ νοσημάτων ἀρχαί· ψυχῆς δὲ νόσημα κακία (the saying that parallels v. 202 immediately follows). Sextus's version lacks δέ in both sayings, and in the second saying uses νόσος in lieu of νόσημα while switching the position of the first and last terms. As the quotations of Philo, *Abr.* 223 and Plutarch, *Sera* 551d above illustrate, it was a commonplace of moral philosophy to liken vices to maladies, moral guides to physicians, and their teaching to therapy for the soul. Another typical example comes from *Sent. Pythag.* 50, which Porphyry cites in *Marc.* 31: "Vain is the discourse of that philosopher by which no human passion (πάθος) is healed. For just as there is no benefit from medicine if it does not heal the diseases (τὰς νόσους) of the body, neither is there from philosophy if it does not purge the passion of the soul." Clement employs this kind of imagery frequently, especially in the opening chapters of the *Paedagogus*, where the Logos is represented as the best healer for the passions of the soul (e.g., *Paed.* 1.1.1.2; 1.1.3.1–3; 1.2.6.1–4; 1.6.51.1). Among the most effective cures in this regard is reproof (ἔλεγχος), which, he says, "is like surgery performed on the passions of the soul, the passions being like a disease of truth, which need to be removed by a surgeon's knife" (*Paed.* 1.8.64.4; cf. Sext. 103, 245). Illnesses of the soul are more serious than those of the body both because they afflict a higher part of the self and because they are more difficult to cure, owing in part to the debilitating influence of deception and self-deception, "for while disease (νόσος) grows in the body through nature, wickedness (κακία) and depravity are the soul's own doing" (Plutarch, *An. corp.* 500c; cf. Menander, *Mon.* 116: "It is indeed better for a body to be sick than a soul"). For passion as a "disease," see also Philo, *Opif.* 150; *Deus* 67; *Spec.* 1.167, 257; Plutarch, *Rect. aud.* 38d; *Tranq. an.* 468b; *Am. prol.* 497d; *Quaest. conv.* 717e, 731b; Dio Chrysostom, *Or.* 77/78.45; SVF 3:421–430. Wickedness, meanwhile, represents a particularly intractable ailment since, "just as an attack of fever is a disease not of a part but of the whole body, so wickedness (κακία) is a malady of the whole soul" (Philo, *Sobr.* 45). It is not surprising, then, to hear it described as "a desperate and deadly disease" (Plutarch, *Lat. viv.* 1128d); cf. Plato, *Soph.* 228e; *Resp.* 444d–e; Philo, *Cher.* 96; *Det.* 123.

Sentence 208b

The vices of the soul are so serious in nature that they can threaten its very existence: "When the soul is 'many,' that is, full of passions and vices (παθῶν καὶ κακιῶν), with her children, pleasures, desires, folly, incontinence, injustice (ἀδικίας), gathered around her, she is feeble and sick and dangerously near to death" (Philo, *Praem.* 159; cf. Plato, *Resp.* 609d, 610c–d). According to Clement, the law "teaches us to avoid the real evils—adultery, shameless behavior, pederasty, ignorance, injustice (ἀδικία), spiritual sickness, death—not the death of separation of soul from body, but the death of separation of the soul from truth" (*Strom.* 2.7.34.2). In *Let. Aris.* 212, meanwhile, one of the Jewish sages suggests that the king "should set before him justice continually in everything and consider injustice a negation of life." Cf. *b. Ber.* 18a: "The righteous are called living even after their death, the sinners dead during their lifetime." The Sextine sage does not fear physical death (v. 323), since it is not this but rather "an evil life" (v. 397) that destroys the soul. Indeed, someone who lives without faith, that is, someone who lives in a way that is unworthy of God (v. 5), is from a spiritual standpoint as good as dead (v. 7b, cf. v. 175). Ironically, injustice leads to the death of the self, even though its origins spring from the love of the self (v. 138, cf. vv. 23, 370, 386). In his translation of v. 208b, Rufinus adds *et inpietas*, expanding on the faith theme identified above.

Sentence 209

What was stated as an indicative in the unit's introduction (v. 204) is now stated as an imperative in its conclusion. Given the realities conveyed by the intervening material, it is incumbent upon the readers to act with regard to the passions in a manner that authenticates their status as the faithful. As Clement explains in the *Stromata*, freedom from the passions is not something simply to be had but is achieved through a process of education and training whose goal is human perfection: "We must therefore raise the gnostic and perfect man above all passion of soul. For knowledge produces training and training habit of disposition, and a state of this kind produces impassibility, not moderation of passion. For complete eradication of desire reaps as its fruit impassibility" (*Strom.* 6.9.74.1; cf. 2.8.39.4; 3.7.57.1). By embracing this regimen, the faithful demonstrate their eagerness to be assimilated to the Lord (*Strom.* 7.12.72.1), who himself was "trained to a habit of impassibility" (*Strom.* 7.2.7.6). For the language of "ridding" oneself of passions, see Posidonius, frag. 409; Clement, *Strom.* 1.28.178.1; and especially *Sent. Pythag.* 2^c (cf. on v. 205), which Porphyry cites in *Marc.* 9: "Being educated should not be considered a matter of acquiring much learning, but of ridding the soul's passions (ἀπαλλάξει δὲ τῶν ψυχικῶν παθῶν)."

Sentences 210a–214

Text

210a ἀνθρώποις χρῶ τοῖς ἅπασιν ὡς ᵃκοινὸς ἀνθρώπων εὐεργέτης^(ab).
210b ὡς θέλεις χρήσασθαί σοι τοὺς πέλας^a, καὶ ᵇσὺ χρῶ αὐτοῖς^b.
211 ἀνθρώποις κακῶς χρώμενος σεαυτῷ κακῶς χρήσῃ.
212 οὐδένα κακῶς ποιήσει^a ὁ πιστός.
213 εὔχου τοὺς ἐχθροὺς δύνασθαι εὐεργετεῖν.
214 φαύλοις φαίνεται ἄχρηστος σοφὸς^a ἀνήρ.

Translation

210a Treat all human beings as though you were a common benefactor of humanity.
210b As you want your neighbors to treat you, so you treat them.
211 In treating human beings badly, you treat yourself badly.
212 The faithful person will act badly toward no one.
213 Pray to be able to confer benefits on your enemies.
214 To the masses a wise man seems useless.

Textual Notes

210a^(a–a) κοινωνοῖς: Υ, sy² • 210a^b εὐεργέτης μετὰ θεόν: lat • 210b omit lat • 210b^a παῖδας: Υ • 210b^(b–b) σὺ τοὺς πέλας χρήσασθαι: Π • 211 omit Υ, sy² • 212^a ποιήσῃ: Π • 214^a ὁ σοφὸς: Π

Commentary

Verse 210a appears to function as a heading for this unit, with the lines that follow elaborating on what it means to be a "common benefactor of humanity." Besides εὐεργέτης in v. 210a and εὐεργετεῖν in v. 213, note the use of χράω in vv. 210a–211. While this section focuses on the readers' relationship with other people, the one that follows focuses on their relationship with God.

Sentence 210a

The title "common benefactor of humanity" was generally reserved for gods, demigods, or kings (e.g., Diodorus Siculus, *Bibl. hist.* 1.13.1; 3.9.1; 3.55.3; 3.72.4; 4.8.5; 5.63.2). Its application here can be interpreted as a variation on the Stoic paradox that the sage alone is king, since he alone knows how to rule to the best benefit of himself and those who heed him (e.g., Philo, *Abr.* 261, 272; Cicero, *Mur.* 61; Musonius Rufus, frag. 8.64.35–8.66.31; Epictetus, *Diatr.* 3.22.63, 72; Clement, *Strom.* 1.26.168.4; 2.4.19.4; Diogenes Laertius, *Vit. phil.* 7.122). In keeping with the general focus of the material in vv. 210a–214 (see above), what is provided here is not a theological perspective on the dynamics of benefaction, such as we have encountered previously (vv. 33, 47, 176), but one that mentions only its human participants, specifically, εὐεργέτης and ἄνθρωποι. For the specific kinds of benefits that the former confers on the latter, see on v. 176. As we will learn shortly, the expected scope of the readers' benefaction is truly universal, extending even to enemies (v. 213, cf. vv. 328, 484). This would be consistent with Clement's insistence that those who imitate God best are those who make their gifts "available for the benefit of all" (*Strom.* 2.19.97.2). A parallel saying in v. 260 (ἐπιτήδευε κοινὸς ἀνθρώποις εὐεργέτης εἶναι) links the sage's role as benefactor with the sage's role as judge (v. 261). For the wording, cf. also v. 478: ἀνθρώποις χρῶ ὡς κοινωνοῖς καὶ πολίταις θεοῦ.

Sentences 210b–211

Verse 210b repeats v. 89 (Rufinus, no doubt aware of this, eliminates the duplication by dropping the line here). As noted in the commentary for that verse, the thought, though not the wording, of this precept is based on Matt 7:12/Luke 6:31, a dominical saying that exercised considerable influence on early Christian morality. In its current context, the reference to "neighbors" (for which see, again, on v. 89) would appear to have fairly broad application, comparable to that of ἄνθρωποι in vv. 210a and 211 (note also the referent of v. 212). As with the first citation of the maxim, Sextus follows it immediately with a negative form of the golden rule. Unlike v. 90 ("What you censure do not do"), however, in v. 211 the element of reciprocity is made explicit, as we see also in v. 179 ("What you do not want to experience, do not do") and v. 327 ("The one who plans evil against another is the first to experience evil"). In certain cases, the reciprocity is spelled out in terms of the negative repercussions awaiting those who break the rule, for example, in *Sent. Pythag.* 11[a]: "By planning evil against another you will cause yourself to be the first to experience evil." Cf. *Syr. Men.* 250–253 ("Everything that is hateful to you, you should not wish to do that to your neighbor. Let not your way of life be arrogant, lest it be harmful to you"); *Instr. Ankh.* 12.6 ("Do not do evil to a man, so as to cause another to do it to you"); 15.23 ("Do not do to a man what you hate, so as to cause another to do it to you").

Sentence 212

According to Philo, the law "does not permit doing wrong to anyone, male or female, even among strangers" (*QE* 2.3). Compare Plato, *Crit.* 49c (cited by Origen in *Cels.* 7.58): "It is not right to do wrong in return or to act badly toward any person (κακῶς ποιεῖν οὐδένα ἀνθρώπων)." Verse 212 is bound to the line that precedes it by the catchword κακῶς. To refrain from treating others badly represents a priority motivated not only by self-interest but also by one's claim to be faithful. Ps.-Clement, *Hom.* 11.4 develops a similar thought, though with more explicitly theological language: "He who wishes to be pious toward God does good to others, because the body of humankind bears the image of God." Acting badly towards someone else would no doubt be counted among the things "unworthy of God" that the faithful strive to avoid in their conduct (v. 5, and cf. the first part of v. 247: "If you want to be faithful, above all do not sin").

Sentence 213

This admonition can be interpreted as a specification and intensification of v. 212. The faithful will not treat anyone badly, including even enemies. More than this, they will pray for opportunities and abilities to do their enemies good. As benefactors of all humanity (vv. 210a, 260), the readers should not allow anything to prevent them from helping others (cf. v. 328). Instead, since they truly belong to God, they are considerate of all persons and pray for their welfare (v. 372), this being one of the things "worthy of God" that they ought to bring to God in prayer (v. 122). Through this practice they show that they in fact consider no one to be their enemy (v. 105).

The principal source for this line is probably Matt 5:44 (ἀγαπᾶτε τοὺς ἐχθροὺς ὑμῶν καὶ προσεύχεσθε ὑπὲρ τῶν διωκόντων ὑμᾶς), though it is noteworthy that, much like Sextus, the parallel in Luke 6:27-28 (cf. 6:35) associates these sorts of practices with "doing good": ἀγαπᾶτε τοὺς ἐχθροὺς ὑμῶν, καλῶς ποιεῖτε τοῖς μισοῦσιν ὑμᾶς, εὐλογεῖτε τοὺς καταρωμένους ὑμᾶς, προσεύχεσθε περὶ τῶν ἐπηρεαζόντων ὑμᾶς. A similar association occurs in *T. Jos.* 18.2: "If anyone wishes to do you harm, you should pray for him, along with doing good." For the particular formulation in the first part of Sext. 213, cf. *Did.* 1.3 (προσεύχεσθε ὑπὲρ τῶν ἐχθρῶν) and Justin Martyr, *1 Apol.* 15.9 (εὔχεσθε ὑπὲρ τῶν ἐχθρῶν). For more general parallels, see Rom 12:14;

1 Cor 4:12; Pol. *Phil.* 12.3; Diogenes Laertius, *Vit. phil.* 8.23 (Pythagoras bade his disciples "so to behave one to another as not to make friends into enemies, but to turn enemies into friends"); Cicero, *Off.* 1.34–40 (on extending justice even to enemies). The *Letter of Aristeas* 227 suggests one possible motive for such efforts: "We must show liberal charity to our opponents so that in this manner we may convert them to what is proper and fitting for them." A rather different approach is recommended by *Syr. Men.* 128–132: "If you have an enemy, do not pray with respect to him that he may die … but pray with respect to him that he may become poor, (then) he will live on and (perhaps may) cease from his evil practices."

The notion of acting as a benefactor to one's enemies was not unheard of. According to a saying attributed to the sage Cleobulus, for instance, "It is right to confer benefits (εὐεργετεῖν) on a friend in order to bind him closer to us, and on an enemy in order to make a friend of him" (Diogenes Laertius, *Vit. phil.* 1.91). In Ps.-Clement, *Hom.* 12.26 (cf. 12.33), meanwhile, the habit of conferring benefits on one's enemies is presented as a distinguishing mark of the humane or "philanthropic" person (ὁ φιλάνθρωπος). Aesop, *Fab.* (vers. 3) 129 manifests a more cynical, and probably more common, perspective: "Many people will not hesitate to confer a benefit on their enemies for the sake of gain." Cf. Sext. 607: "Do what is right even to those who are trying to wrong you."

Sentence 214

This precept is based on Clitarchus, *Sent.* 64: φαύλοις ἄχρηστος δοκεῖ σοφὸς ἀνήρ. Sextus replaces δοκεῖ with φαίνεται, shifting the verb to the second position in the line, perhaps for the sake of alliteration. The term φαῦλος conveys both the "common" and the "base" character of those who discredit the importance of the sage (cf. v. 314). Given the nature of the sage's role in society, it was only to be expected that those embracing this profession would face a fair amount of neglect and rejection. In Plato's *Respublica*, for instance, the majority of the people misunderstand and mistrust the philosopher-rulers even though the latter are the only ones who are truly virtuous (*Resp.* 493e–494a, 498d–500d), a reflection of that fact that to the masses even morally decent philosophers are ἄχρηστοι (489b). Hence Epictetus's advice in *Ench.* 22: "If you yearn for philosophy, prepare at once to be met with ridicule, to have many people jeer at you," and so forth. As Seneca observes, whenever a discussion of how to be good is being held, there will in fact be "very few in attendance, and the majority think that even these few are engaged in no good business, for they have the reputation of being empty-headed idlers" (*Ep.* 76.4). Thus, as Cicero explains, "he who depends upon the caprice of the ignorant rabble cannot be numbered among the great" (*Off.* 1.65), since crowds are morally fickle, assigning praise and blame indiscriminately (Philo, *Spec.* 4.88). Cf. *Sent. Pythag.* 111ᵃ (= v. 82ᵇ): φαῦλος κριτὴς καλοῦ πράγματος ὄχλος. In *Strom.* 2.18.79.3 (cf. Prov 16:21), Clement offers a variation on the theme, declaring that those who are unrighteous "call those who are wise and discerning base (τοὺς σοφοὺς καὶ φρονίμους φαύλους καλοῦσιν)."

For his part, the Sextine sage is more concerned with being virtuous than with seeming virtuous (v. 64), and therefore makes little effort to ingratiate himself with the masses (vv. 112, 241, 354, 360), even to the point of scorning their approval (v. 299, cf. v. 531: φυλάττου φαύλων ἐπαίνους). Ironically, then, even though he is second only to God in conferring benefactions to humanity (v. 176, cf. vv. 210a, 260, 372) and is deserving of the kind of respect that ought to be accorded a living image of God (v. 190, cf. v. 244), it is unlikely that he will be acknowledged for who he truly is except by a very few (vv. 53, 145), that is, by God (e.g., v. 308) and by fellow sages (vv. 218–219, 244). Those who show a lack of appreciation for the sage are actually showing a lack of gratitude to God (v. 229), who is present in the sage, guiding his actions and caring for his soul (vv. 144, 416–424). On the other hand, the individual who is truly ἄχρηστος is the sage's opposite, the man who longs not for God but for pleasure (v. 172).

SENTENCES 215–229

TEXT

215 οὐκ ἄνευ θεοῦ καλῶς ζήσεις.
216 ὑπὲρ τοῦ κατὰ θεὸν ζῆν πάνταᵃ ὑπόμενε.
217 εὐχῆς οὐκᵃ ἀκούει θεὸς τοῦᵇ ᶜἀνθρώπων δεομένωνᶜ οὐκ ἀκούοντος.
218 φιλόσοφος φιλοσόφῳ δῶρον παρὰ θεοῦᵃ.
219 τιμῶν φιλόσοφον τιμήσεις σεαυτόν.
220 πιστὸς ὢν ἴσθι.
221 ὅταν υἱόν ᵃσε λέγῃ τιςᵃ, μέμνησο τίνος ᵇσε λέγει υἱόνᵇ.
222 θεὸν πατέρα καλῶν ἐν οἷς πράττεις τούτου μέμνησο.
223 τὰ ῥήματά σου ᵃτὰ πιστὰᵃ πολλῆς ᵇεὐσεβείας μεστὰ ἔστωᵇᶜ.
224 ἐν οἷς πράττεις πρὸ ὀφθαλμῶν ἔχε τὸν θεόν.
225 δεινόν ἐστιν ᵃθεὸν πατέραᵃ ὁμολογοῦντα πρᾶξαί τι ἄσχημον.

226 σοφὸν ὁ μὴ φιλῶν, οὐδὲ^a ἑαυτόν.
227 ^aμηθὲν ἴδιον κτῆμα^a νομιζέσθω φιλοσόφῳ.
228 ὧν κοινὸς ὁ θεὸς ^aκαὶ ταῦτα ὡς πατήρ^a, τούτων μὴ κοινὰ εἶναι τὰ κτήματα οὐκ εὐσεβές.
229 ἀχαριστεῖ θεῷ ὁ μὴ περὶ πολλοῦ ποιούμενος φιλόσοφον.

Translation

215 Without God you will not live nobly.
216 Endure all things in order to live in accord with God.
217 God does not listen to the prayer of one who does not listen to people in need.
218 To a philosopher a philosopher is a gift from God.
219 By honoring a philosopher you will honor yourself.
220 Know that you are faithful.
221 When someone calls you "son," remember whose son he calls you.
222 In the things you do remember this, that you call God "father."
223 Let your words of faith be full of much piety.
224 In the things you do keep God before your eyes.
225 It is terrible while confessing God as father to do something shameful.
226 The one who does not love a sage does not love himself.
227 Let a philosopher consider no possession his own.
228 It is impious for those who have God in common, indeed as father, not to have possessions in common.
229 The one who does not have much regard for a philosopher shows ingratitude to God.

Textual Notes

216[a] πᾶν: Π • 217[a] omit Υ • 217[b] omit Π • 217[c-c] ἀνθρώπου δεόμενον: lat? • 218[a] θεῷ: Υ • 221[a-a] λέγῃ τίς σε: Π • 221[b-b] λέγει σε υἱὸν εἶναι: Υ • 223[a-a] omit lat • 223[b-b] εὐλαβείας ἤτω μεστά: Υ • 223[c] ἔστωσαν: Π • 225[a-a] πατέρα θεόν: Π • 226[a] οὔτε: Π • 227[a-a] μηδὲν κτῆμα ἴδιον: Υ • 228 omit Υ, sy² • 228[a-a] omit sy¹

Commentary

This block of sayings and the one that immediately precedes it can be interpreted as matching panels. While vv. 210a–214 addressed the readers' relationship with other people, this (much longer) unit addresses their relationship with God. Note references to θεός in vv. 215–218, 222, 224–225, 228–229, as well as to πιστός in vv. 220, 223, and to εὐσέβεια in v. 223 and εὐσεβής in v. 228. In particular, attention is drawn repeatedly to the believer's relationship to God as father (vv. 221–222, 225, 228). Interspersed within this material are two similarly structured sayings on another figure who deserves love and honor, the sage (vv. 219, 226).

Sentences 215–216

In *Leg.* 888b, Plato argued that "the most important matter of all" involves recognizing that it is only possible to live nobly (ζῆν καλῶς) if one holds correct beliefs about the gods (cf. Diogenes Laertius, *Vit. phil.* 10.123). The first line of this couplet (note the catchwords θεοῦ ... ζήσεις and θεὸν ζῆν) serves as motivation for the second: the readers must be willing to endure everything in order to live in accord with God since this is the only way that they can live nobly and, while many things in life are beyond their control, they do possess the freedom to choose to live in this manner (v. 255). This is only possible however, if they have faith (v. 196), since God is the source and guide of everything that is noble (vv. 104, 113, 304, 390), that is, of everything that is good (v. 197). The person committed to doing good not only performs noble works; he himself actually becomes a noble "work" of God (v. 395). Such a person lives in accord with God, which includes acting not only nobly, but also moderately and righteously (v. 399), criteria that lend some specificity to the meaning of ζῆν καλῶς. Another criterion is identified here in v. 216: perseverance. Aristotle defined courage as the endurance of difficulties for what is noble (e.g., *Eth. nic.* 3.7.2; 3.8.14; 3.9.4; cf. Ps.-Plato, *Def.* 412c; Philo, *Migr.* 144). Since, for Sextus, what is noble cannot be achieved without God, the moral life consists of enduring difficulties κατὰ θεόν. As Ignatius promises, "If you endure all things for (God's) sake, you will reach him" (*Smyrn.* 9.2). Perseverance in such endeavors is imperative, since the purpose of life is to live in accord with God (v. 201, cf. vv. 48, 433) or, as Origen explains in *Cels.* 8.75, God unites himself "to everyone who has been persuaded to live in accord with God in all things (τὸ κατὰ θεὸν ἐν πᾶσι ζῆν)." For πάντα ὑπόμενε, cf. also 1 Cor 13:7; Col 1:11; 2 Tim 2:10.

Sentence 217

This saying is repeated in the appendices with slight modification (i.e., with σπουδαίως in lieu of τοῦ ἀνθρώπων) as v. 584 and with significant modification (i.e., with γονέων in lieu of τοῦ ἀνθρώπων δεομένων) as v. 492. The prayer of one who ignores the needy is ignored by God, much like the prayer of a lazy person (v. 126) or the prayer of a person who longs for pleasure (v. 72). A similar principle of serial reciprocity (again expressed negatively) informs the logic of v. 378: "If you do not give to those in need (δεομένοις) when you are able, you will not receive from God when you are in need." This verse also sheds light on what it means to "listen" to the needy. As Origen explains in *Orat.* 11.4, when Christians hear the prayer of a poor man asking God for help, they do not neglect his needs but draw from what resources they have "so as to fulfill the prayer of the poor man, being a minister of the will of the father who brought together at the time of the prayer, into the same place with him who is to pray, him who is able to give." Sextus's readers are expected to give freely to others of what they have freely received from God (v. 242), acting as intermediaries in a divine scheme of benefaction (vv. 33, 176, 210a, 260) by sharing what they have (vv. 82b, 227–228, 295–296), especially with the poor (vv. 266–267) and the needy (vv. 330, 377–379, 382), kindness to those in need being one of the things that makes a person "great" in the eyes of God (v. 52, cf. vv. 340, 382). Presumably the prayers of an individual who enjoys such a status will be heeded by God (cf. vv. 81, 125, 277, 372). In other texts, what God heeds is not the prayer of the giver but the prayer of the recipient offered on behalf of the giver, for example, Herm. *Sim.* 2.5: "So whenever the rich go up to the poor and supply them with their needs, they believe that what they do for the poor will be able to find a reward from God, because the poor are rich in intercession and confession, and their intercession has great power with God." Cf. Clement, *Quis div.* 33–35.

Sentences 218–219

Given the exalted stature accorded the sage in our text, it stands to reason that what Sextus describes as a divine δῶρον is not philosophy or any of philosophy's particular contributions (as is usually the case, e.g., Philo, *Congr.* 146; Libanius, *Orat.* 18.155) but the philosopher himself. Verse 218 contains the first two of fourteen references to φιλόσοφος in our text. While the term appears to be largely interchangeable with σοφός (e.g., compare v. 244 with v. 319), it is noteworthy that all but one of these fourteen references (v. 392) occur between v. 218 and v. 319. In the manner of text's presentation, therefore, the former is made to occupy a not only lesser but also more circumscribed role than the latter.

To the ignorant masses, those who occupy themselves with wisdom appear irrelevant (vv. 53, 145) and worthless (v. 214). As Plato explains in *Resp.* 489a–b, it is precisely because philosophers appear worthless to the general public that they should not expect to be accorded any honors, civic or otherwise. To someone of the same profession, however, a sage is a welcomed gift, since goodness is rare (Sext. 243). That the sage is welcomed as a gift παρὰ θεοῦ (cf. vv. 21, 124, 128, 182, 242, 353, 378, 449) is appropriate, inasmuch as he is not only a servant of God (v. 319) but a living image of God (v. 190). The measure of honor that he has earned is therefore second only to that of God (vv. 244, 319, cf. vv. 176, 292), assuming that he has proven himself to be trustworthy (v. 258). Those who honor the sage bring honor upon themselves insofar as honoring the sage entails accepting the sage's correction, through which they themselves can become wise (vv. 244–246). By learning to honor the sage, the readers learn to honor themselves, especially the highest aspect of themselves, their souls (v. 129), since the sage represents the pinnacle of what the human soul can achieve (v. 403). Conversely, the readers must not dishonor a sage by allowing him to be censured (v. 194) or maligned (v. 259), since such actions show a lack of gratitude to God (v. 229). A negative version of v. 219 occurs in v. 226 (note the substitution of σοφός for φιλόσοφος): "The one who does not love a sage does not love himself." Cf. *Gnom. Vat.* 32: "The veneration of the wise man is a great blessing to those who venerate him."

Sentence 220

This line appears to be Sextus's variant on a precept attributed to the sage Sosiadas: ξένος ὢν ἴσθι (Stobaeus, *Anth.* 3.1.173 = Septem Sapientes, *Praec.* 217.6–7). In its revised form, the verse introduces a cluster of sayings bound together by a fair amount of shared language. Besides πιστός/πιστά in vv. 220 and 223, note also μέμνησο in vv. 221 and 222, θεόν in vv. 222, 224, and 225, πατέρα in vv. 222 and 225, and ἐν οἷς πράττεις in vv. 222 and 224 (cf. πρᾶξαι in v. 225). Read in this context, and especially in conjunction with vv. 221–222, v. 220 serves as a reminder of the relational nature of faith. In the *Sentences*, faith is a matter not only of seeking God (v. 402) but of becoming utterly dependent on God (v. 49). It is not enough, then, to honor being faithful, one must actually "be" faithful (v. 189), especially by doing nothing unworthy of God (v. 5, cf. vv. 234, 247). To those who prove themselves faithful, God in turn bestows a power befitting God (v. 36, cf. v. 60), so that one becomes a god in a living body (v. 7a, cf. vv. 200,

376a). For our author's propensity to insert faith language into his material, see part 4 of the introduction.

Sentences 221–222

The two halves of this couplet are bound not only by the natural juxtaposition of πατήρ and υἱός but also by the repetition of μέμνησο and the reciprocal use of "call" language (λέγῃ, λέγει, καλῶν): the reader is summoned to remember both that God calls him "son" and that he calls God "father" (cf. v. 28). Bringing these acts of mutual naming and the relationship they establish into the reader's awareness is not simply a mental exercise, however, but a habit that should guide all of one's actions. To remember that one is God's son is to remember that one is "next best" to God, and that one should therefore behave in a manner worthy of God (vv. 376a–b, cf. vv. 60, 82c, 135, 225). Regarding this couplet's formulation, comparison should be made especially with vv. 58–59: "Be worthy of the one who deems you worthy to be called son and act always as God's son. In the things you do remember this, that you call God 'father.'" Verse 222 replicates v. 59 exactly (note that Υ omits v. 59), while v. 221 shares the language of being "called son" with v. 58 (εἰπεῖν υἱόν in v. 58, λέγει υἱόν in v. 221), even as it lacks the appeal in v. 58 for moral action commensurate with one's sonship. This is found instead in v. 224, which opens with phrasing familiar from v. 222: ἐν οἷς πράττεις. For more on the background and significance of father–son imagery in the *Sentences*, see the commentary on vv. 58–59. Comparable calls for remembrance are issued also in vv. 82c and 364.

Sentence 223

Cf. v. 84: "Have a reverent tongue, especially concerning God." The language of speech continues from v. 221 (λέγῃ, λέγει) and v. 222 (καλῶν) into this line (cf. ὁμολογοῦντα in v. 225). As a rule, the faithful are more concerned with acts of faith than words of faith (v. 383), and prefer hearing such words to speaking them (vv. 171a–b). However, when they do utter words of faith, that is, words about God (cf. *Const. ap.* 8.32), they are uttered with great piety (e.g., v. 374). Speech about God must be informed by a love of God that demonstrates itself in action. Indeed, works of divine love should precede "every word" about God (vv. 358–359, cf. vv. 173, 356). It is only in this manner that words spoken about God can be considered "true" and therefore deserving of the same honor accorded God himself (vv. 355, 357). Those who fail to speak about God out of a sense of piety run the risk of blasphemy, the "most impious" of all sins (v. 85, cf. vv. 83, 367–368). In Clement, *Paed.* 3.12.96.1, the relationship between words of faith and piety appears to be construed somewhat differently, the former serving not to reflect but to foster the latter: "Be nourished by the words of faith; train yourself in piety" (cf. 1 Tim 4:6–7).

Sentence 224

This line relates to the one that follows insofar as v. 224 identifies a means by which the reader can avoid the scenario that v. 225 depicts. Specifically, by keeping God in his consciousness, he will avoid doing anything that might betray his confession of God as father. Seneca employs similar imagery in *Ep.* 11.8–9: "Cherish some man of high character, and keep him ever before your eyes, living as if he were watching you, and ordering all your actions as if he beheld them.... We can get rid of most sins, if we have a witness who stands near us when we are likely to go wrong." In early Christian circles, this sort of psychagogic technique focuses not on "some man of high character" but on God, as we also see in Clement, *Strom.* 7.7.35.4: "If the presence of some good man always moulds for the better one who converses with him, owing to the respect and reverence that he inspires, with much more reason must he, who is always in the uninterrupted presence of God by means of his knowledge and his life and his thankful spirit, be raised above himself on every occasion, both in regard to his actions and his words" (cf. Philo, *Mut.* 217; Justin Martyr, *Dial.* 20.1; 46.5). Since his intellect is always "with" God (v. 143) and his soul always "sees" God (vv. 417, 445–447), the sage thinks about God constantly (v. 289), especially before every deed (v. 95a), calling upon God to witness what he does (v. 303), thus becoming the sort of person he desires to be when actually present before God (v. 82a).

Sentence 225

This line functions in part to help clarify and extend the meaning of v. 222: believers do not simply "call" God father but in so doing commit themselves not to sin against God (cf. v. 234, also with ὁμολογέω). God's son is expected to remain both holy and sinless (v. 60). To do something shameful, then, that is, to do something that renders one impure (v. 102) and therefore unfit for God, would be truly terrible (cf. v. 75a). Sextus will provide an example of such conduct presently, in v. 228. Reverence for God the father as a motive for unsullied behavior figures as an element in the argumentation of other early Christian texts as well, most notably 1 Pet

1:15–17: "As he who called you is holy, be holy yourselves in all your conduct; for it is written, 'You shall be holy, for I am holy.' Since you call upon a father who judges all people impartially according to their deeds, live in reverent fear during the time of your exile." For the "confession" of God as father, cf. Philo, *Post.* 175; Theophilus, *Autol.* 2.4; Origen, *Frag. Luc.* 162; Hippolytus, *Noet.* 8.1; Ps.-Justin Martyr, *Exp. rect. fid.* 379a.

Sentence 226

According to Lev 19:18, it is necessary to love the neighbor as oneself. As we saw, v. 87 reformulates this as a command to treat a pious person as oneself. Verse 226 represents yet another variation on the theme, naming the sage as the object of one's affection and expressing the command as a negative statement. While the sage treats all people fairly (e.g., v. 89), even aspiring to become a benefactor of all humanity (e.g., v. 210a), he only "loves" that which is like himself (v. 106a), that is, God (v. 106b) and a fellow sage (v. 292, cf. vv. 190, 244, 319), since "like is dear to like" (v. 443) and "what is wise is always like itself" (v. 147). Indeed, the wise are so much "alike" that when one sage honors another sage he also honors himself (v. 219). The use of the verb φιλέω to express the affinity that one ought to have for the sage brings the saying here into the ambit of ancient discussions of φιλία. Forming friendships and explicating the nature of friendship were matters of particular importance to Pythagoras and his followers (e.g., Diodorus Siculus, *Bibl. hist.* 10.8.1–2; Porphyry, *Vit. Pythag.* 59–61; Iamblichus, *Vit. Pythag.* 33.229–240; Diogenes Laertius, *Vit. phil.* 8.10, 16, 23, 33). Care should be observed in choosing friends (e.g., Clitarchus, *Sent.* 88, 141), the best friend being an individual who can help one advance in wisdom (e.g., *Sent. Pythag.* 33). If one fails to love such a friend, this not only hinders one's moral progress, it also demonstrates a failure to love oneself, since the friend is "a second self" (e.g., Porphyry, *Vit. Pythag.* 33). While it lacks the language of friendship, a similar sentiment is expressed in Prov 19:8: "The one who acquires understanding loves himself." For Sextus, as with the Pythagoreans, the friendship sages establish with one another has its basis in the friendship they have with God (see on v. 86b).

Sentences 227–228

The first saying in this couplet is repeated in the appendices as v. 594 with μηδέν in lieu of μηθέν and φιλοσόφου in lieu of φιλοσόφῳ. In its current context it is bound to v. 228 by the repetition of κτῆμα, and, less closely, to v. 229 by the repetition of φιλόσοφος. Similar language is employed in the first part of *Sent. Pythag.* 62 (μηδὲν κτῆμα ἴδιόν ἐστιν τοῦ ἀνδρός, ὃ μὴ καὶ τῆς γυναικός ἐστιν), though for the basic point *Sent. Pythag.* 80 is closer: "Be persuaded that you have no possession (κτῆμα) that is not within your intellect." Sextus's readers are similarly encouraged to acquire for themselves those things that have a share in reason (e.g., v. 277), that is, the things of the soul (v. 77). Being the only things that are truly divine, they are the only things that are truly secure (cf. vv. 118, 121b, 128) and the only things that the sage deems to be his "own" in the sense that their possession contributes to his identity as a person worthy of God. Indeed, he acquires these things to such an extent that "whatever possessions belong to God belong also to a sage" (v. 310). From the realm of the material, on the other hand, the readers are to acquire only enough to meet their physical requirements (vv. 19, 115), anything beyond this representing a source of distraction and impurity that must be expunged (vv. 78, 81, 264a, cf. vv. 137, 274b). Cf. Publilius Syrus, *Sent.* 424: "Think nothing your own that can change." Representing a more philosophical position, Epictetus claimed for himself nothing other than being a friend of God (cf. v. 86b), "not body, not property (οὐ κτήσεως), not office, not reputation—in short, nothing" (*Diatr.* 4.3.10).

Pythagoras similarly instructed his followers "to deem nothing your own (ἴδιον)" (Diogenes Laertius, *Vit. phil.* 8.23). Much like Sextus, this injunction is associated with an ideal of common property. From this perspective, v. 228 can be interpreted as a version of κοινὰ τὰ φίλων, a precept attributed to Pythagoras by Diogenes Laertius in *Vit. phil.* 8.10 (cf. Porphyry, *Vit. Pythag.* 33; Iamblichus, *Vit. Pythag.* 6.32), who goes on to explain how "his disciples put all of their possessions into one common stock" (cf. Diodorus Siculus, *Bibl. hist.* 10.3.5; Iamblichus, *Vit. Pythag.* 6.30; 18.81). The impulse informing the famous precept is reflected also in Sextus's Pythagorean source material, especially *Sent. Pythag.* 97: συγγενεῖ καὶ ἄρχοντι καὶ φίλῳ πάντα εἶχε πλὴν ἐλευθερίας. For Pythagoras, the practice of having possessions in common was motivated not only by his understanding of friendship, but also by a desire to establish a higher form of justice among his followers (Iamblichus, *Vit. Pythag.* 30.168). Sextus, by contrast, is motivated not by the principles of friendship or justice, but by a desire that his readers' substantiate their common confession of God (see on v. 225). In this case, the scenario projected by vv. 227–228 more closely approximates the community of goods depicted in Acts, according to which the Jerusalem Christians "had all things in common (κοινά) …

selling their possessions (κτήματα) and goods and sharing them with all, as anyone might have need ... spending much time together in the temple ... praising God" (2:44–47; cf. 4:32–35). As vv. 59 and 222 make plain, calling God "father" is an affirmation that the readers are to recall especially in their actions. Those who have a common father are not by implication friends, but principally siblings and members of the same household, a reality that according to our author ought to have implications for the decisions his readers make regarding possessions (cf. Plutarch, *Frat. amor.* 483d), specifically, they must share from what they have with the needy (vv. 330, 378–379, 383; and, again, cf. Acts 2:45; 4:34; also *Did.* 4.8: "You shall not turn away from someone in need, but shall share everything with your brother, and do not claim that anything is your own"). Since such priorities are grounded in the believer's filial relationship with God, failure to abide by them is properly represented as a form of impiety (cf. v. 96; Acts 5:1–11).

Sentence 229

This is the fourth saying within a relatively short span of the *Sentences* on the respect that ought to be accorded the philosopher-sage (vv. 218–219, 226, cf. v. 246). It is a fact of life that people will fail to show gratitude for the benefits they receive (v. 328). Those who fail to show gratitude for the philosopher fail to show gratitude to God, since the philosopher is a gift from God (v. 218), the living image of God (v. 190, cf. v. 307), and, as God's servant, deserving of a measure of respect second only to that of God (v. 319, cf. v. 244). Indeed he is the work of which God is most pleased (v. 308), and in the world of human affairs a benefactor second only to God (v. 176), since God actually dwells in his intellect (v. 144, cf. v. 421). It is only to those ignorant of these truths that the sage appears irrelevant (vv. 53, 145) or useless (v. 214, cf. vv. 53, 145). For the problem of ingratitude as a topic of theological reflection in early Christian discourse, see especially Justin Martyr, *Dial.* 19.5; Tatian, *Orat. Graec.* 4.1; Clement, *Strom.* 6.5.40.2; Ps.-Clement, *Hom.* 16.20; *Const. ap.* 6.20. Xenophon describes ingratitude as the "offence for which people hate one another the most but go to law the least," since they believe that "the ungrateful are likely to be most neglectful of their duty toward their gods, their parents, their country, and their friends" (*Cyr.* 1.2.7).

Sentences 230a–240

Text

230a γάμον^a δίδωσίν σοι παραιτεῖσθαι ἵνα ζήσῃς^b ὡς^c πάρεδρος θεῷ.
230b ^aγάμει καὶ παιδοποιοῦ χαλεπὸν εἰδὼς ἑκάτερον^a· εἰ δὲ καθάπερ εἰδὼς πόλεμον ὅτι χαλεπὸν ἀνδρίζοιο, καὶ^b γάμει καὶ παιδοποιοῦ^c.
231 μοιχὸς τῆς ἑαυτοῦ γυναικὸς πᾶς ὁ^a ἀκόλαστος.
232 μηδὲν^a ἕνεκα ψιλῆς ἡδονῆς ποίει.
233 ^aἴσθι μοιχὸς εἶναι κἂν νοήσῃς μοιχεῦσαι^a· καὶ περὶ παντὸς ἁμαρτήματος ὁ^b αὐτὸς ἔστω σοι λόγος^c.
234 πιστὸν εἰπὼν σεαυτὸν ^aὡμολόγησας μηδὲ^b ἁμαρτεῖν θεῷ^a.
235 πιστῇ γυναικὶ κόσμος σωφροσύνη νομιζέσθω.
236 ἀνὴρ γυναῖκα ἀποπέμπων ὁμολογεῖ μηδὲ^a γυναικὸς ἄρχειν δύνασθαι^b.
237 γυνὴ σώφρων ἀνδρὸς εὔκλεια.
238 αἰδούμενος γαμετὴν αἰδουμένην ἕξεις.
239 ὁ τῶν πιστῶν γάμος ἀγὼν ἔστω περὶ ἐγκρατείας.
240 ὡς ἂν γαστρὸς ἄρξῃς, καὶ ἀφροδισίων ἄρξεις.

Translation

230a It is granted you to decline marriage so that you might live as a partner to God.
230b Marry and have children knowing that each is difficult. If you would be brave, like one knowing that a battle will be difficult, then marry and have children.
231 Every intemperate person is an adulterer with his own wife.
232 Do nothing for the sake of mere pleasure.
233 Know that you are an adulterer if you even intend to commit adultery. And let your thought regarding every sin be the same.
234 In calling yourself faithful, you have pledged not to sin against God.
235 Let moderation be considered adornment for a faithful wife.
236 A man who divorces his wife admits to being unable to govern even a woman.
237 A moderate wife is her husband's renown.
238 If you respect your wife you will have her respect.
239 Let the marriage of faithful people be a struggle for self-control.

240 As you govern your stomach, you will also govern your sexual desires.

Textual Notes

230a[a] γάμον γάρ: Υ • 230a[b] ζήσεις: Π • 230a[c] omit Υ • 230b[a-a] omit Υ, sy[2] • 230b[b] omit Υ • 230b[c] ποίει: Υ • 231[a] omit Υ • 232[a] μηδὲ: Π • 233[a-a] μοιχὸς ὢν ἴσθι εἶναι κἂν νοσεῖς τὸ μοιχεύειν: Π • 233[b] omit Υ • 233[c] ὁ λόγος: Υ • 234[a-a] καὶ ὁμολογήσας μηδὲν ἁμαρτήσθω: Υ • 234[b] μήτε: Π • 236[a] μήτε: Π • 236[b] omit lat, sy[2] • 240 ὅταν γαστρὸς ἄρξεις καὶ ὑπογαστρίων ἄρξεις: Π

Commentary

Chadwick (1959, 153) identifies vv. 230a–240 as a section on marriage (note γάμος in vv. 230a, 239 and γαμέω in v. 230b; also γυνή in vv. 231, 235–237 and γαμετή in v. 238). Appropriately enough, the first two sayings (vv. 230a–b) take up the question of whether or not to be married, while subsequent sayings concern conduct within marriage, with a saying nearer to the end of the section (v. 236) speaking to the matter of divorce. Consistent with the ascetical tendencies of the text as a whole, the section's main emphasis is on the need for restraint in sexual relations. Note that two of the sayings (vv. 232 and 234) do not deal with sex and marriage per se but support the overall theme on account of their placement. Additional instruction on women and marriage is offered in the appendices (vv. 499–516).

Sentences 230a–b

The γάρ printed by Elter (1892, 16) and Chadwick (1959, 38) but missing from Π and Rufinus's translation (as well as from the Syriac translation) is, as Chadwick (1959, 172) suggests, probably a vestige from a now-lost source. The suggestion of Edwards and Wild (1981, 42) that it is a secondary redaction meant to join v. 230a to v. 229 seems unlikely since the two verses have nothing in common content-wise (a γάρ inserted into v. 231 or v. 234, for example, would have been more logical) and Sextus does not demonstrate a propensity for such editorial interference elsewhere (see part 4 of the introduction). Pointing to 1 Cor 7:1–6, Chadwick (1959, 172–73) also argues that v. 230a is addressed to married couples, granting them the right to dissolve their unions and live in abstinence. However, as v. 236 makes plain, our author frowns upon on the practice of divorce. If the two lines are read together, an alternative interpretation suggests itself, namely, that Sextus here addresses not married but unmarried readers, offering them permission to leave their status unchanged, provided that this is done for reasons of faith. Note also that while, on rare occasions, παραιτέομαι + γυναῖκα can refer to the situation of a husband leaving his wife (e.g., Ps.-Plutarch, *Reg. imp. apophth.* 206a), the construction παραιτέομαι + γάμον, which Sextus employs here, is used elsewhere of a man who refuses to enter into marriage (e.g., Josephus, *Ant.* 5.294) or of a man who disparages marriage generally (e.g., Clement, *Strom.* 2.23.138.3). If the alternative interpretation is accepted, then v. 230a can be read in conjunction with v. 230b, both lines addressing unmarried readers and presenting them with two basic options: either marry, knowing the difficulties involved, or live as a partner of God by remaining unmarried.

Similar options and priorities are discusses elsewhere in early Christian literature, for example, *Strom.* 7.12.70.7–8. "The prize in the contest of men," says Clement, is won not by the encratite but by "him who has trained himself by the discharge of the duties of marriage and procreation." Through the discipline of supervising a household, and by rising superior to all the tests of pleasure and pain implicated thereby, the married man "shows himself to be inseparable from the love of God" (*Strom.* 7.12.70.7). On the other hand, there is the unmarried man, who by comparison "is in most respects untried" because he cares for himself alone. Nevertheless, in Clement's opinion he is superior to the married man "as regards his own salvation" (*Strom.* 7.12.70.8). Thus, even as he mounts a rigorous defense of marriage (especially in book 3 of the *Stromata*), the Alexandrian concedes that single Christians are better suited to serve God than their married counterparts (cf. 1 Cor 7:8–9, 26, 38).

Looking at vv. 230a–b in light of this parallel, we notice that it is only to the unmarried that Sextus applies the title πάρεδρος θεῷ (literally, "God's assessor"), a designation that would appear to correspond especially with the sage's role as judge, for which see vv. 183–184 (cf. Philo, *Mut.* 194; *Ios.* 48; *Mos.* 2.53). Married life, meanwhile, is depicted as a difficult battle (πόλεμος; cf. Clement's use of νικᾷ in *Strom.* 7.12.70.7), referring presumably to the struggle for self-control (v. 239) that the married couple will engage against the allures of sensual pleasure (v. 232). For the combative dimension, cf. vv. 140 and 205. For descriptions of marriage as χαλεπός, see Antoninus Liberalis, *Metam. syn.* 39.3; Origen, *Comm. Joan.* 1.27.184; Stobaeus, *Anth.* 4.22a.25; 4.22b.64. Marriage for our author may not be preferable, but when observed with self-restraint it is not something to be regarded as shameful or immoral (see v. 202), and may in fact confer a certain degree of respect upon the believing husband (vv. 237–238). Finally, the coupling of γαμέω and παιδοποιέω twice in v. 230b (practically a hendiadys; cf. Clement, *Strom.* 2.23.141.5; 3.6.52.1) points to a further similarity with Clement, who endorses a strictly procreative definition of marriage (e.g., *Paed.* 2.10.83.1–2; *Strom.* 2.18.93.1; 2.23.137.1; 3.7.58.2). For Sextus's instruction on children, see vv. 254–257.

That marital status could create hierarchical divisions within an intentional community is attested in philosophical circles as well, including Pythagorean circles, for example, Philostratus, *Vit. Apoll.* 1.13.3: "Pythagoras was esteemed for the words he spoke, that a man must have relations with no other woman except his wife. Apollonius, however, said that Pythagoras ordained this for others and that he himself would never marry nor even as much as approach having intercourse." As a rule, the Cynic sage will also refrain from marriage for the sake of his mission (Epictetus, *Diatr.* 3.22.67–82; Ps.-Diogenes, *Ep.* 47; Diogenes Laertius, *Vit. phil.* 6.29). In fact, according to Epictetus, the situation facing the Cynic who is deciding whether or not to marry and beget children is "like that of a battlefield," one in which he has been summoned to serve as "the messenger, the scout, the herald of the gods" (*Diatr.* 3.22.69).

Sentence 231

Verses 231–234 constitute a subunit on adultery. Note μοιχός in vv. 231, 233 and μοιχεύω in v. 233; and for the role of ἡδονή (v. 232) in adultery, see below. The source of the first line is Clitarchus, *Sent.* 71: μοιχός ἐστι τῆς αὐτοῦ γυναικὸς πᾶς ὁ ἀκόλαστος. Sextus replaces ἐστι τῆς αὐτοῦ with τῆς ἑαυτοῦ. His saying is in turn cited by Jerome at *Jov.* 1.49 (*adulter est, inquit, in suam uxorem amator ardentior*) and *Comm. Ezech.* 6.18 (*adulter est uxoris propriae amator ardentior*) in translations that differ from one another as well as from the version offered by Rufinus (*adulter etiam propriae uxoris omnis inpudicus*). Cf. Peter Lombard, *Sent.* IV, 31.5.2: *omnis ardentior amator propriae uxoris adulter est.*

It was common knowledge that intemperate men are by nature adulterous (e.g., *Phal. ep.* 4.1; Philo, *Spec.* 3.1; Plutarch, *Adol. poet. aud.* 18f; *Conj. praec.* 144f; cf. *Tu. san.* 126a). For our author, such men are adulterous even when having sex with their wives, a position with which, according to *Paed.* 2.10.99.3, Clement would have agreed: "The one who seeks only sexual pleasure commits adultery against his own marriage (μοιχεύει … τὸν ἑαυτοῦ γάμον)." The Logos therefore instructs husbands "not to treat their wives as sexual objects, making their goal the violation of their bodies, but directing their marriage to ... moderation (σωφροσύνην) at the highest level" (*Strom.* 2.23.143.1). The promotion of such austere norms for marital sexuality would not have been unusual for the era. In Seneca's opinion, for instance, "nothing is more shameful than to love your wife as if she were your mistress" (*Matr.* 85; cf. Plutarch, *Conj. praec.* 142c; and for an extended treatment of the subject, Musonius Rufus, frag. 12). Philo has comparable standards in mind when he condemns individuals whose natural need for pleasure (ἡ κατὰ φύσιν ἡδονή) becomes so immoderate that it deteriorates into lustful and lascivious passion even for their own wives (*Spec.* 3.9, cf. 3.79, 113). For the idea of a man committing adultery with his own wife, see Athenagoras, *Leg.* 33.1–6; Origen, *Comm. Matt.* 14.24 (cf. Matt 5:32; 19:9).

Sentence 232

While this line does not address the topic of marriage per se, a saying on ἡδονή is not unexpected in this context, given the nature of its relationship with ἀκολασία. Specifically, as explained in v. 71b, in order to escape the latter one must stop longing for the former (cf. vv. 68, 451). While conceding that pleasure has a necessary place in human existence (v. 276), Sextus asserts that nothing should be done for the sake of mere pleasure (ἕνεκα ψιλῆς ἡδονῆς; cf. Porphyry, *Marc.* 35: ψιλῆς δὲ ἕνεκα ἡδονῆς μηδέποτε χρήσῃ τοῖς μέρεσι), since the desire for pleasure corrupts both the body (v. 139b) and the soul (v. 411), and those who fail to control their pleasures become the object of reproach (v. 272, cf. v. 70). Thus, one should never have sexual relations under the influence of pleasure, the same sort of rule that applies to eating and drinking (v. 111). Cf. v. 509: "Those who procreate for the sake of pleasure abuse the gifts of procreation." Again, a close parallel can be adduced from the writings of Clement: "Pleasure sought for its own sake (ψιλὴ ... ἡδονή), even within the marriage bonds, is a sin and contrary both to law and to reason" (*Paed.* 2.10.92.2). According to Musonius Rufus, frag. 12.86.7–8, sexual intercourse is "unjust and unlawful when conducted for mere pleasure (ἡδονὴν ... ψιλήν), even in marriage." For the relationship between ἡδονή and adultery, see also Ps.-Plutarch, *Lib. ed.* 5b; Clement, *Paed.* 3.3.22.1; Origen, *Cels.* 7.63; *Act. Thom.* 126.

Sentence 233

For the third member of the subunit (see above), our author turns to Matt 5:28 (for his interaction with Matt 5:29–30, see on vv. 12–14, 273):

"Everyone who looks at a woman with desire for her has already committed adultery with her in his heart" (cf. Exod 20:14; Deut 5:18; 2 Pet 2:14). While the evangelist situates the venue of adulterous sinning in the heart, Sextus characteristically focuses instead on the activity of the mind (for the ἴσθι formula, cf. Sext. 220; *Sent. Pythag.* 47–48). The source of sin is not one's body but one's thoughts (v. 12), and nothing that a human being thinks can escape God's notice (v. 57a). It is therefore necessary to purge the intellect of every evil thought and sinful intention (vv. 57b, 181) so that one does not "even consider doing" what must not be done (v. 178, cf. v. 327). For the generalizing application communicated in the second half of the line, cf. v. 596 ("Let even the intention to sin be considered to be a sin for you") and v. 601 ("Consider it a disgrace to intend a disgraceful action"). Adultery is frequently identified as a sin in the early church (e.g., Herm. *Mand.* 4.1.5; Clement, *Paed.* 3.12.89.1; Origen, *Hom. Jer.* 4.6; Ps.-Clement, *Hom.* 3.68; 5.8, 12). Clement alludes to Matt 5:28 frequently in the *Stromata*, for example, 3.2.8.4–3.2.9.1. Cf. *Strom.* 4.12.82.2: "For as he who wishes to commit adultery is an adulterer, although he does not succeed in committing adultery ... so also, if I see a man without sin, whom I specify, suffering, though he has done nothing bad, I should call him bad, on account of his wishing to sin."

Sentence 234
The reminder here is linked to the line that precedes it by catchword: ἁμαρτήματος (v. 233) and ἁμαρτεῖν (v. 234). To refrain from contemplating sins like adultery is an expression of one's identity and confession as a believer. Only those who are sinless (v. 8, cf. v. 46b) or practically sinless (vv. 247, 283, 298) are truly faithful. Indeed, the highest priority for those who claim the title "believer" is to avoid sin altogether (v. 247). Things like passion, then, should never arise in a believer's heart (vv. 204, 209), much less inform a believer's actions (vv. 75a, 206). Inasmuch as sinning makes one unworthy of God (v. 5), it is properly considered an act of sacrilege (v. 11) committed "against" God (ἁμαρτεῖν θεῷ). While Chadwick (1959, 139, 173) thinks that the pledge mentioned here alludes to "the baptismal promise," given the absence of references in our text to the rite or theology of baptism, the more likely allusion is to the confession of God as father: see especially v. 225, also with ὁμολεγέω. As Sextus stresses repeatedly, the readers' filial relationship with God has concrete implications for their moral comportment, committing them not only to avoiding anything shameful (v. 225), but to doing only that which is worthy of God (v. 58),

even to the point of becoming "holy and sinless" persons (v. 60, cf. vv. 59, 135, 221–222, 228, 376b).

Sentence 235

This line is connected to the one that precedes it by the catchword πιστός and to the two that follow it by the catchword γυνή. In the *Sentences*, moderation, especially as it pertains to meeting the needs of the body (v. 412), constitutes a path to holiness (v. 67). Since living a godly life is impossible without this virtue (v. 399), the readers must be prepared to take even extreme measures in order to observe it (vv. 13, 273). As the quotation from Clement, *Strom.* 2.23.143.1 above illustrates, it was not uncommon for σωφροσύνη to be held up as a matrimonial norm; cf. v. 499: "Nothing is more proper to marriage than moderation." Especially insofar as it was associated with the ideals of modesty and chastity, within such contexts σωφροσύνη was often singled out as a quintessentially "feminine" quality. In the Pythagorean tract "On Women's Moderation" attributed to Phintys, for example, it is said that "fortitude and prudence regard the man more than the woman … but moderation belongs peculiarly to the woman" (frag. 1.152.16–18). Musonius Rufus, meanwhile, while conceding that women will benefit from learning other virtues such as justice and wisdom, argues that "above all a woman must be moderate (σώφρονα); she must, I mean, be pure in respect of unlawful love, exercise restraint in other pleasures, not be a slave to desire, not be contentious, not lavish in expense, nor extravagant in dress…. The person who learns and practices these things would seem to me to have become especially well-ordered (κοσμιώτατος)" (frag. 3.40.17–24). As this quotation suggests, in both its standards and goals, moderation demonstrates a natural affinity for κόσμος ("order"), which can, especially in the case of women, be reflected in the sort of κόσμος ("adornment") they wear, as we learn also from 1 Tim 2:9 (ὡσαύτως γυναῖκας ἐν καταστολῇ κοσμίῳ μετὰ αἰδοῦς καὶ σωφροσύνης κοσμεῖν ἑαυτάς); cf. 1 Tim 2:15; 1 Pet 3:3–5. See further Clitarchus, *Sent.* 75 (= Sext. 513): "A wife fond of adornment is not faithful" (γυνὴ φιλόκοσμος οὐ πιστή).

Instructions such as these would have lent themselves readily to metaphorical application, as is the case here. In the same tract mentioned above, Ps.-Phintys similarly argues that a woman should eschew jewelry, cosmetics, and expensive garments, "adorning herself instead with modesty" (frag. 2.153.27–28), while Clement recommends that she be content with "the adornments the Holy Spirit confers: justice, prudence, fortitude, moderation, love of the good, and modesty" (*Paed.* 3.11.64.1;

cf. 2.12.129.1; 3.1.1.1). See further Plutarch, *Conj. praec.* 141e; Menander, *Mon.* 148: γυναικὶ κόσμος ὁ τρόπος, οὐ τὰ χρυσία. In Ps.-Clement, *Hom.* 13.16, meanwhile, metaphor becomes full-blown *ekphrasis*: "The moderate woman is adorned with the Son of God as bridegroom, clothed in holy light, her beauty lying in a well-governed soul, fragrant with ointment, that is, her good reputation, and arrayed in beautiful vesture, her modesty."

Sentence 236

Verses 235 (γυναικί ... σωφροσύνη) and 237 (γυνὴ σώφρων) are separated by a precept on divorce, which in turn shares a verb with v. 234 (ὁμολογέω), though it is used in a very different way. Chadwick's surprise regarding the absence of "any Christian appeal to divine or dominical sanction" (1959, 173) in v. 236 perhaps would have been more restrained had he recognized that the gnome is based not on any Christian source, but (in part) on Clitarchus, *Sent.* 69: γάμει δυνατὸς ὢν ἄρχειν (note that v. 238 parallels Clitarchus, *Sent.* 72, and that v. 240 parallels Clitarchus, *Sent.* 73). Both this saying and Sextus's expanded version reflect prevailing androcentric standards, according to which the respectable husband exercises control not only over himself (see v. 240, again with ἄρχω) but also over his wife, a perspective that becomes even more pronounced in the appendices to the *Sentences*, where we encounter a whole set of stock themes. See especially v. 506 ("Let a husband govern his wife, but not tyrannize her"), v. 508 ("A moderate man is able to govern his wife"), v. 512 ("The richer she is, the more difficult it will be for you to rule her"), v. 514 ("Let a wife regard her husband as the law of her life"), and v. 515 ("Let a husband make his wife obey him"). Cf. Menander, *Mon.* 300: "Either marry and rule (κράτει), or don't get married at all." For his part, Sextus not only assumes that the sage will govern other human beings, but that the manner in which he does so will reflect the manner in which he himself is governed by God (vv. 42–43, 182, 288). If this principle is applied in a rigorous sense, then the remarks made in v. 422 (that one rejoices in whatever one governs) and v. 423 (that one is joined to whatever one governs) could have some relevance for interpreting Sextus's understanding of marital relations. For ἀποπέμπω used of divorce, see Josephus, *Ant.* 17.48; Plutarch, *Aem. Paul.* 5.2; *Cic.* 41.2; Appian, *Bell. civ.* 2.2.14; Cassius Dio, *Hist. rom.* 37.45.2.

Sentence 237

While a man who is moderate has status before God (v. 67), a woman who is moderate enhances the status of the man to whom she is attached.

For σωφροσύνη as a matrimonial, and particularly feminine, virtue, see on v. 235. Incentive for that injunction is provided here with the observation that a wife's good reputation is a credit to her husband, a point made frequently by gnomic authors, for example, Prov 12:4 ("A virtuous woman is a crown to her husband"); 18:22; 19:14; 31:10; Sir 26:1–3, 15 ("Grace upon grace is a women with a sense of shame, and a soul with self-control has worth beyond all value"); Menander, *Mon.* 149 ("An upright wife is salvation for one's life"), 155 v.l. ("A moderate woman is the rudder of a noble life"). As Clitarchus, *Sent.* 123 points out (cf. Sext. 399), obtaining εὔκλεια is not possible if one does not live moderately (cf. Stobaeus, *Anth.* 4.22b.66).

Sentence 238

This line replicates Clitarchus, *Sent.* 72 exactly, except for replacing τὴν γυναῖκα with γαμετήν. Cf. Sext. 501: "If you respect your wife you will save her." Those who exhibit moderation in their comportment are naturally guided by a sense of shame (e.g., Philo, *Congr.* 124; *Fug.* 5; *Mut.* 217; 1 Tim 2:9; Clement, *Paed.* 2.12.129.2; 3.11.58.1; 3.11.64.1; Plutarch, *Conj. praec.* 139c; *Amat.* 765b). Within marital contexts, αἰδώς is held up as an ideal for the wife more often than it is for the husband (e.g., Dionysius of Halicarnassus, *Ant. rom.* 8.44.2; Plutarch, *Rect. rat. aud.* 37d; Clement, *Paed.* 3.11.58.1; *Strom.* 4.19.120.1), though, as with so many values in the Greco-Roman world, the logic of αἰδώς is generally governed by an ethic of reciprocity, as we see, for example, in Plutarch, *Conj. praec.* 144f–145a: "Plato used to advise the elderly men especially to have a sense of shame before the young, so that the young might be respectful toward them.... The husband ought to bear this in mind, and show no greater respect (αἰδεῖσθαι) for anyone than for his wife, seeing how their bedroom is bound to be for her a school of either orderly behavior or licentiousness" (cf. *Lyc.* 15.6). As this citation indicates, principal responsibility for initiating the cycle of mutual respect rests with the husband, and such respect pertains especially to sexual relations. See also *Conj. praec.* 139c: "Husband and wife bring to their mutual relations the greatest respect (αἰδεῖσθαι) as a token of the greatest love."

Sentence 239

As vv. 234–235 have established, propriety in marital affairs is a reflection of one's identity and commitment as a believer. Since self-control is the foundation of a pious life (v. 86a), it stands to reason that it would also be the foundation of a pious marriage (cf. v. 438). In the exposition on Christian marriage offered in book 3 of the *Stromata*, Clement refers to ἐγκράτεια over thirty times (*Strom.* 3.7.59.4; 3.10.69.3; 3.12.79.1; 3.16.101.5; etc.), often in conjunction with σώφρων or σωφροσύνη (e.g., *Strom.* 3.5.41.2; 3.12.86.1; cf. above on vv. 235, 237). For the Alexandrian, self-control describes an interior disposition that extends to every aspect of one's relationship with the things of the world, limiting their use to what is necessary and assuring that one never acts out of desire. Thus "when a man marries in order to have children he ought to practice self-control. He ought not to have a sexual desire even for his wife, to whom he has a duty to show Christian love. He ought to produce children by a reverent, disciplined act of will" (*Strom.* 3.7.58.3). For the agonistic imagery of Sextus's gnome, cf. Hippolytus, *Frag. Prov.* 10; Epiphanius, *Pan.* 2.361, 383, 503; Ephraem Syrus, *Serm. paraen. mon.* 44. According to v. 282, life ought to be a struggle not for ἐγκράτεια, but for σεμνός (cf. v. 332).

Sentence 240

The source for this line is Clitarchus, *Sent.* 73: ἐφ' ὅσον ἂν γαστρὸς ἄρξῃς, καὶ ἀφροδισίων ἄρξεις. Sextus alters the opening ἐφ' ὅσον to ὡς. In its current location, the maxim supports the admonition in v. 239 by identifying a means by which believers can achieve self-control in their married lives. Cf. v. 428 (= v. 588): "No one is faithful who does not control the stomach and the parts below the stomach." A somewhat different approach is suggested by v. 517: "When you have had enough children, you have had enough sexual desires (ἀφροδισίοις)." That a fundamental connection exists between alimentary and sexual drives is an idea deeply ingrained in gnomic thought, for example, P.Ins. 6.1 ("The evil that befalls the fool, his belly and his phallus bring it"); Menander, *Mon.* 263, 425; *Syr. Men.* 63–66 ("And there is no one who follows his lust and his stomach who will not immediately be dishonored and despised. Blessed is the man who has mastered his stomach and his lust; he is one on whom one can rely at all times"); Porphyry, *Marc.* 28: "Even the gods have prescribed remaining pure from food and sexual desires (ἀφροδισίων)." See further Musonius Rufus, frag. 18a–b; Josephus, *C. Ap.* 2.234; Plutarch, *Tu. san.* 126b; Porphyry, *Abst.* 1.47.2; Hierocles, *In aur. carm.* 8.1. For Sextus, overindulgence in eating impairs the soul (v. 345) by infecting it with impurities (vv. 108a–b), so much so that gluttony degrades one to a practically subhuman status (v. 270, cf. on v. 391). For further instruction on moderation in food and drink, see vv. 109–111, 265–269, and 412–413.

Sentences 241–253b

Text

241 φυλάττου τὸν παρὰ τῶν ἀπίστων[a] ἔπαινον.
242 ἃ προῖκα[a] λαμβάνεις παρὰ θεοῦ, καὶ δίδου προῖκα.
243 πλῆθος πιστῶν οὐκ ἂν ἐξεύροις[a]· σπάνιον γὰρ τὸ ἀγαθόν.
244 σοφὸν τίμα μετὰ θεόν.
245 ἐλεγχόμενος ἵνα γένῃ σοφὸς χάριν ἴσθι τοῖς ἐλέγχουσιν.
246 ὁ τὸν σοφὸν οὐ δυνάμενος φέρειν τὸ ἀγαθὸν οὐ δύναται [a]φέρειν.
247 πιστὸς εἶναι θέλων μάλιστα[a] μὲν μὴ ἁμάρτῃς, εἰ δέ τι, μὴ δισσῶς τὸ αὐτό.
248 ὃ μή ἐστι μάθημα θεοῦ ἄξιον, μὴ μάθῃς.
249 πολυμαθία[a] περιεργία [b]ψυχῆς νομιζέσθω.
250 ὁ τὰ[b] τοῦ θεοῦ [c]ἀξίως εἰδὼς[c] σοφὸς ἀνήρ[d].
251 [a]χωρὶς μαθήματος[b] οὐκ[a] ἔσῃ θεοφιλής· [c]ἐκείνου περιέχου[c] ὡς ἀναγκαίου[d].
252 φείδεται χρόνου σοφὸς[a] ἀνήρ.
253a παρρησίαν ἄγε[a] μετὰ αἰδοῦς.
253b ἔστιν σοφοῦ καὶ ὕπνος ἐγκράτεια.

Translation

241 Guard yourself against the praise of those without faith.
242 Things that you freely receive from God, freely give as well.
243 You will not find a multitude of those with faith, for goodness is scarce.
244 After God, honor a sage.
245 When you are being reproved in order that you might become wise, be grateful to those reproving you.
246 The one who is unable to bear the sage is unable to bear what is good.
247 If you want to be faithful above all do not sin; but if you do, do not commit the same one twice.
248 If something is a teaching unworthy of God, do not learn it.
249 Let excessive learning be considered something superfluous for the soul.
250 The one who knows the things of God in a worthy manner is a wise man.

251 Without learning you will not be dear to God: accept it as necessary.
252 A wise man is thrifty with time.
253a Use outspokenness with respect.
253b For a sage even sleep involves self-control.

Textual Notes
241ᵃ ἀνθρώπων: Π • 242ᵃ προῖκα καὶ δίδου: Υ • 243ᵃ εὕροις: Π • 246–247ᵃ⁻ᵃ φέρειν πιστὸς εἶναι θέλων. μάλιστα κτλ: Υ (Chadwick 1959, 174) • 247 omit Π • 248 ὃ μὴ ἔστι θεοῦ ἄξιον μάθημα μὴ θῇς: Υ • 249ᵃ πολυμάθεια: Υ • 249–250ᵇ⁻ᵇ ψυχῆς. νομιζέσθω σοι ὁ τὰ κτλ: Π (Chadwick 1959, 174) • 250ᶜ⁻ᶜ εἰδὼς ἄξια: Υ • 250ᵈ omit Π • 251ᵃ⁻ᵃ μαθήματος χωρὶς οὗ οὐκ: lat? • 251ᵇ μαθημάτων: Υ • 251ᶜ⁻ᶜ ἀσόφου μὴ περιέχου: Υ • 251ᵈ ἀναγκαῖον: Π • 252ᵃ ὁ σοφός: Π • 253aᵃ ἄγει: Υ, sy² • 253b–254 εἴ τι σοφοῦ καὶ ὕπνος ἀνιάτω σε. μᾶλλον κτλ: Υ

Commentary

The material included in this span of verses contains at least two fairly well-defined clusters of sayings. Bound by the catchword σοφός (cf. vv. 250, 252, 253b), there is, to begin with, vv. 244–46, to which has been attached an admonition on avoiding sin (v. 247). Complementing this is a unit on learning, vv. 248–251. Note μάθημα in vv. 248, 251, μανθάνω in v. 248, and πολυμαθία in v. 249. Verses 241 and 243, meanwhile, separated by an injunction on generosity (v. 242), convey an implicit contrast of believers and nonbelievers. This unit, in turn, is linked to the unit in vv. 244–246 by the repetition of τὸ ἀγαθόν in vv. 243 and 246. Perhaps it is not coincidental that a unit on learning (vv. 248–251) is situated near and between units on marriage (vv. 230a–240) and on children (vv. 254–257). A block of sayings on education (vv. 540–547) can also be found in the appendices.

Sentence 241
This line is repeated as v. 570 in the appendices. If praising the wicked only exacerbates wickedness (v. 150), then cherishing the praise of the wicked constitutes an equally objectionable practice, as we learn from an anecdote attributed to the Cynic sage Antisthenes, who, when informed that he was being commended by depraved men, replied "I am terribly afraid that I have done something wrong" (Diogenes Laertius, *Vit. phil.* 6.5; he has a similar rejoinder in 6.8 when told that he is being commended

by the masses). For Sextus, to be a nonbeliever is to be wicked, since life without faith is a kind of moral death (v. 7b) and therefore deserving of reproach (v. 400). While it is appropriate to welcome praise when it comes from the right source (v. 298), since most people are not believers—that is, good (see on v. 243)—a reasonable person will be reluctant to accept their approval. As we learn from v. 299, such a person will not only scorn the commendations of those he deems unworthy: he will also disregard their censures, a practice that accords with the opinion of Epictetus, according to whom paying attention to what uneducated people have to say by way of praise is just as misguided as paying attention to what they have to say by way of blame, since in both cases they fail to understand the principles upon which moral judgments ought to made (*Diatr.* 1.26.13). Similar discrimination was observed by King Agesilaus, who "whenever he heard people blaming or praising, thought it was no less necessary to inform himself about the ways of those who spoke than of those about whom they spoke" (Plutarch, *Apophth. lac.* 208d). Cf. Ps.-Cato, *Dist.* 1.14: "When someone praises you, remember to be your own judge; refuse to trust others more than yourself." For this use of φυλάττω, cf. vv. 269, 393, and especially v. 531: "Be on guard against the praises of the base" (φυλάττου φαύλων ἐπαίνους). Plutarch advises that upright individuals find for themselves "a defense and a shield" against the approval of flatterers and sycophants (*Adul. am.* 57c), since people become arrogant when they are praised for the wrong reasons (*Adul. am.* 59a).

Sentence 242

Here, as elsewhere in the *Sentences*, God is conceptualized as a benefactor, the readers as stewards and imitators of divine beneficence (see on vv. 33, 176, 210a, 260). Our author's inspiration may come from Matt 10:8 (δωρεὰν ἐλάβετε, δωρεὰν δότε), where the principle is applied to the gift of healing (cf. 4 Kgdms 5:15–16), though the idea is a common one. See Deut 15:14; 2 Cor 9:8; Menander, *Mon.* 198 ("Give to the poor as you receive from God the giver"); Ps.-Phoc. 28–29 ("Having wealth extend your hand to the poor. From what God has given you provide for those in need"); *T. Zeb.* 7.2 ("From what God has provided you, be compassionate and merciful to all without discrimination"); *Did.* 1.5 ("The father wants something from his own gifts to be given to everyone"). As these parallels suggest, and as vv. 52, 217, 330, 379, and 382 indicate, it is to the needy in particular that one should give, since the will to share with them is "something great" in God's sight. The repercussions for failure to follow this rule are spelled out in v. 378, again in reciprocal terms: "If you do not give to those in need when you are able, you will not receive from God when you are in need." Under such circumstances, it is in fact better to receive nothing from God than to receive much and share it with no one (v. 377).

Sentence 243
Logically this line corresponds better with v. 241 than it does with v. 242. The readers should assign no value to the judgment of unbelievers, since they are not "good." Furthermore, there will be very few people whose judgment they should value, since goodness is rare (cf. Publilius Syrus, *Sent.* 412: "You may make many attempts before finding a good man"). For Sextus, being a believer is synonymous with being good, that is, with doing and honoring that which is worthy of God (vv. 131–132, 197, 395) and that which sets one on a path to God (v. 349). Among humankind, the individual who embodies goodness most fully, of course, is the sage (see on v. 246; and cf. v. 535: πλῆθος φιλοσόφων οὐκ ἂν ἐξεύροις). Since being good (that is, being a believer) requires virtual sinlessness (vv. 8, 234, 247), there will not only be few sages, there will be few people who are wise enough even to recognize a sage for who he truly is (vv. 53, 145, 214). As Philo puts it, "The good is scarce, the evil abundant (μὲν σπάνιόν ἐστι τἀγαθόν, τὸ δὲ κακὸν πολύχουν). Thus it is hard to find a single sage, while of inferior persons there is a countless multitude" (*Leg.* 1.102; cf. *Ebr.* 26; *Migr.* 59–61; *Prob.* 63, 72). The multitude (τὸ πλῆθος), therefore, is something that must be approached with extreme caution (vv. 112, 343, 360). For Stoic views on the rarity of the sage, see *SVF* 3:658 (cf. Ps.-Diogenes, *Ep.* 41). Incapable of error or of assenting to anything false (Diogenes Laertius, *Vit. phil.* 7.121–122), even Zeus cannot surpass him in virtue (Plutarch, *Comm. not.* 1076a).

Sentences 244–246
These three sayings are connected by the catchword σοφός, which indicates their main theme. It was a tenet of traditional piety that one's highest obligation is to honor God, who has created and cared for all humanity, and thereafter one's parents, who have created and cared for oneself. See Menander, *Mon.* 322 ("Honor God foremost, and secondly your parents"); Xenophon, *Mem.* 4.4.19–20; Aristotle, *Eth. nic.* 9.2.8; Polybius, *Hist.* 6.4.5; Porphyry, *Abst.* 4.22.2–3; Diogenes Laertius, *Vit. phil.* 1.60 (Solon); 8.23 (Pythagoras); Ps.-Cato, *Dist.* prol. 1–2; Ps.-Phoc. 8: "First of all honor God, and after that your parents." In the *Sentences*, the place of the parents has

been taken over by the sage, the one who, after God, confers the greatest benefits on others (v. 176). In receiving honor second only to that of God, the sage is recognized in his role as a servant of God (v. 319, cf. vv. 219, 229), embodying the character and will of God to such an extent that it is even appropriate for him to be revered as a living image of God (v. 190). Cf. v. 292: ψυχῆς ἀγαθῆς ἔρα μετὰ θεόν.

Verses 245–246 elaborate on this characterization. The particular goodness of the wise man is evident in the fact that not only is he wise himself, but through his admonishments he endeavors to make others wise as well. Therefore the honor that ought to be accorded him is second only to that accorded God, the source of all wisdom (v. 30), while those incapable of enduring the sage's efforts are shown to be incapable of enduring goodness itself. People are ruled by what they honor, and it is always preferable to be ruled by what is best (vv. 41–42). The readers should therefore reject the judgments of the unfaithful (v. 241) but accept the judgments of the sage without complaint (v. 194), since he offers such judgments with the intent of making them wise. Indeed, his words have power to purify the soul (v. 24), especially through the refutation (ἔλεγχος) of irrational beliefs (v. 103), and the readers should expect to be censured for their mistakes, just as they desire to be praised for their accomplishments (v. 298).

Verse 245 (including the use of χάρις) may have been inspired by *Sent. Pythag.* 113ᵃ: "Give welcome to those who reprove you (χαῖρε τοῖς ἐλέγχουσί σε) rather than to those who flatter you." By the same token, the need to accept and appreciate reproof is a constant refrain in the book of Proverbs, for example, 1:23, 25, 30; 3:11–12 ("My son, do not despise the instruction of the Lord, nor faint when you are reproved by him, for whom the Lord loves he reproves, and he afflicts every son whom he receives"); 5:12; 6:23; 9:8 ("Reprove a sage and he will love you"); 10:10; 12:1; 13:18; 15:10, 12; 19:25; 27:5; 28:13; 29:1, 15 (cf. Sir 16:12; 18:13; 21:6). Note in particular Prov 28:23: "The one who reproves (ὁ ἐλέγχων) a person's ways will have more thanks (χάριτας) than one who flatters with the tongue." Insofar as the scene of a father reproving his son would have been a traditional one (as, for example, in Prov 3:11–12), here again we see the sage of the *Sentences* usurping the role of parent. Comparison with Clement's *Paedagogus* suggests that in a Christian context the sage of the *Sentences* might also be seen as usurping the role of the Lord. As the Alexandrian explains in *Paed.* 1.9.78.2, ἔλεγχος "is rebuke for sin expressed publically. (The Lord) employs it in a special way, as a necessity in our education, because of the weakness of faith exhibited by so many." As examples of this mode of instruction, he refers to Isa 1:4; Jer 2:12; Lam 1:9; and Prov 3:11 (*Paed.* 1.9.78.2–4). Since its purpose is to eradicate sin and establish justice, such reproof is properly understood as an expression of the Lord's innate goodness, that is, as an expression of the fact that he is good not only of himself but because he is good he establishes what is good for others (*Paed.* 1.9.88.1; cf. 1.9.85.4). The sage of the *Sentences* similarly represents what is "good" (v. 246), something that is rare and therefore to be treasured (v. 243), though while the aim of the Lord's reproof is to make sure that his listeners are saved (e.g., *Paed.* 1.8.72.1; 1.9.75.1), the aim of the sage's reproof is to make sure that his listeners are wise (cf. Theognis, frag. 7). Compare also v. 543: "If you reprove yourself you will not be reproved by others."

Sentence 247

This saying may have been attracted to the cluster in vv. 244–246 by the use of ἐλέγχω in v. 245. After all, sin is precisely the sort of thing sages are apt to reprove (cf. v. 298; also the quote of Clement, *Paed.* 1.9.78.2 above). This line can even be construed as an incentive for vv. 245–246, insofar as responding properly to reproof constitutes a means by which one can avoid repeating a mistake. Sextus is convinced that true faith is a matter of remaining sinless (v. 8, cf. v. 60), even in one's heart (v. 46b) and mind (vv. 181, 233), and that being faithful means committing oneself not to sin against God (v. 234). The readers should therefore expect to be chastised for their sins (v. 298) no matter how insignificant they might seem (vv. 9–11, 297). Given the gravity of the situation, the appropriate response to sin is not to ignore it, but to acknowledge it (v. 283), believers being more concerned with correcting their mistakes than with defending them: "When you struggle to defend an unjust deed that you have committed, you act unjustly twice (δίς)" (v. 452 = Clitarchus, *Sent.* 54). An equally serious tone is evoked by Sir 7:8: "Do not commit a sin twice; not even for one will you go unpunished." In *Strom.* 2.13, Clement explains that converts, having received pardon for previous sins, must refrain from future sin (*Strom.* 2.13.56.1). However, if they are subsequently "forced or tricked into sin," they may be granted one more chance of "a repentance that brings no regret" (*Strom.* 2.13.57.1; cf. 2 Cor 7:10). On the other hand, "to repeat an action repented is the deliberate accomplishment of an action already condemned" (*Strom.* 2.13.57.4), and for those who sin deliberately, "there is no sacrifice for sins left anymore," only "a fearful prospect of judgment" (*Strom.* 2.13.57.2; cf. Heb 10:25). A believer caught up in a recurring cycle of sin and repentance, then, is no different than an apostate (*Strom.* 2.13.57.3). Cf. Menander, *Mon.* 183 ("To commit the same sin twice is not the mark of a wise man"); Publilius Syrus, *Sent.* 239: "He who is unashamed of his offence doubles his sin."

Sentence 248

Catchword helps to unite the four sayings in vv. 248–251 around the theme of learning: μάθημα ... μάθης (v. 248), πολυμαθία (v. 249), μαθήματος (v. 251); note also ἄξιος in vv. 248 and 250. For a moral philosopher like Seneca, the only teachings worth studying are those that inculcate virtue: "All other studies are puny and puerile" (*Ep.* 88.2). Origen expresses a view somewhat closer to that of our author's when he explains in *Cels.* 3.47 that the opening chapters of 1 Corinthians condemn not wise men as such but only those who "interest themselves in things of sense" and so are "wise men of the world," as opposed to those who study that which is "intelligible, invisible, and eternal." The readers of the *Sentences* are instructed to eschew studies unworthy of God, that is, studies occupied with things of the material world (e.g., vv. 19–21), especially the body, its needs and passions (e.g., vv. 78, 101, 127, 448), as opposed to things proper to the realm of the mind (e.g., vv. 381, 447) and the soul (e.g., vv. 55, 77). Believers must be careful not to believe everything that they hear (v. 409), especially everything that they hear about God, since it is possible for anyone to offer theological speculations, but for only a righteous few to know and speak the truth (v. 410). There is a great deal at stake in such exchanges, since even listening to a novel doctrine can endanger one's faith (v. 338). Examples of μαθήματα unworthy of God would no doubt including teachings that deny divine providence (v. 312) or suggest divine indifference to human affairs (v. 380) or in some fashion constitute blasphemy (vv. 82e–85). According to Origen, the contents of scripture have been organized and presented in such a way that nothing unworthy of God can be learned from them (*Princ.* 4.2.9; *Philoc.* 1.16; cf. *Sel. Lev.* 12.397).

Sentence 249

The readers should be concerned with the extent as well as with the character of their learning. Becoming a polymath is not the same as becoming a sage, a point developed at some length in the pseudo-Platonic dialogue *Amatores* (e.g., 139a). Cf. *Gnom. Democr.* 64–65: "Many who have much learning have no intelligence. One should cultivate much intelligence, not much learning." For Sextus, any knowledge beyond what is necessary for the good of the soul (vv. 24, 97, 103, 167, 195, 413, 441, etc.), that is, beyond what one needs in order to honor and imitate God (e.g., vv. 41–46b), constitutes a περιεργία, or "superfluity" (for the language, cf. Origen, *Frag. Lam.* 29; Ephraem Syrus, *Imit. prov.* 255). A comparable saying in *Sent. Pythag.* 2ᶜ includes a suggestion as to the positive aspects of study as well, something that Sextus will take up in the next two lines: "Becoming educated should not be seen to consist in acquiring much learning (πολυμαθείας), but in discarding one's natural passions" (cf. Porphyry, *Marc.* 9). According to Clement, insofar as it teaches self-control, philosophy is desirable for its own sake, but, when it is pursued with the intent of knowing and glorifying God, it becomes "more majestic and more authoritative" (*Strom.* 1.5.30.2). By the same token, the Alexandrian is aware that philosophical studies can have a certain distracting allure. At *Strom.* 1.19.93.2, for example, he cites with approval the dictum of Heraclitus (= frag. 18): "Much learning (πολυμαθίη) does not teach understanding" (cf. Diogenes Laertius, *Vit. phil.* 9.1). Thus "the one who culls what is useful for the advantage of the catechumens, especially when they are Greeks … must not abstain from erudition (φιλομαθίας) like irrational animals, but he must by no means linger over these studies, except solely for the advantage accruing from them" (*Strom.* 6.11.89.2). For Clement one of the principal advantages of exposure to a broad curriculum is that it better enables one to "protect the faith from all attacks" (*Strom.* 1.9.43.4). In addition, a Christian teacher of wide learning, especially one conversant with the most important philosophical doctrines, will more readily win the confidence of his listeners, even to the point of "creating astonishment in candidates for church membership" (*Strom.* 1.2.19.4).

Sentence 250

A sage is not simply someone who knows teachings that are worthy of God (v. 248); he also knows such teachings in a worthy (ἄξιος) manner (v. 250). Cf. *Sent. Pythag.* 79: "Every person is worthy to the extent that the things he knows or thinks are worthy." What the sage "knows" is himself, that is, the reason for which he exists (v. 398), namely, to know God through the cultivation of his noetic capacities (v. 394), which represent the means by which one can comprehend God's words and deeds and honor God accordingly (v. 439). This last point is crucial, since for the sage it is sufficient not to obtain knowledge about God but to draw on such knowledge in order to honor God, something that he does especially by imitating God, the highest honor that anyone can offer (v. 44). In this way the sage not only knows what is worthy of God—he becomes worthy of what he knows about God by becoming like God (cf. vv. 4–5, 58, 132, 376a). Such a person has truly earned the title "wise," since his wise words are confirmed by his wise actions (cf. vv. 177, 359, 383, 408).

Sentence 251

Cf. *Carm. aur.* 30–31: "Do not do even one thing of which you do not understand, but learn what is necessary, and you will lead a most enjoyable life." For the concept of "necessary" learning, see also Plato, *Resp.* 519c; *Leg.* 818b–d, 967e; Clement, *Paed.* 3.10.52.2; Diogenes Laertius, *Vit. phil.* 6.7; Iamblichus, *Vit. Pythag.* 17.79. Assuming that for Sextus such learning includes the sort of teaching conveyed by the *Sentences* itself, then v. 251 also corresponds to the appeals sometimes conveyed by gnomic documents for the reader to accept the author's instruction, such as we find in Prov 1:1–7; Sir prol. 1–14; *Teach. Silv.* 87.4–15; Epicharmus, frag. (c) 6–9; *Gnom. Democr.* 35; and Ps.-Cato, *Dist.* 3.1: "Equip your mind with precepts: do not fail to learn; for without learning life is like an image of death" (note also the general prologue to Cato's collection, as well as the prologues to books 2, 3, and 4).

For Sextus, there are certain things that derive only from learning (v. 290), including especially knowledge of how to achieve εὐδαιμονία (v. 344). A believer who is fond of learning (φιλομαθής) both knows and does the truth (v. 384), while those who lack learning are a burden to others (v. 285). The endorsement of learning here also supplements the emphasis placed throughout the text on acquiring wisdom (e.g., vv. 167–168, 199, 245, 406, 441) and cultivating the intellect (e.g., vv. 46a, 57b, 61–62, 143–144, 381, 447, 450). In *Strom.* 1.6.35.2, Clement describes the advantages of education to Christian life this way: "Just as we say that it is possible to have faith without being literate, so we assert that it is not possible to understand the statements contained in faith without study. To assimilate the right affirmations and reject the rest is not the product of simple faith, but of faith engaged in learning." Verse 251 differs from the gnomic appeals mentioned above in that it links learning with the goal of becoming someone who is dear to God (θεοφιλής), a term that not only signifies the nature of the sage's relationship to God (v. 419), but as such also serves as the basis for what he says and does (vv. 340, 358–359, 363a). As Clement observes in *Strom.* 7.1.3.6, a person who is dear to God is "someone who knows (ὁ εἰδώς, cf. v. 250) what is fitting both in theory and in life" (cf. *Strom.* 1.26.168.4; 2.5.20.2). Compare also *Sent. Pythag.* 2ª: "Lack of education is the mother of all passions" (cf. Porphyry, *Marc.* 9).

Sentence 252

This line represents our author's variant on the precept χρόνου φείδου, a saying of the seven sages (Septem Sapientes, *Praec.* 217.16; 218.15–16), and attributed specifically to Chilon in Septem Sapientes, *Sent.* 216.31. In Tryphon, Περὶ τρόπων 202.19, it is cited as a Delphic maxim (together with γνῶθι σαυτόν and μηδὲν ἄγαν) under the heading περὶ βραχύτητος. In *Strom.* 5.4.22.1, Clement explains that the saying refers to the fact that "either because life is short, we ought not to expend this time in vain; or on the other hand, it bids you spare your personal expenses, so that, though you may live many years, necessities may not fail you." The latter interpretation accords with the value assigned thrift generally in gnomic literature, for example, Hesiod, *Op.* 368–369; Theognis, *El.* 903–932; *Gnom. Vat.* 43; P.Ins. 4.6–7; 6.17; Ps.-Phoc. 138. In *Contempl.* 16 (cf. *Prob.* 14), Philo links the precept with another well-known aphorism: "For taking care of wealth and possessions consumes time, and to be thrifty with time is a fine thing (χρόνου δὲ φείδεσθαι καλόν), since according to the physician Hippocrates, 'Life is short but art is long.'" According to Iamblichus, it was for the sake of "being thrifty with time" that Pythagoras renounced drinking wine, eating meat, and eating excessively, a regimen that limited his need for sleep (*Vit. Pythag.* 3.13; cf. vv. 109, 253b, 265, 269, 435). For Sextus, the only appropriate use of one's time is thinking about God (v. 54).

Sentence 253a

Drawing on a familiar cultural ideal (e.g., Demosthenes, *Or.* 6.31; Diodorus Siculus, *Bibl. hist.* 12.63.2; Acts 19:8; 26:26; Eph 6:19–20), Clement describes the true gnostic as someone who, on the basis of his extensive study and experience, "has acquired boldness of speech, not the power of a mere random fluency, but the power of straightforward utterance, keeping back nothing that may be spoken at a fitting time before the right audience, either from favor or from fear of influential persons" (*Strom.* 7.7.44.8). The gnostic's training will even inculcate in him a certain frankness when speaking to God, emboldening him to ask for that of which he has made himself worthy (e.g., *Strom.* 7.7.48.5–6; 7.12.71.1–3; 7.12.72.6; 7.13.81.3–4). Outspokenness in talking to others is a value for Sextus as well, though only when combined with respect. While παρρησία is sometimes presented as the opposite of αἰδώς (e.g., Achilles Tatius, *Leuc. Clit.* 1.5.6; Maximus of Tyre, *Dial.* 4.5), to speak to someone openly and frankly without having a sense of shame could be seen as insulting (e.g., *Act. Thom.* 43). As Plutarch explains, frank speech ought to be delivered in a manner that is "friendly and noble," so as to win the approval of one's listeners (*Adul. amic.* 66e). Combining outspokenness with modesty is particularly important when addressing one's superiors (Philo, *Ios.* 222, cf. 107). Although there is nothing that can deprive him of his freedom (vv. 275, 309), the Sextine sage is circumspect when it comes to freedom of speech (e.g., vv. 153–154), especially when in the company of other believers (v. 171b). In particular, a proper sense of reverence governs all his talk about God (vv. 84, 355, 366, cf. v. 22). In the same vein, while he is not reluctant to pray for those things that he has rightly earned (v. 125), such petitions will be tempered by a strong sense of humility regarding his relationship with God (v. 434). Insofar as speaking openly sometimes involves speaking publically (e.g., John 7:26; 18:20), this gnome accords also with warnings such as those expressed in vv. 164a and 360.

Sentence 253b

For the sage, ἐγκράτεια is not only his most valuable asset (v. 294, cf. v. 239), it is the basis for his relationship with God (vv. 86a, 438). While its formulation is quite different, the inclusion of this saying on self-control may have been prompted by Clitarchus, *Sent.* 87: ὕπνον προσίεσο διὰ τὸ ἀναγκαῖον (note the use of Clitarchus, *Sent.* 76 in v. 255). In gnomic literature, maxims urging discipline in sleep are often found contributing to one or both of two prominent sapiential themes, the condemnation of laziness and the commendation of industriousness. See Prov 6:9–11; 10:5; 19:15; 20:13 ("Do not love sleep, or else you will come to poverty; open your eyes, and you will have plenty of bread"); 24:33–34; Menander, *Mon.* 780 v.l.; *Syr. Men.* 67–75; Ps.-Cato, *Dist.* prol. 19; *Carm. aur.* 9–11: "Accustom yourself to have control (κρατεῖν) of the following above all: of your stomach, of sleep, of lust, and of anger." As this final example illustrates, self-control in sleep was thought to be interrelated with self-control in other areas of personal comportment (cf. Hierocles, *In aur. carm.* 8.1), including eating (cf. vv. 109–111, 240, 265), drinking (cf. vv. 110–111, 269), and sex (cf. vv. 239–240). A connection between eating, sleeping, and sex is implied by v. 435 as well: "A person who doubly gorges himself with food and never sleeps alone at night cannot avoid (sexual) couplings." Iamblichus explains that Pythagoras limited his need for sleep by abstaining from wine, meat, and excessive eating, all for the sake of "being thrifty with time" (*Vit. Pythag.* 3.13), suggesting that this line offers some specification as to the observation just made about the sage in v. 252 as well.

In chapter 9 of *Paedagogus* book 2, Clement offers an extended reflection on the proper Christian attitude toward sleep, which he believes ought to be governed by the standards of σωφροσύνη (*Paed.* 2.9.77.1). Accordingly, expensive beds and bedding are frowned upon, sleep being something "taken not as self-indulgence, but as rest from activity" (*Paed.* 2.9.78.5). Even at night, believers should rouse themselves from sleep frequently for times of prayer, like servants alert for the return of their master (*Paed.* 2.9.79.1–4; cf. Prov 8:34; Luke 12:35–37). Citing 1 Thess 5:5–8 as a proof text, he claims that a reasonable person will reserve "only as much time for sleep as his health demands, much sleep not being required, once that little has become a regular habit" (*Paed.* 2.9.80.1–2; cf. Plato, *Leg.* 808c). Not surprisingly, this is supplemented by recommendations about being disciplined in habits of eating and drinking (*Paed.* 2.9.80.3–4).

Sentences 254–257

Text

254 ἀνιάτω σε μᾶλλον τέκνα κακῶς ζῶντα τοῦ μὴ[a] ζῆν.
255 [a]τὸ γὰρ[a] ζῆν μὲν[b] οὐκ ἐφ' ἡμῖν, [c]καλῶς δὲ ζῆν καὶ ἐφ' ἡμῖν[c].
256 τέκνα μὴ πιστὰ οὐ τέκνα.
257 πιστὸς ἀνὴρ εὐχαρίστως φέρει τέκνων ἀποβολήν.

Translation

254 Let it grieve you more that children live badly than that they do not live at all.
255 For to live is not up to us, but to live nobly is indeed up to us.
256 Children who are not faithful are not children.
257 A faithful man bears the loss of children gratefully.

Textual Notes
253b–254 εἴ τι σοφοῦ καὶ ὕπνος ἀνιάτω σε. μᾶλλον κτλ: Υ • 254[a] omit Π • 255[a–a] τέκνα: Π • 255[b] omit Υ • 255[c–c] omit Υ

Commentary

This short section on children (so Chadwick 1959, 153) supplements the instruction on marriage in vv. 230a–240. Note especially τέκνον in vv. 254, 256, 257, as well as ζάω in vv. 254, 255 and πιστός in vv. 256, 257. The author's message in this tightly organized segment (an admonition followed by three supporting explanatory statements) is clear enough: the reader should judge his children by the same standards he judges anyone, including himself.

Sentence 254

It is probably safe to assume that Sextus, like Clement (see on vv. 230a–b), believed that sexual relations in marriage should occur only for the sake of procreation. Also like Clement (e.g., *Strom.* 3.15.98.4; cf. 1 Tim 2:15; Titus 1:5–6; *Did.* 4.9), he probably believed that parents have a responsibility to raise their children in the faith (see also v. 256). A lack of success in this regard, then, is for the parents a cause for grieving. Cf. vv. 519–520: "Raise your children as though they were to be servants of God. Pray to have no children at all rather than to have bad ones." In other early Christian contexts, the prospect of bearing wicked offspring can inform vehement denunciations of both marriage and children, for example, *Act. Thom.* 12: "Abandon this filthy intercourse … and you will not be girt about with cares for life and for children … for the majority of children become unprofitable, possessed by demons … performing useless and abominable deeds … caught either in adultery or murder or theft or unchastity, and by all these you will be afflicted." Gnomic authors, by contrast, are wont to endorse an approach that is less dogmatic and more evaluative in nature, for example, P.Ins. 9.12–15: "The son who is not taught, his <…> causes wonder. The heart of his father does not desire a long lifetime for him. The wise one among the children is worthy of life. Better the son of another than a son who is an accursed fool." Cf. Wis 3:10–4:6 and Sir 16:1–3 (quoted below). From Sextus's perspective, losing a child is less painful than seeing one become morally corrupt, since what kills the soul is not death but an evil life (v. 397, cf. vv. 7b, 175, 208b).

Sentence 255

The source for this verse is Clitarchus, *Sent.* 76: τέκνα ζῆν μὲν οὐκ ἐφ' ἡμῖν, καλῶς δὲ ζῆν ἐφ' ἡμῖν. Sextus replaces τέκνα with τὸ γάρ, so that the line, taken in isolation, expresses a *topos* familiar especially from Stoic philosophy, for example, Musonius Rufus, frag. 38; Epictetus, *Ench.* 1.1 (τῶν ὄντων τὰ μέν ἐστιν ἐφ' ἡμῖν, τὰ δὲ οὐκ ἐφ' ἡμῖν); Seneca, *Ep.* 90.1 ("Life is the gift of the immortal gods, but living well is the gift of philosophy");

93.2 ("We should strive, not to live long, but to live rightly"). Cf. Plato, *Crit.* 48b: "The most important thing is not life, but the good life." Note that in none of these parallels do we find a reference to children. Nevertheless, the application of Sext. 255 to τέκνα is clear enough, not only from the immediate context but also from the way that the line is bound to the one that precedes it by the use of γάρ, the repetition of ζῶντα ... ζῆν (v. 254) ... ζῆν ... ζῆν ... (v. 255), and the juxtaposition of κακῶς (v. 254) with καλῶς (v. 255). For Sextus's conception of the noble life, see on vv. 56, 104, 113, 142, 196–197, 215, 304, 390, and 399.

Sentence 256
Verse 256 offers another explanation as to why one should be more distressed over a child who lives badly than over one who dies: the former, because he or she does not believe, has ceased to be one's child at all. As the previous verse has established, it is within one's power to choose to live nobly, and, as v. 196 has established, it is only possible to live nobly if one chooses to have faith. Those without faith, on the other hand, are as good as dead (v. 7b), their lives fit only for reproach (v. 400). Especially noteworthy for comparative purposes is Sir 16:1–3: "Do not desire a multitude of worthless children, and do not rejoice in ungodly offspring. If they multiply, do not rejoice in them, unless the fear of the Lord is in them. Do not trust in their survival, or rely on their numbers; for one can be better than a thousand, and to die childless is better than to have ungodly children."

Sentence 257
Verse 257 provides a third and final explanation in support of v. 254: a child lost to death is less painful than a child lost to immorality because death is something to be welcomed. Here we encounter another argument familiar from Stoic sources, for example, Seneca, *Ep.* 74.30: "The sage is not distressed by the loss of children or of friends. For he endures their death in the same spirit in which he awaits his own. And he fears the one as little as he grieves for the other." See also Seneca, *Prov.* 3.2; Epictetus, *Diatr.* 2.17.19–28; 3.24.27; *Ench.* 11; Marcus Aurelius, *Med.* 1.8 (cf. Plato, *Resp.* 387e; Teles, frag. 7.56–57). Such statements are reflective of the *praemeditatio futuri mali*, intellectual exercises meant to train the sage to see death not as an evil, but as an opportunity for exercising virtue (e.g., Cicero, *Tusc.* 3.28–32). That comparable practices were observed among Pythagorean tradents is suggested by Iamblichus, *Vit. Pythag.* 31.196 (cf. 32.224): "They had a precept, that no human misfortune should be unexpected

to those with understanding, but that they should expect everything over which they themselves are not in control." Cf. *Carm. aur.* 13–16; Hierocles, *In aur. carm.* 11.6: "The righteous mode of life bears the loss of children mildly (παίδων ἀποβολὴν πράως ἤνεγκεν), being able to say, 'Has the child died? So, it has been given back.'" In the *Sentences*, death is understood as both a blessing and a benefit, insofar as it releases the soul from the chains of the body (vv. 320–322). While the sage will cause neither his own death (v. 321) nor the death of another (v. 324), he does not become angry with those who do (v. 321) but bears the loss of life in the same manner he bears all of the "things that must be" (v. 119), understanding that only someone inexperienced in spiritual matters faces death with fear or grief (v. 323). Clement similarly believes that a believer's attachment to the faith ought to outweigh attachments to his household or any of its members: "We have an obligation to behave as resident aliens: if married, as if we were single; if we have possessions, as if dispossessed; if we have children, doing so in the knowledge that they will die" (*Strom.* 3.14.95.3). Cf. Sext. 522–523: "Remember that you did not beget children for yourself alone, for they are liable to death. If you are unable to bear the loss of children (φέρειν τέκνων ἀποβολήν), do not have them."

Sentences 258–264b

Text

258 μὴ κρίνῃς φιλόσοφον ᾧ μὴ πάντα πιστεύεις.
259 διαβολὰς κατὰ φιλοσόφου[a] μὴ παραδέχου.
260 ἐπιτήδευε κοινὸς ἀνθρώποις[a] εὐεργέτης εἶναι.
261 ἀπευκτὸν[a] ἡγοῦ καὶ τὸ δικαίως τινὰ κολάζειν.
262 μετ' εὐθυμίας[a] εἰ θέλεις ζῆν, μὴ πολλὰ πρᾶττε· πολυπραγμονῶν γὰρ κακοπραγμονῶν ἔσῃ.
263 ὃ μὴ κατέθου, μηδ'[a] ἀνέλῃς, [b]οὐ γὰρ κατὰ τὸν αὐτάρκη πολιτεύῃ[b].
264a ἀφεὶς ἃ κέκτησαι[a] ἀκολούθει τῷ ὀρθῷ λόγῳ.
264b ἐλεύθερος ἔσῃ ἀπὸ πάντων δουλεύων θεῷ.

Translation

258 Do not judge someone in whom you do not have complete trust to be a philosopher.

259 Do not accept slander against a philosopher.
260 Strive to be a common benefactor to humanity.
261 Deem even the just punishment of someone to be deplorable.
262 If you want to live contentedly, do not do many things; for by doing much you will be doing ill.
263 What you have not put down, do not take up, for by doing this you will not conduct yourself in accord with self-sufficiency.
264a Let go of the things that you have acquired and follow right reason.
264b You will be free from all things if you serve God.

Textual Notes
259ᵃ φιλοσόφων: Υ • 260ᵃ ἄνθρωπος: Π • 261ᵃ ἀπευκταῖον: Υ • 262ᵃ εὐθείας: Π • 263ᵃ μηδὲ: Υ • 263ᵇ⁻ᵇ omit Π • 264aᵃ ἐκέκτησο: Π

Commentary

This miscellaneous set of sayings contains three weakly defined subunits. First, in vv. 258–259, we have a pair of prohibitions regarding the treatment of a philosopher. Next, there is a pair of admonitions regarding the treatment of others: the readers should be more concerned with doling out benefits than meting out punishments (vv. 260–261). The maxims in vv. 262–264b, finally, are loosely associated by the theme of distractions from service to God.

Sentences 258–259
These two lines are linked by the catchword φιλόσοφος. The former offers advice regarding one of those situations in which the readers will need to judge others (v. 183), that is, when a determination must be made as to whether or not someone is a philosopher. According to Sextus, an individual should not be so judged unless he has proven himself to be a person in whom the readers can have complete trust. Trust, in turn, should be based not simply on what the person says (v. 409)—especially since philosophers will not talk much about themselves (v. 284)—but on a faithful harmony of words and deeds (vv. 177, 359, 383, 408). It was a cliché among ancient moralists, including Pythagorean moralists, that care ought to be observed when forming friendships, for example, *Carm. aur.* 5; Clitarchus, *Sent.* 88 ("Do not make friends quickly"), 141 ("It is better to have one friend who is worthy than many friends who are not");

Porphyry, *Vit. Pythag.* 13. According to Ps.-Plutarch, *Lib. ed.* 12e, the Pythagorean *akousma*, "Do not give the right hand to everyone," means "Do not become friends with everyone" (cf. Plutarch, *Amic. mult.* 96a). Various gnomic sources also contribute to this theme, such as Sir 6:7 ("If you would gain a friend, put him to the test, and do not put your trust in him quickly"); Isocrates, *Demon.* 24; *Ad Nic.* 27; P.Ins. 12.15, 18; Publilius Syrus, *Sent.* 134 ("Mind you think no man a friend save him you have tried"); Ps.-Cato, *Dist.* 4.15 ("When you seek a companion or a friend, ask about a person's life, not his fortune"). Compare also Seneca, *Ep.* 3.2: "If you consider any man a friend whom you do not trust as you trust yourself, you are mightily mistaken and you do not sufficiently understand what true friendship means." In the hands of our author, advice regarding the φίλος is converted into advice regarding the φιλόσοφος, the latter usurping the role not only of parent (see on v. 244), but also of friend.

Thus, just as one should not accept slander aimed at a friend (e.g., Sir 19:15), one should not accept slander aimed at a philosopher (v. 259). Indeed, the status of the latter is so divine in nature that censuring a wise man is tantamount to censuring God (v. 194). Instead, a philosopher should be honored and esteemed as a servant of God (vv. 219, 229, 319). For his part, the philosopher must both expect slander and become inured to it, since the majority of people have no appreciation for the sage (vv. 53, 145, 214, cf. v. 229) and the sage will make little effort to ingratiate himself with the masses (vv. 112, 241). Cf. v. 299: "Spurn the censures of those whose praises you despise." For the διαβολή that a philosopher must endure, see Plato, *Apol.* 23a; *Resp.* 499d–500d; Xenophon, *Mem.* 1.2.31; Philostratus, *Vit. Apoll.* 1.2. Clement also finds slander unacceptable, though for him this is true regardless of the target. Citing Exod 23:1 he writes, "'You shall not accept (οὐ παραδέξῃ) an idle report, nor consent to an unjust person becoming an unjust witness', whether for slander (εἰς διαβολάς) or for libel or indeed for malice" (*Paed.* 2.7.57.3).

Sentences 260–261

Comparison with Plato, *Gorg.* 476a–477b suggests that these two lines can be read as a couplet. Here Socrates persuades his interlocutor that the just punishment (τὸ κολάζεσθαι δικαίως) of a wrongdoer confers a benefit (ὠφέλεια) on him inasmuch as it removes "something bad in his soul" (*Gorg.* 477a, quoted with approval by Clement at *Paed.* 1.8.67.2; cf. 1.8.70.3). Likewise, in vv. 260–261, disciplining wrongdoers would appear to be among the services rendered by someone who aspires to be a public benefactor (cf. vv. 47, 176, 210a, 213, 260, 328), though for Sextus such actions should be carried out only with great reluctance. For κόλασις as an act of εὐεργεσία, cf. Philo, *Virt.* 41; and note the title for chapter 9 of Clement, *Paedagogus* book 1: Ὅτι τῆς αὐτῆς δυνάμεως καὶ εὐεργετεῖν καὶ κολάζειν δικαίως. As he explains in *Strom.* 7.16.102.5, when God punishes human beings, he does so not out of vengeance but with a view to the good, both public and private (καὶ κοινῇ καὶ ἰδίᾳ), of those who are punished. Ironically, the Sextine sage must endure ill repute (v. 259), even though as a benefactor to humanity he is excelled only by God (v. 176, cf. v. 542). The first saying in our couplet exhorts the readers to strive for this anthropological ideal themselves, essentially repeating the injunction of v. 210a: ἀνθρώποις χρῶ τοῖς ἅπασιν ὡς κοινὸς ἀνθρώπων εὐεργέτης. The notion of "public" beneficence is one that our author takes seriously. The readers are encouraged to treat all people well, even enemies (v. 213) and the ungrateful (v. 328). In this they follow the example of God (v. 372), the ultimate benefactor (v. 33) and the one for whose sake benefits ought to be conferred on others (v. 47).

As v. 63 makes plain, following God's example also includes showing leniency when judging malefactors. The readers should be loath to punish others, even rightly, since when they do so they run the risk of forestalling God's action as postmortem judge (vv. 14, 347), the one in whose hands the ultimate fate of all human souls lies (vv. 373, 436a–b). This risk is significant, since if they judge wrongly they themselves will be judged by God (vv. 183–184). Nevertheless, the sage is deeply aware of the power that injustice possesses to corrupt the soul (v. 208b, cf. v. 138), and so he both honors and practices justice with the purest of intentions (vv. 64–65, 399). Cf. v. 607 ("Do what is right even to those who try to wrong you"); *Sent. Pythag.* 85[a] ("Do not exact justice from those who treat you unjustly").

Sentence 262

Sextus has issued warnings concerning excessive speech (v. 155), excessive learning (v. 249), and, now, excessive activity. The translation of v. 262 given above attempts to render the wordplay created by the juxtaposition of πολυπραγμονῶν and κακοπραγμονῶν. (For the matter of the puzzling dislocation of v. 262 in Π, see Chadwick 1959, 42, 174–75.) Our most extensive critique of the former is preserved in Plutarch's treatise *De curiositate*, where πολυπραγμοσύνη ("meddlesomeness") is defined as a desire to learn the κακά (either "troubles" or "misdeeds") of others, an affliction exacerbated especially by feelings of envy, malice, and pettiness (*Curios.*

515d–e). Cf. Cassius Dio, *Hist. rom.* 46.27.1; Menander, *Mon.* 654: "Don't try to meddle (πολυπραγμονεῖν) in the misdeeds (κακά) of others." For Sextus, by contrast, πολυπραγμοσύνη appears to be not so much a matter of involving oneself in the misdeeds of others but of becoming responsible for misdeeds oneself, in which case comparison can be made with Sir 11:10: "My child, do not busy yourself with many matters (μὴ περὶ πολλὰ ἔστωσαν αἱ πράξεις σου); if you multiply activities, you will not be held blameless. If you pursue, you will not overtake, and by fleeing you will not escape." Philo provides a detailed portrait of the sort of individual inflicted with this vice in *Abr.* 20–21: "He spends his life, one long restlessness, haunting marketplaces, theaters, courts, council halls, assemblies, and every group and gathering of men. His tongue he lets loose for unmeasured, endless, indiscriminate speech.... His ears he keeps alert in meddlesome officiousness (πολυπράγμονος περιεργίας), ever eager to learn his neighbor's affairs, whether good or bad, and ready with envy for the former and joy at the latter." For Sextus's μὴ πολλὰ πρᾶττε, comparison can be made with two more sayings of Menander, specifically, *Mon.* 737 ("Doing too many things is always unpleasant") and 750: "Doing too many things (τὸ πολλὰ πράττειν) brings many griefs." The importance of remaining focused on what matters most is a recurring gnomic theme, as we see also in *Instr. Ankh.* 23.17 ("Do not be active in all sorts of work and slack in your own work") and *m. Avot* 4:10: "Keep your business to a minimum and make your business Torah."

Sentence 263

In *Leg.* 913c, Plato cites "Do not pick up what you did not put down" (ἃ μὴ κατέθου, μὴ ἀνέλῃ) as a saying formulated "by a man of great nobility" and "the finest law there is," while Diogenes Laertius lists ἃ μὴ ἔθου, μὴ ἀνέλῃ as one of the edicts of Solon (*Vit. phil.* 1.57). The injunction's legal character is further reflected in Josephus, *C. Ap.* 2.208 and 216, where ὃ μὴ κατέθηκέ τις οὐκ ἀναιρήσεται is presented as a provision of the Mosaic law, and in Philo, *Hypoth.* 7.6, where ἃ μὴ κατέθηκεν, μηδ' ἀναιρεῖσθαι is presented as one of the "unwritten customs and institutions" of the Jews (cf. Lev 6:2; Deut 22:1–3; Luke 19:21; Aelian, *Var. hist.* 4.1). Sextus's version most closely approximates Plato's, though, as these citations attest, the form of the saying evidences a fair amount of variation. By comparison, what is most distinctive about v. 263 is that the injunction is interpreted as a contribution to αὐτάρκεια, a virtue that the readers of the *Sentences* are repeatedly encouraged to "practice" (vv. 98, 334). This is because self-sufficiency represents a means of becoming more like God, who is entirely self-sufficient (vv. 49–50), and the knowledge and imitation of God are "sufficient" for human well-being (v. 148, cf. v. 466). Consideration for v. 300 (θησαυρὸν κατατίθεσθαι μὲν οὐ φιλάνθρωπον, ἀναιρεῖσθαι δὲ οὐ κατὰ φιλόσοφον) suggests that what one is not to "take up" here is principally money, in which case this may be a warning for the sage not to accept payment for his services. At any rate, the danger posed by the desire for material wealth is noted frequently in our text, for example, vv. 15, 18, 76, 81, 137, 192, and 274b. Cf. Matt 10:8: "You received without payment; give without payment."

Sentence 264a

This perspective carries over into the next verse, a gnomic version of Matt 19:21 (cf. Mark 10:21; Luke 18:22): "If you wish to be perfect, go, sell your possessions (σου τὰ ὑπάρχοντα), and give the money to the poor, and you will have treasure in heaven; then come, follow me (ἀκολούθει μοι)." While v. 263 appears to focus on money, in v. 264a the focus is on possessions, which are not, as in the dominical saying, to be sold for the benefit of the poor (cf. vv. 267, 330, 378–379, 382) but simply relinquished, as in v. 81. While the previous admonition had identified dispossession as a means of becoming pure, here it is carried out for the sake of pursuing ὁ ὀρθὸς λόγος, a concept associated especially with Stoic philosophy (e.g., *SVF* 3:198, 200a, 308, 317, 500–501, 560) and referred to frequently by Clement and other early Christian authors (e.g., *Strom.* 2.4.19.3–4 = *SVF* 3:619). Philo integrates this concept with a number of other philosophical commonplaces using the metaphor of "following" in *Migr.* 128: "The aim extolled by the best philosophers is to live by following nature (ἀκολούθως τῇ φύσει), and it is attained whenever the mind, having entered on virtue's path, walks in the track of right reason (κατ' ἴχνος ὀρθοῦ λόγου βαίνῃ) and follows God (ἕπηται θεῷ), mindful of his injunctions." For Sextus, an individual's reason is "right" when it governs the passions and desires of the soul (see on vv. 74, 123, 205, cf. v. 533), including the desire for material possessions (cf. vv. 137, 228, 274b), even to the extent that one does not consider anything belonging to the world as one's own (v. 227, cf. vv. 15, 17). Indeed, it is through the exercise of reason that one leaves the things of the world behind and "travels" to God (v. 420, cf. v. 349), participating in divine reason (v. 277). Epictetus agrees that attachment to possessions must not determine which path the sage will "follow" in his life: "Everything (Diogenes) had was easily loosed, everything was merely tied on.

If you had laid hold of his property (τῆς κτήσεως), he would have let it go (ἀφῆκεν) rather than followed (ἠκολούθησεν) you for its sake.... His true ancestors, indeed, the gods, and his real country, he would never have abandoned" (*Diatr.* 4.1.153-154).

Sentence 264b

Philo espouses a Stoic position when he argues that only those who obey right reason (ὁ ὀρθὸς λόγος) are truly free, while those who fail to abide by its norms are truly enslaved, regardless of their legal status (*Prob.* 45-47 = *SVF* 3:360). In *Prob.* 20, he couches the same argument in theological terms, drawing on another Stoic paradox, namely, that the sage alone is king: "For in very truth he who has God alone for his leader, he alone is free, though to my thinking he is also the leader of all others, having received charge over earthly things from the great, immortal king, whom he, the mortal, serves as regent" (cf. *Leg.* 3.89; *Spec.* 1.176). For his part, the only thing that the Sextine sage honors, that is, the only thing by which he is governed, is God (vv. 41-42). Because he is governed by God alone, he governs everything except God (v. 43, cf. v. 575), including not only other human beings (v. 182) but especially his body (v. 274a) and its desires (v. 240, cf. vv. 75a-b, 574, 600), exercising the authority that he has received from God (v. 36). From this perspective he can be said to be "free" of all these things (cf. v. 392), enjoying a freedom that is second only to that of God (v. 309) and is thus inalienable (v. 275, cf. v. 17). In his capacity as God's servant (v. 319), the thoughts and deeds of the sage are so fully governed by God (v. 288) that he not only pleases God (v. 422)—he is in fact inseparable from God (v. 423). A similar paradox is echoed in 1 Pet 2:16: "As slaves of God (ὡς θεοῦ δοῦλοι), live as free persons (ὡς ἐλεύθεροι), yet do not use your freedom as a pretext for evil."

Sentences 265-270

Text

265 ἀπαλλάττου τροφῆς [a]ἔτι θέλων.
266 τροφῆς[a] παντὶ κοινώνει.
267 ὑπὲρ τοῦ πτωχὸν τραφῆναι καὶ νηστεῦσαι καλόν.
268 ποτόν σοι[a] πᾶν ἡδὺ ἔστω.
269 [a]μέθην δὲ ὁμοίως μανίᾳ[a] φυλάττου.

270   ἄνθρωπος γαστρὸς[a] ἡττώμενος ὅμοιος θηρίῳ.

Translation

265   Stop eating food while you still want some.
266   Share your food with everyone.
267   In order to feed the poor it is noble even to fast.
268   Let every drink be pleasing to you.
269   But guard yourself against drunkenness like madness.
270   A human being overcome by his stomach is like an animal.

Textual Notes

265–266[a-a] omit lat • 266 τροφὴ παντὶ κοινόν: Υ • 268[a] σου: Π • 269[a-a] μέθην καὶ μανίαν ὁμοίως: Π • 270[a] γαστρὶ: Υ

Commentary

Chadwick (1959, 153) identifies these lines as the second group of maxims in the *Sentences* united by the theme of food (cf. vv. 108a–111). Note τροφή in vv. 265–266 and τρέφω in v. 267. It should be observed, however, that vv. 268–269 do not deal with food as such but address the theme of drink. The first cluster of sayings argues that it is good to refrain from eating in order to provide sustenance for others (vv. 265–267), while the second argues for moderation, especially in the consumption of intoxicants (note ὅμοιος in vv. 269–270).

Sentence 265

Read in isolation, this verse could be interpreted as an example of the sort of banqueting advice proffered by Sir 31:12–19: "Are you seated at the table of the great? Do not be greedy at it.... Do not reach out your hand for everything you see, and do not crowd your neighbor at the dish.... Be the first to stop, as befits good manners, and do not be insatiable, or you will give offense.... How ample a little is for a well-disciplined person!" (For additional examples, see the introductory comments to vv. 108a–111.) Consideration for other sayings in the *Sentences*, however, indicates that the guidance being offered here is informed not by the principles of decorum but by a concern that the desire accompanying eating can defile and impair the soul (vv. 111, 345), thus exacerbating other bodily passions (vv. 240, 428). Accordingly, the intake of nourishment should be limited not by the desire to eat but by the body's physical needs (v. 115), needs that can be met with plain food consumed in moderation (vv. 412–413). This approach is familiar especially from the regimens of self-control and self-sufficiency promulgated among the philosophers, for example, Epictetus, *Gnom.* 17 ("Let the first satisfying of appetite always be the measure to you of eating and drinking, and appetite itself the sauce and pleasure. Thus you will never take more than is necessary"); Plutarch, *Tu. san.* 124e (Socrates taught that "it is by remaining still hungry that we ought to get enjoyment from the necessary or pleasant foods; but we should not stir up in ourselves a second and separate set of appetites after we have appeased the usual ones"); Porphyry, *Abst.* 1.54.5–6 ("We must also make the body unaccustomed, as far as possible, to pleasure from satiety, but accustomed to the repletion which comes from satisfying hunger ... and take as our limit not the unlimited, but the necessary. Thus it too, by self-sufficiency and assimilation to the divine, can obtain the good that is possible for it"); Clitarchus, *Sent.* 94 ("Eat in order to avoid hunger") and 97: "Let the extent of your eating be the avoidance of hunger" (note that Sext. 270 quotes Clitarchus, *Sent.* 95). For Sextus as well, limiting one's bodily needs is a path to holiness (v. 67) and a means of emulating God, who needs nothing (v. 50). The next two verses will suggest another reason for alimentary self-restraint, one not mentioned by the philosophers but one that accords with Sextus's understanding of the divine (e.g., vv. 378–379, 382): eating less leaves one with more to share with others.

Sentences 266–267

The previous unit on food (vv. 108a–111) concentrated on the ramifications of eating for personal purity. Here attention is drawn instead to social considerations. The readers have a responsibility to share possessions in common (κοινὰ ... τὰ κτήματα) with other believers (v. 228). They have a responsibility to share (κοινώνει) food as well, though this is to be done "with all" (παντί), that is, it is to be carried out in a manner consistent with the actions of someone who is a common (κοινός) benefactor "to all" (ἅπασιν) people (vv. 210a, 260). The same spirit of generosity informs texts like *Ep. Barn.* 19.8: "You shall share everything with your neighbor (κοινωνήσεις ἐν πᾶσιν τῷ πλησίον σου), and not claim that anything is your own." Also Justin Martyr, *1 Apol.* 14.2: "We put to common use (εἰς κοινόν) even what we have, and share (κοινωνοῦντες) with everyone in need." As Clement explains in *Quis div.* 13.6, Jesus commanded his followers to practice sharing (κοινωνία) in the use of material wealth, specifically, "to give drink to the thirsty and bread to the hungry, to receive the homeless, to clothe the naked." For the practice of sharing food in early Christianity, see also Matt 25:35; Luke 3:11; 14:13; Acts 6:1; Jas 2:15–16; Clement, *Paed.* 2.1.4.5; Ps.-Clement, *Hom.* 3.69; 11.4; 12.32; Gregory Thaumaturgus, *Met. Eccl. Sal.* 1013. Hermas argues for the practice in *Vis.* 3.9.2–3 by highlighting the contribution it makes to both personal and communal harmony: "Be at peace among yourselves, and be concerned for one another and assist one another; and do not partake of God's creation in abundance by yourselves, but also share (μεταδίδοτε) with those in need. For by overeating some people bring on themselves fleshly weakness and injure their flesh, while the flesh of those who do not have anything to eat is injured because they do not have enough food, and their bodies are wasting away." Cf. Sir 31:23: "People bless the one who is liberal with food, and their testimony to his generosity is trustworthy." Mention may also be made of agricultural statutes like Exod 23:10; Lev 19:9–10; 23:22; 25:3; and Deut 24:19–21, all of which are expounded by Clement in *Strom.* 2.18.85.3–2.18.86.7 as ways of "providing the poor with a chance of food" (2.18.85.3). The reader of Epictetus, *Gnom.* 24, meanwhile, is encouraged to share (κοινωνεῖς) his food with the slaves who prepare and serve his meals.

Although the readers have been instructed to share their food with everyone, the second line in the couplet (especially when taken together with sayings like those in vv. 52, 217, 378–379, 382) makes it apparent that the principal beneficiary of such largesse is to be the needy, here represented by πτωχός, the sole occurrence of the term in the *Sentences*. In contrast to all of the sayings just mentioned, in v. 267 no theological motivation is provided for the desired action, which is simply deemed to be καλόν (cf. v. 330). Ritual fasting is evidenced by a wide assortment of New Testament texts, including Matt 4:2; 6:16–18; 9:14–15; Mark 2:18–20; 9:29 v.l.; 17:21; Luke 2:37; 5:33–35; Acts 10:30 v.l.; 13:3; 14:23; 1 Cor 7:5 v.l.; 2 Cor 6:5; 11:27. Its observance, in various forms, continued to be an important marker of group identity in the early church, for example, *2 Clem.* 16.4; Pol. *Phil.* 7.2; Justin Martyr, *Dial.* 15.1; *1 Apol.* 61.2; *Gos. Pet.* 7.27; *Gos. Heb.* frag. 7; *Prot. Jas.* 1.4; Herm. *Sim.* 5.1.1–2; Tertullian, *De jejunio adversus psychicos*. Unlike many of these texts (cf. *Did.* 8.1; Origen, *Hom. Jer.* 12.13; Eusebius, *Hist. eccl.* 5.24.12–13), Sextus is concerned not with when believers fast but with to what end they fast. Specifically, fasting becomes "noble" when it is carried out in order to provide food for the poor. Hermas spells out the positive consequences of this practice for both the donor and the recipient in *Sim.* 5.3.7: "You must taste nothing except

274   THE *SENTENCES* OF SEXTUS

bread and water on that day on which you fast. Then you must estimate the cost of the food you would have eaten on that day on which you intend to fast, and give it to a widow or an orphan or someone in need. In this way you will become humble-minded, so that as a result of your humility the one who receives may satisfy his own soul and pray to the Lord on your behalf." In the same spirit is Aristides of Athens, *Apol.* 15 ("And if there is among them any that is poor and needy, and if they have no spare food, they fast two or three days in order to supply to the needy their lack of food") and Clement, *Strom.* 7.12.77.6: "Through the perfection of his love, (the gnostic) impoverishes himself that he may never overlook a brother in affliction, especially if he knows that he could himself bear want better than his brother."

Sentences 268–269

Attention now shifts from food to drink. Since it is not what one consumes but the manner in which it is consumed that defiles a person (vv. 110–111), drink of any kind is allowed, and may even be considered something "pleasant" (cf. v. 276). As Xenophon explains, Socrates "found any kind of drink pleasant (ἡδύ), because he drank only when he was thirsty" (*Mem.* 1.3.5; cf. *Ages.* 9.3). At the same time, for our author μέθη is μανία, presumably because the former is the result of being overwhelmed by pleasure (again, see vv. 110–111, also cf. v. 272). According to Stobaeus, Pythagoras proclaimed "drunkenness to be a rehearsal for madness" (τὴν μέθην μανίας εἶναι μελέτην), while Chrysippus called it "a short-term madness" (*Anth.* 3.18.23–24). Comparable assessments are made in Plutarch, *Garr.* 503e ("Drunkenness is madness, shorter in duration, but more culpable, because the will is involved"); Diogenes Laertius, *Vit. phil.* 6.89; Philostratus, *Vit. Apoll.* 2.36.2; *Anth. Gr.* 12.115; Seneca, *Ep.* 83.18: "Drunkenness is nothing but a condition of insanity purposely assumed."

In keeping with their general valorization of self-control and decorum, gnomic sources convey a range of pointed warnings regarding intoxication and its ill effects. See Prov 23:20–21, 29–35; Sir 31:25–26, 30; Theognis, *El.* 467–510; Menander, *Mon.* 417; Publilius Syrus, *Sent.* 12; Ps.-Cato, *Dist.* 2.21; 4.24; P.Iand. 5.77.4; Clitarchus, *Sent.* 116: "There is for no one a good time for drunkenness (μέθης καιρός), since there is for no one a good time to be foolish." A particularly good parallel for the pairing of v. 268 and v. 269 is found in Sir 31:28–29: "Wine drunk at the proper time and in moderation is rejoicing of heart and gladness of soul. Wine drunk to excess leads to bitterness of spirit, to quarrels and stumbling."

Other texts similarly acknowledge the pleasant effects of imbibing along with the unpleasant, discretion making the difference between the two—for example, Theognis, *El.* 211–212 ("Drinking wine in large quantities is indeed a bane, but if one drinks wisely, wine is not a bane but a blessing"); *Syr. Men.* 52–56: "Drink wine moderately and do not boast of it; for wine is indeed mild and sweet, but every man that quarrels and boasts of it will immediately be dishonored and despised."

According to Diogenes Laertius, Pythagoras was never known to be drunk (*Vit. phil.* 8.19; cf. Philostratus, *Vit. Apoll.* 1.8), while according to Iamblichus, he instructed his more advanced students not to drink wine at all (*Vit. Pythag.* 24.107; cf. Diogenes Laertius, *Vit. phil.* 8.13; Clement, *Paed.* 2.1.11.1; Porphyry, *Abst.* 4.6.8). For the evidence that certain encratite movements within early Christianity abstained from wine, see *Orig. World* 109.25–29; *Act. Paul.* 7.4; Clement, *Strom.* 1.19.96.1; Tertullian, *Jejun.* 1.4; 15.2; Epiphanius, *Pan.* 46.2; Eusebius, *Eccl. hist.* 2.23.5. Cf. Lev 10:9; Num 6:3; Jer 35:6; Dan 1:8; Luke 1:15; 7:33; Rom 14:21; Eph 5:8 ("Do not get drunk with wine, for that is debauchery"); 1 Tim 3:8; Titus 1:7. While conceding that wine does possess certain medicinal qualities (*Paed.* 2.2.22.3–2.2.23.2; cf. 1 Tim 5:23), Clement argues that it is best for younger believers to avoid wine as much as possible (*Paed.* 2.2.20.2–3), since the heat it generates can leave the senses "deranged" (*Paed.* 2.2.24.2).

Sentence 270

The source for the final line in this unit is Clitarchus, *Sent.* 95: ἄνθρωπος γαστρὸς ἥσσων ὅμοιος θηρίῳ (Sextus changes ἥσσων to ἡττώμενος). In its Sextine context the saying is connected to the one that precedes it by the catchword ὅμοιος. Drunkenness should be shunned "like" a madness that incapacitates one's reason, because the one who succumbs to gastronomical desires becomes "like" an unreasoning beast. This saying, then, both expands and intensifies the condemnation conveyed by its predecessor. For the problem of controlling the γαστήρ, see also on vv. 240, 345, and 428.

Likening the behavior of gluttons to that of ravenous, irrational animals was a common expedient in ancient moral criticism. Indeed, Musonius Rufus contends that the way such people feed themselves is in fact "much worse than the unreasoning brutes, for even if they, driven by appetite as by a lash, fall upon their food, nevertheless they are not guilty of making a fuss about it and exercising ingenuity about it, but are satisfied with what comes their way, seeking satiety and nothing more" (frag. 18a.112.31–114.3). The sort of excess that goads such individuals is particularly odious because "it makes them greedy like swine or dogs rather than people, and incapable of behaving properly with hands, eyes, or mouth, so completely does the desire for pleasure in eating fine foods pervert them" (frag. 18b.116.12–16). See further Philo, *Abr.* 149; Plutarch, *Tu. san.* 133b; *Quaest. conv.* 746e; Dio Chrysostom, *Or.* 5.16; Athenaeus, *Deipn.* 8.64. From a Christian context, we have Clement, who bewails the extent to which gourmands are willing to sacrifice reason, friendship, and even life itself "for the pleasures of the belly, creeping upon their bellies, beasts that merely resemble human beings, made to the image of their father, the ravening beast" (*Paed.* 2.1.7.4; cf. 2.1.9.3–4; 2.1.11.4). See also the commentary on v. 391.

Sentences 271–277

Text

271 οὐδὲν φύεται ἐκ σαρκὸς^a ἀγαθόν.
272 αἰσχρᾶς ἡδονῆς τὸ μὲν ἡδὺ ταχέως ἄπεισιν, τὸ δὲ ὄνειδος παραμένει.
273 ἀνθρώπους ^aἴδοις ἄν^a ὑπὲρ τοῦ τὸ λοιπὸν τοῦ σώματος ἔχειν ἐρρωμένον ἀποκόπτοντας ἑαυτῶν^b ^cκαὶ ῥίπτοντας^c μέλη^d· πόσῳ βέλτιον ὑπὲρ^e τοῦ σωφρονεῖν;
274a μεγάλην νόμιζε παιδείαν τὸ ἄρχειν σώματος·
274b οὐ γὰρ^a ^bπαύσει ἐπιθυμίαν κτημάτων ἡ^b χρημάτων κτῆσις.
275 φιλόσοφον οὐδέν ἐστιν δ^a τῆς ἐλευθερίας ἀφαιρεῖται^b.
276 ἡδονὰς ἡγοῦ τὰς ^aἀναγκαίας ὡς ἀναγκαίας^a.
277 τὰ ἀγαθὰ ^aμὲν ἔχειν πάντες^a εὔχονται, κτῶνται δὲ οἱ γνησίως τοῦ θείου^b λόγου μετέχοντες^c.

Translation

271 Nothing good stems from the flesh.
272 The sweetness of shameful pleasure quickly departs, but the reproach remains.
273 You may see people cutting off and throwing away their own limbs in order to keep the rest of the body strong. Is it not much better to do this in order to observe moderation?
274a Consider the control of the body to be a major feat of learning.

274b For the possession of goods will not stop a desire for possessions.
275   There is nothing that deprives a philosopher of his freedom.
276   Regard pleasures that are necessary as necessary.
277   All pray to have good things, but those who truly partake of divine reason possess them.

Textual Notes

271ᵃ γαστρός: Π, sy² • 273ᵃ⁻ᵃ ἐὰν ἴδῃς: Υ • 273ᵇ omit Υ • 273ᶜ⁻ᶜ omit Υ, lat • 273ᵈ τὰ μέλη: Π • 273ᵉ omit Υ • 274bᵃ omit Υ • 274bᵇ⁻ᵇ παύσῃ ἐπιθυμία κτημάτων ἤ: Π • 275ᵃ ὅς: Υ • 275ᵇ ἀφαιρήσεται: Υ • 276ᵃ⁻ᵃ ἀναγκαίως ἀναγκαίας: Υ • 277ᵃ⁻ᵃ πάντες μὲν ἔχειν: Π • 277ᵇ θεοῦ: Υ • 277ᶜ μετασχόντες: Υ

COMMENTARY

While vv. 265–270 cautioned against desires of the table, the bulk of material in this unit takes up the problem of physical pleasure more generally. Note ἡδονή in vv. 272 and 276, ἐπιθυμία in v. 274b, σάρξ in v. 271, and σῶμα in vv. 273 and 274a. Interspersed near the end of the section are sayings on the philosopher (v. 275) and those who have a share in divine reason (v. 277), persons who understand that in order to obtain what is "good" one must turn not to the flesh (v. 271) but to God (v. 277), the references to ἀγαθός in vv. 271 and 277 creating an *inclusio* for the unit.

Sentence 271

The inspiration for this line most likely comes from Rom 7:18: οἶδα γὰρ ὅτι οὐκ οἰκεῖ ἐν ἐμοί, τοῦτ᾽ ἔστιν ἐν τῇ σαρκί μου, ἀγαθόν. Nothing good may "dwell" within the flesh (the γαστρός of Π no doubt inspired by the γαστρός of v. 270), but the readers of the *Sentences* know that something good does in fact "dwell" within the human personality, specifically within the intellect, even something divine (v. 144, cf. v. 35). The options are laid out contrastively in vv. 316–317: "Where your ability to reason is, there is your good. Do not seek goodness in the flesh." For our author, only that which befits God is "good" (v. 131) and the only way to obtain what is good is to participate in divine reason (v. 277). It is this alone that governs the life of the sage (v. 42) and which he therefore properly considers his "own" (v. 79). Conversely, what derives from the flesh is not anything good but only physical desires, as exemplified by a saying in one of Sextus's sources,

Sent. Pythag. 98 (cited in Porphyry, *Marc.* 30): "The flesh cries out not to be hungry, not to be thirsty, not to be cold." Cf. *Gnom. Vat.* 20 ("The flesh perceives the limits of pleasure as unlimited.... But the mind, having attained a reasoned understanding of the ultimate good of the flesh ... supplies us with the complete life"); Philo, *Deus* 143 ("There are no two things so utterly opposed as knowledge and fleshly pleasure"); Plutarch, *Cons. Apoll.* 107f: "To pass one's time unenslaved by the flesh and its passions, by which the mind is distracted and tainted with human folly, would be a blessed piece of good fortune." The prudent therefore do not love the flesh (v. 291), just as they do not love the body (v. 101). Rather they love what is truly akin to themselves, especially God (vv. 106a–b, cf. vv. 158, 226, 292, 358, 442).

Sentence 272

As the citations just offered illustrate, σάρξ was frequently associated with pleasure, which is the subject of the next saying. It is a fact that pleasure (ἡδονή) is pleasant (ἡδύς): Aristotle, *Eth. nic.* 2.9.6; Philo, *Leg.* 3.250; Diogenes Laertius, *Vit. phil.* 2.87; Porphyry, *Vit. Pythag.* 39. But it is also a fact that the pursuit of pleasure often instigates conduct thought to be shameful and thus deserving of reproach. See Aristotle, *Eth. nic.* 7.11.5; Ps.-Andronicus Rhodius, *Pass.* 6.3; 9.4; Philo, *Ebr.* 233; *Spec.* 3.49; Musonius Rufus, frag. 12.86.27–32; Plutarch, *Virt. mor.* 447a; *Gen. Socr.* 585a; Dio Chrysostom, *Or.* 4.136. The particular reasoning that informs the expression of this idea here is familiar from the negative half of a Stoic *topos*: "If one accomplishes something noble though with toil, the toil passes, but the noble remains; if one does something shameful with pleasure (αἰσχρὸν μετὰ ἡδονῆς), the pleasure passes, but the shame remains" (Musonius Rufus, frag. 51.144.7–9). Other examples focus less on public venues of moral assessment (as implied by the use of a term like αἰσχρός, cf. v. 286) and more on the element of self-recrimination, such as Seneca, *Ep.* 27.2–3 ("Just as crimes, even if they have not been detected when they were committed, do not allow anxiety to end with them; so with guilty pleasures, regret remains even after the pleasures are over.... Cast about instead for some good which will abide") and Epictetus, *Ench.* 34: "Think of the two periods of time: first, that in which you will enjoy your pleasure, and second, that in which, after the enjoyment is over, you will later repent and revile your own self; and set over against these two periods of time how much joy and self-satisfaction you will have if you refrain. But if you do feel that a suitable occasion has arisen to do the deed, be careful not to allow its enticement and sweetness (ἡδύ) and attractiveness to overcome you." In the *Sentences*, shameful deeds have not only social ramifications, as we learn here, but also religious ones, the latter taking the form of a defilement that attaches to the perpetrator of a shameful action (v. 102, cf. v. 111), rendering him unfit to participate in the divine (v. 429).

Sentence 273

The foregoing precepts (vv. 271–272) create an incentive for compliance with the observation + rhetorical question presented in v. 273. If the pleasures of the flesh expose one to enduring reproach while conferring nothing that is truly good, then it is prudent to take even extreme measures in order to achieve self-control (cf. v. 274a). In *Comm. Matt.* 15.3, Origen cites this verse together with a parallel saying in v. 13 as evidence that certain Christians endorsed a literal reading of Matt 19:12 (for the preponderance of nonliteral interpretations in the early church, see the commentary on v. 13). Both verses present a scenario in which it is necessary to throw away (ῥίπτειν) a limb (μέλος) of the body (σῶμα) in order to observe moderation (σωφρονεῖν), though only the latter mentions the need to cut (ἀποκόπτειν) the limb off first. In addition, while both lines include "better" sayings, the one in v. 13 opens with ἄμεινον γάρ, while the rhetorical question in v. 273 opens with πόσῳ βέλτιον. Finally, while v. 13 recommends removing a body part that prevents one from observing moderation, v. 273 talks about removing a body part in order to preserve one's health, which is then contrasted with the "better" practice of removing a body part in order to preserve one's moderation. As explained above, the wording of v. 13 appears to be based in part on Matt 5:29–30 and 18:8–9. The influence of these dominical sayings on v. 273 is less evident, a more important parallel coming instead from Porphyry, *Marc.* 34: "Often people cut some limb to save their lives; you should be prepared to cut off the whole body to save your soul" (πολλάκις κόπτουσί τινα μέρη ἐπὶ σωτηρίᾳ· τῆς δὲ ψυχῆς ἕνεκα ἕτοιμος ἔσο τὸ ὅλον σῶμα ἀποκόπτειν). In addition to the common verb ἀποκόπτειν (also compare Sextus's σωφρονεῖν with Porphyry's σωτηρία τῆς ψυχῆς), the two sayings are distinctive in their use of the same kind of medical analogy (note that Porphyry uses medical terminology to illuminate philosophical matters also in *Marc.* 9, 27, 31). Given the parallel between v. 274a and Porphyry, *Marc.* 34 (see below), there is a likelihood, then, that this saying is based on the gnomic source that Sextus shares with Porphyry (see further part 4 of the introduction). The point for both authors is not that their readers might have to amputate body parts (much less "the whole body") for the sake of the moral life but rather that they must, as Sextus puts it in v. 78, set aside "the things of the body" as much as possible (cf. vv. 71a, 101, 115, 127). This entails providing for the needs of the body with moderation (v. 412, cf. vv. 67, 399).

Sentence 274a

Moderation, then, is a matter not of throwing away limbs but of learning how to exercise self-control. Directly preceding the parallel for v. 273 in Porphyry, *Marc.* 34 is a saying that closely parallels v. 274a: μεγάλη οὖν παιδεία ἄρχειν τοῦ σώματος. The Sextine construction differs owing to the use of the verb νομίζω, one of our author's favorites (seventeen occurrences in the *Sentences*), in lieu of the particle οὖν. At the same time, it retains παιδεία, even though elsewhere our author demonstrates a propensity to drop that word from his source material (see on vv. 92 and 285, cf. v. 538). Earlier in his letter, Porphyry had explained that true education concerns itself not with acquiring much learning, but with "discarding the passions" (*Marc.* 9 = *Sent. Pythag.* 2ᶜ; cf. on Sext. 209 and 249). In the same vein, the readers of the *Sentences* are taught to "conquer" everything bodily (v. 71a), including especially bodily pleasures (e.g., v. 70), passions (e.g., vv. 75a–b), longings (e.g., v. 136), and desires (e.g., v. 240). The learning that this entails can be considered "major" insofar as self-control provides both the basis (v. 86a) and the sustenance (v. 438) of a believer's relationship with God (cf. vv. 204, 209, 428). As v. 425 indicates, the somatic education of the faithful can sometimes be experienced in the form of divine "testing" (cf. v. 7a).

Sentence 274b

The ensuing precept takes up a particular type of desire in which discipline is needed, namely, the desire for possessions. For this saying Sextus draws on *Sent. Pythag.* 30ᶜ: "For the further acquisition of possessions does not stop a desire for them" (οὐ γὰρ παύσει ποτὲ ἐπιθυμίαν ἡ τῶν κτημάτων ἐπίκτησις). Sextus inserts χρημάτων before ἐπίκτησις, shortens the latter to κτῆσις, and drops ποτέ (Π also drops the γάρ). Worldly things should be acquired only to the extent that they are required to meet essential physical needs (vv. 19, 115), since anything beyond this distracts one from the things of God (vv. 20, 81, 264a, cf. v. 192). Indeed, the sage does not claim anything as his own property (v. 227), since in this he becomes like God (v. 18). However, insofar as desire is by its very nature insatiable

(v. 448), the business of acquiring possessions will cease only once the desire for possessions ceases, and desire in this case is especially intractable because it is attended by the vice of greed (v. 137). As Teles explains in frag. 4a ("A Comparison of Poverty and Wealth"), ironically enough, the acquisition of possessions does not represent a solution to the problem of the desire for possessions, since this does nothing to enhance the moral integrity of the person who acquires them, "for sooner, it seems to me, could one say that the possession of goods (ἡ τῶν χρημάτων κτῆσις) changes skin, size, or appearance than it changes character" (frag. 4a.36). Despite his wealth, then, an insatiable man is ever in want: "He's a slave. He's eager to be free and says, 'If I get this, I have everything'. He becomes free: immediately he longs to acquire a slave. He gets one: he's eager to acquire a second as well.... Then he's eager to acquire a house, a plot of land, then to become an Athenian, then to be a magistrate, then a king" (frag. 4a.43). The readers of the *Sentences*, by contrast, are encouraged to acquire not material possessions but the sorts of possessions that belong to those who share in divine reason (see on v. 277). Cf. Plutarch, *Cupid. divit.* 523d–e: "Having wealth is not the same as being superior to it, nor is possessing luxuries the same as feeling no need of them. From what other ills then does wealth deliver us, if it does not even deliver us from the craving for it?"

Sentence 275

Set within the immediate context of maxims on σῶμα (vv. 273–274a), on ἐπιθυμία (v. 274b), and on ἡδονή (vv. 272, 276), it is fair to assume that the ἐλευθερία mentioned in this verse refers not to liberty in the social or political sense (cf. v. 392), but to freedom of character and moral judgment, including especially freedom from enslavement to the body and its passions (vv. 75a–b, cf. vv. 574, 600). As Clement explains, "to yield in subjection to the passions is the lowest form of slavery, just as to conquer them is the only true freedom" (*Strom.* 2.23.144.3). The only thing that rules the sage is God (vv. 40–42, 422–424). This does not entail a loss of freedom, however, since God shares everything with the sage (v. 310) and what God gives no one can take away (vv. 92, 404). Above all, it is the sage's intellect, the divine that dwells within (vv. 35, 46a, 61, 144), that is properly his "own" (v. 17, cf. v. 227), and as such the aspect of the personality that both achieves and exercises freedom. Because it refers to the life of the mind and not the life of the body, this freedom is unassailable (vv. 363a–b, cf. vv. 118, 130, 321). Having been set free from everything in the world through his relationship with God (v. 264b), the sage is freer than everything in the world except God (v. 309). Similar logic informs Philo, *Prob.* 60: "The good man cannot be compelled or prevented. He therefore cannot be a slave, and that he can be neither compelled nor prevented is evident from the fact that one is prevented when he does not obtain what he desires, but the sage desires things that have their origin in virtue, and these, being what he is, he cannot fail to obtain." Epictetus also offers many contributions to this theme, for example, *Diatr.* 2.2.3–4 ("What else do you care about if you want to secure the things that are completely in one's power and naturally free? … Who has authority over them, who can remove them? If you want to be a person with integrity, who will stop you? If you want to be free from impediment and compulsion, who will compel you to have desires and aversions that don't accord with your judgments?") and 4.1.82: "What is there to be fearful about? About the things that are your own, wherein is the true nature of good and evil for you. And who has authority over these things? Who is able to take them away (ἀφελέσθαι) or hinder them, any more than one can hinder God?" For the Stoic paradox that the sage alone is free, see *SVF* 3:355, 362–364, 544, 593.

Sentence 276

For the structure of this sentence, see v. 119: φέρε τὰ ἀναγκαῖα ὡς ἀναγκαῖα. It is not pleasures themselves that lead to shame and reproach (v. 272) but the failure to moderate them (v. 273) by learning how to control the body (v. 274a) and free oneself from their tyranny (v. 275). Most likely, what Sextus has in mind here are ἡδοναί that derive from the flesh (v. 271), especially those that accompany eating and drinking. This is suggested by comparison with *Resp.* 558d–559a (cf. 560e–561a, 571b), where Plato differentiates unnecessary desires, "whose presence leads to no good" (cf. v. 271), from necessary ones, namely, those "from which we cannot desist," such as "the desire to eat to the point of health." Cf. Plutarch, *Tu. san.* 136e; *Gen. Socr.* 584d–e; *An seni* 786a; *Esu carn.* 999b; Plotinus, *Enn.* 1.2.5; Porphyry, *Abst.* 1.56.4; 3.18.5; Seneca, *Ep.* 116.3: "Nature has intermingled pleasure with necessary things, not in order that we should seek pleasure, but in order that the addition of pleasure may make the indispensable means of existence attractive to us." According to Clement, even the gnostic remains subject to certain passions that exist for the maintenance of the body, such as hunger and thirst (*Strom.* 6.9.71.1; cf. 2.20.118.7). While it is a repeated contention of the *Sentences* that physical pleasures must be curtailed (vv. 70, 232, 411) lest they contaminate the soul (v. 111), it is acknowledged here that they represent not only an unavoidable but also a "necessary" aspect of human existence, insofar as each person has certain minimal physical requirements that must be met (vv. 19, 115, 412). The admonition in v. 388 ("What must be done, do willingly") may be relevant here as well. Since fulfilling such needs is not evil, the pleasures associated with them ought not be included among the things considered shameful (v. 202).

Sentence 277

The section in vv. 271–277 begins by identifying that from which good things never derive (the flesh) and ends by identifying that from which good things always derive (divine reason). Such "goods" contrast with the material wealth denounced in v. 274b, whose possession only inhibits one from becoming more like God (cf. v. 18).

Pythagoras taught his followers to pray not for specific blessings but simply for "good things" (Diodorus Siculus, *Bibl. hist.* 10.9.8). In the *Sentences*, only that which befits God is good (vv. 131, 197), and the only thing that befits God is the life of the mind (vv. 26, 394, 450, cf. v. 316: "Where your ability to reason is, there is your good"). It is apparent, then, that while "all" (presumably all believers) pray for good things, that is, for things worthy of God (v. 122, cf. vv. 88, 128), only those whose intellects are pure enough to serve as an abode for God (vv. 46a, 61, 144, cf. vv. 381, 447) will receive the power they need from God to obtain such things (v. 375, cf. v. 36). This would appear to be what Sextus means by "having a share" of divine reason (cf. Origen, *Sel. Ps.* 12.1164). In *Orat.* 20.2, Origen explains that when someone prays, he "shuts up every door" of the sense-perceptible world and enters into the realm of the mind, "a hidden sanctuary," wherein the father also dwells (cf. also *Orat.* 2.4 and 12.1, both of which include references to 1 Cor 14:15). Clement, meanwhile, describes prayer in its highest form as an endeavor to "detach the body from the earth" and direct the soul "towards the intellectual essence … winged with the desire of better things … magnanimously despising the fetters of the flesh" (*Strom.* 7.7.40.1–2). Cf. Evagrius Ponticus, *Orat.* 53 ("The state of prayer is an imperturbable habit, snatching the philosophic and spiritual mind to the heights by keenest love"), 64, 84, 86 ("Knowledge is exceedingly fair, for it is prayer's collaborator, rousing the mind's mental power to the contemplation of divine knowledge"), 101. Further instruction on prayer is offered in vv. 80–81, 124–128, 213, 217, and 372–375.

Sentences 278–282

Text

278 φιλόσοφος ὢν σεμνὸς ἔσο μᾶλλον ἢ φιλοσκώπτης[a].
279 σπάνιόν σου ἔστω σκῶμμα καὶ τὸ εὔκαιρον.
280a ἄμετρος γέλως σημεῖον ἀπροσεξίας.
280b σεαυτῷ διαχεῖσθαι πέρα τοῦ μειδιᾶν[a] μὴ ἐπιτρέψῃς.
281 σπουδῇ πλείονι ἢ διαχύσει χρῶ.
282 ἀγών[a] [b]ὁ βίος[b] ἔστω σοι περὶ τοῦ[c] σεμνοῦ.

Translation

278 As a philosopher, be serious rather than facetious.
279 Let your jest be rare, even the one that is timely.
280a Immoderate laughter is a sign of inattentiveness.
280b Do not permit yourself any levity beyond a smile.
281 Be more prone to earnestness than to levity.
282 Let your life be a struggle for seriousness.

Textual Notes

278[a] φιλοσκόπτης: Π • 279 omit Π • 280b[a] μηδιᾶν: Π • 282[a] ἀγνῶν: lat • 282[b-b] omit Υ • 282[c] βίου: Π, Υ (cf. v. 573)

Commentary

Chadwick (1959, 153) suggests that vv. 278–281 are unified by the theme of humor, though it is best to include v. 282 in the unit as well. Indeed, the term σεμνός not only better names the topic of this section; it also creates an *inclusio* for its contents.

Sentences 278–279

The philosopher is a person who is fond of wisdom (φιλόσοφος), not a person who is fond of jesting (φιλοσκώπτης), the reserve he demonstrates in this regard (cf. v. 284) being illustrative of his self-control more generally (v. 294). Philosophers as a group were known for their serious (σεμνός) demeanor (e.g., Marcus Aurelius, *Med.* 6.47.1; Ps.-Lucian, *Am.* 23), though they might tell the occasional joke in order to make an audience more attentive (Plutarch, *Quaest. conv.* 614a; for the sort of teasing philosophers themselves had to endure, see Plutarch, *Quaest. conv.* 634a–b; Diogenes Laertius, *Vit. phil.* 7.27). A fondness for joking or mockery was generally something to be avoided, since it could be viewed as a symptom of dissolution (ἀκολασία), as we see, for example, in Ps.-Aristotle, *Virt. vit.* 6.7–8 (cf. Ps.-Andronicus Rhodius, *Pass.* 9.4; Plutarch, *Sulla* 2.2; Clement, *Paed.* 2.5.46.1). As Cicero explains, those who fail to control their desire for jesting give the appearance of doing everything "from mere impulse or at random" (*Off.* 1.29.103). Conversely, it is only after the claims of more serious responsibilities have been satisfied that the virtuous will, in a moment of leisure, allow themselves a jest, and even then it will be of a witty and refined rather than coarse or vicious nature (*Off.* 1.29.103–104). In the same manner, Clement contends that, as a rule, believers should neither make jokes nor make themselves the butt of jokes (*Paed.* 2.5.45.2–3), though on occasion older or more dignified persons may utter a witticism in order to put those around them at ease (*Paed.* 2.5.47.3). As with most things, levity has its own μέτρον as well as its own καιρός (*Paed.* 2.5.46.1). Compare Menander, *Mon.* 144: "Ill-timed laughter (γέλως ἄκαιρος) is as faulty as ill-timed weeping." Indeed, "Ill-timed laughter (γέλως ἄκαιρος) among mortals is a terrible mistake" (*Mon.* 144 v.l.). Epictetus expresses the same sentiment in *Ench.* 33.4: "Do not laugh much, nor at many things, nor boisterously." Compare also *Ench.* 33.15: "Avoid raising a laugh, for this is a kind of behavior that slips easily into vulgarity, and at the same time is calculated to lessen the respect which your neighbors have of you."

Sentences 280a–b

For the form of v. 280a, see v. 157: μακρολογία σημεῖον ἀμαθίας. In Publilius Syrus, *Sent.* 340, levity is seen as a sign of caprice, while in Porphyry, *Marc.* 19, it is seen as a sign of demonic possession. For Sextus, it is a sign of ἀπροσεξία, a term used of people who are easily distracted emotionally (Plutarch, *Adul. amic.* 69f). In a philosophical context, "inattentiveness" categorizes students bent on following their own inclinations, rather than carrying out their duties with moderation and self-respect (Epictetus, *Diatr.* 4.12.6). Origen, meanwhile, uses the term of those who know God's law but neglect to observe it (*Cels.* 7.69; cf. *Comm. Matt.* 10.24; 12.5; *Orat.* 29.13; *Sel. Ps.* 12.1128).

Of all the ancient philosophical movements, Pythagoreanism was the one best known for its mirthlessness. According to Diogenes Laertius, its founder "avoided laughter and all pandering to tastes, such as insulting jests and vulgar tales" (*Vit. phil.* 8.20). Porphyry takes this avoidance as evidence not of Pythagoras's unwillingness to curry favor, but of his sage-like imperturbability: "His soul always revealed through his appearance the same disposition, for he was neither much relaxed (διεχεῖτο) by pleasure nor withdrawn because of pain, nor did he ever seem to be in the grip of joy or grief. Indeed, no one ever saw him laughing or weeping" (*Vit. Pythag.* 35; cf. Athanasius, *Vit. Ant.* 14.3–4). Iamblichus further reports that Pythagoras inspected prospective disciples for signs of "untimely (ἀκαίρους) laughter" (*Vit. Pythag.* 17.71).

The church fathers generally frowned upon laughter, Clement's comments in *Paed.* 2.5.46.1–2.5.47.3 being illustrative. Laughter, the Alexandrian explains, is natural to the human species, and when it occurs at the right moment is a proper part of decorum. Excessive or undue laughter, on the other hand, demonstrates not only a lack of composure but a tendency to dissolution (ἀκολασία). For those who observe moderation, the preferred way to express good humor is with a smile, though even this form of expression should be used tactfully, lest one give the wrong impression. The thought as well as the wording of v. 280b are familiar especially from an aphorism Clement cites in *Paed.* 2.5.46.4, namely, Sir 21:20: "A fool raises his voice in laughter (ἐν γέλωτι), but an intelligent man will smile (μειδιάσει) scarcely a little." Cf. Sir 27:13 ("The talk of fools is offensive, and their laughter is wantonly sinful"); *Syr. Men.* 302 ("Excessive laughter is a true disgrace"); Menander, *Mon.* 165 ("The fool laughs even when there is nothing to laugh at"), 172: "The solemn things of life (τὰ σεμνά) bring a smile to the prudent." For the construction διαχεῖσθαι πέρα τοῦ μειδιᾶν, cf. Plutarch, *Pomp.* 57.5; Heliodorus, *Aeth.* 3.5.5.

Sentences 281–282

If the purpose of life is to harmonize thoughts, words, and deeds (vv. 177, 381) in accordance with the divine (v. 201), even down to the smallest detail (vv. 9–10), then it stands to reason that it must be lived in an earnest and disciplined manner. Verse 281 is linked to the saying that precedes it by catchword: διαχεῖσθαι (v. 280b) and διαχύσει (v. 281). Verse 282, in turn, (which is repeated as v. 573 in the appendices) is linked to v. 281 by the near synonyms σπουδή and σεμνός (Edwards and Wild 1981, 49 even translate both terms as "seriousness"), the latter creating an *inclusio* for the unit with v. 278.

Given the comments made above, it is not surprising that Pythagoras was well known for the σεμνότης of his life and bearing and that in this regard he was emulated by his followers (Diogenes Laertius, *Vit.*

phil. 8.56; Iamblichus, *Vit. Pythag.* 2.10; 3.15-16; 33.234). As evidence of their seriousness, Chaeremon the Stoic, in his account of the priests of Egypt, reports that "their laughter was rare, and if it did happen, did not go beyond a smile" (Porphyry, *Abst.* 4.6.7). According to Philo, the countenance of the sage is neither severe nor flippant but combines seriousness with a tranquil and amiable spirit (*Plant.* 167; cf. Plutarch, *Sept. sav. conv.* 156d). As Cicero explains, when individuals overindulge in levity it shows a lack of perception regarding their true purpose and calling in life: "For nature has not brought us into the world to act as if we were created for play or jest, but rather for earnestness and for some more serious and important pursuits" (*Off.* 1.29.103). Clement makes the additional point that "there is some quality in seriousness (ἡ σεμνότης) that strikes fear into those who approach with immoral intent, simply by its bearing" (*Paed.* 2.5.48.1; cf. *Strom.* 1.3.22.1; 1.25.165.1; 2.18.78.1). On the other hand, foolish talk betrays a foolish character (*Paed.* 2.5.45.1), since "by the repetition of unbecoming words we lose all fear of unbecoming deeds" (*Paed.* 2.5.45.4). For life as a "struggle" for control, cf. v. 239.

Sentences 283-292

Text

283 ἄριστον μὲν τὸ μὴ ἁμαρτεῖν, ἁμαρτάνοντα δὲ γινώσκειν ἄμεινον ἢ ἀγνοεῖν.
284 ἀλαζὼν φιλόσοφος οὐκ ἔστιν.
285 μεγάλην σοφίαν νόμιζε δι' ἧς^a δυνήσῃ φέρειν ἀγνοούντων ἀπαιδευσίαν.
286 αἰσχρὸν ἡγοῦ^a ^{b}λόγον ἔχων^b διὰ στόμα^c ἐπαινεῖσθαι.
287 σοφῶν^a ψυχαὶ ἀκόρεστοι θεοσεβείας.
288 ἀρχόμενος ἀπὸ^a θεοῦ πρᾶττε ^{b}ὃ ἂν πράττῃς^b.
289 συνεχέστερον νόει τὸν θεὸν ἢ ἀνάπνει^a.
290 ἃ μαθόντα δεῖ ποιεῖν, ἄνευ τοῦ μαθεῖν μὴ ἐπιχείρει^a.
291 σαρκὸς μὴ ἔρα.
292 ψυχῆς ἀγαθῆς^a ἔρα μετὰ θεόν.

Translation

283 It is best not to sin, but having sinned, it is better to acknowledge it than to ignore it.

284 A philosopher is not a braggart.
285 Consider that wisdom to be great by which you are able to bear ignorant people's lack of education.
286 Deem it shameful when you have reason to be praised for your speech.
287 The souls of sages are insatiable in their reverence for God.
288 Do whatever you do beginning from God.
289 Think about God more often than you breathe.
290 Things that should be done with learning do not attempt without learning.
291 Do not love the flesh.
292 After God, love a good soul.

Textual Notes
285ᵃ ἦν: Π, sy¹ • 286ᵃ αἰδοῦ: Π • 286ᵇ⁻ᵇ omit lat, sy² • 286ᶜ σῶμα: Υ, sy² • 287ᵃ φιλοσόφων: Π • 288ᵃ ὑπὸ: Π • 288ᵇ⁻ᵇ ὃ πράττεις: Π • 289ᵃ ἀνάπνεε: Π • 290ᵃ ἐγχείρει: Υ • 292ᵃ omit Π

Commentary

The material in this block of sayings appears to be largely uncoordinated, though the instruction in vv. 284–286 would be particularly relevant to the sage's interaction with nonbelievers, while the instruction in vv. 287–289 would be particularly relevant to his interaction with God, vv. 288–289 serving as practical definitions of θεοσέβεια in v. 287. Verse 283, meanwhile, may have been attracted to the former cluster by the linkword ἀγνοέω (vv. 283, 285). Verses 291–292, finally, are an antithetical gnomic couplet on love.

Sentence 283

The source for this line is *Sent. Pythag.* 84: πολλῷ ἄμεινον μὴ ἁμαρτάνειν, ἁμαρτάνοντα δὲ ἄμεινον γινώσκειν ἢ ἀγνοεῖν. Sextus creates a μέν ... δέ ... construction by replacing the initial clause with ἄριστον μὲν τὸ μὴ ἁμαρτεῖν, which also has the effect of eliminating the repetition of ἄμεινον. Given the saying's philosophical provenance, it is safe to assume that the topic under consideration is not inadvertent sins (as, e.g., in Lev 4:13, also with ἀγνοέω) but unacknowledged sins. Compare v. 595: "It is best not to sin, but having sinned, it is better to reveal it than to hide it." In the moral economy of the *Sentences*, even the smallest sin is a sacrilege (vv. 11, 297). Therefore only the sinless can be considered truly faithful (vv. 8, 36, 60). As believers, the readers are obliged not only to refrain from committing sins (v. 234) but also to prevent sin from corrupting their thoughts (vv. 181, 233), since it is in the heart and the mind that God dwells (vv. 46b, 144). As the current verse suggests, such sins should be brought to light, so that they can be properly censured (v. 298) and the perpetrator rendered less likely to repeat an error (v. 247). The opposite scenario is presented in v. 452 (= Clitarchus, *Sent*. 54): "When you struggle to defend an unjust deed that you have committed, you will commit a second injustice" (cf. Sir 7:8; 23:11).

The practice of repentance is commended in a wide range of ancient, especially philosophical, sources. In his commentary on the Pythagorean *Carmen aureum*, for instance, Hierocles of Alexandria identifies repentance as "the very beginning of philosophy: the flight from both senseless deeds and words and the first preparation for a life without regret" (*In aur. carm*. 14.10; cf. Ps.-Apollonius, *Ep*. 42a). Even a Stoic like Seneca concedes that for those who fall short of perfection "the most dependable change toward integrity comes from repentance" (*Nat*. 3, pref. 3; cf. *Ira* 3.36.1–4; *Ep*. 28.9–10), while Plutarch describes μετάνοια as an act of reason working through the conscience to chastise and reform the soul (*Tranq. an.* 476f; cf. *Virt. mor.* 452c). In Philo's moral hierarchy, among humankind the "unbroken perfection of virtues" most nearly approximates the divine, while ranking second after it is repentance, "just as a change from sickness to health is second to a body free from disease" (*Abr*. 26; cf. *Somn*. 1.91; *Virt*. 176). The reason for the latter's subordinate status is that even after the penitent are restored, the "scars and impressions" of their old transgressions remain imprinted on their souls (*Spec*. 1.103; cf. *Abr*. 47; Plato, *Gorg*. 524d–525a). For the particular formulation of v. 283, comparison should be made especially with Clement, *Paed*. 1.9.81.3: "It is noble not to sin at all, but it is good also to repent after sinning." For similar gnomes, see *Instr. Ankh*. 19.8 ("If a stupid man repents he becomes a wise man"); Septem Sapientes, *Praec*. 217.40 (ἁμαρτάνων μετανόει); *Gnom. Democr*. 43, 60; Ps.-Cato, *Dist*. 4.40; Publilius Syrus, *Sent*. 139 ("You could soon avoid a fault, if you repent having run into it") and 343 ("When you've slipped once, be it your fault if you fall again").

Sentence 284

Insofar as boastfulness and imposture can represent obstacles to acknowledging one's faults, this line can be read in conjunction with the one that precedes it. Compare *1 Clem*. 57.1–2: "Accept discipline leading to repentance, bending the knees of your heart. Learn how to subordinate yourselves, laying aside the boastful and proud stubbornness of your tongue." According to Clement, *Strom.* 2.19.97.3, ἀλαζονεία itself is a vice of which believers need to repent. In our sources, ἀλαζών ("boaster, braggart") is used especially of the sophists, notorious for their pretension and arrogance (e.g., Plutarch, *Adv. Col.* 1118d, 1124c; Dio Chrysostom, *Or.* 4.33; Philostratus, *Vit. Apoll.* 7.16), though the term could be employed in a range of polemical situations (cf. Clement, *Strom.* 1.17.87.7; Lucian, *Dial. mort.* 1.2; *Gall.* 4; Dio Chrysostom, *Or.* 66.25; Plutarch, *De laude* 547e). According to Aristotle, the boastful man is similar to the liar in that he deliberately exaggerates his own merits and accomplishments in order to achieve either profit or glory (*Eth. nic.* 4.7.10–13). Epictetus adds that not only is the braggart conceited—he makes pretense to things that in no way concern him (*Diatr.* 3.24.43). The philosopher, on the other hand, does not brag, especially about being a philosopher (*Diatr.* 2.13.23; *Ench.* 46.1), and will refrain from speaking often or at length about his accomplishments (*Ench.* 33.14). As *Gnom. Vat.* 45 asserts, philosophy "does not make individuals productive of boasting or bragging nor apt to display that culture which is the object of rivalry with the many, but people who are high-spirited and self-sufficient, taking pride in the good things of their own minds and not of their circumstances." For his part, the Sextine sage is more concerned with pleasing God than with pleasing the multitudes (vv. 51, 112), and in fact regards the approval of the latter with suspicion (see on v. 286 below). The sage is therefore resigned to the fact that he will have little standing with the general public (vv. 53, 145, 214, 360). He aims instead for the reality rather than the appearance of virtue (v. 64), knowing that in this arena actions count more than words (vv. 177, 198, 383), while self-deceit (v. 199) and the love of reputation (v. 188), especially a reputation for being wise (v. 389b), are constant threats to spiritual progress. For all of these reasons those who belong to God do not boast much (v. 432), preferring to give God the credit for any noble thing they do (v. 390). For the critique of ἀλαζονεία in early Christian literature, see also Rom 1:30; 2 Tim 3:2; Jas 4:16; 1 John 2:16; *1 Clem.* 2.1; 13.1; 14.1; 21.5; 38.2 ("Let the one who is pure in flesh remain so and not boast, recognizing that it is someone else who grants his self-control"); Herm. *Mand.* 6.2.5; Clement, *Paed.* 2.3.36.2–4. For gnomic perspectives, cf. Prov 21:24; Ps.-Phoc. 122.

Sentence 285

The source for this line is *Sent. Pythag.* 64 (μεγάλην παιδείαν νόμιζε δι' ἧς δυνήσῃ φέρειν ἀπαιδευσίαν), which is cited as a saying of Pythagoras in Stobaeus, *Anth.* 3.19.8. Our author ruins the wordplay by changing παιδείαν to σοφίαν (cf. on v. 92), and then inserts by way of clarification ἀγνοούντων before ἀπαιδευσίαν (cf. Clement, *Strom.* 1.6.35.3: "Ignorance involves a lack of education"). This second alteration raises the possibility that in its Sextine context the maxim is best read in the light of v. 174, where ἀγνοούντων is similarly redactional: "The sins of the ignorant are a reproach to those who teach them" (cf. Clitarchus, *Sent.* 45). In this case, the ignorant are fellow believers under the sage's tutelage, and "great" wisdom consists not in making claims regarding one's own education (v. 284), but in showing patience when responding to their lack of it. Such an approach is desirable because the sage is obligated to persuade fellow believers who lack judgment not to act out of ignorance (v. 331, cf. v. 103). The sage, then, demonstrates forbearance in offering correction, just as his followers demonstrate forbearance in receiving correction, as suggested by vv. 245–246: "When you are being reproved in order that you might become wise, be grateful to those reproving you. The one who is unable to bear (οὐ δυνάμενος φέρειν) the sage is unable to bear what is good." The basic disposition encouraged in v. 285 is lauded elsewhere, for instance, in *Gnom. Democr.* 46 ("It is greatness of soul to endure faults easily"), and frequently in the New Testament, for example, Eph 4:2; Col 3:12–13; 1 Thess 5:14 ("Admonish the idlers, encourage the faint hearted, help the weak, be patient with all of them"); 2 Tim 2:24–25; 4:2; Heb 5:2 (The high priest "is able to deal gently with the ignorant and wayward"). In evaluating such texts, it is worth remembering that the willingness to "bear" the ignorant errors of others (φέρειν τὰς ἀλλήλων ἀγνοίας) could be seen as a sign of fraternal love (Polybius, *Hist.* 23.11.3; cf. Plutarch, *Ages.* 8.4). As Clement explains, the gnostic does not keep aloof from "simple" believers, but "stoops to accommodation" for the sake of their salvation, thereby demonstrating Christian "condescendence" (*Strom.* 7.9.53.4–5).

By the same token, it is possible to read v. 285 in tandem with the verse that follows, in which case the ignorant would be coterminous with the unbelieving public, that is, with people who praise the sage not for what he says but for the way that he says it. Certainly, from our author's perspective such a population could be fairly described as lacking in education. In this context, "great" wisdom consists in the sage's ability to bear with people who fail to recognize that he in fact possesses such wisdom. Cf. Sir 22:15: "Sand and salt and a mass of iron are easier to bear than a person without understanding."

Sentence 286

Praising someone for the wrong reasons, a practice generally associated with flatterers, could be considered αἰσχρός (e.g., Dio Chrysostom, *Or.* 1.33; 3.21; Plutarch, *Alex.* 23.7). What makes the sage valuable both to God and to humanity is not his tongue but his prudence (v. 426). It is therefore "shameful" to praise the former while failing to recognize the latter. Presumably, those most apt to do so would be unbelievers, since they by definition lack goodness (v. 243) and it is in the power of reason that the good resides (v. 316). Signs of approbation from unbelievers, then, are to be viewed with suspicion (vv. 241, 299, cf. vv. 530–531). On the other hand, failing to acknowledge the sage's reason is ironic, inasmuch as the way of life he embodies is one guided by λόγος (vv. 69, 74, 123, 205, 264a, 277, 363a, 413), a fact reflected in his habits of speech, where in everything he says he endeavors to bring his tongue under the control of his mind (v. 151, cf. v. 154). Accordingly, in his speech he avoids boasting about himself (vv. 284, 431–432), flattering the wicked (vv. 149–150), or striving to please the multitudes (vv. 112, 360), just as he refrains from everything shameful, that is, from everything that derives from a love of the body (vv. 101–102, and note that in v. 286 Υ replaces στόμα with σῶμα). The sage desires to be praised, not for his words but for his deeds (v. 298). Compare further *Gnom. Vat.* 81 ("The disturbance of the soul cannot be ended nor true joy created either by the possession of the greatest wealth or by honor and respect in the eyes of the multitude") and Seneca, *Ep.* 99.17 ("Crowds are never good advisers in anything"). A more neutral attitude is endorsed by Clitarchus, *Sent.* 111: "Be neither impressed nor dishonored by a crowd's praise." As Isocrates points out, crowds are more likely to praise a speech for its style than for its content (*Phil.* 4).

Sentence 287

The term θεοσέβεια, a near synonym of εὐσέβεια (e.g., Philo, *Spec.* 4.134–135; cf. on Sext. 371), is found only infrequently outside of Jewish and Christian settings, though see Ps.-Plato, *Epin.* 985c, 990a. Here in v. 287 the virtue is identified as an aspect, indeed an "insatiable" aspect, of the sage's very being. As Chadwick (1959, 176) suggests, this saying can be read against the background of Clement's argument regarding the indefectibility (ἀναπόβλητος) of the perfection achieved by the gnostic, especially as expounded in book 7, chapter 7 of the *Stromata* (cf. *Strom.* 4.22.139.2; 7.12.70.5; for the theory's Stoic pedigree, see *SVF* 3:237–238, 537). As the Alexandrian explains, not only does the gnostic pray for the power never to fall away from virtue, but through "discipline based upon knowledge, habit is changed into nature" to such an extent that his perfection can never be lost or taken away (*Strom.* 7.7.46.9). What informs this discipline is not just any knowledge, however, but the knowledge of God. Thus it is the gnostic alone, owing to the nature of this perfection, who can be considered truly εὐσεβής (*Strom.* 7.7.47.3), since he alone is possessed of divine σοφία, and "he who partakes of what has no defect must himself be without defect" (*Strom.* 7.7.47.5). Here as elsewhere, Clement simply assumes that wisdom and reverence represent mutually implicating concepts: "Reverence is the beginning of wisdom" (*Strom.* 2.18.84.1; cf. Prov 9:10), while a love for wisdom leads one to revere God (*Strom.* 1.4.27.3; cf. Josephus, *C. Ap.* 2.140; Origen, *Phil.* 13.3). While Sextus does not use the language of perfection, he does liken the soul of a reverent person to a god in a human body (v. 82d, cf. v. 46a). Like God, such an individual is not only blessed himself (v. 326b); he also communicates blessings to others without discrimination (v. 371, cf. vv. 372–374).

Sentence 288

Insofar as reverence for God entails service to God (e.g., Jdt 11:17; Act. Paul. 38), v. 288 can be interpreted as an elaboration of v. 287 (cf. vv. 43, 182, 236, 240, 274a, 363a, all also with ἄρχω). Accordingly, to have a reverence for God that is indeed "insatiable" entails a passionate commitment to serving God in "whatever" one does. As Sextus explains in vv. 41–42, being governed by God means being governed by what is best, and in order to be governed by what is best it is necessary to honor what is best above all other things. In practical terms, this means living in accord with God, that is, acting moderately, nobly, and righteously (v. 399), doing nothing unworthy of God (v. 4). Those who act under God's governance in all that they do think about God before every action that they take (v. 95a), remembering in particular that they call God father (vv. 59, 222, cf. vv. 58, 225). It is in this sense that they "begin" with God, God operating as the source (vv. 113, 390), guide (vv. 95b, 104), witness (vv. 224, 303), and validator (v. 304) of every noble deed that they accomplish. Through this process those who begin with God finish by becoming "inseparable" from God (vv. 422–424).

Sentence 289

This line can be interpreted as an additional and complementary elaboration on v. 287. Reverence for God pertains not only to one's actions but also to one's thoughts, and those whose souls are ardent in their θεοσέβεια think about God constantly, just as they serve God constantly. Indeed, the former constitutes both a prior and necessary condition for the latter, as suggested by v. 56 ("Think about noble things, so that you may also do noble things") and v. 95a ("Before every action you take, think about God"). Constant attention to God in one's thoughts (with the intention of putting those thoughts into action) doubtless serves as the principal means by which the intellect purges itself of evil (vv. 57b, 181) and becomes suitable as a dwelling place for the divine (vv. 46a, 61, 143–144). Such attentiveness is critical because God, as mind (v. 26), is aware of every thought (v. 57a), and even the intention to disobey God separates one from God (v. 233, cf. v. 82e). Thus the only appropriate and beneficial activity for the human mind is to think about God (v. 54), conforming one's mind to the mind of God as much as possible (v. 381).

Verse 289 appears to have been the source for Gregory Nazianzen's precept, μνημονευτέον θεοῦ μᾶλλον ἢ ἀναπνευστέον (*Eunom.* 4), which in turn is cited by John Chrysostom, *In Ps. 118* 55.703; Ps.-John Damascene, *Sacr. par.* 95.1357; 96.228; and Theodora Palaeologina, *Typ. mon. Lips* 13.28.

Sentence 290

The wording of this gnome may be indebted in part to Clitarchus, *Sent.* 50: ἄρχεσθαι μὴ μαθὼν ἄρχειν μὴ ἐπιχείρει. It is often the case that the accomplishment of some noble deed requires not only effort (v. 125) but also instruction. For those who would be close to God, then, learning must be accepted as necessary (v. 251), while its absence is burdensome (v. 285). Given that the purpose of human existence is to become as much like God as possible (vv. 44–45, 381), the focus of Sextine learning lies in the area of theology strictly speaking (e.g., vv. 25–30). As the saying here in v. 290 indicates, such learning is obtained not for its own sake but so that one will understand what to do (ποιεῖν). Cf. v. 384: "A faithful person fond of learning is a worker of truth." What the readers ought to learn about God is only that which is worthy of God (v. 248). But more than this, the only reason they ought to acquire such learning at all is so that through their conduct they might become worthy of God themselves (vv. 4–5, 58, 132, 376a). One's curriculum in this regard needs to be chosen with care, however, since there is a chance that students will be exposed to faulty theological opinions (vv. 338, 409–410, cf. v. 353) or to forms of learning that distract them from the care of the soul (v. 249).

For the argument that the business of becoming morally good and making others morally good is one that should not be undertaken without the proper teaching and experience, see especially Plato, *Gorg.* 513e–515b. Pythagoreanism, like all ancient philosophies, embraced the need for learning and instruction as well. According to Iamblichus, for example, Pythagoras himself would only accept students who demonstrated an aptitude for learning (*Vit. Pythag.* 20.94–95; cf. 29.164; 30.183; 31.200; 32.227). Such aptitude is important, since those who try to act without learning are unlikely to succeed, as we discover from a saying in the Pythagorean *Carmen aureum* that closely parallels v. 290: "Do not do even one thing of what you do not understand, but learn what is necessary, and thus you will lead a most enjoyable life" (*Carm. aur.* 30–31). In the same vein, Clement asserts that the gnostic not only does what is right; he also understands why it is right to do it: "However admirably people live, if they do so without real knowledge of what they are doing ... they have stumbled into good works by accident, whereas there are those who by means of understanding hit the target of the word of truth" (*Strom.* 1.7.38.1).

Sentences 291–292

Here we have an antithetical pair of sayings bound by the catchword ἔρα. It is taken for granted that the readers will "love" something, though basic alternatives exist as to the direction of their commitment and desire. As Plato explains, ἔρως considered in and of itself is neither honorable nor disgraceful; it only becomes disgraceful when someone "loves the body rather than the soul" (*Symp.* 183d–e). By assigning σαρκός and ψυχῆς the first position in their respective lines, Sextus draws out the contrastive nature of these alternatives, which are presumably to be understood in mutually exclusive terms, as v. 141 suggests: "If you love what is not necessary, you will not love what is necessary." See further Matt 6:24; Luke 16:13; Ps.-Phoc. 67 ("Love of virtue is revered, but love of passion earns shame"). For Sextus, what is "not necessary" to love is the life of the flesh, since from it derives nothing that is good (vv. 271, 317). In a parallel saying, the readers had been similarly implored not to "love" the things of the body (v. 101, cf. v. 76). This requires great effort, however, since the body has many powerful drives (vv. 136, 139b, 274a, 411, etc.). Compare *Evang. Bart.* 5.8: "It is good if he who is baptized preserves his baptism without blame. But the lust of the flesh will practice its allurement (ἐραστή)." Conversely, what is "necessary" to love above all is God, a concept that may be derived indirectly from the Deuteronomic injunction to "love the Lord your God" (Deut 6:5; 11:1; etc.; cf. Matt 22:37; Mark 12:30; Luke 10:27). In order to love God, however, the readers must become like God, that is, they must cultivate "what God wills" within themselves (v. 442, cf. v. 444), since only like is "dear" (φίλος) to like (v. 443) and the goal of the believing life is φιλία with God (v. 86b). Cf. vv. 106a–b: "Love what is akin to you. Love God even more than your own soul." Next to God, the readers should love that which is most like God, a "good soul" (for the expression, see also v. 349), the sort of soul that belongs to the sage, as suggested by another μετὰ θεόν saying in the collection, v. 244 ("After God, honor a sage"). See also v. 226: "The one who does not love a sage does not love himself."

Sentences 293–302

Text

293   οἰκείων^a ὀργὰς δύνασθαι^b φέρειν κατὰ φιλόσοφον^c.
294   πιστοῦ^a πλοῦτος ἐγκράτεια.
295   ^aὅπερ μεταδιδοὺς ἄλλοις αὐτὸς οὐχ ἕξεις, μὴ κρίνῃς ἀγαθὸν εἶναι.
296   οὐδὲν^a ἀκοινώνητον ἀγαθόν.
297   μὴ νόμιζε ^aμικρότερον ἁμάρτημα^a ἄλλο ἄλλου.^b
298   ὡς ἐπὶ τοῖς κατορθώμασιν τιμᾶσθαι^a θέλεις, ^bκαὶ ἐπὶ τοῖς ἁμαρτήμασιν ψεγόμενος ἀνέχου^b.
299   ὧν τῶν ἐπαίνων καταφρονεῖς, καὶ τῶν ψόγων ὑπερόρα.
300   θησαυρὸν ^aκατατίθεσθαι μὲν^a οὐ φιλάνθρωπον, ἀναιρεῖσθαι δὲ οὐ κατὰ^b φιλόσοφον.
301   ὅσα πονεῖς^a διὰ τὸ σῶμα, καὶ διὰ τὴν ψυχὴν πονέσας σοφὸς ἂν εἴης.
302   σοφὸν οὐδέν ἐστιν ὃ βλάπτει.

Translation

293   It befits a philosopher to be able to bear the anger of friends.
294   A faithful person's wealth is self-control.
295   Do not judge something to be good that you cannot share with others and still have yourself.
296   Nothing is good that is unshared.
297   Do not consider one sin smaller than another.
298   Just as you want to be honored for your successes, so tolerate being censured for your sins.

299 Spurn the censures of those whose praises you despise.
300 To hoard wealth is not humane, and even to accept it does not befit a philosopher.
301 If you labor as much for the soul as you labor for the body, you will be wise.
302 There is nothing that can harm a sage.

Textual Notes

293ᵃ αἰκιῶν: Π • 293ᵇ δύνασαι: Υ • 293ᶜ σοφῶν: Π • 294ᵃ φιλοσόφῳ: Π; φιλοσόφων: lat • 295–296ᵃ⁻ᵃ παρ' ὅσον μὴ μεταδιδοὺς (= μεταδίδως) ἄλλοις αὐτὸς οὐκ ἕξεις. μὴ κρίνῃς ἀγαθὸν εἶναι οὐδὲν κτλ: Υ • 297ᵃ⁻ᵃ ἁμάρτημα μικρόν: Υ • 297ᵇ ἄλλου. πᾶν ἁμάρτημα ἀσέβημα ἡγοῦ.: Υ (cf. v. 11) • 298ᵃ ἐπαινεῖσθαι: lat, sy²; ἐπαινεῖσθαι καὶ τιμᾶσθαι: Υ • 298ᵇ⁻ᵇ ἀνέχου καὶ ἐν κακοῖς ψεγόμενος: Υ • 300ᵃ⁻ᵃ μὲν καταθέσθαι: Υ • 300ᵇ omit Π • 301ᵃ πονέσας: Π, Υ

Commentary

This block of sayings demonstrates little thematic coherence, though note that it begins (v. 293, cf. v. 294 v.l.) and ends (vv. 300–302) with references to the philosopher-sage, anticipating a major theme in the unit that follows (vv. 303–311). In between is a gnomic cluster on sharing (vv. 295–296, both with ἀγαθόν), followed by a cluster dealing with praise and blame (vv. 297–299). Within the latter, vv. 297 and 298 are linked by the catchword ἁμάρτημα, while vv. 298 and 299 are linked by the related terms ψέγω and ψόγος.

Sentence 293

The reader of the Sermon on the Mount is instructed to reconcile promptly with a brother who "has something against you" (Matt 5:23–24; cf. 18:21–22), while Prov 22:24–25 recommends that one not associate with people given to anger in the first place. The advice offered the readers of the *Sentences*, by contrast, is not to resolve or avoid the anger of others, but to bear (φέρειν) it, in keeping with their philosophical aspirations, much like they "bear" the ignorance of the uneducated, in keeping with their understanding of wisdom (v. 285, cf. v. 119). Moralists of varying backgrounds agreed in identifying the ability to tolerate a friend's mistakes and faults as an essential component of friendship, for example, Sir 19:13–17; Septem Sapientes, *Sent.* 216.1; Theognis, *El.* 323–328; Plato, *Phaedr.* 233c. Aristotle opines that we should tolerate even badness in friends, that is, tolerate it so long as they have not become incurably bad, since "it is incumbent on us to help them morally as long as they are capable of reform" (*Eth. nic.* 9.3.3). Among the things that must be tolerated is a friend's fit of anger, as we hear in Theognis, *El.* 97–99 (cf. 1164a–d): "May I have the sort of friend who knows his comrade and, like a brother, puts up with his anger (ὀργή) even when he is hard to bear (φέρει)." Cf. Isocrates, *Demon.* 31 ("You must not oppose harshly the angry moods of your associates, even if they happen to be angry without reason, but rather give way to them when they are in the heat of passion and rebuke them when their anger has cooled"); Menander, *Mon.* 99 ("Be slow to anger and disciplined to bear it"), 604: "Try to bear the anger of a comrade and friend" (ὀργὴν ἑταίρου καὶ φίλου πειρῶ φέρειν). For evidence of the theme's impact on Pythagorean thought, see *Carm. aur.* 7–8: "Do not hate your friend for a small fault, for as long as you are able to do so." Of particular interest for the interpretation of v. 293 is the argument preserved in Iamblichus, *Vit. Pythag.* 22.101: since anger and similar emotions tend to undermine the preservation of friendship, it is important not only to master anger oneself, but also to "draw back" from a friend's anger, especially when that friend happens to be a social superior (cf. *Vit. Pythag.* 33.230–232). Note that although the problem of anger represents one of the more prominent themes of gnomic literature, it is raised in the *Sentences* only infrequently (see on v. 343), and even on those occasions it is not the readers' anger that is under discussion, but their responsibilities regarding the anger of others.

Sentence 294

The idea for this line may have been inspired by *Sent. Pythag.* 89, a saying that is preserved in Stobaeus, *Anth.* 3.17.11 as well: "Procure for yourself the greatest strength and wealth, namely, self-control" (ῥώμην μεγίστην καὶ πλοῦτον τὴν ἐγκράτειαν κτῆσαι). Cf. Porphyry, *Marc.* 28: "The philosophers say that nothing is as necessary as perceiving clearly what is not necessary, and that the greatest wealth of all is self-sufficiency (πλουσιωτάτην … πάντων τὴν αὐτάρκειαν)." Verse 294, in turn, may have been the source for *Apophth. patr.* [sy.] 4.87: ψυχῆς πλοῦτος ἐγκράτεια. By the same token, the paradox being expressed here was not uncommon. Consider, for instance, Musonius Rufus, frag. 34 ("One man and one alone shall we consider rich, the man who has acquired the ability to want for nothing always and everywhere"); Philo, *Somn.* 2.40 ("He that makes it his object to be rich in nature's riches will lay his hands on self-control and thrift"); Stobaeus, *Anth.* 3.5.31 (αὐτάρκεια γὰρ φύσεώς ἐστι πλοῦτος). In *Strom.* 6.2.24.8, Clement cites with approval a saying of Epicurus (πλουσιώτατον αὐτάρκεια πάντων), which is most likely the teaching to which Porphyry refers in *Marc.* 28. For his part, the sage of the *Sentences* does not consider material wealth of any kind to be his own possession (v. 227, cf. v. 300), since it represents an obstacle to salvation (v. 193). Instead, the only thing that he regards as his "own" is that which is good (v. 79), in other words, that which befits God (vv. 131, 197). One of the means by which he obtains this good—indeed, it is the very foundation of his relationship with God—is ἐγκράτεια, or self-control (v. 86a, cf. vv. 239, 253b, 438). By limiting his acquisition of material things to a bare minimum (vv. 78, 115, etc.), the philosopher not only becomes like God (v. 18); he also comes into possession of whatever God possesses (vv. 310–311), things that can be obtained only from God (v. 124), the sorts of "goods" acquired only by those who have a share in divine reason (v. 277).

Sentences 295–296

This pair of sayings is linked by the theme of sharing as well as by the catchword ἀγαθόν. The source of the first line is Clitarchus, *Sent.* 105: "Something is not your possession to the extent that you cannot share it with others and still have it yourself (μεταδίδως τοῖς ἄλλοις αὐτὸς οὐχ ἕξεις)." Sextus drops the first part of the saying, replacing it at the end with μὴ κρίνῃς ἀγαθὸν εἶναι, perhaps under the influence of *Sent. Pythag.* 32: "Deem to be especially good (ἀγαθόν εἶναι) that which increases all the more to you even as you share it (μεταδιδόμενον) with another." The thought behind Clitarchus, *Sent.* 105, in turn, may be indebted ultimately to Plato, *Leg.* 730e, according to which praise should be bestowed on "moderation and good judgment and all the other good things (ἀγαθά) which the possessor is able not only to have himself (αὐτὸν ἔχειν) but also to share with others (ἄλλοις μεταδιδόναι)." Note that while Plato names particular virtues, Clitarchus and Sextus leave what ought to be shared with others unidentified.

In the *Sentences*, such a high premium is placed on the practice of sharing that it is considered better to have nothing at all than to have many things and share them with no one (v. 377, also with ἀκοινώνητος), though it is also important that sharing be done in the proper spirit (vv. 329, 342). Sextus's readers are to demonstrate their disdain for the things of the world by sharing them (v. 82b), deeming it more appropriate to serve others (ἄλλοι) than to be served by them (v. 336, cf. vv. 210a, 260, 266). In particular, they are to share their possessions with the needy (v.

330), since this meets with God's approval (vv. 379, 382) and accords with the generosity that God expressed to the giver in the first place (v. 242). The sort of "good" that one can share with others and still have oneself would appear to refer in the first place to reason (vv. 277, 316), which the sage both possesses himself and imparts to others, especially in the form of prudent teaching and counsel (vv. 24, 331, 358, etc.). This ought to be distributed in a spirit of generosity as well, even if instruction about God is something that must not be "shared" with everyone (v. 401, cf. v. 350).

Sentences 297–298

In keeping with its monistic psychology, Stoic doctrine made no allowance for degrees or intermediate states of virtue and vice (e.g., Diogenes Laertius, *Vit. phil.* 7.127). Those who have yet to achieve the perfection of the sage "are all in the same degree vicious and unjust and unreliable and foolish" (Plutarch, *Comm. not.* 1062e; cf. *Stoic. rep.* 1038c). Hence the Stoic paradoxes that "whoever has one vice has them all" (e.g., Seneca, *Ben.* 5.15.1) and that "all sins are equal" (e.g., Diogenes Laertius, *Vit. phil.* 7.120; cf. Cicero, *Acad.* 2.132–137; *Fin.* 3.48; 4.21, 56, 63, 75, 77; *Parad.* 3.20–26). In the *Sentences*, the sentiment expressed here is familiar especially from vv. 8–11 (apparently recognizing this, Υ repeats v. 11 as a gloss on v. 297, which Chadwick 1959, 46 prints as v. 297b *seclusi*), where the author's reliance on biblical perspectives is somewhat clearer. For additional remarks, see the commentary on those verses, and note in particular the language of v. 10: οὐ γὰρ μικρὸν ἐν βίῳ τὸ παρὰ μικρόν. See further Philo, *Leg.* 3.241 ("He that exercises perfect self-control must shun all sins, both the greater and the lesser, and be found implicated in none whatsoever"); Origen, *Cels.* 3.60; 4 Macc 5:20–21: "To transgress the law in matters either small (μικροῖς) or great is of equal seriousness, for in either case the law is equally despised." Among the sorts of sins one might be persuaded to deem "smaller" than others would be sins of intention, a notion that Sextus rejects in v. 233. As believers, the most serious pledge that the readers make is not to sin (vv. 234, 247) even in their thoughts (v. 181).

When sins are committed, therefore, it is imperative that they be acknowledged, not ignored (v. 283), since failure in this regard increases the likelihood that they will be committed again (v. 247). The seriousness attached to the problem of sin is reflected in v. 298 as well, which should be interpreted especially in the light of v. 245: the readers are advised not only to tolerate being censured for their sins, but to be grateful for the person, presumably a fellow believer, who offers reproof in an effort to make them wise (cf. v. 609). Indeed, as we learn here, such reproof is so valuable that they should accept it to the same degree that they desire to be honored for their successes, a rather high degree of desirability, since being honored for one's successes was an important mark of virtue (Aristotle, *Eth. nic.* 2.6.12; in *Abr.* 186, Philo adds that a κατόρθωμα is praiseworthy only when it is performed voluntarily, rather than out of fear; cf. Sext. 121a). On the other hand, it was considered one of the responsibilities of friendship to censure a comrade when he sinned (e.g., Plutarch, *Ages.* 5.1). For the particular configuration of these ideas in v. 298, comparison can be made with *Mos.* 1.154, where Philo explains how "censures (ψόγοι) and reprimands are prescribed by the law for sinners (ἁμαρτανόντων), praises and honors (ἔπαινοι καὶ τιμαί) for those who succeed (κατορθούντων)" (note that Υ reads ἐπαινεῖσθαι καὶ τιμᾶσθαι). See also Plutarch, *An seni* 795a and, for a gnomic formulation, P. Louvre 2377 no. 3: "No deed brings honor to him whom they cannot reprove." The appropriate, that is, therapeutic, use of censure in a Christian context is spelled out by Clement in *Paed.* 1.8.74.2: "It is not inconsistent for the word that brings salvation to make use of reproof (λοιδορεῖσθαι) in its providential care. For this is the remedy supplied by the divine love of humanity, because it awakens the blush of reverence and shame for sins committed. For if it is necessary to censure (ψέξαι) and reprove, then there is also occasion to wound, not to death, but to its salvation, a soul grown callous" (cf. Origen, *Princ.* 3.1.21).

Sentence 299

Even if some people offer reproof in the proper spirit, that is, in order to make others wise (v. 245), this does not mean that all people do so. Presumably, the individuals referred to here are unbelievers, people not only who lack wisdom themselves but who fail to recognize or cultivate it in others as well. It is thus inappropriate, even shameful, either to praise unbelievers (v. 150) or to accept their praise (v. 241). For the composition of v. 299, our author turns to *Sent. Pythag.* 111[b]: ὧν τῶν ἐπαίνων καταφρονεῖς, καὶ τὸν ψόγον καταφρόνει. Sextus alters τὸν ψόγον to τῶν ψόγων, perhaps under the influence of Clitarchus, *Sent.* 106: ὃς ἂν τῶν ἐπαίνων καταφρονῇ, οὗτος καὶ τῶν ψόγων καταφρονεῖ (note that Sext. 295 parallels Clitarchus, *Sent.* 105). Sextus also alters (perhaps for the sake of variation) καταφρόνει to ὑπερόρα. A similar saying is attributed to Pythagoras in Stobaeus, *Anth.* 4.5.42: ὧν ἂν τῶν ἐπαίνων καταφρονῇς, καὶ τῶν ψόγων καταφρόνει. Cf. *Sent. Pythag.* 35[a]: "Deem both the blame and the censure of every thoughtless person to be ridiculous." Also similar is *Gnom. Democr.* 48: "The good man takes no account of the reproaches of the bad." It is best to despise (καταφρονεῖν) the opinions of worldly people just as one despises the attractions of worldly things (vv. 82b, 121a, 127). Such an attitude is necessary, since as vv. 53, 145, 214, 322, and 363b indicate, the sage can expect to be ignored, misunderstood, and mistreated by "the world." A typical scenario in this regard is sketched by Seneca in *Ep.* 76.4: "Where the question discussed is: 'What is a good man?' and the lesson to be learned is 'How to be a good man,' very few are in attendance, and the majority think that even these few are engaged in no good business, giving them the name of empty-headed idlers. I hope that I may be blessed with that kind of mockery. For one should listen in an unruffled spirit to the railings of the ignorant. When one is marching toward the goal of honor, one should scorn scorn itself" (cf. Epictetus, *Diatr.* 1.26.13; Plutarch, *Apophth. lac.* 208d).

Sentence 300

In v. 263 (also with ἀναιρέω and κατατίθημι), we learn that accumulating more than what one has "put down" does not accord with the virtue of self-sufficiency. Here, we learn that the accumulation of wealth (literally, "treasure") does not accord with the virtue of humanity, or φιλανθρωπία (cf. v. 371). Presumably, this is because such hoarding conflicts with the practice of sharing, for which see above on vv. 295–296, the danger posed by the desire for riches being something that is noted frequently in our text (vv. 15, 18, 76, 81, 137, 192, 274b, etc.). For "philanthropic" attitudes towards the use of wealth, see also Menander, *Mon.* 182; *Chion. ep.* 10.1; Clement, *Quis div.* 1.4; *Paed.* 3.6.34.1; *Strom.* 2.18.84.4–2.18.86.7; Dio Chrysostom, *Or.* 7.90; Plutarch, *Pelop.* 3.2–4. In his treatise *De humanitate*, Philo explains that in comparison to those who possess virtues like humanity and kindness, "even the Great King appears to be the poorest of all … for his wealth is soulless, buried underground in treasuries and vaults, while the wealth of virtue is in the governing part of the soul; and it is to this that both the purest realm of existence, heaven, and the parent of all things, God, lay claim" (*Virt.* 85). Much like v. 300, the Alexandrian's comments evoke the ancient critique of illiberality, according to which riches ought to be put to good use (e.g., to help others), not vainly hoarded (Aristotle, *Eth. nic.* 4.1.37–44; Teles, frag. 4A.67–75; Sir 14:3–16; etc.). Cf. Seneca, *Ben.* 6.3.4: "The wealth that you esteem, that you think makes you rich and powerful, is buried under an inglorious name so long as you keep it." The miser who would rather hide his money than spend it was something of a cliché in parables and comedy (e.g., Antiphon, frag. 54).

The second half of the verse goes beyond this observation, suggesting that for a philosopher, given the basic stance towards worldly things that he is supposed to exemplify, even accepting money, presumably for his services, is not permissible. For Socrates's debate with the sophists over teaching for pay, see Plato, *Apol.* 33a–b; *Hipp. maj.* 282b–d; *Protag.* 313c–314b; Xenophon, *Apol.* 16; *Cyn.* 13.8–9; *Mem.* 1.2.6–8. Many subsequent philosophers both refused to accept money for their services and criticized those who did (e.g., Musonius Rufus, frag. 11; Plutarch, *Alex. fort.* 333b; *Stoic. rep.* 1043e–1044a; Clement, *Strom.* 4.22.137.1; *SVF* 3:686; Dio Chrysostom, *Or.* 32.9–11; 66.1; Lucian, *Nigr.* 24–26). From the Pythagorean tradition, we have Ps.-Apollonius, *Ep.* 42 ("If someone gives money to Apollonius, and the giver is someone considered respectable, he will take the money if he needs it. But he will not accept a fee for philosophy even if he does need it") and 51 ("Some criticize you for having accepted money from the emperor. That would not be immoral if you did not appear to have done so as a fee for philosophy"). According to Diogenes Laertius, Pythagoras himself taught that a philosopher "seeks for truth," not "for fame and gain" (*Vit. phil.* 8.8). In the same vein, we also have the example of Paul foregoing financial support, for which see 1 Cor 9:11–12; 2 Cor 11:7; 12:14 (with θησαυρίζω); 1 Thess 2:5–9; 2 Thess 3:7–9; cf. Matt 10:8.

Sentence 301

The basis for this line is *Sent. Pythag.* 95: "A person who is intelligent (συνετός) and beloved of God will be as eager to labor on behalf of the soul (ὑπὲρ τῆς ψυχῆς πονῆσαι) as others struggle on account of the body" (cf. Porphyry, *Marc.* 32). Sextus replaces συνετός with his favorite, σοφός (creating a catchword with σοφόν in v. 302 and a partial catchword with φιλόσοφον in v. 300), emphasizes the concept of labor by employing the verb πονέω twice, and turns a comparative statement into an integrative one: the sage toils on behalf of both the body, struggling to bring its desires under control (vv. 70–71a, 239–240, 274a, etc.), and on behalf of the soul, training it in reason (vv. 97, 123, 264a, 413, 420, etc.) and cleansing it of its vices and passions (vv. 205, 208a–209, etc.). The former, in fact, complements the latter, since the soul cannot know God if the body is distracted with longings (v. 136), and it is through the body that God tests the soul (v. 425; for more on the body–soul connection, see vv. 139a, 345–347, 411, 449). Cf. also v. 125 ("Pray that after your labors those things that labors lead to might be yours") and v. 216 ("Endure all things in order to live in accord with God"). For the image of the philosopher as a "soul-worker" doing moral "labor," see Plato, *Ep.* 340b–341a; Xenophon, *Mem.* 2.1.25; Philo, *Mos.* 1.48; 4 Macc 7:21–22; Iamblichus, *Vit. Pythag.* 8.40–42; 16.68; 32.223–225; Ps.-Justin Martyr, *Quaest. Christ. gent.* 212d; Clement, *Strom.* 2.20.126.4. Note also that the language of labor is employed regularly by both Clitarchus (*Sent.* 21, 47, 100, 119) and Porphyry (*Marc.* 6–7, 11–12, 31–32). For the anthropological division of labor conveyed here, comparison can be made with Musonius Rufus, who argues that philosophers must engage in two kinds of ἄσκησις (cf. vv. 51, 64, 69, 98, 120, 334), one which concerns both the body and the soul, and one which concerns the soul alone. While the former disciplines its adherents in self-control and the avoidance of pleasures, the latter trains them to distinguish that which is truly good from that which only seems to be good (frag. 6.54.10–25).

Sentence 302

It is possible to interpret this line as complementing the one that precedes it: the sage accepts the hardships obligatory to his profession, confident in the knowledge that none of the afflictions attendant upon them can injure him, that is, injure his soul. Cf. v. 318: "Whatever does not harm a soul does not harm a human being." It was a tenet especially among the Stoics that since the only thing of any consequence to the sage is his moral reason, and this lies completely under his control, he ought to be superior to all injuries, insults, and adversities. Besides *SVF* 3:567–581, see Musonius Rufus, frag. 10.76.16–10.80.6; Seneca, *Ben.* 2.35.2; *Const.* 7.3; *Ep.* 85.37 ("The wise man is not harmed by poverty, or by pain, or by any other of life's storms, for not all of his functions are checked, but only those which pertain to others; he himself is always in action, and is greatest in performance at the very time when fortune has blocked his way"); 92.24; Plutarch, *Stoic. abs.* 1057d–e; Epictetus, *Ench.* 20; *Diatr.* 3.6.5–7; 3.19.1–3; 3.22.100–106; 4.1.127: "How then does it come about that he is not harmed (βλάπτεται), even though he is soundly flogged or imprisoned or beheaded? Is it not thus, if he bears it all in a noble spirit, and comes off with increased profit and advantage?" Cf. Plato, *Apol.* 30d ("I do not think that it is permitted that a better man be harmed by a worse"); Philo, *Conf.* 153. For his part, the Sextine sage is unaffected by the loss of anything relating to the physical world (vv. 15, 91b, 130), even his own life (vv. 321–323). What concerns him instead is his moral freedom (vv. 17, 275, 306, 309), since it is not death but an evil life that can destroy his soul (v. 397, cf. vv. 7b, 208a–b). By the same token, the sage possesses the ability to harm the souls of others with his speech (v. 185), especially his speech about God (v. 195).

Sentences 303–311

Text

303 ὧν ἂν πράττῃς[a] θεὸν ἐπικαλοῦ μάρτυρα.
304 ὁ[a] θεὸς ἀνθρώπων[b] βεβαιοῖ καλὰς πράξεις.
305 κακῶν πράξεων κακὸς δαίμων ἡγεμών ἐστιν.
306 οὐκ ἀναγκάσεις σοφὸν [a]πρᾶξαι ὃ μὴ βούλεται[a] μᾶλλον ἤπερ[b] θεόν.
307 σοφὸς ἀνὴρ θεὸν ἀνθρώποις συνιστᾷ.
308 ὁ[a] θεὸς τῶν ἰδίων[b] ἔργων[c] μέγιστον φρονεῖ ἐπὶ σοφῷ.
309 [a]οὐδὲν οὕτως ἐλεύθερον[a] μετὰ θεὸν ὡς σοφὸς ἀνήρ.
310 ὅσα θεοῦ κτήματα, καὶ σοφοῦ.
311 [a]κοινωνεῖ βασιλείας[a] θεοῦ σοφὸς ἀνήρ.

Translation

303 Call upon God as witness of whatever you do.
304 God confirms the noble actions of human beings.
305 An evil demon is a guide of evil actions.
306 You will not compel a sage to do what he does not want any more than you can compel God.
307 A wise man presents God to human beings.
308 Of all his works God is most proud of a sage.
309 After God, nothing is as free as a wise man.
310 Whatever possessions belong to God belong also to a sage.
311 A wise man shares in God's kingdom.

Textual Notes

303[a] πράττῃς: Υ¹; πράττεις: Π, Υ* • 304[a] omit Υ • 304[b] ἀνθρώποις: Υ • 306[a-a] ὃ μὴ βούλεται πρᾶξαι: Υ • 306[b] περὶ: Π • 308[a] omit Υ • 308[b] ἤδη: Π • 308[c] omit Υ • 309[a-a] οὐδεὶς οὕτως ἐλεύθερος: co • 310–311 omit Υ • 311[a-a] κοινωνοῖ βασιλεία: Π

Commentary

The first four lines in this section form a unit bound by actions terms. Note πράττω in vv. 303, 306 and πρᾶξις in vv. 304–305. The final verse in this string (v. 306) mentions the sage, who then is the subject of six lines

(vv. 306–311). The entire unit is further bound together by the word θεός, which is used in every verse except v. 305.

Sentence 303

This line has a partial parallel in Porphyry, *Marc.* 12: "Let God be present as overseer and guardian of every action (πάσης πράξεως) and of every deed and word." For God as ἐπόπτης of human deeds, see 2 Macc 3:39; *Let. Aris.* 16; Philo, *Hypoth.* 7.9; *1 Clem.* 59.3; Musonius Rufus, frag. 15.96.30–31; Epictetus, *Diatr.* 3.11.6. For God as ἔφορος, cf. *Sent. Pythag.* 26 (quoted in Porphyry, *Marc.* 20): "Remember that wherever your body and your soul complete a deed, God stands by as guardian." God's role as ἔφορος τοῦ παντός is a prominent feature of the *corpus Philonicum*, where it is associated especially with the execution of divine justice in human affairs (*Ios.* 48, 170, 265; *Decal.* 95, 177; *Spec.* 3.19, 129; 4.200; *Virt.* 57, 200; cf. Epictetus, *Diatr.* 1.14, entitled ὅτι πάντας ἐφορᾷ τὸ θεῖον). Philo is also acquainted with the biblical image of God as witness (e.g., *Ebr.* 139; *Mos.* 2.284; *Dec.* 86; *Spec.* 2.10; cf. Gen 31:44; Judg 11:10; 1 Kgdms 12:5–6; 20:23), a concept that appears in early Christian writings as well (e.g., Rom 1:9; Phil 1:8; 1 Thess 2:5; Justin Martyr, *2 Apol.* 12.4; Origen, *Cels.* 1.46). The language of v. 303 is reminiscent especially of 2 Cor 1:23 (ἐγὼ δὲ μάρτυρα τὸν θεὸν ἐπικαλοῦμαι ἐπὶ τὴν ἐμὴν ψυχήν), though similar formulae can be found in texts like Polybius, *Hist.* 11.6.4; Josephus, *Ant.* 1.243; Galen, *Reb. bon. mal.* 6.755; Heliodorus, *Aeth.* 1.25.1. For Sextus, it is important to invoke God as witness not only when making an oath but when making a moral decision of any kind. Comparison can again be made with Philo:

> For when the tutor is present his charge will not go amiss; the teacher at the learner's side brings profit to him; the company of his senior gives to the youth the grace of modesty and self-control; the mere sight of father or mother can silently prevent the son from some intended wrongdoing. Imagine then the vastness of blessings which we must suppose will be his who believes that the eye of God is ever upon him, for if he reverences the dignity of him who is ever present, he will in fear and trembling flee from wrongdoing with all his might. (*Mut.* 217; cf. Seneca, *Ep.* 11.8–9)

See further on vv. 82a and 224.

Sentences 304–305

These two lines are paralleled in both wording and order by a pair of sayings in Porphyry, *Marc.* 16: θεὸς δὲ ἄνθρωπον βεβαιοῖ πράσσοντα καλά. κακῶν δὲ πράξεων κακὸς δαίμων ἡγεμών. The source of the latter is *Sent. Pythag.* 49 (Π): κακῶν πράξεων κακὸς δαίμων ἡγεμών ἐστιν (for the ἡγεμών ἐστιν ending, cf. Clitarchus, *Sent.* 126b and Sext. 104). As for the former, the two versions differ only slightly, Porphyry's perhaps preserving the more original phrasing, with Sextus's καλὰς πράξεις representing an editorial effort to make the gnome correlate better with v. 305, which has κακῶν πράξεων. For the parallels between Porphyry, *Marc.* 16 and vv. 312–314, see below.

Paul sometimes speaks of God as ὁ βεβαιῶν ἡμᾶς, "the one who confirms us" (2 Cor 1:21; cf. 1 Cor 1:8), while the Philonic sage interprets the gifts of grace he receives from God as confirmation (βεβαίωσις) of his virtue, which, like all good things, originates with God (*Mut.* 155; cf. *Abr.* 273). Relevant to the interpretation of both v. 304 and v. 305 is v. 104: ὁ θεὸς ἀνθρώπων καλῶν πράξεων ἡγεμών ἐστιν. God "confirms" what people do when they participate in divine reason (vv. 277, 413, cf. vv. 315–316) to such an extent that God dwells within their minds (vv. 46a, 61, 144), guiding their thoughts, words, and deeds. Reason, then, can be similarly described as something that should "guide" the faithful (v. 74, cf. v. 95b) and that they should "follow" (v. 264a, cf. vv. 123, 167, 349, 420). It is only through such participation that someone can perform noble actions, or guide others to noble actions (v. 106), since without God the noble would not exist (vv. 113, 197, 215, 390).

If God is the guide of what is noble and not its opposite (cf. vv. 29–30), then the guide of evil actions cannot be God, in whom there is no evil (vv. 114, 314, 440), but something that is itself evil, namely, an evil demon (cf. vv. 39, 349, 604). Just as God dwells within the mind of the sage, that is, within an intellect that has been cleansed of sins (vv. 46a–b, 57b, 181), then an intellect that has not been so cleansed, one rendered impure by shameful thoughts and actions (vv. 82e, 102, 356), becomes the abode of "evil things" (v. 62) and the property of demons, who by their nature are morally "unclean" (v. 348). Such statements are fairly indicative of ancient anthropological speculation. Porphyry, for example, takes it for granted that "the soul is a dwelling place either of gods or demons. Accordingly, when gods are present it will do good in both words and deeds, but if it receives the evil partner, the soul does everything in a state of wickedness" (*Marc.* 21; and for an elaboration of his demonology, see *Abst.* 2.37.1–2.43.5). Early Christian authors could also analyze morality as a cooperative effort. With Origen, for example, it is clear that just as in regard to things that are good the mere human will is by itself incapable of completing the good act (for this is in all cases brought to perfection by divine help), so also in regard to things of the opposite kind we derive the beginnings and what we may call the seeds of sin from those desires which are given to us naturally for our use. But when we indulge these to excess ... then the hostile powers, seizing the opportunity of this first offence, incite and urge us on in every way, striving to extend the sins over a larger field. (*Princ.* 3.2.2; cf. 3.2.4; *Hom. Num.* 20.3; *Hom. Jer.* 1.3)

For the language of v. 305, cf. Evagrius Ponticus, *Spirit. sent.* 30: ζωῆς ἀλόγου δαίμων ἡγεμών. For a description of a demon as ὁ τῆς κακίας ἡγεμών, see Ps.-Clement, *Hom.* 7.3.

Sentence 306

For the form of this saying, compare v. 403: "You will not discover the greatness of a sage's soul any more than (μᾶλλον ἤπερ) the greatness of God." The sage is as incoercible as God because, through the divine reason that dwells within him, it is God and God alone who guides, governs, and empowers him (see on v. 304, cf. vv. 36, 43, 288). Since the sage accords the things of the world no value (vv. 82b, 227, etc.), his will can be compelled neither by internal desires (vv. 70–71a, 274a) nor by external threats to his physical possessions (v. 15) or his physical well-being (vv. 320–322). Neither tyrants (vv. 363b) nor demons (v. 349) have power over him, since nothing can control his reason and prevent him from following God (v. 363a). The sage's incoercibility in this regard is a manifestation of his freedom (see on v. 309), the one thing that he will never relinquish (v. 17, cf. vv. 264b, 275, 392). Thus whatever it is that reason determines is necessary, this he does willingly (v. 388, cf. vv. 88, 141).

Such assertions regarding the sage are familiar especially from Stoic philosophy, and especially from the writings of Epictetus, for example, *Diatr.* 2.17.22 ("Give up wanting anything but what God wants. And who will prevent you, who will compel you? No one, any more than anyone prevents or compels God") and 4.1.89–90: "I have never been hindered in the exercise of my will, nor have I even been subjected to compulsion against my will. And how is this possible? I have submitted my freedom of choice unto God.... Who can hinder me any longer against my own views, or put compulsion upon me? That is no more possible in my case than it would be with God" (see further *Diatr.* 1.1.23; 1.17.20–29; 1.25.17; 2.2.4; 2.5.8; 3.13.11; *Ench.* 1.3; *SVF* 3:567; Plutarch, *Stoic. abs.* 1057e; Clement, *Strom.* 4.7.50.1). Philo builds on such ideas in *Prob.* 60, declaring that it is impossible for a sage to be compelled, since someone who is compelled acts against his will, and the sage not only always performs virtuous actions—he always performs them willingly, since virtue is the only thing he holds to be desirable.

Sentence 307

The sage not only shares certain attributes with God, he imitates God to such an extent that he is actually "a god in a living human body" (v. 7a, cf. vv. 82d, 376a), which, as such, provides humanity with a "mirror" (v. 450) and "living image" of God (v. 190). Thus it is possible to say that the sage "presents" or "exhibits" God to others (for this use of συνίστημι, cf. Philo, *Contempl.* 90; Ps.-Clement, *Hom.* 17.5; Diogenes Laertius, *Vit. phil.* 7.122), language that draws attention especially to the former's actions, which would accord with the preponderance of "action" terms in the preceding four lines (see the introduction to vv. 303–311 above). Other sayings in the collection suggest that the sage is godlike particularly in his self-sufficiency (e.g., v. 18), his beneficence (e.g., v. 176), his sinlessness (e.g., v. 60), and his impassivity (e.g., v. 15), not to mention his just-mentioned incoercibility (v. 306). Cf. Seneca, *Vit. beat.* 16.1: "You should stand unmoved both in the face of evil and by the enjoyment of good to the end that, as far as is allowed, you may represent God (*deum effingas*)." Of Pythagoras, meanwhile, it was said that "there was such persuasion and charm in his words that every day almost the entire city turned to him, as to a god present among them, and everyone ran in crowds to hear him" (Diodorus Siculus, *Bibl. hist.* 10.3.2). See further on v. 7a.

Sentence 308

In the biblical ambit, ἔργα τοῦ θεοῦ can refer to manifestations of the divine in the realm of human affairs (e.g., Josh 24:29; Ps 66:5 [65:5]; John 5:20, 36; 9:3; Heb 3:9; Rev 15:3; cf. Sir 42:15–17; Matt 11:2, 19; Epictetus, *Diatr.* 3.5.10). In the ambit of the *Sentences*, nothing manifests God to humanity more fully than the sage (see above). Thus of everything in the world he represents that which is "most pleasing" to God (v. 45, cf. vv. 51, 422) and the work of which God is most proud (for the expression μέγιστον φρονεῖ ἐπί, see Xenophon, *Cyr.* 4.2.6; Dio Chrysostom, *Or.* 8.32; 31.58). As v. 359 suggests, the sage is not only himself a divine "work" (cf. v. 395): he is also an instrument through whom divine works, specifically divine works of love, are accomplished (cf. v. 383).

Sentence 309

Since God is greater than everything (vv. 27–28), those who serve God alone are free from everything except God (v. 264b), those who are governed by God alone govern everything except God (v. 43), and those who take God alone as their guide can serve as a guide for everyone except God (vv. 104, 166). Cf. Philo, *Prob.* 20: "He who has God alone for his guide, he alone is free, though to my thinking he is also the guide of all others, having received charge over earthly things from the great, the immortal king, whom he, the mortal, serves as regent." The ἐλευθερία exercised by the sage includes freedom from submission both to internal forces, such as bodily desires (vv. 75a–b), as well as to external forces, such as public opinion (v. 299) or the threats of a tyrant (v. 363b). Since this liberty derives from God, it cannot be restricted or annulled (v. 275, cf. vv. 17, 392). Compare Epictetus, *Diatr.* 2.17.22; 4.1.89–90 (both quoted above under v. 306); also *Diatr.* 2.14.13; 4.7.16–17: "No one has authority over me, I have been set free by God. I know his commands, no one has power any longer to make a slave of me. I have the right kind of emancipator, the right kind of judges." Mention may also be made of Origen's formulation of the Stoic paradox that the sage alone is free in *Comm. Joan.* 2.16.112 (= *SVF* 3:544): "The sage alone is free of all things, having received power of independent action from divine law." For other μετὰ θεόν sayings in the collection, see vv. 34, 82c, 129, 176, 244, 292, and 319.

Sentence 310

The Stoic paradox that the sage alone is king (see below) generated a number of correlates, including the claim that "all things belong to the wise" (Diogenes Laertius, *Vit. phil.* 7.125; cf. *SVF* 3:589–603; Cicero, *Fin.* 3.22.75: "Rightly will he be said to own all things, who alone knows how to use all things"). Among the major witnesses to this tenet is Philo, who draws on it, for example, in an exposition of Deut 10:9 ("for the Lord is their portion") preserved in *Plant.* 62–72. The wise, he says, accumulate for themselves possessions not from the material realm, which they in fact renounce, but from the noetic realm, judging God to be the only source of true wealth. Such things they obtain not with their bodies, of course, but with minds "perfectly cleansed and purified" (*Plant.* 64), which, as such, both know God and are known by God. The assertion that "everything belongs to the sage," then, is really not such a paradox after all, since through these pursuits the wise have become "great kings" (*Plant.* 68), greater than any earthly sovereign, since the source of their sovereignty is "the very Lord of all" (*Plant.* 69).

Similar priorities guide the Sextine sage, who "purifies" himself of material things (v. 81, cf. v. 227), relinquishing his possessions in order to follow right reason (v. 264a), the means by which he can obtain instead things in which one can be rightly confident (v. 121b, cf. v. 118), that is, the things of the soul (v. 77), knowing that only those who have a share in divine reason acquire "good," that is, divine things (v. 277). Because the sage not only follows divine reason but purifies his intellect to such an extent that the divine can actually abide there (vv. 46a–b, 57b, 61, 144, 181), directing and empowering his every thought and action (vv. 36, 60, 74, 95a–b, 104), it is possible to say that all such things are truly his.

An important variation of the Stoic paradox was attributed to the Cynic philosopher Diogenes, who reasoned that all things belong to the wise because all things belong to the gods, and the gods are friends to the wise, and friends share everything in common (Diogenes Laertius, *Vit. phil.* 6.72). Such thoughts also resonate with the aspirations of the Sextine sage, who, as we learn from v. 86b, in his piety endeavors to obtain friendship with God. As documented in the commentary on that verse, it was widely understood that friends not only share everything in common (e.g., Iamblichus, *Vit. Pythag.* 6.32); they even go so far as to share "one soul" (e.g., Aristotle, *Eth. nic.* 9.8.2), and it is precisely in the realm of the soul that the sage can be said to acquire divine "possessions," not only by perceiving God (v. 417, cf. v. 97) and following God (vv. 349, 402) but by uniting itself (v. 418, cf. v. 55) and attuning itself (v. 416) to God to such an extent that the soul actually becomes a "god" in a living human body (v. 82d, cf. v. 403).

Sentence 311

According to the Gospels, the kingdom of God belongs to the poor (Luke 6:20), or to the poor in spirit (Matt 5:3). According to the *Sentences*, it belongs to the sage, an assertion that reflects yet another correlate of the Stoic paradox that the sage along is king, for which again Philo provides evidence: "Other kingdoms are established among men through wars and campaigns and numberless ills which those ambitious for power inflict on one another … but the kingdom of the sage comes as a gift from God, and the virtuous person who receives it brings no harm to anyone, but the acquisition and enjoyment of good things to all his subjects, to whom he is the herald of peace and order" (*Abr.* 261). As he explains elsewhere, this is a kingship to be found not in any earthly realm but in the intellect of the virtuous (*Mut.* 152). Such ideas may also be reflected in Origen's comment that "the kingdom of God means the mind's state of blessedness and the ordering of wise thoughts" (*Orat.* 25.1). For his part, the sage in v. 311 can be said to share in God's kingdom insofar as the rule that he exercises in the world constitutes a reflection and extension of the rule of God (vv. 41–44, 182, 288, 423–424). Accordingly, his intellect governs both his body, so as to control its impulses (e.g., vv. 70, 151, 240, 274a), as well as other people, so as to confer as many benefits upon them as possible (e.g., vv. 47, 176, 210a, 260). With regard to the latter priority, it is important to note that just as the sage shares in the kingdom of God, he shares what he has with others (vv. 82b, 228, 266, 295–296, 330, 377, 379, 382). For more on the sage's kingdom, see Philo, *Migr.* 197; *Somn.* 2.243–244; Clement, *Strom.* 2.4.19.3–4; Diogenes Laertius, *Vit. phil.* 7.122; *SVF* 3:615, 617–618. And for the Stoic paradox that the sage along is king, see further on vv. 210a and 264b.

Sentences 312–319

Text

312 κακὸς ἀνὴρ πρόνοιαν θεοῦ^a εἶναι οὐ θέλει.
313 ψυχὴ κακὴ θεὸν φεύγει.
314 πᾶν τὸ φαῦλον θεῷ πολέμιον.
315 τὸ ἐν σοὶ φρονοῦν τοῦτο νόμιζε εἶναι ἄνθρωπον.
316 ὅπου σου τὸ φρονοῦν^a, ἐκεῖ^b σου τὸ ἀγαθόν.
317 ἀγαθὸν ἐν σαρκὶ μὴ ἐπιζήτει^a.
318 ὃ μὴ βλάπτει ψυχήν, οὐδὲ^a ἄνθρωπον.
319 φιλόσοφον^a ἄνθρωπον ὡς^b ὑπηρέτην θεοῦ τίμα μετὰ θεόν.

Translation

312 An evil man does not want God's providence to exist.
313 An evil soul flees from God.
314 Everything base is hostile to God.
315 Consider the ability to reason within you to be what a human being is.
316 Where your ability to reason is, there is your good.

317   Do not seek goodness in the flesh.
318   Whatever does not harm a soul does not harm a human being.
319   After God, honor a philosophical human being as a servant of God.

Textual Notes

312ᵃ omit lat • 313 omit Υ • 316ᵃ φρονεῖν: Υ • 316ᵇ ἐκεῖ καὶ: lat, sy² • 317ᵃ ζήτει: Υ • 318ᵃ οὔτε: Π • 319ᵃ πιστὸν: Υ • 319ᵇ omit Π

Commentary

The two triads of sayings in vv. 312–314 and vv. 315–317, while having little in common thematically, are similar in being contrastive in nature. In the former, the divine is contrasted with what is evil (vv. 312–313, with the catchword κακός) and base (v. 314). In the latter, reason, which is "good" (vv. 316–317, with the catchword ἀγαθός), is contrasted with the flesh (v. 317), which is then further contrasted with the soul (v. 318).

Sentences 312–313

In Porphyry, *Marc.* 16, immediately following the pair of sayings that parallel vv. 304–305 (see above) is a set of sayings that parallel vv. 312–314, though they differ as to both wording and arrangement: "Therefore a wicked soul flees from God, and does not wish God's providence to exist; it completely rejects the divine law which punishes everything base" (ψυχὴ οὖν πονηρὰ φεύγει μὲν θεόν, πρόνοιαν δὲ θεοῦ εἶναι οὐ βούλεται. νόμου τε θείου τοῦ πᾶν τὸ φαῦλον κολάζοντος ἀποστατοῖ πάντως). What Sextus presents in vv. 312–313 as independent maxims is combined in Porphyry's version by a μέν ... δέ ... construction, with the order of the statements reversed. The parallel to v. 313 is particularly close, the only noteworthy difference being that Sextus uses κακή while Porphyry has πονηρά (the order of φεύγει and θεόν is also different). As for the parallel with v. 312, Sextus's θέλει essentially matches Porphyry's βούλεται, while the former has κακὸς ἀνήρ preceding πρόνοιαν, so that the sentence's subject is not a wicked soul but an evil man. Verse 314, finally, has in common with *Marc.* 16 only the phrase πᾶν τὸ φαῦλον, which in Sextus's (shorter) gnome serves as the subject of the sentence, while in Porphyry's construction the subject ("a wicked soul") remains unchanged.

A bit later in his letter, Porphyry elaborates on both what it is from which the soul that denies providence tries to escape and how futile such

314   THE *SENTENCES* OF SEXTUS

efforts are: "Those who believe that neither the gods nor the universe are managed by God's providence have suffered the punishment of justice.... And assuredly the gods avoid these people because of their ignorance and lack of faith, though they themselves are not able to flee (φυγεῖν) or elude the gods and justice, the attendant of the gods" (*Marc.* 22). For a more multifaceted explication of πρόνοια, we can turn to Clement, according to whom divine providence not only disposes all things; it does so in a manner illustrative of "authoritative excellence" insofar as its power dispenses salvation in two ways: "as our sovereign it brings us to our senses through punishment; as benefactress, it helps us by positive action for us" (*Strom.* 1.27.173.5). Various sayings in the *Sentences* suggest that its author would concur with such sentiments. For the former type of providential "power," see vv. 14, 63, and 347; and for the latter, vv. 33 and 176. As Clement explains elsewhere, even when providence manifests itself in the form of punishment, its execution should still be understood as an act of mercy, since God punishes sinners not out of vengeance but in order to benefit those being disciplined, much like teachers or fathers discipline those under their care (*Strom.* 7.11.61.5; 7.16.102.5; cf. 1.17.86.1–2; 7.7.42.3–7). Individuals who deny the existence of providence, on the other hand, deprive themselves of divine justice, divine mercy, and divine beneficence (*Strom.* 4.12.82.2–4.12.88.2).

A more methodical assessment of such individuals is provided by Theophilus, who in *Autol.* 3.7 surveys a variety of positions that in his estimation fall under the auspices of either atheism or agnosticism. Among those who "deny the existence of religion and destroy providence" he specifically mentions Euhemerus, Epicurus, and—somewhat surprisingly—Pythagoras. Cf. Iamblichus, *Vit. Pythag.* 28.145: "They thought that nothing happens spontaneously and by chance, but according to divine providence, especially to good and pious human beings" (cf. *Vit. Pythag.* 30.174; 32.217). Sextus's point in vv. 312–313 would seem to be not that evil people necessarily embrace a particular philosophical position regarding providence (cf. v. 380), but that their actions demonstrate a disregard for divine justice generally. Efforts on their part to "flee" from God (for the imagery, cf. Origen, *Schol. Cant.* 17.269; Plotinus, *Enn.* 1.2.1; 2.9.6) contrast with the orientation of the faithful, who in everything they do endeavor to follow God (vv. 95b, 104, 264a, 349, 402).

Sentence 314

As noted above, the final element of the cluster preserved in vv. 312–

314 is not as well integrated into the overall composition in Sextus's version as it is in Porphyry's version, where the same subject ("a wicked soul") is retained throughout (*Marc.* 16). Instead, we have a theological statement of broader application, reminiscent especially of efforts elsewhere in the collection to disassociate God from evil, particularly v. 114 ("God is not the cause of evil things") and v. 440 ("Regard nothing that is evil as belonging to God"); cf. also vv. 29–30. Here the argument appears to be that an evil soul flees from God and denies God's providence, not because it rejects the idea that God punishes "everything base" (as in Porphyry's version) but because it is itself something "base" and as such finds itself in opposition to God. One of the reasons for this enmity is suggested by v. 82e: by attributing evil to God, the evil soul becomes such a potent source of impurity that it threatens to defile even the divine (cf. v. 194). For comparable statements, see Sir 15:11–13; Philo, *Conf.* 45 ("Is not every sage a mortal enemy to all things base?"); *Mut.* 30 ("God did not create the soul of a base man, since evil is God's enemy"); Josephus, *Bell.* 2.582; Plutarch, *An. procr.* 1015c; Arius Didymus, *Lib. phil. sect.* 82.1 (= *SVF* 3:661): "Those who are base are at variance with the gods when it comes to their way of life, on which account every fool is an enemy to the gods. For if all those who think the opposite of what the gods think are their enemies, and the base person thinks the opposite of what is respectable, then the base person is an enemy to the gods (ὁ φαῦλος θεοῖς ἐστιν ἐχθρός)." See further on v. 114. For φαῦλος, see also vv. 214, 468, and 531.

Sentences 315–316

For Sextus, the goal of human existence is to honor and imitate God as much as possible (vv. 44–45, 48). Since God is mind (v. 26), this means conforming one's mind to God as much as possible (v. 381). The highest aspects and activities of the human personality, then, those with the greatest affinity for the divine, are those that contribute to the life of the mind, referred to in our text by means of various terms, not only as νοῦς (e.g., vv. 151, 181) but also as διάνοια (e.g., vv. 57b, 143), λόγος (e.g., vv. 363a, 420), εὐλογιστία (v. 69), τὸ νοοῦν (v. 394), and, here, τὸ φρονοῦν, "the ability to reason," for which cf. v. 447; *Sent. Pythag.* 79: "Every human being is worthy insofar as he thinks or reasons (φρονεῖ) worthy things." In order to achieve one's full potential as a human being, then, it is necessary to participate in divine reason (v. 277), that is, to follow (v. 264a) and practice (v. 69) reason, making it the norm of one's life (v. 123) and the nourishment for one's soul (v. 413). The application of ἐν σοί to τὸ φρονοῦν in v. 315

reminds the reader that the ability to reason does not constitute the totality of the human self but rather represents the "something godlike" (v. 35, cf. v. 394) that has been established as a part or capacity of the self, which thus can be likened to a temple (v. 46a), or to a temple-worshiper, whose purpose is to venerate that which is "within" (v. 448). See further on vv. 61, 144, and 450.

It is possible that v. 316 is based upon a logion first attested in Justin Martyr, *1 Apol.* 15.16: ὅπου γὰρ ὁ θησαυρός ἐστιν ἐκεῖ καὶ ὁ νοῦς τοῦ ἀνθρώπου ("For where the treasure is, there also is the mind of a human being"). Later versions of the logion, that is, those preserved by Clement in *Quis div.* 17.1 (ὅπου γὰρ ὁ νοῦς τοῦ ἀνθρώπου, ἐκεῖ καὶ ὁ θησαυρὸς αὐτοῦ) and *Strom.* 7.12.77.6 (ὅπου γὰρ ὁ νοῦς τινος, φησίν, ἐκεῖ καὶ ὁ θησαυρὸς αὐτοῦ), better approximate the structure, though not the wording, of Sextus's gnome, which has τὸ φρονοῦν in lieu of ὁ νοῦς, and τὸ ἀγαθόν in lieu of ὁ θησαυρός. While definitive proof regarding our author's source(s) at this juncture is elusive, these comparative texts do provide evidence that noetic variants on Matt 6:21/Luke 12:34 were circulating in the early church, and such dependence would help to account for Sextus's use of ἄνθρωπον at the end of v. 315. See further on v. 41. The specific inspiration for Sextus's choice of terminology here may have come from *Sent. Pythag.* 107—"everyone declares prudence (τὴν φρόνησιν) to be the greatest good (μέγιστον ἀγαθόν)"—though it would not have been unusual to identify τὸ φρονεῖν and φρόνησις as "goods," for example, Plato, *Euthyd.* 281e; *Resp.* 505b; *Ceb. Tab.* 41.3 (τὸ φρονεῖν μόνον ἀγαθόν); Plutarch, *Comm. not.* 1064b; Diogenes Laertius, *Vit. phil.* 2.31, 91; 10.132 (cf. also Prov 19:8: ὃς δὲ φυλάσσει φρόνησιν, εὑρήσει ἀγαθά). For additional statements on the nature and location of "the good," see vv. 79, 131, 197, and 246.

Sentence 317

In vv. 291–292, the flesh was contrasted with the soul. In vv. 316–317, it is contrasted with reason. To search for something good in the former amounts to a both senseless and futile act, since "nothing good stems from the flesh" (v. 271). More than this, the flesh represents a potentially destructive force within the personality, insofar as its longings can divert the soul from its true purpose, which is knowing God (v. 136, cf. v. 55). Similar concerns about σάρξ are voiced elsewhere, for example, Philo, *Deus* 143 ("There are no two things so utterly opposed as knowledge and fleshly pleasure"); Plutarch, *Cons. Apoll.* 107f ("To pass one's time unenslaved by the flesh and its passions, by which the mind is distracted and tainted with human folly, would be a blessed piece of good fortune"); and *Gnom. Vat.* 20: "The flesh perceives the limits of pleasure as unlimited.... But the mind, having attained a reasoned understanding of the ultimate good of the flesh ... supplies us with the complete life." As a practical matter, then, it is necessary not only to refrain from any attachment to the flesh (v. 291) or the body (v. 101) but to "conquer the body in everything" (v. 71a), renouncing the things of the body as much as humanly possible (v. 78). On the other hand, as Aristotle explains in *Eth. nic.* 6.7.5–6, it is a central preoccupation of those possessed of φρόνησις that they "seek the things that are good for humankind" (τὰ ἀνθρώπινα ἀγαθὰ ζητοῦσιν). For Sextus, τὸ φρονοῦν not only manifests itself in the search for what is good, it is itself the object of that search (v. 316). Cf. Epictetus, *Diatr.* 2.5.4–5 ("The principal task in life is this, to distinguish matters and weigh them against one another, and say to yourself, 'Externals are not under my control; moral choice is under my control. Where am I to look for the good and the evil? Within me, in that which is my own'") and 3.22.43–44: "But to desire, to avoid, to choose, to refuse, to prepare, or to set something before yourself, who among you can do these things without first conceiving an impression of what is profitable and what is not fitting? ... Develop this, pay attention to this, here seek the good (ζητεῖτε τὸ ἀγαθόν)."

Sentence 318

The claim made in this line can be seen as drawing an inference from the preceding observations: if that which is truly good for humankind, that is, the ability to reason, resides in the soul (vv. 315–316), and the flesh contributes nothing to this good (v. 317), then nothing that can harm the body can harm a human being, that is, the essence of what a human being ought to be. In the *Sentences*, the apex of human possibility in this regard is represented by the sage, who is both unconcerned with and impervious to the loss of anything belonging to the physical world (vv. 15, 91b), even his own body (vv. 321–323). This is because his soul has achieved such a level of "greatness" (v. 403) and become so godlike in nature (v. 82d, cf. v. 418) that there is literally nothing that can harm it (v. 302), so long as he continues to shun the only thing that can injure, or even kill, the soul, namely, an evil life (v. 397, cf. vv. 7b, 208a–b). As Philo explains, what causes harm to a person are not such things as the loss of money or status, or even physical punishment, but the vices of the soul and the sins that they incite (*Prob.* 55; cf. *Det.* 109; *Virt.* 13, 211; Plato, *Leg.* 863e–864a; Dio Chrysostom, *Or.* 14.15). At the same time, the sage possesses the ability to harm the souls of others with his speech (v. 185), especially when such speech is intended to shape their understanding of God (v. 195). According to Ps.-Plutarch, *Lib. ed.* 12e, the Pythagorean *akousma*, "Do not eat your heart," was interpreted as advice "not to harm the soul by wasting it with worries" (cf. *Mant. prov.* 2.10).

Sentence 319

Chadwick (1959, 177) suggests that the source for this line is *Sent. Pythag.* 105: "After God, honor the one who confers benefits on your soul as a servant of God" (τὸν εὐεργετοῦντά σε εἰς ψυχὴν ὡς ὑπηρέτην θεοῦ μετὰ θεὸν τίμα). To be sure, there is a strong resemblance between the two sayings, especially in the final six words (though with a slight difference in order). If this is indeed Sextus's source, however, it is something of a mystery as to why he would replace τὸν εὐεργετοῦντά σε εἰς ψυχήν with φιλόσοφον ἄνθρωπον, when the concept of benefiting the soul would have formed a natural juxtaposition to that of harming the soul in v. 318. A more likely candidate, then (as noted by Chadwick 1959, 83), is Clitarchus, *Sent.* 134, which not only has the same final six words (and in the same order) as v. 319, but also includes a reference to ἄνθρωπον while lacking any reference to the soul: εὐεργετοῦντά σε ἄνθρωπον ὡς ὑπηρέτην θεοῦ τίμα μετὰ θεόν ("After God, honor a human being who confers benefits on you as a servant of God"). Sextus simply alters εὐεργετοῦντά σε ἄνθρωπον to φιλόσοφον ἄνθρωπον, perhaps in order to make the statement accord better with v. 244: σοφὸν τίμα μετὰ θεόν (note also the parallel between Sext. 325 and Clitarchus, *Sent.* 132). While the sage is a benefactor, indeed a benefactor second only to God (v. 176), not all benefactors are necessarily sages and therefore deserving, in our author's opinion, of honor. For the reasons why the sage/philosopher ought to be honored and the nature of the honor he ought to be accorded, see the commentary on vv. 190, 219, and 244. While elsewhere the sage is to be honored as "a living image of God" (v. 190) or "a gift from God" (v. 218), here he is to be honored as a ὑπηρέτης θεοῦ, a title employed also in v. 32, where we learn that each angel is a servant of God πρὸς ἄνθρωπον, a qualification that would seem to apply to the sage as well, who, in keeping with his role as a benefactor second only to God, aspires to become a benefactor to all humanity (vv. 210a, 260). As such, the sage deems it better to serve others than to be served by them (v. 336), doing so not out of a need for approval (v. 341) but with the sort of freedom that comes from serving only God (v. 264b, cf. v. 575). In the early church, believers were sometime referred to as ὑπηρέται θεοῦ (e.g.,

Ign. *Trall.* 2.3; *Pol.* 6.1; cf. Luke 1:2), while in *Diatr.* 3.22.82, Epictetus uses ὑπηρέτης τοῦ Διός of the Cynic sage. Cf. Sext. 519: τοὺς παῖδας τρέφε ὡς ὑπηρέτας θεοῦ ἐσομένους. It would not have been uncommon for slaves or servants to become implicated in the dynamics of honor and shame, usually as intermediaries or proxies, as we see, for instance, in Philo, *Dec.* 119: "Parents are the servants of God (θεοῦ ... ὑπηρέται) for the task of begetting children, and he who dishonors the servant dishonors also the Lord."

Sentences 320–324

Text

320   τὸ σκήνωμα ᵃτῆς ψυχῆςᵃ σουᵇ βαρύνεσθαι μὲν ὑπερήφανον, ἀποθέσθαι δὲ πραέωςᶜ ὁπότε χρὴ δύνασθαι μακάριον.
321   θανάτου μὲν σαυτῷᵃ παραίτιος μὴ γένῃ, τῷ δὲ ἀφαιρουμένῳ σε τοῦ σώματοςᵇ μὴ ἀγανάκτει.
322   σοφὸν ὁ τοῦ σώματος ἀφαιρούμενοςᵃ τῇ ἑαυτοῦ κακίᾳ εὐεργετεῖ, λύεται γὰρ ὡς ἐκ δεσμῶν.
323   ἄνθρωπον θανάτου φόβος ᵃλυπεῖᵇ ἀπειρίᾳ ψυχῆς.
324   σίδηρον ἀνδροφόνον ἄριστον μὲν ἦν μὴ γενέσθαι, γενόμενον δὲ σοὶ μὴ νόμιζε εἶναιᵃ.

Translation

320   To be distressed by the tent of your soul is arrogant, but to be able to lay it aside gently when need be is blessed.
321   Do not become the cause of your own death, but do not become indignant with the one who would deprive you of your body.
322   The one who by his own wickedness deprives a sage of his body confers a benefit on him, for he releases him as though from chains.
323   Fear of death grieves a human being with no experience of soul.
324   It would be best for there to be no such thing as a murderous weapon, but since there is, do not consider it to be for you.

Textual Notes

320ᵃ⁻ᵃ τοῦ σώματος: lat, sy²? • 320ᵇ omit Π, lat • 320ᶜ πράως: Υ • 321ᵃ ἑαυτῷ: Π • 321ᵇ co adds: "and kills you" • 322ᵃ ἀφαιρούμενος βίᾳ: co?, sy² • 323-324ᵃ⁻ᵃ λυπεῖ. ἀπειρία ψυχῆς σίδηρον ἀνδροφόνον. ἄριστον μὲν ἦν ... σὺ μὴ νόμιζε εἶναι: Υ • 323ᵇ λυπῇ: Π

COMMENTARY

Chadwick (1959, 153, 177) labels vv. 320–324 as a group of sayings on death. Note θάνατος in vv. 320, 323 as well as ἀφαιρουμένῳ σε τοῦ σώματος in v. 321 and τοῦ σώματος ἀφαιρούμενος in v. 322. According to the commands in vv. 320–321, the reader should not become so troubled by the body that he would either cause his own death or harbor resentment against the one who would deprive him of it. Supporting statements in vv. 322–323 argue that death is a benefit, since it releases the soul from the confines of the body. To be grieved by a fear of death, then, is the mark not of the sage, but of someone unproven in matters of the soul. Verse 324, finally, draws an inference from v. 321: the use of lethal weapons is incompatible with the life of faith.

Sentence 320

In v. 449, the body will be imaged as the soul's garment. Here it is imaged as its σκήνωμα ("tent, dwelling"), for which cf. Ps.-Plato, *Axioch.* 365e–366a; *Ep. Diogn.* 6.8; *Corp. herm.* 13.12; *PGM* 4.1951, 1970 (σκῆνος is also used frequently in Neopythagorean writings, e.g., Ps.-Archytas, *Educ.* 43.19–23; Ps.-Aresas, *Nat. hom.* 49.8–11). In this particular instance, the metaphor probably derives from 2 Cor 5:4 (cf. 5:1): καὶ γὰρ οἱ ὄντες ἐν τῷ σκήνει στενάζομεν βαρούμενοι (v.l. βαρυνόμενοι), "For while we are still in this tent, we groan, being burdened (v.l. being distressed)." Perhaps the copyists responsible for the variant reading (D*·ᶜ F G 1505 *pc*) were influenced by Wis 9:15, which may be part of the background for Sextus as well: "For a perishable body distresses a soul (βαρύνει ψυχήν), and this earthy tent (σκῆνος) encumbers a mind full of cares" (cf. Plato, *Phaed.* 81c). At any rate, our author probably would have agreed with Paul's declaration that "we would rather be away from the body and at home with the Lord" (2 Cor 5:8; cf. v. 322), though for Sextus it is wrong, even arrogant, to be distressed by the body, since what causes trouble for the soul is not the body as such (v. 139a), but the longing for bodily pleasures (v. 139b). The body then, is something that the person of faith endeavors to control (e.g., vv. 71a, 274a), not destroy. Cf. v. 411: "Do not torture the body with your soul nor your soul with the pleasures of the body." The person whom God does not release from the body, then, should not be distraught (v. 337). As

Origen explains in an exposition of 2 Cor 5:1–4 preserved in *Cels*. 7.32–33, while human beings do not require a body to know God, they do require a body for a variety of other purposes, all of which are appropriate to the "material place" in which God has placed them, and thus the body "needs to be of the same character as the material place, whatever that may be" (*Cels*. 7.33; cf. *Res*. 1.22.4–5). Similarly, in an exposition of Phil 1:20–24, Clement explains that with these words the apostle is not disparaging life in the body but showing that "love of God is the crowning reason for leaving the body, whereas to remain behind gratefully for those in need of salvation is the reason for being in the flesh" (*Strom*. 3.9.65.3).

By the same token, according to v. 320, the faithful should also be able to surrender the body when necessary (χρή), and, moreover, they should be able to do so "gently" (πραέως), the latter corresponding with the command μὴ ἀγανάκτει in v. 321. Surrendering the body gently, then, means not becoming indignant with those who would take it, just as one should not become indignant with those who would take any of one's physical possessions (vv. 15, 91b, both also with ἀγανακτέω and ἀφαιρέω), even when such deprivation constitutes an act of evil (v. 322, cf. v. 130). This sort of a "blessed" end to life would be in keeping with a blessed life itself, that is, the life of a person who fears and follows God and nothing else (vv. 326b, 424, cf. v. 40). But under what circumstances "must" the faithful lay aside the body, and who is the evil person who would deprive them of it? Sextus provides no answers here, though in vv. 363a–364 he presents the scenario of a powerful tyrant threatening the sage with bodily harm. Cf. also vv. 387–388: "A tyrant cannot take away (ἀφαιρεῖται) happiness. What must be done, do willingly."

Sentence 321

As Chadwick (1959, 177) notes, an injunction not to cause one's own death would have been applicable to debates in the early church regarding voluntary martyrdom. According to Clement, for example, the gnostic does not try to evade martyrdom, but "when called, obeys easily, and gives up his body to him who asks" (*Strom*. 4.4.13.1). Since "he will most gladly depart from this life" (*Strom*. 4.4.14.1), he expresses to his persecutors not resentment (*Strom*. 4.4.13.1), but gratitude, since such a noble death affords him the opportunity to demonstrate his love for God (*Strom*. 4.4.14.1). On the other hand, those who "have rushed into death" and "are in haste to give themselves up" are in fact giving themselves up only to "a vain death" inasmuch as their actions demonstrate not a love of God, but "a hatred for the Creator" (*Strom.* 4.4.17.1-3). A bit later, he interprets the dominical saying in Matt 10:23 as instruction for Christians neither to flee persecution nor to present themselves to the authorities for arrest, arguing that those who opt for the latter are guilty of their own deaths as accomplices, and "the one who kills a man of God sins against God" (*Strom.* 4.10.76.1-4.10.77.3; cf. 7.11.66.3-7.11.67.2). See further *Pass. Pol.* 4; Origen, *Cels.* 1.65; 8.44; Tertullian, *Cor.* 1.4. For an actual example of this *via media*, we have Anthony, who neither fled nor sought martyrdom but openly expressed his solidarity with persecuted Christians by attending their trials and executions or by ministering to them in prison (Athanasius, *Vit. Anth.* 46.1-7).

These arguments are familiar from the philosophical debate regarding suicide, especially as it was conducted in Stoic circles (see *SVF* 3:757-768). Seneca, for example, was open to the possibility that a life guided by reason and freedom might appropriately end in suicide (*Ep.* 70.14-16). Yet, "we need to be warned and strengthened in both directions, that is, not to love or to hate life overmuch. Even when reason advises us to make an end of it, the impulse is not to be adopted without reflection or at headlong speed. The brave and wise man should not beat a hasty retreat from life" (*Ep.* 24.24). He thus finds himself in agreement with Epicurus, who "upbraids those who crave, as much as those who shrink from death" (*Ep.* 24.22; cf. 12.10; 26.10; 66.13; 77.15).

Sentences 322-323

If Clement's martyr receives a benefit from his persecutor insofar as the former's death affords him an opportunity to demonstrate his love for God (*Strom.* 4.4.14.1), Sextus's sage sees his killer as a benefactor because death liberates him from the greatest threat to his freedom (vv. 17, 264b, 275, 309, 392). Ironically, then, the one who after God benefits others the most (v. 176) receives one of his most important benefits from a person who acts of out wickedness (cf. vv. 150, 208a, 469, 474). For the image of the soul being released from the "chains" of the body, see also Epictetus, *Gnom.* 32-33; Philo, *Det.* 158; *Her.* 68; *Somn.* 1.181; *Legat.* 324; Hippolytus, *Haer.* 7.38.5; Iamblichus, *Protr.* 65. Cf. also vv. 39, 127, 337. In *Marc.* 33, Porphyry speaks of how human beings "have been enchained with nature's chains (δεσμοῖς) with which she has surrounded us: the belly, the genitals, the throat, the other bodily members, both in respect to our use and passionate pleasure in them and our fears (φόβοις) about them."

As this statement illustrates, one of the things that turns the body into a chain that burdens and confines the soul are the fears that people allow themselves to entertain about it. The observation in v. 323 offers additional support for the admonitions in vv. 320 and 321 by addressing such concerns. Only someone inexperienced in matters of the soul, says Sextus, allows the fear of death to cause him grief. Indeed, if the sage could be said to "fear" anything, it would not be physical death, which frees the soul from the body for its ascent to God (v. 40), but rather an evil life, since this is what can destroy his soul (v. 397). Cf. v. 473 (= Clitarchus, *Sent.* 62): "Death is not evil, but the inability to die nobly." Thus, when he must, he accepts death "gently," that is, without any emotions that might cause reluctance or resentment. As Clement explains in *Strom.* 4.4.13.2, when called upon, the gnostic will give up his body "easily" because his fear of death is no match for his love of God (cf. Heb 2:15). Insofar as the observation here in its critique of fear implicates a condemnation of grief, comparison can also be made with Stoic doctrine, where φόβος and λύπη were not only categorized as two of the four most basic of the irrational passions (i.e., movements of the soul contrary to nature and therefore incompatible with the life of wisdom) but were thought to affect the soul in comparable ways, the former involving its "shrinking," the latter its "contraction" (*SVF* 3:391, cf. 3.377–420). As Epictetus explains, the unwanted influence of irrational passions like fear on the soul can be attributed in part to the lack of proper training (cf. v. 431). Specifically, while most people are "thoroughly experienced" in material things, in their actions they are "dejected, unseemly, worthless, and cowardly" because they have not bothered to understand the true causes of appropriate and inappropriate conduct: "Yet, if we were afraid, not of death or exile, but of fear itself, then we would practice how not to encounter those things that appear evil to us" (*Diatr.* 2.16.18–19).

Sentence 324

This line functions as a corollary to the command in v. 321. Just as the reader should not cause his own death, he should not cause the death of anyone else. Indeed, it would be "best" if the means of killing others did not exist at all. Although Chadwick (1959, 177) describes Ps.-Phoc. 32–34 ("Gird on your sword not for murder but for defense. But may you not need it at all, unlawfully or justly. For if you slay a foe, you stain your hand") as a near parallel, it should be noted that while Pseudo-Phocylides (reluctantly) allows his readers to carry weapons for protection, Sextus rules them out altogether, presumably because his reader will have no "foe" to begin with (v. 105, cf. v. 386). At any rate, both texts can be interpreted as extensions both of the Decalogue's prohibition of murder (Exod 20:15; Deut 5:18; cf. Matt 5:21; 19:18; Mark 10:19; Luke 18:20; Rom 13:9; Jas 2:11) and, more generally, of the negative version of the golden rule, for which see on vv. 179 and 211 (cf. vv. 90, 327). For gnomic perspectives on the subject, see Prov 28:17; *Ahiqar* 126, 128; *Syr. Men.* 15–19; *Instr. Ankh.* 22.21–25; P.Ins. 29.18–19; 33.19; Ps.-Cato, *Dist.* 1.6. The faithful will not act badly towards anyone (v. 212) because the mistreatment of a fellow human being would be the "greatest" impiety that they could commit against God (v. 96). For the form of this saying (ἄριστον μέν κτλ), see v. 283. For the expression ἀνδροφόνος σίδηρος, see Manetho, *Apotel.* 1.136.

Sentences 325–338

Text

325 οὐδεμία προσποίησις ᵃἐπὶ πολὺν χρόνονᵃ λανθάνει, μάλιστα δὲᵇ ἐν πίστει.
326a οἷον ἄνᵃ ᾖ σου τὸ ἦθος, τοιοῦτος ἔσταιᵇ σου καὶ ὁ βίος.
326b ἦθος θεοσεβὲς ποιεῖ βίον μακάριον.
327 ὁ βουλευόμενοςᵃ κατ' ἄλλου κακῶς, φθάνει κακῶς πάσχων.
328 μή σε παύσῃ τοῦ εὐεργετεῖν ἀχάριστος ἄνθρωπος.
329 μηθὲνᵃ ὧν παραχρῆμαᵇ αἰτούμενος δῷςᶜ, ᵈπλείονος ἄξιον κρίνῃςᵈ τοῦ λαμβάνοντος.
330 ᵃκάλλιστα οὐσίᾳᵃ χρήσῃ τοῖς δεομένοις προθύμως μεταδιδούς.
331 ἀδελφὸν ἀγνωμονοῦντα πεῖθε μὴ ἀγνωμονεῖν καὶ ἀνιάτως ἔχοντα συντήρει.
332 εὐγνωμοσύνῃ πάντας ἀνθρώπους νικᾶν ἀγωνίζου.
333 νοῦν οὐ πρότερον ἕξεις ᵃπρὶν ἢ γνῷςᵃ οὐκ ἔχων.
334 αὐτάρκειαν ἄσκει.
335 τὰ μέλη τοῦ σώματος τοῖς οὐ χρωμένοις φορτία.
336 ὑπηρετεῖν κρεῖττον ἑτέροις ἢ πρὸς ἄλλων ὑπηρετεῖσθαι.
337 ὃνᵃ οὐκ ἀπαλλάττει ὁᵇ θεὸς τοῦ σώματος μὴ βαρυνέσθωᶜ.
338 δόγμα ἀκοινώνητον οὐ μόνον ἔχειν ἀλλὰ καὶ ἀκούειν χαλεπὸν ἡγοῦ.

Translation

325 No pretense escapes notice for very long, especially in faith.
326a Whatever your character, so also will be your way of life.

326b A reverent character produces a blessed way of life.
327 The one who plans evil against another is the first to experience evil.
328 Do not let an ungrateful person prevent you from conferring a benefit.
329 When upon being asked you promptly give something, do not judge it to be worth more than the one receiving it.
330 You will put what there is to best use by sharing it willingly with those in need.
331 Persuade an ignorant brother not to act ignorantly and protect him if he is incurable.
332 Strive to surpass all people in goodwill.
333 You will not have intelligence until you know that you do not have it.
334 Practice self-sufficiency.
335 The members of the body are burdens to those who do not put them to use.
336 It is better to serve others than to be served by others.
337 Let the one whom God does not release from the body not become distressed.
338 Deem it dangerous not only to hold a dissonant opinion but even to listen to one.

Textual Notes

325^{a-a} ἐν πολλῷ χρόνῳ: Υ; ἐπὶ πολλῷ χρόνῳ: Π • 325^b omit Π • 326a^a ἐὰν: Π, Υ • 326a^b ἔστω: Π, lat • 327^a βουλόμενος: Π, Υ • 329^a μηδὲν: Υ • 329^b omit lat • 329^c δώσεις: Π • 329^{d-d} πλεονεξίαν κρίνεις: Π • 330^{a-a} καλλίστῃ οὐσίᾳ: co, sy²; τῇ περιουσίᾳ: Π • 333^{a-a} πρηνὶ γνῷς: Π • 337^a ὧν: Π • 337^b omit Υ • 337^c βαρύνεσθαι: Π

Commentary

Within this miscellaneous block of material we find a couplet of sayings on moral character (vv. 326a–b), a triad of different rules on benefaction (vv. 328–330), a rule on fraternal correction (v. 331) accompanied by maxims promoting a pair of virtues relevant to that practice (vv. 332–333), and an admonition to practice self-sufficiency (v. 334) followed by sayings on the body and its use (vv. 335–337). Otherwise there are few signs of topical organization.

Sentence 325

This line is based on Clitarchus, *Sent.* 132 (οὐδεμία προσποίησις ἐπὶ πολὺν χρόνον λανθάνει), to which has been appended μάλιστα δὲ ἐν πίστει (note that Sext. 319 depends on Clitarchus, *Sent.* 134). A version of the saying also appears in *Sent. Pythag.* 47 (ἴσθι ὡς οὐδεμία προσποίησις πολλῷ χρόνῳ λανθάνει), which differs most notably in its opening imperative (ἴσθι ὡς), for which cf. *Sent. Pythag.* 48; Sext. 233. While Chadwick (1959, 157) is no doubt correct that the final four words of v. 325 represent a "characteristic addition of the Christian reviser" (for our author's editorial proclivity for πίστις language, see part 4 of the introduction), it is worth noting that the Pythagoreans were sometimes mocked for "the pretended trustworthiness" (ἡ προσποίητος πίστις) that they allegedly extended to one another (Iamblichus, *Vit. Pythag.* 33.234). Read against this background, Sextus's gnome can be interpreted as a warning not only against imposture in faith, but also against imposture in friendship, a moral problem that occupied a variety of authors in antiquity. See Demosthenes, *Aristocr.* 163, 193; Aristotle, *Eth. nic.* 8.8.1; *Eth. eud.* 7.1.17; Strabo, *Geogr.* 6.3.2; 11.2.11; 13.1.57; Dio Chrysostom, *Or.* 74.2; Chariton, *Call.* 1.11.2; *Acts Andr.* 49–50 (and note the story about φιλία that immediately follows Iamblichus, *Vit. Pythag.* 33.234 in 33.235–236). As for imposture in matters of faith, Sextus can assert that no pretense will go unnoticed for very long (though cf. the Coptic version: "Someone who says, 'I believe,' even if he spends a long time pretending," etc.) because for him faith is a matter not of claims (vv. 284, 389b, 392, 433–434) but of actions that confirm those claims (vv. 177, 359, 408–409), of actually "being" faithful (vv. 188–189, cf. v. 220). Under such conditions, it will not be long before a test of faith exposes pretended faith for what it truly is (vv. 7a, 200). Cf. Ps.-Cato, *Mon.* 68: "The mind's pretenses will not long endure."

Sentences 326a–b

The sayings in vv. 326a–327 are based on *Sent. Pythag.* 11, though with important differences in order and composition. For the first line, Sextus draws on *Sent. Pythag.* 11ᶜ (οἷον γὰρ τὸ ἦθος ἑκάστου, τοιοῦτος καὶ ὁ βίος καὶ αἱ δόσεις), dropping the final three words (perhaps for the sake of symmetry), and personalizing the aphorism by omitting ἑκάστου while inserting σου before both τὸ ἦθος and καὶ ὁ βίος. In its current location, the saying can perhaps be interpreted as a commentary on v. 325: a pretense to faith cannot remain hidden for long, since eventually one's true character will be revealed in one's way of life. *Sent. Pythag.* 11ᶜ continues in 11ᵈ (=

Sent. Pythag. 117) with: "For the soul is a treasury, of good things if it is good, of bad things if it is bad." Given the saying's strong similarity to the dominical logion in Matt 12:35/Luke 6:45 (note that the Coptic translation of both v. 326a and v. 326b changes "character" to "heart"), we might have expected our author to follow his source material more closely here, but in v. 326b he offers instead what appears to be his own gnome, repeating the ἦθος–βίος format (so as to create a couplet) and restricting himself to a positive illustration of the concept articulated in the first line. For a negative illustration of the concept, see v. 110. For the affirmation that a "reverent" (θεοσεβής) person is blessed, see Maximus of Tyre, Dial. 14.6; Origen, Frag. Ps. 49.3; 118.158; Ps.-Clement, Hom. 3.60; cf. 2 Clem. 19.4: "The godly person (ὁ εὐσεβής), then, should not be grieved if he is miserable at the present time; a time of blessing awaits him." While Sextus is not unacquainted with the idea of future blessings (v. 40), for him the pious person is already blessed (v. 424) because his intellect has already been blessed by the presence of God (v. 46a, cf. v. 86b), his soul having achieved a godlike status (v. 82d, cf. vv. 287, 412).

Sentence 327

This line is based on Sent. Pythag. 11ᵃ: βουλευόμενος περὶ ἄλλου κακῶς φθάνεις αὐτὸς πάσχων ὑπὸ σεαυτοῦ κακῶς ("By planning evil against another you yourself will cause yourself to be the first to experience evil"). Sextus not only rearranges the order of his material (see above), presenting the first member of Sent. Pythag. 11 last; he also alters its second-person formulation to the third person, dropping ὑπὸ σεαυτοῦ in the process, thus leaving the source of the evil being "experienced" unspecified. The source of the Pythagorean gnome, in turn, may be Hesiod, Op. 265–266: "The man does mischief to himself who does mischief to another, and evil planned harms the planner most (ἡ δὲ κακὴ βουλὴ τῷ βουλεύσαντι κακίστη)." All three versions of the maxim are governed by a similar logic of reciprocity, though while for Hesiod the plotter of evil suffers evil "most," in the later texts he suffers evil "first." In any event, the basic thought is consistent with the negative version of the golden rule, for which see on v. 179 (also with πάσχω) and v. 211. Cf. Menander, Mon. 764 ("The one who acts terribly also comes to suffer badly"); Seneca, Ep. 81.22: "When we do wrong, only the least and lightest portion of it flows back upon the other; the worst and, if I may use the term, densest portion of it stays at home and troubles the owner." For biblical parallels, see Pss 7:15–16; 9:15–16; 57:6 [56:7]; Prov 26:27; Qoh 10:8. Insofar as it is not actually doing evil but simply planning evil that is said to initiate negative consequences, the thought in this verse is consistent also with sayings elsewhere in the collection that emphasize the importance of intentionality, such as vv. 12, 57a, 178, 181, and 233.

Sentence 328

For this line our author turns to *Sent. Pythag.* 104: τοῦ εὐεργετεῖν μή ποτέ σε παύσῃ ἀχάριστος ἄνθρωπος. Sextus alters the word order in the first part of the saying slightly, dropping ποτέ. The topic of reciprocity continues from the preceding verse, though here the problem is not the reality of reciprocity but its absence.

It was a given among Greco-Roman elites that it is necessary to be discriminating with one's largesse, bestowing it only on the morally worthy, specifically, on those who would show proper gratitude, including the will to make a return (e.g., Cicero, *Off.* 2.61-63; Seneca, *Ben.* 1.10.5; 2.35.1; 3.2.2). For Aristotle, "the very existence of the state" depends on the reciprocal obligation of its citizens "not only to repay a kindness done one (χαρισαμένῳ), but at another time to take the initiative in performing a kindness oneself (χαριζόμενον)," with the understanding that "one ought to return services rendered … just as one ought to pay back a loan" (*Eth. nic.* 5.5.6-7; 9.2.3; cf. 9.7.1). This entailed no inconsiderable social obligation for the recipient of a "gift." The Romans in particular seem to have been virtually obsessed with the moral problem of *ingratia* (e.g., Seneca, *Ep.* 81.23, 28, 32; *Ben.* 1.1.9-10; 3.1.1-2; 4.18.1-4). In their moral world, requiting a kindness outranked even showing affection for family members, since "no duty is more imperative than that of proving one's gratitude" (Cicero, *Off.* 1.47), and so one must be ever "watching for an opportunity to repay" (Seneca, *Ben.* 3.17.4). Requital was especially important in dealing with one's social superiors. Clients, for example, were obliged to exchange χάριτες with their patrons so as to strengthen φιλανθρωπία between them, even if the long-term nature of the relationship was asymmetrical (Dionysius of Halicarnassus, *Ant. rom.* 2.10.2-4). For the problem (in some instances, the crime) of ingratitude to benefactors, see Xenophon, *Ages.* 11.3; Dionysius of Halicarnassus, *Ant. rom.* 8.49.1; Strabo, *Geogr.* 14.6.6; Dio Chrysostom, *Or.* 31.27, 37, 125; Lucian, *Abdic.* 13, 19; Philo, *Ios.* 99; Ps.-Clement, *Hom.* 10.13; *Sent. Pythag. Dem.* 6: "Conferring a benefit on an ungrateful person has the same effect as anointing a corpse." For further gnomic reflections on the topic, see Menander, *Mon.* 12, 42, 49, 655.

Against such a background, the willingness of the sage to confer benefits even on the ungrateful would have been seen as exemplary (cf. Seneca,

Ben. 1.1.11–13; 4.26.1; 7.26.1–5). As Seneca explains in *Ep.* 81.10–13, "the sage alone knows how to confer a benefit," not only because he knows the best kind of benefit to confer in any situation and the best way to confer it but because he confers benefits for the right reason, that is, not out of an expectation of a return but as an act of virtue. For him, therefore, "it is better to get no return than to confer no benefits" (*Ep.* 81.1). The Sextine sage sets for himself similar standards, insofar as he follows God's example (vv. 47, 176) and endeavors to become a common benefactor to all humanity (vv. 210a, 260). The person who shows ingratitude to him, then, is actually showing ingratitude to God (v. 229).

Sentences 329–330

For Sextus, none of the things of the world are "good" unless they are shared (vv. 295–296, cf. vv. 82b, 377), especially with the needy (vv. 52, 217, 266, 378–379, 382). He would therefore no doubt agree with the dominical injunction παντὶ αἰτοῦντί σε δίδου (Luke 6:30; cf. Matt 5:42; *Did.* 1.5), though he also stipulates certain conditions under which such giving ought to occur: the readers should give whenever they can (v. 378), without discrimination (v. 266) or reproach (v. 339) or in order to attract attention (v. 342) but for the sake of humanity (v. 342) and to please God (vv. 379, 382). In v. 329, it is further assumed that the readers' giving will be done promptly (παραχρῆμα), for which compare Ps.-Phoc. 22 ("To a beggar give at once, and do not tell him to come tomorrow"); *Ep. Barn.* 19.11 ("You shall not hesitate to give"); Herm. *Sim.* 9.24.2; Septem Sapientes, *Praec.* 217.23 (ὃ μέλλεις, δός); Publilius Syrus, *Sent.* 274 ("To do a kindness to the needy at once is to give twice"). The readers are also admonished not to assign more value to what they give than the person receiving it would. This addresses an important consideration, since "as a rule, those who possess a thing value it differently than those who want to obtain it. This is because one's own possessions and gifts always seem to one worth a great deal (πολλοῦ ἄξια); nevertheless it is the recipients (οἱ λαμβάνοντες) whose valuation determines the repayment" (Aristotle, *Eth. nic.* 9.1.9). For his part, the ideal benefactor does not concern himself with the value of his gifts at all, since he does not give with a view to receiving in return (e.g., Seneca, *Ep.* 81.19–20). In their obedience to this precept the readers not only act in a manner consistent with such an ideal (see above), they also demonstrate their contempt for and freedom from worldly possessions (cf. vv. 15, 82b).

Verse 330 identifies yet another criterion for appropriate giving, namely, willingness. Cf. v. 379: "The gift of one who with his whole heart shares food with a person in need is small, but before God his willingness (προθυμία) to share is great." In both cases canonical precedent can be found in Paul's appeal to the Christians in Achaia regarding the collection for the poor in the Jerusalem church, especially 2 Cor 8:11–12: "But now finish doing it also, so that just as there was the willingness (ἡ προθυμία) to desire it, so there may be also the completion of it by your ability. For if the willingness is present, it is acceptable according to what a person has, not according to what he does not have." A statement found a bit later in the appeal intimates what the apostle may have understood such willingness to entail: "Each of you must give as you have made up your mind, not reluctantly or under compulsion, for God loves a cheerful giver" (2 Cor 9:7; cf. LXX Prov 22:8; Sir 35:9). According to Irenaeus, the precedent in this regard was set by the Lord himself, who in passages like Luke 6:29–31 commands his followers to give in such a way "so that we may not grieve as those who are unwilling to be defrauded, but may rejoice as those who have given willingly, and as conferring a favor upon our neighbors rather than yielding to necessity" (*Haer.* 4.13.3). In reference to Irenaeus's final comment, it is worth noting that προθυμία is often used of benefactors in Greco-Roman inscriptions (see BDAG s.v., and cf. *SEG* 53.1312; Musonius Rufus, frag. 19.122.28–30; Aelian, *Var. hist.* 9.1). Aristotle sums up the expected comportment in *Eth. nic.* 9.11.5: "Since it is noble to bestow benefits, we ought to invite our friends to share our good fortune willingly (προθύμως), but be reluctant when asking them to aid us in our misfortune." In all these cases, we see that importance is assigned not only to appropriate action but also to the intentionality that informs such action, for which see the references mentioned above in the discussion of v. 327.

Sentence 331

Sextus assumes that his readers will be implicated in processes of moral persuasion and correction (vv. 91a, 245–246, 358). He further assumes that they have a responsibility not only to tolerate the participation of ignorant people in such processes (v. 285) but to serve as their instructors. Consequently, the readers shoulder at least part of the blame when such individuals fail: "The sins of the ignorant are a reproach to those who teach them" (v. 174). Verse 103 identifies one means for addressing such pedagogical predicaments, namely, the refutation of "senseless" opinions, which is said to purify the soul, while v. 298 mentions the censure of sins. Verse 331 identifies another means, namely, persuasion, specifically persuading someone who lacks judgment not to act out of ignorance. Taken together, the different strategies mentioned in these sayings can be understood as contributing to a "mixed" method of moral instruction, one that adapts it pedagogical approach to the suit the learner's particular disposition and needs. Accordingly, more compliant students receive mild forms of instruction like praise and encouragement (see vv. 121a, 298), while recalcitrant students receive more stringent forms like censure and correction (cf. Clement, *Paed.* 1.9.75.1–1.9.88.3). According to Philo, such an approach was adopted by Moses, whose teachings as a whole were set forth with the purpose of "persuading (ἀναπείθουσαι) the obedient more gently, the disobedient more strictly" to pursue a life of virtue (*Virt.* 15; cf. Plato, *Leg.* 718b, 722b–c). Regardless of the form it takes, in order for such instruction to be effective, and least likely to cause harm or resentment, it has to be offered in a spirit of goodwill (see v. 332), that is, out of a genuine desire to benefit the recipient. Given such priorities, it is not surprising that this is an occasion (indeed, the only occasion) on which Sextus uses the term ἀδελφός of a fellow believer, though from the appendices we have v. 497: "Other friendships are begrudged, but brother corrects (εὐθύνεται) brother without loving (to do so)."

For the idea that persuasion is a cure for ignorance, see Dio Chrysostom, *Or.* 8.8; Athanasius, *Ep. Max.* 26.1089. For ἀνιάτως ἔχειν, see Plato, *Phaed.* 113e; *Ep.* 322b, 326a; *Resp.* 615e; Dionysius of Halicarnassus, *Ant. rom.* 7.48.2; 8.56.1; Philo, *Ebr.* 28; *Conf.* 163; *Mos.* 2.167; *Spec.* 4.152; *Praem.* 149. In most of these cases, the "incurable" are, as such, simply to be punished, rejected, or both—though, according to Philo, Joseph displayed before those around him a life of such exceeding virtue that "he converted even those who seemed to be quite incurable (τοὺς πάνυ δοκοῦντας ἀνιάτως ἔχειν), who, as the long-standing maladies of their souls abated, reproached themselves for their past and repented" (*Ios.* 87; cf. *Spec.* 1.324). For its part, the Coptic version replaces "if he is incurable" with "if he is mad."

Sentence 332

The life of a believer should be a struggle (ἀγών) for self-control (v. 239), for seriousness (v. 282), and, here, for εὐγνωμοσύνη, a concept that attracted interest from various philosophical schools. In the Aristotelian tradition, for example, it is associated with the virtues of honesty, reasonableness, and hopefulness (*Virt. vit.* 8.3; cf. *Mag. mor.* 2.2.1), while in the Stoic schema of virtues, it is classified (together with ἰσότης) as a species of justice (*SVF* 3:295), specifically, as ἑκούσιος δικαιοσύνη (*SVF* 3:273). In a

Pythagorean tractate on kingship, meanwhile, it is held up together with kindness, justice, and reasonableness as one of the traits of the ideal ruler (Ps.-Diotogenes, *Regn.* 2.74.19–27). The term's application to the political realm is consistent with what we find in historical writings, where it is used of kings and generals who show consideration for their inferiors (e.g., Polybius, *Hist.* 5.10.2; Diodorus Siculus, *Bibl. hist.* 13.22.2; 13.23.5; Plutarch, *Arist.* 23.1). In concert with this, the term is sometimes employed in parallel constructions with φιλανθρωπία (e.g., Plutarch, *Dem.* 17.1; *Marc.* 20.1). As Plutarch explains in *Them.* 7.3, the security of a nation is achieved when its leaders have earned a reputation "for surpassing their enemies in courage and their allies in goodwill (εὐγνωμοσύνῃ δὲ τῶν συμμάχων περιγενομένους)." It is possible to interpret εὐγνωμοσύνη as a political virtue within the context of the *Sentences* as well, insofar as the sage is understood to exercise a certain authority, indeed, the ultimate sort of authority, since it has been conferred on him by God (v. 36, cf. vv. 60, 375). In the execution of this authority, the surpassing goodwill of the sage comes to expression in numerous ways, for example, in his eagerness to benefit as many people as possible (v. 210a), in his willingness to share with the needy (v. 330), in his compassion for his enemies (v. 213), and in his desire to be a merciful judge (v. 63). As suggested above, this virtue would be germane to his role as teacher and corrector as well.

Sentence 333

The next verse implicates another virtue that would be germane to this role, namely, humility. Even as he presumes to advise the ignorant, the sage remains cognizant of his own ignorance. Indeed, as this saying maintains, it is only such cognizance that counts as "intelligence" for the sage, insofar as he remains attentive to the problems of self-conceit and self-deception in knowledge, aware that God alone is truly and fully wise (v. 30). The sage, therefore, does not boast about himself (vv. 284, 432) or claim to be wise (v. 389b). What he seeks is not a reputation for wisdom but the reality of it (cf. vv. 53, 64, 145, 214). For the Socratic background of these concepts, and for parallels from gnomic literature, see the commentary on v. 199. The source for the line here is Clitarchus, *Sent.* 109: οὐ πρότερον γνώσῃ ὃ μὴ οἶσθα, πρὶν ἂν γνώσῃς οὐκ εἰδώς ("You will not know what you have not known until you know that you do not know it"). Sextus abandons the symmetry of the γνώσῃ–γνώσῃς construction in favor of a ἕξεις–ἔχων one, replacing ὃ μὴ οἶσθα with νοῦν, for which see vv. 26, 151, 154, and 181. The assertion here can be compared with the warning in 1 Cor 3:18 ("Do not deceive

yourselves. If you think that you are wise in this age, you should become fools so that you may become wise"), though it lacks Paul's reference to the "folly" of the cross (1 Cor 1:18–25). Cf. Epictetus, *Ench.* 13: "If you wish to make progress, then be content to appear senseless and foolish in externals, and do not make it your wish to give the appearance of knowing anything."

Sentences 334–336

The reader of the *Sentences* is summoned to practice (ἀσκεῖν) justice (v. 64), discretion (v. 69), greatness of soul (v. 120), and here, self-sufficiency. The first line in this triad repeats v. 98, where, as the ensuing admonitions indicate, αὐτάρκεια is a matter of eschewing the things in life that are not appropriate (v. 99), while ascertaining the things that are (v. 100). Here the saying is followed by a gnomic observation on the conditions under which the members of the body become burdensome (cf. v. 101) and an assertion that serving others is better than being served by them. Cf. Porphyry, *Marc.* 35: "Practice doing many things for yourself (τὰ πολλὰ ἄσκει αὐτουργεῖν), since doing things for yourself is simple and expedient. And people should use each of their members (τῶν μερῶν) for what nature fashioned it, nature demanding nothing else. To those who do not use (χρωμένοις) their own members but abuse those of others it is a double burden (φορτίον) and ungrateful to nature, which has given them their limbs." The parallels in language and thought are sufficient to support the conclusion that Sextus and Porphyry are here drawing on a common source, though any attempt at reconstruction would be tentative. The latter's comments are made within the context of an exhortation on manual labor and the treatment of slaves, in which it is argued that relying on oneself rather than on others to perform simple tasks accords better with the principles of "nature," a criterion that may represent Porphyry's addition, φύσις being used over twenty times in *Ad Marcellam*. From his perspective, failure in this regard constitutes a "double burden" for the perpetrator, insofar as it subverts the "natural" purpose of both one's own bodily members and those of another human being. In the *Sentences*, by contrast, the manual labor in question is not that of a slave (cf. the Coptic version of v. 336: "It is better to serve others than to make others serve you"), but that of a sage, who is elsewhere depicted as a servant (ὑπηρέτης), indeed, as a servant of God (v. 319), who through his beneficence, generosity, and teaching ministers to as many people as he can (vv. 210a, 260).

As Chadwick (1959, 139, 178) suggests, v. 336 may be modeled after Matt 20:26–27/Mark 10:43–44, though it is important to note that Sextus's formulation conveys no promise about the servant becoming "first" or "great" among his peers (for other "better" sayings in the collection, see vv. 165a, 283, 345, 362, 377). Instead, the gnome is accompanied by an observation about bodily members and their use (v. 335), the implication being that the more one allows one's body to be served by others, rather than used to serve them, the more of a burden (φορτίον) it will become, presumably because doing so makes it more difficult to observe moderation in one's bodily comportment (cf. vv. 13 and 273, both also with μέλος). As Sextus explains elsewhere, it is not the body as such but the longing for bodily pleasures that makes it burdensome, even "intolerable" for the soul (vv. 139a–b), since such longings make it impossible for the soul to know God (v. 136). Hence the urgent need to control the body (vv. 78, 115, 274a, etc.). When read together, vv. 336 and 337 suggest that using the body to serve others represents a means for achieving such control. Accordingly, while Porphyry presents his advice as a way for Marcella to practice self-reliance (ἄσκει αὐτουργεῖν), Sextus presents his advice as a way for the reader to practice self-sufficiency (αὐτάρκειαν ἄσκει), that is, as a way for the reader to become more like God, who is entirely self-sufficient (vv. 49–50), something that is accomplished by divesting oneself of material encumbrances, including especially those associated with physical desires (see the commentary on vv. 98 and 263). This godlike state is not simply to be had, however, but must be "practiced" through disciplined habits, including habits of the body such as those indicated in vv. 335–336.

Sentence 337

According to Athanasius, when Anthony realized that his prayers to die as a martyr would not be answered, "he seemed distressed (λυπουμένῳ ἐῴκει) ... but it was the Lord who was protecting him for our benefit ... so that he might become a teacher to many" (*Vit. Ant.* 46.6; cf. Eusebius, *Hist. eccl.* 6.2).

This line, which has no obvious thematic connection with the surrounding material, may have been attracted to the trio of maxims in vv. 334–336 by catchword, τοῦ σώματος occurring in both vv. 335 and 337. A more logical location for the injunction would have been the paragraph of sayings on death in vv. 320–324. The verb βαρύνω is also used in v. 320, while the construction ἀπαλλάττω + σῶμα (for which see also vv. 39 and 127) is paralleled by λύω + σῶμα in v. 322. There the readers were instructed to be neither distressed by life in the body (v. 320) nor indignant with the one who would deprive them of that life (v. 321). Here the rejected object of their resentment is God, when God does not "release" them from the body. Such resentment is misguided because, as Sextus explains elsewhere, the readers' souls are not their own, but something that they have received as a trust from God (v. 21). Accordingly, it is God who determines when this "loan" must be returned, just as it is God who determines the soul's final destiny (v. 373). It is the will of God, then, not human desire or fate (vv. 92, 436b), that determines what is "necessary" for the soul. As faithful servants of God (vv. 182, 288), the readers must adapt themselves to this and every necessity (vv. 88, 385, 388), even as they affirm that God's providential care will ultimately bring about what is good, not what is evil (vv. 31, 114, 312, 423). To accuse God of doing otherwise, or to think that God is unconcerned with human welfare, would be a sin (vv. 194, 380).

Sentence 338

Logically, this line would be better placed elsewhere as well, specifically, in the paragraph of sayings on education in vv. 248–251. There the reader was encouraged to embrace learning as ingredient to the life of faith (cf. vv. 290, 384), but to eschew teachings unnecessary or improper to the development of the soul. For the sorts of ideas that our author may have considered "dangerous," see the commentary on those verses. While in vv. 296 and 377 ἀκοινώνητος is used of material goods that the reader does not share in common with others (cf. the Coptic version of v. 338: "Not only do not hold an opinion which does not benefit the needy, [but also do not] listen to it"), here the term is applied to a δόγμα that has nothing in common with other opinions that the reader holds (cf. Nicomachus, *Theol. arith.* 59; Ps.-Alexander of Aphrodisias, *Prob.* 2.72; Gregory of Nyssa, *Eunom.* 1.1.360). For Sextus, the danger posed by an unusual or incompatible opinion extends even to those who merely hear it, in which case comparison can also be made with the cluster of sayings in vv. 408–410, where the readers are warned not to believe everything that they hear (v. 409), especially everything that they hear about God, since practically anyone can spout forth theological suppositions, but only a righteous few both know and speak the truth (v. 410). In such matters it is crucial that the readers be discriminating, since when they listen to speech about God, they are placing their very souls into the hands of the person who speaks (v. 195, cf. vv. 171a–b). One of the principal criteria to be applied in this process is identified by another saying in the cluster, v. 408 ("Make a test of a man's works before a man's words"), which is reminiscent of the advice offered in v. 177: "Let your life confirm your words among those who hear you (παρὰ τοῖς ἀκούουσιν)." Cf. also v. 547 (= Clitarchus, *Sent.* 49): "Let your works be a demonstration of your opinions (τῶν δογμάτων)." Presumably, one of the things that makes an opinion "dissonant," and hence objectionable, is that the manner in which it informs moral action remains unclear, thus leaving those who embrace it liable to judgment. As Ps.-Clement, *Hom.* 2.38 asserts, those "who dare to listen to things written against God" are rightly convicted, while those who love God "should not only disbelieve the things spoken against him, but should not even endure to hear them at all." Cf. Menander, *Mon.* 48: "Neither hear nor see things that are not proper."

Sentences 339–349

Text

339 ὁ διδοὺς ᵃὁτιοῦν μετ'ᵃ ὀνείδους ὑβρίζειᵇ.
340 ᵃκηδόμενος ὀρφανῶνᵃ πατὴρ ἔσῃ πλειόνων τέκνων θεοφιλήςᵇ.
341 ᾧᵃ ἂν ὑπουργήσῃς ἕνεκα δόξης, μισθοῦ ὑπούργησας.
342 ἐάν ᵃτι δῷςᵃ ἐπὶ τὸ αὐτὸ γνωσθῆναι, οὐκ ἀνθρώπῳ δέδωκας, ἰδίᾳ δὲ ἡδονῇ.
343 ὀργὴν πλήθους μὴ παρόξυνε.
344 μάθε τοίνυνᵃ τί δεῖᵇ ποιεῖν τὸν εὐδαιμονήσονταᶜ.
345 κρεῖττον ἀποθανεῖν λιμῷ ἢ διὰ γαστρὸς ἀκρασίαν ψυχὴν ἀμαυρῶσαι.
346 ἐκμαγεῖονᵃ τὸ σῶμά σου νόμιζε τῆς ψυχῆς· καθαρὸν οὖν τήρει.
347 ὁποῖαᵃ ἂν ἐπιτηδεύσῃ ψυχὴ ἐνοικοῦσα τῷ σώματι, τοιαῦτα μαρτύρια ἔχουσα ἄπεισιν ἐπὶ τὴν κρίσιν.
348 ᵃἀκαθάρτου ψυχῆςᵃ ἀκάθαρτοι δαίμονες ἀντιποιοῦνται.
349 πιστὴν ψυχὴν καὶ ἀγαθὴν ἐν ὁδῷ θεοῦ κακοὶ δαίμονες οὐκ ἐμποδίζουσιν.

Translation

339 The one who in any way gives with reproach acts insolently.
340 One who cares for orphans will be a God-pleasing father of many children.
341 Whomever you serve for glory you serve for pay.
342 If you give something in order for it to become known, you have given not for the person's sake but for your own pleasure.

343 Do not incite the anger of a multitude.
344 Learn, then, what a happy person should do.
345 It is better to die of hunger than to impair a soul through overindulgence of the belly.
346 Consider your body to be an imprint of the soul. Therefore keep it pure.
347 Whatever a soul strives for while dwelling in the body will accompany it as evidence when it departs for judgment.
348 Impure demons lay claim to an impure soul.
349 Evil demons do not impede a faithful and good soul on its way to God.

Textual Notes

339ᵃ⁻ᵃ ὁτιοῦν ὅτῳ μετὰ: Υ • 339ᵇ ὑβρίζει καὶ εἰς θεὸν ἁμαρτάνει: Υ • 340ᵃ⁻ᵃ φειδόμενος παίδων: Υ • 340ᵇ θεοφιλῶν: sy²; κατὰ θεόν: lat? • 341 omit Υ • 341ᵃ δ: lat, sy² • 342 omit Υ, sy² • 342ᵃ⁻ᵃ δίδως: Π • 344ᵃ omit Π, lat • 344ᵇ χρὴ: Υ • 344ᶜ εὐδαιμονήσαντα: Υ, lat; εὐγνωμονοῦντα: Π, sy² • 346ᵃ ἱμάτιον: lat, co, sy² • 347ᵃ ὁποῖα δ': Π • 348ᵃ⁻ᵃ ἀκαθάρτῳ ψυχῇ: Π

Commentary

The first unit (vv. 339–342) in this block of sayings offers advice on providing for others (note δίδωμι in vv. 339, 342), with particular attention drawn to the question of motive (vv. 341–342). After a couplet contrasting anger and happiness (vv. 343–344), there is a unit on the soul (with ψυχή in every line), dealing first with its relationship to the body (vv. 345–347), and then its relationship with demons (vv. 348–349), vv. 347–349 offering perspectives relevant to the readers' understanding of postmortem judgment.

Sentence 339

The readers of the *Sentences* are bid not only to share what they have (vv. 82b, 295–296, 377) and give to the needy (vv. 52, 217) but to give freely (v. 242) and willingly (vv. 329–330), in order to please God (vv. 379, 382) and not themselves (v. 342). Here another condition is stipulated: giving should never be accompanied by reproach (cf. vv. 174, 272, 400), since in so doing one acts in a way that is insolent and insulting, and, as v. 203 tells us, "the result of insolence is ruin." Sextus's advice is familiar from another wisdom text that emphasizes the importance of sharing with the needy,

Ben Sira. Of particular interest is Sir 18:15, 18: "My child, do not mix reproach with your good deeds, or spoil your gift by harsh words.... A fool reproaches (ὀνειδιεῖ) ungraciously, and the gift of a grudging giver dims the eyes." Sirach 20:14–15 dilates on the theme: "A fool's gift will profit you nothing, for he looks for recompense many times over. He gives little and reproaches much (ὀλίγα δώσει καὶ πολλὰ ὀνειδίσει)." As these sayings imply, the fool may give to the right people, and even in appropriate amounts, but he gives in the wrong way, for the wrong reason, and with the wrong result. Cf. Sir 41:25: "Do not be reproachful after making a gift" (μετὰ τὸ δοῦναι μὴ ὀνείδιζε). This theme informs early Christian instruction on giving as well. According to Herm. *Sim.* 9.24.2, for example, the faithful "are always having compassion for everyone, and from their labors they supply everyone's needs without reproach (ἀνονειδίστως) and without hesitation." See also *Ep. Barn.* 19.11 ("You shall not hesitate to give, nor shall you grumble when giving") and *Sib. Or.* 2.272–273 (Among the most wicked are those who "make reproach when they give from the fruit of their labors"). In Jas 1:5, meanwhile, God is held up as a model of the ideal giver, that is, as one "who gives to all generously and without reproach (μὴ ὀνειδίζοντος)" (note that in v. 339 Υ adds καὶ εἰς θεὸν ἁμαρτάνει). Read within this context, Sextus's point would seem to be that the readers have an obligation not only to provide concrete assistance to others, but to do so with a generous spirit, which means being compassionate to those in need, that is, being kind to them (v. 52), listening to them (v. 217), and helping them out of a sense of humanity (v. 342). For a Greco-Roman parallel, see Plutarch, *Adul. amic.* 64a: "In the flatterer's favors the reproach (τὸ ἐπονείδιστον) and mortification that he feels do not occur at some later time, but at the very moment when he performs the favor."

Sentence 340

It is probable that this line entails an allusion to Sir 4:10 (cf. 35:17): "Be like a father to orphans (γίνου ὀρφανοῖς ὡς πατήρ), and be like a husband to their mother; you will then be like a son of the Most High, and he will love you (ἀγαπήσει σε) more than does your mother" (for another early allusion to Sir 4:10, see Cyprian, *Quir.* 3.113). Regardless of their precise relationship, the two texts are distinctive in the assertion that caring for orphans like a father will make one beloved of God (in Clement, *Quis div.* 34.2, by contrast, it is orphans who are said to be God-beloved). Cf. Job 31:18: "From my youth I reared the orphan like a father, and from my mother's womb I guided the widow." Here, as often, orphans are grouped with widows as categories of individuals typically in need of assistance and protection (Exod 22:22; Deut 10:18; 24:17, 19–21; 27:19; etc.). Sextus lacks the second command in Sir 4:10, perhaps so as to avoid the potentially confusing idea that the reader should be "like a husband" to an unmarried woman (cf. vv. 230a–240).

Early Christian discourse is rife with admonitions to support rather than abuse orphans, for example, Ign. *Smyrn.* 6.2; Pol. *Phil.* 6.1; *Ep. Barn.* 20.2; Herm. *Mand.* 8.10; *Sim.* 1.8; 5.3.7; 9.26.2; Aristides of Athens, *Apol.* 15; Justin Martyr, *1 Apol.* 67.6 (cf. Mark 12:40 v.l.). The most prominent proof-text in this regard, however, is not Sir 4:10 but Isa 1:16–20 (e.g., *1 Clem.* 8.4; Justin Martyr, *1 Apol.* 44.3; 61.7). In Jas 1:27, meanwhile, caring for widows and orphans is a definitional practice of the sort of "pure" religion (cf. vv. 23, 46b–47, 81) that keeps one unstained by "the world" (cf. vv. 20, 82b).

Sentences 341–342

For Sextus, it is imperative that sharing be done not only in the right way (see on v. 339 above) but also with the proper motive. Edwards and Wild (1981, 56), following Chadwick (1959, 178), suggest that the source for this couplet is Matt 6:1–4. There is nothing in the *Sentences*, however, that corresponds to Matthew's idea that giving should be done and seen "in secret" (6:3–4), and so it is probably best to see the influence as being restricted to Matt 6:1–2, v. 341 corresponding to 6:1 as a general heading on how not to practice acts of piety, v. 342 corresponding to 6:2 as an application of this principle to a specific case, namely, the practice of giving to others. Beyond this, our author's utilization of the dominical material is both flexible and selective. For example, the construction ἕνεκα δόξης in v. 341 (cf. v. 351) draws not on Matt 6:1 but on Matt 6:2 (ὅπως δοξασθῶσιν), while the formula ἐπὶ τὸ αὐτὸ γνωσθῆναι in v. 342 finds its closest match not in Matt 6:2, but in Matt 6:1 (πρὸς τὸ θεαθῆναι). Likewise, the μισθός to which our author refers in v. 341 is not the heavenly reward of Matt 6:1, but the "pay" that, according to Matt 6:2, individuals receive when they perform acts of piety in order to be seen and praised by other people. In addition, Sextus ignores the trumpet imagery of Matt 6:2 (including its references to where the trumpet is sounded), drops the language of doing (i.e., ποιεῖν in Matt 6:1, ποιῇς in Matt 6:2) in favor of the language of serving (v. 341, cf. vv. 264b, 319, 336), and broadens the application beyond almsgiving (Matt 6:2) to anything that one gives (v. 342; for this use of δίδωμι, cf. vv. 242, 329, 378). Perhaps most important, for Sextus the underlying moral problem, that which prevents one from giving ἀνθρώπῳ (for the sake of the recipient him- or herself), is not hypocrisy (Matt 6:2) but pleasure, a major theme for our text (vv. 70, 111, 232, 272, 276). Verse 342 makes a distinctive contribution to the development of this theme insofar as it indicates an understanding of ἡδονή that encompasses not only pleasures of the body (as in v. 411), but also those of the ego. Cf. P.Ins. 10.11: "Do not vaunt what you have done as a service, for then you annoy." For other references to Matt 6:1–2 in early Christian literature, see Aristides of Athens, *Apol.* 15; Justin Martyr, *1 Apol.* 15.17; Clement, *Strom.* 1.1.9.3; 4.22.138.2.

Sentence 343

The source for this line is Clitarchus, *Sent.* 110: <ὀργὴν πλήθους> μὴ παρόξυνε. Crowds should be approached with caution, since in them one will find few believers (v. 243). Accordingly, the reader is advised against trying to speak to the multitudes about God (v. 360) or trying to win their approval (vv. 112, 241, 299, cf. vv. 530–531, 570–71). By the same token, he should avoid doing or saying anything that outsiders might deem offensive (vv. 38, 51, 396) or that might give "the world" reason to condemn (v. 16) rather than to revere (v. 37) his way of life (see further on v. 16). Presumably, this would include doing or saying anything that might incur the anger of others (cf. v. 293), a concern of particular importance when dealing with a large gathering, "for a crowd is another name for everything that is disorderly, indecorous, discordant, and culpable" (Philo, *Praem.* 20), always "in a state of confusion and anger … just as a wild rough sea is whipped this way and that" (Dio Chrysostom, *Or.* 3.49). For the general reputation that crowds had for volatility and impulsiveness, see further Sir 16:6; Menander, *Mon.* 372; Philo, *Ebr.* 113; *Mos.* 2.169; *Spec.* 4.88; *Flacc.* 33; *Legat.* 67; Ps.-Socratics, *Ep.* 24.1–2. While steering clear of crowds altogether is usually the best option, it was considered the mark of a good leader that he "should be prepared to withstand absolutely all those things which are considered difficult or vexatious, and especially the vilifications and anger of the mob" (Dio Chrysostom, *Or.* 34.33; cf. Sext. 293). No doubt taking measures to avoid inciting the anger of the mob in the first place (for the formula παροξύνω + πλῆθος, see Polybius, *Hist.* 15.25.36; 38.12.10; 38.13.6; Diodorus Siculus, *Bibl. hist.* 11.57.3; 11.77.6; 15.58.1; Josephus, *Ant.* 4.63; *Vita* 298; Ps.-Clement, *Hom.* 20.18) would be even more commendable. As Seneca puts it, in a thronging multitude, "you may be sure that just as many vices are gathered there as men" (*Ira* 2.8.1).

Sentence 344

Clitarchus, *Sent*. 110 (see above) is joined to the saying that follows it by catchword: "Be neither impressed nor dishonored by the praise of the multitude" (Clitarchus, *Sent*. 111). Sext. 343 is apparently joined to v. 344 by τοίνυν, though note that the term is missing in both Π and the Latin manuscripts, while the Coptic version at this point is corrupt. There is a possibility, then, that the connecting particle was added by the copyist responsible for Υ, which would accord with his activity elsewhere in the text (cf. the apparatus for vv. 10, 230a). In addition, retaining τοίνυν creates problems of interpretation, since its logical force here is not apparent. Perhaps the assumption is that εὐδαιμονία entails an absence of anger and/or actions that provoke anger in others, in which case comparison can be made with Teles, frag. 7.56. On the other hand, decoupling v. 344 from v. 343 facilitates the task of reading the former in the light of other sayings in the collection. Thus, just as learning is necessary for those who would be dear to God (v. 251), it is also necessary for those who would be happy, the basis of human happiness lying with the divine (v. 133). As v. 148 emphasizes, the sort of learning that is necessary—and sufficient—for happiness concerns itself not only with the knowledge of God but also with the imitation of God. Proper learning, therefore, entails both knowing (vv. 353, 394) and doing (vv. 250, 274a, 384) what is worthy of God.

Sentence 345

Chadwick (1959, 147, 178) identifies as the source of this line *Sent. Pythag*. 103 (τεθνάναι πολλῷ κρεῖττον ἢ δι' ἀκρασίας τὴν ψυχὴν ἀμαυρῶσαι), which is cited as a saying of Pythagoras in Stobaeus, *Anth*. 3.17.26 (cf. Nicolaus Catascepenus, *Vit. Cyr. Phil*. 20.4). Despite the obvious similarities, a better candidate is Clitarchus, *Sent*. 114 (κρεῖττον ἀποθανεῖν ἢ διὰ γαστρὸς ἀκρασίαν ψυχὴν ἀμαυρῶσαι), which v. 345 matches exactly, except for the insertion of explanatory λιμῷ after ἀποθανεῖν. The version preserved in Porphyry, *Marc*. 35 (πολλῷ γὰρ κρεῖττον τεθνάναι ἢ δι' ἀκρασίαν τὴν ψυχὴν ἀμαυρῶσαι), meanwhile, appears to be based on *Sent. Pythag*. 103, both of which lack γαστρός while having τεθνάναι rather than ἀποθανεῖν, though the word order is slightly different.

In gnomic literature, overindulgence in food and drink is said to diminish one's health (Prov 23:29–32; Sir 37:29–30; P.Ins. 6.8–19; *Carm. aur*. 33–34) and one's reputation (Prov 23:20–21; *Syr. Men*. 52–66; Ps.-Phoc. 67–69B; Theognis, *El*. 467–502). In the *Sentences*, it is said to diminish one's soul. It does so by creating impurities that inhibit holiness (vv.

108a–b), turning it into a source of defilement (v. 429). Given this body-soul connection (cf. vv. 346–347), maintaining control over the γαστήρ is for the faithful a major priority (vv. 240, 270, 428). Cf. Epictetus, *Gnom.* 20 ("In every feast remember that there are two guests to be entertained, the body and the soul; and that what you give the body you presently lose, but what you give the soul you keep forever") and 26: "If you want to be a musical and harmonious person, whenever you are at a drinking party and your soul is bedewed with wine, suffer it not to go forth and defile itself." The damage or "impairment" that overindulgence causes the soul is in fact lamented by a variety of ancient moralists. Clement even goes so far as to say that "every depravity of soul" is accompanied by ἀκρασία (*Strom.* 5.13.86.3; cf. Dio Chrysostom, *Or.* 4.103). Comparable is Philo, *Leg.* 3.62: "We can note also the overindulgent man inclined to pleasure of the belly (τὸν ἀκρατῆ ἐπὶ τὴν γαστρὸς νενευκότα ἡδονήν); he welcomes as a good thing the abundance of strong drink and a well-spread table, though taking harm from them in both body and soul" (for γαστρὸς ἀκρασία, see also Athenaeus, *Deipn.* 4.19; John Chrysostom, *Hom. Matt.* 57.209, 211). Similar disapproval is heaped upon those who overindulge in drinking alone: "Wine must be regarded as very unprofitable for every part of life, since it presses hard upon the soul, impairs the senses (αἰσθήσεων ἀμαυρουμένων), and weighs down the body, leaving none of our faculties free and untrammeled, but hampering the natural activity of each" (Philo, *Spec.* 1.100). As Plutarch explains in *Tu. san.* 125c, for those who overindulge, "there is no way to prevent their leaving as a residue the most violent and serious injuries caused by weak and injurious pleasures (ἐφ' ἡδοναῖς ἀσθενέσι καὶ ἀμαυραῖς)." For an additional Pythagorean perspective, we can turn to Ps.-Pythagoras, *Ep.* 2.185.25–28: "A good disposition is not engendered by the desire for sex or for food, but by privation leading to manly virtue. For pleasures manifold and overindulgent (ἡδοναὶ ποικίλαι καὶ ἀκρατεῖς) enslave the souls of weak people."

Sentence 346

This saying can be understood as elaborating an unstated premise of the preceding line, namely, that the body and the soul are not only related to one another—they also affect one another. The soul, for its part, is affected through (διά) what one does with or to one's body (v. 345), while the body, as we learn here, is affected by the soul insofar as it has been marked by the soul's "imprint" (ἐκμαγεῖον). Given the mutually implicating nature of this relationship, the admonition in the second half of the verse follows naturally. Even though it represents a higher aspect of the human personality (vv. 129, 318, 320, 403, etc.), it is not sufficient to keep only the soul "pure," that is, sinless (vv. 46b, 57b, 181—or, as the Coptic puts it, "pure, since it is innocent"): the same must be done for the body as well (cf. vv. 23, 81, 356). Although a different anthropological metaphor is employed (cf. v. 320), the same thought can be seen at work in v. 449: "Keep unstained your body, the garment of the soul that is from God, just as you keep unstained your coat, the garment of the flesh." Maintaining somatic purity is crucial, since it is through the body that one's soul is tested (v. 425), and whatever the soul pursues while inhabiting the body will accompany it as evidence when it goes to judgment (v. 347).

Plato had famously imagined that "we have an imprint of wax (κήρινον ἐκμαγεῖον) in our souls" (*Theaet.* 191c, cf. 194d–e, 196a–b). The metaphor was subsequently utilized in a wide variety of ways, as evidenced perhaps most fully in the writings of Philo. On some occasions, he employs the imagery of the seal and impression to explain the relationship between intelligible and sense-perceptible realities, for example, to explain how the latter are created or shaped as copies of the models provided by the former (e.g., *Her.* 179–181; *Spec.* 1.47–48). The human being modeled after the divine image, for instance, can be construed as "a kind of idea or genus or seal" (*Opif.* 134). The Alexandrian can also speak of the model of the sanctuary being "stamped" on the mind of Moses (*Mos.* 2.76) or of divine virtues and moral truths being "impressed" on the soul through obedience to Moses and his laws (*Spec.* 1.30, 59; 2.104; 4.137). For the particular application of the metaphor here, however, we must turn to Plutarch, *Fac.* 945a (= Posidonius, frag. 398): "The soul receives the impression of its shape through being molded (τυπουμένη) by the mind and molding in turn and imprinting (ἐκμάττεται) the body, enfolding it on all sides, so that, even if it be separated from either one for a long time, since it preserves the likeness and the stamp it is correctly called an image." The body is given its form by the imprint of the soul, then, which itself has been molded by the mind. For comparable anthropological speculations, see Proclus Diadochus, *Plat. rem publ. comm.* 2.327.21–2.328.18; Macrobius, *Somn. Scip.* 1.14.8.

Sentences 347–349

Sextus envisions human life as a time during which the soul is tested by God through the body (v. 425), followed by a time when the soul, separated from the body, is judged by God on the basis of this testing, with the things for which it strived while in the body serving as witnesses against it (cf. v. 303). For the imagery, see Plato, *Gorg.* 524d: "Everything that's in the soul becomes evident after it has been stripped naked of the body, both things that are natural to it and things that have happened to it, that is, things that the person came to have in his soul as a result of his pursuit (ἐπιτήδευσιν) of each object." Cf. Jas 5:3: "Your gold and your silver have rusted; and their rust will be evidence against you (εἰς μαρτύριον ὑμῖν) and will consume your flesh like fire." While for James it is the objects of one's greed that condemn the soul at judgment (cf. *1 En.* 96.7), the proximity to v. 345 suggests that for Sextus it is principally the objects of one's gluttony that do so. The scenario of judgment, then, can be seen as relating to the verses that precede as motivation (cf. vv. 12–14), though it relates to the verses that follow as well, insofar as they elaborate further on how bodily pursuits are thought to "accompany" the postmortem soul (cf. v. 421). While in v. 39 the souls of those who led an evil life were envisioned as being "called to account" by evil demons after death, here the demons are said to "lay claim" to such souls (for this use of ἀντιποιέω, see also Ephraem Syrus, *Virt.* prol. 27–28). The conceptualization that Sextus employs here is familiar from other early Christian texts, for example, Ps.-Clement, *Hom.* 9.9, where we learn that during its earthly life demons attempt to infiltrate and corrupt the soul through the body, blending their essence with immoral souls to such an extent that even after the soul's release from the body, demonic forces burden and impede it like a "strong chain" (for additional examples, see the commentary on vv. 39–40; and cf. v. 604: "A person enslaved by pleasure is enslaved by an evil demon").

According to Diogenes Laertius, *Vit. phil.* 8.31, students of Pythagoreanism imagined the postmortem soul being "claimed" by otherworldly beings as well. Specifically, when the soul "is cast out upon the earth, it wanders in the air like a body" (alluding perhaps to the notion that after death the soul retains the appearance of the body; cf. Lucian, *Vera hist.* 2.12), being accompanied by Hermes, the "steward" and "keeper" of souls, who "brings in the souls from their bodies both by land and sea." Souls that are "pure," that is, souls unencumbered by bodily desires, are taken to the uppermost region, while impure souls "are bound by the Furies in bonds unbreakable." Purity functions as an eschatological determinant in the *Sentences* as well, unclean souls being claimed by unclean demons (cf. Luke 4:33; 9:42; Rev 16:13–14), while souls that are "faithful and good" (cf. v. 243), that is, souls cleansed of impure thoughts and deeds (cf. vv. 23, 57b, 102, 108b, 356, 407), are immune to demonic interference. Specifically, the demons are unable to block a soul that is ἐν ὁδῷ θεοῦ, an allusion to the soul's heavenly ascent, a topic addressed also in v. 40: "Blessed is the man whose soul no one will seize when it journeys to God" (note that the version of v. 349 in v. 591 uses ἐν ἐννοίαις θεοῦ in lieu of ἐν ὁδῷ θεοῦ). Just as those who are evil follow an evil "guide" (v. 305), the faithful have as their guide the divine (v. 104, cf. v. 582), that is, reason (v. 74, cf. v. 95b), through which the soul ascends to God (v. 420). It is thus possible to speak of souls that "follow" reason (v. 264a), thereby being "led" to God (v. 167) and "accompanied" by God (v. 421). For the expression ὁδός θεοῦ, cf. Acts 13:10; 18:26; Heb 3:10; *Apoc. Pet.* 20.34. According to the evangelists, it is Jesus who teaches "the way of God in truth" (Matt 22:16; Mark 12:14; Luke 20:21). The idea that evil forces endeavor to block the soul's ascent to heaven was common in early Christianity. Athanasius, for example, describes a vision of Anthony's ascent in which the latter sees an enormous, terrible being blocking "the pathway for souls" and "seizing those who were accountable to him and preventing them from passing by" (*Vit. Ant.* 66.5; for additional examples, see the commentary on vv. 39–40). Non-Christian authors utilized such imagery as well. Porphyry, for example, is familiar with the concept of "the blessed way (ὁδός) to the gods," by which "ascents to God are made" (*Marc.* 8). Those who follow this way avoid anything having to do with "the nature of a base soul and the kinship and pleasure which it feels for the body," doing so in order that they should not be "disturbed by alien souls, violent and impure … and not be impeded (μηδὲ ἐμποδίζοιντο) in their solitary approach to God by disruptive demons" (*Abst.* 2.47.3). For this use of ἐμποδίζω, see also *T. Sol.* 18.42; Origen, *Frag. Luc.* 124; Evagrius Ponticus, *Orat.* 79.1176.

SENTENCES 350–368

TEXT

350 λόγου^a περὶ θεοῦ μὴ παντὶ κοινώνει.
351 οὐκ ἀσφαλὲς ἀκούειν περὶ θεοῦ τοῖς ὑπὸ δόξης διεφθαρμένοις.
352 περὶ θεοῦ καὶ τἀληθῆ^a λέγειν κίνδυνος οὐ μικρός.
353 περὶ θεοῦ μηδὲν εἴπῃς μὴ μαθὼν παρὰ θεοῦ.
354 ἀθέῳ δὲ^a περὶ θεοῦ μηδὲν εἴπῃς.
355 ^aπερὶ θεοῦ^a λόγον ἀληθῆ ὡς θεὸν^b τίμα.
356 μὴ καθαρεύων ἀνοσίων ἔργων μὴ φθέγξῃ περὶ θεοῦ λόγον.

357 λόγος ἀληθὴς περὶ θεοῦ λόγος ἐστὶν θεοῦ.
358 πεισθεὶς πρότερον θεοφιλὴς εἶναι ᵃπρὸς οὓς ἂν πεισθῇςᵃ λέγε περὶ θεοῦ.
359 τάᵃ ἔργα σου θεοφιλῆ προηγείσθω παντὸς λόγου περὶ θεοῦ.
360 ἐπὶ πλήθουςᵃ λέγειν περὶ θεοῦ μὴ ἐπιτήδευε.
361 λόγου περὶ θεοῦ ᵃφείδου μᾶλλονᵃ ἢ περὶ ψυχῆς.
362 ψυχὴν αἱρετώτερον ἢ λόγον εἰκῇ ᵃπροέσθαι περὶᵃ θεοῦ.
363a θεοφιλοῦς ἀνδρὸς σώματος μὲν ἄρξεις, λόγου δὲ οὐ κυριεύσεις.
363b σοφοῦ σώματος καὶ λέων ἄρχειᵃ, ᵇτούτου δὴ μόνου καὶ τύραννοςᵇ.
364 ὑπὸ τυράννου γινομένηςᵃ ἀπειλῆς τίνοςᵇ ᶜεἶ τότεᶜ μάλισταᵈ μέμνησο.
365 λόγονᵃ οἷς οὐ θέμις ὁ λέγων περὶ θεοῦ προδότης θεοῦ νομιζέσθω.
366 λόγον περὶ θεοῦ σιγᾶν ἄμεινον ἢ προπετῶς διαλέγεσθαι.
367 ὁ λέγων ψευδῆ περὶ θεοῦ καταψεύδεται θεοῦ.
368 ἄνθρωπος μηδὲν ἔχων ᵃλέγειν περὶ θεοῦᵃ ἀληθὲς ἔρημός ἐστιν θεοῦ.

Translation

350   Do not share a word about God with everyone.
351   It is not safe for those corrupted by fame to hear about God.
352   To speak even the truth about God entails no small risk.
353   Say nothing about God without having learned it from God.
354   Say nothing about God to a godless person.
355   Honor a true word about God as you would God himself.
356   If you are not cleansed of unholy works, do not utter a word about God.
357   A true word about God is a word of God.
358   Once you are persuaded that you are God-pleasing, then speak about God to those whom you would persuade.
359   Let your God-pleasing works precede every word about God.
360   Do not strive to speak to a multitude about God.
361   Be more sparing with a word about God than with one about a soul.
362   It is preferable to relinquish a soul without purpose than a word about God.
363a You may have control over the body of a man dear to God, but you will not rule over his reason.
363b Over a sage's body both a lion and a tyrant have control, but over this alone.

364 When a tyrant makes a threat, then especially remember whose you are.
365 Consider the one who speaks a word about God to those who have no right to hear it a betrayer of God.
366 It is better to keep silent with a word about God than to utter it recklessly.
367 The one who speaks lies about God speaks lies against God.
368 A person having nothing true to say about God is bereft of God.

Textual Notes

350ᵃ λόγῳ: Π, Υ • 352ᵃ τἀληθὲς: Υ • 354ᵃ omit Π, co • 355ᵃ⁻ᵃ omit lat • 355ᵇ θεοῦ: Υ, sy² • 358 πιστοῖς λέγε περὶ θεοῦ: Υ • 358ᵃ⁻ᵃ omit sy¹ • 359ᵃ omit Π • 360ᵃ πλήθει: Υ • 361ᵃ⁻ᵃ μᾶλλον φείδου: Υ • 362ᵃ⁻ᵃ προθέσθαι περὶ: Π • 363bᵃ ἄρξει: Π • 363bᵇ as the beginning of v. 364: Υ • 364ᵃ γενομένης: Υ • 364ᵇ τινὸς: Π, Υ • 364ᶜ⁻ᶜ εἴποτε: Υ • 364ᵈ μάλιστα: Π • 365ᵃ λόγου attached to v. 364: Υ • 368ᵃ⁻ᵃ περὶ θεοῦ λέγειν: Υ

Commentary

According to Chadwick (1959, 153), vv. 350–362 are on caution in making theological statements. It may be preferable to see vv. 350–368 as the unit, with vv. 363a–364 representing an aside on the sage and the tyrant (note the catchword λόγος in vv. 361–363a, as well as θεοφιλής in vv. 358–359, 363a). In contrast to the previous section on speech-ethics (vv. 149–165g), which lacked references to God altogether, here the phrase περὶ θεοῦ runs as a thread through the section, occurring no less than seventeen times (vv. 350–362, 365–368). Note also the use of λόγος in vv. 350, 355–357, 359, 361–363a, 365–366 and of λέγω in vv. 352–354, 358, 360, 365, 367–368. While a variety of priorities and perspectives are expressed, the overall point is that integrity must be observed with regard to all elements of the theological speech-act, that is, with regard to the one who speaks (vv. 356, 358–359, 365, 367–368), the one who hears (vv. 350–351, 354, 360), and what is spoken (vv. 353, 355, 357, 361–362). The seriousness with which our author approaches this subject is dramatized especially by the final four sayings (vv. 365–368), which in their strongly negative orientation can be understood to function as warnings.

Sentences 350–352

A phenomenon widely attested in both ancient philosophy and ancient religion is the practice of esotericism, according to which the dissemination of certain theological truths is purposefully restricted to an intellectual or moral elite, the justification being that divulging such truths to those unworthy or unable to hear them poses a danger to the listeners, to the speaker, and to the truth itself. The speaker must take an accounting of his listeners before discussing such truths, then, lest their imprudent revelation have unintended consequences. As Clement explains, this process of "distinguishing the one who is capable of hearing from the rest" (*Strom.* 1.1.9.1) is critical, since "it is difficult to present arguments which are truly pure and lucid and concern the true light to people who are like pigs in their lack of education. There is almost nothing which seems more ridiculous to the man in the street than these addresses, or more marvelous and divinely inspired to those of noble natures" (*Strom.* 1.12.55.4, alluding to a quotation of Matt 7:6 in *Strom.* 1.12.55.3). As this citation illustrates, the observance of esotericism in teaching scriptural principles could be validated by appeals to scripture itself (cf. *Const. ap.* 3.5, cited below under v. 365). After all, there were occasions when Jesus taught the disciples privately (Clement, *Strom.* 1.1.2.2–3; 1.1.13.2; 6.15.124.3; Origen, *Cels.* 3.21; 4.36; 6.6; *Princ.* 3.1.17; cf. Matt 13:13, 36; Mark 4:11, 34), while Paul reserved the "solid food" of divine wisdom for those who were mature enough to digest it (Clement, *Strom.* 5.4.25.2–5.4.26.5; Origen, *Cels.* 3.60; *Comm. Joan.* 13.18; cf. 1 Cor 2:6–7, 14; 3:1–2). Origen also observes that "the existence of certain doctrines, which are beyond those that are exoteric and do not reach the multitude, is not a peculiarity of Christian doctrine only, but is shared by the philosophers. For they had some doctrines which were exoteric and some which were esoteric. Some hearers of Pythagoras only learnt of the master's *ipse dixit*, while others were taught secret doctrines which could not deservedly reach ears that were uninitiated and not yet purified" (*Cels.* 1.7; cf. Clement, *Strom.* 2.5.24.3). That the Alexandrian would turn first to Pythagoreanism as an example in this regard is hardly surprising, given that its founder was widely admired for the "mysterious" nature of his pedagogy (Plutarch, *Is. Osir.* 354e), a fact evident not only in the division (to which Origen alludes here) of his followers into ἀκουσματικοί and μαθεματικοί (e.g., Iamblichus, *Vit. Pythag.* 18.80–89; Clement, *Strom.* 5.9.59.1) but also in the promulgation of the enigmatic σύμβολα, to which Clement devotes an entire chapter in his extended discussion of esotericism in book 5 of the *Stromata* (5.5.27.1–5.5.31.5; cf. 5.9.57.2–5.9.58.1; Plutarch, frag. 202).

An appeal to Pythagoreanism is evidenced here as well, with v. 350 being derived from the now-lost material that our author apparently shared with Porphyry (see part 4 of the introduction). Cf. *Marc.* 15: "With the person from whose opinions you cannot profit share neither a life nor a word that concerns God" (μήτε βίου μήτε λόγου τοῦ περὶ θεοῦ κοινώνει). Sextus's use of the more indeterminate μὴ παντί makes the saying an appropriate heading for the section. The sage may share his food with everyone (v. 266), but he does not share God's word with everyone.

The saying from *Marc.* 15 just cited continues immediately with: "For it is not safe to speak a word about God to those who have been corrupted by fame. For, indeed, to speak either truly or falsely about God with such persons carries with it equal danger" (λόγον γὰρ περὶ θεοῦ τοῖς ὑπὸ δόξης διεφθαρμένοις λέγειν οὐκ ἀσφαλές. καὶ γὰρ καὶ τἀληθῆ λέγειν ἐπὶ τούτων περὶ θεοῦ καὶ τὰ ψευδῆ κίνδυνον ἴσον φέρει). The source for both Sextus and Porphyry is clearly *Sent. Pythag.* 55[a–b]: λόγον περὶ θεοῦ τοῖς ὑπὸ δόξης διεφθαρμένοις λέγειν οὐκ ἀσφαλές. καὶ γὰρ τὰ ἀληθῆ λέγειν ἐπὶ τούτων καὶ τὰ ψευδῆ κίνδυνον φέρει. With regard to the first saying, except for the connective γάρ, Porphyry, *Marc.* 15 reproduces *Sent. Pythag.* 55[a] exactly, while in v. 351 Sextus moves οὐκ ἀσφαλές from the last position to the first, and replaces λόγον ... λέγειν with ἀκούειν (despite the fact that λόγον would have created a catchword with the saying that precedes and λέγειν would have created a catchword with the saying that follows), thus shifting the object of concern from the speaker to the listener. The latter redaction has the effect of creating a more balanced couplet with the verse that follows: there is risk both for those who hear about God (v. 351) and for those who talk about God (v. 352). While in its original setting δόξα here may have referred to "opinion" (as in vv. 28, 103), comparison with vv. 112, 188, and 341 suggests that for Sextus it means "glory," an interpretation supported also by the Latin and (apparently) Coptic translations. The distinction between those who are worthy to learn divine truths and those who are unworthy (see above) is not primarily epistemological, but moral. Cf. v. 401: "Never unknowingly share a word about God with someone of a sordid nature." For the "corrupting" effects of fame, see Diodorus Siculus, *Bibl. hist.* 24.3.1; Plutarch, *Ag. Cleom.* 18.2; Dio Chrysostom, *Or.* 11.6.

With regard to the second saying, again, Porphyry, *Marc.* 15 reproduces *Sent. Pythag.* 55[b] almost exactly (the most notable change being the addition of ἴσον after κίνδυνον), while in v. 352 we see numerous alterations.

To begin with, Sextus drops both ἐπὶ τούτων (broadening the gnome's scope of application) and καὶ τὰ ψευδῆ. With regard to the latter, no doubt he found the notion of false speech about God to be objectionable (cf. vv. 83–85, 165a–f). By the same token, while our author expects that the readers will be committed to the truth (v. 158), especially when it comes to theological discourse (vv. 355, 368, 410, 441), speaking the truth about God to those who are unworthy may represent for him one of the occasions when one would actually "sin by speaking the truth," that is, an occasion when it would be better to speak falsely (v. 165e). In addition, Sextus changes κίνδυνον φέρει to κίνδυνος οὐ μικρός, in which case comparison can be made with Clitarchus, *Sent.* 144: ὃ μὴ θέλεις ἀκούειν μηδὲ εἴπῃς· ὃ μὴ θέλεις λέγειν μηδ' ἄκουε. ὤτων καὶ γλώττης μέγας ὁ κίνδυνος. Finally, on one of the few occasions when he agrees with Porphyry against *Sententiae Pythagoreorum*, Sextus also adds περὶ θεοῦ, though he places the clause at the beginning of the line, while the Tyrian inserts it after ἐπὶ τούτων.

Verse 352 is cited by Origen on three occasions in his extant corpus. It is cited verbatim, together with v. 22, in the preface to his commentary on the first psalm (*Sel. Ps.* 12.1080a [= Epiphanius, *Pan.* 2.416]) in support of the argument that one ought to observe discretion when speaking and (especially) writing about sacred matters (see Chadwick 1959, 115). He cites it again in *Comm. Joan.* 20.6 with reference to theological concepts difficult to explain: "since such things would trouble some people who have an inkling of these matters but do not understand them thoroughly, we will expose ourselves to danger concerning such matters where it is precarious to mention and disclose such things, even if one speaks the truth." Finally, we have the following from *Hom. Ezech.* 1.11: "I gladly profess the opinion uttered by a wise and believing man which I often quote: 'To speak even the truth about God is dangerous' (*de deo et vera dicere periculum est*). For not only false statements about him are risky; there is also danger to the speaker in true statements if they are made at an inopportune time" (translation from Chadwick 1959, 114). It is interesting that the Alexandrian comments on the risky nature of false statements about God even though, as we have seen, Sextus dropped καὶ τὰ ψευδῆ from his source, while *periculum est* would seem to accord better with κίνδυνον φέρει in *Sent. Pythag.* 55^b than with κίνδυνος οὐ μικρός in v. 352. Rufinus has *de deo etiam quae vera sunt dicere periculum est non parvum*.

Sentence 353

If it is dangerous to say things about God that are true, then it is certainly dangerous to say things about God that have been obtained from dubious sources (cf. v. 338). Compare Ps.-Clement, *Hom.* 2.12: "If you would know the things pertaining to God, you have to learn them from him alone, because he alone knows the truth." Despite their best efforts, says Athenagoras, the poets and the philosophers have been unable to apprehend this truth, "because they thought fit to learn, not from God concerning God, but each one from himself; hence they came each to his own conclusion respecting God, and matter, and forms, and the world. But we have for witnesses of the things we apprehend and believe the prophets, men who have pronounced concerning God and the things of God, guided by the Spirit of God" (*Legat.* 7.2–3). The position on this matter endorsed by our author, who of course makes no mention of prophets or the Spirit, would probably accord more closely with that of Athenagoras's philosophers. See especially v. 394: τίς θεὸς γνῶθι· γνῶθι δὲ τί τὸ νοοῦν ἐν σοί. One knows God by knowing oneself, specifically, by knowing the power of reason that resides within the human mind (vv. 35, 46a, 61, 144), which reflects the true nature of God as mind (vv. 26, 450). Presumably, this provides the basis not only for learning but also for speaking (v. 352) the truth about God.

Sentences 354–355

The readers are instructed to say nothing about God to the multitudes (v. 360), to the depraved (v. 401), to the impure (v. 407), to the intemperate (v. 451), or, as we learn here, to the "godless" (cf. vv. 380, 599), a designation that no doubt overlaps with the other four. As Clement emphasizes in *Strom.* 5.9.56.3, "the real philosophy and the true theology" should be disseminated only to those who have proven themselves in "a trial by faith in their whole way of life." Those lacking such credentials must not hear such teaching, lest they "receive harm in consequence of taking in the wrong sense the things declared for salvation" (*Strom.* 6.15.126.1), deceiving both themselves and anyone who listens to them (*Strom.* 1.2.21.2; 5.9.56.4). Clement explains that in communicating his own teachings in the *Stromata*, he has been at least as refrained in his writing as he is in his speaking, out of a fear that people "might misunderstand them and go astray and that I might be found offering a dagger to a child" (*Strom.* 1.1.14.3). A major consequence of such misunderstanding is that unbelievers will fail to demonstrate proper reverence for what they are being taught (as well as, we can presume, for the one who teaches it; see on vv. 244, 319). As Origen puts it, "the unworthy and irreligious are not able to understand the deep meaning and the sacredness of the doctrine of God" (*Cels.* 6.18). From this perspective, we can see that v. 355 rests on a premise that provides a rationale for the command in v. 354: it is wrong to talk about theology with the godless because they are no more likely to accord a word about God the honor it deserves than they are to accord such honor to God himself. Elsewhere Sextus urges the readers not only to honor God (vv. 135, 244, 319, 427), but to honor God by learning God's word (v. 439), the knowledge of God forming the basis for the imitation of God (vv. 41–44), which represents the highest honor that one can pay to God (v. 381). It is by the divine λόγος that the soul is purified (v. 24) and nourished (v. 413), and through which the soul ascends to God (v. 420). Regarding the "truth" of this word, see below on v. 357. The Coptic version ("Speak concerning the word about God as if you were saying it in the presence of God") appears to integrate elements from other sayings in the collection; cf. vv. 82a, 350, 356.

Sentence 356

Immediately following the saying that parallels v. 352 (see above), Porphyry, *Marc.* 15 has: "Neither is it fitting for any of these people to speak about God if he has not been cleansed from unholy deeds" (οὔτε αὐτῶν τινα προσῆκεν ἀνοσίων ἔργων μὴ καθαρεύοντα φθέγγεσθαι περὶ θεοῦ). As discussed in part 4 of the introduction (and, again, cf. above on v. 352), it is probable that this saying ultimately derives from a now-lost portion of the *Sententiae Pythagoreorum*. While in *Marc.* 15 the prohibition is applied to "these people," (that is, people corrupted by glory), in v. 356 it is applied to the readers themselves. While their ordering differs somewhat, both sayings are composed of the same basic elements: μὴ καθαρεύ– + ἀνοσίων ἔργων + φθέγ– περὶ θεοῦ in v. 356, ἀνοσίων ἔργων + μὴ καθαρεύ– + φθέγ– περὶ θεοῦ in *Marc.* 15 (for the language, cf. also Porphyry, *Abst.* 4.13.2). For the final verb, Sextus utilizes the imperative μὴ φθέγξῃ, balancing μὴ καθαρεύων at the beginning of the line, while Porphyry has an infinitival construction with οὔτε ... προσῆκεν. Sextus is also alone in appending λόγον, which has the effect of creating a catchword with the sayings that immediately precede and immediately follow.

Our author is well aware of the dangers that attend both speech (vv. 152, 185) and impurity (vv. 346–348). Theological speech is particularly dangerous insofar as the nature of God is not only pure (v. 36), it admits of nothing that is impure (v. 30). If one is to honor a word about God as one would honor God himself (v. 355), then, such words must be approached in the same way that one would approach God, that is, in a state of purity (cf. vv. 46b, 81). To attain this state, however, it is necessary not only to cleanse the mind of evil thoughts (vv. 57b, 181); one must also refrain from shameful actions (vv. 23, 102), thus achieving within oneself a harmony of words and deeds (vv. 177, 408). Thus, just as the readers would never contemplate speaking about God to a person whose soul they deemed to be impure (v. 407), before presuming to speak about God they must also inspect themselves for impurities. This way it is less likely that they will bring any disrepute on the word that they speak (v. 396) or corrupt the souls of those who hear that word (v. 195). Cf. v. 590: "Only when you have a soul pure from unholy deeds speak and hear about God." For a similar admonition without the purity language, see v. 173.

Sentence 357

According to Deut 18:22, a word is to be considered a word of God if it "comes true" (cf. Num 11:23). According to Sextus, a word is to be considered a word of God if it declares the truth "about" (περί) God. Bearing in mind that several Pauline texts identify the gospel as the "word of truth" (2 Cor 6:7; Eph 1:13; Col 1:5; 2 Tim 2:15; cf. Jas 1:18), comparison can also be made with 1 Thess 2:13: "We also constantly give thanks to God for this, that when you received the word of God that you heard from us, you accepted it not as a human word but as what it really is, God's word, which is also at work in you believers." That speech about God is or must be "true" is asserted no less than four times in this section (vv. 352, 355, 357, 368). Truth is a desideratum for those who would be wise insofar as there is nothing that is more conducive to wisdom than the truth (v. 168). Indeed, it is even possible to describe the sage as a prophet of divine truth, though before he can don this mantle his soul must become not only wise but also "pure" (v. 441), that is, pure of the sort of "unholy deeds" just mentioned. The relation of v. 357 to v. 356 is further suggested by v. 410, where we learn that speaking the truth about God is only possible for those who are righteous.

Sentences 358–359

The one who would speak the truth about God must be in a right relationship not only with others, however, but also with God. Specifically, one must be "dear" to God, or θεοφιλής (cf. vv. 251, 340, 359, 363a, 419, 487), a concept of some significance for understanding the spirituality of the *Sentences*. For Sextus, the whole basis of piety is φιλία with God (v.

86b). Without loving God—indeed, without loving God more than one's own soul (v. 106b)—it is impossible to be "with" God (v. 444). Such love is construed principally not as an emotion or as an act but as a process of recognizing what is "of" God or "like" God within oneself (vv. 442–443, cf. vv. 106a, 251), that is, within one's intellect (see above on v. 353), while disassociating from that which is not divine, especially from the things of the body (v. 101, cf. v. 141). The use of πεισθείς in this saying suggests that such recognition is not something simply to be had but must be accomplished through a regimen of self-reflection and self-persuasion (cf. vv. 25, 91a). Verse 540 makes the point even more succinctly: "Educate yourself, then others." Only those who have themselves navigated this regimen of self-persuasion to a point of conviction can effectively persuade others about divine truths (cf. v. 331).

As the next saying (v. 359) makes clear, however, in matters of faith self-persuasion is not sufficient. In order to persuade others, the faithful person must also demonstrate that he is θεοφιλής (note the catchword with v. 358) through appropriate "works" (cf. v. 356, for which this serves as a positive counterpart), such as caring for orphans (v. 340). This is a major priority for the speaker, since his listeners are unlikely to trust him until they see proof that his conduct is consistent with his speech (vv. 408–409). Hence the appeal, "Let your life confirm your words among those who hear you" (v. 177, cf. vv. 325, 383).

Sextus's source for this line is *Sent. Pythag.* 56: λόγου τοῦ περὶ θεοῦ προηγείσθω τὰ θεοφιλῆ ἔργα. Besides inverting the overall word order, the only significant changes are the insertions of σου after τὰ ἔργα, and of παντός before λόγου. The version of the saying preserved in Porphyry, *Marc.* 15 (προηγείσθω οὖν τοῦ περὶ θεοῦ λόγου τὰ θεοφιλῆ ἔργα) occurs after the maxim that corresponds with v. 356 (see above), with two sayings intervening, the latter being based on *Sent. Pythag.* 112. For the concept of "God-pleasing works," see also Philo, *Leg.* 3.130; *Mos.* 2.160. For the form of the saying, see vv. 74, 95b, and 160.

Sentence 360

Immediately following the saying from *Marc.* 15 just cited, Porphyry writes: "Let a word about him be silenced before a multitude" (σιγάσθω ὁ περὶ αὐτοῦ λόγος ἐπὶ πλήθους). While the verbal correspondence is not extensive, the two aphorisms having only ἐπὶ πλήθους in common, the similarities in content and sequence suggest that once again the two authors are drawing from a now-lost portion of *Sententiae Pythagoreorum* (see above on vv. 350, 356; also part 4 of the introduction). In lieu of Porphyry's σιγάσθω, Sextus uses one of his favorite expressions, μὴ ἐπιτήδευε. Just as one should "strive" neither to please the multitude (v. 112) nor to be first when addressing the multitude (v. 164a), one should not strive to speak to the multitude about God, since there is no telling how many unbelievers might be present in such a gathering (cf. v. 243) and therefore no possibility of controlling the different ways in which they might misconstrue or misrepresent what has been said. This refusal to discuss divine truths in public represents one of the most basic tenets of the esotericism described above, under vv. 350–352. See also Clement, *Strom.* 5.9.57.2: "It is not wished that all things should be exposed indiscriminately to all and sundry, or the benefits of wisdom communicated to those who have not even in a dream been purified in soul (for it is not allowed to hand to every chance comer what has been procured with such laborious efforts); nor are the mysteries of the word to be expounded to the profane." As the Alexandrian explains elsewhere, crowds assess intelligence and rectitude "not by the truth, but by whatever they are delighted with," for they are "not yet pure and worthy of the pure truth, but still discordant and disordered and material" (*Strom.* 5.4.19.1–2). In the *Sentences*, this sort of attitude is reflective of the circumspection that the sage displays generally regarding both crowds and their opinions (cf. vv. 145, 214, 241, 299, 530–531). Cf. *Gnom. Vat.* 81: "The disturbance of the soul cannot be ended nor true joy created either by the possession of the greatest wealth or by honor and respect in the eyes of the mob or by anything else that is associated with causes of unlimited desire."

Sentences 361–362

These two gnomes are joined to form a couplet not only by the repetition of λόγος περὶ θεοῦ (see the introductory comments for the section), but also by the catchword ψυχή, which is used as the last word of the first line and the first word of the second. Attention is called to the significance and value of the soul by a host of sayings in the *Sentences*. The soul, we learn, is not only of divine origin (v. 21), it represents that part of the human personality bequeathed with the capacity to become divine (v. 82d), the part that can know God (vv. 136, 417), revere God (v. 287), ascend to God (vv. 167, 394, 402, 420), and join with God (vv. 418, 421, cf. vv. 415b–416). Given the exalted status to which it has been assigned, it is not surprising to see the soul referred to in comparative statements as a way of dramatizing the even more exalted status that ought to be accorded God himself—

for example, vv. 106b ("Love God even more than your own soul"), 129, 292, and 403. A similar sort of comparison is drawn here, though it is not between the soul and God, but between the soul and a word about God. For the idea that one should be "sparing" with a word, cf. Dionysius of Halicarnassus, *Ant. rom.* 10.5.1; Plutarch, *Cons. Apoll.* 114c.

The source for v. 362 is *Sent. Pythag.* 115: ψυχὴν νόμιζε αἱρετώτερον εἶναι προέσθαι ἢ λόγον βλάσφημον περὶ θεοῦ. The version of the saying preserved in *Marc.* 15 (νόμιζε αἱρετώτερον εἶναι σιγᾶν ἢ λόγον εἰκῆ προέσθαι περὶ θεοῦ) occurs after the maxim that corresponds with v. 360 (see above), with one saying intervening. Porphyry agrees with *Sent. Pythag.* 115 against Sextus in retaining the νόμιζε ... εἶναι construction, though he stands alone in dropping ψυχήν and adding σιγᾶν (again, see above on v. 360). In what is a fairly rare occurrence (see above on v. 352), Porphyry agrees with Sextus against their Pythagorean source in replacing βλάσφημον after λόγον with εἰκῆ. It is possible that in making this editorial decision the two authors were influenced by a saying with a very similar construction that occurs elsewhere in their source, namely *Sent. Pythag.* 7 (αἱρετώτερόν σοι ἔστω λίθον εἰκῆ βάλλειν ἢ λόγον ἀργόν), a version of which occurs in both Sext. 152 (αἱρετώτερον λίθον εἰκῆ βάλλειν ἢ λόγον) and Porphyry, *Marc.* 14 (αἱρετωτέρου σοι ὄντος λίθον εἰκῆ βαλεῖν ἢ λόγον); cf. also Clitarchus, *Sent.* 28. For the use of προίημι in constructions meaning to "let slip" or "let drop" a word, see Homer, *Od.* 14.466; 20.105; 2 Macc 10:34; Clement, *Paed.* 2.5.45.1; Plutarch, *Alex.* 49.2; Lucian, *Pod.* 81.

Sentences 363a–364

This three-line digression is loosely linked to the surrounding material both by the use of λόγος in v. 363a (cf. vv. 361–362, 365–366), though the meaning of the term is different, and, more remotely, by the use of θεοφιλής in the same verse (cf. vv. 358–359). Internally, the first line is connected to the second by the repetition of σῶμα + ἄρχω, while the second is connected to the third by the repetition of τύραννος. Its sequence of thought confronts the audience with an interesting rhetorical progression: the first saying addresses the reader directly as someone who might have control over the body of a faithful person; the second then identifies this "someone" as a tyrant; the third, in conclusion, returns to directly addressing the reader, though not as a tyrant but as someone threatened by a tyrant.

With regard to the section's overall message, it may not be too much of an exaggeration to say that what is presented here by Sextus in gnomic form is presented by the author of 4 Maccabees in narrative form. We learn that Eleazar, for example, when "buffeted by the threats of the tyrant (ταῖς τοῦ τυράννου ἀπειλαῖς)," did not give up the fight for religion (4 Macc 7:1–3), but even when "he fell to the ground because his body (σῶμα) could not endure the agonies, he kept his reason (λογισμόν) upright and unswerving" (4 Macc 6:7), raising his eyes to heaven and praying to God (4 Macc 6:6, 26–29). Later, the martyrs mock the tyrant: "If you take our lives because of our religion, do not suppose that you can injure us by torturing us; for we, through this severe suffering and endurance, shall have the prize of virtue and shall be with God, on whose account we suffer" (4 Macc 9:7–8). Holding fast to reason (4 Macc 9:17; 11:27; 13:3; 15:1; etc.), they use their "bodies as a bulwark for the law" (4 Macc 13:13), nobly fulfilling their service to God (4 Macc 12:14) through a supreme demonstration of piety (4 Macc 13:10).

In these portrayals, as elsewhere, 4 Maccabees betrays the influence of Stoicism, where the victory of the sage's reason over the tyrant's threats was a stock theme, as we see, for example, in Epictetus, *Diatr.* 1.19 (entitled, Πῶς ἔχειν δεῖ πρὸς τοὺς τυράννους;). As he explains in *Diatr.* 1.29.1–7, for the sage, the essence of the good, and the only thing that matters for his own virtue, is to be found solely in the correct execution of his own moral volition as a rational being. As for everything else, "when the tyrant threatens (ἀπειλῇ ὁ τύραννος) and summons me, I answer, 'Whom are you threatening?' If he says, 'I will put you in chains,' I reply 'He is threatening my hands and my feet.' ... If he says, 'I will throw you into prison,' I say, 'He is threatening my whole paltry body.' ... Does he, then, threaten *you* at all? If I feel that all of this is nothing to me, then not at all." Thus when tyrants "think that they have some power over us because of the paltry body and its possessions," the readers must "show them that they have power over no one" and heed the call to "wait upon God" instead (*Diatr.* 1.9.15–17; cf. 1.18.17; 1.19.8–9; 4.5.33–34; 4.7.1–5). The antityrant *topos* is evidenced in other philosophical traditions as well. Philostratus's presentation of Apollonius as a Pythagorean sage, for instance, includes a sustained narration of his contest with the tyrannical Domitian (*Vita Apollonii* books 7–8), who is at one point likened to a lion (*Vit. Apoll.* 7.30.2–3; for the comparison, see also Prov 19:12; 20:2; 28:15; Dio Chrysostom, *Or.* 6.59; Aelian, *Var. hist.* 1.29). During the trial, he challenges the emperor: "Send someone to seize my body, because you cannot seize my soul, or rather, you can never even seize my body; you will not kill me, since I am not mortal" (*Vit. Apoll.* 8.5.3; cf. 7.34.1). For Pythagoras's own manner of dealing with tyrants, see Iamblichus, *Vit. Pythag.* 32.214–221 (cf. 31.189–194).

Clement, meanwhile, prefaces a discussion of Christian martyrdom with references to pagan philosophers who boldly defied tyrants, including the Pythagoreans Theodotus and Zamolxis (*Strom.* 4.8.56.1–4.8.58.1). Of his coreligionists he writes, "though threatened (ἀπειλῆται) by death at a tyrant's hands, and brought before the tribunals, and all their substances imperiled, they will by no means abandon piety" (*Strom.* 4.8.67.2). In the *Sentences*, the tyrant who would go so far as to kill a sage would actually confer on him a benefit, since this releases the sage from the "chains" of his body (v. 322), leaving the freedom of his moral reason intact (vv. 275, 309). After all, "a tyrant cannot take away happiness" (v. 387) and "the heart of one who is dear to God (θεοφιλής) is secure in God's hand" (v. 419). For the sort of divine "remembering" encouraged in v. 364, see also vv. 59, 82c, 182, 221, and 222 (all also with μέμνησο).

Sentences 365–366

After a brief digression (vv. 363a–364), the theme of esotericism resumes from vv. 350–62, with emphasis falling on the negative implications attending failure to observe proper caution in theological discourse. Those who speak about God to the unworthy are traitors (v. 365), while those who speak about God falsely are slanderers (v. 367) and God-forsaken (v. 368). It is better to say nothing at all than to engage in such recklessness (v. 366).

In early Christian circles, προδότης is used of Judas (e.g., Luke 6:16; Clement, *Paed.* 2.8.62.3), as well as of those who betray the faith, either by sinful conduct (e.g., Origen, *Comm. Joan.* 1.11.71) or by actual apostasy (e.g., Origen, *Comm. Joan.* 28.23.195). Herm. *Sim.* 8.6.4 groups betrayers together with apostates as those who are "ashamed of the Lord's name by which they were called," while *Sim.* 9.19.1–3 identifies as the sins for which there is no repentance apostasy, blasphemy, and "betrayal of God's servants." In a passage that sheds some light on the connection between v. 365 and v. 366, in *Const. ap.* 3.5, the term is used of those who violate *disciplina arcani* in a "reckless" fashion:

> But of the rest let (the widow) not answer anything recklessly (προπετῶς), lest by speaking unlearnedly she should cause the word to be blasphemed.... For in the mystical points one must not be a traitor (προδότην), but cautious; for the Lord exhorts us, saying: "Cast not your pearls before swine, lest they trample them with their feet, and turn again and maul you." For unbelievers, when they hear the doctrine concerning Christ not explained as it ought to be, but defectively, and especially that con-

cerning his incarnation and his passion, will rather reject it with scorn, and laugh at it as false, than praise God for it. And so the aged woman will be guilty of recklessness (προπετείας), and of causing blasphemy, and will inherit woe.

Some sort of relationship between traitorous and reckless behavior is implied also by the vice list in 2 Tim 3:3–4 (... ἀφιλάγαθοι, προδόται, προπετεῖς, τετυφωμένοι ...). The reference to those who have no "right" to hear, meanwhile, is redolent of the mystery cults; see Euripides, *Bacc.* 474; Diodorus Siculus, *Bibl. hist.* 5.48.4; Lucian, *Alex.* 43; Clement, *Strom.* 4.25.162.4.

When the subject matter is a word about God (note the use of λόγον + περὶ θεοῦ in both v. 365 and v. 366), then, silence is preferable to carelessness. After all, one should only speak when it is not appropriate to keep silent (v. 161). The formulation in v. 366 is familiar from the saying in *Marc.* 15 that parallels v. 360 (σιγάσθω ὁ περὶ αὐτοῦ λόγος ἐπὶ πλήθους) and especially the saying in *Marc.* 15 that parallels v. 362: "Consider silence to be preferable to proffering a word about God without purpose" (νόμιζε αἱρετώτερον εἶναι σιγᾶν ἢ λόγον εἰκῆ προέσθαι περὶ θεοῦ). Given Porphyry's extended reliance on Pythagorean traditions in composing his letter, it is probable that this emphasis reflects that school's teachings on the practice of silence, for which see the commentary on v. 427. Cf. Didymus Caecus, *Frag. Ps.* 1229: "Speaking is not as beneficial as keeping silent in all situations; for to the one who is able to open his mouth with a word of God it is not appropriate to keep silent, but to the one who utters idle speech and words condemning the good there should be silence." For other "better" sayings in the collection, see vv. 13, 165a, 283, 336, 345, 362, and 377.

Sentences 367–368

The members of this couplet are joined by the repetition of λέγω + περὶ θεοῦ, as well as by the antithetical juxtaposition of ψευδῆ (v. 367) and ἀληθές (v. 368). If false words attest to evil intentions (v. 165c, cf. vv. 159, 393), then the one who speaks false words about God harbors evil intentions against God, much like the one who blasphemes against God (vv. 82e–85). The gist of v. 367 is conveyed by the wordplay between ψευδῆ and καταψεύδεται. In translating the latter, the force of the κατα- prefix ought to be taken seriously: "tell lies (against) τινός, in contradiction or in opposition to someone" (BDAG s.v). For parallels to the usage here, see Philo,

Mos. 1.90; *Spec.* 4.52; Josephus, *Ant.* 10.178; *Bell.* 6.288; Dio Chrysostom, *Or.* 6.17; *Ep. Diogn.* 4.3; Ps.-Clement, *Hom.* 5.22; 6.1.

To be against God is to be without God. Chadwick (1959, 156, 178) suggests that v. 368 is an adaptation of the first sentence of *Sent. Pythag.* 50 (cf. Porphyry, *Marc.* 31): "Vain is the word of that philosopher by which no human passion is healed" (κενὸς ἐκείνου φιλοσόφου λόγος ὑφ' οὗ μηδὲν ἀνθρώπου πάθος θεραπεύεται). Note, however, that verbally the two sayings have only the words ἄνθρωπος and μηδέν in common, that in v. 368 the speech in question is about God and truthtelling, not about human beings and their πάθος (for which see vv. 204–209), and that in v. 368 the judgment rendered on such speech is not that it is vain, but that it leaves one ἔρημος θεοῦ.

This last item was an expression capable of various applications in early Christian discourse. The author of *2 Clement*, for instance, interprets the "desolate" one of Isa 54:1 (cf. Gal 4:27) as a reference to the Gentiles, "who seemed to be bereft of God, but now that we have believed, have become more numerous than those who seemed to have God" (*2 Clem.* 2.3; cf. Origen, *Hom. Jer.* 9.3), while Justin Martyr describes the Gentiles as those bereft not of God himself but of the knowledge of God (*Dial.* 69.4–6). In Origen, *Cels.* 6.43, meanwhile, the expression is used of individuals who, having fallen under the power of Satan, "are opposed to the people of God's inheritance" (cf. Deut 32:9), most likely a reference to persecutors. In the usage that most closely approximates the one here, Clement applies ἔρημος θεοῦ to those who espouse heretical doctrines (*Strom.* 1.19.95.7). Having abandoned the God who truly exists, it is as though they were trekking "through a waterless desert" (δι' ἐρημίας ἀνύδρου), an allusion to Prov 9:12. Among non-Christian texts, mention may be made of Plotinus, *Enn.* 5.5.11, according to which what leaves one bereft of God is not heresy but the (erroneous) assumption that all things are perceived by the senses (cf. Plato, *Leg.* 908c).

Sentences 369–376b

Text

369 θεὸν οὐκ ἔστιν γινώσκειν μὴ σεβόμενον[a].
370 οὐκ ἔστιν ὅπως ἀδικῶν τις ἄνθρωπον σέβοι τὸν θεόν.
371 κρηπὶς[a] θεοσεβείας φιλανθρωπία.

372 ὁ προνοῶν ἀνθρώπων εὐχόμενός τε ὑπὲρ πάντων οὗτος ἀληθείᾳ θεοῦ νομιζέσθω[a].
373 θεοῦ μὲν ἴδιον τὸ σῴζειν οὓς ἄν[a] προαιρῆται.
374 εὐσεβοῦς δὲ τὸ[a] εὔχεσθαι θεῷ σῴζειν.
375 ὁπόταν εὐξαμένῳ σοι γένηται ὑπὸ τοῦ[a] θεοῦ, τότε ἐξουσίαν ἔχειν ἡγοῦ παρὰ θεῷ.
376a ἄξιος ἄνθρωπος θεοῦ[a] θεὸς ἐν ἀνθρώποις.
376b θεὸς καὶ υἱὸς θεοῦ τὸ μὲν ἄριστον, τὸ δὲ ἐγγυτάτω[a] τοῦ ἀρίστου.

Translation

369 It is not possible to know God without revering God.
370 It is not possible that someone could revere God while wronging a human being.
371 The foundation of reverence for God is love for humanity.
372 Let the one who takes thought for all human beings and prays for them be considered truly of God.
373 It is a prerogative of God to save those whom he would choose.
374 But it is a prerogative of a pious person to pray to God to save.
375 Whenever there is an answer to your prayer by God, then consider that you have power before God.
376a A human being worthy of God is a god among human beings.
376b God is the best, and God's son is nearest to the best.

Textual Notes

369[a] σεβόμενος: Π • 370 omit Π • 371[a] ἀρχὴ: co; κρηπὶς καὶ ἀρχὴ: lat • 372[a] omit co • 373[a] ἐάν: Π • 374[a] omit Υ • 375[a] omit Υ • 376a[a] omit Π • 376b[a] ἐγγύτατον: Π

Commentary

The maxims in this block are joined by the themes of piety and godliness. Note σέβομαι in vv. 369–370, θεοσέβεια in v. 371, and εὐσεβής in v. 374. Observations are made regarding acts of godliness, especially prayer (note εὔχομαι in vv. 372, 374–375), the godly person (vv. 376a-b), and godliness itself (vv. 369–371). Appropriately enough, consideration for this theme presents an opportunity to discuss salvation as well (vv. 373–374, both with σῴζω).

Sentence 369

The three sayings in the opening cluster (vv. 369–371) are bound together by the use of similar terminology, σέβομαι + θεόν in the first two lines, θεοσέβεια in the third. The first two are also alike in employing an οὐκ ἔστιν construction.

According to *Sent. Pythag.* 92[a], the one "who reveres God is known by God." According to Sextus, the one who reveres God knows God. In the *Sentences*, the reverence that ought to be shown to God is an expression of the reverence that ought to be shown to that aspect of the human personality in which the divine is to be found, namely, the intellect (vv. 61, 144, 450). As God's temple (v. 46a), the intellect is not only the medium through which one venerates God but, as something divine and holy itself, is worthy of veneration as well—hence the summons to "revere that which is within you" (v. 448). The cultivation of intellectual capacities implied by such a summons can be appropriately understood as a form of piety, then, insofar as it represents the means by which one comes to "know who God is" (v. 394, also with γινώσκω). Accordingly, the person of the sage represents a focal point for the expression of such piety, not only because he is exemplary in his reverence for God (v. 287) but also because he himself ought to be revered as "a living image of God" (v. 190, cf. v. 319) on account of his superior intellect (vv. 143, 450). In this he is similar to Clement's gnostic, who alone is truly pious, because he alone is truly possessed of divine wisdom (*Strom.* 7.7.47.5). In such a scheme, wisdom and reverence are seen to function as mutually implicating concepts. Indeed, "reverence is the beginning of wisdom" (*Strom.* 2.18.84.1; cf. Prov 9:10), while a love for wisdom leads one to revere God (*Strom.* 1.4.27.3; cf. Josephus, *C. Ap.* 2.140; Origen, *Phil.* 13.3).

Sentence 370

Such wisdom, however, precisely because it has God as its object, concerns itself not only with the good of the mind but with the good of humanity as well. To revere God means not only to know God but through such knowledge to imitate God (v. 44), and it is impossible to imitate God without acting in accord with the principles of justice (v. 399; cf. vv. 64–65). Conversely, since only those who are just can know and speak the truth about God (v. 410, cf. v. 582), injustice can be construed as a kind of spiritual death (v. 208b), a practice predicated on a love of self, rather than a love of God (v. 138). Indeed, for Sextus the greatest impiety that one can commit against God is the mistreatment of another human being (v. 96), while the best way to become "pure"—that is, godlike—is to abstain from ἀδικία (v. 23).

In identifying the renunciation of injustice as a precondition and expression of piety, Sextus taps into a deep vein of ancient spirituality. Compare, for example, Sir 35:3: "To keep from wickedness is pleasing to the Lord, and to refrain from wrongdoing (ἀπὸ ἀδικίας) an atonement." Moralists often pair injustice and impiety together (e.g., Plato, *Protag.* 324a; Philo, *Conf.* 152; Josephus, *Bell.* 7.260; Rom 1:18; Justin Martyr, *1 Apol.* 4.7; *Dial.* 46.5; Ps.-Apollonius, *Ep.* 58.6; Marcus Aurelius, *Med.* 9.1.1; Diogenes Laertius, *Vit. phil.* 6.17), the implication being that those guilty of the former are also guilty of the latter. As the author of Ps.-Clement, *Rec.* 5.23 puts it, "to injure others is a great impiety toward God." For the formulation here, see especially Clitarchus, *Sent.* 6: "Pious (εὐσεβής) is not the one who offers many sacrifices but the one who does no wrong (ὁ μηδὲν ἀδικῶν)." This accords with the teaching of Pythagoras, who insisted that those approaching the altar for sacrifice be "pure of every wrongful deed" (Diodorus Siculus, *Bibl. hist.* 10.9.6). Cf. also Minucius Felix, *Oct.* 32 ("He who cultivates justice makes offerings to God; he who abstains from fraudulent practices propitiates God ... among us he who is most just is he who is most religious"); *Corp. herm.* 12.23: "The only worship of God is not to be evil" (θρησκεία δὲ τοῦ θεοῦ μία ἐστί, μὴ εἶναι κακόν).

Sentence 371

According to v. 86a, the foundation of piety is ἐγκράτεια. According to this saying, the foundation of piety is φιλανθρωπία, v. 371 forming a positive counterpart to v. 370, much like v. 47 ("The only offering suitable for God is beneficence to humanity for God's sake") can be interpreted as a positive counterpart to v. 23 ("Realize that the best purification is to wrong no one"). If the greatest form of impiety is the mistreatment of fellow human beings (v. 96), then it stands to reason that the greatest form of piety is the love of fellow human beings. While our author's source for v. 86a was Clitarchus, *Sent.* 13, here he relies on *Sent. Pythag.* 51: κρηπὶς εὐσεβείας ἡ φιλανθρωπία σοι νομιζέσθω. Cf. Porphyry, *Marc.* 35: κρηπὶς εὐσεβείας σοι νομιζέσθω ἡ φιλανθρωπία. Sextus renders the saying in a more compressed, less personalized form, replacing εὐσεβείας (for which see v. 374) with the near synonym θεοσεβείας (cf. on v. 287). Regardless of the particular terminology, all three variants of the gnome reflect the common procedure in antiquity of abstracting moral obligation in terms of two primary virtues, the first (usually εὐσέβεια or ὁσιότης) encompassing obligations owed to one's superiors, especially the gods, parents, and the dead, the second (usually δικαιοσύνη or φιλανθρωπία) encompassing obligations owed to one's peers, especially friends, neighbors, and fellow citizens. Philo, for instance, speaks of the two together as "queens" of the virtues (*Virt.* 95), the two "main heads" of human responsibility (*Spec.* 2.63), and summaries of the two tables of the Decalogue (*Her.* 168). Virtue in its full sense, he thinks, necessarily attends to both (*Decal.* 110), and so the two are mutually implicating: "The nature that is pious is also humane, and the same person will exhibit both qualities, holiness towards God and justice towards others" (*Abr.* 208; cf. Demosthenes, *Or.* 21.12; Polybius, *Hist.* 4.20.1; Diodorus Siculus, *Bibl. hist.* 3.56.2; 21.17.4; Pausanius, *Graec. descr.* 1.17.1). Just as the body requires food to survive, the soul requires a way of life that is θεοσεβής in nature (v. 412), through which it becomes both blessed (v. 326b) and godlike (v. 82d). For φιλανθρωπία, see also on v. 300.

Sentence 372

The next line provides an illustration of how the principle just articulated can be put into practice. If reverence for God is predicated upon love for humanity, then it is fitting that the latter be communicated through acts of piety. The readers should pray to God for what is truly "good" (v. 277), not only for themselves, or for those in need (cf. vv. 217, 378) but even for their enemies (v. 213) and, as we learn here, for all people, a Christian obligation extending back at least as far as 1 Tim 2:1: "I urge that supplications, prayers (προσευχάς), intercessions, and thanksgivings be made for all human beings (ὑπὲρ πάντων ἀνθρώπων)." Evagrius Ponticus, meanwhile, contends that it is just to pray "for the sake of all one's kinfolk (περὶ παντὸς ὁμοφύλου)," mediating salvation to others in imitation of the angels (*Orat.* 40). See further Pol. *Phil.* 12.3; Athenagoras, *Suppl.* 37; Clement, *Strom.* 6.9.77.4–5 (quoted below); Origen, *Cels.* 8.73; *Orat.* 14.2. According to Asterius, the person who prays on behalf of his neighbors is φιλάνθρωπος καὶ φιλάλληλος (*Comm. Ps.* 4.13). In "taking thought" for others, the readers demonstrate their solidarity with them (cf. v. 423), expressions of πρόνοια and φιλανθρωπία being especially apropos when dealing with individuals who have experienced some sort of misfortune (Josephus, *C. Ap.* 1.283).

Sentences 373–374

Encouragement to pray for all people (including of course all unbelievers) engenders reflection on the dynamics of prayer and salvation (vv.

373–375). The first saying in this couplet makes reference to the role of προαίρεσις in this regard, a concept utilized also by Clement, though usually with reference to the "choice" that human beings themselves make to be saved (e.g., *Protr.* 10.105.1; 11.117.2; *Paed.* 1.6.33.3; cf. *SVF* 1:216; 3.173; Epictetus, *Diatr.* 1.29.1–3; 2.16.1; etc.). Nevertheless, although

> the person who is being saved will not be saved without his will ... hastening to salvation willingly and inclined to choose (προαιρετικῶς) ... God does not do good out of necessity, but according to his own choice (κατὰ προαίρεσιν) he befriends those who turn to him of their own accord. For the providence that comes to us from God is not ministrative, as though it proceeded from inferiors to superiors; rather it is from pity for our weakness that the nearer dispensations of providence are set in motion. (*Strom.* 7.7.42.4–7; for the mutuality of choice, cf. Deut 26:17–18; Philo, *Virt.* 184–185)

In *Princ.* 3.1.18, Origen reports as a position based on Rom 9:16 the idea that "salvation does not come from what lies in our power ... but from the choice (ἐκ προαιρέσεως) of him who has mercy when he pleases" (cf. *Frag. 1 Cor.* 39). Such a position could also be justified by appeal to Deut 7:6–7, where we learn that it is God who "chooses" who his people will be (cf. Origen, *Hom. Jer. II* 3.6). In the *Sentences*, the soul is imaged as a "deposit" that belongs not to the one in whom it resides, but to the one from whom it originates (v. 21). Accordingly, its fate is ultimately determined by divine judgment (vv. 14, 347) and divine grace (vv. 436a–b). Cf. v. 565: "By God's judgment all things are saved; by God's power all things are possible."

Verse 374 continues and completes the thought, being connected to v. 373 by a μέν ... δέ ... construction. Prayers for salvation are strewn throughout scripture (e.g., 1 Kgdms 7:8; 4 Kgdms 19:19; Ps 116:4 [114:4]; Joel 3:5; Bar 2:14; Rom 10:1, 13; Acts 2:21; Heb 5:7; Jas 5:15; cf. Cassius Dio, *Hist. rom.* 62.6.4; Plutarch, *Them.* 13.2; *Thes.* 8.2; *Comm. not.* 1075d). In the *Sentences*, the offering of such prayers is understood as a particular responsibility of the pious person (cf. vv. 46a, 87), while salvation itself would no doubt be among the "advantageous" (v. 88), "worthy" (v. 122), and "good" (vv. 213, 277) things for which one should pray. Both the scope (see above on v. 372, and cf. the Coptic version of v. 374: "It is the business of the pious man to beseech God to save everyone") and the intent informing the prayer of Clement's gnostic are comparable: "He will pray that as many as possible may become like him, to the glory of God, which is perfected through knowledge. For he who is made like the savior is also devoted to saving" (*Strom.* 6.9.77.4–5).

Sentence 375

As we have seen, when describing the nature of divine ἐξουσία in v. 36 ("To one who is faithful God gives power that accords with God; what he gives, then, is pure and sinless") and v. 60 ("A man holy and sinless has power in the eyes of God as God's son"), Sextus seems intent on drawing its moral dimensions into relief. In presenting the concept here, he focuses on its character as a dimension of piety, prayer functioning as the medium through which divine authority is bestowed upon humankind. In his treatise on prayer, Origen takes it for granted that Christians pray in order to receive spiritual power from God (e.g., *Orat.* 25.3). At one point he encourages his readers to follow the example of Jonah and pray to "have power by the goodness of the Spirit" so that they might preach repentance to unbelievers and become an instrument of their salvation (*Orat.* 13.4; cf. above on v. 372). Much like Sextus's sage (vv. 143–144, 416–418, etc.), the mind of Clement's gnostic is so fully conformed to the will of God that "he no sooner prays than he receives, being brought close to the almighty power and, by his earnest striving after spirituality, united to the Spirit through the love that knows no bounds" (*Strom.* 7.7.44.5). Clement elsewhere highlights the ability of pious prayers to disarm the power of evil in both its human and demonic forms (*Quis div.* 34.3; cf. Evagrius Ponticus, *Orat.* 50, 63, 94). For an example of a non-Christian praying for divine ἐξουσία, see Polybius, *Hist.* 5.104.11. In the *Sentences*, divine power principally takes the form of divine reason, the possession of which enables human beings not only to know the "good things" for which they should pray, but to acquire them as well (v. 277).

Sentences 376a–b

Talk about receiving divine power leads to talk about the one who receives such power, the latter referred to in v. 60 both as "a man holy and sinless" and as "a son of God" (cf. v. 36). Such a person not only prays for what is worthy of God (v. 122); he is himself worthy of God, because he does nothing unworthy of God (v. 4). Cf. Porphyry, *Marc.* 15: "Neither to speak nor to do nor to ask to know anything at all unworthy of God will make you worthy of God. And the human being worthy of God would be a god" (ὁ δὲ ἄξιος ἄνθρωπος θεοῦ θεὸς ἂν εἴη). The source for both v. 376a and Porphyry's second gnome is *Sent. Pythag.* 4: ἄξιος ἄνθρωπος θεοῦ θεὸς ἂν εἴη ἐν ἀνθρώποις (which is cited as a saying of Pythagoras by Stobaeus; see Wachsmuth and Hense 1884–1912, 5.vii). While Porphyry drops ἐν ἀνθρώποις from his version of the saying, Sextus drops ἂν εἴη. The "worthy" person here, of course, is the sage, whose intellect is so fully occupied and directed by the divine that in his comportment he actually "presents" (v. 307) and "images" (v. 190) God to others (cf. vv. 7a, 82d). As Clement explains, all those worthy of being called faithful are "noble and godlike" (*Quis div.* 36.1). This is because the one who obeys God "is fully perfected after the likeness of his teacher, and thus becomes a god while still moving about in the flesh" (*Strom.* 7.16.101.4).

The one who is worthy of God is worthy to be called God's son, because he always comports himself as such (v. 58; cf. the Coptic version of v. 376a: "[A man who] is worthy of God, [he] is God among [men], and [he is] the son of God"). Sons are naturally "close" (ἐγγύς) to their fathers (e.g., Eusebius, *Dem. evang.* 4.6.3). However, as Clement explains, because the heavenly father is so distant, "hard to catch and hard to hunt down," he only draws "close" to those who have ascended to him by following the path of wisdom (*Strom.* 2.2.5.3–4). Compare Origen, *Cels.* 4.96: "Only those who are truly wise and genuinely pious are closer (ἐγγυτέρω) to communion with God." According to Pythagorean traditions, meanwhile, the way of life that is ἐγγυτάτω θεοῦ is the one governed by αὐτάρκεια (Ps.-Pythagoras, *Ep.* 2.185.23–25; cf. Sext. 98, 263, 334). See further Ps.-Crates, *Ep.* 11; Diogenes Laertius, *Vit. phil.* 2.27; Philo, *Migr.* 57: God "himself will draw near (ἐγγυτέρω) those worthy (τῶν ἀξίων) to receive his benefits." For more on the language of divine filiation in the *Sentences*, see the commentary on vv. 58–60, 135, and 221–222.

Sentences 377–382

Text

377 ἀκτήμονα κρεῖττον ἢ ἀκοινώνητον εἶναι πολυκτήμονα.
378 μὴ διδοὺς δεομένοις δυνατὸς ὢν οὐ[a] λήψῃ δεόμενος παρὰ θεοῦ[b].
379 τροφῆς δεομένῳ μεταδιδόντος [a]ἐξ ὅλης[a] ψυχῆς[b] δόμα μέν τι βραχύ, προθυμία δὲ μεγάλη [c]παρὰ θεῷ[c].
380 θεὸν οὐ [a]νομίζοντος ὁ νομίζων[a] καὶ [b]οὐδὲν εἶναι πρὸς αὐτὸν ἡγούμενος[b] οὐχ [c]ἧττον ἄθεος[c].
381 τιμᾷ θεὸν ἄριστα ὁ τὴν ἑαυτοῦ διάνοιαν ἐξομοιώσας θεῷ εἰς δύναμιν.

382 θεὸς δεῖται μὲν οὐδαμῇᵃ οὐδενόςᵇ, χαίρει δὲ τοῖς μεταδιδοῦσι τοῖς δεομένοις.

Translation

377 It is better to possess nothing than to possess much without sharing it.
378 If you do not give to those in need when you are able, you will not receive from God when you are in need.
379 A gift from one who with his whole heart shares food with a person in need is small, but before God his willingness to share is great.
380 The one who acknowledges God while thinking that nothing matters to God is no less godless than one who does not acknowledge God at all.
381 The one who conforms his intellect to God as much as possible honors God best.
382 God needs nothing in any way, but rejoices in those who share with those in need.

Textual Notes

378ᵃ οὐ μὴ: Υ • 378ᵇ θεῷ: Υ • 379ᵃ⁻ᵃ omit Π • 379ᵇ ψυχή: Π • 379ᶜ⁻ᶜ omit lat • 380ᵃ⁻ᵃ νομιζόντως ὀνομάζων: Π • 380ᵇ⁻ᵇ μηδὲν ἡγούμενος εἶναι πρὸς αὐτόν: Υ • 380ᶜ⁻ᶜ ἧττον ἢ ἄθεος: Υ; ἥττονα θεός: Π • 382ᵃ omit co, sy² • 382ᵇ omit lat

Commentary

The basic framework for this section is provided by *Sent. Pythag.* 70, with v. 378 being based on *Sent. Pythag.* 70ᵇ and v. 382 on *Sent. Pythag.* 70ᶜ⁻ᵈ. Sextus prefaces the former with an additional saying on sharing (v. 377) and then inserts between the two elements a triad of sayings that together provide theological warrant for the expected comportment (vv. 379–381). Note the use of δέομαι in vv. 378–379, 382.

Sentence 377

The desire for worldly goods not only engenders vice (v. 137); it inhibits one from remaining pure (v. 81) and following right reason (v. 264a). The sage therefore relinquishes himself of all material possessions beyond what his body requires (vv. 81, 115, 227, 264a), especially by sharing them (vv. 82b, 266, 330, 379, 382), following God's example (vv. 33, 47, 176, 210a, 260), convinced that leaving something "unshared" (ἀκοινώνητος) represents not only a failure to do what is good (v. 296) but an act of impiety against God (v. 228). For the wordplay here, comparison can be made with a saying of Evagrius Ponticus: "The monk who possesses much (πολυκτήμων) delights in many profits, the one who possesses nothing (ἀκτήμων) in crowns of upright deeds" (*Oct. spirit. malit.* 79.1153; cf. Ephraem Syrus, *Corr. vit. viv.* 283; *Hom. meretr.* 88). Sextus coins similar "better" sayings in v. 336 ("It is better to serve others than to be served by others") and v. 345 ("It is better to die of hunger than to impair the soul through overindulgence of the belly"). It is indeed "better" to be ἀκτήμων, since in this one becomes like God (v. 18, cf. vv. 49–50).

Sentence 378

Cf. Menander, *Mon.* 198: "Give to the poor so that you will find God giving to you." Those who receive freely from God should give freely as well (v. 242), acting as brokers in a divine regime of benefaction (vv. 33, 176, 210a, 260). A similar principle of serial reciprocity (also expressed negatively) informs the logic behind v. 217: "God does not listen to the prayer of one who does not listen to people in need." Here we have the first of three references in the section to οἱ δεόμενοι (cf. vv. 379, 382), the source in this case being *Sent. Pythag.* 70[b]: "For the one who does not share with good people in need will not receive from the gods when he is in need" (ὁ γὰρ μὴ μεταδιδοὺς ἀγαθοῖς δεομένοις οὐ λήψεται δεόμενος παρὰ θεῶν. Cf. v. 70[a]: ξένοις μεταδίδου καὶ σοφοῖς ἀνδράσι κἀγαθοῖς. For v. 70[c-d], see below on v. 382). Sextus switches from third person to second person, changes μεταδιδούς to διδούς (perhaps for the sake of alliteration; cf. vv. 379, 382), and replaces παρὰ θεῶν with παρὰ θεοῦ. More important is the deletion of ἀγαθοῖς and the addition of δυνατὸς ὤν (cf. v. 78). In the Sextine economy of giving, no moral assessment is made of the recipient, his or her worthiness being determined by need alone (cf. on v. 382). On the other hand, a means assessment must be made of the donor, who is expected to give (only) when he or she is able. For similar provisos, see Prov 3:27 ("Do not abstain from doing good to the needy, whenever your hand can help"); Sir 14:13; *Syr. Men.* 229–239; Ps.-Phoc. 28–29 ("When you have wealth, extend your hand to the poor. From what God has given you provide for those in need"); Septem Sapientes, *Praec.* 217.18–19 (ἔχων χαρίζου); Menander, *Mon.* 478 ("Remember when you are rich to aid the poor"). Note that none of these parallels stipulates the amount to be given or the frequency with which the giving occurs, sharing with the needy being viewed instead as a general obligation of those with the capacity to do so. The thematic connection of v. 377 to v. 378 is made explicit by the Coptic translator: "It is better for man to be without anything than to have many things while not giving to the needy; so also you, if you pray to God, he will not give to you" (for the reference to prayer here, see v. 217).

Sentence 379

This perspective continues in v. 379, which not only serves as a positive counterpart to v. 378 but also expands the discussion by adding the principle of προθυμία, or willingness (for which see on v. 330), by specifying food as one of the things that should be shared with the needy (cf. vv. 266–267) and by motivating the prescribed behavior with the promise that it makes one "great" before God (cf. vv. 51–52). Tobit 4:6–9 is a particularly instructive parallel for vv. 378–379 insofar as its instruction on giving to the poor also combines the criteria of ability, willingness, serial reciprocity, and divine acknowledgement: "To all those who practice righteousness give alms from your possessions, and do not let your eye begrudge the gift when you make it. Do not turn your face away from anyone who is poor, and the face of God will not be turned away from you. If you have many possessions, make your gift from them in proportion; if few, do not be afraid to give according to the little you have. So you will be laying up a good treasure for yourself against the day of necessity." The idea that one accumulates heavenly "riches" by giving to the poor figures in a number of dominical sayings as well, for example, Matt 6:19–21; 19:21; Mark 10:21; Luke 12:33; 18:22 (cf. Luke 14:13–14; 19:8–9). See also P.Ins. 16.10–13: "Giving food without dislike removes all dislike. The god gives a thousand for one to him who gives it to another. The god lets one acquire wealth on account of doing the good deed of mercy. He who gives food to him who is poor, the god credits it to him for an offering of millions." Cf. Prov 28:27 ("Whoever gives to the poor will lack nothing, but one who turns a blind eye will get many a curse"); Sir 12:3 ("No good comes to one who persists in evil or to one who does not give alms"). For the expression ἐξ ὅλης ψυχῆς, see Epictetus, *Diatr.* 2.23.42; 3.22.18; 4.1.131; cf. Deut 6:5; Matt 22:37; Mark 12:30; Luke 10:27.

Sentences 380–381

Although both of the sayings in this antithetical couplet relate to broader theological positions developed elsewhere in the text (see below), in their current position they can be interpreted as supplying motivation for the surrounding material on sharing. To think that God is unconcerned with anything, including the basic needs of human beings and the responsibility that believers have to meet them, is the mark of a godless person, while his counterpart, the godly person, not only follows God's example by trying to meet such needs but also conforms himself to God by reducing his own needs as much as possible. As v. 312 indicates, the existence of God's providential regard for the world is something that only a person committed to evil would deny (cf. v. 25). The readers of the *Sentences*, on the other hand, affirm that God's involvement in the course of human affairs comes to expression in various ways, for example, through benefaction (vv. 33, 176), through judgment (vv. 14, 63, 347), and, above all, through the actions of the sage, who is infused with and guided by divine power (vv. 421–424, etc.). For Sextus's critique of those who deny providence, see the commentary on vv. 312–313. For the construction ἡγούμενος οὐχ ἧττον, see Dio Chrysostom, *Or.* 8.35. There is a fair amount of textual instability in this verse (see above), which may account for the divergent Coptic translation: "He who thinks that no one is in the presence of God, he is not humble towards God."

The second line in the couplet can be read as a summation of the argument in vv. 41–46a. Note in particular the use of τιμάω in vv. 41, 42, of τιμή and ὁμοίωμα in v. 44, of ἐξομοιόω and εἰς δύναμιν in v. 45, and of διάνοια in v. 46a (see further the commentary on those verses). Its particular source, however, is *Sent. Pythag.* 102ᵃ: τιμήσεις τὸν θεὸν ἄριστα, ὅταν τῷ θεῷ τὴν διάνοιαν ὁμοιώσῃς. Porphyry preserves a similar version of the saying (immediately followed by *Sent. Pythag.* 102ᵇ⁻ᶜ) in *Marc.* 16: τιμήσεις μὲν ἄριστα τὸν θεόν, ὅταν τῷ θεῷ τὴν σαυτῆς διάνοιαν ὁμοιώσῃς. The Sextine version, by contrast, differs in a number of particulars, altering the initial verb from the second-person future to the third-person present (perhaps in order to reinforce the contrast with v. 380), dropping the definite articles before θεόν and θεῷ and inserting ἑαυτοῦ between τήν and διάνοιαν, in partial agreement with Porphyry, who inserts in the same location σαυτῆς. More important, our author changes ὁμοιώσῃς in his source to ἐξομοιώσας and adds εἰς δύναμιν, the latter bringing the gnome into closer conformity with middle Platonic and Neoplatonic identifications of the *telos*, for which see, again, on vv. 44–45. *Sententiae Pythagoreorum* 102ᵃ is also cited (independently of *Sent. Pythag.* 102ᵇ⁻ᶜ) by Hierocles, *In aur. carm.* 1.17: τιμήσεις τὸν θεὸν ἄριστα, ἐὰν τῷ θεῷ τὴν διάνοιαν ὁμοιώσῃς. For our author, honoring God is more than a matter of knowing God (v. 439). Rather, such knowledge must serve as the basis for becoming "like" God (cf. vv. 147–148), that is, for conforming one's intellect so fully to the divine that it becomes an "abode" (v. 61) and "mirror" (v. 450) of God. Cf. v. 447: "If you see God you will make the ability to reason within of the same sort as God's." For *Sent. Pythag.* 102ᶜ, see on v. 402. An abbreviated version of *Sent. Pythag.* 102ᵃ⁻ᶜ is cited also in the *Gnomologium Byzantinum* ἐκ τῶν Δημοκρίτου Ἰσοκράτους Ἐπικτήτου (Wachsmuth 1882, 168).

Sentence 382

Coming on the heals of v. 381 and its echoes of vv. 41–46a, the declaration in the first part of v. 382 brings to mind the appeal in vv. 48–50 to become like God by needing as little as possible (cf. v. 18), the sort of aspiration that earns God's favor (cf. v. 45). Here we learn that the criterion of "need" draws one closer not only to God, who needs nothing, but also to other human beings when they are in need. For the divine approval conferred on those who assist this group, see Prov 22:9 ("Those who are generous are blessed, for they share their bread with the poor"); Tob 4:10–11 ("For almsgiving delivers from death and keeps you from going into the Darkness. Indeed, almsgiving, for all who practice it, is an excellent offering in the presence of the Most High"); Sir 17:22–23 ("One's almsgiving is like a signet ring with the Lord, and he will keep a person's kindness like the apple of his eye. Afterward he will rise up and repay them, and he will bring their recompense on their heads"); 29:12–13; Matt 6:3–4; 25:34–40; Acts 10:4, 31; P.Ins. 16.3 ("The heart of the god is content when the poor man is sated before him"), 14–15 ("The giving of food contents the heart of the god <more than> the heart of him who finds it. He who loves to give food to another will find it before him in every house").

Sententiae Pythagoreorum 70ᵇ, the source for v. 378 (see above), continues in v. 70ᶜ⁻ᵈ with the following: "Since it is indeed correctly said that the divine needs nothing at all in any way, but rejoices in the one who shares with those who are just and laboring for God" (ἐπεὶ καὶ λέγεται ὀρθῶς δεῖσθαι μὲν οὐδαμῇ οὐδαμῶς τὸ θεῖον οὐδενός, χαίρειν δὲ τῷ μεταδιδόντι τοῖς δικαίοις καὶ διὰ θεὸν πενομένοις). Sextus drops both the introductory formula and (as redundant) the adverb οὐδαμῶς, substituting θεός for τὸ θεῖον, perhaps to preserve better continuity with the other verses in the unit. He also replaces the rather awkward τοῖς δικαίοις καὶ διὰ θεὸν πενομένοις with τοῖς δεομένοις, thus creating the wordplay with δεῖται and continuing the redactional excision of moral criteria observed in v. 378. God "rejoices" in such giving because it reflects the behavior of those who participate in God's rule (v. 422). For this use of μεταδίδωμι, cf. vv. 82b, 295, and 330.

Sentences 383–392

Text

383 πιστῶν ὀλίγοι μὲν ἔστωσαν οἱ^a λόγοι, ^bἔργα δὲ πολλά^b.
384 πιστὸς φιλομαθὴς ἐργάτης ἀληθείας.
385 ἁρμόζου^a πρὸς τὰς περιστάσεις ἵνα εὐθυμῇς.
386 μηδένα ἀδικῶν οὐδένα φοβηθήσῃ^a.
387 τύραννος εὐδαιμονίαν οὐκ ἀφαιρεῖται.
388 ὃ δεῖ ποιεῖν, ἑκὼν ποίει.
389a ὃ ^aμὴ δεῖ^a ποιεῖν, μηδενὶ τρόπῳ ποίει.
389b πάντα μᾶλλον ἢ τὸ^a σοφὸς εἶναι ὑπισχνοῦ.
390 οὗ καλῶς πράττεις ^bτὴν αἰτίαν ἀνάφερε^b εἰς θεόν.
391 οὐδεὶς σοφὸς ἀνήρ^a ^bκάτω που^b βλέπων εἰς γῆν καὶ τραπέζας^c.
392 τὸν φιλόσοφον ^aοὐ τὸν^a χρηματισμὸν ἐλευθεροῦν^b δεῖ, ἀλλὰ τὴν ψυχήν.

Translation

383 Let the words of faithful people be few but their works many.
384 A faithful person fond of learning is a worker of truth.
385 Adapt to circumstances in order to be content.
386 If you wrong no one you will fear no one.
387 A tyrant cannot take away happiness.
388 What should be done, do willingly.
389a What should not be done, by no means do.
389b Claim everything except to be wise.
390 Assign the responsibility for whatever you do nobly to God.
391 No one is a wise man who looks down upon the ground and tables.
392 The philosopher must be free not in name but in spirit.

Textual Notes

383[a] omit Υ • 383[b-b] πολλὰ δὲ τὰ ἔργα: Π • 385[a] ἁρμόττου: Υ; ἀγωνίζου: sy² • 386[a] φοβήσῃ: Υ • 388 omit Υ • 389a[a-a] δεῖ μὴ: Υ • 389b[a] omit Π •

390^{b-b} ἀνάφερε τὴν αἰτίαν: Υ • 391^a omit Υ • 391^{b-b} κατώπου: Υ • 391^c τράπεζαν: Υ • 392^{a-a} αὐτὸν: Π • 392^b ἐλευθεροῖν: Π

Commentary

This block of sayings can be divided into four short segments. The first, in vv. 383–384, is a couplet on faith and works. Next comes a triad of maxims on securing happiness (vv. 385–387), followed by a pair of structurally similar precepts on the readers' responsibilities regarding what they "should" and "should not" do (vv. 388–389a). Finally, there is a couplet on the humility that accompanies wisdom (vv. 389b–390), loosely linked to the sayings in vv. 391–392 by the use of σοφός in vv. 389b, 391 and φιλόσοφος in v. 392.

Sentences 383–384

These two sayings are bound by the anaphoric repetition of πιστός, as well as by the similarity of ἔργα ("works") in v. 383 and ἐργάτης ("worker") in v. 384.

In the *Sentences*, faith has repercussions both for one's actions (e.g., v. 212) and for one's speech (e.g., vv. 171a–b), though in terms of scale priority is assigned to the former. In keeping with the gnomic tradition generally, Sextus associates loquaciousness with sin (v. 155) and taciturnity with wisdom (v. 156). Because actions confirm words, and not vice versa (vv. 177, 356, 359, 408), what matters most is what people do, not what they promise to do (v. 198). The readers should therefore never see speech as a substitute for action (v. 163b), being cautious never to speak too quickly (vv. 153, 164a), too much (vv. 157, 431), or to the wrong kinds of people (vv. 350–351, 360). Compare Sir 4:29 ("Do not be hasty with your tongue but slack and remiss with your deeds") and *m. Avot* 1:15 ("Say little and do much"). According to Maximus of Tyre, the discourses of Pythagoras "were short and concise, like laws; the lengthy sequence of his deeds, however, saw no interruption" (*Dial.* 25.2). That doing ought to take precedence over speaking is a theme of several New Testament texts as well, for example, 1 John 3:18: "Let us love, not in word or speech, but in truth and action." James, meanwhile, highlights the potential for self-deception in this regard, a reality that persists even—or perhaps especially—among the faithful: "But be doers of the word, and not merely hearers who deceive themselves.… If any think they are religious, and do not bridle their tongues but deceive their hearts, their religion is worthless" (Jas 1:22, 26).

Cf. *Gnom. Democr.* 82: "People who do everything in word but nothing in deed are fraudulent hypocrites."

Believers are committed to action, then, though as v. 384 indicates, they are committed not to action as such but to action that accords with truth. Put differently, the truth is not only something that one should speak (vv. 165a, 352, 355, 357, 368, 410); it is also something that one should do. Acting in accord with the truth is consistent with acting in accord with the divine (vv. 95a–b, 104, 224, 304), since "nothing is more akin to wisdom than truth" (v. 168), and wisdom defines both the nature of God (v. 30) and the means by which human beings ascertain that nature (v. 167). Indeed, it is incumbent upon those who consider themselves to be wise and faithful not only to undertake actions informed by the truth but to uphold and manifest the truth so fully that they can be properly called prophets of truth (v. 441, cf. vv. 158, 169). Such truth is not simply to be had, however, but is acquired only through "work," that is, through deliberation (v. 93) and instruction (v. 290). Hence the need for the right kind of learning (vv. 248–250, 344, 353): one cannot become θεοφιλής without first becoming φιλομαθής (v. 251; cf. Melito, frag. 3.1). For the designation of early Christians as "workers of truth," see *Const. ap.* 3.19; Ephraem Syrus, *Serm. virt. vit.* 10, 14; Gregory of Nyssa, *Inst. Christ.* 8.1.85; Ps.-Macarius, *Serm.* 25.4. Cf. Sir 27:9: "Birds roost with their own kind, so truth comes home to those who work at it (καὶ ἀλήθεια πρὸς τοὺς ἐργαζομένους αὐτὴν ἐπανήξει)."

Sentence 385

The group of sayings in vv. 385–387 is based on Clitarchus, *Sent.* 120–121: ἁρμόζου πρὸς τὰς περιστάσεις ἵνα εὐθυμῇς. περιστάσεις εὐδαιμονίαν οὐδαμῶς ἀφαιροῦνται. Verse 385 replicates Clitarchus, *Sent.* 120 exactly, while v. 387 replaces the catchword περιστάσεις with τύραννος, and οὐδαμῶς with οὐκ. In between Sextus inserts what appears to be his own saying, v. 386.

In frag. 6 (Περὶ περιστάσεων), Teles suggests that, in responding to the vicissitudes of fortune, "a good man must play well any part she assigns him. You have been shipwrecked, play the shipwreck well. From a prosperous man you have become poor, play the poor man well, equipped in adversity and equipped in prosperity, being content with any chance garment, diet, or service" (frag. 6.52, cf. frag. 2.9–10). On the same subject, Ps.-Plutarch, *Cons. Apoll.* 116e recommends several poetic selections (including *Carm. aur.* 17–18) for consideration: "If one keeps these in mind … he will be able to adapt (ἐφαρμόζειν) easily to all the circumstances of life, and to bear with such circumstances readily," the ultimate lesson being that "we should maintain a cheerful frame of mind, since we know that we cannot escape destiny" (*Cons. Apoll.* 117e). See also Seneca, *Ep.* 107.6–9: "An equal law consists, not of that which all have experienced, but of that which is laid down for all.... It is to this law that our souls must adapt (*aptandus*) themselves, this they should follow, this they should obey." In v. 385, Sextus similarly encourages his readers to adopt what we might call a spirit of accommodationism, that is, of adjusting amenably to whatever possibilities the exigencies of one's situation allow. This sort of outlook is what enables the sage to "bear the things that must be as things that must be" (v. 119), remaining content (cf. v. 262) with the loss of his property (v. 15), loved ones (v. 257), or even his own life (v. 321), confident in the knowledge that it is not fate (vv. 436a–b) but divine providence that guides the course of human affairs (vv. 31, 114, 380, 419), and that such "circumstances" provide an opportunity for him to demonstrate the true character of his faith (v. 200, cf. vv. 7a, 425). For further gnomic reflections relevant to the topic, see Sir 2:4; Ps.-Phoc. 55–56, 118–121; *Syr. Men.* 453–457; Theognis, *El.* 591–592, 657–658; Menander, *Mon.* 15, 223, 392, 721, 813; Publilius Syrus, *Sent.* 206, 218, 220, 256, 411, 473, 479, 648; Ps.-Cato, *Dist.* 2.24; 4.35, 39; Diogenes Laertius, *Vit. phil.* 1.93. Cf. also *Ceb. Tab.* 26.2–3; 31.1–6.

Sentence 386

This verse is repeated as v. 608 in the appendices. In its current location, it is possible to interpret the saying as a gloss on v. 385. Part of what accommodationism requires, and one of the ways in which it contributes to the readers' happiness, is that they refrain from responding to adverse circumstances out of anger or resentment (cf. vv. 15, 91b, 321), that is, in a manner that might engender acts of injustice (cf. vv. 23, 138, 208b, 370). Such restraint is especially in order for those who agree with Publilius Syrus that "a wrong done to one means a threat to many" (*Sent.* 351) and that "many must he fear whom many fear" (*Sent.* 379). It was common knowledge that criminals live in fear of retribution, whether it be from human or divine sources (e.g., Xenophon, *Hell.* 2.4.23; Iamblichus, *Vit. Pythag.* 30.179). As Plutarch puts it, "fear for the next moment lies so heavily on them that it precludes any delight or confidence in their present situation" (*Suav. viv.* 1090d). On the other hand, those who have done nothing wrong have nothing to fear (e.g., Plutarch, *Apophth. lac.* 219f). Indeed, those "who have never done wrong to anyone, or only to a few, or not to such as are to be feared" are more likely to be "reassured" and "confident" in their state of mind (Aristotle, *Rhet.* 2.5.18–20). In this light, v. 386 can be seen as relating to v. 385 through the contrast of (epistrophic) εὐθυμῆς and φοβηθήσῃ (cf. Diodorus Siculus, *Bibl. hist.* 8.12.13; Philo, *Praem.* 71; Ephraem Syrus, *Serm. adv. haer.* 133). For the formulation of his own contribution to this theme, Sextus may be relying (perhaps indirectly) on Isa 54:14: "Abstain from wrongdoing and you shall not fear" (ἀπέχου ἀπὸ ἀδίκου καὶ οὐ φοβηθήσῃ). For other appropriations of the Isaian verse, see *Const. ap.* 4.7; Eusebius, *Comm. Isa.* 2.43; Ephraem Syrus, *Virt.* prol. 20–21.

Sentence 387

Here Sextus drops περιστάσεις in his source (see above) in favor of a more specific reference, one to a typical agent of such adverse "circumstances," namely, the tyrant, for whom see the commentary on vv. 363a–364. While the ideal ruler endeavors to augment the εὐδαιμονία of his subjects, the tyrant attempts to obtain it for himself at the expense of others (Isocrates, *De pace* 91). Nevertheless, even though he may take away the sage's property (v. 15) or his life (v. 321), he cannot take away the sage's happiness, any more than he can take away his freedom (vv. 17, 275; cf. Plutarch, *Exil.* 607e). This is because εὐδαιμονία derives not from human sources but from God (v. 133), that is, from the knowledge and imitation of God (v. 148), and what God gives no one can take away (vv. 92, 404). Insofar as the sage concentrates his efforts on acquiring what is secure (v. 118) rather than the things that evil people might take from him (v. 130), he remains undismayed when deprived of the latter (vv. 15, 91b, 321). In ancient philosophy, the image of the sage "happy in adversity" (Seneca, *Ep.* 41.4) is familiar especially from Stoic sources, such as Epictetus, *Diatr.* 2.19.24: "Show me a man who though sick is happy, though in danger is happy, though dying is happy, though condemned to exile is happy, though in disrepute is happy. Show him! By the gods, I would fain see a Stoic." Indeed, as Cicero explains, the power of virtue in the Stoic sage is so great that he "can never be otherwise than happy" (*Pis.* 18.42). Even tyrants cannot alter this condition, since they lack the power either to procure good for the sage or to involve him in evil, authority over these matters lying exclusively within the sphere of his own moral will (Epictetus, *Diatr.* 4.12.7–9). Cf. Epictetus, *Gnom.* 8: "Examine yourself, whether you had rather be rich or happy; and, if rich, be assured that this is neither a good, nor altogether in your own power; but, if happy, that this is both a good and in your own power, since the one is a temporary loan of fortune and the other depends on choice."

Sentences 388–389a

Exhibiting both similar beginnings (ὃ δεῖ ποιεῖν/ὃ μὴ δεῖ ποιεῖν) and similar endings (ποίει), these two sayings mirror one another structurally. Together they expand on the thought of v. 387: the sage is always happy because whatever he does he does willingly. This is because, as a sage, he always knows and does that which is necessary (ἃ δεῖ), in other words, he always knows and does that which is dictated by an intellect assimilated to the divine (vv. 381, 447, cf. vv. 45–46a, 61, 143–144, 450). This is, accordingly, that which he most dutifully learns (v. 344), desires (v. 141), and prays for (v. 88), graciously accepting whatever "must be" (v. 119), even his own death (v. 320).

It was a truism that the most upright and admirable people do what is right willingly (ἑκών), rather than out of fear or compulsion (e.g., Isocrates, *Nic.* 47; Xenophon, *Cyr.* 8.1.4; Demosthenes, *1 Aristog.* 93; *Chers.* 48). For the fullest discussion, however, we must turn again to the Stoa. Central to Stoic ethics was the tenet that "conduct will not be right unless the will to act is right" (Seneca, *Ep.* 95.57), correct action in any circumstance being a matter not of compliance but of volition, that is, of exercising one's reason. The sage, then, is not simply resigned to what is necessary—he consents to it. From this perspective it is more correct to say that he does not so much obey God as agree with God: "I follow him because my soul wills it, not because I must" (Seneca, *Ep.* 96.2; cf. *Prov.* 5.6). He can therefore say to God: "Have I ever found fault with you? Have I ever blamed your governance at all? I fell sick when it was your will; so did others, but I willingly (ἑκών). I became poor, it being your will, but with joy.... Have I not always come before you with a radiant countenance, ready for any injunctions or orders that you might give?" (Epictetus, *Diatr.* 3.5.8–9). For more on the assent of the sage, see Epictetus, *Diatr.* 4.3.10; 4.7.6–14; *Ench.* 31.1; Seneca, *Ep.* 90.34; Marcus Aurelius, *Med.* 4.34.1. For a non-Stoic perspective, cf. Xenophon, *Mem.* 2.1.18: "He who endures hardship willingly enjoys his toils because he is comforted with good hope." Chadwick (1959, 179) also refers to John Chrysostom, *Hom. Rom.* 9.4.

As the similarly worded v. 141 indicates (φιλῶν ἃ μὴ δεῖ οὐ φιλήσεις ἃ δεῖ), divided loyalties in this regard are not to be tolerated: doing what one must is only possible when one refrains from doing what one must not. If the sage carries out the former willingly, his resolution in desisting from the latter can be described as godlike (v. 306). Because all of his actions are guided by reason, to do what should not be done (ὃ μὴ δεῖ ποιεῖν) is something that he will not even contemplate (v. 178, cf. v. 93). As Epictetus explains, the greatest injury that a person can cause himself consists not in doing something that brings harm or discomfort to one's body, but in doing what must not be done (τὸ μὴ ποιῆσαι ἃ δεῖ), since the latter corrupts not only one's sense of honor and decorum, but also one's commitment to reason (*Diatr.* 3.7.36). Cf. v. 471: "Do not do by preference what should be done (ἃ δεῖ πράττειν) in a moment of crisis."

Sentences 389b–390

Cf. v. 433: "A person who is chosen does all things in accord with God but does not claim (ὑπισχνεῖται) to be chosen." This maxim provides a clue as to the logic connecting the couplet in vv. 389b–390 with the one in vv. 388–389a: wisdom is about action, not about claims, an assertion consistent with vv. 198–199: "Do great things without promising (ὑπισχνούμενος) great things. You will not become wise thinking that you are wise before you are." The sage strives to surpass others not in reputation, but in good judgment (v. 332, cf. vv. 53, 64, 145, 188, 214), mindful of the fact that the beginning of wisdom is the recognition that one does not yet possess it (v. 333) and that no pretense remains hidden for long (v. 325). See further *Instr. Ankh.* 8.3 ("Do not say 'I am learned'; betake yourself to become wise"); Prov 3:7 ("Do not be wise in your own eyes"); Qoh 7:16 ("Do not be too righteous, and do not act too wise; why should you destroy yourself?"); Rom 12:16 ("Do not claim to be wiser than you are"); Epictetus, *Ench.* 46.1 ("On no occasion call yourself a philosopher"); Seneca, *Helv.* 5.2 ("Do I say that I am a wise man? By no means. For if I could make that claim, I should thereby not only deny that I am unhappy, but should also declare that I am the most fortunate of all men and had been brought into nearness with God"); Sext. 470: "To perform noble deeds is noble, but to make a claim (ὑπισχνεῖσθαι) of doing so is presumptuous."

As the human being who knows and appreciates the greatness of the divine most fully, then, the sage boasts not about himself (v. 432, cf. v. 284), his own destiny in the scheme of salvation remaining uncertain (v. 434), but about God. Having searched out the causes of noble things (v. 100), he deems God to be not only the source (v. 113), but also the guide (v. 104) and the upholder (v. 304) of everything that human beings do right, while uninvolved in anything that they do wrong (v. 114). To live nobly, then, is impossible without the divine (v. 215), God being both the standard for and creator of everything noble, including the sage himself (vv. 197, 395). For the composition of v. 390, comparison can be made with a saying attributed to the sage Bias in Diogenes Laertius, *Vit. phil.* 1.88: "Whatever good thing you do, ascribe it to the gods" (ὅ τι ἂν ἀγαθὸν πράττῃς, εἰς θεοὺς ἀνάπεμπε). For this particular use of ἀναφέρω + αἰτία, cf. Aesop, *Fab.* 112; Isocrates, *Bus.* 41; Polybius, *Hist.* 10.5.8. As for the couplet as a whole, comparison can be made with Jer 9:23–24 [9:22–23] ("Do not let the wise boast in their wisdom ... but let those who boast boast in this, that they understand and know me"), a text popular in early Christian circles; see 1 Cor 1:31; 2 Cor 10:17; *1 Clem.* 13.1; Clement, *Paed.* 1.6.37.2; *Strom.* 1.11.50.2; Origen, *Comm. Matt.* 10.19; *Hom. Jer.* 11.4; 17.5.

Sentence 391

In the course of a discussion regarding how Christians should conduct themselves while dining, Clement exclaims, "Unquestionably, it is contrary to reason, utterly useless, and beneath human dignity for people to feed themselves like cattle being fattened for the slaughter, for those who come from the earth to keep looking down to the earth (κάτω βλέπονψας εἰς γῆν) and ever bent over their tables (κεκυφότας εἰς τραπέζας)." Those who partake of such gluttony "practice a life only of greed, burying the good of this life in a way of life that will not last" (*Paed.* 2.1.9.4). The Alexandrian's likely source is Plato's description of pleasure lovers in *Resp.* 586a: "Like cattle they are always looking down at the ground, and with their heads bent over their tables (κάτω ἀεὶ βλέποντες καὶ κεκυφότες εἰς γῆν καὶ εἰς τραπέζας), they feed, fatten, and fornicate." For Sextus, the person who cannot control his desire for food defiles (vv. 108a–b, 111) and degrades (v. 345) his soul to such an extent that he actually becomes like an animal (v. 270), the very antithesis of the rational, disciplined sage (vv. 294, 438, cf. vv. 265–267, 412–413). For further illustrations of animal imagery being applied to the overindulgent, see the commentary on v. 270. For a different way of "looking" at tables, see Sir 40:29.

Sentence 392

The basis of the sage's freedom is his exclusive service to God (v. 264b, cf. vv. 40–42, 422–424), who shares everything with his servant (v. 310), including his freedom from all worldly concerns and distractions (v. 309, cf. v. 36). This freedom, then, pertains not to life in the body, that is, to one's social or legal standing (though note that χρηματισμός could be used of a public document, including a slave's title-deed: see LSJ s.v. I.4), but to the life of the soul, which represents the sphere within which the sage achieves and exercises his freedom (cf. v. 55). This and only this constitutes true freedom, because this is the one thing of which the sage can never be deprived (v. 275, cf. vv. 17, 77, 363a–b). Ancient moralists agreed that freedom ought to be understood as a matter not of status, titles, or rank but of virtue. The Stoics, for instance, held that "the sage alone is free, the morally bad are slaves," since slavery consists not in subordination to or possession by another human being, as most people think, but in the absence of αὐτοπραγία (Diogenes Laertius, *Vit. phil.* 7.121–122; cf. *SVF* 3:349–366). Epictetus tells his students that if they do not conquer their fears and desires, "you will be a slave among slaves, even if you are consul ten thousand times, even if you go up to the palace; you will be a slave none the less" (*Diatr.* 4.1.173). Cf. Ps.-Heraclitus, *Ep.* 9.5: "Evil alone makes one a slave; virtue alone frees, but no man can do either. Even if you happen to command others who are virtuous, you yourselves are slaves on account of your desire, and you are ordered around by your own masters." If v. 392 is read together with v. 391, freedom here may be understood as referring in the first instance to freedom from alimentary desires, in which case comparison can be made with texts like v. 75b ("All the soul's passions are just so many despots"); *Sent. Pythag.* 77 ("No one is free who does not master himself"); Clement, *Strom.* 2.23.144.3 ("To yield in subjection to the passions is the lowest form of slavery, just as to conquer them is the only true freedom"). See also the commentary on v. 275. For its part, the Coptic version of Sext. 392 ("The philosopher who is an outer body, he is not the one to whom it is fitting to pay respect, but (the) philosopher according to the inner man") appears to combine elements familiar from previous sayings in the collection; cf. vv. 192, 219, 319.

SENTENCES 393–399

TEXT

393 ψεύδεσθαι φυλάττου· ἔστιν γὰρ ἀπατᾶν καὶ ἀπατᾶσθαι.
394 τίς θεὸς γνῶθι· μάθε[a] τὸ νοοῦν[b] ἐν σοί[c].
395 θεοῦ καλὸν ἔργον ἀγαθὸς ἄνθρωπος.
396 ἄθλιοι[a] δι' οὓς ὁ λόγος ἀκούει κακῶς[b].
397 ψυχὴν θάνατος οὐκ ἀπόλλυσιν ἀλλὰ κακὸς βίος.
398 πρὸς ὃ γέγονας εἰδὼς γνώσῃ σαυτόν.

399 οὐκ ἔστιν κατὰ θεὸν ζῆν ᵃἄνευ τοῦ σωφρόνως καὶ καλῶς καὶ δικαίωςᵃ πράττειν.

Translation

393 Be on guard not to lie, for to deceive is to be deceived.
394 Know who God is; understand the ability to reason within you.
395 A good person is a noble work of God.
396 Wretched are those through whom the word suffers ill repute.
397 Not death but an evil life destroys a soul.
398 When you know for what purpose you have been born, you will know yourself.
399 It is not possible to live in accord with God without acting moderately and nobly and justly.

Textual Notes

394ᵃ τι: Π; γνῶθι δὲ τί: co • 394ᵇ νοοῦν ἔστιν: Π • 394ᶜ σοὶ τὸν θεόν: lat, sy² • 396ᵃ ἄθεοι: lat • 396ᵇ κακός: Π • 398 omit Π • 399ᵃ⁻ᵃ ἄνευ τοῦ σωφρόνως καὶ δικαίως: Π; ἄνευ τοῦ δικαίως καὶ σώφρονος: Υ; καὶ δικαίως ἄνευ τοῦ σωφρόνως: sy²

Commentary

The sayings in this block show few signs of organization. Verses 396 and 397 are linked by the catchword κακός (cf. καλός in vv. 395, 399), while vv. 398 and 399 are connected logically: one knows and fulfills the purpose of human existence (v. 398) by living in accord with God (v. 399). Here we also discover two Sextine variations on the famous Delphic precept, "Know thyself" (vv. 394, 398).

Sentence 393

As Plato observed, where there is falsehood there is deception (*Soph.* 260c), and those who defend the practice of lying and deceit do "nothing but harm both to themselves and to others" (*Leg.* 916e). For his part, the Stoic sage neither deceives nor is deceived, just as he neither harms others nor is harmed by them (*SVF* 3:567). According to Jas 1:16, the person who does not "bridle" his tongue "deceives his own heart" (ἀπατῶν καρδίαν αὐτοῦ), and comparison with Philo, *Mut.* 240 suggests that lying and deception are precisely the sorts of speech-acts that are "better to bridle" (cf. Jas

3:2, 14; 4:11). A clearer parallel comes from *Instr. Ankh.* 21.11: "There is none who engages in deceit who is not deceived." The observation here in v. 393 is consistent not only with admonitions elsewhere in the *Sentences* against falsehood and deception (see on vv. 159, 165a–f, 186, 367) but also with sayings that assert the logic of moral reciprocity (e.g., vv. 179, 211, 327), especially v. 165b: "The one who conquers with deceit is conquered in character." Cf. Evagrius Ponticus, *Sent. mon.* 127: "A man who lies will fall away from God; one who deceives his neighbor will fall victim to evils." For the problem of self-deception, see also on vv. 199, 333, and 389b.

Sentence 394

This line is the first of two variants offered in this section (cf. v. 398) on the Delphic maxim γνῶθι σαυτόν, frequently cited (and variously ascribed) by ancient authors. Besides Clitarchus, *Sent.* 2, see Septem Sapientes, *Sent.* 216.9, 30; Plato, *Phil.* 48c; *Charm.* 164d–165b; *Prot.* 343b; Menander, *Mon.* 762; Epictetus, *Diatr.* 1.18.17; 3.1.18; 3.22.53; Plutarch, *Sept. sap. conv.* 164b; *E Delph.* 385d, 392a, 394c; *Pyth. orac.* 408e; Clement, *Strom.* 1.14.60.3; 2.15.70.5; 2.15.71.3; 5.4.23.1 (quoted below); 5.8.45.4; 7.3.20.7; Diogenes Laertius, *Vit. phil.* 1.40. Its appropriation in the *Sentences* resonates especially with Clement's statement in *Paed.* 3.1.1.1: "To know oneself has always been, so it seems, the greatest of all lessons. For if anyone knows himself, he will know God; and, in knowing God, he will become like him." For Sextus, one knows God by knowing the ability to reason (τὸ νοοῦν) within oneself, no doubt a reference to the operation of the mind (ὁ νοῦς), otherwise known as the intellect (ἡ διάνοια). Insofar as God subsists as mind (v. 26), the cultivation of one's noetic faculties represents not only the means by which one comes to "know" God most fully, but also the means by which one comes to be "like" God most fully (vv. 44, 148, 381), the intellect thereby being distinguished as that aspect of the human personality with the capacity to accommodate and communicate the divine (vv. 46a, 61, 143–144, 450). It is in this light that we can appreciate Sextus's repeated commands for the readers to think (νοεῖν) about the divine as much as humanly possible (vv. 54, 56, 95a, 289, cf. vv. 181, 333). See further v. 577: ("Know God, so that you may also know yourself"); Evagrius Ponticus, *Spirit. sent.* 26 ("You want to know God? First know yourself").

Sentence 395

Thinking about God entails thinking about what is noble (v. 197, cf. v. 100), and one thinks about what noble in order to do what is noble (v.

56, cf. v. 255). A good person (cf. v. 132) embodies this process to such an extent that he not only performs noble works (e.g., vv. 267, 330): he actually becomes a noble "work" (ἔργον) himself, indeed, the work with which God is most pleased (v. 308), and as such is both a manifestation of the divine in the realm of human affairs and an exemplum for others in nobility of conduct (v. 166). From this perspective, it is possible to say that faith is a necessary precondition of and guide for any noble act or any noble person (v. 196, cf. vv. 104, 113, 304, 390) or, as Sextus puts it in v. 215: "Without God you will not live nobly." Verse 399 will suggest something of the content of such "noble" living, aligning it with the virtues of moderation and righteousness (see below). For the human person as a "work of God," see also *Const. ap.* 7.2; Clement, *Strom.* 4.13.93.3; 7.14.86.2.

Sentence 396
Ill-considered speech not only manifests evil (vv. 163a, 165c), it can give what is spoken of an evil reputation, especially when that speech is about God. For Sextus, the word of God suffers disrepute especially when it is spoken by those who are morally unworthy (vv. 173, 356) or to those who are morally unworthy (vv. 350, 366). For his part, the sage honors God's word in the same way that he honors God himself (v. 355, cf. v. 357), that is, by bringing his life into conformity with his speech (vv. 177, 358–359), seeing the souls of his listeners as a divine trust (v. 195, cf. vv. 24, 361–362). In all of this, the sage is careful to refrain from anything that might give unbelievers reason to censure him or his message (vv. 16, 38, 51, 343). Note in particular the comparably structured warning in v. 175, which Chadwick (1959, 170) describes as a "Christian version" of this verse: "Dead before God are those through whom (δι' οὕς) the name of God is reviled." While that aphorism entailed a possible allusion to Rom 2:24 (for the problem of blasphemy in our text, see also vv. 82e–85), here the closest biblical analogy appears to come from 2 Pet 2:2: "Even so, many will follow their licentious ways, and because of these teachers the way of truth will be maligned" (cf. *Apoc. Petr. graec.* 1; Clement, *Protr.* 10.106.2; Eusebius, *Hist. eccl.* 5.1.48). For other attempts to dissuade early Christians from conduct that might incur the negative judgment of outsiders, see the commentary on v. 16.

Sentence 397
Causing the name of God to be defamed is so reprehensible that those who do so are, as we have just seen, νεκροὶ παρὰ θεῷ (v. 175). The sage,

by contrast, enjoys true βίος, since he only "lives" in accord with God (v. 201) and reason (v. 123), impervious to the loss of anything relating to the material world, including his possessions (vv. 15, 91b, 130), his loved ones (v. 254), even his own life (vv. 320–322), confident in the knowledge that "whatever does not harm a soul does not harm a human being" (v. 318, cf. v. 302; for the argument that death cannot "destroy" the soul, see Plato, *Phaed.* 106b–e). What he fears, then, are not threats to his physical existence (vv. 323, 363b, 387, cf. v. 473) but moral malignancies like wickedness, which can plague his soul (v. 208a), injustice, which can cause his soul's death (v. 208b), and faithlessness, which can render him "a dead human being in a living body" (v. 7b, cf. v. 400). See also Philo, *QG* 1.70 ("But from the prayers of evil men God turns away his face, considering that—even though they enjoy the prime of life—they are dead to true life"); *b. Ber.* 18a ("The righteous are called living even after their death, the sinners dead during their lifetime"); Clement, *Strom.* 3.9.64.1: "Sin is called the death of the soul." Also relevant is a saying of Democritus recorded by Porphyry in *Abst.* 4.21.6: "To live badly, without intelligence or temperance or piety, is not bad life, but long death." For the concept of moral or spiritual death, see further 1 Tim 5:6; Rev 3:1; Herm. *Sim.* 9.21.2–4; 9.28.6; Musonius Rufus, frag. 53. Mention may also be made of the Pauline concept of being "dead" in one's sins (Col 2:13; Eph 2:1, 5). See further on vv. 7b and 208b.

Sentence 398

This line is best understood in conjunction with both the other variant on γνῶθι σαυτόν offered in this section (see above on v. 394) and the gnome that immediately follows. Human beings come to "know" themselves, that is, to know the reason for their existence (cf. v. 201), by knowing God (through the cultivation of one's noetic capacities) and becoming like God (through a life lived in conformity to that knowledge). The command to "know yourself" was sometimes taken as a reminder of human creatureliness and mortality (e.g., Plutarch, *E Delph.* 394c, cf. 392a–b). The statement here accords especially with Clement's interpretation (cf. the quote of *Paed.* 3.1.1.1 above), according to which the Delphic maxim in fact "shows many things: both that you are mortal and that you are a human being; also that, in comparison with the other excellences of life, you are of no account, because you say that you are rich or renowned…. And it says, Know for what purpose you have been born (εἰς τί γέγονας), and whose image you are, and what is your essence, and what your creation, and what your relation to God" (*Strom.* 5.4.23.1; cf. 7.3.20.7: τὸ γνῶθι σαυτὸν ἐνταῦθα, εἰδέναι ἐφ᾽ ᾧ γεγόναμεν). Philo, meanwhile, sees the maxim as encouraging a more diagnostic anthropological process: to "know yourself" means "to know the parts of which you consist, what each is, and for what purpose it was made (πρὸς τί γέγονε), and how it is meant to work, and who it is that invisibly sets the puppets in motion and pulls their strings, whether it be the mind that is within you or the mind of the universe" (*Fug.* 46; cf. *Somn.* 1.57–58). For a different kind of variant on the famous precept, see *Sent. Pythag.* 27: "Insofar as you do not know yourself, deem yourself to be mad."

Sentence 399

The source for this line is Clitarchus, *Sent.* 123: οὐκ ἔστιν εὐκλεῶς ζῆν ἄνευ τοῦ σωφρόνως καὶ καλῶς καὶ δικαίως <πράττειν> (note that Sext. 385 is based on *Sent.* 120, and Sext. 387 on *Sent.* 121). Sextus replicates his source exactly, except for replacing εὐκλεῶς ("illustriously") with one of his favorite expressions, κατὰ θεόν (cf. vv. 36, 48, 63, 201, 216, 433), though note that the reading καὶ καλῶς is supported only by the Latin witnesses. Verse 201 is of particular interest here, since it provides the logic connecting v. 399 with v. 398: the *telos* of human existence, that is, the reason for which human beings exist, is "to live in accord with God" (cf. vv. 48, 216). The character of such a life is delineated at this point with reference to three moral criteria, each of which is deemed to be essential. The readers of the *Sentences* have been reminded repeatedly about the importance of comporting themselves "nobly" (vv. 56, 100, 142, 166, 255, 267). Such conduct indeed "accords" with God insofar as God is understood to be its ultimate source and standard (vv. 104, 113, 215, 304, 390, 395). Sextus here fleshes out the content of this rather generic standard by associating it with two well-known virtues, σωφροσύνη (cf. vv. 13, 67, 235, 237, 273, 412) and δικαιοσύνη (cf. vv. 64–65, 261, 410). Compare Clement, *Paed.* 2.12.121.4: "It is the just and moderate or, in a word, the good man who is noble, and not the wealthy one" (cf. Isocrates, *Nic.* 43; Plotinus, *Enn.* 1.6.4; 2.9.15; 6.7.33). Earlier, Plato had held that characters shaped by "justice, nobility, and moderation" belong to "human beings that the gods love as much as possible" (*Resp.* 501b, cf. 364a).

Sentences 400–410

Text

400 ἀνθρώπων ἀπίστων βίος ὄνειδος.
401 μήποτε λάθης^a σαυτὸν ἀγενεῖ^b φύσει μεταδιδοὺς λόγου θεοῦ.
402 ψυχὴν ^aἀπὸ γῆς^a πίστις ἀνάγει^b παρὰ θεόν.
403 σοφοῦ ψυχῆς μέγεθος οὐκ ἂν ἐξεύροις μᾶλλον ἤπερ^a καὶ θεοῦ.
404 ὅσα δίδωσιν ὁ θεὸς οὐδεὶς ἀφαιρεῖται.
405 ὃ παρέχει κόσμος βεβαίως οὐ τηρεῖ.
406 θεία σοφία ^aἡ ^bτοῦ^a θεοῦ^b γνῶσις.
407 ἀκαθάρτῳ ψυχῇ μὴ τόλμα λέγειν περὶ θεοῦ.
408 ἀνδρὸς ^aπεῖραν πρότερον^a ἔργων ἢ λόγων ποίει^b.
409 τὰ ὦτά σου μὴ παντὶ πίστευε.
410 οἴεσθαι μὲν περὶ θεοῦ εὐμαρές, λέγειν δὲ ἀληθὲς μόνῳ τῷ δικαίῳ^a συγκεχώρηται.

Translation

400 The life of people without faith is a reproach.
401 Never unknowingly share a word of God with someone of a sordid nature.
402 Faith leads a soul from earth to God.
403 You will not discover the greatness of a sage's soul any more than the greatness of God.
404 Whatever God gives, no one takes away.
405 What the world provides, it does not keep secure.
406 Divine wisdom is the knowledge of God.
407 Do not dare to speak to an impure soul about God.
408 Make a test of a man's works before a man's words.
409 Do not believe your ears in everything.
410 To speculate about God is easy, but to speak the truth has been granted to the just one alone.

Textual Notes

401^a λάθῃ: Π • 401^b ἀπηνεῖ: Υ • 402^{a–a} omit sy² • 402^b ἄγει: Υ • 403^a περ ἤ: Π • 406^{a–a} omit Υ • 406^{b–b} omit lat • 408^{a–a} πρότερον πεῖραν: Π • 408^b ποιοῦ: Π • 410 omit Υ • 410^a δικαίῳ: Π

Commentary

A gnomic observation on the faithless (v. 400) leads naturally to a precept regarding those of a "sordid" nature (v. 401), both of which contrast with a soul led by faith (v. 402, note ἄπιστος in v. 400 and πίστις in v. 402). The gnome in v. 402, in turn, seems to have attracted the saying in v. 403 by means of the catchwords ψυχή and θεός. This is followed by a couplet contrasting divine and worldly goods (vv. 404–405), a precept describing an example of the former (v. 406), and a set of maxims on caution in speaking and listening (vv. 407–410, cf. v. 401) reminiscent of the instruction in vv. 350–368.

Sentence 400

The source for this line is the second part of *Sent. Pythag.* 35: "Consider both the blame and the praise of every thoughtless person to be ridiculous, and the life of the ignorant to be a disgrace (τῶν ἀμαθῶν ὄνειδος εἶναι τὸν βίον)." Sextus drops εἶναι and τόν, reverses the order of the remaining two final words, and changes βίον to βίος. More important, he replaces τῶν ἀμαθῶν (cf. v. 157) with ἀνθρώπων ἀπίστων, in keeping with his redactional proclivity for faith language (see the introduction, part 4). Those guilty of faithlessness are worthy of reproach, as Mark 16:14 suggests: ὠνείδισεν τὴν ἀπιστίαν αὐτῶν (cf. Demosthenes, *Lept.* 10). Here the target is not faithlessness but the faithless, a group which, judging from v. 243, constitutes in Sextus's context the majority population, or what he sometimes refers to as "the world" (vv. 16, 37). Presumably, what makes the life of unbelievers such a "reproach" is that they engage in reproachful behaviors, including especially sin (v. 174) and acts of disgraceful pleasure (v. 272), to such an extent that morally they are as good as dead (v. 7b, see also above on v. 397). The βίος of the faithful, by contrast, is so impervious to sin (vv. 8, 234, 247) and passion (vv. 204, 209), indeed, to anything unworthy of God (v. 5), that even "the world" views it with admiration (v. 37).

Sentence 401

Given the risks involved (v. 352), it is important to deliberate carefully before saying anything (vv. 153–154), especially anything about God (vv. 361–362). The reader is therefore warned not to discuss theology with everyone (v. 350), especially the impure (v. 407), the immoderate (v. 451), and the godless (v. 354), the last of these categories being particularly relevant for understanding the connection between this verse and v.

400, with its reference to ἄπιστοι. Heeding these warnings is imperative because the dissemination of a word about God to such persons constitutes an act of betrayal against God (v. 365), even, as we learn here, if it is done unintentionally. Among the situations in which such a mistake might be most likely to occur would be when the reader is speaking about God to a multitude (v. 360, cf. v. 112), since unbelievers are bound to be present (v. 243). In such circumstances it is better to keep silent than to say anything recklessly (v. 366). As Clement explains in *Strom.* 5.9.56.3, "true theology" should be shared only with those who have proven themselves in "a trial by faith in their whole way of life." Those lacking such credentials must not hear such instruction, lest they "receive harm in consequence of taking in the wrong sense the things declared for salvation" (*Strom.* 6.15.126.1), deceiving both themselves and anyone who listens to them (*Strom.* 1.2.21.2; 5.9.56.4). For more on the practice of esotericism in the early church, see the commentary on vv. 350–352.

Sentences 402–403

This couplet takes up the topic of the soul and its relationship to God. Note the presence of ψυχή and θεός in both sayings. Chadwick (1959, 180, cf. pp. 150–51) suggests that v. 402 is a "Christian version" of *Sent. Pythag.* 102ᶜ (cf. Porphyry, *Marc.* 16): "For virtue alone draws the soul upward and toward what is kindred" (μόνη γὰρ ἀρετὴ τὴν ψυχὴν ἄνω ἕλκει πρὸς τὸ συγγενές). Note, however, that the two sayings demonstrate very little verbal correspondence.

Regarding the Pythagoreans, Iamblichus explains that "their whole way of life is arranged in order to follow God (πρὸς τὸ ἀκολουθεῖν τῷ θεῷ), and this is the rationale for their philosophy" (*Vit. Pythag.* 28.137). It was for this reason that the dictum ἕπου θεῷ came to be associated with Pythagoras (e.g., Arius Didymus, *Lib. phil. sect.* 59.1), its significance as a kind of heading or summary for the Pythagorean way of life being evidenced also by Clitarchus, who chose it as the initial saying of his collection (*Sent.* 1; cf. Septem Sapientes, *Praec.* 217.3). By the same token, it should be noted that both the saying and the ideal it communicates can be found in a wide variety of contexts. For examples, see Ps.-Demetrius, *Eloc.* 9; Diogenianus, *Paroem.* 3.31; Alexander Filius Numenii, *Fig.* 28; Philo, *Migr.* 131, 146; *Abr.* 60; *Decal.* 98; *Spec.* 4.187–188; Clement, *Strom.* 2.15.70.1; Hierocles, *In aur. carm.* 23.11; Plutarch, *Rect. rat. aud.* 37d: "You have often heard that to follow God and to obey reason are the same thing." In his myth of the charioteer, Plato describes how "a soul following a god (θεῷ ἑπομένη) most closely, making itself most like that god" is able to "rise" (ὑπεράραι) into the heavens and achieve a view of reality (*Phaedr.* 248a; cf. *Leg.* 716b). Sextus's gnome similarly identifies both the means and the direction of the soul's ascent, though the former is identified not as ἐπιστήμη (as in *Phaedr.* 247d–e), but as πίστις (cf. vv. 6, 7a–b, 170, 188, 325). The imagery here accords generally with that of other sayings in the collection that depict wisdom "leading" a soul to God (v. 167), for instance, or God "guiding" human beings (v. 104, cf. vv. 74, 95b, 582), or the sage "following" reason (v. 264a, cf. v. 349). For more on the ascent of the soul, see the commentary on vv. 40 and 420.

In Plutarch's imagining, as it ascends towards the heavens, the soul in Plato's myth of the charioteer acquires certain ennobling qualities, most notably "greatness (μέγεθος) and high-mindedness, mingled with joy" (*An seni* 786d). If faith guides a soul to God (v. 402), then the soul of a faithful person not only ascends to God—it has actually achieved its destination, being "with" God (v. 55) and "united" to God (v. 418) so much so that it is possible to claim that "the soul of a God-fearing person is a god in a body" (v. 82d, cf. vv. 7a, 144, 307, 376a). It is not simply the case, then, that a faithful person (that is, the sage) is "like" God (e.g., vv. 18, 44–45) or "next best" to God (e.g., vv. 34, 82c, 376b). With regard to certain qualities, he is in fact indistinguishable from God. See vv. 306 (also with μᾶλλον ἤπερ), 310, cf. v. 194. This pertains in particular to the "greatness" of his soul, which, having been purified and enlightened by divine reason, is no more ascertainable than the greatness of God himself (cf. v. 27, also with ἐξευρίσκω + μέγεθος). For the virtue of μεγαλοψυχία, see the commentary on v. 120. Ps.-Aristotle, *Virt. vit.* 5.6 defines it as the ability "to bear nobly both good fortune and bad, honor and disgrace, and not to think highly of luxury or attention or power or victories in contests, but to possess a certain depth and greatness of soul (τι βάθος τῆς ψυχῆς καὶ μέγεθος)." See further Philo, *Abr.* 199; *Virt.* 216; Origen, *Hom. Luc.* 4.24; Iamblichus, *Vit. Pythag.* 2.3.

Sentences 404–405

This couplet contrasts the inviolability of spiritual acquisitions ("what God gives") with the transitoriness of material possessions ("what the world provides"). The first line essentially repeats v. 92 (ἃ δίδωσιν ὁ θεός, οὐδεὶς ἀφαιρεῖται), which in turn represents a modified version of Clitarchus, *Sent.* 15: ἃ δίδωσι παιδεία, ταῦτα οὐδείς σε ἀφαιρήσεται (see further the commentary on v. 92). In framing the previous gnome, Sextus may have retained the opening ἃ in order to create better parallelism with v. 91b (ἃ δέδοταί σοι, κτλ), while the use of ὅσα here may reflect the influence of a similarly structured saying in Clitarchus, *Sent.* 122: "Whatever fortune gives, circumstances take away" (ὅσα δίδωσι τύχη, ταῦτα περιστάσεις ἀφαιροῦνται). Comparison can also be made with *Sent. Pythag.* 3, which is cited in Porphyry, *Marc.* 12: "Do not ask God for things you will not retain once you have acquired them. For every gift of God is irrevocable. Consequently he will not give you what you will not retain." In the *Sentences*, what God (and only God) gives, and what the readers are urged to acquire, are "things that no one can take from you" (v. 118), identified in v. 77 as the things of the soul, a fact that may account for the placement of v. 404 immediately adjacent to a couplet on God and the ψυχή (vv. 402–403). The readers can be rightly confident in such things (v. 121b), because they are not only divine in origin (v. 128) but also divine in nature (vv. 36, 277, 310).

The only thing that the readers truly need, then, is God (v. 49), and the only thing necessary for their happiness is the knowledge of God (v. 148). Worldly acquisitions, by contrast, are insecure (for the use of βέβαιος here, cf. v. 77), contributing nothing to the life of the soul (v. 116, cf. v. 603). The sage is therefore not only unimpressed by such things (vv. 130, 227) and those who possess them (v. 192), he actively divests himself of material goods (vv. 82b, 264a), and remains untroubled at their loss (vv. 15, 91b), mindful that riches are an obstacle to salvation (v. 193, cf. v. 137). For gnomic reflections on the instability of wealth, see Theognis, *El.* 318; Isocrates, *Demon.* 42; *Carm. aur.* 16; Qoh 2:18–21; 5:10–14; 6:1–2; Sir 11:18–19; 18:25–26; 20:9; P.Ins. 17.2; Ps.-Phoc. 27; Publilius Syrus, *Sent.* 160, 424. For the opposition of θεός and κόσμος, see also vv. 18–20.

Sentence 406

This line can be read in conjunction either with vv. 404–405, in which case it offers an illustration of the sort of "secure" acquisition that comes from God, or with v. 407, in which case it offers an observation in support of its speech-injunction: if knowledge about God is something "divine," and as such pure (see below), then it would be sacrilegious to expose it to anything or anyone that is impure. Although the verbal correlations are not extensive, the verse is analogous to a saying preserved in *Sent. Pythag.* 94: σοφίαν ἀσκῶν ἐπιστήμην τὴν περὶ θεὸν ἀσκεῖ. Porphyry explicates the gnome as follows: "The one who practices wisdom practices the knowledge of God, not by continually praying and offering sacrifice, but by practicing piety toward God through his deeds" (*Marc.* 17). In lieu of ἐπιστήμη (cf. vv.

164b, 187, 578), Sextus has γνῶσις (cf. vv. 44, 148), and, instead of talking about the one who practices wisdom, he makes a claim regarding wisdom itself. For him, wisdom that is "divine" (cf. vv. 277, 413), that is, wisdom in its highest and most important sense, is knowledge not of the world or of anything in the world (cf. v. 405), but of God. This is the wisdom that "leads a soul to God" (v. 167), enabling it to know God (cf. vv. 394, 398), the "wise light" (v. 30). Cf. Clement, *Ecl.* 32.3: "The wisdom that is truly divine (ἡ τῷ ὄντι θεία σοφία) is untainted light, illuminating those who are pure among humankind (τοὺς καθαροὺς τῶν ἀνθρώπων), just as the pupil of an eye provides sight and a secure (cf. v. 405) apprehension of the truth."

Sentence 407

This line introduces a cluster of sayings on speech (vv. 407–410). Note the use of λέγω in vv. 407 and 410, and of λόγος in v. 408. In terms of tone and content it is reminiscent of the much longer section in vv. 350–368.

As Origen explains, "the mysteries of the religion of Jesus" are "delivered only to the holy and pure," that is, to those "who have been purified in soul" (*Cels.* 3.60). Clement expresses similar sentiments in *Strom.* 1.12.55.2: "We too ought to be purified in hearing as well as in speech, if we are to try to have a share in the truth." Most important, "it is not wished that all things should be exposed indiscriminately to all and sundry, or the benefits of wisdom communicated to those who have not even in a dream been purified in soul" (*Strom.* 5.9.57.2; cf. 5.4.19.2–4). A word about God from a sage may purify the soul (vv. 24, 103), but the soul of an unclean person has been so polluted by shameful actions (v. 102) that it has become the property of unclean demons (v. 348), and is therefore unfit for interaction with the divine (cf. v. 429). The saying in v. 407 is repeated in v. 451, the final line of the collection, though with ἀκολάστῳ used in lieu of the opening ἀκαθάρτῳ. For more on the practice of esotericism in early Christianity, see the commentary on vv. 350–352.

Sentence 408

The remaining lines in the cluster (see above) urge discretion not in speaking but in hearing. As v. 356 indicates, it is not only those hearing words about God who must be "cleansed" of immorality, but those speaking such words as well (cf. v. 590). Hence the reader's need to put potential teachers to the test by scrutinizing their moral actions, or "works" (cf. vv. 356, 359, 383, 547, 590, 606). The thought, though not the form, of v. 408 derives from *Sent. Pythag.* 83[a]: "Test a human being based on his works rather than on his words" (πεῖραν ἀνθρώπου ἐκ τῶν ἔργων μᾶλλον λάμβανε ἢ τῶν λόγων). From his source Sextus retains only the basic elements: πεῖραν, ἔργων, ἤ, and λόγων. *Sent. Pythag.* 83^b continues: "For there are many who are evil in their way of life but most persuasive in their speech." Cf. *Gnom. Democr.* 82: "People who do everything in word but nothing in deed are fraudulent hypocrites." Of a scoundrel, Ps.-Demosthenes writes: "Since you have already put his works to the test, what need is there to trust his words?" (*2 Aristog.* 21). Compare also Aesop, *Fab.* 33.1: "When a test of one's works is ready to hand, every word about them is superfluous." In the *Sentences*, integrity of word and deed serves as a standard not only for the evaluation of others, but for the practice of self-evaluation as well (vv. 90, 177, 359, 383). See further Clitarchus, *Sent.* 48–49; Porphyry, *Marc.* 8 ("Deeds provide the positive demonstration of each person's beliefs; and whoever has acquired certainty must live in such a way that he himself can be a faithful witness to the things about which he speaks"); Musonius Rufus, frag. 32; Seneca, *Ep.* 20.1-2; *Syr. Men.* 2–3; Zenobius, *Paroem.* 1.74. For a Christian parallel, we have *Did.* 2.5: "Your word must not be false or meaningless, but confirmed by action."

Sentence 409

The next line appears to be based on Clitarchus, *Sent.* 126a: <τὰ ὦτά σου μὴ> πᾶσιν ὕπεχε (note the use of *Sent.* 123 in Sext. 399). Sextus alters the final word to πίστευε, bringing the advice of vv. 407–410 to bear on the question of the readers' πίστις. It is unwise to put one's trust in a teaching (or a teacher) until it becomes plain how what is being taught informs the moral comportment of those who espouse it. In an environment where listeners place their very souls into the hands of the person who speaks to them about God (v. 195), and where even listening to a novel opinion is considered dangerous (v. 338, cf. vv. 248–249), wariness in such matters would be only sensible. The advice here reflects one of the rudiments of gnomic wisdom, namely, that human beings are easily deceived in affairs of personal loyalty. Thus the need for warnings like Sir 6:7 ("When you gain friends, gain them through testing, and do not trust them hastily"); 19:4; 36:24 ("As the palate tastes the kinds of game, so an intelligent mind detects false words"); *Instr. Ankh.* 16.22; P.Ins. 11.23; 12.6; Theognis, *El.* 75–82; Isocrates, *Demon.* 24–25; *Gnom. Democr.* 67; Menander, *Mon.* 460. The problem of gullibility is of special interest in the *Collectio distichorum* attributed to Cato, for example, 1.27; 2.20 ("Refuse to trust those who are often reporting news; slight faith is due those who utter many things"); 3.2; 4.20.

Sentence 410

It was universally agreed that a righteous person can be relied upon to speak the truth regardless of either the topic or the circumstances (e.g., Plato, *Resp.* 589b-c; Ps.-Plato, *Alc. maj.* 122a; Marcus Aurelius, *Med.* 12.29.1; Herm. *Sim.* 9.25.2; Clement, *Strom.* 1.18.90.2; 7.11.67.5; Origen, *Sel. Ps.* 12.1157, 1429, 1545). In our text, the *only* person who can be relied upon to speak the truth is a righteous person (v. 410), since only someone who is righteous can live in accord with God (v. 399, cf. vv. 64–65) and therefore be entrusted with something as pure and valuable as a word about God (vv. 352, 355, 357). In making this identification, Sextus offers a realistic view of human nature: the reader must be prepared to interact not only with people who speak falsely (vv. 159, 165a, c, f, 169, 393), but with people who speak falsely about God (vv. 83, 85, 367–368). Cf. Clement, *Strom.* 1.7.38.4: "Someone talking about truth and truth giving an account of itself are very different matters. The former is an attempt at truth, the latter is truth. The former is a likeness, the latter the actuality. The former survives by learning and discipline, the latter by power and faith." In the *Sentences*, a commitment to both speaking and doing the truth is similarly understood as a manifestation of a believer's faith (vv. 384, 441, cf. v. 168). Hence the appeal to "love the truth" (v. 158).

SENTENCES 411–425

TEXT

411 [a]μὴ βασανίσῃς σου[a] τῇ ψυχῇ τὸ σῶμα μηδὲ[b] τὴν ψυχήν σου βασανίσῃς ταῖς τοῦ σώματος ἡδοναῖς.

412 ἔθιζε σεαυτὸν τῷ μὲν σώματι παρέχειν τὰ τοῦ σώματος σωφρόνως, τῇ δὲ ψυχῇ θεοσεβῶς.

413 τρέφε[a] σου τὴν μὲν[b] ψυχὴν [c]λόγῳ θείῳ[c], τὸ δὲ σῶμα σιτίοις λιτοῖς[d].

414 χαίρειν ἔθιζέ σου τὴν ψυχὴν ἐφ' οἷς καλὸν χαίρειν.

415a ψυχὴ χαίρουσα ἐπὶ μικροῖς ἄτιμος παρὰ θεῷ.

415b σοφοῦ ψυχὴ ἀκούει θεοῦ.

416 σοφοῦ ψυχὴ ἁρμόζεται πρὸς θεὸν ὑπὸ θεοῦ.

417 [a]σοφοῦ ψυχὴ[a] ἀεὶ θεὸν ὁρᾷ.

418 ψυχὴ σοφοῦ σύνεστιν[a] ἀεὶ θεῷ.

419 καρδία θεοφιλοῦς ἐν χειρὶ θεοῦ ἵδρυται.

420 ψυχῆς ἄνοδος πρὸς θεὸν διὰ λόγου θεοῦ[a].

421 σοφὸς ἕπεται θεῷ καὶ ᵃὁ θεὸς ψυχῇ σοφοῦᵃ.
422 χαίρει τῷ ἀρχομένῳ τὸ ἄρχον, καὶ ὁᵃ θεὸς οὖνᵇ σοφῷ χαίρει.
423 ἀχώριστόν ἐστινᵃ τοῦ ἀρχομένου τὸ ἄρχον, καὶ θεὸς οὖν ᵇτοῦ σοφοῦᵇ προνοεῖ καὶ κήδεται.
424 ἐπιτροπεύεταιᵃ σοφὸς ἀνὴρ ὑπὸᵇ θεοῦ, διὰ τοῦτο καὶ μακάριος.
425 ψυχὴ σοφοῦ δοκιμάζεται διὰ σώματοςᵃ ὑπὸ θεοῦᵇ.

Translation

411 Do not torture the body with your soul nor your soul with the pleasures of the body.
412 Accustom yourself to provide the things of the body for the body with moderation, and (the things of the soul) for the soul with reverence.
413 Nourish your soul with divine reason, and your body with plain food.
414 Accustom your soul to rejoice in things in which it is noble to rejoice.
415a A soul rejoicing in petty things is dishonored before God.
415b A sage's soul hears God.
416 A sage's soul is attuned to God by God.
417 A sage's soul always sees God.
418 The soul of a sage is always joined to God.
419 The heart of one dear to God is secure in God's hand.
420 A soul's ascent to God occurs through God's word.
421 A sage accompanies God and God accompanies a sage's soul.
422 That which governs rejoices in that which is governed, and so God rejoices in a sage.
423 That which governs is inseparable from that which is governed, and so God provides and cares for the sage.
424 A wise man is under the guardianship of God, and for this reason is blessed.
425 A sage's soul is tested through the body by God.

Textual Notes

411ᵃ⁻ᵃ μὴ βασανίζου: Υ • 411ᵇ μήτε: Π • 412 omit Υ • 413ᵃ ἀρχῇ τρέφε: Π • 413ᵇ omit Υ • 413ᶜ⁻ᶜ θείῳ λόγῳ: Π • 413ᵈ ὀλίγοις: Υ • 414 omit Υ, sy² • 415a omit Υ • 416 omit Υ • 417ᵃ⁻ᵃ ψυχὴ σοφοῦ: Υ • 418ᵃ ἐστιν: Υ • 420ᵃ θείου: Υ • 421ᵃ⁻ᵃ θεὸς σοφοῦ ψυχῇ χαίρει: Υ • 422ᵃ omit Υ • 422ᵇ omit Π

- 423ᵃ ἀεί: Υ • 423ᵇ⁻ᵇ σοφοῦ καί: Υ • 424ᵃ ὑποτροπεύεται: Υ • 424ᵇ τοῦ: Υ
- 425ᵃ τοῦ σώματος: Υ • 425ᵇ τοῦ θεοῦ: Υ

Commentary

The presence of ψυχή in vv. 411–418, 420–421, and 425 signals the theme of this section, vv. 411–413 concentrating on the soul's relationship with the body, vv. 414–421 on its relationship with God, and the final verse of the unit, v. 425, mentioning both. Overlapping this are two groups of sayings on the sage, the first (vv. 415b–418) focusing on the sage's perception of God, the second (vv. 421–425) on his governance by God (note the structurally similar use of ἄρχω in v. 422 and v. 423).

Sentences 411–412

Cf. *Sent. Pythag.* 52: "The unjust person suffers greater ills when being tortured (βασανιζόμενος) by his conscience than when being scourged by blows to his body (τῷ σώματι)." For the image of a person being "tried" by pleasure, see Plato, *Resp.* 413d–e, 503a (cf. *T. Ash.* 6.5). In *Or.* 30.14–15, Dio Chrysostom utilizes the concept in constructing an anthropology: "We are composed of the very things that torture us (τῶν βασανιζόντων), namely, soul and body. For the one has within it desires, pains, angers, fears, worries, and countless such feelings ... while the body is subject to vertigo, convulsions, epilepsy, and other diseases." While Sextus would no doubt agree that conditions of the soul like desire can prove vexatious (vv. 146, 448), he would probably disagree that the same should be said regarding conditions of the body like illness, since for him what causes trouble for the soul is not the body as such (v. 139a), but the longing for bodily pleasures (v. 139b). Thus, while release from physical existence is desirable (v. 322), the believer does not see the body as something to escape (vv. 320, 337) but as something to control (vv. 70–71a, 240, 274a, etc.), its members being burdensome only to those incapable of using them properly (v. 335).

This proper "use" is explicated in the second (v. 412) and third (v. 413) lines of the cluster. The readers should not torment the body by depriving it altogether, certain physical pleasures being necessary and therefore unavoidable (v. 276), but provide for it with moderation (σωφρόνως), just as they "provide" for their souls with godly reverence (θεοσεβῶς). It is necessary to make the body "at home" on the earth (v. 55) by acquiring enough to meet its minimum requirements (vv. 19, 115). At the same time, one must renounce bodily things as much as possible (vv. 78, 101,

127, 347), since the body not only provides a temporary abode for the soul (vv. 320, 449) but actually bears its "imprint" (v. 346). The practice of somatic moderation (cf. vv. 13, 272), then, supports the development of spiritual reverence (cf. vv. 82d, 287): the soul cannot know God if the body is distracted by desires (v. 136) and becomes impaired when it succumbs to them (v. 345), self-control constituting the very foundation of piety (v. 86a, cf. v. 399). Discipline in such affairs, then, represents one of the ways in which the readers are to be "strict in rendering the things of the world to the world and the things of God to God" (v. 20). Cf. Ps.-Crates, *Ep.* 3.1 ("Take care of your soul, but take care of the body only to the degree that necessity requires, and of externals not even that much"); Athanasius, *Vit. Ant.* 45.5: "He used to say that it is necessary to give all one's time to the soul rather than to the body, but to concede a little time to the body for its necessities; all the rest of the time, however, one ought to devote to the soul and what is profitable for it." For more on Sextus's anthropological division of labor, see the commentary on v. 301. For σωφροσύνη and θεοσέβεια as complementary virtues, see *Jos. Asen.* 4.9; Clement, *Paed.* 2.10.109.4; Origen, *Comm. Rom.* frag. 14; Ps.-Didymus Caecus, *Trin.* 39.808.

Sentence 413
The substance of the "provisions" mentioned in v. 412 is specified here. For its part, the soul is to be "nourished" in divine reason (for the language, cf. Philo, *Plant.* 114; Origen, *Cels.* 4.18; *Orat.* 27.5) to such an extent that it becomes the norm of one's life (vv. 74, 123, 264a, 277), leading the soul to God (v. 420, cf. v. 167). The body, meanwhile, is to be nourished with simple food, λιτότης representing a standard generally conducive to σωφροσύνη (e.g., Dionysius of Halicarnassus, *Ant. rom.* 6.96.2; Strabo, *Geogr.* 4.1.5; 7.3.4; Plutarch, *Sept. sap. conv.* 150d; Porphyry, *Abst.* 3.1; Socrates, *Hist. eccl.* 6.22). Among Hellenistic philosophers, the Cynics were particularly keen to advertise their satisfaction with "the simplest fare" as a sign of their freedom and self-sufficiency (Ps.-Socrates, *Ep.* 6.2; cf. Ps.-Crates, *Ep.* 13; Ps.-Diogenes, *Ep.* 27, 46; Epictetus, *Diatr.* 3.22.87; Diogenes Laertius, *Vit. phil.* 6.31). The standard also figures prominently in a tract with Pythagorean leanings,Porphyry's *De abstinentia*—for example, *Abst.* 1.49.4: "Ordinary foods suffice to provide what nature necessarily requires, and because they are simple and small in quantity, they are easy to acquire" (cf. *Abst.* 1.37, 48, 50; 3.1; 4.5). Indeed, at one point the entire treatise is characterized as an "investigation into simplicity and holiness" (*Abst.* 2.1), a pairing of complementary virtues reminiscent of

the one found in v. 412. As Clement observes, "those who live on plain foods are stronger and healthier and more alert" (*Paed.* 2.1.5.2). He therefore recommends, "let the meal be plain and restrained, of such a sort to quicken the spirit" (*Paed.* 2.1.7.3). For further instructions on alimentary self-restraint, see vv. 108a–111, 267, and 435. In *Cap. paraen.* 17 (ῥώννυσι μὲν οἶνος τὸ σῶμα, τὴν δὲ ψυχὴν λόγος θεοῦ), Evagrius Ponticus appears to combine Sext. 413 with *Sent. Pythag.* 90 (ῥώννυσι μὲν οἶνος κτλ).

Sentences 414–415a

This couplet is about the soul's rejoicing, with χαίρω and ψυχή occurring in both lines. It is linked to the preceding cluster by the repetition of ψυχή in vv. 411–414 and (more loosely) of ἐθίζω in vv. 412 and 414.

Clement reports the Stoic definition of χαρά in *Strom.* 2.16.72.1 (= *SVF* 3:433, cf. 3.431–442, 434–436, 438–439): "They say that joy and sorrow are passions of the soul. They describe joy as a rational elation, and the state of delight that likes to rejoice in noble things (χαίρειν ἐπὶ καλοῖς)." The final element in this description reflects a more general view, according to which taking pleasure in what is noble represents a basic component of moral education. According to Aristotle, *Eth. nic.* 10.9.6, for instance, before it is possible to begin teaching someone about virtue, "the soul of the pupil must have been prepared through the cultivation of habits (τοῖς ἔθεσι) so that it has the inclination both to rejoice and to hate in accord with what is noble (καλῶς χαίρειν καὶ μισεῖν)." In the same way, for Plutarch it is a characteristic of those well schooled in virtue that they "have become accustomed to rejoice in noble things" (*Dion* 9.1). Elsewhere he notes that those who delight in worthwhile endeavors such as philosophy are less likely to find enjoyment in carnal pleasures or frivolous pursuits (*Tu. san.* 136c–e). For the particular formulation of Sextus's gnome, we can turn to Maximus of Tyre, *Dial.* 25.7: just as there are many pleasures associated with vice, there are also "pleasures that console the labors of virtue, pleasures that do not accrue via the flesh or the senses, but which grow spontaneously from inside, when the soul becomes accustomed to rejoice in noble deeds and habits and words" (ἐθιζομένης τῆς ψυχῆς χαίρειν τοῖς καλοῖς καὶ ἔργοις καὶ ἐπιτηδεύμασιν καὶ λόγοις). In the *Sentences*, to rejoice in what is noble is to rejoice in what befits God (v. 197), God being the source and guide of everything and everyone that is noble (vv. 104, 113, 215, 304, 390, 395). Presumably, this would include rejoicing in whatever God rejoices in (cf. v. 135), for example, the sage (v. 422) and those who share with the poor (v. 382).

From this perspective, it stands to reason that those who fail to rejoice in what is noble, that is, in what accords with God, are less likely to think and do noble things (v. 56), and are therefore less likely to be honored by God (cf. vv. 32, 426), since what pleases God most are those who become like him (v. 45). Indeed, as we learn here, the one who rejoices in trivial, that is, ignoble things (cf. vv. 9–10, 297), is dishonored (ἄτιμος) before God, the latter action most likely entailing a reference to the soul's post-mortem judgment. Cf. v. 14: "Consider that both the honors (τὰς τιμάς) and the punishments given to you at the judgment will be unending." As Dio Chrysostom explains in *Or.* 38.37, it is only those with a childish outlook on life who concern themselves not with matters of import like freedom and justice but "in their ignorance of what is truly valuable take their pleasure in what is of least account (τὰ ἐλάχιστα) and rejoice in mere nothing (χαίρει τῷ μηδενί)."

Sentences 415b–416

Like other lines in this unit (vv. 415a, 420–421, 425, cf. v. 413), all of the sayings in the next cluster (vv. 415b–418) have references to both ψυχή and θεός. The first three sayings are further bound to one another by anaphora: σοφοῦ ψυχὴ ἀκούει (v. 415b), σοφοῦ ψυχὴ ἁρμόζεται (v. 416), σοφοῦ ψυχὴ ἀεί (v. 417). The fourth saying (v. 418) has a similar opening (ψυχὴ σοφοῦ) and is further connected to the third saying by the catchword ἀεί. The second, third, and fourth sayings are paralleled in Porphyry, *Marc.* 16: ψυχὴ δὲ σοφοῦ ἁρμόζεται πρὸς θεόν, ἀεὶ θεὸν ὁρᾷ, σύνεστιν ἀεὶ θεῷ. Sextus (apparently) turns a single maxim into three by repeating the initial ψυχὴ σοφοῦ, reversing the word order in vv. 416 and 417, but maintaining it for v. 418. (Note that there are further parallels with Porphyry, *Marc.* 16 in vv. 422–424, 426–427, and 429.)

In Judaism, Moses especially is known as one who hears God (e.g., Deut 5:22–33; cf. Philo, *Leg.* 3.142; *Mos.* 1.83), while the early Christians could portray themselves as those who "hear" (that is, obey) God rather than men (Acts 4:19). See also John 8:47 (ὁ ὢν ἐκ τοῦ θεοῦ τὰ ῥήματα τοῦ θεοῦ ἀκούει) with the comments in Origen, *Comm. Joan.* 20.284–292, 304–308. For his part, the Sextine sage generally honors listening above speaking (vv. 171a–b). Insofar as God is understood as τὸ νοοῦν ἐν σοί (v. 394, cf. vv. 46a, 61, 143–144), in order to "listen" to God it is necessary to think (νοεῖν) about God as much as possible (vv. 54, 289), a process that illuminates the soul (v. 97) and guides one's actions (vv. 56, 95a, 233). Those who hear and obey God, then, are those who hear and obey reason (see on v.

413 above). Like its human counterpart, listening in this theological sense can be conceptualized in reciprocal terms. Just as the sage hears and obeys God, God hears and honors the entreaties of the sage, since he is someone who participates in divine reason (v. 277, cf. v. 375). On the other hand, God does not listen to those who fail to observe reason, those who long for pleasure (v. 72), or those who refuse to help the needy (v. 217, cf. vv. 126, 492).

The soul that can "hear" the divine is most likely to be "attuned" to it (v. 416). In Pythagorean writings, the sage attunes himself to God by harmonizing his mind to the harmony of the cosmic spheres (Iamblichus, *Vit. Pythag.* 15.64–67; cf. Plato, *Tim.* 36e–37c, 47a–e, 90c–d; Aristides Quintilianus, *Mus.* 1.1). In the *corpus Philonicum*, the sage attunes himself to God (ἁρμόζεσθαι θεῷ) by achieving a "harmony" of virtues (*Conf.* 198), thereby joining the ranks of their heavenly "choir" (*Spec.* 1.269; 2.259; 4.134). In the *Sentences*, the sage attunes himself to God by knowing and imitating God (vv. 44, 148), conforming his mind to God (v. 381) and living κατὰ θεόν as much as humanly possible (vv. 48, 201, 216, 399). Such assimilation is said to be accomplished "by" God insofar as God is the ultimate source both of everything that the sage knows about God (e.g., v. 353) and of everything that the sage does in accord with God (e.g., v. 113). For more concerning the doctrine of ἐξομοίωσις, see the commentary on vv. 44–45.

Sentences 417–418

Verse 417 belongs to a trajectory of religious thought according to which the prospect of seeing God is presented not as an impossibility (as in Exod 33:20; John 1:18; 1 Tim 6:16; etc.) but as an appropriate aspiration of human spirituality (e.g., Pss 11:7 [10:7]; 17:15 [16:15]; Job 19:26; Matt 5:8; Heb 12:14). When the soul of the Sextine sage is said to "see" God, however, this is not to be construed as part of a cultic (cf. Ps 63:2 [62:3]) or visionary (cf. Philo, *Contempl.* 11–12) or eschatological (cf. Rev 22:4) scenario but represents yet another way of saying that he knows and imitates the divine (vv. 445–447). In this case, comparison can be made with 1 Cor 13:12, where "seeing face to face" is aligned with "knowing fully" (cf. Clement, *Strom.* 1.19.94.4–7; 7.11.68.4; Origen, *Comm. Rom.* 1.1, 4; 4.8; 7.4–6) and 1 John 3:2, where "seeing him as he is" is aligned with "becoming like him" (cf. Origen, *Hom. Ezech.* 13.2; *Princ.* 3.6.1). As with the act of hearing (v. 415b), seeing in its theological sense is understood in reciprocal terms. The readers are ordered not only to "keep God before your eyes" (v. 224) but also to summon God "as witness of whatever you do" (v. 303).

The process of the soul's "union" with God, addressed in v. 418, is similarly noetic and similarly reciprocal. God, as mind (v. 26), dwells in the intellect of the sage (v. 144, cf. vv. 46a, 61), while the intellect of the sage is always "with" God (v. 143, cf. vv. 55, 444). As v. 423 will soon explain, the inseparability of the sage from God is a product of God's rule over the sage (cf. vv. 41–43, 182, 422, 424), who is committed to serving God in everything that he does (v. 288). With this line of thought comparison can be made with Clement, *Strom.* 7.10.57.1–2: when the gnostic finally looks upon God "face to face," that is, with full understanding and certainty, then his soul, having achieved perfection, "is with the Lord (σὺν τῷ κυρίῳ γίγνεσθαι) where he is, in immediate subordination to him." In the Greco-Roman world, those serving a divinity, for example, in the capacity of a priest, were sometimes said to be "joined" (συνεῖναι) to the deity (e.g., Plutarch, *Pyth. orac.* 405d; *Numa* 15.2). Plotinus, apparently familiar with the concept, adapts it to a philosophical context, identifying such union as the object of the soul's contemplative activity (*Enn.* 2.2.2; cf. Philostratus, *Vit. Apoll.* 1.16.3).

Sentence 419

The soul that is joined to God is safe with God (cf. *Sent. Pythag.* 20[b]; Porphyry, *Marc.* 19). In reference to Sext. 419, Chadwick (1959, 180) draws attention to Wis 3:1 ("But the souls of the righteous are in the hand of God"), though for a greater density of verbal correlations we can turn to another sapiential text, Sir 2:16–18: "Those who fear the Lord seek to please him, and those who love (οἱ ἀγαπῶντες) him are filled with his law. Those who fear the Lord prepare their hearts (καρδίας), and humble themselves before him. Let us fall into the hands (εἰς χεῖρας) of the Lord, but not into the hands of mortals; for equal to his majesty is his mercy, and equal to his name are his works" (cf. Sir 34:19). In the *Sentences*, the person who is θεοφιλής, because he is ruled solely by reason (v. 363a), learns (v. 251) and speaks (v. 358) and acts (vv. 340, 359) in ways that are pleasing to God. Because his heart, that is, his moral intention, is pure, that is, sinless (v. 46b, cf. v. 204), it can be said to be secure with God. Cf. also Ps 31:5 [30:6]; Luke 23:46.

Sentences 420–421

Images of proximity are supplemented with images of movement: the sage's soul is not only with God, hearing and seeing God (vv. 415b–419); it is guided by God in its journey to God. In depicting this movement,

Sextus draws on two common concepts, the ascent of the soul and the injunction to "follow God."

In v. 402, it is faith that guides a soul from the earth to God. Here it is God's λόγος, that is, the divine reason (v. 277) or wisdom that "leads a soul to God" (v. 167) and that the readers are therefore supposed to "follow" (v. 264a) as the norm (v. 123) and the "guide" (v. 74) for their lives (cf. vv. 95b, 104). Accordingly, and is often the case, the ascent of the soul is understood in noetic terms. The use of ἄνοδος here is familiar especially from Plato's myth of the cave, which describes "the upward journey of the soul to the intelligible realm" (*Resp.* 517b), that is, the realm of truth, beauty, and understanding, the soul fleeing from the realm of the senses as though it were a prison (cf. v. 322). In the same vein, of the virtuous Philo writes, "while their bodies are firmly planted on the land … in mind and thought … they provide their souls with wings, so that they may traverse the upper air and gain full contemplation of the powers that dwell there" (*Spec.* 2.45; cf. *Opif.* 69–71; *Sacr.* 5–8; *Conf.* 95; *Her.* 280; *Spec.* 1.37; 3.1–2; *QG* 1.86; 3.11; *QE* 2.40). Through the activity of the mind the soul is capable not only of contemplating divine realities, but of actually joining such realities (cf. v. 418), anticipating its disassociation from the body and ascent after death (vv. 39–40). Indeed, much like Philo's sage, even while in the body, the soul of the Sextine sage aspires to be "always with God," his body alone being at home on the earth (v. 55).

If v. 421 is taken together with v. 420, it can be read as an assertion that in its ascent to God through divine λόγος the soul is attended by God himself. As Philo explains, whenever the human mind "walks in the track of right reason" it in fact "follows God" since in doing so the mind comes to a knowledge of God's will (*Migr.* 128; cf. Plutarch, *Rect. rat. aud.* 37d: "You have often heard that to follow God and to obey reason are the same thing"). If Sextus's precept has a direct source, the most likely candidate is Clitarchus, *Sent.* 1 (ἕπου θεῷ), though, as shown by the commentary on v. 402, while they were sometimes associated with Pythagoreanism, both the dictum "follow God" and the concept it represents were broadly represented in ancient thought. In Plato's myth of the charioteer, for instance, the soul ascending into the intelligible realm is said to be "following a god (θεῷ ἑπομένη) most closely, making itself most like that god" (*Phaedr.* 248a). Using somewhat different language, in *Det.* 114 Philo observes how souls that "follow" virtue are "raised high above that which is earthly and mortal … having God to guide their ascent (ἡγεμόνι χρησάμενοι τῆς ἀνόδου θεῷ)." Once again, in interpreting Sextus's meaning it is appropriate to make reference to the principle of reciprocity, though in contrast to vv. 415b and 417–418, here the principle is made explicit in the saying itself (hence the translation of ἕπεται as "accompanies"). Presumably, it is God's presence with the sage's soul that makes it impossible for evil demons to prevent his soul "from following God's way" (v. 349, cf. v. 40). For more on the ascent of the soul, see the commentary on vv. 40 and 402.

Sentences 422–424

In *Marc.* 16, immediately after the saying that parallels vv. 416–418 (see above), Porphyry writes: "And if that which governs rejoices in what is governed, God too cares and provides for the sage. And for this reason the sage is blessed, because he is under the guardianship of God" (εἰ δὲ χαίρει τῷ ἀρχομένῳ τὸ ἄρχον καὶ θεὸς σοφοῦ κήδεται καὶ προνοεῖ· καὶ διὰ τοῦτο μακάριος ὁ σοφός, ὅτι ἐπιτροπεύεται ὑπὸ θεοῦ). Verse 424 matches the latter saying rather closely (though with the order of the clauses reversed; cf. Clitarchus, *Sent.* 135: μακάριος οὗ ὁ θεὸς κηδεμών ἐστιν), while vv. 422–423 present as a pair of structurally analogous gnomes what the former saying conveys in a more compressed fashion. Verse 422 lacks the opening εἰ δέ, in effect turning a general condition into a general principle, which is then applied to the specific case of God's relationship with the sage by means of a second clause that repeats the main verb, χαίρει. By repeating (with slight modification) τῷ ἀρχομένῳ τὸ ἄρχον in the first clause of v. 423, Sextus creates a parallel construction with the first clause of v. 422, this time describing (in a way that Porphyry does not) the govern-governed relationship as "inseparable" (ἀχώριστος), and then applying this principle to the relationship of God to the sage with a pair of verbs that parallel the second half of Porphyry's first saying, though with the order of the verbs reversed.

In the *Sentences*, the sage is governed by God (for this use of ἄρχω, cf. vv. 182, 288) in the sense that he obeys God just as a son obeys his father (vv. 58–59, 222, 225), taking God into consideration before doing anything (e.g., vv. 95a, 224, 289), attributing to God all the good that he does (vv. 113, 390), and constantly striving to know, honor, and emulate God (vv. 41–44, 148, 355, 439). Indeed, as that which emulates God most fully, the sage represents that which is "most pleasing" to God (v. 45). It is not surprising, then, to hear that God "rejoices" in the sage (cf. vv. 382, 414–415a). It is also not surprising to hear that God "provides and cares" for the sage, since this is precisely what a father is expected to do for his children (cf. v. 340; Epictetus, *Diatr.* 3.24.15; Plutarch, *Praec. ger. rei publ.* 802f–803a), the use of προνοεῖ in v. 423 serving as a reminder that divine πρόνοια ("providence") extends to the care of specific individuals (see the commentary on v. 312; cf. also v. 372). Sextus takes all of this as evidence both for the sage's "inseparability" from God (cf. Rom 8:39; Ign. *Trall.* 7.1; *Mart. Pet.* 37) and for the sage's blessedness (cf. vv. 40, 320, 326b). Because the sage is governed by what is best, he participates in a regime of divine power that enables him, in turn, to govern whatever he chooses (vv. 42–43, cf. vv. 36, 310–311, 363a–b, 375). For this use of ἐπιτροπεύω, cf. Musonius Rufus, frag. 14.94.20–22. For God as ἐπίτροπος ("manager, guardian"), see Philo, *Deus* 30 (also cf. Gal 4:2).

Sentence 425

The unit in vv. 411–425 concludes, appropriately enough, with a saying that includes references to the soul (cf. vv. 411–418, 420–421), the body (cf. vv. 411–413), the sage (cf. vv. 415b–418, 421–424), and God (cf. vv. 415a–425). Note also that v. 425 has the same opening as v. 418: ψυχὴ σοφοῦ.

In keeping with biblical perspectives (e.g., Ps 66:10 [65:10]; 1 Thess 2:4; both also with δοκιμάζω), Sextus attributes any hardship the sage endures not to fortune (cf. vv. 436a–b), but to God. Such hardship is not to be interpreted as a sign of divine hostility or neglect, however, but as an extension of God's fatherly, providential care for the sage (see above; cf. Wis 11:10). The divine "testing" that this hardship represents occurs through the body (cf. Origen, *Cels.* 1.69; *Comm. Joan.* 10.39.266; *Frag. Luc.* 101c; Athanasius, *Vit. Ant.* 7.3), because it is in the body that the sage reveals God to others (v. 82d, cf. vv. 190, 307), including when his soul resists the temptations of the body (cf. vv. 136, 347, 411, 449). See especially v. 7a: "One who is faithful in a test (δοκιμῇ) of faith is a god in a living human body." In an environment where "an extreme situation reveals a faithful man" (v. 200), such adversity, then, is best understood as a reflection of God's designs for the sage as a sage, who in this way mediates divine benefactions to humankind (cf. v. 176). As documented in the commentary on vv. 7a, 257, 306, 363a–364, and 387, our author's teaching on the hardships of the sage accords generally with Stoic doctrine, and in light of the comments above, it is worth noting that a fair number of statements relevant to the topic can be found in Seneca's treatise, *De providentia* (e.g., 1.5–6; 2.5–7; 3.2; 4.5–8, 11–12; 5.3, 9).

Sentences 426–434

Text

426 οὐχ ἡ γλῶττα ᵃτοῦ σοφοῦ τιμία παρὰ θεῷᵃ, ἀλλ' ἡ φρόνησις.
427 σοφὸς ἀνὴρ καὶ σιγῶν τὸν θεὸν τιμᾷᵃ.
428 γαστρὸς καὶ τῶν ὑπὸ γαστέρα [ὁ] μὴ κρατῶν οὐδεὶς πιστός.
429 ἄνθρωπος ἀκρατὴς μιαίνει τὸνᵃ θεόν.
430 ἄνθρωπον θεοῦᵃ γνῶσις βραχύλογον ποιεῖ.
431 πολλοὺς λόγους ᵃπερὶ θεοῦᵃ ἀπειρία ποιεῖ.
432 θεὸν ἄνθρωπος εἰδὼς οὐ πολλὰ κομπάζει.
433 ἐκλεκτὸς ἄνθρωπος ποιεῖ μὲν πάντα κατὰ θεόν, εἶναι δὲ οὐχ ὑπισχνεῖται.
434 * * *

Translation

426 It is not the sage's tongue that is honored before God, but his prudence.
427 A wise man honors God even while silent.
428 No one is faithful who does not control the stomach and the parts below the stomach.
429 A person lacking self-control defiles God.
430 Knowledge of God produces a person of few words.
431 Inexperience produces excessive words about God.
432 A person who knows God does not boast much.
433 A person who is chosen does all things in accord with God but does not claim to be chosen.
434 A faithful man is always in fear until he goes to God.

Textual Notes

426ᵃ⁻ᵃ σοφοῦ παρὰ τῷ θεῷ τίμιον: Υ • 427 omit Υ • 427ᵃ τιμᾷ εἰδὼς διὰ τίνα σιγᾷ: Π • 428 omit Υ • 429ᵃ omit Υ • 430ᵃ omit Υ • 431–434 omit Π • 431ᵃ⁻ᵃ omit sy² • 434 omit Υ

Commentary

The major feature of this block of material is the presence of two sets of sayings on the need for discretion in speech (cf. vv. 149–165g, 350–368), with an emphasis on the virtues of taciturnity and humility (vv. 426–427 and vv. 430–433, with v. 434 added as support to v. 433). Intervening is a pair of sayings on the need to control the stomach and sex organs (vv. 428–429). Cf. Diogenes Laertius, *Vit. phil.* 1.104 (γλώσσης, γαστρός, αἰδοίων κράτει) and Clement, *Strom.* 1.5.30.2 (quoted below under v. 428).

Sentences 426–427

In *Marc.* 16, immediately after the sayings that parallel vv. 422–424 (see above), Porphyry writes: "It is not the tongue of the sage that is honored before God, but his works. For a wise man honors God even when silent" (οὐχ ἡ γλῶττα τοῦ σοφοῦ τίμιον παρὰ θεῷ, ἀλλὰ τὰ ἔργα. σοφὸς γὰρ ἀνὴρ καὶ σιγῶν τὸν θεὸν τιμᾷ). The source for both Porphyry and Sextus is *Sent. Pythag.* 14[a–b]: γλῶττα σοφοῦ οὐ προηγουμένως τίμιον παρὰ θεῷ, ἀλλὰ τὰ ἔργα· σοφὸς γὰρ καὶ σιγῶν τὸν θεὸν τιμᾷ.

With regard to the first saying, Porphyry and Sextus agree against *Sent. Pythag.* 14[a] in opening with οὐχ ἡ and dropping οὐ προηγουμένως. Our author departs from both *Sent. Pythag.* 14[a] and *Marc.* 16 in using τιμία in lieu of τίμιον (note the catchword with τιμᾷ in the next line) and, more noticeably, dropping τὰ ἔργα in favor of ἡ φρόνησις (cf. *Sent. Pythag.* 13[a] = Sext. 457). The latter has the effect of altering an observation about the proper relationship between words and works (as in vv. 356, 359, 383, 408) to one about the need to observe good sense in one's speech. For parallels, see the commentary on v. 151 ("Let your tongue obey your mind") and v. 154 ("Words without thought are blameworthy"). Expressing what may have been an Epicurean view (cf. Diogenes Laertius, *Vit. phil.* 10.132), Philo declares that not only is φρόνησις "honored" (τιμία) before God: it is also acknowledged to be "God's fairest treasure" (*Leg.* 1.67; cf. *Ebr.* 86). See further Matt 7:24; 10:16; 24:45; Luke 12:42; 16:8.

With regard to the second saying, the three renderings are more nearly identical, though Sextus and Porphyry agree against *Sent. Pythag.* 14[b] in adding ἀνήρ (cf. v. 424), while Sextus is alone in dropping the γάρ. Where all three agree is in including the element of reciprocity: God honors the sage's prudence, while the sage honors God in everything he does, even when silent. This is because honoring God is not so much a matter of speech (though cf. vv. 83–84) but of knowing and imitating God so as to conform one's mind, or τὸ φρονοῦν (v. 447), to God as much as possible (vv. 44, 381, cf. v. 439).

The observance of silence was an especially prominent aspect of the regimen promoted by the Pythagorean movement. See Diogenes Laertius, *Vit. phil.* 8.10; Plutarch, *Quaest. conv.* 728d–f; Philostratus, *Vit. Apoll.* 1.14–16; Iamblichus, *Vit. Pythag.* 20.94. Indeed, being a Pythagorean was virtually synonymous with being silent, as the opening lines of the *Vita Secundi* attest: "Secundus was a philosopher. This man cultivated wisdom all his days and observed silence religiously, having chosen the Pythagorean way of life" (*Vit. Sec.* 68.1–3). The silence of the Sextine sage, like everything he does, is informed by ἐπιστήμη (v. 164b). He therefore avoids speaking at the wrong time (v. 161) or about what he does not know (v. 162a), especially when the topic is God (v. 366). As Chadwick (1959, 180) suggests, unease at the implication that in v. 427 silence is being admired for its own sake may have prompted the addition of εἰδὼς διὰ τίνα σιγᾷ in Π (the phrase is absent from the Latin and Syriac versions). The longer version of the saying is cited in Ps.-John Damascene, *Sacr. par.* 95.1341, while the shorter version is repeated as v. 589 in the appendices, without the τόν before θεόν. Cf. also v. 578 ("The greatest honor paid to God is knowledge of him in silence"); Aesop, *Prov.* 37 (στόματος σιγῶντος θεὸς ἔκδικος); Clement, *Strom.* 7.1.2.3; Ign. *Eph.* 15.1: "Now there is one teacher, who spoke and it happened; indeed, even the things that he has done in silence are worthy of the Father."

Sentence 428

The treatment of speech-ethics (vv. 426–427, 430–434) is interrupted by a pair of sayings on ἐγκράτεια. Note the juxtaposition of κρατῶν (v. 428) and ἀκρατής (v. 429). Verse 428 is repeated (with minor modifications) in the appendices as v. 588.

Both the connection between alimentary and sexual drives and their bearing on the life of faith were established by Sextus in vv. 239–240: "Let the marriage of faithful people be a struggle for self-control. As you govern your stomach, you will also govern your sexual desires." The negative ramifications attending failure in this area of comportment are amplified here. The person deficient in self-control is deemed to be not only unfaithful but also a source of defilement to God, much like the one who thinks evil of God (v. 82e). On the other hand, for Sextus ἐγκράτεια represents both the basis (v. 86a) and the sustenance (v. 438) of faith (cf. v. 294). Hence the appeal in v. 70 to "control pleasures" (κράτει τῶν ἡδονῶν). For the specific formulation here, see Clement, *Paed.* 2.10.90.2: "We must keep a firm control over the pleasures of the stomach, and an absolutely uncompromising control over the parts below the stomach." In *Strom.* 1.5.30.2, he places such observance within a more explicitly theological context: "If philosophy advertises control of the tongue, the stomach, and the parts below the stomach, and is desirable for its own sake, then it will appear more majestic and more authoritative if it is practiced for the glory and true knowledge of God" (cf. Philo, *Congr.* 80). For the expression τῶν ὑπὸ γαστέρα, see also Philo, *Spec.* 1.192; *Virt.* 208; Ps.-Musonius Rufus, *Ep.* 1.4; Clement, *Strom.* 2.20.106.2. For γαστρὸς κρατεῖν, see *Carm. aur.* 9–10; Menander, *Mon.* 137, 425 (καλόν γε γαστρὸς κἀπιθυμίας κρατεῖν). Cf. also *Syr. Men.* 65: "Blessed is the man who has mastered his stomach and his lust." That the observance of ἐγκράτεια supports the life of faith is maintained by a variety of early Christian texts (e.g., Acts 24:24–25; Gal 5:22–23; 2 Pet 1:5–6; Herm. *Mand.* 6.1.1). Those who are γαστέρες ἀργαί, meanwhile, should be rebuked, "so that they might become sound in faith" (Titus 1:12–13).

Sentence 429

In *Marc.* 16, immediately after the sayings that parallel vv. 426–427 (see above), Porphyry writes: "A foolish person, even while praying and sacrificing, defiles the divine" (ἄνθρωπος δὲ ἀμαθὴς καὶ εὐχόμενος καὶ θύων μιαίνει τὸ θεῖον). His source is *Sent. Pythag.* 15ᵃ: γλώτταλγος ἄνθρωπος καὶ ἀμαθὴς εὐχόμενος καὶ θύων τὸν θεὸν μιαίνει. Given the number and sequence of parallels between the *Sentences*, *Sententiae Pythagoreorum*, and *Marc.* 16 at this juncture of the text (see above on vv. 416–418, 422–424, 426–427), we can safely assume that *Sent. Pythag.* 15ᵃ is Sextus's source as well, though he offers a drastically simplified version of the saying, dropping γλώτταλγος and εὐχόμενος καὶ θύων, reversing the order of τὸν θεὸν and μιαίνει, and, most notably, replacing ἀμαθής with ἀκρατής, thereby drawing attention to the polluter's moral rather than intellectual deficiencies (cf. below on v. 431). For our author, what defiles a person above all are shameful thoughts (v. 57b) and actions (v. 102), brought about especially when one succumbs to the desire for physical things (vv. 108a–b, 110–111). This view can be compared with what we find in texts like Porphyry, *Marc.* 28 ("Even the gods have prescribed remaining pure by abstinence from food and sex … as though any excess, by being contrary to nature's intent, is defiled and deadly") and Plutarch, frag. 200, which censures people whose lives have been made "sullied and impure by love of pleasure and gluttony." In the *Sentences*, by contrast, such individuals are said to defile not only themselves, but also God, in which case comparison can be made with Epictetus, *Diatr.* 2.8.13: "Do you suppose that I am speaking of some external god, made of silver or gold? It is within yourself that you bear him, and you do not perceive that you are defiling him with impure thoughts and filthy actions." The person who lacks self-control is so polluted by immorality, so unfit for communion with the divine, that it is shameful for him to speak or even hear a word about God (vv. 356, 407; cf. Plotinus, *Enn.* 2.9.15: the ἀκρατής man cannot see God or know God's name, being in the grip of his passions). As elsewhere in the text, the language of defilement is employed here both morally and metaphorically, as a way of signifying that which inhibits a human being's assimilation to the divine (vv. 102, 108a–b, 110–111, 181; cf. vv. 23–24, 46b–47, 57b). For more on the theological anthropology informing v. 429, see the commentary on v. 82e.

Sentences 430–431

The source for these lines is *Sent. Pythag.* 10ᵃ⁻ᵇ: βραχύλογον μάλιστα ἡ θεοῦ γνῶσις ποιεῖ· πολλῶν δὲ λόγων περὶ θεοῦ ἡ πρὸς θεὸν ἀμαθία αἰτία (*Sent. Pythag.* 10ᵃ is cited verbatim by Stobaeus; see Wachsmuth and Hense 1884–1912, 5.vii). Comparison can also be made with *Sent. Pythag.* 16 (γνῶσις θεοῦ ποιεῖ βραχύλογον), which appears to be the source for Porphyry, *Marc.* 20: θεοῦ γὰρ γνῶσις ποιεῖ βραχὺν λόγον. With regard to the first saying, Sextus drops μάλιστα and ἡ from his source, moves βραχύλογον to the penultimate position, and in its place inserts ἄνθρωπον, creating an anaphoric catchword with v. 429. With regard to the second saying, our author drops both the connecting δέ and ἡ πρὸς θεόν, replaces πολλῶν λόγων with πολλοὺς λόγους and αἰτία with ποιεῖ (creating an epistrophic catchword with v. 430), and, most notably, uses ἀπειρία in lieu of ἀμαθία, thereby drawing attention to the experiential rather than the intellectual nature of the problem at hand (cf. above on v. 429).

In v. 156, brevity of speech was attributed to σοφία. Here it is attributed to γνῶσις (cf. vv. 44, 148, 406, 578), specifically, to knowledge of God. The one who knows God knows that it is dangerous to talk indiscriminately (vv. 152–154), especially about God (v. 352), and especially when those hearing such talk are morally impure (v. 407, cf. above on v. 429). One must therefore be "sparing with a word about God" (v. 361). For examples of the sort of laconic discourse Sextus has in mind here, we can turn, of course, to the *Sentences* themselves, as well as to the Pythagorean σύμβολα (for which see Clement, *Strom.* 5.5.27.1–5.5.31.5), including in particular the saying, "Rule your tongue before all else, when following the gods" (Iamblichus, *Protr.* 21; cf. Jas 1:26). Plutarch would add that not only is speaking concisely appropriate to discourse about the divine—it also imitates divine discourse itself (*Garr.* 511b). For more on βραχυλογία, see the commentary on v. 156.

On the other hand, for Sextus the opposite of knowledge is not ἀμαθία but ἀπειρία (cf. vv. 323, 567). Among early Christians, ἄπειρος could be used of an immature believer (e.g., Irenaeus, *Her.* 1.8.1). In the *Stromata*, for example, those "inexperienced" in faith are characterized as being prone to speak about God either inadequately or confusingly (Clement, *Strom.* 1.11.53.3; 6.14.112.4; 7.16.100.5; cf. Heb 5:12–13). In the *Sentences*, such individuals are characterized as being prone to speak about God excessively, a significant problem, since prolonged speech is seen as both a sign of ignorance (v. 157) and a gateway to sin (v. 155). Presumably, speaking excessively about God also increases the odds that one will say something unworthy of God (vv. 84, 353) or say something about God to those who are unworthy to hear it (vv. 350–351, 365, 407, 451). The "experienced" instructor, by contrast, has proven himself worthy to speak about God through his god-pleasing way of life (vv. 173, 356, 358–359, 383, 410). Cognizant of the stakes involved both for himself (v. 22) and for those to whom he speaks (vv. 195, 352), he prefers listening about God to speaking about God (vv. 171a–b, 366). For more on πολυλογία, see the commentary on v. 155; and for the theme of esotericism, vv. 350–352.

Sentence 432

Speaking excessively also increases the odds that one will speak immodestly. Cf. Herm. *Mand.* 11.12: "The person who seems to have a spirit exalts himself and wants to have a seat of honor, and immediately is arrogant and shameless and talkative." Among ancient moralists the κομπαστής was detested as much for his obstinacy as for his conceit (e.g., Aesop, *Fab.* 33; Philo, *Spec.* 2.18; Plutarch, *Crass.* 16.1; Philostratus, *Vit. Apoll.* 7.14.7). Abstaining from this sort of behavior was one of the ways in which sages differentiated themselves from sophists (e.g., Aelius Aristides, *Or.* 28.81; cf. on v. 284). As part of an appeal for his readers to demonstrate the proper communal spirit, the author of *1 Clement* holds up the example of Christ, who "did not come in the boasting (ἐν κόμπῳ) of imposture or pride, though he could have done so, but in humility" (*1 Clem.* 16.2). The critique of boasting, that is, of verbally asserting oneself at the expense of others, is also a recurring sapiential theme. See Prov 11:7 ("The boast of the ungodly perishes"); 20:9; 25:14; 27:1–2; Sir 10:26–27; 11:4; 32:12; Jas 3:5, 14; 4:16; Ps.-Phoc. 122; Theognis, *El.* 159–160; Menander, *Mon.* 778; P.Ins. 3.10–11; Diogenianus, *Paroem.* 6.70b; Publilius Syrus, *Sent.* 597. Because the sage is more concerned with pleasing God than with pleasing others (vv. 51, 112), he is not a braggart (v. 284) and is often uncomfortable when receiving praise (v. 241), preferring instead to give God the credit for everything he does nobly (vv. 113, 390). Cf. Jer 9:23–24 [9:22–23]; 1 Cor 1:31; 2 Cor 10:17.

Sentences 433–434

Because the sage is more concerned with pleasing God than with pleasing others, it is also the case that he aspires to the reality rather than the appearance of virtue (vv. 64–65). As someone who is chosen, that is, as someone who belongs to God (v. 2), this means that he aspires to a life worthy of God (v. 3, cf. v. 35), a life whose sole purpose is to live κατὰ θεόν (vv. 48, 201, 216). Armed with constant reminders that the true measure of such a life is not speech but action (vv. 163b, 177, 356, 359, 383, 408), the sage safeguards himself against such vices as love of reputation (v. 188), overpromising (v. 198), and self-deceit (v. 199). He will therefore never claim to be wise (v. 389b, also with ὑπισχνέομαι, cf. v. 470) or, as we learn here, chosen. The same spirit informs Ign. *Eph.* 14.2: "Those who profess to be Christ's will be recognized by their actions. For the work is a matter not of what one promises now, but of persevering to the end in the power of faith." Likewise, Clement asserts that the truly faithful are truly the salt of the earth, being "more elect in proportion as they are less conspicuous." Accordingly, they "do not wish to appear holy and are ashamed if someone calls them so ... scorning to let their nobility of nature be seen in the world" (*Quis div.* 36; cf. *Strom.* 6.17.149.5).

Apprehension regarding one's final status in the scheme of salvation safeguards against such vices as well, the observation in v. 434 serving as a motivation for the implicit imperative in v. 433. The appeal to fear at this point is consistent with the function of this emotion in certain wisdom texts, where it is presented as an antidote to arrogance and self-deceit, such as Prov 3:7 ("Do not be wise in your own eyes; fear the Lord, and turn away from evil"); 8:13 ("The fear of the Lord is hatred of evil. Pride and arrogance and the way of evil and perverted speech I hate"); Qoh 5:7; Sir 1:27 ("For the fear of the Lord is wisdom and discipline, fidelity and humility are his delight"), 30; 2:17; *m. Avot* 2:4: "Do not have confidence in yourself until the day you die." A variety of New Testament texts concur, advising that the spirituality appropriate for believers is one informed by fear, for example, Matt 10:28; Luke 12:5; 2 Cor 5:11; 7:1; Eph 5:21; Phil 2:12–13 ("Work out your own salvation with fear and trembling; for it is God who is at work in you, enabling you both to will and to work for his good pleasure"); 1 Tim 5:20; 1 Pet 1:17. This perspective continues in the apostolic period (e.g., *1 Clem.* 3.4; 19.1; 21.6–7; 22.1; 23.1; 28.1; 51.2; 57.5; 64.1; Pol. *Phil.* 2.1; 4.2; 6.3; *Ep. Barn.* 2.2; 4.11; 10.11; 19.2), with Herm. *Mand.* 7.1–5 conveying perhaps the most fully developed treatment of "the fear you must have to be saved" (*Mand.* 7.1; cf. 1.2; 6.1.1; 10.1.6; 12.2.4; *Sim.* 5.1.5; 8.11.2).

Verse 434 is absent from both Greek manuscripts (cf. vv. 437, 440), the translation above being based on the Latin text (Chadwick 1959, 140).

Sentences 435–440

Text

435 ἄνθρωπος δὶς ἐμπιπλώμενος τροφῇ καὶ μηδέποτε[a] μόνος[b] κοιμώμενος νύκτωρ συνουσίας οὐ φεύγει.
436a εἱμαρμένη πιστὸν οὐ ποιεῖ.
436b εἱμαρμένη θεοῦ χάριτος οὐκ ἄρχει· εἰ δὲ μή, καὶ θεοῦ.
437 * * *
438 πιστὸς ἀνὴρ τρέφεται ἐγκρατείᾳ.
439 γνῶθι ῥήματα καὶ κτίσματα θεοῦ καὶ τίμα[a] κατ' ἀξίαν τὸν[b] θεόν.
440 * * *

Translation

435 A person who doubly gorges himself with food and never sleeps alone at night cannot avoid (sexual) couplings.
436a Fate does not produce a faithful person.
436b Fate does not govern God's grace, otherwise it would govern God as well.
437 A faithful man welcomes bodily desires with reluctance.
438 A faithful man is nurtured in self-control.
439 Know God's words and works, and honor God accordingly.
440 Regard nothing that is evil as belonging to God.

Textual Notes
435–440 omit Π • 435[a] omit sy² • 435[b] omit lat • 437 omit Υ • 439[a] τίμα ἕκαστον: lat, sy² • 439[b] μετὰ: lat, sy² • 440 omit Υ

Commentary

Two elements in this block of sayings address the problem of somatic self-control, an isolated saying in v. 435 and a couplet on ἐγκράτεια in vv. 437–438, the latter being loosely bound to a couplet on fate (vv. 436a–b) by the use of faith language. Rounding out the unit is a contrastive couplet on the appropriate way to honor God (vv. 439–440).

Sentence 435

Regarding the final words of this line, Chadwick (1959, 62) reports as a conjecture of H. Lloyd-Jones συνουσίαν θεοῦ φεύγει. If adopted, comparison could then be made with v. 136: "Insofar as the body has longings, the soul is ignorant of God" (cf. v. 72). Staying with the text as printed by Elter (1892, 28) and Chadwick (1959, 62), on the other hand, presents problems of translation. Edwards and Wild (1981, 71) try "[he] does not avoid becoming like his passions," though comparison with the Latin (*concubitum non effugit*) suggests instead something more specifically sexual (the Syriac is unfortunately of little help at this point: "Every man who eats and satisfies himself twice in one day—and will even sleep by himself—will not acquire anything without fatigue and struggle"). In this case, comparison can be made with other places in the text where our author draws a connection between alimentary and sexual desires (see on vv. 239–240, 428). Cf. *T. Benj.* 6.3: The good man "does not gorge himself with food (οὐκ ἐμπιπλᾶται τροφῆς), nor is he led astray by visual excitement." For this use of συνουσίας φεύγει, mention can be made of Plutarch, *Amat.* 768a, which refers to slave girls who "flee" from sexual liaisons with their masters (cf. *T. Jos.* 8.2–3).

In *Ep.* 326b–c, Plato describes his first encounter with the "happy" life as observed in Italy and Sicily: "Men were gorging themselves twice a day and never sleeping alone at night (δίς τε τῆς ἡμέρας ἐμπιμπλάμενον ζῆν καὶ μηδέποτε κοιμώμενον μόνον νύκτωρ), and following all the other customs that go with this way of living." In his opinion, no young man cultivated in such practices could possibly grow up to be wise, moderate, or virtuous. Clement cites this passage in *Paed.* 2.1.18.1–4 as evidence of the sort of extravagance condemned by Paul in Phil 3:19.

Sentences 436a–b

In *Migr.* 179, Philo offers his critique of the Chaldeans, people who imagined that this visible universe was the only thing in existence, either being itself God or containing God in itself as the soul of the whole. And they made fate (εἱμαρμένη) and necessity divine, thus filling human life with much impiety by teaching that apart from phenomena there is no originating cause (αἴτιον) of anything whatever, but that the circuits of sun and moon and of the other heavenly bodies determine for every being in existence both good things and their opposites.

What is being offered here, of course, is a thinly veiled reference to the Stoics, many of whom were committed to a view of providence that was tantamount to determinism. Chrysippus, for example, held that "all things are enforced and linked through fate by a certain necessary and primary rationale" (*SVF* 2:1000) and defined fate itself as "the rationale of providence's act of government in the universe" (*SVF* 2:913; cf. *SVF* 1:532; 2:774, 917, 921, 944–945, 974, 997). While Sextus would agree that the universe is providentially ordered (v. 312, cf. vv. 380, 423), he would disagree with any explanation of this order that could be construed as fatalistic. God is not "the world" (vv. 20, 405–406), nor is he "governed" by anything (cf. vv. 42–43, 182, 288, 422–423), but is himself the "cause" of all things (cf. vv. 100, 113, 390). What "produces" a believer, on the other hand, is not fate but an individual's decision to live a life worthy of God (v. 5, and for the concept of freedom: vv. 17, 275, 309, 392), his or her place in the scheme of salvation being determined ultimately by God's grace (cf. vv. 35–36) and God's will (v. 373). As Clement explains, a person is faithful not by nature, but by "instruction, purification, and the beneficence of good works" (*Strom.* 5.1.3.3–4; cf. Justin Martyr, *1 Apol.* 43.1–8). Chadwick (1959, 181) also draws attention to Clement, *Exc.* 78: "Until baptism, they (the Valentinians) say, Fate is real; but after it the astrologists are no longer right. But it is not only the washing that is liberating, but the knowledge of who we were."

Sentences 437–438

This couplet is loosely connected to the one that precedes it by the repetition of faith language. Note πιστός in vv. 436a and 438, and *vir fidelis* in v. 437. Like vv. 434 and 440, v. 437 is absent from both Greek manuscripts, the translation above being based on the Latin text. Its reference to *libidines corporis* invites comparison with sayings like those in vv. 136, 204, and 209, which disassociate the pursuit of bodily pleasures from the life of faith (cf. vv. 72, 448). The sage accepts the fact that certain pleasures are necessary to his survival and therefore unavoidable (v. 276), but he does so only begrudgingly, since they represent forces that can enslave (vv. 75a–b), defile (v. 111), and corrupt (vv. 205–207) the human will. He therefore does nothing for the sake of pleasure (v. 232), seeing the body not as something to be loved (v. 101), but as something to be controlled (vv. 70–71a, 274a). As the Syriac translation puts it, "If a wise man falls suddenly into the lusts of the body, he quickly stifles them."

Accordingly, the sage is intent on nourishing himself not with too much food, since this impedes holiness (v. 108a, cf. vv. 265, 267), but with self-control, since this represents not only the source of his self-worth (v. 294), but also the basis upon which his piety is established (v. 86a, cf. v. 239), ἐγκράτεια providing a means by which he assimilates himself to God (vv. 49–50). The remark in v. 438 accords with another saying in the collection in which the verb τρέφω is used metaphorically, v. 413: "Nourish your soul with divine reason, and your body with plain food" (cf. Ephraem Syrus, *Paen.* 28.14–15). Employing a different kind of metaphor, Herm. *Vis.* 3.8.4 elucidates the relationship between self-control and faith by imaging the former as the daughter of the latter (cf. *Vis.* 3.8.7; Clement, *Strom.* 2.6.31.1). Elsewhere, the obligation "to protect faith and fear and self-control" is held up as a "foremost commandment" (Herm. *Mand.* 6.1.1; cf. Acts 24:24–25; 2 Pet 1:5–6). See also Clement, *Strom.* 2.18.80.5: "If we exercise self-control we continue on our journey in purity toward piety."

Sentences 439–440

As members of the faith, the readers' obligation to honor God is taken for granted (vv. 244, 319). The best way for them to fulfill this obligation, in the author's opinion, is to conform themselves to God as far as possible (v. 381) through the knowledge and imitation of God (vv. 41–44; cf. Porphyry, *Marc.* 11: "Appropriate honor has been rendered to God by the one who has firm knowledge of God"). Here the content of that knowledge is identified as ῥήματα καὶ κτίσματα θεοῦ (cf. Ps 33:4 [32:4]; Sir 42:15; John 14:10). For the former, cf. Matt 4:4; Luke 3:2; John 3:34; 8:47; Eph 6:17; Heb 1:3; 6:5; 11:3; 1 Pet 1:25. For the latter, cf. Wis 9:2; 13:5; 1 Tim 4:4; Jas 1:18. As Matt 22:29/Mark 12:24 indicates, those who "know neither the scriptures nor the power of God" find themselves incapable of understanding, much less honoring God appropriately (cf. Tertullian, *Res.* 36.2; Origen, *Comm. Matt.* 17.34–36; Ps.-Clement, *Hom.* 2.51; 3.50; 18.20; *Testim. Truth* 37.5–9). For this use of κατ' ἀξίαν, cf. Sext. 575. Note that the Latin translation of v. 439 ("Recognize who are God's children among his creatures and who alone are accordingly honored after God") departs substantially from the Greek (again, cf. vv. 244, 319), a point to bear in mind when interpreting vv. 434, 437, and 440.

Those who know God's words and works know that nothing evil can be ascribed either to them or to God himself. The source of evil things, then, is not God (v. 114) but something that is itself evil, such as an evil demon (v. 305, cf. vv. 39, 348–349). God is not only opposed to everything evil (v. 314)—the nature of the divine is such that it does not admit of anything except what is wise and good (v. 30). God does not cause evil; God judges evil (vv. 14, 39–40, 347). It is therefore never right for a human being to "think" evil of God (v. 82e, cf. v. 29). Compare Porphyry, *Marc.* 24 ("No god causes evils for a man; rather he himself causes them by the choices he makes for himself"); Ps.-Clement, *Hom.* 19.11 ("Men may be both good and evil, but God can be only incomparably good … while men beget evil and good, God can beget good alone; and while men do evil and good, God rejoices only in doing good … thus he alone is the cause of all good things"); Clement, *Strom.* 7.4.22.2: "The conceptions which the wicked form about God must naturally be bad, and those of the good must be excellent. And on this account he who is gnostic and truly royal in soul is both devout and free from superstition, persuaded that the only God is alone meet to be honored and reverenced, alone glorious and beneficent, abounding in well-doing, the author of all good and of nothing that is evil." For additional parallels, see the commentary on vv. 113–114. As with vv. 434 and 437, v. 440 is absent from both Greek manuscripts, the translation above being based on the Latin text. In his rendering, the Syriac translator appears to have been influenced by Jas 1:13–15: "Never admit in your mind that the evil of man is from God. Rather, man is tested either by his sin or by his lusts."

Sentences 441–451

Text

441 ψυχὴ πιστὴ ἁγνὴ καὶ σοφὴ καὶ[a] προφῆτις ἀληθείας θεοῦ.
442 οὐκ ἀγαπήσεις κύριον[a] τὸν θεὸν οὐκ ἔχων ἐν ἑαυτῷ οἷον ὁ θεὸς θέλει[b].
443 φίλον ἡγοῦ τὸ ὅμοιον τῷ ὁμοίῳ.
444 οὐκ ἀγαπῶν τὸν θεὸν οὐκ ἔσῃ παρὰ θεῷ.
445 ἔθιζε σεαυτὸν ἀεὶ ἀφορᾶν[a] πρὸς τὸν θεόν.

446 ὁρῶν τὸν θεὸν ὄψῃ σεαυτόν[a].
447 ὁρῶν τὸν θεὸν ποιήσεις τὸ ἐν σοὶ φρονοῦν ὁποῖον ὁ[a] θεός.
448 σέβου τὸ ἐν σοὶ καὶ ταῖς τοῦ σώματος ἐπιθυμίαις μὴ καθυβρίσῃς[a].
449 ἀσπίλωτόν[a] σου τὸ σῶμα τήρει ὡς ἔνδυμα τῆς[b] ψυχῆς παρὰ θεοῦ[c], ὡς καὶ τὸν χιτῶνά σου τηρεῖς[d] ἀσπίλωτον[a] ἔνδυμα ὄντα τῆς σαρκός.
450 σοφοῦ[a] διάνοια θεοῦ ἔνοπτρον.
451 ἀκολάστῳ ψυχῇ μὴ τόλμα λέγειν περὶ θεοῦ.

Translation

441 A faithful soul is holy and wise and a prophet of God's truth.
442 You will not love the lord God if you do not have within yourself what God wills.
443 Realize that like is dear to like.
444 If you do not love God, you will not be with God.
445 Accustom yourself to look always toward God.
446 If you see God you will see yourself.
447 If you see God you will make the ability to reason within you of the same sort as God's.
448 Revere that which is within you and do not insult it with the desires of the body.
449 Keep unstained your body, the garment of the soul that is from God, just as you keep unstained your coat, the garment of the flesh.
450 A sage's intellect is a mirror of God.
451 Do not dare to speak to an intemperate soul about God.

Textual Notes

441–443 omit Π • 441[a] omit lat • 442[a] omit sy² • 442[b] omit lat, sy² • 445[a] ἐφορᾶν: Υ • 446 omit Υ • 446[a] αὐτόν: lat, sy² • 447[a] omit Π • 448 omit Υ • 448[a] καθυβρίσεις: Π • 449[a] ἄσπιλον: Π • 449[b] omit Υ • 449[c] θεῷ: Υ • 449[d] τηρήσεις: Υ • 450[a] σοφή: Υ • 451 omit Π, sy²

Commentary

The final segment of the *Sentences* recapitulates a fair number of its more prominent themes: abiding by the truth (v. 441, cf. vv. 158, 168, 384), loving God by becoming like God (vv. 442–444, 447, cf. vv. 35, 44–45, 106a–b, 147–148, 292, 381), seeing God (vv. 445–447, cf. v. 417), recognizing the divine character of the intellect (vv. 447, 450, cf. vv. 46a, 61, 143–144, 394), keeping bodily desires in check (v. 448, cf. vv. 146, 240, 437), maintaining moral holiness (vv. 441, 449, cf. vv. 46b, 57b, 67, 81, 346), and, finally, practicing esotericism (v. 451, cf. vv. 350–351, 354, 407).

Sentence 441

According to Diogenes Laertius, Pythagoras was so greatly admired for his insight that his disciples were called "prophets of God's voice" (*Vit. phil.* 8.14). Here, the faithful (or, more specifically, their souls; cf. Origen, *Cels.* 3.81) are called prophets of God's truth, a description consistent with biblical expectations expressed in texts like Deut 18:22 and Jer 28:9. Cf. Origen, *Cels.* 7.15: "The prophets of the great God must necessarily speak the truth." Since nothing is more akin to wisdom than the truth (v. 168), the Sextine sage loves a true word (v. 158), especially a true word about God (v. 357), something that he honors as much as he honors God himself (v. 355, cf. v. 368). The addition of ἁγνή as a criterion of faith would appear to be particularly significant, drawing attention as it does to the matter of moral rectitude (cf. vv. 60, 67, 108a). Sextus would no doubt have agreed with the rule laid down in *Did.* 11.10: "If any prophet teaches the truth, yet does not practice what he teaches, he is a false prophet" (cf. v. 410). More generally, the declaration here accords with the elements of the basic profile of the prophetic vocation laid down by Clement in the *Stromata*, where we learn that prophets speak not only about faith (e.g., 2.2.8.2) but by faith (e.g., 1.9.45.2), not only about wisdom (e.g., 1.4.25.3) but through wisdom (e.g., 1.18.88.3), and not only about holiness (e.g., 4.25.159.1) but in a state of purity, so as "to have a share in the truth" (1.12.55.2; cf. 2.4.17.4).

Sentences 442–444

The three lines in this cluster are bound by the language of affection: ἀγαπάω in vv. 442 and 444, and φίλος in v. 443. In terms of their internal argument, the second line specifies the means for the first (it is not possible to love God without being like God), while the third offers its motivation (it is not possible to experience God's presence without loving—that is, being like—God).

In Deuteronomy, the faithful express their love for God by keeping his commandments (e.g., Deut 11:1). In the *Sentences*, they express their love for God by having that which God wills within themselves. At first sight, the latter approximates what we find in a text like 1 John 4:16 ("God is love, and those who abide in love abide in God, and God abides in them"), though it is important to note that for John the indwelling of God is thought to manifest itself especially in the love that believers have for one another (e.g., 1 John 4:20), while for Sextus it manifests itself especially in the sage's efforts to conform his intellect to the divine (vv. 381, 447), the διάνοια constituting the "something godlike" within (v. 35), the aspect of the human personality that houses (vv. 46a, 61, 144) and mirrors (v. 450) the divine in such a manner that it is always "with" God (v. 143). Loving God, then, can be understood as a process of recognizing and cultivating one's "kinship" with the divine (vv. 106a–b) both as mind (v. 26) and as wisdom (v. 30). After all, "what is wise is always similar to itself" (v. 147). The language of affection is appropriate for describing the level of seriousness attached to this process insofar as the commitment it entails allows of no compromises (v. 141). The sage must love God, not the body or anything that pertains to it (v. 101). Indeed, he must love God more than his own soul (v. 106b).

As Chadwick (1959, 181) notes, Aristotle quotes the proverb "like is dear to like" in *Eth. nic.* 8.1.6 and 9.3.3 (cf. Homer, *Od.* 17.218). A more relevant usage occurs in a passage quoted with approval by Clement in *Strom.* 2.22.133.1, namely, Plato, *Leg.* 716c–d, a *locus classicus* on assimilation to the divine: "What conduct, then, is dear to God and in his steps? One kind of conduct, expressed in the ancient saying that 'like is dear to like' when it is moderate.... He, then, that is to become dear to such a one must become, as far as he possibly can, of a like character; and, according to the present argument, he among us that is moderate is dear to God, since he is like him (θεῷ φίλος, ὅμοιος γάρ)." In the *Sentences*, that which is "dearest" (προσφιλέστατον) to God is that which becomes "like" (ὅμοιος) him as far as possible (v. 45, cf. v. 48), "likeness" (ὁμοίωμα) to God representing the greatest honor one can bestow on him (v. 44, cf. v. 148). While Plato conceptualizes friendship with God in terms of moral comportment (i.e., observing virtues like moderation), here Sextus conceptualizes it in terms of moral anthropology, drawing attention as he does in v. 442 to that which is like God within the human self. In this case comparison can be made with *Sent. Pythag.* 20[b–c] (cf. Porphyry, *Marc.* 19): "The god-filled intellect, firmly established, is joined to God, for like must gravitate to like (χωρεῖν γὰρ ἀνάγκη τὸ ὅμοιον πρὸς τὸ ὅμοιον)." Verse 443 is repeated as v. 592 in the appendices. For the theme of friendship with God, see also on v. 86b. For more on Sextus's doctrine of assimilation, see on vv. 44–45.

While *Sent. Pythag.* 20[b] speaks of the intellect that is like God being "joined" to God (συνάπτει θεῷ), and 1 John 2:5 speaks of those who love

God being "in" God, the final verse in this triad speaks of the readers being "with" God, παρὰ θεῷ representing for our author a signature expression (besides the references below, see vv. 32, 175, 375). Of particular interest is vv. 143–144, where we learn that what is always "with" God is not the sage as such but the sage's intellect, since this is the part of the sage in which God is said to abide. This reality is reflected in the conduct of the sage, who makes all of his decisions with reference to the divine presence (vv. 51–52, 55, 60, 82a, 426). Because the sage loves God in this manner, his life is "secure in the hand of God" (v. 419), that which is governed being "inseparable" from that which governs it (v. 423). For a similar use of this expression, see *1 Clem.* 21.8 (quoted by Clement in *Strom.* 4.17.108.4), which orders that everyone "learn what pure love is able to accomplish before God (παρὰ τῷ θεῷ), how the fear of him is noble and great and saves all those who live in it in holiness with a pure intellect." Cf. also Clement, *Quis div.* 27.5: "For in proportion as someone loves God, he slips more fully within the presence of God."

Sentences 445–447

The three lines in this cluster are held together by the use of the language of visual perception to describe the appropriation of the divine. Note ἀφορᾶν πρὸς τὸν θεόν in v. 445 and anaphoric ὁρῶν τὸν θεόν in vv. 446–447. Note also σεαυτόν in v. 445 and v. 446.

In 4 Macc 17:10, the martyrs are described as "looking to God" (εἰς θεὸν ἀφορῶντες) for strength, while the readers of Heb 12:1–2 are told that they should be "looking to" (ἀφορῶντες εἰς) the pioneer and perfecter of their faith. For a directive more in keeping with the one offered here, we must turn to *Diatr.* 2.19.29, where Epictetus explains to his students that his aim as their instructor is "to make of you a perfect work, secure against restraint, compulsion, and hindrance, free, prosperous, happy, looking to God (εἰς τὸν θεόν ἀφορῶντας) in everything both small and great" (cf. Plato, *Leg.* 804b; Clement, *Strom.* 1.25.165.3; Ps.-Justin Martyr, *Quaest. Christ. gent.* 195d). The Sextine sage, because he fixes his attention exclusively and continuously on the divine and conforming himself to it, is similarly free from all worldly constraints and distractions (e.g., vv. 264b, 275, 309, 392). Thus his soul not only "looks to" God, it "always sees God" (v. 417, cf. v. 224). For the form of the saying, cf. vv. 129, 412, and 414.

The second line can be interpreted as another Sextine variation on the Delphic maxim, γνῶθι σαυτόν (for discussion, see the commentary on vv. 394 and 398, and cf. v. 577: "Know God, so that you may also know yourself"). That self-knowledge can be obtained through a visually conceived perception of the divine is attested also by Clement, *Strom.* 2.15.70.5, which contends that the dictum, "Know thyself," in fact derives from an extracanonical saying of Jesus, namely, "You have seen your brother, you have seen your God" (cf. Tertullian, *Orat.* 26). According to Ps.-Gregogry of Nyssa, *Imag. dei sim.* 44.1332, meanwhile, the believer sees God when he sees himself, because when he truly "sees" himself what he sees is the image and likeness of God. In the *Sentences*, to know God is to know τὸ νοοῦν ἐν σοί (v. 394). To "see" or perceive God, then, involves perceiving not the self as such, but the highest aspect of the self, that is, the intellect, or "that which is of God" within the self (see above on v. 442). More than this, the sage not only sees God: he makes it possible for others to see God as well, insofar as his intellect images or "reflects" God to others (see below on v. 450).

Divine perception does not culminate in self-perception, however, but informs a process of bringing the self into conformity with the divine. Cf. Clement, *Paed.* 3.1.1.1: "To know oneself has always been, so it seems, the greatest of all lessons. For if anyone knows himself, he will know God; and, in knowing God, he will become like him." Insofar as it is τὸ ἐν σοὶ φρονοῦν that constitutes the true essence or "good" of the human self (vv. 315–316), it constitutes the proper object of self-perception. Accordingly, in the *Sentences* what is assimilated to the divine is not the self per se but the intellect (v. 381, cf. vv. 44–45, 148), such assimilation representing the ultimate purpose for which human beings are created and therefore the ultimate form of self-knowledge (v. 398). The idea that divine perception, conceptualized metaphorically as "seeing" the divine, is the basis for assimilating to the divine is variously attested in our source material. In *Phaedr.* 252e–253a, for instance, Plato similarly links the process of assimilation with a process of self-inquiry, explaining that those who love (cf. above on v. 442) and emulate a particular god, "when they search eagerly within themselves to find the nature of their god, they are successful, because they have been compelled to look towards the god (πρὸς τὸν θεὸν βλέπειν), and as they reach and grasp him by memory they are inspired and receive from him character and habits, so far as it is possible for a human being to have a share in god … and become like (ὁμοιότατον) their god as far as possible" (see also the quotation of Ps.-Plato, *Alc.* 133c below). For a Pythagorean formulation, we have Hierocles, *In aur. carm.* 21.5: "Virtue is in fact an image of God in the rational soul, and every image needs a model for its genesis, and the acquired image does not suffice unless it sees (βλέπῃ) that by the assimilation to which it will acquire its nobility." Paul, finally, develops a Christological application of the conceptual field in 2 Cor 3:18: "And all of us, with unveiled faces, seeing the glory of the Lord as though reflected in a mirror, are being transformed into the same image from one degree of glory to another" (cf. Origen, *Comm. Joan.* 32.336, 340, 357; *Comm. Rom.* 4.8; 5.8). For more on Sextus's visual imagery, see the commentary on v. 417. For his contribution to the doctrine of ὁμοίωσις θεῷ, see on vv. 44–45.

Sentences 448–449

This cluster of sayings is linked to the one that precedes it by the repetition of τὸ ἐν σοί in v. 447 and v. 448. If v. 447 describes the implications of proper self-perception for the intellect, then vv. 448–449 can be said to do the same for the body. Just as God, being divine, is to be revered by human beings (vv. 287, 369–370), "that which is within you," being "akin" to the divine (vv. 442, 447), is to be accorded due reverence as well (cf. v. 190). The intellect, then, is appropriately likened to a temple (vv. 35, 46a), and the self to a temple-worshiper, whose responsibility it is to keep both the temple and himself pure, that is, sinless (vv. 23, 46b, 57b, 102, 356, cf. v. 590). As readers of the *Sentences* already know, one of the principal obstacles to the fulfillment of this responsibility is the body and its desires (for ἐπιθυμία, see on vv. 146, 274b). It was common knowledge that those unable to control their lusts are more likely to act insolently (e.g., Xenophon, *Rep. Lac.* 3.2; Plato, *Resp.* 572c; Plutarch, *Brut. anim. rat.* 990f; Clement, *Paed.* 2.10.89.2). What is being insulted here, however, is not another human being but the aspect of the human self that ought to be honored and cared for (for the juxtaposition of σέβω and καθυβρίζω, cf. *Ep. Diogn.* 2.7; Theophilus, *Autol.* 3.30). Self-control, conversely, can be construed as a form of worship (v. 86a, cf. v. 412). Paul employs similar imagery in his appeal for holiness in 1 Cor 3:16–17, though for him God's temple is not the Christian self but the Christian community, and what "dwells within" is not the intellect but the Holy Spirit (cf. 1 Cor 6:19–20; 2 Cor 6:14–16). More in keeping with the usage here is Philo's discussion of Gen 1:26 in *Opif.* 69, where he explains that "it is in respect of the mind, the sovereign element of the soul, that the term 'image' is used.... It is in a fashion a god to him who carries and enshrines it as an object of reverence. For the human mind evidently occupies a position in the self precisely answering to that which the great Ruler occupies in all the world" (cf. *Somn.* 1.215). For an effort to draw out the imagery's moral implications, see Cicero, *Leg.*

1.59: "For he who knows himself will realize, in the first place, that he has a divine element within him, and will think of his own inner nature as a kind of consecrated image of God; and so he will always act and think in a way worthy of so great a gift of the gods." See further the commentary on vv. 35 and 46a.

Assumed in Sextus's statements is the reality of a body–soul connection: the soul cannot know God if the body is distracted with longings (v. 136), and it is through the body that God tests the soul (v. 425), whatever it pursued while in the body accompanying it as evidence when it goes to judgment (v. 347). As our author explains in v. 346, it is necessary to keep the body pure because it bears the "imprint" of the soul (cf. vv. 139a, 301, 345, 411). Using different metaphors, he also imagines the body enveloping the soul like a tent (v. 320) or, as we see here, like an article of clothing. For the body (or the flesh) as the "garment" of the soul, see Empedocles, frag. 126; Plato, *Cratyl.* 403b; *Gorg.* 523c; Plutarch, *Def. orac.* 415c; Sir 14:17; Philo, *Leg.* 2.55–59; Origen, *Cels.* 7.32. The metaphor is similarly integrated with temple imagery by Porphyry in *Abst.* 2.46.1: "In the shrines which people have allocated to gods, even footwear must be clean and sandals spotless; in our father's temple, this universe, should we not keep our last external garment, the skin tunic (χιτῶνα τὸν δερμάτινον), and live with it holy in the temple of the father?" The word ἀσπίλωτος, an extremely rare term (elsewhere only in Dioscorides Pedanius, *Mat. med.* 2.167.1; Oribasius, *Coll. med.* 11.1.64; 13.11.10), is equivalent in meaning to ἄσπιλος, which is used regularly in constructions with τηρέω, for example, Jas 1:27; 1 Tim 6:14; 2 Clem. 8.6; *Act. Just. Sept. Sod.* 3.3. Cf. Herm. *Sim.* 5.6.7: "For all flesh in which the holy spirit has lived will, if it proves to be undefiled and unstained, receive a reward." For this use of παρὰ θεοῦ, see v. 21.

Sentences 450–451

While the *Sentences* does not have a carefully constructed conclusion to match its introduction (see the commentary on vv. 1–5), the final couplet does at least pull together two important themes for our text, contrasting the sage and his godlike intellect (v. 450) with the undisciplined masses, who should not even be allowed to hear a word about God (v. 451).

In Wis 7:26 it is σοφία that "mirrors" the divine (cf. Philo, *QG* 1.57), while for Philo it is the words of scripture (*Contempl.* 78), and for Paul it is Christ (2 Cor 3:18; cf. 1 Cor 13:12; *Act. Joan.* 95). Here it is the intellect, an idea that may have been inspired by Ps.-Plato, *Alc.* 133c: "The way that we can best see and know ourselves is to use the finest mirror available and look at God." And that mirror is nothing other than the part of the human personality that most fully resembles the divine, namely, the part "where knowing and understanding take place." Thus "someone looking at that and grasping everything divine … would have the best grasp of himself as well" (cf. Philo, *Dec.* 105; Plutarch, *Plat. quaest.* 1002a). As in the *Sentences*, "seeing" God through the activity of the mind is said to inform the process of self-understanding (see above on vv. 445–447; for the mirror as a metaphor for self-examination and self-knowledge, see Philo, *Migr.* 98; *Mos.* 2.139; Epictetus, *Diatr.* 2.14.21; 3.22.51; Plutarch, *Rect. rad. aud.* 42a–b; Ps.-Plutarch, *Lib. ed.* 14a; Jas 1:23). However, for Sextus it is not the intellect as such but the intellect of the sage that mirrors God since his διάνοια is "pure" and "good" enough to become the abode of God (vv. 46a, 57b, 61, 143–144, cf. v. 381). Moreover, the vocation of the sage does not culminate in such self-knowledge, but through this he becomes humanity's benefactor (v. 176). Most important, through his rationally informed conduct, he actually "exhibits" (v. 307) and "images" (v. 190) God to others, providing an embodiment of the godly life for them to emulate (see on vv. 7a, 82d, 376a).

Given the importance Sextus assigns to the practice of esotericism (see on vv. 350–352), it is not surprising that he concludes on this theme. Perhaps the warning here even functions as a final reminder regarding the appropriate use of the text itself, in which case comparison can be made with concluding disclosure statements such as *Melch.* 27.4–6 ("These revelations do not reveal to anyone in the flesh, since they are incorporeal, unless it is revealed to you to do so"); *Apoc. Adam* 8.16–17; *Ap. John* 31.32–32.5; *Gos. Eg.* 68.1–69.17; *Disc. 8–9* 63.16–32. The readers of the *Sentences* have been instructed to say nothing about God to the multitudes (v. 360), to the depraved (v. 401), to the impure (v. 407), or, in a word, to the godless (v. 354). As Clement puts it, "the real philosophy and the true theology" should be disseminated only to those who have proven themselves in "a trial by faith in their whole way of life" (*Strom.* 5.9.56.3). The admonition here is in fact the twin of the one in v. 407, except that the latter uses ἀκάθαρτος in lieu of ἀκόλαστος (for which cf. vv. 68, 71b, 231; *Sent. Pythag.* 48: "Know that not only is the act of intemperance something wrong, but even to associate with that given to such acts"). Presumably, what makes such persons unworthy to hear even a word about God is that the intemperance that guides their lives engenders shameful pleasures that pollute the soul (e.g., vv. 102, 108b, 429), rendering it fit to house not God (as in vv.

46a–b) but demons (v. 348). Once again we can turn to Clement for a parallel: "It is not wished that all things should be exposed indiscriminately to all and sundry, or that the benefits of wisdom be communicated to those who have not even in a dream been purified in soul" (*Strom.* 5.9.57.2).

Bibliography

1. Sextus: Texts and Translations

Chadwick, Henry. 1959. *The Sentences of Sextus: A Contribution to the History of Early Christian Ethics*. TS 5. Cambridge: Cambridge University Press.
Conybeare, F. C. 1910. *The Ring of Pope Xystus*. London: Williams and Norgate.
Edwards, Richard A. and Robert A. Wild. 1981. *The Sentences of Sextus*. SBLTT 22. Chico: Scholars.
Elter, Anton. 1892. *Sexti Pythagorici, Clitarchi, Evagrii Pontici sententiae*. Vol. 1 of *Gnomica*. Leipzig: C. George.
Gildemeister, Johann. 1873. *Sexti Sententiarum recensiones latinam, graecam, syriacas*. Bonn: Marcus.
Kroll, J. 1924. Die Sprüche des Sextus. Pages 625–43 in *Neutestamentliche Apokryphen*. 2nd ed. Edited by Edgar Hennecke. Tübingen: Mohr-Siebeck.
Lagarde, Paul de. 1858. *Analecta Syriaca*. Leipzig: Teubner. Repr., Osnabrück: Otto Zeller, 1967.
Paola, Ferdinando de. 1937. *Le sentenze di Sesto*. Milan: Società anonima editrice Dante Alighieri.
Poirier, Paul-Hubert. 1983. *Les sentences de Sextus (NH XII,1)*. Bibliothèque copte de Nag Hammadi: Section "Textes" 11. Québec: Les Presses de l'Université Laval.
Ryssel, V. 1895–1897. Die syrische Übersetzung der Sextussentenzen. ZWT 38:617–30; 39:568–624; 40:131–48.
Wisse, Frederik. 1988. The Sentences of Sextus (XII,*1*). Pages 503–8 in *NHL*. San Francisco: Harper & Row.

2. STUDIES

Baumstark, Anton. 1922. *Geschichte der syrischen Literatur*. Bonn: Marcus & Weber.

Bogaert, P.-M. 1972. La Préface de Rufin aux Sentences de Sexte et à une œuvre inconnue: Interprétation, tradition du texte et manuscrit remembré de Fleury. *Revue Bénédictine* 82:26–46.

———. 1982. Les sentences de sexte dans l'ancien monachisme latin. Pages 337–40 in *Gnosticisme et monde hellénistique: Actes du colloque de Louvain-la-Neuve (11–14 mars 1980)*. Edited by J. Ries, Yvonne Janssens, and Jean-Marie Sevrin. Louvain-La-Neuve: Université catholique de Louvain, Institut orientaliste.

Bostock, Gerald. 2003. Origen and the Pythagoreanism of Alexandria. Pages 465–78 in *Origeniana Octava: Origen and the Alexandrian Tradition*. Edited by L. Perrone. BETL 164. Leuven: Leuven University Press.

Bouffartigue, Jean. 1979. Du grec au latin. La traduction latine des Sentences de Sextus. Pages 81–95 in *Etudes de littérature ancienne*. Edited by Suzanne Saïd. Paris: Presses de l'Ecole normale supérieure.

Caner, Daniel F. 1997. The Practice and Prohibition of Self-Castration in Early Christianity. *Vigilae christianae* 51:396–415.

Centrone, Bruno. 1996. *Introduzione a i pitagorici*. Rome: Laterza.

Cribiore, Raffaella. 1996. *Writing, Teachers, and Students in Graeco-Roman Egypt*. ASP 36. Atlanta: Scholars.

Davies, W. D., and Dale C. Allison. 1988–1997. *The Gospel According to Saint Matthew*. ICC. 3 vols. London: T&T Clark.

Delling, Gerhard. 1961. Zur Hellenisierung des Christentums in den "Sprüchen des Sextus." Pages 208–41 in *Studien zum Neuen Testament und zur Patristik: Erich Klostermann zum 90. Geburtstag dargebracht*. Deutsche Akademie der Wissenschaften zu Berlin. TU 77. Berlin: Akademie-Verlag.

Dillon, John M. 1977. *The Middle Platonists: 80 B.C. to A.D. 220*. Ithaca: Cornell University Press.

Dodds, E. R. 1965. *Pagan and Christian in an Age of Anxiety: Some Aspects of Religious Experience from Marcus Aurelius to Constantine*. Cambridge: Cambridge University Press.

Dörrie, Heinrich. 1963. Pythagoras 1C: Der nachklassische Pythagoreismus. PW 24.1:268–77.

Evans, G. R. 1983. The Sentences of Sextus in the Middle Ages. *JTS* 34:554–55.
Francis, James A. 1995. *Subversive Virtue: Asceticism and Authority in the Second-Century Pagan World*. University Park: Pennsylvania State University Press.
Garitte, Gérard. 1959. Vingt-Deux 'Sentences de Sextus' en Géorgien. *Le Muséon: Revue d'études orientales* 72:355–63.
Gildemeister, Johann. 1870. Pythagorassprüche in syrischer Überlieferung. *Hermes* 4:81–98.
Hermann, Th. von. 1938. Die armenische Überlieferung der Sextussentenzen. *ZKG* 57:217–26.
Kirk, Alan. 1998. *The Composition of the Sayings Source: Genre, Synchrony, and Wisdom Redaction in Q*. NovTSup 91. Leiden: Brill.
Köhler, Wolf-Dietrich. 1987. *Die Rezeption des Matthäusevangeliums in der Zeit vor Irenäus*. WUNT 2/24. Tübingen: Mohr-Siebeck.
Küchler, Max. 1979. *Frühjüdische Weisheitstraditionen: Zum Fortang weisheitlichen Denkens im Bereich des frühjüdischen Jahweglauben*. OBO 26. Freiburg: Universitätsverlag; Göttingen: Vandenhoeck & Ruprecht.
Lazaridis, Nikolaos. 2007. *Wisdom in Loose Form: The Language of Egyptian and Greek Proverbs in Collections of the Hellenistic and Roman Periods*. Mnemosyne 287. Leiden: Brill.
Meeks, Wayne A. 1993. *The Origins of Christian Morality: The First Two Centuries*. New Haven: Yale University Press.
Morgan, Teresa. 1998. *Literate Education in the Hellenistic and Roman Worlds*. Cambridge: Cambridge University Press.
———. 2007. *Popular Morality in the Early Roman Empire*. Cambridge: Cambridge University Press.
Murphy, Francis X. 1945. *Rufinus of Aquileia (345–411): His Life and Works*. Washington, D.C.: Catholic University of America Press.
Muyldermans, J. 1929. De discours de Xystus dans la version arménienne d'Evagrius le Pontique. *Revue des études arméniennes* 9:183–201.
Outtier, Bernard. 1978. Deux mots des 'Sentences de Sextus' en Géorgien. *Le Muséon: Revue d'études orientales* 91:153–54.
Riedweg, Christoph. 2002. *Pythagoras: Leben, Lehre, Nachwirkung*. München: Beck.
Rocca-Serra, G. 1971. La Lettre à Marcella de Porphyre et les Sentences des Pythagoriciens. Pages 193–99 in *Le néoplatonisme*. Edited by Pierre

M. Schuhl and Pierre Hadot. Paris: Centre national de la recherche scientifique.

Rubenson, Samuel. 2004. Wisdom, Paraenesis and the Roots of Monasticism. Pages 521–34 in *Early Christian Paraenesis in Context*. Edited by James Starr and Troels Engberg-Pedersen. Berlin: de Gruyter.

Russell, Norman. 2004. *The Doctrine of Deification in the Greek Patristic Tradition*. Oxford: Oxford University Press.

Schenkl, Heinrich. 1886. Pythagoreersprüche in einer Wiener Handschrift. *Wiener Studien* 8:262–81.

Silvestre, Hubert. 1963. Trois nouveaux témoins latins des *Sentences* de Sextus. *Scriptorium* 17:128–29.

Thesleff, Holger. 1961. *An Introduction to the Pythagorean Writings of the Hellenistic Period*. Acta Academiae Aboensis: Humaniora 24:3. Åbo: Åbo Akademi.

Valantasis, Richard. 1995. Constructions of Power in Asceticism. *JAAR* 63:775–821.

———. 2001. Nag Hammadi and Asceticism: Theory and Practice. Pages 172–90 in *Ascetica, Gnostica, Liturgica, Orientalia*. Edited by M. F. Wiles and E. J. Yarnold. StPatr 35. Leuven: Peeters.

Vogel, C. J. de. 1966. *Pythagoras and Early Pythagoreanism*. Assen: Van Gorcum.

Vogüé, Adalbert de. 1973. "Ne juger de rien par soi-même": Deux emprunts de la Règle colombanienne aux Sentences de Sextus et à saint Jérôme. *Revue d'histoire de la spiritualité* 49:129–34.

———. 1986. Deux Sentences de Sextus dans les oeuvres de Césaire d'Arles. *SacEr* 29:19–24.

Waerden, B. L. van der. 1979. *Die Pythagoreer: Religiöse Bruderschaft und Schule der Wissenschaft*. Die Bibliothek der Alten Welt. Zürich: Artemis.

Wilken, Robert L. 1975. Wisdom and Philosophy in Early Christianity. Pages 143–68 in *Aspects of Wisdom in Judaism and Early Christianity*. Edited by Robert L. Wilken. Notre Dame: University of Notre Dame Press.

Wisse, Frederik. 1975. Die Sextus-Sprüche und das Problem der gnostischen Ethik. Pages 55–86 in *Zum Hellenismus in den Schriften von Nag Hammadi*. Edited by Alexander Böhlig and Frederik Wisse. Wiesbaden: Harrassowitz.

3. Texts and Translations

Where available, the editions used for Greek and Latin texts (including Philo and Josephus) are from the Loeb Classical Library; for patristic texts, from Jacques-Paul Migne, *Patrologiae cursus completus: Series Graeca* (161 vols.; Paris: Migne, 1857–1866). Translations for texts from the Old Testament Pseudepigrapha are from James H. Charlesworth, *Old Testament Pseudepigrapha* (2 vols.; Garden City: Doubleday, 1983, 1985). Note also the following:

Aelius Aristides
    Charles A. Behr. *Aelius Aristides: The Complete Works.* 2 vols. Leiden: Brill, 1981–1986.

Aesop, *Fabulae*
    August Hausrath and Herbert Hunger. *Corpus fabularum Aesopicarum.* 2nd ed. Leipzig: Teubner, 1959.

Aesop, *Proverbia*
    Ben E. Perry. *Aesopica.* Urbana: University of Illinois Press, 1952. Pages 265–91.

Aesop, *Sententiae*
    Ben E. Perry. *Aesopica.* Urbana: University of Illinois Press, 1952. Pages 248–58.

Anecdota Graeca
    Jean-François Boissonade. ΑΝΕΚΔΟΤΑ: *Anecdota Graeca e codicibus regiis.* 5 vols. Paris: F. G. Levrault, 1833. Repr., Hildesheim: Georg Olms, 1962.

Ankhsheshonqy
    Miriam Lichtheim. *Late Egyptian Wisdom Literature in the International Context: A Study of Demotic Instructions.* OBO 52. Freiburg: Universitätsverlag; Göttingen: Vandenhoeck & Ruprecht, 1983. Pages 13–92.

Apophthegmata patrum (collectio alphabetica)
    Jacques-Paul Migne. *Patrologiae cursus completus: Series Graeca.* Paris: Migne, 1857–1866. Vol. 65. Pages 72–440.

Apophthegmata patrum (collectio anonyma)
    François Nau. Histoires des solitaires égyptiens. *Révue de l'Orient Chrétien* 12 (1907): 48–68, 171–81, 393–404; 13 (1908): 47–57, 266–83; 14 (1909): 357–79; 17 (1912): 204–11, 294–301; 18 (1913): 137–46.

Apophthegmata patrum (collectio systematica)
: Jean-Claude Guy. *Les apophtegmes des pères: collection systématique, chapitres i–ix*. Sources chrétiennes 387. Paris: Cerf, 1993.

Ps.-Archytas
: Holger Thesleff. *The Pythagorean Texts of the Hellenistic Period*. Acta Academiae Aboensis: Humaniora 30:1. Åbo: Åbo Akademi, 1965. Pages 2–48.

Ps.-Aresas
: Holger Thesleff. *The Pythagorean Texts of the Hellenistic Period*. Acta Academiae Aboensis: Humaniora 30:1. Åbo: Åbo Akademi, 1965. Pages 48–50.

Arsenius, *Apophthegmata*
: E. L. von Leutsch and F. G. Schneidewin. *Corpus paroemiographorum Graecorum*. 2 vols. Göttingen: Vandenhoeck & Ruprecht, 1839. Repr., Hildesheim: Georg Olms, 1958. Vol. 2. Pages 240–744.

Babylas of Antioch, *Passio*
: Johannes Bolland. *Acta sanctorum quotquot toto orbe coluntur, vel à catholicis scriptoribus celebrantur: Januarii Tomus II*. 2nd ed. Venice: S. Coleti et J. B. A. Hieron, 1734. Pages 571–76.

Carmen aureum
: Johan C. Thom. *The Pythagorean Golden Verses*. Religions in the Graeco-Roman World 123. Leiden: Brill, 1995.

Chionis epistulae
: Ingemar Düring. *Chion of Heraclea: A Novel in Letters*. New York: Arno, 1979.

Clementina
: Johannes Irmscher, Franz Paschke, and Bernhard Rehm. *Die Pseudoklementinen I: Homilien*. 2nd ed. Die griechischen christlichen Schriftsteller 42. Berlin: Akademie Verlag, 1969.

Clitarchus, *Sententiae*
: Henry Chadwick. *The Sentences of Sextus: A Contribution to the History of Early Christian Ethics*. TS 5. Cambridge: Cambridge University Press, 1959. Pages 73–83.

Corpus Hermeticum
: A.-J. Festugière and A. D. Nock. *Corpus Hermeticum*. 4 vols. Paris: Belles Lettres, 1945–1954. Repr., 1972.

Democritus and Ps.-Democritus
: Hermann Diels and Walther Kranz. *Die Fragmente der Vorsokratiker*. 6th ed. 3 vols. Berlin: Weidmann, 1951–1954. Vol. 2. Pages 81–230.

Ps.- Diotogenes
   Holger Thesleff. *The Pythagorean Texts of the Hellenistic Period*. Acta Academiae Aboensis: Humaniora 30:1. Åbo: Åbo Akademi, 1965. Pages 71–77.
Ps.-Ecphantus
   Holger Thesleff. *The Pythagorean Texts of the Hellenistic Period*. Acta Academiae Aboensis: Humaniora 30:1. Åbo: Åbo Akademi, 1965. Pages 78–84.
Epicurus
   Graziano Arrighetti. *Epicuro: Opere*. Rev. ed. Biblioteca di cultura filosofica 41. Turin: Einaudi, 1973.
Epiphanius, *Panarion*
   Philip R. Amidon. *The Panarion of St. Epiphanius, Bishop of Salamis: Selected Passages*. Oxford: Oxford University Press, 1990.
Evagrius Ponticus
   Robert E. Sinkewicz. *Evagrius of Pontus: The Greek Ascetic Corpus*. Oxford: Oxford University Press, 2003.
Gnomologium Byzantinum ἐκ τῶν Δημοκρίτου Ἰσοκράτους Ἐπικτήτου
   Curt Wachsmuth. *Studien zu den Griechischen Florilegien*. Berlin: Weidmannsche Buchhandlung, 1882. Pages 162–207.
Gnomologium Democrateum
   Hermann Diels and Walther Kranz. *Die Fragmente der Vorsokratiker*. 6th ed. 3 vols. Berlin: Weidmann, 1951–1954. Vol. 2. Pages 153–65.
Gnomologium Epictetum
   Heinrich Schenkl. *Epicteti dissertationes ab Arriano digestae*. Leipzig: Teubner, 1916. Repr., 1965. Pages 476–92.
Gnomologium Vaticanum
   Graziano Arrighetti. *Epicuro: Opere*. rev. ed. Biblioteca di cultura filosofica 41. Turin: G. Einaudi, 1973. Pages 139–57.
Iamblichus, *De vita Pythagorica*
   John M. Dillon and Jackson P. Hershbell. *Iamblichus: On the Pythagorean Way of Life*. SBLTT 29. Atlanta: Scholars, 1991.
Justin Martyr
   Dennis Minns and Paul Parvis. *Justin, Philosopher and Martyr: Apologies*. Oxford: Oxford University Press, 2009.
Mantissa proverbiorum
   E. L. von Leutsch and F. G. Schneidewin. *Corpus paroemiographorum Graecorum*. 2 vols. Göttingen: Vandenhoeck & Ruprecht, 1839. Repr., Hildesheim: Olms, 1958. Vol. 2. Pages 745–79.

Maximus of Tyre
> M. B. Trapp. *Maximus of Tyre: The Philosophical Orations*. Oxford: Clarendon, 1997.

Menander, *Collectio monostichorum*
> S. Jaekel. *Menandri Sententiae*. Leipzig: Teubner, 1964.

Mishnah
> Jacob Neusner. *The Mishnah: A New Translation*. New Haven: Yale University Press, 1988.

Musonius Rufus
> Cora E. Lutz. *Musonius Rufus: "The Roman Socrates."* YCS 10. New York: Yale University Press, 1947.

Origen, *Contra Celsum*
> Henry Chadwick. *Origen: Contra Celsum*. Cambridge: Cambridge University Press, 1953.

Origen, *Homiliae in Lucam*
> Joseph T. Lienhard. *Origen: Homilies on Luke; Fragments on Luke*. Fathers of the Church 94. Washington, D.C.: Catholic University of America Press, 1996.

Origen, *De principiis*
> G. W. Butterworth and Henri de Lubac. *Origen: On First Principles*. Gloucester: Peter Smith, 1973.

Papyrus Insinger
> Miriam Lichtheim. *Late Egyptian Wisdom Literature in the International Context: A Study of Demotic Instructions*. OBO 52. Freiburg: Universitätsverlag; Göttingen: Vandenhoeck & Ruprecht, 1983. Pages 107–234.

Papyrus Louvre 2377
> Miriam Lichtheim. *Late Egyptian Wisdom Literature in the International Context: A Study of Demotic Instructions*. OBO 52. Freiburg: Universitätsverlag; Göttingen: Vandenhoeck & Ruprecht, 1983. Pages 100–3.

Ps.-Phintys
> Holger Thesleff. *The Pythagorean Texts of the Hellenistic Period*. Acta Academiae Aboensis: Humaniora 30:1. Åbo: Åbo Akademi, 1965. Pages 151–55.

Ps.-Phocylides
> Walter T. Wilson. *The Sentences of Pseudo-Phocylides*. Commentaries on Early Jewish Literature. Berlin: de Gruyter, 2005.

Pistis Sophia
  Carl Schmidt and Violet MacDermot. *Pistis Sophia*. NHS 9. Leiden: Brill, 1978.
Porphry, *De abstinentia*
  Gillian Clark. *Porphry: On Abstinence from Killing Animals*. London: Duckworth, 2000.
Porphyry, *Ad Marcellam*
  Kathleen O'Brien Wicker. *Porphyry the Philosopher: To Marcella*. SBLTT 28. Atlanta: Scholars, 1987.
Posidonius
  Willy Theiler. *Poseidonios: Die Fragmente*. Texte und Kommentare 10. 2 vols. Berlin: de Gruyter, 1982.
Ps.-Pythagoras
  Holger Thesleff. *The Pythagorean Texts of the Hellenistic Period*. Acta Academiae Aboensis: Humaniora 30:1. Åbo: Åbo Akademi, 1965. Pages 155-86.
Regula Magistri
  Adalbert de Vogüé. *La Régle du Maître*. Sources chrétiennes 105-7. 3 vols. Paris: Cerf, 1964-1965.
Regula Sancti Benedicti
  Timothy Fry, et al. *The Rule of St. Benedict in Latin and English with Notes*. Collegeville: Liturgical Press, 1981.
Scholia in Aeschylum
  Ole L. Smith. *Scholia Graeca in Aeschylum quae exstant omnia*. 2 vols. Leipzig: Teubner, 1976-1982.
Secundus, *Vita et sententiae Secundi*
  Ben Edwin Perry. *Secundus the Silent Philosopher*. Philological Monographs 22. Ithaca: Cornell University Press, 1964.
Sententiae Pythagoreorum
  Henry Chadwick. *The Sentences of Sextus: A Contribution to the History of Early Christian Ethics*. TS 5. Cambridge: Cambridge University Press, 1959. Pages 84-94.
Sententiae Pythagoreorum (fort. auctore vel collectore Demophilo)
  Anton Elter. *Gnomica homoeomata*, pt. 5. Programm zur Feier des Geburtstages seiner Majestät des Kaisers und Königs am 27. Januar 1904. Bonn: Georg, 1905. Coll. 1-36.
Septem Sapientes, *Apophthegmata* (ex collectione Demetrii Phalerei)
  Hermann Diels and Walther Kranz. *Die Fragmente der Vorsokratiker*. 6th ed. 3 vols. Berlin: Weidmann, 1951-1954. Vol. 1. Pages 63-66.

Septem Sapientes, *Praecepta* (sub auctore Sosiade)
    F. W. A. Mullach. *Fragmenta philosophorum graecorum*. 3 vols. Paris: Didot, 1860–1881. Repr., Aalen: Scientia, 1968. Vol. 1. Pages 217–18.
Septem Sapientes, *Sententiae*
    F. W. A. Mullach. *Fragmenta philosophorum graecorum*. 3 vols. Paris: Didot, 1860–1881. Repr., Aalen: Scientia, 1968. Vol. 1. Pages 215–16.
Sophocles, *Fragmenta*
    S. L. Radt. *Tragicorum Graecorum fragmenta*, vol. 4. Göttingen: Vandenhoeck & Ruprecht, 1977.
Stoa
    Hans F. A. von Arnim. *Stoicorum veterum fragmenta*. 4 vols. Leipzig: Teubner, 1903–1924. Repr., New York: Irvington, 1986.
Stobaeus
    Curt Wachsmuth and Otto Hense. *Ioannis Stobaei Anthologium*. 5 vols. Berlin: Weidmann, 1884–1912. Repr., Zürich: Weidmann, 1999.
Teles
    Edward N. O'Neil. *Teles, the Cynic Teacher*. SBLTT 11. Missoula: Scholars, 1977.
Theophilus, *Ad Autolycum*
    Robert M. Grant. *Theophilus of Antioch: Ad Autolycum*. Oxford: Clarendon, 1970.
Tryphon, Περὶ τρόπων
    Leonhard von Spengel. *Rhetores graeci*. 3 vols. Leipzig: Teubner, 1853–1856. Repr., Frankfurt a.M.: Minerva, 1966. Vol. 3. Pages 191–206.
Ps.-Zaleucus
    Holger Thesleff. *The Pythagorean Texts of the Hellenistic Period*. Acta Academiae Aboensis: Humaniora 30:1. Åbo: Åbo Akademi, 1965. Pages 225–29.
Zenobius
    E. L. von Leutsch and F. G. Schneidewin. *Corpus paroemiographorum Graecorum*. 2 vols. Göttingen: Vandenhoeck & Ruprecht, 1839. Repr., Hildesheim: Georg Olms, 1958. Vol. 1. Pages 1–175.

Index of Greek Words

Numbers refer to verses in the *Sentences*, not pages in the commentary. The follow terms are not included: ἄν, ἀνήρ, ἄνθρωπος, ἀπό, αὐτός, δέ, διά, εἰμί, εἰς, ἐκ, ἐν, ἤ, θεός, καί, κατά, μέν, μετά, μέχρι, μή, μηδεῖς, ὁ, ὅς, οὐ, οὗτος, παρά, πᾶς, περί, πρό, πρός, σύ, τίς, ὑπέρ, ὑπό, ὡς.

ἀγαθός	13, 23, 28, 42 bis, 43, 46b, 61, 79, 91a, 131, 132, 165a, 197, 243, 246, 271, 273, 277, 283 bis, 292, 295, 296, 316, 317, 324, 336, 345, 349, 366, 376b bis, 377, 381, 395
ἀγανακτέω	15, 91b, 321
ἀγαπάω	101, 106a, 106b, 158, 442, 444
ἄγγελος	32 bis
ἀγενής	401
ἅγιος	46a
ἁγνεία	108a
ἀγνοέω	136, 174, 283, 285
ἁγνός	60, 67, 441
ἀγνωμονέω	331 bis
ἄγω	253a
ἀγών	239, 282
ἀγωνίζω	332
ἀδελφός	331
ἀδιάφορος	109
ἀδικέω	23, 63 bis, 370, 386
ἀδικία	138, 208b
ἄδικος	66
ἀδύνατος	186
ἀεί	55, 80, 143, 147, 417, 418, 445
ἀείδω	53
ἀθάνατος	14
ἄθεος	354, 380
ἄθλιος	396
αἰδέομαι	37, 238 bis
αἰδώς	253a
αἱρετός	152, 362
αἰσχρός	102, 180 bis, 202, 272, 286
αἰτέω	81, 124, 128, 329
αἴτιος	100, 113, 188, 390
ἀκάθαρτος	102, 108b, 348 bis, 407
ἀκοινώνητος	296, 338, 377
ἀκολασία	68, 71b
ἀκόλαστος	231, 451
ἀκολουθέω	264a
ἀκόρεστος	287
ἀκούω	72, 171a, 171b, 177, 195, 217 bis, 338, 351, 396, 415b
ἀκρασία	108b, 345
ἀκρατής	429
ἀκριβής	9, 20
ἀκτήμων	18, 377
ἀλαζών	284
ἀλήθεια	8, 168, 372, 384, 441
ἀληθής	158, 165a, 165e, 352, 355, 357, 368, 410
ἀλλά	12, 28, 64, 88, 110, 338, 392, 397, 426
ἄλλος	12, 32, 88, 295, 297 bis, 327, 336, 426
ἀμαθία	157
ἁμαρτάνω	12, 107, 165e bis, 234, 247, 283 bis
ἁμάρτημα	11, 174, 181, 194, 233, 297, 298
ἁμαρτία	155
ἁμαρτωλός	107
ἀμαυρόω	345

ἀμείνων	13, 165a, 283, 366	ἀποδίδωμι	20
ἄμετρος	280a	ἀποθνήσκω	345
ἀναβαίνω	204	ἀποκόπτω	273
ἀναγκάζω	306	ἀπολαμβάνω	39
ἀναγκαῖος	19, 50, 119 bis, 165e, 251, 276 bis	ἀπόλλυμι	54, 397
		ἀποπέμπω	236
ἀνάγω	402	ἄπορος	146
ἀναιρέω	263, 300	ἀποτάσσω	78
ἀναίσθητος	25	ἀποτίθημι	320
ἀναίτιος	114	ἀποχή	109
ἀναμάρτητος	8, 36, 46b, 60	ἀπροσεξία	280a
ἀνάξιος	4, 5	ἀρέσκω	112
ἀναπείθω	13	ἄριστος	23, 42 bis, 43, 46b, 283, 324, 376b bis, 381
ἀναπνέω	289		
ἀναφέρω	390	ἁρμόζω	385, 416
ἀναχόω	298	ἀρχή	137, 207
ἀνδρίζω	230b	ἄρχω	42, 43 bis, 182 bis, 236, 240 bis, 274a, 288, 363a, 363b, 422 bis, 423 bis, 436b
ἀνδροφόνος	324		
ἀνελεύθερος	170		
ἀνεπίδεκτος	30	ἀσέβεια	96
ἀνεπίφθονος	51	ἀσέβημα	11
ἄνευ	154, 215, 290, 399	ἀσεβής	85
ἀνεύθυνος	173	ἀσκέω	51, 64, 69, 98, 120, 334
ἀνίατος	331	ἀσπίλωτος	449 bis
ἀνιάω	254	ἀσφαλής	351
ἄνοδος	420	ἀσχήμων	225
ἀνόητος	103	ἄτιμος	415a
ἀνόσιος	356	ἄτοπος	99
ἀντιποιέω	348	αὐγή	30
ἄξιος	3, 4, 58, 122, 132, 248, 250, 329, 376a, 439	αὐτάρκεια	98, 334
		αὐτάρκης	148, 263
ἀξιόω	58	αὐτοκίνητος	26
ἀπαιδευσία	285	ἀφαιρέω	15, 17, 64, 91b, 92, 118, 130, 275, 321, 322, 387, 404
ἀπαλλαγή	39		
ἀπαλλάττω	63, 127, 209, 265, 337	ἀφίημι	264a
ἅπας	109, 166, 185, 210a	ἀφοράω	445
ἀπατάω	165b, 165f, 186, 393 bis	ἀφόρητος	139b, 150
ἀπάτη	165a	ἀφροδίσιος	240
ἀπειλή	364	ἀχαριστέω	229
ἄπειμι	272, 347	ἀχάριστος	328
ἀπειρία	323, 431	ἄχρηστος	172, 214
ἀπευκτός	261	ἀχώριστος	423
ἄπιστος	6, 7b, 241, 400		
ἀπλήρωτος	146	βάλλω	152
ἀποβολή	257	βαρύνω	320, 337

INDEX OF GREEK WORDS

βασανίζω	411 bis
βασιλεία	311
βέβαιος	77, 405
βεβαιόω	177, 304
βελτίων	91a, 273
βίος	10, 37, 123, 177, 201, 282, 326a, 326b, 397, 400
βιόω	9, 34, 196
βλάπτω	185, 302, 318
βλασφημέω	85
βλάσφημος	83
βλέπω	391
βόρβορος	81
βουλεύω	327
βούλομαι	88, 306
βραχυλογία	156
βραχύλογος	430
βραχύς	379
γαμετή	238
γαμέω	230b bis
γάμος	230a, 239
γάρ	13, 28, 32, 64, 66, 85, 243, 255, 262, 263, 274b, 322, 393
γαστήρ	240, 270, 345, 428 bis
γέλως	280a
γῆ	55, 391, 402
γίνομαι	88, 107, 117, 125, 149, 150, 165c, 199, 245, 321, 324 bis, 364, 375, 398
γινώσκω	145, 283, 333, 342, 369, 394, 398, 439
γλῶσσα	83, 84, 151, 426
γνήσιος	196, 277
γνῶσις	44, 148, 406, 430
γυμνός	191
γυνή	231, 235, 236 bis, 237
δαίμων	39, 305, 348, 349
δείκνυμι	200
δειλός	170
δεινός	75a, 225
δέομαι	49, 50 bis, 52, 88, 93, 127, 141 bis, 153, 162b, 163b, 165f, 171a, 178, 217, 290, 330, 344, 378 bis, 379, 382 bis, 388, 389a, 392
δεσμός	322
δεσπότης	75b
δεύτερος	33
δή	32, 363b
διαβολή	259
διαλέγομαι	366
διανοέω	66
διάνοια	46a, 57b, 61, 62, 83, 143, 144, 163a, 381, 450
διαφθείρω	351
διαχέω	280b
διάχυσις	281
διδάσκω	174
δίδωμι	36 bis, 38, 91b, 92, 195, 230a, 242, 329, 339, 342 bis, 378, 404
δικάζω	184
δίκαιος	64, 65, 261, 399, 410
δικαστής	184
δίς	93, 435
δισσός	247
δόγμα	338
δοκέω	64 bis, 191, 209
δοκιμάζω	425
δοκιμή	7a
δόμα	379
δόξα	28, 103, 341, 351
δουλεύω	75a, 264b
δύναμαι	213, 236, 246 bis, 285, 293, 320
δύναμις	45, 48, 381
δυνατός	78, 85 bis, 169, 186, 378
δῶρον	218
ἑαυτοῦ	129, 147, 226, 231, 273, 322, 381, 442
ἐγγύς	376b
ἐγκράτεια	86a, 239, 253b, 294, 438
ἐγώ	255 bis
ἐθίζω	129, 412, 414, 445
εἰκῇ	152, 362
εἰκών	190
εἱμαρμένη	436a, 436b
εἴσειμι	110
ἕκαστος	64
ἑκάτερος	230b
ἐκεῖ	316

ἐκεῖνος	41, 251	ἔσχατος	39
ἐκλεκτός	1, 2, 35, 433	ἕτερος	180, 336
ἐκμαγεῖον	346	ἔτι	265
ἐκπονέω	100	εὐγνωμοσύνη	332
ἐκφεύγω	71b, 155	εὐδαιμονέω	344
ἑκών	388	εὐδαιμονία	133, 148, 387
ἔλεγχος	76, 83, 103, 163a	εὐεργεσία	47
ἐλέγχω	245 bis	εὐεργετέω	33 bis, 213, 322, 328
ἐλευθερία	17, 275	εὐεργέτης	176, 210a, 260
ἐλεύθερος	264b, 309	εὐθυμέω	385
ἐλευθερόω	392	εὐθυμία	262
ἐμπίπλημι	435	εὐθύνω	39
ἐμποδίζω	108a, 349	εὔκαιρος	279
ἔμψυχος	109	εὔκλεια	237
ἐναντίος	30	εὐλογιστία	69
ἔνδυμα	449 bis	εὔλογος	81, 121a, 121b
ἕνεκα	232, 341	εὐμαρής	410
ἔννοια	57a, 97	εὑρίσκω	28
ἐνοικέω	144, 347	εὐσέβεια	86a, 86b, 223
ἔνοπτρον	450	εὐσεβής	46a, 87, 228, 374
ἐνοχλέω	139a	εὔφημος	84
ἐντρυφάω	117	εὐχάριστος	257
ἔξειμι	110	εὐχή	126, 217
ἐξευρίσκω	27, 243, 403	εὔχομαι	80, 88, 122, 125, 213, 277, 372, 374, 375
ἐξομοιόω	45, 381		
ἐξουσία	36, 60, 375	ἐχθρός	105, 213
ἐπαινέω	121a, 150, 286	ἔχω	15, 21, 35, 60, 192, 224, 238, 273, 277, 286, 295, 331, 333 bis, 338, 347, 368, 375, 442
ἔπαινος	241, 299		
ἐπιδημέω	55		
ἐπιζητέω	115, 317		
ἐπιθυμία	146, 274b, 448	ζάω	7a, 7b, 13, 39, 48, 53, 190, 201, 215, 216, 230a, 254 bis, 255 bis, 262, 399
ἐπικαλέω	303		
ἐπιλαμβάνω	40	ζηλόω	50
ἐπιλήψιμος	16, 38	ζητέω	28, 29
ἐπίσταμαι	187		
ἐπιστήμη	164b	ἡγεμών	104, 125, 166, 305
ἐπιτηδεύω	5, 112, 164a, 260, 347, 360	ἡγέομαι	11, 23, 79, 105, 113, 131, 197, 201, 202, 261, 276, 286, 338, 375, 380, 443
ἐπιτρέπω	280b		
ἐπιτροπεύω	424		
ἐπιχειρέω	290	ἤδη	82a
ἕπομαι	151, 421	ἡδονή	70, 111, 232, 272, 276, 342, 411
ἐράω	291, 292	ἡδύς	268, 272
ἐργάτης	384	ἦθος	110, 165b, 326a, 326b
ἔργον	308, 356, 359, 383, 395, 408	ἤπερ	171b, 306, 403
ἔρημος	368	ἡττάομαι	111, 165a, 270

INDEX OF GREEK WORDS

ἥττων	380
θάνατος	208b, 321, 323, 397
θεῖος	277, 406, 413
θέλω	80, 82a, 89, 94, 134 bis, 179, 210b, 247, 262, 265, 298, 312, 442
θέμις	365
θεοσέβεια	287, 371
θεοσεβής	82d, 326b, 412
θεοφιλής	251, 340, 358, 359, 363a, 419
θηρίον	270
θησαυρός	300
θυσία	47
θυσιαστήριον	46b
ἴδιος	227, 308, 342, 373
ἰδρύω	419
ἱερόν	35, 46a
ἵνα	28, 42, 56, 93, 153, 230a, 245, 385
ἴσος	194
καθαίρω	24, 103
καθάπερ	230b
καθαρεύω	181, 356
καθαρμός	23
καθαρός	36, 46b, 57b, 81, 346
καθήκω	161
καθό	26
καθυβρίζω	448
καιρός	160, 163a
κακία	150, 208a, 322
κακοδοξία	188
κακοπραγμονέω	262
κακός	12, 39 bis, 62 bis, 57b, 82e, 83, 85, 110, 114, 116, 130, 149 bis, 163a, 165c, 202, 203, 211 bis, 212, 254, 305 bis, 312, 313, 327 bis, 349, 396, 397
κάκωσις	96
καλέω	28, 59, 222
καλός	56 bis, 81, 100, 104, 113, 142 bis, 166, 196, 197 bis, 215, 255, 267, 304, 330, 390, 395, 399, 414
καρδία	46b, 204, 419
κατατίθημι	263, 300
καταφρονέω	82b, 121a, 127, 299
καταψεύδομαι	367
κατέχω	128
κατόρθωμα	298
κάτω	391
κήδω	340, 423
κίνδυνος	184, 352
κλέος	53
κοδράντης	39
κοιμάομαι	435
κοινός	210a, 228 bis, 260
κοινωνέω	266, 311, 350
κολάζω	63, 261
κολακεύω	149
κομπάζω	432
κοσμικός	19
κόσμος	15, 16, 20 bis, 37, 82b, 235, 405
κρατέω	70, 428
κρείσσων	28, 336, 345, 377
κρηπίς	86a, 371
κρίνω	22, 183 bis, 258, 295, 329
κρίσις	14, 347
κτάομαι	77, 84, 115, 118, 121b, 128, 264a, 277
κτῆμα	81, 227, 228, 274b, 310
κτῆσις	137, 274b
κτίσμα	439
κυριεύω	41, 363a
κύριος	442
λαμβάνω	124, 242, 329, 378
λανθάνω	57a, 66, 142, 325, 401
λέγω	22, 58, 153 bis, 161, 162b, 164a, 164b, 165a, 165e bis, 165g, 171a, 171b, 221 bis, 234, 352, 353, 354, 358, 360, 365, 367, 368, 407, 410, 451
λέων	363b
λίθος	152
λιμός	345
λιτός	413
λογικός	109
λόγος	24, 53, 74, 123, 126, 152, 160, 163a, 163b, 165c, 173, 177, 185, 186, 187, 195, 205, 233, 264a, 277, 286, 350, 355, 356, 357 bis, 359, 361, 362, 363a, 365, 366, 383, 396, 401, 408, 413, 420, 431

λοιδορέω	175	νομίζω	14, 21, 54, 195, 227, 235, 249, 274a, 285, 297a, 315, 324, 346, 365, 372, 380 bis
λοιπός	273		
λυπέω	323		
λύω	322	νόμος	123
		νόσημα	207
μάθημα	248, 251	νόσος	208a
μακάριος	40, 320, 326b, 424	νοῦς	26, 151, 154, 181, 333
μακρολογία	157	νύκτωρ	435
μάλιστα	84, 165f, 247, 325, 364		
μᾶλλον	165g, 171b, 185, 254, 278, 306, 361, 389b, 403	ὁδηγέω	167
		ὁδός	349
μανθάνω	248, 290 bis, 344, 353, 394	οἶδα	94, 162a, 162b, 220, 230b bis, 233, 245, 250, 398, 432
μανία	269		
μαρτύριον	347	οἰκεῖος	79, 168, 293
μάρτυς	165c, 303	οἴομαι	199, 410
μάταιος	126	οἷος	326a, 442
μεγαλοφρονέω	121b, 129	ὀλέθριος	13
μεγαλοψυχία	120	ὄλεθρος	73, 203
μέγας	44, 51, 52, 96, 165d, 184, 198 bis, 200, 274a, 285, 308, 379	ὀλιγόπιστος	6
		ὀλίγος	50, 53, 139a, 145, 383
μέγεθος	27, 403	ὅλος	379
μέθη	269	ὅμοιος	12, 18, 45, 147, 269, 270, 443 bis
μειδιάω	280b	ὁμοίωμα	44, 148
μέλος	13 tris, 273, 335	ὁμολογέω	225, 234, 236
μέντοι	186	ὁμόφυλος	106a
μεστός	223	ὄνειδος	174, 272, 339, 400
μεταδίδωμι	82b, 295, 330, 379, 382, 401	ὄνομα	28 bis, 175
μετανοέω	206	ὀνομάζω	28 tris
μέτειμι	170	ὁποῖος	35, 80, 82a, 447
μετέχω	277	ὁπόσος	15
μηδέποτε	435	ὁπόταν	375
μήποτε	401	ὁπότε	163b, 165e, 320
μιαίνω	82e, 110, 111, 429	ὁράω	165g, 273, 417, 446 bis, 447
μικρός	9, 10 bis, 297a, 352, 415a	ὀργή	293, 343
μιμνήσκω	59, 82c, 182, 221, 222, 364	ὀρέγω	99
μισθός	341	ὄρεξις	137
μοιχεύω	233	ὀρθός	264a
μοιχός	231, 233	ὁρμή	74
μόνος	47, 49, 55, 79, 131, 135, 197 bis, 338, 363b, 410, 435	ὀρφανός	340
		ὅσος	31, 75b, 78, 136, 301, 310, 404
		ὅσπερ	295
νεκρός	7b, 175	ὅταν	81, 209, 221
νηστεύω	267	ὅτε	22, 161, 162b
νικάω	71a, 165b bis, 187, 332	ὁτιοῦν	339
νοέω	54, 56, 82e, 95a, 233, 289, 394	οὐδαμός	382

INDEX OF GREEK WORDS

οὐδέ	12 bis, 66, 133, 226, 318
οὖν	5, 28, 29, 32, 35, 36, 346, 422, 423
οὖς	409
οὐσία	25, 330
ὀφθαλμός	12 bis, 224
πάθος	75a, 75b, 204, 205, 206, 207, 209
παιδεία	274a
παιδοποιέω	230b bis
παραδέχομαι	259
παραθήκη	21, 195
παραιτέω	230a
παραίτιος	321
παρακολουθέω	156
παραμένω	272
παρασκευή	117
παραχρῆμα	329
πάρεδρος	230a
παρέχω	16, 405, 412
παροξύνω	343
παρρησία	253a
πάσχω	179, 327
πατήρ	59, 222, 225, 228, 340
παύω	274b, 328
πείθω	25, 91a, 331, 358 bis
πεῖρα	408
πέλας	17, 89, 210b
πέρα	280b
πέρας	73, 203
περιγίνομαι	165a
περιεργία	249
περιέχω	121a, 251
περίστασις	165d, 200, 385
πέτομαι	27
πιστεύω	196, 258, 409
πίστις	6, 7a, 7b, 170, 188, 325, 402
πιστός	1, 5, 7a, 8, 36, 49, 166, 169, 171a, 171b, 189, 200, 204, 209, 212, 220, 223, 234, 235, 239, 243, 247, 256, 257, 294, 349, 383, 384, 428, 436a, 438, 441
πλείων	115, 140, 165g, 281, 329, 340
πλεονεξία	137
πλῆθος	112, 243, 343, 360
πλουτέω	193
πλοῦτος	294
ποθέω	136
ποιέω	31 bis, 85 bis, 90, 91a, 93, 102, 108b, 123, 139b, 178 bis, 179, 180, 198, 212, 229, 232, 290, 326b, 344, 388 bis, 389a bis, 408, 430, 431, 433, 436a, 447
πολέμιος	140, 205, 314
πόλεμος	230b
πολιτεύω	263
πολυκτήμων	377
πολυλογία	155
πολυμαθία	249
πολυπραγμονέω	262
πολύς	108a, 115, 140, 165g, 192, 223, 229, 262, 281, 325, 329, 340, 383, 431, 432
πονέω	301 bis
πόνος	125 bis
πορεύομαι	40
πόσος	273
πότε	25
ποτόν	110, 268
ποῦ	391
πρᾶγμα	19
πρᾶξις	95b, 102, 104, 166, 304, 305
πρᾶος	320
πράττω	4, 5, 48, 56, 58, 59, 66, 93 bis, 94 bis, 95a, 113, 163b, 206, 222, 224, 225, 262, 288 bis, 303, 306, 390, 399
πρέπον	131, 165d, 197
πρίν	333
προαιρέω	43, 373
προδότης	365
προηγέομαι	74, 95b, 160, 359
προθυμία	379
πρόθυμος	330
προίημι	362
προίξ	242 bis
προνοέω	372, 423
πρόνοια	312
προπετής	366
προσηνής	47
προσποίησις	325
προστάσσω	180
προσφέρω	111
προσφιλής	45

πρότερος	33, 164a, 333, 358, 408	συνουσία	435
προτιμάω	171a	συντηρέω	331
προφῆτις	441	σύστασις	35 bis
πτερόν	27	σῴζω	193, 373, 374
πτωχός	267	σῶμα	7a, 7b, 13, 39, 55, 71a, 78, 82d, 101, 115, 127, 136, 139a, 139b, 273, 274a, 301, 321, 322, 335, 337, 346, 347, 363a, 363b, 411 bis, 412 bis, 413, 425, 448, 449
ῥᾴθυμος	126		
ῥῆμα	154, 223, 439		
ῥίπτω	13, 81, 273		
ῥύομαι	116	σωφρονέω	13, 273
ῥώννυμι	273	σωφροσύνη	235
		σώφρων	13, 67, 237, 399, 412
σάρξ	271, 291, 317, 449		
σαυτοῦ	16, 38, 87, 211, 219, 234, 280b, 321, 398, 401, 412, 445, 446	ταχύς	272
		τέκνον	254, 256 bis, 257, 340
σέβομαι	190, 369, 370, 448	τελευτάω	53
σεμνός	278, 282	τέλος	86b, 201
σημεῖον	157, 280a	τηρέω	346, 405, 449 bis
σιγάω	161, 366, 427	τιμάω	41, 42, 65, 130, 135, 189, 192, 219 bis, 244, 298, 319, 355, 381, 427, 439
σίδηρος	324		
σιτίον	108b, 110, 111, 413	τιμή	14, 44
σιωπάω	162a, 164b	τίμιος	32, 426
σκέπτομαι	93, 153	τιμωρία	14
σκήνωμα	320	τοιγάρ	34
σκῶμμα	279	τοίνυν	344
σοφία	156, 167, 168, 285, 406	τοιοῦτος	326a, 347
σοφός	18, 24, 30, 53, 143, 144, 145, 147, 176, 190, 191 bis, 194, 199, 214, 226, 244, 245, 246, 250, 252, 253b, 287, 301, 302, 306, 307, 308, 309, 310, 311, 322, 363b, 389b, 391, 403, 415b, 416, 417, 418, 421 bis, 422, 423, 424, 425, 426, 427, 441, 450	τολμάω	407, 451
		τοσοῦτος	75b
		τότε	81, 165e, 209, 364, 375
		τράπεζα	391
		τρέφω	267, 413, 438
		τρόπος	389a
		τροφή	108a, 265, 266, 379, 435
σπάνιος	243, 279	τρυφή	73
σπουδάζω	142	τύραννος	363b, 364, 387
σπουδή	281		
στόμα	110, 286	ὑβρίζω	339
συγχωρέω	410	ὕβρις	203 bis
σύλλογος	164a	υἱός	58 bis, 60, 135, 221 bis, 376b
συμβάλλω	133	ὑπακούω	28
συμβουλία	165f	ὑπείκω	17
συμφέρω	88, 165g	ὑπερήφανος	320
σύνειμι	418	ὑπεροράω	299
συνεχής	289	ὑπηρετέω	336 bis
συνίστημι	307	ὑπηρέτης	32, 319

INDEX OF GREEK WORDS

ὑπισχνέομαι	198, 389b, 433
ὕπνος	253b
ὑπομένω	216
ὑπονοέω	178
ὑπουργέω	341 bis
ὑφίστημι	26
φαίνω	214
φάρμακον	159
φαῦλος	214, 314
φείδομαι	252, 361
φέρω	119, 246 bis, 257, 285, 293
φεύγω	68, 313, 435
φθάνω	327
φθέγγομαι	356
φιλανθρωπία	371
φιλάνθρωπος	300
φιλαυτία	138
φιλέω	141 bis, 226
φιληδονία	71b, 139b
φιλήδονος	72, 172
φιλία	86b
φιλοδοξία	188
φιλομαθής	384
φίλος	443
φιλοσκώπτης	278
φιλόσοφος	218 bis, 219, 227, 229, 258, 259, 275, 278, 284, 293, 300, 319, 392
φιλοσωματία	76
φιλοχρηματία	76
φιλοψευδής	169
φοβέω	386
φόβος	323
φορτίον	335
φρονέω	308, 315, 316, 447
φρόνησις	426
φυλάττω	241, 269, 393
φύσις	169, 170, 401
φύω	138, 139a, 271
φῶς	95b
φωτίζω	97
χαίρω	382, 414 bis, 415a, 422 bis
χαλεπός	107, 187, 193, 230b bis, 338
χαρίζω	48
χάρις	245, 436b
χείρ	12 bis, 419
χειρίζω	195
χιτών	449
χράω	12, 19, 35, 87, 89 bis, 159, 163b, 173, 210a, 210b bis, 211 bis, 281, 330, 335
χρή	320
χρῆμα	192, 274b
χρηματισμός	392
χρῆσις	109
χρηστός	52
χρόνος	54, 252, 325
χρυσός	116
χωρίς	13, 17, 251
χῶρος	61, 62
ψέγω	90, 194, 298
ψευδής	165c, 165e, 367
ψεῦδος	159, 165d
ψεύδω	393
ψιλός	232
ψόγος	299
ψόφος	154
ψυχή	21, 24, 40, 55, 75b, 77, 82d, 97, 103, 106b, 116, 129, 136, 139a, 167, 195, 205, 208a, 208b, 209, 249, 287, 292, 301, 313, 318, 320, 323, 345, 346, 347, 348, 349, 361, 362, 379, 392, 397, 402, 403, 407, 411 bis, 412, 413, 414, 415a, 415b, 416, 417, 418, 420, 421, 425, 441, 449, 451

Index of Texts Cited

The contents of this index are organized as follows: 1. Old Testament; 2. Deuterocanonical Writings; 3. New Testament; 4. Old Testament Pseudepigrapha; 5. Josephus and Philo; 6. Rabbinic Literature; 7. Christian Writers and Works; 8. Gnostic Tractates; 9. Greek and Roman Writers and Works; 10. Ancient Egyptian Writings.

1. Old Testament

Leviticus
  19:18 — 28, 125

Deutonomy
  10:9 — 310
  18:22 — 353

Job
  31:18 — 338

Psalms
  13:3 — 185
  51:6 — 184
  51:17 — 84
  74:18 — 200
  139:4 — 185

Proverbs
  3:7 — 379, 411
  3:11–12 — 254
  3:27 — 369
  8:13 — 411
  9:8 — 254
  10:19 — 27, 182
  11:14 — 193
  12:4 — 248
  12:18 — 180
  12:21 — 133
  12:26 — 192
  14:25 — 184
  15:23 — 185
  17:27–28 — 182
  18:18 — 189
  18:21 — 178
  19:8 — 237, 316
  19:17 — 91
  20:13 — 260
  22:9 — 372
  26:12 — 218
  26:18–19 — 208
  26:28 — 184
  28:23 — 254
  28:27 — 370

Qoheleth
  7:16 — 379

Isaiah
  54:14 — 377

Jeremiah
  9:23–24 — 380

2. Deuterocanonical Writings

Tobit
  4:5 — 203
  4:6–9 — 370
  4:7 — 91
  4:10–11 — 372

4:18	193	31:5	214
		31:6	173
Wisdom		31:12–19	271
3:1	401	31:15	128
3:5	47	31:23	273
9:15	320	31:28–29	274
		32:9	188
Sirach		33:4	181
1:27	411	35:3	63, 363
2:4	156	36:24	393
2:16–18	401	37:7–8	192
4:10	338	37:16	111, 131
4:23	186	41:25	338
4:29	188, 374	42:18	95
5:12	187	42:20	95
5:13–6:1	190		
6:1	141	4 Maccabees	
6:7	266, 393	1:3	110
7:8	255	1:26	210
9:18	181	1:30–31	110
10:13	170	3:17	107
11:7–9	188	5:20–21	300
11:10	268	5:20	50
12:3	370	5:22–23	106
13:15–16	141	6:7	357
16:1–3	263	6:35	106
16:6	142	7:1–3	357
17:22–23	372	9:7–8	357
17:22	91	13:7	106
18:15	338	13:13	357
18:18	387	17:10	420
18:19	181		

3. New Testament

20:5	189		
20:6–7	185	Matthew	
20:7	186	5:23–24	297
20:14–15	338	5:26	26
20:18	180	5:28	244
20:20	185	5:29–30	52
21:20	286	5:29	28
21:25	183	5:39	101
22:15	291	5:44	228
26:15	248	5:48	101
27:9	375	6:1–4	339
27:13	286	6:19–20	165
28:17–18	207		

Matthew (cont.)
- 6:19 — 28
- 7:2 — 206
- 10:8 — 28, 252, 269
- 15:11 — 147
- 18:8–9 — 52
- 18:8 — 53
- 19:21 — 269
- 19:23 — 214
- 20:26 — 28
- 22:21 — 60
- 22:29 — 415

Mark
- 4:40 — 197
- 12:24 — 483
- 16:14 — 388

Luke
- 6:27–28 — 228
- 6:30 — 55, 329
- 16:10 — 50

John
- 8:47 — 399

Acts
- 2:44–47 — 239
- 10:4 — 91

Romans
- 2:24 — 200
- 7:18 — 277
- 12:16 — 379
- 14:21 — 147

1 Corinthians
- 3:18 — 332
- 13:12 — 400

2 Corinthians
- 1:21 — 307
- 1:23 — 306
- 3:18 — 422
- 5:4 — 320
- 5:8 — 320
- 8:11–12 — 330
- 9:7 — 330

Ephesians
- 4:24 — 219
- 4:25 — 184
- 5:1 — 96
- 5:8 — 275

Philippians
- 2:12–13 — 411
- 4:11 — 135

1 Thessalonians
- 2:13 — 353
- 5:14 — 291

2 Thessalonians
- 2:10 — 184

1 Timothy
- 2:1 — 364
- 2:9 — 246

2 Timothy
- 3:2 — 170
- 3:3–4 — 359
- 4:2 — 187

Titus
- 1:12–13 — 408

Hebrews
- 1:14 — 70
- 5:2 — 291
- 12:1–2 — 420
- 13:7 — 195

James
- 1:5 — 338
- 1:16 — 382
- 1:27 — 339
- 3:1 — 63
- 3:8 — 185

5:3	344	142	141

1 Peter

1:15–17	237
2:12	56, 75
2:16	270
3:14	56
4:6	28, 219

2 Peter

1:5–6	124
2:2	384

1 John

1:5	28, 68
3:2	400
3:18	188, 374
4:16	418

Sentences of Syriac Menander

2	202
52–56	275
63–66	249
65	408
128–32	229
250–53	227
302	286
312	189

Testaments of the Twelve Patriarchs

T. Benj. 6.3	413
T. Gad 5.5	203
T. Jos. 18.2	228
T. Zeb. 7.2	252

4. OLD TESTAMENT PSEUDEPIGRAPHA

Aristeae epistula

132–33	96
212	225
227	229
234	84
281	201

Oracula Sibyllina

2.272–73	338

Ps.-Philo, *L.A.B.*

33.2–3	61

Ps.-Phocylides, *Sent.*

8	253
11	206
22	329
28–29	252, 369
32–34	323
43	155
60	172
61	108
67	295
69b	172

5. JOSEPHUS AND PHILO

Josephus, *Ant.*

1.14	166

Josephus, *C. Ap.*

2.160	140
2.208	268
2.216	268

Josephus, *Vita*

80	90

Philo, *Abr.*

20–21	268
26	289
208	364
223	223
261	311

Philo, *Cher.*

86	166

Philo, *Conf.*

45	315
65	208

Philo, *Congr.*		Philo, *Migr.*	
130	170	57	367
		128	269, 402
Philo, *Contempl.*		179	413
16	259		
		Philo, *Mos.*	
Philo, *Dec.*		1.154	301
73	175	1.185	174
119	319	1.299	112
122	171	2.24	205
170	64		
		Philo, *Mut.*	
Philo, *Det.*		13	67
114	402	30	315
170	63	217	306
		240	382
Philo, *Deus*			
3	68	Philo, *Opif.*	
143	278, 316	69	422
		75	140
Philo, frag.		81	111
2.649	172	134	343
		144	86
Philo, *Fug.*			
85	122	Philo, *Plant.*	
		64	310
Philo, *Gig.*		167	287
63–64	43		
		Philo, *Praem.*	
Philo, *Hypoth.*		20	340
7.6	204	123	173
		159	224
Philo, *Ios.*			
87	331	Philo, *Prob.*	
		20	195, 270, 310
Philo, *Leg.*		60	282
1.102	253		
2.1	81	Philo, *QE*	
3.62	342	2.3	228
3.185	111		
3.238	115	Philo, *QG*	
3.241	300	1.70	49, 385
3.242	107		
		Philo, *Sobr.*	
		45	224

Philo, *Somn.*
1.124	124, 155
2.40	298
2.100	80

Philo, *Spec.*
1.100	342
1.103	289
1.287	84
4.191	51

Philo, *Virt.*
8–9	59
15	331
85	302
164	68

6. Rabbinic Literature

m. Avot
1:13	211
1:15	374
1:17	182, 189
2:1	50
4:10	268

b. Berakot
18a	225, 385

7. Christian Writers and Works

Acta et martyrium Apollonii
44	85

Acta Philippi
111	169

Acta Thomae
12	262

Apophthegmata patrum [al.]
116.22–24	129

Apophthegmata patrum [an.]
379	117

Apophthegmata patrum [sy.]
4.87	298

Aristides of Athens, *Apol.*
15	274

Asterius, *Comm. Ps.*
4.13	364

Athanasius, *Vit. Ant.*
20.9	61
45.5	155, 397
46.6	334
65.3	76
66.5	76, 345

Athenagoras, *Legat.*
7.2–3	351
16.3	68

Athenagoras, *Res.*
21.3	169

Augustine, *Nat. grat.*
64.77	98

Barnabae epistula
6.15	84
19.8	272
19.11	329, 338

1 Clement
16.2	410
21.8–9	96
21.8	420
38.2	290
57.1–2	289

2 Clement
1.3–4	97
2.3	360
19.4	327
20.4	101

Clement, *Ecl.*		Clement, *Protr.*	
32.3	392	10.105.3	87
Clement, *Exc.*		Clement, *Quis div.*	
78	414	13.6	272
		17.1	316
Clement, *Paed.*		18.3	52
1.8.64.4	224	23.1	200
1.8.74.2	342	27.5	420
1.9.78.2	254	28.1	142
1.9.81.3	289	29	71
1.9.82.2	139	36	411
1.9.82.3	139	36.1	43, 49, 367
1.10.91.3	137		
1.12.98.4	136	Clement, *Strom.*	
2.1.1.4	148	1.1.9.1	348
2.1.5.2	398	1.1.14.3	351
2.1.7.3	398	1.1.18.1	27
2.1.7.4	276	1.2.19.4	257
2.1.8.4–9.1	146, 148	1.5.30.2	257, 407
2.1.9.4	380	1.6.35.2	258
2.1.11.1	147	1.6.35.3	291
2.1.16.3	146	1.7.38.1	295
2.1.16.4	136	1.7.38.4	394
2.1.17.3	144	1.9.43.4	257
2.2.24.2	275	1.12.55.2	392, 418
2.3.39.1	136	1.12.55.4	348
2.3.39.4	176	1.12.56.3	40
2.5.45.4	287	1.19.93.2	257
2.5.46.1–47.3	286	1.19.95.7	360
2.5.48.1	287	1.27.173.5	314
2.6.52.4	182	2.2.4.2	196
2.7.57.3	298	2.2.5.3–4	367
2.9.78.5	261	2.7.34.2	225
2.9.80.1–2	261	2.7.57.3	266
2.10.90.2	407	2.8.40.2	222
2.10.92.2	244	2.9.45.3	184
2.10.99.3	243	2.11.51.6	110
2.12.121.4	386	2.13.57.1	255
3.1.1.1	87, 104, 383, 421	2.13.57.2	255
3.7.39.2	155	2.13.57.4	255
3.11.55.2	138	2.13.59.6	222
3.11.64.1	246	2.15.70.5	421
3.12.96.1	236	2.16.72.1	398
		2.18.79.3	230

INDEX OF TEXTS CITED

2.18.80.5–81.1	87	7.1.3.6	165, 258
2.18.80.5	124, 415	7.2.7.6	225
2.18.84.1	293, 362	7.2.10.1	221
2.18.85.3	273	7.3.13.3	222
2.19.97.1	81, 85	7.3.14.1	85
2.19.97.2	85, 227	7.3.14.3	222
2.19.100.3	166, 175	7.3.16.3–4	206
2.19.102.2	201	7.3.16.5	212
2.20.119.5	108	7.3.20.7	386
2.23.143.1	244	7.4.22.2	416
2.23.144.3	111, 281, 381	7.4.27.4	64
3.5.41.2	111	7.6.32.5	84
3.5.42.5	82	7.6.32.8	146
3.5.43.1	168	7.6.33.6	146
3.7.58.3	249	7.7.35.4	118, 236
3.9.64.1	385	7.7.38.4	161
3.9.65.3	321	7.7.40.1–2	283
3.14.95.3	264	7.7.41.5	160
4.4.13.1	321	7.7.42.4–7	365
4.4.17.1–3	322	7.7.44.3–4	115
4.8.67.2	358	7.7.44.5	366
4.10.76.1–77.3	322	7.7.44.8	259
4.12.82.2	245	7.7.46.9	293
4.18.117.2	76	7.7.47.5	293
4.20.127.2	140	7.9.53.1	179
4.25.162.5	65	7.9.53.2	191
5.1.3.3–4	414	7.9.53.4–5	291
5.4.19.1–2	355	7.10.57.1–2	401
5.4.22.1	259	7.11.64.6	212
5.4.23.1	386	7.11.67.2	210
5.5.28.3	214	7.12.70.7–8	242
5.9.56.3	351, 389, 424	7.12.70.7	242
5.9.57.2	355, 392, 425	7.12.70.8	242
5.12.81.5–6	66	7.12.72.6	126
5.14.98.5–8	94	7.12.77.6	274, 316
5.14.118.2	161	7.12.78.5	117
6.7.60.2–3	85	7.13.82.1	200
6.9.71.4	222	7.16.101.4	49, 367
6.9.74.1	225	7.16.102.5	267
6.9.77.4–5	366	7.16.105.5	192
6.11.89.2	257		
6.12.99.6–100.1	59	Ps.-Clement, *Hom.*	
6.15.116.3	186	2.12	351
6.15.126.1	351, 389	2.38	336
7.1.3.4–6	119	9.9	76, 344

Ps.-Clement, Hom. (cont.)		*Evagrius Ponticus, Oct. spirit. malit.*	
11.3	198	79.1153	369
11.4	228		
11.29	134	*Evagrius Ponticus, Orat.*	
13.16	247	17	117
15.9	55	19	162
18.10	152	31	126
19.8	122	37	117
19.11	416	39	160
		40	364
Ps.-Clement, Rec.		53	283
5.23	133, 363	84	160
7.37	53		
8.56	204	*Evagrius Ponticus, Sent. mon.*	
		66	222
Constitutiones apostolicae		127	383
3.5	358		
6.5	123	*Evagrius Ponticus, Spirit. sent.*	
6.27	148	26	383
		30	308
Didache		48	170
1.3	228		
1.5	252	*Evangelium Bartholomaei*	
2.5	202, 393	5.8	295
3.6	122		
4.8	239	*Gregory Nazianzen, Eunom.*	
5.2	184	4	294
11.10	418		
		Hermas, Mand.	
Didymus Caecus, Frag. Ps.		6.1.1	415
1229	186, 359	7.1	412
		11.12	410
Ephraem Syrus, Virt.			
3	198	*Hermas, Sim.*	
		2.5	233
Evagrius Ponticus, Al. sent.		5.3.7	273
54	112	5.6.7	423
		8.6.4	358
Evagrius Ponticus, Cap. paraen.		9.19.1–3	358
2	180	9.20.2	214
10	112	9.24.2	338
13	211		
17	398	*Hermas, Vis.*	
20	107	3.9.2–3	273
23	214		

INDEX OF TEXTS CITED

Hippolytus, *Haer.*
1.19.17 — 175

Ignatius, *Eph.*
8.1 — 219
14.2 — 216, 411
15.1 — 407
15.3 — 96

Ignatius, *Trall.*
6.2 — 185

Ignatius, *Smyrn.*
9.2 — 232

Irenaeus, *Haer.*
4.13.3 — 55, 330

Jerome, *Comm. Ezech.*
6.18 — 243

Jerome, *Comm. Jer.*
4.41 — 10

Jerome, *Ep.*
133.3 — 1, 9

Jerome, *Jov.*
1.49 — 243

Justin Martyr, *1 Apol.*
14.2 — 272
15.9 — 228
15.16 — 27, 316
21.6 — 70

Justin Martyr, *2 Apol.*
5.1–3 — 67

Justin Martyr, *Dial.*
82.3 — 63
123.9 — 96

Ps.-Justin Martyr, *Quaest. Christ. gent.*
161b — 133

Maximus Confessor, *Schol. libr. myst. theol.*
4.429 — 11, 67

Minucius Felix, *Oct.*
18.8 — 66
32 — 83, 85, 363

Origen, *Cels.*
1.7 — 348
1.62 — 152
3.45 — 183
3.47 — 256
3.60 — 392
3.72 — 114
4.74 — 70
4.80 — 71
6.18 — 352
6.43 — 360
6.63 — 73
7.15 — 418
7.23 — 214
7.33 — 321
7.48 — 108
7.58 — 228
8.17 — 84, 165
8.25 — 44
8.28 — 147
8.30 — 1, 7, 147
8.38 — 66, 200
8.75 — 232

Origen, *Comm. Joan.*
2.16.112 — 310
2.23.149–51 — 68
20.6 — 350

Origen, *Comm. Matt.*
15.3 — 7, 52
15.4 — 53
17.27 — 59

Origen, *Exp. Prov.*
17.201 — 195

Origen, *Hom. Ezech.*
1.11   7, 11, 350

Origen, *Hom. Jer.*
14.12.2   165
17.4.5   173
20.3.5   191

Origen, *Hom. Luc.*
35.9   76

Origen, *Hom. Num.*
11.9   85

Origen, *Mart.*
39   44

Origen, *Orat.*
8.2   117, 118
11.4   233
12.2   117
13.4   366
17.2   160
19.3   108
20.2   283
25.1   312
26.2   160
28.2   171

Origen, *Princ.*
1.1.6   66
3.1.18   365
3.2.2   308

Peter Lombard, *Sent.*
IV, 31.5.2   243

Polycarp, *Phil.*
4.3   84, 95

Regula Magistri
10.81   174
11.62   180

Regula Sancti Benedicti
7.61   174

Tertullian, *Pat.*
7   57

Theophilus, *Autol.*
1.3   66
1.8   195
2.15   68
3.7   314

8. Gnostic Tractates

Melchizedek
27.4–6   424

Pistis Sophia
113   77

Teachings of Silvanus
108.18–30   45
115.27–29   154

Testimony of Truth
30.12–17   76

9. Greek and Roman Writers and Works

Aelian, *Var. hist.*
14.24   158

Aeschines, *Ctes.*
249   201

Aesop, *Fab.*
33.1   393
56.3   216

Aesop, *Sent.*
40   112

Anecdota Graeca
1.96   155

3.470	58	Arius Didymus, *Epit.*	
		5b9	172
Ps.-Apollonius, *Ep.*			
42	303	Arius Didymus, *Lib. phil. sect.*	
51	303	82.1	315
82	138		
83	184, 197	Babrius, *Fab.*	
92	181	1.20	162
93	182		
		Carmen aureum	
Aristotle, *Eth. eud.*		7–8	298
1.7.2	166	9–11	260
		15–18	56
Aristotle, *Eth. nic.*		25–26	129
1.7.1	137	27	131
3.1.4	204	30–31	258, 295
4.3.18	158	35–36	90
4.3.28	192	48–49	162
4.6.1	151		
4.7.8	184	Cassius Dio, *Hist. rom.*	
5.5.6–7	328	60.4.2	100
6.7.5–6	317		
6.7.5	137	Ps.-Cato, *Dist.*	
7.8.4–5	111	1.10	179
7.9.6	110	1.14	252
9.1.9	329	1.30	128
9.2.3	328	2.20	183, 393
9.3.3	298	3.1	258
9.8.4	170	4.15	266
9.8.7	173		
9.11.5	330	Ps.-Cato, *Mon.*	
10.2.4	115	50	179
10.9.6	398	68	326
Aristotle, *Pol.*		*Cebetis Tabula*	
3.7.13	80	41.3	316
3.8.1	80		
		Chionis epistulae	
Aristotle, *Rhet.*		16.7	141
2.5.18–20	377		
2.6.19	128	Cicero, *Fin.*	
2.23.7	128	3.22.75	310
Ps.-Aristotle, *Virt. vit.*		Cicero, *Leg.*	
5.6	390	1.59	212, 423

Cicero, *Off.*
1.47	328, 375
1.65	101, 230
1.103	285, 287

Cicero, *Pis.*
18.42	377

Clitarchus, *Sent.*
1	402
3	60
4	86
5	90
6	63, 363
7	94
8	95
9	212
10	24, 107
11	86
12	112
13	124
14	126
15	129, 390
16	131
17	64, 133
18–19	153
21	23, 161
24	170
25	171
26	24, 174
27	178
29	180
30	181
34	184
37	187
40	191
44	198
45	199
48	201
50	294
53	24, 208
54	289
63	85, 200
64	229
66	51
69	247
71	243
73	249
75	246
76	262
85	110
86	110
87	24, 260
88	265
94	272
95	275
97	272
105	299
106	301
109	332
110	340
111	292, 341
113	144
114	24, 341
116	274
120–21	375
122	129, 391
123	386
125	65
126a	393
132	25, 326
134	201, 318
135	403
137	92
141	265
143	171
144	350

Corpus hermeticum
4.6	172
12.23	363

Ps.-Crates, *Ep.*
3.1	397
11.1	59, 87

Ps.-Democritus, frag.
302.185	45

INDEX OF TEXTS CITED

Ps.-Demosthenes, *2 Aristog.*
21 — 393

Dio Chrysostom, *Or.*
1.35 — 141
3.49 — 340
3.53 — 133
4.99 — 114
6.27 — 171
7.132 — 183
8.35 — 371
10.27 — 205
30.14–15 — 396
34.33 — 340
36.19 — 187
38.37 — 399

Diodorus Siculus, *Bibl. hist.*
10.3.2 — 309
10.9.6 — 64, 363
10.9.8 — 283
10.10.2 — 90
10.12.2–3 — 93
34/35.2.35 — 220

Diogenes Laertius, *Vit. phil.*
1.35 — 184
1.36 — 102, 128
1.57 — 268
1.58 — 185
1.59 — 220
1.70 — 179, 190
1.88 — 153, 213, 380
1.91 — 229
1.92 — 106, 131
1.97 — 53
1.104 — 406
2.73 — 213
3.78 — 175
5.41 — 211
6.5 — 251
6.51 — 212
7.93 — 157
7.102 — 145
7.121–22 — 381
7.125 — 310
8.10 — 238
8.14 — 418
8.20 — 285
8.23 — 140, 229, 238
8.31 — 344

Ps.-Diotogenes, *Regn.*
2.72.22–23 — 201

Ps.-Ecphantus, *Regn.*
82.7–30 — 87

Epictetus, *Diatr.*
1.6.28 — 157
1.9.15–17 — 357
1.24.1 — 218
1.29.1–7 — 357
2.2.3–4 — 282
2.5.4–5 — 317
2.8.2 — 66
2.8.11–13 — 72
2.8.13 — 121, 408
2.14.11 — 102
2.14.12 — 82
2.16.18–19 — 323
2.17.22 — 308
2.19.24 — 377
2.19.29 — 420
3.1.7 — 137
3.5.8–9 — 378
3.7.36 — 379
3.22.43–44 — 317
3.22.47–49 — 57
3.22.69 — 243
3.24.2 — 166
3.26.20 — 152
4.1.82 — 282
4.1.89–90 — 308
4.1.103 — 56
4.1.127 — 304
4.1.130–31 — 58, 116
4.1.133 — 219
4.1.153–54 — 270
4.1.173 — 381

Epictetus, Diatr. (cont.)
4.7.16–17   310

Epictetus, *Ench.*
1.1   262
5   128
22   229
33.2   186
33.4   285
33.7   156
33.15   285
34   278
42.1   186
46.1   379

Epictetus, *Gnom.*
8   377
17   272
20   342
26   342
28   190
55   206

Epicurus, *Ep. frag.*
131   151

Galen, *Prop. an.*
6   34

Gnomologium Democrateum
46   291
48   301
62   203
66   131
72   172
82   375, 393
112   94
113   179

Gnomologium Vaticanum
20   278, 317
32   234
45   290
67   117
74   209
81   292, 355

Ps.-Heraclitus, *Ep.*
9.5   381

Hesiod, *Op.*
265–66   327

Hierocles, *In aur. carm.*
1.17   81, 371
7.11   141
11.6   264
14.10   289
21.5   421

Iamblichus, *Protr.*
2.10.1–3   205

Iamblichus, *Vit. Pythag.*
3.13   145, 259, 260
16.68–70   96, 205
17.74   64
22.101   298
24.107–9   146
28.137   389
28.145   314
28.149   122
29.162   183
30.171   108, 220
31.196   263
32.218   154
33.229   125
33.234   326
33.240   125

Isocrates, *Demon.*
31   298
41   179, 187

Isocrates, *Phil.*
22   174

Juvenal, *Sat.*
14.138–40   170

INDEX OF TEXTS CITED

Lucian, *Dem.*		392	157
64	189	425	408
		478	369
Ps.-Lucian, *Cyn.*		531	66
12	87	540	161
		546	207
Marcus Aurelius, *Med.*		597	189
7.3	79	604	298
7.44.1	131	621	180
9.1.1	133	654	268
9.40	162	690	186
10.8	81	710	187
10.12.1	131	737	268
		750	268
Maximus of Tyre, *Dial.*		764	327
8.3	90	840	185
11.10	171	846	184
14.6	125	849	184
25.2	188, 374		
25.7	398	Musonius Rufus, frag.	
33.6	198	3.40.17–24	246
		4.44.21–22	105, 107
Menander, *Mon.*		8.62.10–16	109
7	128	12.86.7–8	244
48	336	15.96.28–98.1	51
59	151	16.102.14–16	205
68	110, 161	18a.112.8–29	145
78	151	18a.112.20–22	146
99	298	18a.112.31–114.3	276
102	151	18b.116.4–22	144
116	224	18b.116.22–32	149
144	285	20.126.15–17	108
144 v.l.	187, 285	51.144.7–9	278
148	247		
149	248	Philostratus, *Vit. Apoll.*	
155 v.l.	248	1.8.1	146
165	286	1.13.3	243
172	386	7.3.2	178
183	256	8.5.3	357
198	252, 369		
250	170	Ps.-Phintys, frag.	
300	247	1.152.16–18	246
322	253	2.153.27–28	246
324	173		
383	142		

Plato, *Apol.*		Plato, *Resp.*	
21c	217	361a	101
21d	217	361b-c	102
29a	217	362e	101
30d	304	366c-e	102
38d-e	208	379b-c	153
		459c	191
Plato, *Crit.*		485c-d	196
48b	263	486b	197
49c	228	501b	386
		517b	402
Plato, *Ep.*		555c	172
326b-c	413	558d-59a	282
		586a	380
Plato, *Gorg.*		730c	184
477a	266		
523b	76	Plato, *Soph.*	
524d	344	227c	96
524e-25a	76	230d	139
Plato, *Leg.*		Plato, *Symp.*	
716c-d	82, 419	183d-e	295
716c	141		
730e	299	Plato, *Theaet.*	
863c	199	173d-e	94
888b	232	176a-b	81
913c	268	191c	343
916e	382		
		Ps.-Plato, *Alc.*	
Plato, *Phaed.*		133c	423
67c-d	164		
68c	114	Ps.-Plato, *Min.*	
107e-8c	75	318e-19a	215
Plato, *Phaedr.*		Plotinus, *Enn.*	
246c	66	3.1.9	111
247c	66		
248a	402	Plutarch, *Adul. amic.*	
252e-53a	421	61d	196
254b	104	64a	338
273e	85	66e	260
248a	467		
		Plutarch, *Amat.*	
Plato, *Phil.*		768a	413
45e	172		

Plutarch, *An. corp.*
  500c   224

Plutarch, *An seni*
  786d   390

Plutarch, *Apophth. lac.*
  208d   252
  223d   183

Plutarch, *Comm. not.*
  1062e   300

Plutarch, *Conj. praec.*
  139c   248
  144f-45a   248

Plutarch, *Cons. Apoll.*
  107f   278, 316
  116e   375

Plutarch, *Cupid. divit.*
  523d-e   158, 281

Plutarch, *Dion*
  9.1   398

Plutarch, *Fac.*
  945a   343

Plutarch, *Garr.*
  502e   210
  503e   274
  504c   185
  504f   181
  505f   189
  506c   189
  510a   179
  510e   183
  515a   182

Plutarch, *Is. Os.*
  382b   65

Plutarch, *Lat. viv.*
  1128d   224

Plutarch, *Lyc.*
  20.2   186

Plutarch, *Per.*
  39.2   153

Plutarch, *Rect. rat. aud.*
  37d   389, 402
  41b   215

Plutarch, *Reg. imp. apophth.*
  199a   90

Plutarch, *Sept. sap. conv.*
  159c   63

Plutarch, *Sera*
  551d   223

Plutarch, *Suav. viv.*
  1090d   376

Plutarch, *Superst.*
  164f-65a   185

Plutarch, *Them.*
  7.3   332

Plutarch, *Tu. san.*
  124e   272
  125c   342

Plutarch, *Virt. mor.*
  444b   111
  445b   110

Plutarch, frag.
  200   144, 408

Ps.-Plutarch, *Lib. ed.*
  6b   151
  6c   182

Ps.-Plutarch, Lib. ed. (cont.)
12e	266, 318

Porphyry, *Abst.*
1.37.4	59, 87
1.46.1	149
1.49.4	397, 461
1.54.5–6	145, 272
2.1	397
2.34.2–3	83
2.45.4	83, 145
2.46.1	423
2.47.3	345
3.26.1	133
4.6.7	287
4.20.3–4	149
4.21.6	49, 385

Porphyry, *Marc.*
7	155
8	201, 345, 393
9	138, 205, 219, 222–23, 225, 280
11	64, 72–73, 81, 83, 86, 133, 173, 212, 415
12	23, 118, 129, 153, 160–62, 306, 391
13	166, 169, 174
14	113, 180, 190–91, 356
15	22, 44, 63, 349, 352, 354, 356, 359, 366
16	21, 307, 313, 371, 399, 403, 406, 408
17	45, 391
18	123, 137
19	83
20	134, 409
21	99, 103, 307
22	103, 314
24	153, 416
27	136
28	124, 135, 145, 249, 298, 408
29	136, 171
31	224
33	322
35	133
34	28, 109, 279, 280
35	244, 333, 341, 363

Porphyry, *Vit. Pythag.*
32	90, 211
35	286

Posidonius, frag.
309a	138

Publilius Syrus, *Sent.*
2	128
32	131
134	266
139	289
141	193
175	143
226	179
239	256
251	185
274	329
343	289
411	157
412	253
424	238
603	154
706	192
710	148

Ps.-Pythagoras, *Ep.*
2.185.23–25	367
2.185.25–28	342

Scholia in Aeschylum Eumenides
278	189

Secundus, *Sent.*
16	174

Seneca, *Ben.*
3.17.4	328
6.3.4	302

Seneca, *Const.*
5.4–5	57

INDEX OF TEXTS CITED

Seneca, *Ep.*		*Sententiae Pythagoreorum*	
3.2	266	2^a	258
11.8–9	236	2^b	222
14.1	112	2^c	225, 257
24.22	322	3^b	130
24.24	322	4	24
27.2–3	278	6a	53
31.11	48	7	180, 356
41.4	48, 377	9	92
74.30	263	10^{a-b}	409
76.4	230, 302	11^a	227, 327
79.14	93	11^c	326
79.17	93	11^d	327
80.9–10	213	13^{a-b}	205
81.1	329	13^c	205
81.10–13	329	14^{a-b}	406
81.22	327	15^a	408
83.18	274	16	409
85.2	42	17	117, 213
85.37	304	20^{b-c}	419
88.2	256	21	109
90.1	262	23	109
93.2	263	26	306
95.57	378	27	386
96.2	378	30^{a-b}	58, 135
99.17	292	30^c	280
107.6–9	376	32	299
108.14	145	35	388
116.3	282	35^a	301
		39^a	86
Seneca, *Helv.*		40	44
5.2	379	42a	75
		47	326
Seneca, *Ira*		48	424
2.8.1	340	49	21, 307
		50	224, 360
Seneca, *Matr.*		51	363
85	244	52	396
		55	21
Seneca, *Nat.*		55^{a-b}	349
3, pref. 3	289	56	22, 354
		57	110, 161
Seneca, *Vit. beat.*		62	238
16.1	309	64	290
		65^a	122

Sententiae Pythagoreorum (cont.)		Septem Sapientes, *Praec.*	
66ª	83	217.6–7	234
70ª	369	217.18–19	369
70ᵇ	24, 369	217.23	329
70ᶜ⁻ᵈ	372		
71	109	Septem Sapientes, *Sent.*	
76	141	216.7–8	179
77	381	216.32	151
79	79, 257, 315		
80	238	*Socraticorum epistulae*	
83ª	392	8.1	135
83ᵇ	393		
84	288	Sophocles, frag.	
85ª	267	247	167
86	24, 217		
89	298	Stobaeus, *Anth.*	
90	398	2.15.28	183
91	114	3.1.173	234
92	173	3.5.31	299
92ª	362	3.13.54	143
94	391	3.18.23–24	274
95	303	3.36.14a	180
97	57, 238	4.1.80	220
98	278	4.5.42	301
102ª	371	4.23.61	220
102ᶜ	389	4.34.71	220
103	341		
104	328	*Stoicorum veterum fragmenta*	
105	318	2.913	414
107	316	2.1000	414
108	49	3.554	184, 192
110ᶜ	113		
110ᵈ	170	*Sylloge inscriptionum graecarum*	
111ª	230	3.1268.1.5	106
111ᵇ	301		
112	62	Teles, frag.	
113ª	254	4a.36	281
115	123, 356	4a.43	281
116	222	6.52	375
120	56, 129		
121ª	162	Theognis, *El.*	
		97–99	298
Septem Sapientes, *Apophth.*		211–12	275
2.6	184	295–97	183
		523–24	155

591–92	157	Papyrus Insinger	
1031–32	216	5.8	95
1185–86	179	6.1	249
		9.12–15	262
Theophrastus, *Char.*		10.11	340
5.1	152	12.5	191
		16.3	372
Vitae Aesopi (G)		16.10–13	370
88	189	16.14–15	372
		22.20–21	188
Vita Secundi		25.21	192
68.1–3	407	27.9	56
		30.3	95
Xenophon, *Apol.*		30.19	98
14	90	31.3	103
Xenophon, *Cyr.*		Papyrus Louvre 2377	
1.2.7	239	no. 2	193
		no. 3	301
Xenophon, *Mem.*			
1.2.23	53		
1.3.5	274		
1.5.4	124		
1.5.6	107		
1.6.10	87		
2.1.18	378		
Zenobius, *Paroem.*			
1.50	187		

10. Ancient Egyptian Writings

Instruction of Ankhsheshonqy

7.23–24	181
8.3	379
8.4	131
12.6	227
12.24	186
13.14–15	184
15.23	228
19.8	289
21.11	383
23.17	268

Index of Authors

Allison, Dale C. 101
Baumstark, Anton 6
Bogaert, P.-M. 5, 8, 10
Boissonade, Jean-François 12
Bolland, Johannes 66
Bouffartigue, Jean 5
Caner, Daniel F. 53
Chadwick, Henry 2, 4, 5, 7, 8–13, 18, 20–21, 23, 25, 28–30, 32, 41, 53, 55–56, 60, 62, 67, 71, 73, 75, 79, 83, 86, 109, 129, 130–31, 142, 148, 150, 159, 181, 189, 195, 198, 200, 211, 214, 219, 220, 241, 245, 247, 251, 261, 267, 271, 284, 292, 300, 318, 320–21, 323, 326, 333, 339, 341, 347, 350, 360, 378, 384, 389, 401, 407, 412–14, 419
Conybeare, F. C. 6, 9
Cribiore, Raffaella 1
Davies, W. D. 101
Delling, Gerhard 25, 27
Dillon, John M. 67
Dodds, E. R. 2
Dörrie, Heinrich 4
Edwards, Richard A. 2, 181, 220, 241, 286, 339, 413
Elter, Anton 4, 11–12, 142, 181, 189, 198, 220, 241, 413
Evans, G. R. 10
Francis, James A. 2
Garitte, Gérard 6
Gildemeister, Johann 5, 10–12
Hense, Otto 130, 367, 409
Hermann, Th. von 6
Jaekel, S. 42
Kirk, Alan 31, 104
Köhler, Wolf-Dietrich 26
Küchler, Max 2, 29

Lagarde, Paul de 6, 10, 12
Lazaridis, Nikolaos 31
Lichtheim, Miriam 29
Meeks, Wayne A. 2
Morgan, Teresa 1
Mullach, F. W. A. 12
Murphy, Francis X. 8
Muyldermans, J. 6
Outtier, Bernard 6
Poirier, Paul-Hubert 5, 6
Rocca-Serra, G. 12
Rubenson, Samuel 11
Russell, Norman 10
Ryssel, V. 6
Schenkl, Heinrich 12
Silvestre, Hubert 5
Sinkewicz, Robert E. 8
Valantasis, Richard 2
van der Waerden, B. L. 4
Vogüé, Adalbert de 10
Wachsmuth, Curt 130, 367, 372, 409
Wicker, Kathleen O'Brien 12, 87
Wild, Robert A. 2, 181, 220, 241, 286, 339, 413
Wilken, Robert L. 43, 79, 148
Wisse, Frederik 2, 5

Index of Subjects

Abraham, 218
abstinence, 64, 124, 143, 145–46, 241, 408
accountability, 76, 194, 198, 345
acquisitiveness, 31, 114, 151, 159
adornment, 87, 104, 240, 246
adultery, 133, 224, 240, 243–45, 262
afflictions, 304
Agesilaus, 252
agnosticism, 314
akousmata, 214, 266, 318
alliteration, 229, 369
almsgiving, 85, 91, 118, 339, 370, 372
a minore ad maius, 102
anaphora, 30, 122, 127, 138, 374, 399, 409, 420
angels, 36, 70, 71, 103, 364
anger, 57, 84, 91, 93, 152, 157, 170, 174, 215, 221, 260, 296–97, 337, 340–41, 376
animals, 105, 110, 144–47, 149, 257, 271, 275, 380
Antisthenes, 251
antithesis, 2, 30, 49, 60, 98, 123, 178, 196, 288, 295, 359, 370, 380
Apollonius of Tyana, 146, 183
apostasy, 358
Aristippus, 213
arrogance, 122, 210, 227, 252, 290, 319–20, 410–11
ascent (of the soul), 323, 345, 390, 395, 402
assimilation, 34, 49, 55–56, 58–59, 79, 81, 85–87, 145–46, 148–49, 173, 272, 400, 409, 419, 421
atheism, 314
atonement, 63, 363

authority, 2, 6, 35, 38, 73, 80, 90, 97–98, 100, 198, 206, 215, 270, 282, 310, 332, 366, 377
avarice, 155
Avita, 8

banqueting, 108, 144, 271
benefaction, 31–32, 38, 67, 70, 75, 78, 84, 90, 92, 102, 116, 145, 200–1, 226–27, 229–30, 233, 254, 265, 267, 312, 318, 322, 325, 328, 330, 355, 367, 369, 371, 392, 404, 425
benefactors, 38, 71, 84, 128, 174, 194, 201, 212, 226, 228–29, 237, 239, 252, 265, 267, 272, 318, 322, 328–30, 424
"better" sayings, 52, 180, 279, 334, 359, 369
Bias, 153, 213, 380
blasphemy, 39, 63, 120–23, 133, 187, 200, 236, 256, 358–59, 384
blessedness, 56, 114, 123, 184, 201, 211, 278, 283, 293, 302, 306, 317, 319, 321, 325, 327, 345, 364, 372, 395, 403–4
boasting, 39, 91, 181, 186, 211, 216–17, 275, 289–90, 292, 379–80, 410
the body, 3, 26–28, 33, 36–37, 44, 46–49, 51–54, 58–60, 64, 74–77, 85, 94, 96, 103, 105–6, 108, 112–15, 117, 119, 122, 124, 134–35, 137–38, 142, 145–48, 150, 154–59, 162, 164–65, 167–69, 171–73, 175, 205, 224, 228, 244, 246, 256, 264, 272, 276, 278–79, 281–83, 292, 295, 297, 303, 317, 320–22, 325, 333–34, 337, 340, 342–44, 346, 354, 356, 364, 380, 395–96, 402, 404, 413, 415, 417, 419, 422–23

body-soul dichotomy, 94, 113, 169, 303, 342, 423
braggart, 288, 290, 410

catchword, 24, 30, 51, 67, 78, 121–22, 149, 164, 170, 178, 196–98, 203, 207–8, 211, 216, 219, 221, 228, 232, 245–46, 251, 253, 265, 275, 286, 295, 297, 299, 303, 313, 334, 341, 347, 349, 352, 354–55, 375, 382, 388, 399, 406, 409
censure, 57, 91–92, 127–28, 136, 171, 179, 209, 214–15, 227, 234, 254, 289, 296, 300–1, 330, 384
Chaeremon, 287
children, 31, 79, 87, 96, 114, 204, 211, 224, 240, 243, 249, 251, 261–63, 319, 336, 404, 415
Chilon, 151, 172, 179, 190, 259
choice, 365
Chrysippus, 274, 414
cleansing, 39, 62, 65, 117, 122, 138–39, 148, 199, 205, 307, 310, 344, 346, 352, 392
Cleobulus, 106, 229
clusters, 27, 51–53, 67, 100, 113, 120, 123, 179, 181, 205, 234, 255, 271, 288, 297, 314, 335, 362, 392, 396, 398–99, 418, 420, 422
conscience, 6, 84, 117, 179, 289, 396
consolation, 60
consultativeness, 193
contentment, 135, 157
correction, 38, 40, 128–29, 143, 152, 192, 197, 206, 215, 234, 255, 291, 325, 330–31
couplets, 30, 96, 178, 186, 191–93, 196–97, 208, 211, 216, 232, 235, 237, 266, 273, 288, 325, 327, 337, 339, 349, 355, 359, 365, 370–71, 374, 379–80, 388–90, 398, 413–14, 423
covetousness, 169
cowardice, 133, 194, 197, 323
crowds, 152, 211, 230, 292, 340, 355
Cynics, 31, 59, 87, 135, 212, 243, 251, 311, 319, 397

dear to God, 82, 119, 141, 165, 251, 258, 341, 346, 353, 358, 395, 419
death, 1, 31, 33, 46, 48–49, 52, 54, 60–61, 65, 75–76, 92–93, 148, 162, 178, 200, 211, 221, 224–25, 252, 258, 262–63, 301, 304, 319–23, 334, 344, 358, 362, 364, 373, 378, 382, 385, 388, 402
Decalogue, 204, 324, 364
deception, 123, 177, 185, 190–92, 197, 207–8, 217, 224, 290, 332, 374, 382, 389, 411
decorum, 188, 271, 274, 286, 379
defilement, 64, 72, 98, 106, 120–21, 124, 138, 143–44, 146–49, 171, 205, 274, 279, 342, 380, 405, 407–9
deification, 34, 48
deliberation, 132
Delphic wisdom, 171, 183, 259, 382–83, 385, 420
Demonax, 189
demons, 3, 33, 75–76, 98–99, 121–22, 138, 147, 154, 168, 191, 262, 285, 307–8, 337, 344, 366, 392, 403, 425
deposits, 54, 60–61, 201, 210, 215, 365
desires, 35, 37, 48, 59, 80, 92, 96, 106–8, 110, 113, 116, 124–25, 136, 138, 146, 158, 170–74, 185, 192, 198, 224, 236, 241, 249, 269–70, 275, 277, 280, 282, 303, 308, 310, 334, 344, 378, 381, 396–97, 407, 412–13, 417–18, 422
diet, 3, 31, 37, 145–46, 375
digression, 89, 356, 358
Diogenes, 311
discretion in speech, 63, 405
dispossession, 157, 269
dissolution, 285–86
divorce, 241–42, 247
drinking, 9, 117, 143–45, 147–48, 155–56, 244, 249, 259–61, 271–75, 282, 341
drunkenness, 174, 271, 274–75
duplicity, 190–91

eating, 117, 144–45, 147–49, 244, 249, 259–61, 271–72, 276, 282

INDEX OF SUBJECTS

education, 1, 31, 139, 152, 182, 189, 225, 251, 254, 258, 280, 288, 291, 335, 348, 398
election, 43, 217
emulation, 4, 80, 85, 115, 154, 206, 213, 272, 403, 421, 424
endurance, 55, 86, 92, 124, 157, 162, 215, 218, 232, 266–67, 285, 291, 326, 336, 357
enemies, 38, 100, 116, 140–41, 161, 169, 190–91, 200–1, 226–29, 267, 315, 332, 364
enlightenment, 93, 130, 134, 155, 390
envy, 80, 88, 90–91, 93, 178, 211, 267
Epicurus, 299, 314
epistrophe, 30, 377, 409
equanimity, 56
eschatology, 52–53, 77, 344, 400
esotericism, 39, 348, 355, 358, 389, 392, 410, 418, 424
Euhemerus, 314

facetiousness, 284
faith, 27, 38, 43–44, 46–50, 84–85, 94, 106, 111, 119, 123–24, 183, 188, 194–98, 200, 206, 209–11, 216–18, 221–22, 225, 231–32, 234–35, 242, 250, 252, 254–58, 262–64, 314, 320, 324, 326, 335, 351, 354, 358, 374, 376, 384, 387–89, 390, 393–94, 402, 404, 407, 410–11, 413–15, 418, 420, 424
the faithful, 6, 36, 47–48, 50, 70, 73, 76, 78, 80, 87, 96, 115, 132, 171, 184, 191, 194–95, 225, 228, 235, 280, 307, 314, 321, 338, 342, 345, 354, 374, 388, 418
the faithless, 36, 92, 142, 388
faithlessness, 49, 206, 210, 385, 388
falsehood, 39, 121, 178, 184–85, 190–91, 194, 196–97, 350, 382, 394
fame, 39, 88, 91–93, 101, 145, 174, 211, 303, 346, 349
fasting, 104, 273–74
fate, 335, 413–14
father imagery, 9, 29, 35, 66–68, 86, 89, 96–97, 101, 166–67, 205, 231–33,
235–36, 239, 245, 252, 254, 262, 276, 283, 293, 306, 336, 338, 367, 403, 423
fittingness, 119, 165, 258
flattery, 81, 152, 178, 185, 252, 254, 292
the flesh, 49, 107, 111, 136–37, 142, 145, 147, 149, 163, 171, 273, 276–77, 279, 282–83, 288, 295, 313, 316–17, 321, 343, 367, 398, 417, 423–24
following God, 71, 129, 314, 389, 402
following nature, 269
food, 31, 59–60, 92, 96, 105, 107, 124, 138, 143–48, 155–56, 219, 249, 260, 271–75, 330, 341, 349, 364, 368, 370, 372, 380, 395, 397, 408, 412–13, 415
foolishness, 131, 135, 137, 172, 274, 287, 300, 333, 408
fools, 197, 249, 338
fortitude, 157, 246
fortune, 48, 56–57, 129, 157, 266, 278, 304, 317, 330, 375, 378, 390–91, 404
freedom, 10, 35, 37, 54, 57–58, 73, 85, 111, 113, 116, 118–19, 185, 225, 232, 260, 270, 277, 281, 304, 308, 310, 318, 322, 329, 358, 377, 380, 397, 399, 414
friendship, 35, 51, 58, 114, 120, 125–26, 140–42, 184, 190, 192, 218, 229, 237–39, 263, 265–66, 276, 296–98, 301, 311, 326, 330, 364, 393, 419

generosity, 32, 118, 251, 272, 300, 333
gluttony, 144, 174, 249, 344, 380, 408
godliness, 37, 164–65, 361
gold, 155
the golden rule, 38, 100, 127–28, 204, 227, 324, 327
goodness, 67, 101, 115, 124, 137, 165, 174, 215, 234, 250, 253–55, 277, 292, 313, 366
governance, 35, 74, 78–82, 97, 104, 109, 180, 203, 206, 223, 247–48, 261, 270, 293, 302, 310, 367, 378, 395–96, 403, 414, 420
gradatio, 78
gratitude, 118, 185, 215, 230, 234, 239, 321, 328

the great commandment, 140–41
greatness of soul, 150–51, 157, 291, 333, 390
greed, 37, 167, 169, 281, 344, 380
grief, 155, 216, 221, 264, 286, 323
guided by God, 132, 140, 195, 401
gullibility, 393
Gymnosophists, 213

happiness, 114, 163, 166, 168, 175, 321, 337, 341, 358, 373–74, 376–78, 391
hardship, 48, 162, 203, 208, 304, 378, 404
high-mindedness, 390
Hippocrates, 259
Hippodamus, 125, 220
holiness, 37, 70–72, 78, 83–84, 89, 96–98, 103–5, 117–18, 121, 133, 143, 145–46, 173, 212, 215, 219, 236, 246–47, 272, 341, 362, 364, 366, 392, 397, 411, 415, 417–18, 420, 422–23
homoioteleuton, 171
honor, 4, 35, 65, 78–80, 83, 102, 122, 155, 164–65, 167, 172, 174–75, 181, 194, 196, 198, 201, 206, 209–11, 213–15, 231–32, 234–35, 250, 253–54, 257, 292–93, 296, 301–2, 313, 315, 318, 352, 355, 379, 390, 403, 407, 410, 412–13, 415, 419
hubris, 210
humility, 104, 210, 217, 260, 274, 332, 374, 406, 410–11
humor, 284, 286
hypocrisy, 47, 128, 340, 375, 393

idleness, 162
idols, 65
ignorance, 10, 111, 129, 157, 177, 183, 187, 195, 199, 206, 225, 291, 297, 314, 330, 331–32, 399, 410
illiberality, 184, 194, 197
illness, 111, 136, 396
illumination, 32, 62, 68, 131, 134, 196, 279, 392

image of God, 29, 48, 59, 73, 81, 133, 142, 174, 201, 209, 212, 215, 228, 230, 234, 239, 254, 318, 362, 421, 423
imitation, 79–80, 85, 87, 96, 128, 166, 173, 195–96, 201, 227, 252, 257, 269, 315, 341, 352, 362, 364, 377, 400, 406, 415
immoderation, 52
impassibility, 221–22, 225
imperturbability, 57, 286
impiety, 31, 38, 46, 51, 64, 95, 103, 120, 123, 130, 133, 148, 200, 213, 215, 218, 231, 236, 239, 324, 362–63, 369, 414
imposture, 39, 289, 326, 410
imprint imagery, 342, 397, 410, 423
impurity, 51, 64, 72, 75, 105, 117, 121, 133–34, 138–39, 143–44, 146, 148–49, 219, 236, 238, 249, 307, 315, 337, 341, 344, 351–53, 387–88, 391, 408–9, 424
inattentiveness, 284–85
inclusio, 30, 221, 277, 284, 286
incoercibility, 308–9
indefectibility, 292
indifferents, 143, 145, 148, 219
indignation, 54–57, 127, 319, 321, 334
industriousness, 260
ingratitude, 201, 215, 231, 239, 328–29
injustice, 64, 100–1, 103, 133, 148, 170, 224, 267, 289, 362–63, 376, 385
insensibility, 105
inseparability, 401, 404
insolence, 3, 108, 210, 219, 337
integrity, 84–85, 153, 178, 190–91, 194, 202, 208, 281–82, 289, 347, 393
intellect, 3–4, 34–36, 48–49, 51, 72, 78, 81–84, 86, 89, 93–94, 96, 98, 102, 120, 122, 134, 167–68, 173, 177, 205, 212, 236, 238–39, 245, 258, 277, 281, 294, 307, 311–12, 327, 354, 362, 367–68, 372, 378, 383, 401, 417–19, 421–24
intemperance, 37, 52, 103–7, 109, 115, 139, 198, 240, 243, 351, 417, 424
intentionality, 37, 50, 52, 79, 84, 95, 99, 101–2, 107, 113, 121, 123, 152, 191, 267, 328, 330, 359

INDEX OF SUBJECTS   473

intercession, 233
interlocking devices, 30, 47, 131
intoxication, 3, 271, 274
irrationalness, 70, 111, 136, 138, 144, 254, 257, 275, 323

joy, 268, 278, 286, 292, 355, 378, 390, 398
Judas, 358
judgment, 5, 27, 34, 36, 39, 46, 52, 54, 56, 61, 63, 65, 72, 74–77, 83, 94, 100, 118, 123, 131–32, 182, 186, 189, 199–200, 203, 206, 209, 216, 253, 255, 265, 267, 291, 299, 336–37, 343–44, 360, 365, 371, 399, 423
justice, 31, 63, 85, 99–101, 103, 140, 147, 170, 211, 223, 225, 229, 238, 246, 255, 267, 306, 314, 331, 333, 362–64, 386, 399

kindness, 91, 187, 233, 302, 328, 329, 332, 372
kingdom, 160–61, 214, 305, 312
kingship, 57, 59, 86–87, 108, 133, 183, 195, 197, 201, 212–13, 225, 227, 270, 281, 310, 311–12, 332

labor, 304, 333
laughter, 3, 187, 284–87
laziness, 108, 159, 162, 233, 260
learning, 31, 34, 107, 139, 196, 199, 225, 234, 246, 250–51, 256, 258, 267, 276, 280, 282, 288, 294–95, 335, 341, 351–52, 373, 375, 394
levity, 284–85, 287
licentiousness, 154, 169, 248
light imagery, 68
likeness to God, 4, 33, 35, 38, 45, 48, 54, 74, 78, 81, 83, 85–87, 90, 93, 119, 125, 135, 142, 155, 165–66, 168–69, 175, 199, 201, 216, 219, 221, 258, 269, 280, 283, 294, 296, 299, 334, 369, 372, 383, 385, 390, 417–19, 421
listeners, 39, 63, 91, 199, 202, 207, 210, 215, 255, 257, 260, 348, 354, 384, 393

longings, 33, 37, 136, 167–68, 171, 280, 303, 316, 334, 413, 423
loquaciousness, 183, 374
love, 3, 28, 35, 37–38, 60, 64, 90–91, 97, 112, 114, 126, 134, 137, 140–41, 144, 167–68, 170–72, 174, 177, 184, 188, 190, 192, 209–10, 222, 225, 231–32, 234–35, 237, 242, 244, 246, 248–49, 254, 260, 274, 278, 283, 288, 290–93, 295, 301, 309, 321–23, 338, 354, 356, 361–64, 366, 374, 386, 394, 401, 408, 417–19, 421
love of God, 60, 141–42, 172, 211, 219, 222, 235, 242, 296, 321, 323, 336, 354, 362, 417, 419
love of humanity, 38, 64, 301, 361, 364
love of money, 37, 114, 170, 210
lust, 53, 108, 170, 221, 249, 260, 295, 408
luxury, 104, 108, 156, 219, 390

magnanimity, 85, 192
marriage, 1, 31, 105, 204, 240–44, 246, 249, 251, 262, 264, 407
martyrdom, 48, 321, 358
the masses, 36, 75, 174, 198, 226, 229–30, 252, 266
material possessions, 3, 37, 55, 57, 94, 117, 161, 213, 269, 281, 368, 390
meat, 145, 147, 149, 155, 219, 260
meddlesomeness, 267–68
mercy, 91, 143, 252, 314, 332, 365, 370, 401
meticulousness, 47, 50, 219
the mind, 27, 34, 36, 51, 65–66, 72, 81, 83–84, 90, 95, 121, 134, 146, 160, 179, 203, 205, 207, 212, 245, 256, 269, 278, 281, 283, 289, 294, 307, 312, 315–16, 343, 353, 362, 366, 383, 386, 402, 422, 424
mind-body imagery, 95, 203
mirror imagery, 36, 212, 309, 372, 423
moderation, 1, 27–28, 31, 37, 46, 52–53, 60, 87, 94, 103–8, 110, 115, 119, 136, 139–40, 145, 154, 156, 172, 219, 221, 225, 232, 240, 244, 246–49, 271–72,

274–75, 276, 279, 282, 285–86, 293, 299, 334, 382, 384, 386, 395–96, 413, 419
modesty, 246, 260, 306
money, 58, 112–14, 155, 170, 213–14, 269, 302–3, 317
the multitudes, 39, 91, 151–52, 290, 292, 340, 351, 355, 424
murder, 133, 262, 323
mysteries, 189, 355, 359, 392
myth of the cave, 402
myth of the charioteer, 66, 104, 389–90, 402

nakedness, 344
namelessness of God, 67
necessities, 58–59, 78, 86, 135, 155, 259, 397
the needy, 38, 86, 88, 91–92, 108, 116, 118, 152, 158, 201, 206, 233, 239, 252, 273, 299, 325, 329, 332, 335, 337–38, 364, 369–70, 400
neighbors, 28, 54–55, 58, 75, 118, 126–27, 141, 148, 184, 187, 192, 200, 208, 226–27, 237, 268, 271–72, 285, 330, 364, 383
nobility, 32, 49, 53, 66, 89, 90, 94–95, 132, 134, 137, 138–40, 145, 153, 161, 165, 168, 170, 173, 189, 194–96, 204, 210, 216–17, 231–32, 248, 260–61, 263, 271, 273, 278, 289–90, 293–94, 304–5, 307, 321, 330, 367, 379, 382–84, 386, 395, 398–99, 420
the noble lie, 191
nonbelievers, 36, 158, 251, 288

obsequiousness, 39, 151, 178
offerings, 38, 64, 78, 84–85, 127–28, 133, 192, 201, 206, 291, 337, 363, 365, 370, 372
omniscience, 95, 103
orphans, 92, 274, 336, 338–39, 354
outsiders, 56, 75, 92, 140, 199, 340, 384
outspokenness, 188, 251, 260

overindulgence, 39, 138, 144–45, 149, 219, 249, 337, 341, 369

paradox, 300
parallelism, 124, 132, 161, 173, 180, 391
parents, 2, 31, 204–5, 239, 253–54, 262, 266, 302, 319, 364
passions, 10, 31, 34, 37, 44, 50–51, 53, 76, 84–85, 87, 90, 104, 106–12, 116, 124, 145, 149, 155, 163, 168, 171, 174, 178, 198, 205, 221–25, 244–45, 256–58, 269, 271, 278, 280–82, 295, 298, 303, 316, 323, 359–60, 381, 388, 398, 409, 413
patience, 55, 104, 157, 291
perfection, 9, 10, 50, 114, 221, 225, 274, 289, 292, 300, 308, 401
philanthropy, 85, 229, 302
Phintys, 220
piety, 31, 36–37, 49, 72–73, 78, 81, 83, 85, 87–88, 91, 101, 106, 119–22, 124–26, 133, 141, 173, 182, 216, 218, 228, 231, 235, 237, 248, 253, 311, 314, 327, 339, 353, 357, 358, 361–67, 385, 391, 397, 415
pleasures, 33, 36–37, 53, 76, 82, 94, 103–8, 110, 116, 137, 143–45, 147–49, 151–52, 155, 157, 168–72, 194, 198, 211, 224, 230, 233, 240, 242–44, 246, 272, 274, 276–80, 282, 286, 304, 316, 320, 322, 334, 336, 340, 342, 344–45, 380, 388, 395–96, 398–400, 407–8, 411, 414–15, 424
pollution, 64, 122, 124, 145, 148–49, 205, 424
the poor, 38, 85, 92, 117, 119, 141, 158, 233, 252, 269, 271, 273, 311, 330, 369–70, 372, 375, 398
possessions, 37, 55, 57–58, 85, 92–93, 113, 115, 117, 119, 136, 151, 154, 156–58, 161, 164, 166, 169, 175, 209, 213–14, 231, 238, 259, 264, 269, 272, 277, 280, 299, 305, 308, 310–11, 321, 329, 357, 370, 385
poverty, 260, 304

INDEX OF SUBJECTS

power, 6, 8, 34, 37–38, 48–49, 51, 62, 64–65, 67–70, 73, 76, 80, 89, 96–98, 106–7, 110, 116, 118, 123, 133, 139, 146, 161–62, 165, 175, 178, 180, 185, 196, 198, 204, 211–12, 217, 233–34, 254, 259, 263, 267, 282–83, 292, 308, 310–11, 314, 351, 357, 360–61, 365–66, 371, 377, 390, 394, 404, 411, 415

Praecepta Delphica, 106

praemeditatio futuri mali, 263

praise, 39, 90–91, 93, 101, 150, 152, 158, 178–79, 184, 192, 213, 230, 250–52, 266, 291–92, 297, 299, 301, 331, 341, 359, 388, 411

prayer, 31, 34, 44, 49, 84–85, 91, 97, 104, 107–8, 112–13, 115–18, 126, 159–62, 169, 175, 198, 228, 231, 233, 261, 283, 334, 357, 361, 364–66, 369, 385, 391, 408

pre-deliberation, 131

presumptuousness, 379

pretense, 326, 379

procreation, 242, 244, 262

programmatic maxim, 104

prophets, 2, 9, 196, 351, 353, 375, 417, 418

providence, 33, 65, 70, 121, 200, 256, 301, 312–15, 335, 365, 371, 376, 404, 414

psychagogy, 236

public opinion, 310

public speaking, 75, 207, 211

punishment, 27, 46, 53, 76, 206, 211, 265–66, 314, 317, 399

purity/purification, 37, 39, 43–44, 52, 58, 61–65, 70, 73, 79, 84–85, 90, 98, 117, 122, 124, 133–35, 138–39, 145, 205, 213, 223, 272, 310–11, 343, 348, 352–53, 355, 363, 390, 414–15, 418, 425

Pythagoras, 12, 34, 64, 90, 93, 96, 113, 122, 125, 130, 140, 143, 145–46, 151, 154, 162, 180, 183, 188, 204–5, 211, 217, 220, 222, 229, 237–38, 243, 253, 259–60, 274–75, 283, 286, 291, 295, 301, 303, 309, 314, 341, 348, 357, 363, 367, 374, 389, 418

Pythagoreanism, 3–4, 9–11, 18–19, 21, 29, 42, 49, 55–56, 60, 81, 87, 90, 101, 109, 125, 129, 131, 146, 148, 169, 178, 183, 186, 201, 212, 214, 220, 222, 238, 243, 246, 263, 265, 285, 289, 295, 298, 303, 318, 327, 332, 342, 344, 348–49, 356–57, 359, 367, 389, 397, 400, 402, 406, 409, 421

reason (divine), 35, 107, 116, 126, 140, 160, 196, 269, 277, 281, 283, 299, 307–8, 311, 315, 366, 390, 395, 397, 400, 402, 415

reciprocity, 128, 143, 204, 227, 233, 248, 327–28, 369–70, 383, 400, 403, 406

refutation, 64, 121, 139, 254, 330

rejoicing, 398–99

remembrance, 90, 93, 96, 235

repentance, 61, 131, 142, 198, 221, 223, 255, 278, 289–90, 358, 366

reproach, 38, 47, 128, 140–41, 149, 170, 172, 181, 190, 194, 199, 218, 244, 252, 263, 276, 278–79, 282, 291, 329–30, 336–37, 387–88

reproof, 38, 143, 224, 250, 254–55, 291, 300–1

reputation, 3, 7, 89, 91–92, 94, 101, 152, 174, 190, 209–11, 217, 230, 238, 247–48, 290, 332, 340–41, 379, 384, 411

resentment, 90, 174, 320–21, 323, 331, 335, 376

reverence, 38–39, 48, 64, 75, 85, 118–20, 123, 164, 200, 212, 216, 235–37, 249, 260, 288, 293, 301, 325, 327, 351, 361–62, 364, 395–96, 422

rewards, 27, 46, 53, 126

righteousness, 56, 60, 63, 76, 100, 160, 219, 221, 370, 384

Rufinus, 5, 7–10, 30, 71, 74, 84, 95, 98, 116, 142, 148, 174, 180–81, 189, 207, 220, 225, 227, 241, 243, 350

sacrifice, 64, 83, 85, 255, 363, 391, 408

sacrilege, 245, 288

salvation, 32, 71, 114, 126, 155, 161, 201, 206, 214–15, 242, 248, 291, 299, 301, 314, 321, 351, 361, 364–66, 379, 389, 391, 411, 414
Satan, 191, 360
self-awareness, 72, 118
self-castration, 7, 53
self-conceit, 218, 332
self-control, 37, 106, 115, 120, 124, 138, 144, 154, 156, 169, 179, 213, 240, 242, 248–49, 251, 257, 260, 272, 274, 279–80, 284, 290, 296, 298, 300, 304, 306, 331, 397, 405, 407, 409, 412–13, 415
self-deception, 217, 224, 383
self-indulgence, 108, 261
self-knowledge, 34, 421, 424
self-perception, 217, 421–22
self-persuasion, 354
self-reflection, 153, 354
self-restraint, 42, 144, 242, 272, 398
self-scrutiny, 40, 202, 207, 393
self-sufficiency, 31–32, 37, 57–59, 63, 87, 113, 134–39, 145, 154, 158, 265, 269, 272, 290, 298, 302, 309, 325, 333–34, 397
self-visualization, 116
seriousness, 31, 50, 284, 286, 287, 300, 331, 419
Sermon on the Mount, 101, 297
servant of God, 38, 69, 201, 212, 234, 239, 254, 266, 270, 313, 318, 333
sex, 37, 106–7, 124, 145–46, 241, 243–44, 248–49, 260, 262, 342, 406–8, 412–13
shame, 75, 134–35, 137–39, 141, 144, 148, 190, 202, 204, 206, 210, 214, 219, 231, 236, 243–45, 248, 259, 276, 278, 283, 288, 292, 301, 307, 319, 353, 392, 408, 424
sharing, 169, 272–73, 299, 311, 329, 349, 368–70
silence, 3, 83, 93, 177–78, 181–83, 185–87, 189, 198, 347, 354, 359, 389, 405–7
simplicity, 397
sin, 26, 28, 31, 34, 37, 39, 46–53, 55, 57, 64, 74, 76, 84, 96, 98, 100, 133, 140, 142–43, 147, 154, 171, 177–78, 182–83, 192, 194, 198–200, 202–3, 205, 209, 211, 214, 216, 218, 222–23, 228, 236, 240, 244–45, 250–51, 254–55, 272, 286–89, 291, 296, 300, 307–8, 317, 322, 330, 335, 339, 350, 358, 374, 385, 388, 393, 410, 416
sinlessness, 6, 10, 36, 46–47, 49–50, 64, 69, 73, 78, 84, 89, 97, 215, 222, 236, 245, 253, 255, 289, 309, 343, 366, 401, 422
sinners, 49, 76, 96, 100, 133, 140, 142, 190, 194, 203, 205, 225, 301, 314, 385
slander, 39, 121, 181, 215, 265–66, 358
slaves, 57, 60, 111–12, 156, 197, 213, 246, 270, 273, 281–82, 310, 319, 333, 380–81, 413
sleep, 3, 37, 59, 106, 185, 251, 259–61, 413
Socrates, 90, 208, 215, 217, 266, 272, 274, 303, 332, 397
Solon, 63, 172, 185, 220, 253, 268
son of God, 35, 72, 89–90, 97–98, 102, 164, 166, 174, 235–36, 361, 366–67
sophists, 151, 290, 303, 410
sorites, 31, 42, 45
Sosiadas, 234
the soul, 3, 31, 33–35, 37, 39, 44, 48–50, 52–54, 59–61, 63–64, 66, 68, 73, 75–76, 86, 94–96, 98, 102, 104, 107–15, 117, 119, 121–22, 124–25, 129, 134, 136–39, 142, 145–46, 149, 154–58, 161–62, 164–65, 167–68, 170–73, 175, 193, 196, 207, 221–22, 224–25, 238, 244, 249–50, 254, 256, 262, 264, 267, 269, 271, 283, 289, 292–95, 297, 302–3, 307, 311, 313, 315–18, 320, 322–23, 327, 330, 334–35, 337, 342–44, 352, 355, 364–65, 369, 381, 385, 389–92, 395–402, 404, 413–14, 417, 422–24
sound reasoning, 103, 106, 110
speech, 1, 3, 31, 38, 57, 62–63, 91, 96, 118, 122–23, 134, 162, 177–92, 194, 198, 200, 203, 207–8, 215, 235, 259, 267, 288, 292, 304, 318, 335, 347, 350,

352–54, 359–60, 374, 382, 384, 391–93, 406–7, 409–11
the Spirit, 351, 366
Stoicism, 3, 10, 50, 58, 65, 70, 95, 110, 136, 145, 157, 174, 191–92, 216, 222, 227, 253, 262–63, 269–70, 278, 282, 287, 289, 292, 300, 303–4, 308, 310–11, 322–23, 331, 357, 377–78, 381–82, 398, 404, 414
the stomach, 145, 149, 241, 249, 260, 271, 405–7
strangers, 51, 213, 228
strictness, 50
suicide, 322
the sun, 68
superstitiousness, 125

taciturnity, 178, 181, 183–84, 374, 406
talkativeness, 178, 181, 184
teachers, 49, 63, 145–46, 188–89, 195, 199–200, 257, 306, 314, 332, 334, 367, 384, 392–93, 407
teaching, 3, 10, 38, 40, 67, 129, 141, 211, 215, 217, 222, 224, 250, 258, 295, 299, 300, 303, 333, 351, 363, 393, 398, 404, 414
teleological anthropocentrism, 70
the *telos*, 79, 81–82, 85–86, 218, 371, 386
temple, 37, 44, 69, 72, 78–79, 83–85, 96, 98, 121, 173, 205, 212, 239, 316, 362, 422–23
temptations, 155, 404
testing, 33, 48, 94, 218, 280, 343, 393, 395, 404, 416
thankfulness, 84, 118, 236
Theodotus, 358
therapy, 224
thrift, 259, 299
the tongue, 64, 98, 120–23, 176, 178–80, 182, 184–85, 187–88, 190, 192, 207, 235, 254, 268, 290, 292, 374, 382, 405–6, 408–9
torture, 396

training, 8, 37, 52–53, 93, 96, 126, 135, 137, 189, 205, 222, 225, 242, 259, 303, 323
transmigration of souls, 147
trials, 47, 119, 126
trustworthiness, 215, 234, 273
truth, 27, 40, 63, 68, 114, 123, 134, 153, 173, 177, 183–84, 186, 188, 190, 192, 194, 196–97, 199, 201, 208, 216, 224–25, 256, 258, 270, 294–95, 303, 335, 345–46, 348, 350–53, 355, 362, 373–75, 384, 387, 392, 394, 402, 417–18
tyrants, 93, 109, 112, 204, 220, 308, 310, 321, 346, 347, 356–57, 373, 377

unbelievers, 39, 152, 253, 292, 301, 351, 355, 358, 364, 366, 384, 388–89
uncleanness, 39, 98, 122, 138, 144, 148, 307, 344, 392
the ungodly, 39, 410
ungratefulness, 38, 239, 267, 325, 328, 333
unnaturalness, 135, 222
untimeliness, 122, 177, 178, 286
unworthiness, 8, 39, 41–42, 44–45, 47, 152, 166, 192, 208, 211, 213, 225, 228, 234, 245, 250, 252, 256, 293, 348–51, 358, 366, 384, 388, 410, 424

vaingloriousness, 211
vegetarianism, 3, 146
veneration, 234, 362
vengeance, 267, 314
verbosity, 182
vice lists, 169, 210
virtue(s), 35, 38, 49–50, 57, 59, 63, 68, 71, 80–81, 93, 103–5, 110, 121, 124, 133, 135, 137, 140, 146, 157–58, 160–61, 165, 172, 175, 189, 195, 212–13, 219, 221, 246, 248, 253, 256, 263, 268–69, 282, 289–90, 292, 295, 299–302, 307, 309, 325, 329, 331–32, 342–43, 357, 363, 377, 381, 384, 386, 389–90, 397–98, 400, 402, 406, 411, 419

warnings, 136, 169, 190, 192, 198, 218, 260, 267, 274, 347, 389, 393

wealth, 1, 56, 58, 113, 115, 135–36, 145, 151, 155, 158, 164–65, 170, 172, 174, 213–14, 219, 252, 259, 269, 272, 281, 283, 292, 296–98, 302, 310, 355, 369–70, 391

weapons, 320, 323

wickedness, 63, 99, 152, 171, 176, 179, 224, 251, 307, 319, 322, 363, 385

widows, 84, 339

willingness, 329–30, 337, 378, 370

wine, 260, 274–75

wisdom, 1, 2, 8, 11, 29–30, 32–33, 43, 51, 61–63, 67–68, 72–73, 83, 92, 95, 113–14, 119, 122, 141, 145, 165, 168, 174–75, 182–83, 188–90, 194–95, 196, 212–13, 217–18, 234, 237, 246, 254, 258, 284, 288, 291, 293, 297, 301, 323, 332, 337, 348, 353, 355, 362, 367, 374–75, 379–80, 387, 390–92, 402, 407, 418–19, 425

witnesses, 4, 12, 122, 132, 184, 195, 199, 202, 207, 236, 266, 293, 305–6, 393, 400

wives, 12, 105, 206, 240, 242–44, 246–49

word of God, 64, 68, 122, 129, 195, 349, 352–53, 384, 395

wordplay, 51, 151, 158, 180, 196, 267, 291, 359, 369, 372

the world, 31, 33, 36–37, 39, 54–57, 59–60, 70–71, 74–76, 91, 96, 100, 113–14, 116, 118, 129, 158, 165, 172, 211, 239, 249, 256, 269, 282, 287, 299, 302, 308–9, 312, 329, 339–40, 351, 371, 387–88, 390, 392, 397, 411, 414, 422

worldly things, 36, 54, 58–59, 76, 86, 113, 168, 302–3

work, 35, 232, 309, 384

worthy (of God), 41, 43–44, 47–48, 97, 107, 116, 126, 155, 159–60, 163–64, 166, 228, 235, 238, 245, 253, 257, 283, 294, 341, 361, 365–67, 369, 411, 414

Xystus, 8–10, 42, 98

Zamolxis, 358

www.ingramcontent.com/pod-product-compliance
Lightning Source LLC
Chambersburg PA
CBHW021349290426
44108CB00010B/173